ASIAN LAW SERIES

ASIAN LAW CENTER
SCHOOL OF LAW
UNIVERSITY OF WASHINGTON
NUMBER 17

The Asian Law Series was initiated in 1969, with the cooperation of the University of Washington Press and the Institute for Comparative and Foreign Area Studies (now the Henry M. Jackson School of International Studies).

The members of the editorial committee are Donald C. Clarke, Toshiko Takenaka, and Veronica L. Taylor (chair).

Asian Law Series

1. *The Constitution of Japan: Its First Twenty Years, 1947–67*, edited by Dan Fenno Henderson
2. *Village "Contracts" in Tokugawa Japan*, by Dan Fenno Henderson
3. *Chinese Family Law and Social Change in Historic and Comparative Perspective*, edited by David C. Buxbaum
4. *Law and Politics in China's Foreign Trade*, edited by Victor H. Li
5. *Patent and Know-how Licensing in Japan and the United States*, edited by Teruo Doi and Warren L. Shattuck
6. *The Constitutional Case Law of Japan: Selected Supreme Court Decisions, 1961–70*, by Hiroshi Itoh and Lawrence Ward Beer
7. *Japan's Commission on the Constitution: The Final Report*, translated and edited by John M. Maki
8. *Service Regulations in Korea: Problems and Recommendations for Feasible Reforms*, by Young Moo Shin
9. *Order and Discipline in China: The Shanghai Mixed Court, 1911–27*, by Thomas B. Stephens
10. *The Economic Contract Law of China: Legitimation and Contract Autonomy in the PRC*, by Pitman B. Potter
11. *Japanese Labor Law*, by Kazuo Sugeno, translated by Leo Kanowitz
12. *Constitutional Systems in Late Twentieth Century Asia*, edited by Lawrence W. Beer
13. *Constitutional Case Law of Japan, 1970 through 1990*, edited by Lawrence W. Beer and Hiroshi Itoh
14. *The Limits of the Rule of Law in China*, edited by Karen Turner, James V. Feinerman, and R. Kent Guy
15. *Legal Reform in Taiwan under Japanese Colonial Rule, 1895–1945: The Reception of Western Law*, by Tay-sheng Wang
16. *Antitrust in Germany and Japan: The First Fifty Years, 1947–1998*, by John O. Haley
17. *The Great Ming Code / Da Ming lü*, translated and introduced by Jiang Yonglin

The Great Ming Code /
Da Ming lü

Translated and introduced by
JIANG YONGLIN

University of Washington Press
Seattle and London

© 2005 by the University of Washington Press
First paperback edition © 2014 by the University of Washington Press
Printed in the United States of America
18 17 16 15 14   5 4 3 2 1

All rights reserved. No part of this publication may be reproduced or transmitted in any form or by any means, electronic or mechanical, including photocopy, recording, or any information storage or retrieval system, without permission in writing from the publisher.

University of Washington Press
PO Box 50096, Seattle, WA 98145
www.washington.edu/uwpress

Library of Congress Cataloging-in-Publication Data

Jiang, Yonglin.
 The Great Ming Code / Da Ming lü (1397) / translated and introduced by Jiang Yonglin.
   p. cm.—(Asian law series ; no. 17)
 Includes bibliographical references and index.
 ISBN 978-0-295-99374-4 (pbk. : alk. paper)
 1. Law—China—Sources. I. Ming lü. English. II. Title. III. Series.
 KNN 33. A4E55   2004
 349.51'09'023—dc22

2004013591

The paper used in this publication meets the minimum requirements of American National Standard for Information Sciences-Permanence of Paper for Printed Library Materials, ANSI Z39.48–1984. ∞

To my parents

JIANG DELIANG and XUE RUIYING

and my teachers

EDWARD FARMER, ANN WALTNER, and ROMEYN TAYLOR

Contents

Acknowledgments xxvii
Note on the Translation xxix
Ming Units of Measure and Money xxxi
Introduction: The Making of *The Great Ming Code* xxxiii

The Great Ming Code

The Imperial Preface to *The Great Ming Code* 3
Diagrams 5
    The Five Punishments 6
    The Penal Instruments 7
    General Mourning Degrees 8
    Formal Mourning Degrees for the Relatives of Nine Generations and Five Mourning Degrees within One's Own Lineage 9
    Wife's Mourning Degrees for Husband's Relatives 11
    Concubine's Mourning Degrees for Household Head's Relatives 12
    Married Daughter's Reduced Mourning Degrees for Her Own Lineage 12
    Mourning Degrees for External Relatives 13
    Mourning Degrees for Wife's Relatives 13
    Mourning Degrees for Three Fathers and Eight Mothers 14
    Six Types of Illicit Goods 15
    The Meanings of Eight Characters as Used in the General Principles 16

CHAPTER 1
Laws on Punishments and General Principles 17

    1   The Five Punishments 17
    2   The Ten Abominations 18
    3   The Eight Deliberations 19

Contents

4. Committing Crimes by Those Entitled to the Eight Deliberations 20
5. Committing Crimes by Officials 20
6. Committing Crimes by Military Officers 21
7. Committing Public Crimes by Civil or Military Officials 21
8. Committing Private Crimes by Civil or Military Officials 22
9. Committing Crimes by the Parents or Paternal Grandparents of Those Entitled to the Eight Deliberations 23
10. Committing Crimes by Military Officers or Soldiers Who Shall Be Exempted from Penal Servitude or Life Exile 24
11. Committing Crimes for Which Penalties May Be Cumulatively Reduced 24
12. Leaving Offices for Legitimate Reasons 25
13. Committing Crimes by Those Who Have Not Yet Become Officials 25
14. Disenrollment and Labor Service 26
15. Families of Those Punished by Life Exile 26
16. Crimes That Shall Not Be Pardoned under the General Amnesty 27
17. Those Punished by Penal Servitude or Life Exile Are En Route When the Amnesty Is Proclaimed 28
18. Committing Crimes and Remaining at Home to Care for Relatives 28
19. Committing Crimes by Government Artisans, Musicians, and Women 29
20. Committing Crimes Again by Those Punished by Penal Servitude or Life Exile 29
21. Redeeming Punishment by Those Who Are Aged, Juvenile, or Disabled 30
22. Committing Crimes before Becoming Aged or Maimed 31
23. Restitution and Confiscation of Illicit Goods 32
24. Voluntary Confession of Crimes 34
25. Sentencing on the Basis of the Punishment for the More Serious Crime When Two Crimes Are Discovered Together 36
26. Fleeing Together after Committing Crimes 37
27. Committing Public Crimes by Those in the Same Office 38
28. Making Errors in Public Matters 39
29. Distinguishing Principals and Accessories in Joint Crimes 40

30	Fleeing When Crimes Are Discovered 41	
31	Mutual Concealment by Relatives 41	
32	Committing Capital Crimes by Functionaries 42	
33	Executing Military Personnel Guilty of Treason 42	
34	Killing Military Personnel 43	
35	Military Personnel and Civilians Residing in the Capital Who Commit Crimes 43	
36	Committing Crimes by Persons beyond the Pale of Civilization 43	
37	Specific Articles Having Different Regulations for Punishment 43	
38	Principles for Increasing and Reducing Punishments 44	
39	The Terms "Sedan Chair" and "Carriage" 45	
40	The Terms "Relatives of Mourning for One Year" and "Paternal Grandparents" 45	
41	The Term "Shall Be Punished by the Same Penalty" 45	
42	The Terms "Supervisors " and "Custodians" 46	
43	The Term "Day" as Being One Hundred Units 46	
44	The Terms "Daoist Priests" and "Daoist Nuns" 47	
45	Deciding Penalties in Accordance with the Newly Promulgated *Code* 47	
46	Deciding Cases without Specific Articles 47	
47	Places for Penal Servitude, Life Exile, and Banishment 47	

CHAPTER 2

Laws on Personnel 52

SECTION 1 *Administrative Institutions* 52

48 Selecting Military Posts 52
49 Selecting Officials by High Officials without Authorization 52
50 Civil Officials Shall Not Be Designated as Dukes or Marquises 53
51 Officials' Protection Privilege 53
52 Appointing Too Many Officials or Functionaries 54
53 Recommending Inappropriate Persons 54
54 Recommending Officials or Functionaries Who Have Transgressed 55
55 Leaving Official Appointments or Employments without Authorization 55
56 Exceeding the Time Limit by Officials When Going to Their Posts 55

x   Contents

      57   Failing to Attend Audiences at the Court or to Fill Official Posts without Reason 56
      58   Summoning Subordinate Officials without Authorization 56
      59   Career Records of Officials or Functionaries 57
      60   Treacherous Cliques 58
      61   Associating with Court Attendant Officials 58
      62   Memorializing in Praise of the Virtues and Achievements of High Officials 58

SECTION 2   *Official Documents* 59

      63   Explaining and Reading the *Code* and *Commandment* 59
      64   Violating Imperial Edicts 59
      65   Discarding or Destroying Imperial Edicts or Official Seals 60
      66   [Losing Imperial Edicts] 60
      67   Mistakenly Violating Name Taboos in Memorials or Statements to the Throne 61
      68   Not Memorializing Matters That Ought to Be Memorialized 61
      69   Not Returning after Being Sent on Missions with Imperial Edicts 62
      70   Divulging Important Military Information 63
      71   Delaying Transmitting Official Documents 63
      72   Inspecting Documentary Files 64
      73   Reviewing Documentary Files 64
      74   Colleagues Affixing Dates or Signatures to Documentary Files on Others' Behalf 65
      75   Adding to or Subtracting from Official Documents 65
      76   Covering Up and Keeping Seals 66
      77   Omitting to Affix Seals 66
      78   Omitting to Employ Seals on Paper Currency 67
      79   Employing Seals of Transferring Troops without Authorization 67
      80   Warrants 67

CHAPTER 3

Laws on Revenue 69

SECTION 1   *Households and Corvée Services* 69

      81   Omitting to Register Households or Household Members 69

Contents   xi

   82   Households Should Be Established according to the Registers   70
   83   Establishing Buddhist or Daoist Monasteries without Authorization and Ordaining Buddhist or Daoist Priests without Authorization   71
   84   Illegally Designating Wives' Sons [as Heirs]   71
   85   Taking Stray Children   72
   86   Unequally Levying Taxes and Corvée Services   73
   87   Unequally Assigning [Corvée Services to] Able-Bodied Adult Males   73
   88   Hiding [Persons from] Corvée Services   73
   89   Prohibition [against Fraudulently Claiming to Be] Security Group Chiefs or Community Heads   74
   90   Fleeing to Evade Corvée Services   74
   91   Appointing Prison Guards   75
   92   Privately Employing Commoners or Government Artisans under One's Jurisdiction to Perform Services   75
   93   Establishing Separate Household Registers or Dividing the Family Property   76
   94   Inferior or Younger Family Members Making Use of Family Property without Authorization   76
   95   Supporting Orphans and Elderly Persons   76

SECTION 2   *Fields and Houses*   76

   96   Fraudulently Concealing Fields and Their Produce   76
   97   Inspecting Fields and Their Produce Damaged by Natural Calamities   77
   98   Meritorious Officials' Fields   78
   99   Fraudulently Selling Fields and Houses   78
   100   Purchasing Fields or Houses [by Officials or Functionaries] in the Locations of Their Service   79
   101   Purchasing Fields or Houses by Mortgage   79
   102   Fraudulently Cultivating Government or Private Land   80
   103   Allowing Land to Go Uncultivated   80
   104   Discarding or Destroying Things Such as Utensils or Crops   81
   105   Eating Melons or Fruits of Gardens or Orchards without Authorization   81
   106   Borrowing Government Carriages or Boats without Authorization   81

SECTION 3 Marriages 82

- 107 Marriages of Men and Women 82
- 108 Mortgaging or Renting Out Wives or Daughters 83
- 109 Disordering Wives and Concubines 83
- 110 Expelling Sons-in-Law and Marrying Off Daughters 84
- 111 Marrying Off or Taking in Marriage during the Mourning Period 84
- 112 Marrying Off or Taking in Marriage While Parents Are Imprisoned 85
- 113 Marrying Persons with the Same Surname 85
- 114 Marrying Superior or Inferior Relatives 85
- 115 Marrying Relatives' Wives or Concubines 85
- 116 Marrying Women or Daughters of Those under [the Officials'] Jurisdiction as Wives or Concubines 86
- 117 Marrying Runaway Women 86
- 118 Forcibly Seizing Wives or Daughters of Honorable Families 87
- 119 Marrying Musicians as Wives or Concubines 87
- 120 Buddhist or Daoist Priests Taking Wives 87
- 121 Marriages between Honorable and Mean Persons 87
- 122 Marriages by Mongols and Semu People 88
- 123 Repudiating Wives 88
- 124 Punishments for Matchmakers and Others Who Arrange Marriages That Violate the *Code* 89

SECTION 4 Granaries and Treasuries 90

- 125 Rules of Paper Currency 90
- 126 Rules of Coinage 91
- 127 Violating the Time Limits in Collecting Grain Taxes 91
- 128 Collecting Too Much Grain Tax above the Level of the Grain Measures 92
- 129 Concealing or Consuming Tax Paid in Grain or Other Taxable Materials 92
- 130 Monopolizing Payment of Tax Paid in Grain 92
- 131 Fraudulently Issuing Invoices or Receipts 93
- 132 Secretly Using Excess Money or Grain to Make Up Deficits 93
- 133 Borrowing Money or Grain without Authorization 94
- 134 Borrowing Government Objects without Authorization 94
- 135 Diverting [Items] in Expenditures or Receipts 94

Contents xiii

	136	Deceitfully Embezzling by Weighers in Granaries and Employees 95
	137	Fraudulently Issuing Government Grain 95
	138	Watching Each Other for Money and Grain 95
	139	Failing to Discover Theft in Granaries and Treasuries 96
	140	Waiting for Money and Grain to Be Expended and Opening Official Seals without Authorization 96
	141	Violating [Rules] in Issuing or Receiving Government Goods 96
	142	Creating Obstructions in Receiving or Issuing [Government Goods] 97
	143	Delivering Gold or Silver in Standard Purity 97
	144	Damaging Goods in Granaries or Treasuries 97
	145	Transmitting Government Goods 98
	146	Deciding the Seizure of Illicit Goods Improperly 99
	147	Guarding Goods in the Hands of the Government 99
	148	Concealing Household Goods That Go to the Government 99
SECTION 5		*Taxes* 100
	149–60	The Salt Rules [Twelve Articles] 100
		[Untitled articles] 100–103
	161	Supervisory [Officials or Functionaries] or Powerful Persons Engaging in Salt Transactions 103
	162	Obstructing the Salt Laws 103
	163	Illegal Transactions in Tea 104
	164	Illegal Transactions in Alum 104
	165	Evading Taxes 104
	166	Maritime Merchants Hiding Goods 104
	167	Households Failing to Pay Taxes 104
SECTION 6		*Monetary Obligations* 105
	168	Taking Interest in Violation of Prohibitions 105
	169	Consuming Property Received in Deposit 106
	170	Finding Lost Objects 106
SECTION 7		*Markets* 107
	171	Filling Positions of Commission Agents or Port Masters without Authorization 107
	172	Assessing Prices of Merchandise by Market Authorities 107

- 173 Monopolizing Markets 108
- 174 Manufacturing Volume Measures, Weights, or Linear Measures without Authorization 108
- 175 Failing to Manufacture Utensils and Textiles in Accordance with the Rules 109

CHAPTER 4
Laws on Rituals 110

SECTION 1 Sacrifices 110

- 176 Sacrifices and Imperial Ancestor Worship 110
- 177 Destroying Mounds or Altars for Great Sacrifices 111
- 178 Performing Sacrifices to Spirits Recorded in *The Sacrificial Canon* 111
- 179 The Mausoleums of Rulers of Previous Dynasties 111
- 180 Profaning the Spirits 112
- 181 Prohibiting Sorcery of Wizards and Witches 112

SECTION 2 Ceremonial Regulations 113

- 182 Preparing Imperial Medicine 113
- 183 Clothing or Personal Objects of the "Sedan Chair" 113
- 184 Collecting and Keeping Proscribed Books and Practicing Astronomy without Authorization 114
- 185 Clothing and Objects Bestowed by the Emperor 114
- 186 Making Errors in Imperial Audiences or Congratulatory Ceremonies 114
- 187 Misbehaving during Ceremonies 114
- 188 Failing to Observe the Proper Procedure in Making Responses to the Throne 115
- 189 Obstructing Others from Attending Court Audiences 115
- 190 Sending Memorials or Making Statements to the Throne 115
- 191 Incumbent Officials Erecting Stele without Authorization 116
- 192 Prohibition against Greeting and Bidding Farewell 116
- 193 Official Messengers Insulting Senior Officials 116
- 194 Violating Sumptuary Regulations on Clothing and Houses 116
- 195 Buddhist and Daoist Priests Honoring Parents 117
- 196 Failing to Prophesy Heavenly Portents 117
- 197 Soothsayers Recklessly Predicting Disaster or Good Fortune 117

Contents

198	Concealing the Death of Parents or Husbands 118
199	Abandoning Relatives to Take Government Offices 118
200	Funerals 119
201	Community Wine-Drinking Ceremonies 119

CHAPTER 5
Laws on Military Affairs 120

SECTION 1 *Guarding Palaces* 120

202	Entering the Gates of the Imperial Ancestral Temple without Authorization 120
203	Entering the Gates of Palaces and Halls without Authorization 120
204	Substituting Imperial Bodyguards or Palace Guards without Authorization 121
205	Delaying in Escorting the "Carriage" 121
206	Walking on the Imperial Pathway 122
207	Substituting Services by Craftsmen Working in the Palace Treasury 122
208	Failing to Leave Palaces or Halls after the Constructions or Manufactures Are Completed 122
209	Leaving or Entering Palace or Hall Gates without Authorization 123
210	Controlling Identification Passes of Palace Eunuchs Who Enter or Leave 123
211	Shooting Arrows at Palaces or Halls 124
212	Arms of Imperial Guards 124
213	Prohibiting Those Who Have Been Convicted from Serving as Imperial Guards 124
214	Intruding into the Imperial Procession: [Failing to Avoid the Imperial Procession] 125
215	Intruding into the Imperial Procession: [Appealing for Redress of Wrongs That Are Not True] 125
216	Intruding into the Imperial Procession: [Failing to Guard against Domestic Animals] 125
217	The Camp Gates of the Imperial Traveling Palaces 125
218	Climbing over City Walls 126
219	Locking Gates through Which Passing Is Prohibited 126
220	Carrying Identification Tablets 126

SECTION 2 Military Administration 127

- 221 Moving Government Troops without Authorization 127
- 222 Reporting Military Matters 128
- 223 Reporting Military Information at Full Speed 129
- 224 Requesting Military Supplies at the Frontiers 129
- 225 Losses or Mistakes in Military Operations 129
- 226 Violating the Time Limit in Following [Orders] to Go on Campaigns 130
- 227 Arranging for Substitutes in Service by Military Soldiers 130
- 228 Commanding Officers Failing to Defend [Their Positions] Tenaciously 131
- 229 Allowing Troops to Pillage 131
- 230 Failing to Train Soldiers 132
- 231 Provoking Honorable Persons to Revolt 132
- 232 Selling Military Horses without Authorization 133
- 233 Selling Military Equipment without Authorization 133
- 234 Destroying or Discarding Military Equipment 133
- 235 Possessing Prohibited Military Equipment without Authorization 133
- 236 Allowing Military Soldiers to Abandon Service 134
- 237 Employing Military Officers or Soldiers by Dukes or Marquises without Authorization 135
- 238 Officers or Soldiers Fleeing from Campaigns or Defense 135
- 239 Treating Military Dependents Preferentially 137
- 240 Curfews 137

SECTION 3 Guard Posts and Fords 138

- 241 Passing Guard Posts or Fords without Authorization, by Circumvention, or by Deception 138
- 242 Deceitfully Issuing Travel Passes 138
- 243 Causing Difficulties at Checkpoints 139
- 244 Sending Wives or Daughters of Military Deserters out of Cities 140
- 245 Interrogating Spies 140
- 246 Crossing Frontiers without Authorization or Going to Sea in Violation of the Prohibitions 140
- 247 Employing Constables without Authorization 141

Contents

SECTION 4		*Stables and Herds* 141
	248	Raising Livestock Contrary to Law 141
	249	Breeding Horses 142
	250	Verifying Livestock Incorrectly 142
	251	Raising or Treating Emaciated or Sick Livestock Contrary to Law 142
	252	Injuring Government Livestock on Their Backs or Necks When Riding Them 142
	253	Failing to Break and Train Government Horses 143
	254	Slaughtering Horses and Cattle 143
	255	Livestock Biting and Kicking People 145
	256	Hiding Newborn Government Livestock 145
	257	Borrowing or Lending Government Livestock without Authorization 145
	258	Government Messengers Demanding to Borrow Horses 146
SECTION 5		*Postal Relay Stations* 146
	259	Delivering Government Documents: [Speed of Delivery] 146
	260	Delivering Government Documents: [Damaged Documents] 146
	261	Delivering Government Documents: [Inspection of Postal Relay Stations] 147
	262	Intercepting Sealed Government Documents 147
	263	Damaged Postal Relay Station Buildings 148
	264	Employing Postal Relay Station Soldiers without Authorization 148
	265	Government Messengers Delaying in Their Mission 148
	266	Excessively Using Postal Horses 149
	267	Accepting Excessive Supplies 149
	268	Documents That Should Be Provided with Postal Relay Station Services [for Delivery] but Are Not Provided 150
	269	Delaying Government Affairs That Should Be Carried Out 150
	270	Occupying the Best Rooms of Postal Relay Stations 151
	271	Carrying Private Articles While Riding on Post Horses 151
	272	Making Commoners Carry Sedan Chairs without Authorization 151
	273	Family Members of Officials Deceased from Illness Returning to Their Home Villages 151

274 Receiving Assignments but Hiring or Sending Others to Perform Them 151
275 Carrying Private Goods While Riding on Government Animals, Carriages, or Boats 152
276 Borrowing Post Horses without Authorization 152

CHAPTER 6
Laws on Penal Affairs 154

SECTION 1 *Violence and Robbery* 154

277 Plotting Rebellion and Great Sedition 154
278 Plotting Treason 154
279 Making Magical Inscriptions and Magical Incantations 155
280 Stealing Sacred Objects of the Spirits Devoted to the Great Sacrifices 155
281 Stealing Imperial Decrees 156
282 Stealing Seals 156
283 Stealing Property from the Palace Treasury 156
284 Stealing Keys to City Gates 156
285 Stealing Military Equipment 156
286 Stealing Plants or Trees within the Imperial Mausoleum 157
287 Supervisors or Custodians Themselves Stealing Money or Grain from Granaries or Treasuries 157
288 Ordinary Persons Stealing Money or Grain from Granaries or Treasuries 158
289 Forcible Robbery 159
290 Rescuing Prisoners by Force 159
291 Forcibly Taking in Daytime 160
292 Theft 160
293 Stealing Horses, Cattle, and Other Livestock 162
294 Stealing Rice and Wheat from Fields 162
295 Relatives Stealing from Each Other 162
296 Obtaining Property by Threats 163
297 Obtaining Government or Private Property by Deceit or Cheating 163
298 Kidnapping Persons or Kidnapping and Selling Persons 164
299 Uncovering Graves 165
300 Entering Others' Houses at Night without Reason 167

	301	The Harborers of Thieves and Robbers 167
	302	Jointly Plotting to Commit Robbery 168
	303	Taking Goods Openly or Secretly Each Constitutes Robbery 169
	304	Removing Tattoos 169

SECTION 2 *Homicide* 169

	305	Plotting to Kill Others 169
	306	Plotting to Kill Imperial Emissaries or One's Own Superior Officers 170
	307	Plotting to Kill Paternal Grandparents or Parents 170
	308	Killing Adulterous Lovers 171
	309	Plotting to Kill the Parents of a Deceased Husband 171
	310	Killing Three Persons from One Household 171
	311	Extracting Vitality by Dismembering Living Persons 172
	312	Killing Others by Making or Keeping *Gu* Poison 172
	313	Killing Others in Affrays or by Intention 173
	314	Depriving Others of Clothes or Food 173
	315	Killing or Injuring Others in Play, by Mistake, or by Negligence 173
	316	Husbands Striking Transgressing Wives or Concubines to Death 174
	317	Killing Sons, Sons' Sons, or Slaves and Putting the Blame on Others 174
	318	Injuring Others with Bows and Arrows 175
	319	Killing or Injuring Others with Carriages or Horses 175
	320	Incompetent Physicians Killing or Injuring Others 176
	321	Killing or Injuring Others with Spring Bows 176
	322	Using Coercion to Cause Others to Die 176
	323	Making Private Settlements When Superior or Older Relatives Are Killed by Others 177
	324	Knowing Companions Plot to Harm 177

SECTION 3 *Affrays and Batteries* 177

	325	Affrays and Batteries 177
	326	The Period of Responsibility for Crimes 179
	327	Quarreling within the Palace 180
	328	Striking the Imperial Relatives within the Sixth Degree of Mourning 180
	329	Striking Imperial Emissaries or One's Own Head Officials 180

	330	Associate or Other Subordinate Officials Striking Head Officials 181
	331	Superior Officials and Subordinate Officials Striking Each Other 181
	332	Officials of the Ninth Rank or Above Striking Head Officials 182
	333	Resisting or Striking Persons Sent to Collect Taxes or to Direct Official Tasks 182
	334	Striking Teachers from Whom [the Offenders] Receive Their Education 182
	335	Using Coercion or Physical Strength to Restrain or Bind Others 182
	336	Honorable and Mean Persons Striking Each Other 183
	337	Slaves Striking Household Heads 183
	338	Wives or Concubines Striking Husbands 185
	339	Relatives of the Same Surname Striking Each Other 186
	340	Striking Superior or Older Relatives of the Third Mourning Degree or More Distant 186
	341	Striking Superior or Older Relatives of the Second Mourning Degree 187
	342	Striking Paternal Grandparents or Parents 187
	343	Wives or Concubines and Husbands' Relatives Striking Each Other 188
	344	Striking Sons of Wives by Their Former Husbands 189
	345	Wives or Concubines Striking Parents of Deceased Husbands 190
	346	When Father or Paternal Grandfather Is Struck 190
SECTION 4		*Cursing* 190
	347	Cursing Others 190
	348	Cursing Imperial Emissaries or One's Own Head Official 190
	349	Associate or Other Subordinate Officials Cursing Head Officials 191
	350	Slaves Cursing Household Heads 191
	351	Cursing Superior or Older Relatives 191
	352	Cursing Paternal Grandparents or Parents 192
	353	Wives or Concubines Cursing Husbands' Superior or Older Relatives of the Second Mourning Degree 192
	354	Wives or Concubines Cursing Parents of Deceased Husbands 192

Contents

SECTION 5   *Accusations and Suits*   192

355   Litigation Bypassing Appropriate Jurisdiction   192
356   Making Anonymous Written Accusations of Offenses against Others   193
357   Not Accepting and Acting on Accusations   193
358   Withdrawing from Trying Cases   194
359   Making False Accusations   195
360   Violating Status and Offending against Righteousness   198
361   Sons or Sons' Sons Violating Instructional Orders   200
362   Prisoners Are Not Permitted to Make Accusations Regarding Others' Matters to the Authorities   200
363   Instigating Litigation   201
364   Coordinating Litigation Involving Military Personnel and Civilians   201
365   Family Members Lodging Accusations on Behalf of Officials or Functionaries   201
366   False Accusations of Offenses Punishable by Military Exile or Banishment   202

SECTION 6   *Accepting Illicit Goods*   202

367   Officials or Functionaries Accepting Property   202
368   Committing Crimes Involving Illicit Goods Obtained through Malfeasance   204
369   Accepting Property after Completing the Matters   205
370   Seeking Favorable Decisions of Matters by Offering Property   205
371   Officials Extorting or Borrowing Property from Others   206
372   Household Members [of Officials] Extorting [Property]   207
373   Surveillance Officials or Functionaries Committing Offenses Involving Illicit Goods   207
374   Making Unauthorized Collections for Public Benefit   207
375   Privately Accepting Property from Dukes or Marquises   207
376   Retaining Stolen Goods   208
377   Officials or Functionaries Permitting Promises of Property   208

Contents

SECTION 7 *Deceiving and Counterfeiting* 208

- 378 Counterfeiting Imperial Rescripts 208
- 379 Deceitfully Transmitting Imperial Decrees 209
- 380 Replying to or Memorializing the Emperor Untruthfully 210
- 381 Counterfeiting Items Such as Seals and Almanacs 210
- 382 Counterfeiting Treasure Paper Currency 210
- 383 Privately Casting Copper Cash 211
- 384 Deceitfully Impersonating Officials 212
- 385 Deceitfully Claiming to Be Palace Attendants or Other Officials 212
- 386 Court Attendants Deceitfully Claiming to Be on Private Missions 213
- 387 Deceitfully Making False Auspicious Portents 213
- 388 Avoiding Duties by Feigning Illness, Death, or Injury 213
- 389 Deceitfully Enticing Others to Violate the Law 213

SECTION 8 *Committing Fornication* 214

- 390 Committing Fornication 214
- 391 Facilitating and Tolerating Wives or Concubines to Commit Fornication 214
- 392 Committing Fornication with Relatives 215
- 393 Falsely Accusing Fathers-in-Law of Fornication 216
- 394 Slaves or Hired Laborers Committing Fornication with Household Heads' Wives 216
- 395 Committing Fornication with Wives or Daughters of Subordinates 216
- 396 Committing Fornication during the Period of Mourning or by Buddhist or Daoist Clergy 217
- 397 Honorable and Mean Persons Committing Fornication with Each Other 217
- 398 Officials or Functionaries Sleeping with Entertainers 217
- 399 Purchasing Honorable Persons to Be Entertainers 217

SECTION 9 *Miscellaneous Offenses* 218

- 400 Destroying Exhibition Pavilions 218
- 401 Furnishing Medical Care and Medicine to Artisans and Soldiers Who Are Sick 218
- 402 Gambling 218
- 403 Castrating Others 218

Contents xxiii

	404	Seeking Favors in Public Matters 218
	405	Privately Settling Public Matters 219
	406	Accidentally Setting Fires 219
	407	Deliberately Setting Fires and Burning Others' Houses 220
	408	Theatrical Performances 220
	409	Violating the *Commandment* 221
	410	Doing What Ought Not to Be Done 221

SECTION 10 *Arrests and Escapes* 221

- 411 Pursuing and Arresting Criminals by Those Who Are Charged with the Duty of Arrest 221
- 412 Criminals Resisting Arrest 222
- 413 Imprisoned Criminals Escaping from Prisons or Using Force to Break out of Prisons and Running Away 222
- 414 Criminals under Penal Servitude or Life Exile Running Away 222
- 415 Delaying in Sending Prisoners 223
- 416 Custodians Not Discovering the Escape of Prisoners 224
- 417 Knowing the Circumstances and Concealing Criminals 225
- 418 Time Limit for Arresting Robbers and Thieves 225

SECTION 11 *Judgment and Imprisonment* 226

- 419 Not Imprisoning Criminals Who Should Be Imprisoned 226
- 420 Deliberately Imprisoning or Interrogating Innocent Persons 226
- 421 Prolonging Imprisonment 227
- 422 Mistreating Prisoners 228
- 423 Giving Prisoners Edged Metal Tools That Can Be Used to Free Themselves 228
- 424 Custodians Instructing Prisoners to Contradict Their Confessions 229
- 425 Prisoners' Clothing and Food 229
- 426 When Meritorious Officials Are Imprisoned, Their Relatives May Visit Them 230
- 427 Prisoners Sentenced to Death Ordering Others to Kill Them 230
- 428 Old and Young Persons Are Not Put to Judicial Torture 230

429 Detaining Prisoners during Interrogations to Wait for Direct Confrontation 231
430 Judging Cases in Accordance with the Specifications in the Complaints 232
431 Complainants Not Being Released after the Trial Is Completed 232
432 Prisoners Falsely Accusing Innocent Persons 232
433 Officials Exonerating the Guilty or Implicating the Innocent 233
434 Reversing Unjust Judgments 235
435 The Degrees of Competence of Officials Having Jurisdiction for Executing [Sentences] of Prisoners 235
436 Examining Wounds on Corpses and Making Untrue Reports 236
437 Administering Penalties Not in Accordance with the Law 237
438 Head Officials or Emissaries Committing Offenses 238
439 Citing the *Code* and the *Commandment* in Deciding Penalties 238
440 Obtaining Prisoners' Acceptance of Punishment or Petition for Revision 238
441 Incorrectly Deciding Penalties before Amnesties 239
442 Hearing That There Will Be Amnesties and Deliberately Committing Crimes 239
443 Prisoners Sentenced to Penal Servitude Failing to Perform Labor Services 239
444 Women Committing Crimes 240
445 Awaiting Replies to Memorials concerning Prisoners Sentenced to Death 240
446 Deciding Penalties Incorrectly 241
447 Functionaries Writing Confessions for [the Accused] 241

CHAPTER 7
Laws on Public Works 243

SECTION 1 *Constructions and Manufactures* 243

448 Engaging in Constructions and Manufactures without Authorization 243
449 Wasting Labor in Procuring [Things] That Cannot Be Used 243
450 Engaging in Constructions and Manufactures Contrary to the Law 244

	451	Fraudulently Taking Excessive Materials 244
	452	Bringing in [Private] Materials and Manufacturing Them into Silk Cloth 244
	453	Weaving Silk Cloth with Prohibited Designs of Dragons and Phoenixes 245
	454	Exceeding Time Limits for Manufacture 245
	455	Repairing Granaries or Treasuries 245
	456	Officials or Functionaries Having Authority but Not Residing in Public Office Buildings 246
SECTION 2		*Dikes* 246
	457	Breaching Dikes through Theft 246
	458	Failing to Repair Dikes at the Proper Time 246
	459	Encroaching on Public Streets and Roads 247
	460	Repairing Bridges and Roads 247

Glossary 249
Bibliography 293
General Index 301

Acknowledgments

During the past decade as I worked on this project, I accumulated enormous intellectual, emotional, and financial debts to a number of individuals and institutions. Three circumstances prepared me for the translation of *The Great Ming Code*. In the early 1980s, while I was studying for the LL.M. degree at East China Institute of Politics and Law in Shanghai, I had the chance to read volume 1 of the English translation of *The Tang Code* by Wallace Johnson, who later introduced me to Harvard Law School's East Asian Legal Studies Program and encouraged me to engage in the translation of *The Great Ming Code*. In 1988, after I came to the Law School and Department of History of the University of Minnesota as a visiting scholar, I audited Stephen Young's seminar on Chinese legal history and began to assist Edward Farmer on revising his translations of Ming legal documents. In 1990, just before I entered the Ph.D. program at the University of Minnesota, I assisted William Jones at Washington University School of Law in St. Louis with his translation of *The Great Qing Code*. These activities not only enhanced my English-language skills and inspired me to fill in a gap in the existing scholarly literature but also provided me with new perspectives from which to study Chinese legal history, and even made me read the Chinese text more judiciously. After I started the project, these scholars' works on Tang, Ming, and Qing law became the major references for the translation.

At various stages of the work, I received insightful suggestions and criticisms from Tahirih Lee, Joachim Savelsberg, Byron Marshall, John Langlois, Jr., Martin Heijdra, Tom Nimick, Zhou Yuan, John Dardess, Timothy Brook, Benjamin Elman, Karen Turner, Robin Yates, Melissa Macauley, Yuan Zujie, Joe and Lorrie Dennis, Hsu Pi-ching, Jennifer Downs, Jeff Hornibrook, Zhu Li, Wang Yuh-shiow, Zhang Dexin, and Wang Xi. Yang Yifan kindly provided me with a copy of the Korean text *The Great Ming Code Directly Explicated* (Taemyong yul chehae) in the early stage of the work. William Alford at Harvard Law School recommended me to the National Endowment for the Humanities when I applied for a fellowship to support work on this translation. David Ihrman, my colleague at Grand Valley State University, Allendale, Michigan, commented on the complete draft of the Introduction. Other colleagues at Grand Valley State University, especially Fran

Kelleher, Tony Travis, Jim Smither, Gretchen Galbraith, Carolyn Shapiro-Shapin, Cliff Welch, and Jim Goode, and my new colleagues at Oklahoma State University offered valuable help of various kinds, including text editing and computer assistance. I am particularly grateful to Dr. Wu Yanhong at the History Institute of the Chinese Academy of Social Sciences, who provided me with a punctuated manuscript of the earliest annotated edition of the *Code—Code with Commentaries and Explication of Questions* (Lü jie bianyi)—and critically read the draft of the Introduction. I am deeply indebted to my wife, Wang Yonglan, and my daughters, Elizabeth and Angela, without whose contribution I might never have completed this work.

Research support over the years came from different sources. Several travel grants from the Center for East Asian Studies at the University of Chicago and Friends of the Library at Princeton University made it possible for me to collect various editions of the *Code*. A Summer Research Stipend from Grand Valley State University in 1998 and a National Endowment for the Humanities Fellowship for College Teachers in 2001 enabled me to complete the manuscript. I have also benefited from the comments of three anonymous readers. And I am obliged to Lorri Hagman, Michael Duckworth, Marilyn Trueblood, and Pamela Bruton for editorial help.

This work is dedicated to my parents and my teachers. My parents have given me valuable spiritual support and patiently encouraged my career, both in China and in the United States. I am most grateful to three of my teachers at the University of Minnesota: Edward Farmer, Ann Waltner, and Romeyn Taylor. In fact, the first part of the translation was accomplished as a course assignment when I took their yearlong "Yuan-Ming-Qing" seminar in the early 1990s. Over the years, they have been extremely generous with their time in offering me diverse perspectives on Chinese and world history, editing my writings, and sharing their personal libraries. Most important, they have served as positive personal models as well as caring teachers and learned scholars. Their profound effect on me as a person and teacher/scholar is beyond description. I am solely responsible for the errors and shortcomings that remain in the book.

Note on the Translation

This translation is based on the text of *The Great Ming Code* contained in Gao Ju, ed., *Da Minglü jijie fuli* (*The great Ming code* with commentaries attached by regulations), originally published during the Wanli reign (1573–1619) and reprinted in five volumes by Taiwan Xuesheng Shuju in 1970. I have also consulted other editions as listed in the Bibliography.

The translation contains the text of *The Great Ming Code* as it was finalized in 1397: "The Imperial Preface"; diagrams on the five punishments, punishment instruments, mourning degrees, the Six Illicit Goods, the meanings of eight characters used in the general principles; and the main body of the document. The 382 regulations (*li*) that were attached to the *Code* during the Wanli reign are not translated. The text that appears in parentheses ( ) refers to the interlinear legal notes, which are an integral part of the *Code*. The text that appears in square brackets [ ] and chapter, section, and article numbers were not originally part of the *Code* but are my own explanatory material.

In rendering English equivalents for Chinese legal and official terms, I have referred, among many other works, to the usage of Wallace Johnson (*The T'ang Code*), Edward Farmer (*Zhu Yuanzhang and Early Ming Legislation*), William Jones (*The Great Qing Code*), Derk Bodde and Clarence Morris (*Law in Imperial China*), Charles Hucker (*A Dictionary of Official Titles in Imperial China*), and E-tu Zen Sun (*Ch'ing Administrative Terms*). The pinyin system of romanization of Chinese terms is used throughout.

Ming Units of Measure and Money

1. Length	1 *fen*	=	10 *li*
	1 *cun*	=	10 *fen*
	1 *chi*	=	10 *cun*
		=	12.3 inches (approx.)
		=	31.8 centimeters (approx.)
	1 *zhang*	=	10 *chi*
	1 *li*	=	1/3 mile
		=	572.4 meters (approx.)
2. Weight	1 *qian*	=	1/10 *liang* = 0.13 ounces
	1 *liang* (tael)	=	1.3 ounces
	1 *jin*	=	16 *liang*
		=	1.3 pounds (approx.)
		=	590 grams
3. Capacity	1 *sheng*	=	0.99 quart (approx.)
	1 *dou*	=	10 *sheng*
		=	9.635 liters
	1 *shi/dan* (picul)	=	10 *dou*
		=	99 quarts
		=	3.1 bushels
4. Area	1 *mu* (mou)	=	0.14 acre
		=	607.7 square meters (approx.)
	1 *qing*	=	100 *mu*
5. Money	1 *guan*	=	1,000 *wen*

SOURCES: "Ming Weights and Measures," in Mote and Twitchett, *Cambridge History of China*, vol. 8, pt. 2; Zheng Tianting et al., *Zhongguo lishi da cidian*, 3458–62.

Introduction: The Making of *The Great Ming Code*

The Great Ming Code (Da Ming lü) is one of the most important law codes in Chinese history.[1] An essential part of the social reform efforts of the early Ming dynasty (1368–1644),[2] the *Code* provided the empire with a definitive statement of values and social norms. It was inherited by the subsequent Manchu Qing dynasty (1644–1911) and also copied to a significant extent by China's neighboring countries: Korea, Vietnam, and Japan. The *Code*, therefore, is a significant source for understanding not only Chinese history and law but also East Asian cultural interactions. This introduction examines this legal milestone's historical context, codification process, structure and basic principles in terms of criminal law, and status as the fundamental law of the Ming dynasty.

Background: The Founding of the Ming Dynasty

The Ming dynasty was founded by Zhu Yuanzhang (1328–98),[3] the second of only two commoners to become emperor of China. The Ming dynasty marked an era of Chinese cultural restoration after the Mongol Yuan dynasty (1271–1368). The restoration, however, was by no means a replica of earlier Han Chinese models; it also signified a time of reform and redefinition. The Ming reforms, in turn, strongly influenced Chinese government and society for nearly six centuries. As the last native dynasty to rule China, the Ming inspired the Chinese revolutionaries who overthrew the Qing dynasty and founded China's first republic at the turn of the twentieth century.[4]

The Ming founder, Zhu Yuanzhang, was born near Fengyang (in present-day Anhui) at a time of weak government and social disorder.[5] During the first half of the fourteenth century, the Mongol Yuan court was plagued with factional strife. Frequent palace coups and regicides were the results of competition between the Mongolia-based faction, orientated toward Mongol interests in the Central Asian part of the empire, and the China-based group, which was more concerned with the Confucian way of governing the realm.[6] While the Yuan government failed to function at both the central and local levels, the country was gradually torn apart by regional warlords and bandits, and the people's livelihood deteriorated due to exploitation by local elites and to plague and other natural disasters. In 1351, when Toghto, chancellor of the Yuan government, conscripted about 150,000 peasants to work on rechanneling the Yellow River and reopening the Grand Canal, some workers led by Han Shantong rose in rebellion. Under the influence of the White Lotus sect of Buddhism, which centered on the worship of the messianic figure of the Buddha Maitreya, and Manicheism, which stressed the struggle between the forces of light and darkness, the rebels (known as the Red Armies because of the red turbans they wore) swept through the Huai and Yangzi Valleys. Before long, three major branches of rebels emerged: the western Red Turbans, led by Xu Shouhui (d. 1360)[7] and Chen Youliang (d. 1363);[8] the northern Red Turbans, headed by Han Liner (d. 1367),[9] Liu Futong, and Guo Zixing (d. 1355);[10] and the non–Red Turban rebels, under Zhang Shicheng (1321–67)[11] in Suzhou and under Fang Guozhen (d. 1374)[12] in Zhejiang. The Yuan Empire was shattered.[13]

Emerging from this background, Zhu Yuanzhang eventually became the victor who conquered and united the realm. A boy from a poor family of tenant farmers, as he often acknowledged later on, the future emperor experienced the hardship of the common people (*buyi*) and witnessed the corruption of government officials during his youth.[14] In 1344, when he was only sixteen years old, Zhu was orphaned as a result of the natural disasters of locusts, drought, and plague. Unable to support himself by farming, he entered the Huangjue Temple as a novice. But he was soon sent out by the monks to beg for his own food. For three years before he returned in 1347, Zhu wandered the Huai River region, where he might have encountered and been influenced by adherents of White Lotus Buddhism and Manicheism. In 1352, after the Huangjue Temple was burned by the Yuan armies, Zhu joined the Red Turban rebels under Guo Zixing.[15]

Zhu Yuanzhang's road to the imperial throne was long and tortuous. He began as a soldier—at the very bottom rank—and gradually moved up to squad leader, to low-ranking officer, and to regional commander. During his military career, time and again he faced the threat of death either from the internal strife of the rebels or on the battlefield. Several crucial steps marked his rise to supremacy. Thanks to his ability and personality, in 1352, only a few months after he had joined Guo Zixing, he was married to Guo's adopted daughter, the future Empress Ma (1332–82),[16] which tied him to the local rebel authority. In 1356, Zhu captured Jiqing City and renamed it Yingtian (In Response to Heaven); this city would eventually become his capital. As regional commander, Zhu involved himself on several fronts. In military affairs, he relied on such able generals as Xu Da (1332–85),[17] Deng Yu (1337–77),[18] and Chang Yuchun (1330–69)[19] to expand his territory. In statecraft, civil servants such as Li Shanchang (1314–90)[20] provided him with ideas for constructing administrative institutions. On intellectual issues, he

Introduction: The Making of The Great Ming Code

acquainted himself with Confucianism and other schools of thought by consulting advisors such as Song Lian (1310–81)[21] and Liu Ji (1311–75).[22] Even as a regional leader, Zhu involved himself with multiple aspects of government, including the establishment of various levels of government offices, construction of hydraulic works, collection of taxes on tea and salt, and issuance of copper coins. In 1364, Zhu Yuanzhang declared himself the prince of Wu and intensified his campaigns to eliminate various local rivals. In that year, his troops took Wuchang, the capital of the Han regime founded by Chen Youliang. And after several more years of fighting, Zhu destroyed two other powerful local forces in 1367: Zhang Shicheng in Suzhou and Fang Guozhen in Zhejiang. At the same time, Zhu's troops launched decisive military expeditions against the Mongol Yuan regime in the north and Chen Youding's forces in Fujian. By the end of 1367, Zhu had almost wiped out any meaningful enemy forces and was ready to declare the birth of the new dynasty.[23]

An important aspect in founding the new regime was to name the dynasty. Zhu Yuanzhang and his followers decided to adopt the title Ming ("radiance" or "brightness"), derived from Mingjiao (lit., "Religion of Radiance [Brightness]"; i.e., Manicheism), which advocated the triumph of "bright" forces over "dark" forces. By the time the Red Turbans rebelled in the mid-1350s, Manicheism had been spreading in China for over five centuries, and the Red Turban rebels turned to it for spiritual justification. One of the rebel leaders, Han Shantong, claimed to be the Prince of Radiance (Ming Wang). When he died, his son Han Liner was called the Young Prince of Radiance (Xiao Ming Wang). Zhu Yuanzhang was subordinate to Han Liner and used Han's reign title Longfeng (Dragon and Phoenix) until the end of 1366, at which time he had the puppet emperor drowned in a river and became an independent leader. By adopting the title Ming, Zhu Yuanzhang intended to declare to "all under Heaven" that his dynasty was the long-awaited "bright" world and he himself the promised savior. The character *ming*, which combines the symbols for sun and moon, also bore special meanings in Confucian cosmology. It was associated with the cosmic yang force and the southern direction and thus granted the new dynasty cosmological legitimacy to conquer the Mongol Yuan, who were located in the north and thus were associated with the yin force. The sun and moon were also essential aspects of Confucian rituals. By representing the intellectual inclinations of both the peasant rebels and Confucian scholars, therefore, the title Ming unified the different forces under Zhu Yuanzhang. On January 23, 1368, Zhu declared the founding of the Ming dynasty, adopted Hongwu (Grand Military Achievement) as his reign title, and seated his central government at Yingtian, which was renamed Nanjing later in the same year and Jingshi in 1378.[24]

During the Hongwu period (1368–98), one of the first urgent tasks for the new dynasty was to pacify the realm. When the dynasty was founded in early 1368, the Ming only controlled most parts of the south. It took the Ming founder 20 more years to expand and consolidate the empire. The Ming armies first launched the northern expedition, and on September 20, 1368, they seized the Yuan capital, Dadu (Great Capital), which was renamed Beiping (Pacified North). They then marched northwest and defeated the Yuan forces in Shanxi and Shaanxi by mid-1369. In 1371, the Ming armies invaded Sichuan and quickly destroyed the Xia regime, which had been founded by Ming Yuzhen (1331–66)[25] in 1362.[26] Another major territorial conquest took place in 1381, when the Ming forces marched to Yunnan and wiped out the local Yuan remnants there.[27] The final major military campaign to consolidate the empire occurred in the late 1380s. The Ming gathered some 200,000 troops and launched a heavy blow against the Mongols beyond the Great Wall.[28] By the end of the Hongwu reign, Ming authority was gradually extended into Outer Mongolia in the north, Hami in the northwest, Manchuria in the northeast, Guangdong and Guangxi in the south, Sichuan in the west, and Guizhou and Yunnan in the southwest. In addition, the Ming regime established tributary relations with a number of foreign countries, especially the neighboring Liuqiu, Korea, Champa, Siam, and Vietnam.[29]

The Hongwu reign also witnessed major institutional reconstructions. The military system took shape along with the military operations even before the founding of the dynasty. In 1364 the basic *weisuo* (lit., guard-battalion) units were created according to the Mongol Yuan model. Each guard contained about 5,000–5,600 soldiers, who were subdivided into 5 battalions and 10 companies. In 1393, the *weisuo* units included 326 guards and 65 independent battalions, a total of 1,200,000 soldiers. The occupation of soldier was made hereditary, and soldiers were assigned farmlands to grow crops. This "colony farm system," which combined both military and civilian duties, functioned effectively through the mid-1400s.[30]

In the early years of the Hongwu reign, the central government agencies also followed the Yuan structure. The Secretariat (Zhongshu Sheng) was the administrative agency and presided over the Six Ministries: the Ministries of Personnel, Revenue, Rites, War, Justice, and Public Works. The Censorate (Yushi Tai) was created to maintain disciplinary surveillance over officialdom, and the Chief Military Commission (Dudu Fu) commanded the armies. In 1380, the senior grand councilor, Hu Weiyong (d. 1380),[31] was charged with plotting rebellion and executed along with thousands of others. The emperor then abolished the Secretariat and took direct control of the Six Ministries into his own hands. Meanwhile he splintered the Chief Military Commission into five coequal agencies known as the Five Commissions (Wufu), each of which was responsible directly to the throne. In addition, the authority of the Censorate, which was abolished in 1380 and reinstituted under the name Du Chayuan, was fragmented and placed in the hands of low-ranking investigating censors who were also responsible directly to the emperor. The reorganization of the central government during the mid–Hongwu reign signified the growth of imperial authority and is sometimes labeled "Ming despotism" in the scholarly literature.[32]

Local administration also underwent a series of reforms. During the early years of the Hongwu period, the central provincial administrative agency was named the Branch Secretariat (Xing Zhongshu Sheng). Created in the Yuan pattern, it exercised political, economic, and military authority within its jurisdiction. In 1376, it was replaced by the Provincial Administration Commission (Chengxuan Buzheng Shi Si). The new provincial agency was primarily charged with civil, especially fiscal, affairs. Parallel to it were the Provincial Surveillance Commission (Tixing Ancha Shi Si) and the Regional Military Commission. These three agencies, known as the Three Provincial Offices (Sansi), were independent of each other and responsible directly to the central government. Below the provincial administrative level were prefectures (*fu*), subprefectures (*zhou*), and districts (*xian*). Below the district level, the commoners were organized into "communities and tithings" (*lijia*), whose heads were charged with maintaining order, settling disputes, collecting taxes, and promoting morality.[33] Furthermore, in local areas, "senior and worthy" elders were chosen to judge minor law cases involving marriage, land, and brawls.[34] Even commoners were empowered to fight corrupt officials by taking them directly to the capital.[35] Indeed, the early Ming witnessed tremendous imperial efforts to penetrate local communities to effect thorough societal reform.

Government officials were recruited through three major channels: recommendation, schooling, and civil service examinations. From time to time, "worthies" or "talents" throughout the empire were recommended to fill official posts, some of whom in a single step became ministers in the central government or provincial administration commissioners in local areas. The school that could directly produce officials was the National University (Guozi Xue; or Directorate of Education, Guozi Jian, after 1382) in the capital. The students, who numbered in the hundreds at first and then thousands in later years, were either assigned by the court from official households or recommended by local schools (hence their designation as "tribute students"). They studied a wide range of materials, such as Confucian classics and legal texts and were appointed to various government posts after graduation. Local schools, the so-called Confucian schools that were established in prefectures, subprefectures, and districts, provided candidates for the National University or for the civil service examinations. The examinations took place every three years in three stages. Students from public Confucian schools or private academies across the empire, generally known as "cultivated talents" (*xiucai*), took the examination at their provincial capitals. Those who passed the examination, the so-called provincial graduates (*juren*), who usually numbered about five hundred each time during the Hongwu reign, would then take the metropolitan examination the next year at Nanjing. Soon after that, the men who passed the metropolitan examination would be tested by the emperor himself at the imperial palace. Winners of the final examination, the metropolitan graduates (*jinshi*), would be appointed to government posts of various ranks, such as magistrates in local subprefectures and districts and senior compilers in the Hanlin Academy, the agency that was responsible for drafting and editing imperial documents. The examination subjects included Confucian classics, literary skills, history, and statecraft. The civil service examinations were first instituted at the beginning of the dynasty but were suspended from 1373 through 1384 due to the emperor's dissatisfaction with the exam results. Beginning in the mid-1380s, as a major institutional development of the Hongwu reign, the civil service examinations became a predominant way to recruit new officials and eventually led to the domination of Confucian scholar-officials in the Ming political landscape.[36]

The Ming founder, Zhu Yuanzhang, envisioned a world of frugality and simplicity based on an agricultural economy.[37] After surveying the entire population, he had his subjects classified into hereditary occupational household registers such as civilians, military, artisans, physicians, and diviners. The household registers, called "yellow books" (*huangce*), functioned not only to restrict population movement but also to assign labor tax (corvée) duties to the hereditary households. To ensure effective collection of land taxes, the emperor had the cultivated fields throughout the empire measured and had land registers known as the "fish-scaled plot books" (*yulin tuce*) compiled. Tax captains (*liangzhang*) were selected from affluent families to collect grain taxes during the summer and autumn. Although the emperor established policies unfavorable to trade, he initiated a number of measures to revive the agricultural production, which had been devastated by war. He reduced taxes for peasants, relocated people to the thinly populated areas for farming, encouraged wasteland reclamation and the building of irrigation works, and severely punished local officials who harassed the common people. By the end of the Hongwu reign, the agrarian economy had recovered, as evidenced by the increase in cultivated land, the growth of the population, and the accumulation of wealth.[38]

For Zhu Yuanzhang, the founding of the dynasty not only was a chance to increase territory and expand production but was even more an enterprise of restoring Confucian values and Chinese culture after the Mongol conquest. Indeed, when the Ming was founded, China had not been unified by a Han government for over three centuries. Zhu believed it was his mission to eliminate "barbarian" influences and reconstruct the ideal Chinese world order.[39] To be sure, during his lifetime, Zhu was influenced by many belief systems, including Buddhism, Taoism, and Manicheism,[40] and he copied Mongol government institutions to a considerable extent.[41] Nevertheless, his thought in essence embraced Neo-Confucianism, the new interpretations of Confucian ideas by scholars of the Song dynasty (960–1279).[42] Particularly in the course of seizing imperial power and establishing and consolidating his authority, Zhu was actively influenced and even taught by his Confucian advisors in various governmental posts. As early as 1358, the Jinhua Confucian Fan Zugan presented Zhu with a copy of *The Great Learning* (Daxue), one of the several core classics held in great esteem by the Song Neo-Confucians. Fan advised the future emperor to comprehend the principles of the kingly way, including the steps necessary to investigate things, extend knowledge, make the will sincere, rectify the mind, cultivate personal life, regulate the family, bring order to the state, and pacify the world. These steps were essential to obtaining and preserving the Mandate of Heaven.[43] During the Hongwu reign, despite the fact that Zhu evinced a certain distrust of the elite scholar-officials[44] (he even arbitrarily had 85 sections from the Confucian classic *Mencius* expunged),[45] the emperor predominantly drew on Neo-Confucian doctrines as sources of wisdom to interpret his world. At the court, a large number of well-known Confucian scholars assisted the emperor. Song Lian was his main Confucian advisor and introduced him to *Expanded Meaning of the Great Learning* (Daxue yanyi), by the Song Neo-Confucian Zhen Dexiu (1178–1235); Song headed several influential offices, such as the Hanlin Academy and the National University.[46] Tao An (d. 1368)[47] and Cui Liang[48] designed ritual institutions as chancellor of the Hanlin Academy and minister of rites, respectively.[49] Zhang Meihe, who wrote *The Classified Encyclopedia on the Learning of Principle* (Lixue leibian), served as a compiler in the Hanlin Academy.[50] Wu Chen (d. 1386), the grand academician of the East Hall, presented to the throne *The Record of Absolute Sincerity* (Jingcheng lu), which consisted of excerpts from Confucian classics in three categories: "Reverence of Heaven," "Loyalty to the Ruler," and "Filial Piety to Parents."[51] Through the efforts of Confucian officials, the "Four Books" and "Five Classics" with Neo-Confucian interpretations were issued to schools as standard textbooks.[52] The achievements of Confucian scholarship in the Hongwu reign led to the formation of a mature state religious orthodoxy in the Yongle period (1403–21).[53]

In order to carry out the dynasty-building programs, Zhu Yuanzhang placed enormous stress on legal constructions. He attributed the collapse of the Mongol Yuan dynasty to the relaxation of its legal system and believed that to uphold the principles of government and save the world, a network of legal institutions had to be soundly established and vigorously enforced. During his thirty-year rule, the emperor had many legal regulations produced, including *The Great Ming Code* (Da Ming lü), *The Great Ming Commandment* (Da Ming ling), *The Grand Pronouncements* (Da gao),

August Ming Ancestral Instruction (Huang Ming zuxun), and *Placard of People's Instruction* (Jiaomin bangwen).⁵⁴ He himself handled many major law cases such as those of Hu Weiyong, prestamped documents (*kongyin*), Guo Huan (d. 1385), and Lan Yu (d. 1393),⁵⁵ and he had several tens of thousands of people executed.⁵⁶ According to Edward Farmer, the legal institutions and their enforcement were essential to the founding of the dynasty and reflected the emperor's desire to save the world through comprehensive moral reform, to discipline his followers and govern the realm, to eliminate evil, and to resist the ravages of time.⁵⁷

In summary, the Ming founding was a time of enormous political, social, and cultural reconstruction under the emperor Zhu Yuanzhang. Zhu succeeded in driving out the Mongols and restoring Han rule. By restructuring government agencies, he increased imperial authority to an unprecedented degree. His socioeconomic policies created a rigid yet stable social order and restored the agrarian economy. And his efforts to purify Chinese culture resulted in the revival of Han values and the development of Confucian studies. In achieving all this, law played a significant role. The making of *The Great Ming Code*, in particular, was rooted in, and at the same time facilitated, these reform programs.

The Codification: Evolution of *The Great Ming Code*

During the Hongwu reign, the early Ming ruling elite, headed by Zhu Yuanzhang, devoted a considerable amount of attention to the compilation of the *Code*. Prior to its final promulgation in 1397, the *Code* underwent a number of revisions, and many officials and court advisors participated in the codification projects.

THE MING CODE OF 1367 (WU 1)

As early as 1364, when Zhu Yuanzhang defeated the Han regime and conquered Wuchang,⁵⁸ he began to discuss the establishment of law codes.⁵⁹ In the first month of that year, Zhu assumed the title of prince of Wu and established his own bureaucratic organization. In the next month, the Han regime was eliminated, clearing the way for Zhu to found a new dynasty. Zhu understood that "the first thing that should be done when founding a dynasty is to mend the cords of the law and the net-ropes of administration [*jigang*]."⁶⁰ Indeed, he viewed the chaotic situation at the end of the Yuan as the result of a weak government that had no authority over its subjects.

In 1367 (Zhizheng 27 of the Mongol Yuan dynasty, or Wu 1 according to Zhu Yuanzhang's calendar), the warlord Zhang Shicheng (1321–67) was destroyed by Zhu Yuanzhang, and the richest agricultural and commercial area of the country, the Jiangnan area, fell into Zhu's hands.⁶¹ This brought

Introduction: The Making of The Great Ming Code   xli

Zhu closer to the establishment of a new dynasty and made it more urgent to enact a new set of legal rules. On November 1, 1367, the Censorate, the organization in charge of disciplinary surveillance over officialdom, together with the Provincial Surveillance Commissions, was created, and surveillance commissioners were ordered to inspect local circuits in the provinces. This placed the law-compiling project higher up on the government agenda because, without clearly enacted law codes, the censors would find it difficult to maintain discipline and impeach wayward officials. This was one of the reasons that, two days later, on November 3, the Secretariat received the order from the emperor to begin compiling both the *Code* (Lü) and the *Commandment* (Ling).[62]

According to *The Veritable Records of Ming Taizu* (Ming Taizu shilu), as early as 1361, laws regarding salt, copper cash, and tea were created.[63] Later, regulations on military forces and activities were enacted.[64] By 1368, when the first fundamental *Code* was promulgated, three legal principles could be found in Zhu's remarks. First, law and ritual were viewed as basic elements in governing the realm. Only when law and ritual were established could the people's minds and hearts be at ease and the social order stabilized. It was law and ritual that enabled an extremely weak child to live in the world and not be afraid of being bullied by strong adults. It was also the failure of law enforcement that had caused the Yuan ruling house to lose the realm.[65]

Second, law should be lenient. Law was an instrument to carry out the Heavenly will, which advocated growth and abhorred death. The purpose of law was to save people rather than to kill them. Especially in a newly conquered realm, implementing a lenient law code was the appropriate way to govern.[66]

Third, law should be simple. In 1367, when Zhu Yuanzhang ordered Li Shanchang (1314–90)[67] and others to compile the basic *Code*, he instructed them that it was important to make the law simple, with straightforward words and clear meanings, so that people would easily understand it and thus avoid getting trapped, and so that evil functionaries (*li*) would find no loopholes to practice fraud. If the meshes of a net were too close, no big fish would be left; likewise, if the meshes of law were too close, no good people would be left in the country. One of the reasons that the Yuan lost control over the realm, said Zhu, was that the functionaries played with numerous regulations and badly harmed the people.[68]

Zhu Yuanzhang not only laid out the principles for drafting the law but also took an active part in some specific codification decisions. He ordered members of the code-drafting commission to consider each article with all their hearts and then to present them to him daily so he could discuss the articles with them.[69] For fifty days, Zhu often summoned his officials to the Western Pavilion to discuss the contents of the law codes. During the discussions, whenever he considered an article inappropriate and changed it, his officials offered no opposition. This sometimes concerned him. He hoped that they would argue against him so that the important law codes (*xingfa*) would achieve the "happy medium" (*zhong*). But still nobody opposed his "wise judgment." After the draft was finished, Zhu and his officials once again examined the law codes, changing the complex articles into simple ones and many severe punishments into light ones.[70]

We do not have much evidence concerning Zhu Yuanzhang's specific recommendations during the codification process, although two episodes give us some clues. On October 18, 1367, about two weeks before a group of officials were formally ordered to draft the codes, Zhu Yuanzhang ordered that the regulation on "collective prosecution" (*lianzuo*) be eliminated from the law code except in the case of some particularly heinous crimes. In the *Veritable Records*, this story was cited as evidence of Zhu's "lenient law code" principle.[71]

Another episode occurred on December 21 of the same year, two days before the draft law codes were completed. Since Zhu Yuanzhang believed that the complex and numerous Yuan regulations made it possible for functionaries to find opportunities to do evil, he wanted the *Code* of the new dynasty to be simple. The example he mentioned on that day was the "Seven Homicides" (*qisha*): killing by plotting, killing with intention, killing in affrays and blows, killing by mistake, killing in play, killing by negligence, and killing while forcibly taking away prisoners. These seven crimes had already been listed in *The Tang Code*.[72] To Zhu, the first three kinds of homicide all deserved the death penalty and thus did not need to be distinguished, and the fourth one was not really different from the fifth and sixth. It seemed that at most these six actions could be defined as two crimes.[73] We do not know how court officials responded to these opinions; the remnants of the early *Ming Code* and the extant texts of its later versions tell us that both the "collective prosecution" and "seven homicides" still existed in the Ming fundamental law.

The specific task of compiling the law codes was taken up by officials from the Secretariat, the top-echelon policy-making agency in the central government, and other offices. On November 3, 1367, Left Grand Councilor (Zuo Xiangguo) Li Shanchang was appointed to be the chief legislator (*zongcai guan*) to lead a commission for drafting the law codes.[74] Twenty-nine other officials served on this commission;[75] they came from the following institutions:

SECRETARIAT:

 Yang Xian (d. 1370), assistant administrator[76]
 Fu Huan, assistant administrator[77]
 Xu Ben, director of the Right Office[78]

Introduction: The Making of The Great Ming Code

CENSORATE:

Liu Ji (1311–75), vice censor-in-chief (and concurrently director of the Astrological Commission)[79]
Wen Yuanji, secretarial censor[80]
Fan Xianzu, secretarial censor[81]
Qian Yongren, registrar[82]
Sheng Yuanfu, investigating censor[83]
Wu Quji, investigating censor
Zhao Lin, investigating censor
Cui Yongtai, investigating censor
Zhang Chuncheng, investigating censor
Xie Ruxin, investigating censor

HANLIN ACADEMY:

Tao An (1312?–68), Hanlin academician[84]

COURT OF JUDICIAL REVIEW:

Zhou Zhen, chief minister[85]
Liu Weijing, vice minister[86]
Zhou Zhen, assistant minister[87]
Chen Min, case reviewer[88]
Sun Zhong, case reviewer

LOCAL SURVEILLANCE COMMISSIONS:

Li Xiang, surveillance commissioner of Zhejiang and other places
Pan Fu, surveillance commissioner of Hudong Circuit, Jiangxi[89]
Teng Yi, surveillance commissioner of Huguang and other places[90]
Liu Chengzhi, assistant surveillance commissioner of Zhejiang and other places[91]
Cheng Kongzhao, assistant surveillance commissioner of Zhejiang and other places[92]
Fu Minxue, assistant surveillance commissioner of Zhejiang and other places
Wang Zao, assistant surveillance commissioner of Zhejiang and other places
Lu Yongzhen, assistant surveillance commissioner of Huguang and other places
Zhang Yin, assistant surveillance commissioner of Huguang and other places
Wu Tong, assistant surveillance commissioner of Huguang and other places[93]

Among these commission members, three officials played a crucial part in completing the law codes: Li Shanchang, Liu Ji, and Zhou Zhen.

Li Shanchang had the overall authority for institutional establishments. Even before the codification work started, he petitioned Zhu Yuanzhang to eliminate collective prosecution for ordinary crimes, which reportedly initiated the drafting of the law code.[94] It is also said that in the "early Ming" Li memorialized Zhu Yuanzhang: "All law codes in previous dynasties were based on the *[Code of the] Nine Chapters* of the Han; they were not synthesized until the Tang [618–907]. Our present institutions should follow the tradition of the Tang." Zhu Yuanzhang accepted his suggestion.[95] It is not clear to what time the "early Ming" refers: did Li propose to follow the Tang tradition in drafting the *Code* of 1367 or in revising the *Code* of 1373, which copied *The Tang Code* more than the *Code* of 1367 did?[96] But *The Veritable Records of the Ming* tells us that the *Code* of 1367 was made on the basis of *The Tang Code*.[97] At any rate, Li must have played a dominant role in drafting the law codes.

Liu Ji's role in the code drafting was unique because he participated in the project as both the vice censor-in-chief of the Censorate and the director of the Astrological Commission. An advisor and strategist for Zhu Yuanzhang, Liu was closely involved in policy making at the early Ming court. He took charge of drawing a plan for enlarging the city of Nanjing, compiling the dynastic calendar (*da tongli*), and making the regulations for the new military system (*weisuo*, or guard-battalion system).[98] As a leading theorist at the court, he also had a deep impact on Zhu's thinking about the dynastic founding.[99] In legal matters, he handled law cases so successfully that Zhu appointed him the vice censor-in-chief.[100]

Zhou Zhen also had expertise in legal affairs. He was specifically ordered to draft the law codes with other high-ranking officials. According to his biography in *The History of the Ming Dynasty* (Ming shi), *The Ming Code* and *The Ming Commandment* are referred to as "[Zhou] Zhen's books" (*Zhen shu*), which clearly indicates Zhou's role in the codification work.[101] As soon as the codes were finished, Zhou was ordered to select from the codes the regulations that were directly relevant to common people and to compile them in different categories. On January 6, 1368, only fourteen days after the codes were promulgated, the simplified version of the two legal documents, *The Code and Commandment Directly Explained* (Lü ling zhijie), was promulgated.[102]

The Ming Code was completed on December 23, 1367. Unlike *The Great Ming Commandment*, which is still extant, *The Ming Code* of 1367 was lost. We are informed by surviving accounts that the whole body of law was based on *The Tang Code*. It consisted of 285 articles: 18 on "administrative rules," 63 on "revenue regulations," 14 on "rituals," 32 on "military affairs," 150 on "penal affairs," and 8 on "public works."[103] What should be noted is its struc-

Introduction: The Making of The Great Ming Code

ture. First, it did not contain a section on "punishments and general principles." Such a section had a long history in Chinese legislation. In *The Tang Code*, for example, under the title "Ming li," it deals with general principles of the law.[104] *The Ming Code* left this section out but might have placed articles on general principles in the law of "penal affairs." Second, the *Code* was constructed in six sections, each pertaining to one of the Six Ministries. This structure is dramatically different from that of *The Tang Code* and was maintained in most of the later versions of *The Ming Code*. This structure might have been influenced by *The Institutes of the Yuan Dynasty* (Yuan dianzhang) and have been intended to make the regulations easy for new officials to understand and preserve.[105]

That the first *Ming Code* was lost causes some problems in studying early Ming law. For instance, do the Chinese characters *lü ling* refer to two different codes or only one document? In other words, did the law compilers during the dynastic founding write both the *Code* and the *Commandment* or only the latter? Charles Hucker states that the *Code* and *Commandment* refer to the same document: the law, *lüling*, "was the rudimentary, one-volume Ming Law Code (*Ta Ming ling*) of 1368, which underwent several revisions thereafter and achieved final form, in 460 articles, in 1397 (entitled *Ta Ming lü*)."[106] This, however, contradicts several key historical records. First, in "The Imperial Preface" to promulgate *The Great Ming Commandment*, Zhu Yuanzhang viewed the *Code* and *Commandment* as separate texts with different functions. The former, he stated, was a set of stipulations to rectify deviates; the latter was a set of rules to lead people.[107] This is verified by the extant *Great Ming Commandment*, in which the articles do not contain any specific penalties for violators. The penalties are supposed to be stipulated in the *Code*.[108] Second, the *Code* and *Commandment* are distinguished in the historical materials. According to *The Veritable Records of the Ming*, for example, the *Commandment* formed an independent text that consisted of 145 articles; the *Code* was another document and was composed of 285 articles.[109] It is not clear whether the two codes were promulgated together or separately. In either case, however, *The Ming Code* was an independent set of statutes that served as the fundamental legal basis for the administration of justice in the early Ming.[110]

Information from surviving historical sources help us gain a sketchy idea about the first *Ming Code*. Immediately after the law codes were finished and promulgated, Zhu Yuanzhang ordered Chief Minister of the Court of Judicial Review Zhou Zhen to compile simplified versions. This resulted, on January 6, 1368, in *The Code and Commandment Directly Explained*.[111] Then, in the summer of 1373, another compilation of the law codes, entitled *Lü ling*, was completed and issued to various government offices.[112] These shortened versions of the law code give us some idea of the content of *The Ming Code*. These law compilation activities suggest that in the early Ming *The Ming Code* and *The Great Ming Commandment* served as the fundamental law of the newly established regime and were intended to function as the basic code of conduct for both officials and common people.

THE GREAT MING CODE OF 1374 (HONGWU 7)

The first *Ming Code* and *The Great Ming Commandment* were compiled in only fifty days, from November 3 to December 23, 1367. The first *Code* met the needs of administering justice in the first years of the dynasty, but the Ming founder was aware of its flaws. In the eighth month of 1368, believing that some stipulations in the *Code* and *Commandment* were still inappropriate in meting out punishments, Zhu Yuanzhang began preparation for code revision. He ordered four Confucian scholars and officials from the Ministry of Justice to explain *The Tang Code* to him. Twenty articles from the Tang law were selected for discussion every day: the ruler and the officials of the new regime tried very hard to keep the essence of past laws and to establish a durable law code.[113]

The revision was a long process. On April 27, 1372, an elaborate article entitled "Intruding into the Imperial Procession" was written.[114] In 1373, the article "Mutual Concealment by Relatives" was revised.[115]

On January 6, 1374, Minister of Justice Liu Weiqian was formally ordered to revise the old version of *The Ming Code*.[116] As usual, the emperor played a key role in the codification. As soon as a chapter was drafted, it was presented to the throne; then Zhu Yuanzhang had it pasted on the walls of the corridors and personally deliberated on it.[117] By the second month of 1374 (March 14–April 12), the revised version of the law code was completed and presented to the throne with a memorial written by the academician of Hanlin Academy Song Lian.

The text of the new law code is also lost. Its general contents can be reconstructed only on the basis of some scattered sources.

For the first time in Ming legal history, the basic law code was entitled *The Great Ming Code*.[118] This title was also adopted by the final (1397) version of the *Code* and was copied by *The Great Qing Code*.[119]

The 606 articles of the new *Code* derived from several sources: 288 were adopted from the old *Code*,[120] 128 from subsequent stipulations (*lü*) that were separate from the *Code*, 36 from the old *Commandment* (*ling*), 31 from concrete circumstances, and 123 from *The Tang Code*.[121]

The *Code* entirely followed the structure of *The Tang Code*. Its 30 sections (*juan*) were grouped within 12 chapters: "Punishments and General Principles" (Mingli), "Imperial Guard and Prohibitions" (Weijin), "Administrative Regulations" (Zhizhi), "Households and Marriage" (Huhun), "Government Stables and Granaries" (Jiuku), "Unauthorized Moving of

Troops and Levying of Labor Services" (Shanxing), "Violence and Robbery" (Zeidao), "Assaults and Accusations" (Dousong), "Fraud and Counterfeit" (Zhawei), "Miscellaneous Articles" (Zalü), "Arrest and Flight" (Buwang), and "Judgment and Imprisonment" (Duanyu).[122] An obvious structural change from the *Code* of 1367 was that a chapter on "general principles" was restored to the basic law, which fits the tradition of Chinese legal culture.

The "Punishments and General Principles" chapter explicitly stipulated five types of punishments, with 20 degrees of severity. While the penal system emphasized an age-old tradition, it differed from the Tang system in that the additional punishment of beating with a heavy stick was attached to the punishments of penal servitude and life exile.[123]

THE GREAT MING CODE OF 1376 (HONGWU 9)

In 1376, the *Great Ming Code* underwent another major revision, and once again, the process was initiated by the emperor. On November 22, 1376, Zhu Yuanzhang informed Left Grand Councilor Hu Weiyong (d. 1380)[124] and Censor-in-Chief Wang Guangyang (d. 1380)[125] that he was still concerned about the "happy medium" (*zhongdao*) of the *Code*, and he ordered them to revise it in accordance with the principles of "leniency" (*kuan*) and "simplicity" (*jian*).

The *Great Ming Code* of 1376 does not survive either, which again leaves a number of problems for later historians. One problem concerns the total number of articles *The Great Ming Code* contained after this revision. Supposedly, 13 articles were changed,[126] and the remaining 446 articles stayed the same as those in the *Code* of 1374.[127] Huang Chang-chien notes that the meaning of the reference in *The Veritable Records of the Ming* is rather ambiguous: was 446 the total number of articles of the *Code* or the number of remaining articles (as opposed to the number of revised articles)? Huang argues for the latter case: in 1376, 13 articles were revised, the rest (446 articles) remained the same, and so the total number of articles in the *Code* was 459. He supports his proposition by arguing that an article concerning "court audience tablets" was added to the *Code* in 1386,[128] and the book *The Code with Commentaries and Explication of Questions* (Lü jie bianyi) shows that at least in 1389 the *Code* contained 460 articles. Therefore, the *Code* in 1376 should have 459 articles, which would accord with the number of articles in the *Code* of 1389.[129]

Huang Chang-chien's hypothesis remains problematic. According to *The Veritable Records of the Ming*, on April 22, 1378, the government had already begun to produce audience tablets for civil and military court officials, and there already existed some stipulation in the *Code* to punish any violation of the regulated usage of the tablets (*lun ru lü*).[130] It seems that the regulation regarding court audience tablets already existed in the *Code* in 1376, but it was not enforced until 1378. The Hongwu reign was a period of institutional creation, in which new regulations emerged from time to time. Consequently, the contents of *The Great Ming Code* might have been constantly changing. For example, on January 18, 1382, the system of "matching tallies" (*kanhe*) was first introduced in government offices.¹³¹ We are not informed explicitly that this was related to the establishment of the article "Transferring Expenditures or Receipts" (Nuoyi chuna) in the *Code*,¹³² but because the system was not initiated until 1382, it would seem unlikely that the article could exist before that year. In a word, it is hard to argue that during the 10 years between 1376 and 1386, only one article was added to the *Code*. Huang himself has noticed that several articles were changed in 1380 that were recorded in neither *The Veritable Records of the Ming* nor *The History of the Ming Dynasty*.¹³³ In any case, *The Great Ming Code* had gone through another substantial change only about two years after it was revised in 1374.

Another problem is how the *Code* was transformed from its 1374 version to that of 1376. According to *The Veritable Records of the Ming*, the latter contained only 459 articles (as Huang Chang-chien argues), of which 13 were changed and the rest (446 in Huang's formula) remained the same as their 1374 versions (*yurugu*). But the *Code* of 1374 was composed of 606 articles; no matter how we calculate, the "rest" would not be 446. It seems that before the revision of 1376, the *Code* had already been substantially changed. But no evidence is presently available and we must await new materials to clarify this point.

The Great Ming Code in The Code with Commentaries and Explication of Questions

The Great Ming Code of 1376 is also lost, but Huang Chang-chien suggests that the text of that *Code* is preserved in *The Code with Commentaries and Explication of Questions* (Lü jie bianyi), written by He Guang, a native of Songjiang Prefecture, during the mid–Hongwu period.¹³⁴ According to the author's preface and Que Jing's postscript dated spring 1386, the work was made to solve problems in understanding the *Code*.¹³⁵ Because it was published before 1389, when another substantial revision took place, Huang argues that *The Great Ming Code* copied in this book was almost identical to that of 1376.¹³⁶

The Great Ming Code in *The Code with Commentaries and Explication of Questions* contains 30 sections and 460 articles. Its chapter and article titles and sequence are identical to those in the *Code* of 1397. The major differences between the earlier text and its final version are some specific crimes and punishments in only several articles. In the article "Fornication between Rel-

Introduction: The Making of The Great Ming Code   xlix

atives," for instance, the early *Code* has the stipulation "In case of fornication with adopted daughters, the penalty shall be increased by one degree,"[137] but this is eliminated from the *Code* of 1397 (Art. 392). Despite the minor differences, we may tentatively conclude that before 1389, *The Great Ming Code* had taken its basic form.

THE GREAT MING CODE OF 1389 (HONGWU 22)

The Great Ming Code underwent another change in 1389. This time, the reform was initiated by officials instead of the emperor. In the eighth month of that year, officials from the Ministry of Justice memorialized that in recent years, articles in the *Code* were constantly being added or deleted. It was very difficult for local judicial officers and newly appointed officials to keep track of all the changes and this caused unjust judgments to be made. The officials suggested that new regulations be added to the *Code* in appropriate categories so people would know where to find them. Zhu Yuanzhang accepted the proposal and ordered the officials of Hanlin Academy and the Ministry of Justice to revise the *Code*.[138]

This *Code* still consisted of 460 articles.[139] The titles of its seven chapters and 30 sections and the total number of articles in each chapter and section are identical to the *Code* quoted in *The Code with Commentaries and Explication of Questions* and its final version of 1397.

According to *The Veritable Records*, a major structural change was made: previously the chapter "Punishments and General Principles" (Minglü) was placed after "Judgment and Imprisonment" (Duanyu), that is, at the end of the law. In 1389, however, it was moved to the beginning of the text.[140] Some confusion is caused by this entry in *The Veritable Records*. First, we have noted that "Punishments and General Principles" had already been made the first chapter in the *Code* of 1374. Was the code structure changed after 1374 or is this entry mistaken?[141] Second, the record implies that the chapter "Judgment and Imprisonment" was the penultimate one in the previous *Code*. This indicates that the revision of the *Code* in 1389 was based on its 1374 version, which followed the structural model of *The Tang Code*. This apparently contradicts the structure of the *Code* of 1386 that we observe in He Guang's *Code with Commentaries and Explication of Questions*. Thus, we wonder: is this entry an error, or are the dates of the preface and postscript in He Guang's book mistaken? All these doubtful points need to be clarified by further evidence.

The History of the Ming Dynasty tells us of five basic characteristics of *The Great Ming Code* of 1389.[142] First, there are five punishments. The least severe is beating with the light stick (*chi*), for which there are five degrees of severity, from 10 to 50 strokes. Then there is beating with the heavy stick (*zhang*), with five degrees of severity, from 60 to 100 strokes. Next comes penal servitude (*tu*), from one to three years, including beating with the heavy stick for 60 to 100 strokes; there are five degrees of punishment depending on number of years of servitude and number of strokes. Then there are the three degrees of life exile (*liu*), from 2,000 to 3,000 *li*, with beating with the heavy stick for 100 strokes. The death penalty (*si*) had two degrees, depending on whether death was by strangulation or decapitation. Some other punishments, such as military exile (*chongjun*) and sentencing to death by slicing (*lingchi*), were stipulated in some specific articles but not listed in the five punishments diagram.

The second characteristic is the mourning-degree (*sangfu*) system. Eight diagrams concerning mourning requirements according to one's relationship to the deceased were placed in front of the text.[143] Crimes among relatives were to be punished in accordance with the degree of their mourning relationship. Concealment of crimes by relatives would not be punished, or the punishments would be reduced. Relatives could not marry each other.

The third characteristic is the specification of the Ten Abominations (Shie): plotting rebellion, plotting great sedition, plotting treason, contumacy, depravity, great irreverence, lack of filial piety, discord, unrighteousness, and incest. Such crimes would not be pardoned even when a general amnesty had been proclaimed.

The fourth characteristic is the specification of the Six Illicit Goods (Liuzang): supervisors or custodians themselves stealing from granaries or treasuries, ordinary people stealing from granaries or treasuries, theft, taking illicit goods by perverting the law, taking illicit goods without perverting the law, and obtaining illicit goods through malfeasance.

The fifth characteristic is the specification of the Eight Deliberations (Bayi): deliberation of crimes on the basis of imperial relatives, old retainers of the emperor, heroic achievement, the morally worthy, those with great ability, those who are diligent, those in high positions, and guests of the dynasty.

THE GREAT MING CODE IN *THE GREAT MING CODE DIRECTLY EXPLICATED*

Insofar as *The Great Ming Code* was influential in China's neighboring countries, the Korean *Great Ming Code Directly Explicated* (Taemyong yul chehae) will help us understand the evolution of the *Ming Code*. In 1392, Yi Song-gye (1355–1408) established the long-lasting Yi dynasty (1392–1911).[144] The new Korean regime considered *The Great Ming Code* a model law code and decided to use it in governing its territory. Only three years after the founding of the dynasty, a Korean version of *The Great Ming Code* entitled *The Great Ming Code Directly Explicated* was finished by Ko Sa-Kyong and Kim Chi[145] and was promulgated in 1395. Because it was made after 1389

Introduction: The Making of The Great Ming Code

(Hongwu 22) but before 1397 (Hongwu 30), it is very likely that the Korean law code copied *The Great Ming Code* of 1389.[146]

The Great Ming Code quoted in *The Great Ming Code Directly Explicated* has the same number of sections and articles and the same chapter and section titles as recorded in *The Veritable Records of the Ming* and *The History of the Ming Dynasty*. When compared to the *Code* in the *Code with Commentaries and Explication of Questions*, *The Great Ming Code* of 1389 shares a great deal in common with its early version: they have the same seven chapters, 30 sections, and 460 articles. Their contents are almost identical. Only 7 articles in the *Code* of 1389 are arranged in a different sequence (but still within the same sections as those in the early text).[147]

Although there are many literary differences between the two versions of the *Code* (i.e., the Korean version and *The Code with Commentaries*), the major changes appear in only four articles (still under the same article titles). In the article "Plotting Rebellion or Great Sedition," the *Code* of 1389 changed the penalty for the criminal's father and sons of 16 years of age and older from "decapitation" in the earlier document to "strangulation."[148] In the article "Counterfeiting Imperial Rescripts," the new law distinguishes the principal criminals from accessories: the latter shall be strangled instead of being decapitated as in the old law. In the article "Fraudulently Transmitting Imperial Orders," the penalty for fraudulently transmitting orders of imperial princes is changed from "strangulation" in the old law to "100 strokes of beating with the heavy stick and life exile to 3,000 *li*." Finally, in the article "Officials or Functionaries Accepting Property" the penalty of "banishment" for those who act as intermediaries and deliver the money in the old law is eliminated.[149] Huang Chang-chien asserts that *The Great Ming Code* of 1389 was based more on *The Tang Code*, and thus some penalties became lighter.[150]

THE GREAT MING CODE OF 1397 (HONGWU 30)

According to *The History of the Ming Dynasty*, before it was finalized in 1397, *The Great Ming Code* underwent its last revision. Imperial Grandson-Heir Zhu Yunwen, a person of compassionate character, started the project. He memorialized that law should aid in the transformation of the people, and thus all the penalties for crimes concerning the "five relationships" (i.e., ruler–minister, father–son, husband–wife, older brother–younger brother, and friend–friend) in the *Code* should be reduced so as to foster "human sentiment." His proposal was approved by the emperor. Consequently, the imperial grandson-heir referred to the ritual classics and law codes in previous dynasties and changed 73 articles in the *Code* which contained extraordinarily severe penalties.[151]

When did this revision take place? *The Veritable Records of the Ming* does not give an account of the event.¹⁵² The "Treatise on Punishments" in *The History of the Ming Dynasty* records that the imperial grandson-heir proposed the revision in 1389,¹⁵³ but Zhu Yunwen was only 12 years old at this time, and Heir Apparent Zhu Biao (1355–92) was still living. Therefore, it is not likely that Zhu Yunwen could have made such a proposal and led the work. The "Basic Annals of Gongmin di" in *The History of the Ming Dynasty* has a slightly different account but does not give a specific date. I suspect that this revision might have occurred sometime between the ninth month of 1392, when Zhu Yunwen was appointed the imperial grandson-heir,¹⁵⁴ and the fifth month of 1397, when the final version of *The Great Ming Code* was officially promulgated.¹⁵⁵ We do not have any evidence concerning exactly what penalties were changed in this project.¹⁵⁶

The Great Ming Code was finalized in 1397. On May 29, 1397, Zhu Yuanzhang ascended the Meridian Gate and issued the following decree to announce *The Great Ming Code with Pronouncements* (Da Ming lü gao) to his officials:

> I have the realm and govern it by imitating antiquity. Rituals are manifested to guide the people; law codes are established to restrain the wayward. They were promulgated in statutes and carried out for a long time. Nevertheless, there were still many who violated them. Therefore, in my spare time, after dealing with governmental affairs, I wrote *The Grand Pronouncements* [Dagao; see disc] and clearly displayed it among the people, causing them to know the way to pursue good fortune and avoid bad luck. People in antiquity referred to "[carrying out] punishments" as "carefully employing punishments." Don't I hope that people can live between Heaven and Earth?¹⁵⁷ But since law is kept in government offices, people cannot understand all the stipulations. So I ordered judicial officials to look up the articles in *The Grand Pronouncements* and select the most important ones to attach to the *Code*. All [laws posted on] placards and interdicts shall be eliminated. Except for plotting rebellions and what is stipulated in *The Code with Pronouncements*, all the miscellaneous major or minor crimes shall be judged in accordance with the *Regulation on Redemption of Crimes*. Now the law is codified and promulgated to the capital and local areas, so that the realm will know what to observe. The purpose of punishments is to stop using punishments. Accord with my intention of careful employment of punishments.¹⁵⁸

The text of *The Great Ming Code* of 1397 has survived to the present.¹⁵⁹ The titles of the seven chapters, 30 sections, and 460 articles in the new *Code* are the same as in the Korean edition, although the sequence of several articles is different.¹⁶⁰ As mentioned in the imperial proclamation, an obvious change in the new text is the attachment of a regulation entitled

The Imperially Approved Code and Pronouncements (Qin ding lü gao).¹⁶¹ This regulation contains a list of "true capital crimes" (*zhenfan sizui*) and "miscellaneous capital crimes" (*zafan sizui*). The former cannot be redeemed but the latter can (i.e., the punishment can be commuted to a monetary or labor penalty). The capital crimes were selected from both *The Great Ming Code* and *The Grand Pronouncements*, which accounts for why the *Code* is called *The Great Ming Code and Pronouncements* (Da Ming lü gao) in some historical records.¹⁶²

The new regulation is an appendix to *The Great Ming Code* and is not a part of the basic law.¹⁶³ To a certain extent, however, it does change the way in which the capital crimes in the *Code* are treated. In most cases, the punishment in the new regulation is similar to that stipulated in the law code. The differences appear in 45 articles, of which 9 alleviate death penalties in the *Code*. Although the crimes remain punishable by death, they can be redeemed with money or labor.¹⁶⁴ The remaining 36 articles, on the other hand, increase the severity of the penalties in the *Code*. They either increase the penalty from beating with the light or heavy stick or penal servitude to death¹⁶⁵ or add new crimes.¹⁶⁶ After the death of Zhu Yuanzhang in 1398, this regulation was no longer taken seriously by later emperors.¹⁶⁷

Other differences between *The Great Ming Code* of 1397 and of 1389 appear in seven articles.¹⁶⁸ In "Redeeming Punishment by Those Who Are Aged, Juvenile, or Disabled" (Art. 21), certain conditions for punishing those who are 80 years of age or older, 10 years of age or younger, or incapacitated are changed: if such persons commit crimes involving homicide or other actions punishable by the death penalty, the matter shall be considered and a provisional sentence shall be proposed, and petition shall be made to the emperor for decision by the throne. But in the old law, the crimes for which petition can be made to the throne on behalf of these persons include rebellion and great sedition (i.e., acts that endanger the emperor and destroy imperial ancestral temples, etc.). In other words, the conditions in the new law have become stricter.

In "Reporting Military Information at Full Speed" (Art. 223), prefecture and district magistrates are no longer permitted to take advantage of the government relay station system to report military affairs to the throne. Instead, they shall send the reports to their provincial offices, which in turn are responsible for sending the reports to the central government offices and the emperor.

In "Plotting Rebellion and Great Sedition" (Art. 277), the penalty for the criminal's close relatives is increased:

> Their paternal grandfather, father, sons, sons' sons, brothers, those living in the same household whether or not their surnames differ [from the criminal's], paternal uncles and brothers' sons whether or not they are in different

household registers, and [male] relatives of 16 years of age and older, including those who are incapacitated or disabled, shall all be punished by decapitation.

In "Officials or Functionaries Accepting Property" (Art. 367), the penalty of banishment for those who act as intermediaries and deliver the money is restored. In "Counterfeiting Imperial Rescripts" (Art. 378), the distinction between the principals and the accessories in the old text is left out. In "Deceitfully Transmitting Imperial Decrees" (Art. 379), the penalty for fraudulently transmitting orders of imperial princes is increased from 100 strokes of beating with the heavy stick and life exile of 3,000 *li* to strangulation. In "Committing Fornication with Relatives" (Art. 392), the stipulation in the old text that "the penalty for fornication with adopted daughters shall be increased one degree" is eliminated.[169]

We can conclude that *The Great Ming Code* of 1397 was fundamentally the same as the 1389 version. Only several minor changes were made. First, a regulation was attached to the law to affect the enforcement of death penalties in the *Code*. Second, certain articles (e.g., Art. 223) were revised to respond to the institutional reforms. Third, the new law restored some harsher punishments that were mitigated in its 1389 version (e.g., Art. 277). The newly restored harsher punishments, however, only concerned a few articles and did not change the severity of the *Code* as a whole.

The codification of *The Great Ming Code* was a long process. In imperial China, no other law code had undergone so many changes in a single reign (and then remained unchanged for several centuries). "After a considerable period of time and careful deliberation, the law of the whole dynasty [*yidai fa*] began to take form."[170] These legislative events demonstrate a number of points about the early Ming empire-building enterprise. First of all, Emperor Zhu Yuanzhang's active role in composing the *Code* was impressive. He provided guiding principles for legislation, initiated codification projects, appointed law-making officials, and personally participated in drafting specific legal provisions. Nevertheless, although—as Zhu Yuanzhang himself asserted—"it is the ruler who makes the law,"[171] the ruler's decision-making power was limited. The officials might not accept every order he issued, as illustrated in drafting the stipulations on the Seven Homicides. So from time to time he would have to make compromises with his subordinates in order to implement their "collective goals."[172] The many versions of the *Code* illustrate a constant and conscious search: the early Ming ruling elite strove to reach their goal in legal culture—the "happy medium" (*zhong*). Zhu Yuanzhang often proclaimed that he endeavored to "establish the law by examining the past [*jigu lifa*]"[173] so that he could guide the people in eliminating Mongol influence. Nevertheless, the times had changed. It was impossible for all the "present institutions to follow the traditions of

Introduction: The Making of The Great Ming Code

the Tang."[174] What traditions should be kept and what rejected? What new elements should be drawn from the present or even from Yuan institutions? These were not easy questions for the early Ming ruling elite, but through their rigorous efforts, they eventually created a new legal identity for the Chinese empire.

The Great Ming Code as a Penal Code: Its Structure and General Principles

The Great Ming Code stipulates Ming legal norms. To be more specific, it is a codification of criminal norms—a penal code. A systematically organized legal document, the *Code* defines crimes, specifies punishments, and stipulates general principles by which the punishments are applied. This section outlines the *Code*'s structure and basic principles in terms of criminal law.

STRUCTURE

The *Code* starts with the "The Imperial Preface" (Yuzhi). Originally issued by the founding emperor in the fifth month of 1397, the preface expressed the emperor's understanding of the function of the law and his intent to promulgate the combination of the *Code* and *Grand Pronouncements*.[175]

The body of the *Code* consists of seven chapters (*lü*), 30 sections, and 460 articles. All but the first three articles start with "In all cases [*fan*]." When necessary, regular-character-sized circles are used to mark separate items in a given article. In terms of criminal justice theory, the first chapter, "Laws on Punishments and General Principles" (Minglilü), which is also the first section, can be understood as the "general part" of the law code. In 47 articles, it lists basic penalties, establishes components of criminal liability, classifies crimes, and lays out general principles that are applied to all crimes.

The second through seventh chapters constitute the "special provisions" of criminal law. They are arranged in accordance with the six major categories of government functions: Personnel, Revenue, Rites, War, Justice, and Public Works. The chapters are further divided into 29 sections. They define specific crimes and stipulate relevant punishments. Generally speaking, the second chapter, "Laws on Personnel" (Lilü), deals with crimes that violate regulations on administrative operations and official documents. The third chapter, "Laws on Revenue" (Hulü), is concerned with the dynastic economic order and harmonious family relations. The fourth chapter, "Laws on Rituals" (Lilü), punishes crimes involving communication with spirit worlds, court ceremonies, and sumptuary rules. The fifth chapter, "Laws on Military Affairs" (Binglü), safeguards the security of imperial palaces and the normal functioning of military operations and transportation networks.

The sixth chapter, "Laws on Penal Affairs" (Xinglü), which constitutes nearly 40 percent of the entire *Code,* deals with crimes against the emperor, the dynasty, personal safety, property, dignity, and judicial procedure. The last chapter, "Laws on Public Works" (Gonglü), punishes violations in constructing government buildings, manufacturing goods, and maintaining dikes and roads. In 413 articles, then, these six chapters protect a whole spectrum of important social relations that could be damaged by crimes ranging from plotting rebellion to cursing others.

Each article of the *Code* starts with an unnumbered title. The titles in the first chapter clearly summarize the topics they cover. Article 29, for example, is entitled "Distinguishing Principals and Accessories in Joint Crimes." The contents of the article specify five different circumstances in which the principals and accessories are distinguished. The article titles in the second through seventh chapters are structured in two ways. Most of them name criminal acts, and they all contain a verb, with either a subject-verb, verb-object, or subject-verb-object structure. Entitled "Expelling Sons-in-Law and Marrying Off Daughters," for instance, Article 110 straightforwardly points out the accusation. Another type of title does not use verbs to designate acts but simply mentions a topic, such as "Marriages of Men and Women" (Art. 107) and "Community Wine-Drinking Ceremonies" (Art. 201).

By defining specific crimes and specifying relevant punishments, the individual articles in the second part of the *Code* (i.e., chapters 2–7) state criminal legal norms. "Criminal legal norm" refers to a government statement binding people within its jurisdiction and serving to guide, control, or prohibit their behavior. A criminal legal norm consists of three elements. (1) Rule: the regulation that permits, requires, or prohibits people's behavior. Namely, it informs people what can, should, or should not be done. (2) Conditions: the situations or circumstances under which the violation of a rule will be corrected. (3) Sanction: the remedies or punishments used to correct the violation of the rule or to guarantee the enforcement of the rule.[176] Although all criminal legal norms are composed of these three elements, their statements in formal documents sometimes differ in structure. While some articles express complete norms, others often omit certain parts for the sake of conciseness or convenience. They all, however, share one common characteristic: they all contain criminal charges and penalties.

The individual articles in the second part of the *Code* give either complete or incomplete norms. Let us first look at the first item of Article 82 as an example of a complete norm:

> In all cases [of household registration,] the various households of military people, civilians, post couriers, salt workers, physicians, diviners, artisans,

Introduction: The Making of The Great Ming Code

and musicians shall be established according to their [original] registers. For those who deceitfully claim or falsely claim [to be another sort of household] so as to escape [from their own household registers] and to avoid their heavier obligation and assume [others'] lighter obligation, they shall be punished by 80 strokes of beating with the heavy stick.

In this article, the first sentence sets up the "rule," instructing people to maintain their household registrations. The first part of the second sentence defines the "conditions" (i.e., some violations occur and thus damage the prescribed social order). The remedy of "80 strokes of beating with the heavy stick" announces the "sanction"—the legal consequence assigned to the socially deviant act. Together, these three parts make up a complete criminal legal norm.

Most articles in the *Code* express incomplete norms. Let us take Article 393 as an example:

> In all cases where sons' wives falsely accuse fathers-in-law or where younger brothers' wives falsely accuse husbands' brothers of fornication by deceit, they shall be punished by decapitation.

This article comprises two elements: "conditions" and "sanction." That is to say, under the condition that sons' or younger brothers' wives falsely accuse fathers-in-law or husbands' elder brothers of fornication, the penalty of decapitation will be inflicted. The "rule" is omitted but implied: no women shall falsely accuse their fathers-in-law or husbands' elder brothers of fornication. In this way, the law eliminates unnecessary words, but the reader is still aware of what the government permits, requires, or prohibits.

In stating "incomplete norms," the *Code* sometimes derives "rules" from other legal sources. For instance, when the *Code* forbids people to violate "sumptuary regulations" on clothing and houses (Art. 194), those regulations are established in *The Great Ming Commandment*.[177] Similarly, when it commands people to follow the "rules" on community wine-drinking ceremonies (Art. 201), those rules are laid out in the separately issued "Diagram of Community Wine-Drinking Ceremonies" (Xiang yinjiu li tushi).[178] The references to other legal texts extend the *Code*'s binding authority.

With regard to "conditions," they are not limited to the criminal charges described in the second part of the *Code*. In finding a person's criminal liability and deciding the appropriate penalty, the judge also has to invoke the general principles provided in the first chapter regarding such circumstances as time, place, status, gender, age, mental state, physical ability, and the purpose of the act. For example, Article 117 prohibits marrying runaway women:

In all cases of marrying as wives or concubines women who commit crimes and who run away, if the men know the circumstances, they shall be punished by the same penalty. If the penalty amounts to death, it shall be reduced one degree. The marriages shall be dissolved. If they do not know the circumstances, they shall not be punished. If the women do not have husbands, and amnesties are issued that exempt them from penalties, the marriages shall not be dissolved.

In order to punish the act, the law sets up several "conditions" in this article: (1) The woman commits a crime and runs away. (2) The man knows she is a runaway criminal but marries her. (3) The woman commits a capital crime by running away. (4) The man does not know her true status. (5) The woman does not have a husband. (6) An amnesty is issued. Different circumstances will decide whether or not the man shall be punished, what penalty shall be inflicted, and whether or not the marital relationship shall be maintained. In order to make a correct decision, however, these conditions are not sufficient. The judge will have to look up the conditions (general principles) dictated in the first chapter. For example, is the man a person belonging to one of the eight groups of people whose cases shall be handled specially (Arts. 3–4)? Is he a relative of those eight groups of people (Art. 9)? Is he a civil or military officer (Arts. 5–8, 12–14)? Is he a soldier (Art. 10)? Does he have old or disabled parents or paternal grandparents to take care of (Art. 18)? Is he a government artisan or musician or student of astronomy (Art. 19)? Was this crime committed after he had already been punished by penal servitude or life exile (Art. 20)? Is he old or disabled (Arts. 21–22)? Does he confess the crime voluntarily (Art. 24)? Does he commit the crime with other people (Art. 20)? Does he commit the crime at the capital (Art. 33)? Only after having deliberated on all such circumstances can a judge make an appropriate decision.

Of the 413 articles in the second part of the *Code*, all but 4 stipulate penalties for criminal acts.[179] The penalties prescribed in the *Code* are all fixed. Once crimes and conditions are determined, there will be no room for a judge's discretion and no alternative remedies to select. In stipulating penalties, three structural patterns exist in the document. The first is to use a single penalty to punish one crime. Forming "treacherous cliques," for example, will result in straightforward penalties of decapitation of the criminals themselves and enslavement of their wives and children (Art. 60). The second pattern is to set up a fixed range of punishment in three categories: the minimum penalty, penalties determined according to legally prescribed circumstances, and the maximum penalty. The penalties for theft are illustrative. If theft is committed but no goods are taken, the criminal shall be punished by 50 strokes with the light stick (the minimum penalty). If goods are taken, the penalty shall be increased. Depending on the value of the

Introduction: The Making of The Great Ming Code

property, the penalties range from 60 to 100 strokes with the heavy stick and life exile to 3,000 *li*. Although such a wide range of penalties (13 degrees) is provided, the judge has no room to exercise discretion, for each degree strictly matches the value of the stolen goods. The maximum penalty is limited to (*zuizhi*) 100 strokes with the heavy stick and life exile to 3,000 *li*. For this single crime, in other words, the death penalty is not an option (Art. 292). Many articles in the *Code* provide such a fixed penalty range, with the specific penalty determined by number of days (Art. 71), deficiencies in document files (Art. 73), plots of land (Art. 96), employed persons (Art. 247), prohibited military weapons (Art. 235), government animals (Art. 252), postal horses or boats (Art. 266), value of illicit goods (Art. 367), and so forth.

The third pattern of stipulating penalties is to invoke penalties from other articles. Here, a distinction is made between "on the basis of" (*yi*) and "as comparable to" (*zhun*). If crime A is punished "on the basis of" crime B, then all the penalties prescribed to crime B (including the death penalty) will be applicable to crime A. If crime A is punished "as comparable to" crime B, the maximum penalty cannot exceed 100 strokes with the heavy stick and life exile to 3,000 *li*.[180] The most frequently cited crimes in the *Code* include "supervisors or custodians themselves stealing" (Art. 287), "theft" (Art. 292), "officials or functionaries accepting property" (Art. 367), "committing crimes involving illicit goods obtained through malfeasance" (Art. 368), and "officials exonerating the guilty or implicating the innocent" (Art. 433). Article 436 states, for example, that if officials who examine wounds on corpses in judging cases make untrue reports, the head officials shall be punished by 60 strokes with the heavy stick. If, as a result, the penalty for the person who committed the original crime is increased or reduced because of such untrue reports, the officials who made the untrue reports shall be punished as "negligently exonerating the guilty or implicating the innocent" (Art. 433). Furthermore, if they accept property and deliberately make untrue reports on the examination, they shall be punished as "deliberately exonerating the guilty or implicating the innocent" (Art. 433). Finally, if the value of the illicit goods entails a heavier penalty than that for making an untrue report, they shall be punished by the heavier penalty as "[accepting property and] subverting the law" (Art. 367). Due to more severe social damage and their corrupt tricks, therefore, the officials are punished more harshly by comparing their actions to other crimes, and the penalty could amount to death.

Besides penalties, the *Code* also provides "reward clauses" in about 20 articles. The rewards are granted to the people who either report crimes to the government or capture criminals by themselves. The types of reward include the salt that is illegally obtained by criminals (Art. 149), others' lost goods (Art. 170), part or all of the criminals' property (Arts. 246, 277–78), and silver from the government treasury (Arts. 311–12, 381, 383). Most of the articles with reward clauses deal with grave crimes that are punished by the death penalty. The most generous rewards go to those who report to the authorities the crimes of "forming treacherous cliques" (2,000 *liang* of silver, Art. 60) and "counterfeiting paper money" (250 *liang* of silver, Art. 382). The reward clauses are apparently used to mobilize the whole society to protect the dynastic order.

In addition to the formal legal norms, the *Code* contains three types of "legal interpretation," which bear the same binding authority as the legal text. The diagrams (*tu*) provided between "The Imperial Preface" and the body of the *Code* are one type of legal interpretation. Since 1389, the Ming court had compiled the diagrams "The Five Punishments," "The Penal Instruments," and "Six Types of Illicit Goods," eight diagrams on mourning garments and mourning degrees among relatives, and the diagram "The Meanings of Eight Characters as Used in the General Principles."[181] These diagrams clarify the basic penal institution and emphasize family relationships, which guide the punishments for crimes among relatives.[182]

Another type of legal interpretation appears as part of the main text in the first chapter. Some of these articles extend the contents of legal terms. When the *Code* refers to "paternal grandparents," for example, the paternal great-grandparents and great-great-grandparents shall be considered the same (Art. 40). In Buddhist and Daoist monasteries, for another example, the disciples' relationship to their masters shall be considered the same as that to their paternal uncles and their wives (Art. 44). Other articles define the connotation of legal terms. Article 42, for instance, clarifies which people the law includes in such terms as "supervisors" and "custodians." Article 43 explains how to calculate a "day" and a "year." These legal interpretations become an essential part of the legal principles in applying the *Code* to specific law cases.

The interlinear notes within the body of the *Code* make up a third type of legal interpretation. These notes have several functions. One is to define crimes. On "public crime," for example, the note defines it as "making mistakes without private motives" (Art. 27). Another function is to clarify the scope of a term. "Living together," for instance, is explained as the situation in which "relatives have common property and dwell together" (Art. 31). The legal notes also add new meanings to the main text. "Plotting," for example, is usually considered an act by two or more persons. However, the note adds, "if the circumstances of the plot are clear and evident, although there is only one person, it shall be considered the same as two persons" (Art. 43). A fourth function of the interlinear notes is to stipulate a proviso. Children will be punished if they establish separate household registers while their parents are living. But the note provides a condition: they shall be punished only if their parents accuse them to the court in person (Art. 93). Finally,

Introduction: The Making of The Great Ming Code

the legal notes extend the connotation of crimes. Article 203 punishes both those who enter the gates of imperial palaces without authorization and the guards who are on duty. The legal note adds: "Other articles shall follow this provision." This means that when other articles punish crimes of illegally entering imperial palaces, although they do not specifically mention the responsibility of the "guards on duty," they automatically include them. Obviously, these legal notes not only clarify the meaning of the text but also add new provisions to the *Code*.

"Crime" as a Concept

What is crime? Although the *Code* does not provide a straightforward legal definition, it stipulates the key elements that define a crime. First, it prohibits commission of an act that is harmful to the envisioned social order, and it prohibits omission of an act that would uphold that social order. Commission of an act refers to active behavior such as killing or injuring. Omission of an act means failure to perform legal duties. In the *Code*, the liability of omission lies in either official duties[183] or social obligation.[184] Second, the *Code* rules that the commission or omission is forbidden by law. It requires that in judging law cases, judicial officials must cite the specific articles of the *Code* or *Great Ming Commandment*; the imperial decrees that decide individual cases cannot be used by analogy (Art. 439). Officials, therefore, are forbidden to decide crimes without specific stipulations in the written law codes. In other words, crime is viewed as an act that violates established laws.

Nevertheless, the *Code* does dictate a principle of analogy. Article 46 states that when a harmful act is regulated by neither the *Code* nor *Commandment*, officials may cite a closely analogous article in the *Code* to decide the case, but the punishments proposed have to be sent to the Ministry of Justice for deliberation and memorialized to the throne for final approval. This provision indicates that decisions based on analogies must always use the *Code* as a guide, and at the same time it mandates a stringent process to obtain approval. Therefore, although the principle seems a deviation from the above-mentioned dictum that no act is considered a crime without being specifically defined as such by written law, it is used under strict regulation intended to reduce the risk of arbitrary decisions while defending the dynastic order.

To determine one's criminal liability, the *Code* also establishes time limitations of the law, namely, the time when the law goes into effect. Article 45 reads: "The *Code* shall take effect from the day it is promulgated. If crimes are committed before then, they shall all be judged in accordance with the new *Code*." By authorizing the new *Code* to regulate something that happened before its existence, the article appears to make certain acts criminal retroactively. In fact, as John Langlois observes, this rule intends only to "change the punishment for actions which had already been deemed criminal" instead of incriminating people for what they had done earlier.[185] Furthermore, the spirit of this principle is to reduce penalties for earlier crimes rather than increase them. While Article 119, for example, forbids government officials or functionaries from marrying musicians or taking them as concubines, it allows those who married before 1368 (Hongwu 1) to maintain the relationship and be exempt from punishment.[186] For another example, Article 90 prohibits peasants from fleeing to other subprefectures or districts to evade corvée services, but it exempts from punishment those who moved away before 1374 (Hongwu 7) as long as they have registered themselves and performed the services.[187] With retroactive effect, these regulations benefit the defendants instead of increasing their suffering.

The *Code* applies to every person living in the Ming Empire, including a special group of people—"persons beyond the pale of civilization" (*huawai ren*). The concept of *huawai ren* is first found in *The Tang Code*, in which they are officially interpreted as "foreigners" of the "barbarian countries."[188] Their treatment in *The Tang Code* is differentiated: those of the same nationality who commit crimes against each other shall be dealt with according to their own customary laws, but when the crime involves people of different nationalities, they shall be dealt with by Chinese law.[189] The Ming concept of *huawai ren* is not officially explained. The "incorporated commentary" to the *Code* interprets them to be either "foreign barbarians" (*waiyi*) who surrender to the Ming court or "barbarian bandits" (*yikou*) who are captured by the Ming government. Although they are not of the same "ethnic identity" (*zulei*) as the Han, as long as they submit themselves to the Ming authority, they are subjects of the dynasty. The equal application of the dynastic law to these "naturalized" persons becomes a way to show that "the emperor does not treat them as outsiders [*wangzhe wu wai*]."[190]

MENTAL STATES

Mental states are among the key factors in deciding criminal liability and penal severity. Looking through the *Code*, we can find four mental conditions: deliberation (*gu* or *guyi*), negligence (*shi, guo,* or *guoshi*), mistake (*wu* or *cuowu*), and lack of knowledge (*buzhi*).

Deliberation is a state of mind in which acts are done or not done knowingly and purposely. Unless otherwise stipulated, all crimes described in the *Code* are deliberate ones. For many crimes, deliberation is an essential component. For instance, in cases of mortgaging or renting out wives, concubines, or daughters, if the buyers know the circumstances but purchase them and then marry them, they commit the same crime as the original offenders. If they do not know the circumstances, they are not guilty.

Introduction: The Making of The Great Ming Code

Although the marriage must be dissolved, they will still get the betrothal gifts back (Art. 108).

Negligence refers to an unconscious mental state. In the *Code*, the meaning of "negligence" is broadly defined by a "legal note" in Article 315. It says: "'Negligence' refers to the circumstances where ears or eyes cannot perceive the result [*ermu suo buji*] or where thought or planning cannot contemplate the consequence [*silü suo budao*]." The interlinear note lists several examples: (1) When one is shooting birds or animals or tossing bricks or tiles, he unexpectedly kills others. (2) When one is climbing to a dangerous height, he loses his footing and thus harms his partners. (3) When one is sailing a boat, the boat is driven by the wind; when one is riding a horse, the horse runs wildly; or when one is driving a carriage at a rapid speed on a descent, he cannot stop. (4) When one is carrying a heavy object with others, the other persons are injured because his strength is insufficient to control the object. The legal note concludes that negligence refers to cases involving "those who initially do not intend to harm others but who accidentally [*ou*] cause death or injury." According to present-day criminal justice theory, this provision includes two types of situations. One, as illustrated by the first example, is "negligence" in the sense that the wrongdoers create social damages when they *should* know the risks but fail to know them. The other, as illustrated by the second through fourth examples, refers to "accident" or "irresistible force" that *cannot* be foreseen or controlled by humans.

The state of "mistake" is harder to define, for neither explanation nor example is given in the text. In Article 315, the crime of "killing or injuring by mistake" is described as "killing or injuring others in play or, because of being in affrays, killing or injuring bystanders by mistake." According to this provision, a criminal mistake might be an act in which the criminal has an original intention to harm a given person but unexpectedly harms another. This provision, however, is concerned only with mistakes in killings and injuries. In fact, the distinction between negligence and a mistake in general is often blurred in the *Code*. For example, criminal liability does not require an original intention to do wrong if someone mistakenly (*wu*) does not follow the correct prescription when preparing imperial medicine (Arts. 2, 182). At any rate, the bottom line for both negligence and mistake is that actors do not consciously commit crimes but inflict damage on prescribed social relations.

A mental state of not knowing the actual circumstances is an element that often determines whether a person should be held responsible for criminal liability. The general rule for those who break the law without any knowledge of the circumstances is that they will either be punished according to lighter penalties or be exempted from punishment. Article 37 of the *Code* stipulates that if the law prescribes heavier penalties for the crimes under special circumstances, but the offenders do not know that those circumstances pertain to the situation when they commit the crimes, they shall be punished as ordinary persons (i.e., as if the special circumstances did not pertain). If the law prescribes lighter penalties, however, the criminals who do not know the special circumstances will be treated by the provisions that entail lighter penalties. For instance, the "legal note" of the article explains that if a paternal uncle and his nephew do not know each other at all and the nephew strikes and injures the uncle, then the nephew shall be punished according to the provision on affrays between ordinary persons (Art. 325) instead of that on striking superior relatives (Art. 341). On the contrary, if a father strikes his son without being aware of the relationship, he shall be dealt with according to the law on striking one's son (Art. 342) instead of ordinary persons (Art. 325).

This general rule applies to most cases in the *Code* where being aware of the situation constitutes a critical requirement for assessing criminal liability. In other words, if the actors know the circumstances and commit the act, they shall be punished according to the regular law. If they do not know, they will not be prosecuted at all. For example, in recommending others for official positions, if the recommended persons know they are fraudulently recommended, they shall be punished the same as those who recommend them; if they do not know the circumstance, they shall not be responsible for the act (Art. 53). By the same token, if a person knows a husband wants to marry off his wife and then takes the woman as a wife, he shall be punished the same as the husband. If the person does not know the circumstance, however, he shall not be punished (Art. 108).

There are three major exceptions to the general rule on crimes committed with lack of knowledge. One is "collective prosecution" (*yuanzuo*), which incriminates the criminal's family members regardless of their knowledge about the criminal's act. Another has to do with "public crimes" (*gongzui*), the acts done for public matters or without private motives. (For brief explanations of both collective prosecution and public crimes, see below.) A third exception is concerned with conspiratorial acts. When two persons conspire to commit a crime, and during the process of the act one person commits an unplanned crime, the other shall be considered to have done the same thing even though he or she is not aware of the situation. An example is if killings ensue when inferior relatives lead outsiders to steal family property (Art. 295). If the inferior relatives commit the killings, the outsiders who are engaging in "theft" will be punished as if they had committed "forcible robbery" (cf. Art. 289) regardless of their knowledge about the killing. Likewise, if the outsiders commit the killings, the inferior relatives shall be punished according to the law on killing superior relatives (e.g., Art. 342) whether or not they know about the outsiders' acts. This is the same for adulterous

Introduction: The Making of The Great Ming Code   lxv

wives: they shall be strangled even though they do not know that their lovers have killed their husbands (Art. 308).

The legal consequences differ according to the state of mind of the actors. Deliberate crimes are punished more severely than negligent and mistaken ones. Under a general amnesty, public crimes by officials and negligent and mistaken crimes shall be pardoned, whereas deliberate ones shall not (Art. 16). Public crimes by officials and ordinary negligent killing can be redeemed with cash, but private crimes cannot (Arts. 7–8, 13, 315).

AGE AND CAPACITY FOR CRIMINAL LIABILITY

Age and capacity are other elements that determine whether or not a person can be found liable for crimes. In *The Great Ming Code*, the criminal liability for the young, aged, and disabled is substantially limited. As far as age is concerned, the younger or older the persons who commit criminal acts, the less liability they will hold for criminal charges. The *Code* divides them into four groups. (1) People 70–79 and 11–15 years of age: if they commit crimes punishable by life exile or lighter penalties, they may redeem their punishments. (2) People 80–89 and 8–10 years of age: if they commit crimes involving rebellion, great sedition, or homicide punishable by the death penalty, they may petition the throne. For crimes of robbery or injury to others, they may redeem the punishments. All other acts shall not be prosecuted. (3) People 90 years of age or older: even though they commit crimes punishable by the death penalty, they shall not be prosecuted (with the exception of committing rebellion or great sedition). (4) Children of 7 years of age or younger are completely exempted from criminal liability (Art. 21).

With respect to the disabled, the *Code* deals with two types of people: the maimed (*feiji*) and the incapacitated (*duji*). People who are maimed may be blind in one eye or broken in one limb.[191] When they commit crimes, they are treated the same as those who are 70–79 years of age. Those who are incapacitated may be blind in two eyes or broken in two limbs.[192] They are handled the same as those who are 80–89 years of age (Art. 21). The *Code* does not specify the situation of insanity. Possibly the law gave discretionary power to district magistrates or other judicial officials to handle the insane in terms of either the maimed or the incapacitated.

Moreover, if people commit crimes before they become aged or disabled, they shall be judged according to the provisions on those who are aged or maimed when their crimes are discovered. This also applies to those who become aged or disabled within their term of years of penal servitude. If the young commit crimes that are not discovered until they are grown up, they shall still be judged in accordance with the provisions concerning the young. In addition, because the aged and the young lack intelligence and strength, if others instigate them to commit crimes, only the instigators shall be punished (Art. 22).[193]

THE TEN ABOMINATIONS

In order to punish some crimes more effectively, *The Great Ming Code* devises special crime classifications. The most important grouping of crimes is the "Ten Abominations" (Shie). These are the 10 kinds of heinous crimes listed in Article 2 of the *Code:* plotting rebellion, plotting great sedition, plotting treason, contumacy, depravity, great irreverence, lack of filial piety, discord, unrighteousness, and incest. This group is especially important because it indicates the major target of the Ming law—the crimes that endanger the fundamental hierarchical order. Nine of these crimes involve behavior against the members of the upper level of the hierarchy: Heaven, Earth, gods of soil and grain, and imperial ancestor spirits in the world of spirits; the ruler of the dynasty; high officials in each administrative jurisdiction; parents, husband, elder brothers and sisters; and teachers. These acts are therefore severely punished in the *Code*. For example, of the 13 crimes that are punishable by the severest penalty, "sentencing to death by slicing" (*lingchi*), 9 are among the Ten Abominations.

Furthermore, the Ten Abominations deprive the offenders of all their legal privileges. For instance, when such cases occur, the privileges of "Eight Deliberations" (Bayi) and "petitions" (*qing*) (see below) are eliminated (Arts. 3–4, 9). Those who commit any of the Ten Abominations lose the privilege of having their death sentences commuted so they can serve their old (80 years or older) or severely handicapped parents or paternal grandparents at home (Art. 18). The crimes are also excluded from the provisions of general amnesties (Art. 16). Even if in special circumstances they are pardoned for crimes of rebellion, great sedition, and treason, any property confiscated by the government would not be returned (Art. 23). And although people were entitled to conceal a crime committed by a close relative, this was forbidden with respect to one of the Ten Abominations.

In addition, for the crimes of plotting rebellion, great sedition, treason, making or keeping insect poisons, mutilating living persons, and killing three persons in a family, the *Code* stipulates particularly harsh treatment. For instance, when the criminals die at the places of their exile, their families who have accompanied them shall not be allowed to return to their hometown (Art. 15). Also, when the criminals are punished by penal servitude or life exile, they shall not be pardoned even though an amnesty is proclaimed (Art. 17). When old (70 years of age or older), young (15 years of age or younger), or disabled people commit such crimes and are punished by life exile or less, they shall not be allowed to redeem their crimes (Art. 21).

Joint Crimes

The *Code* stipulates a general rule in dealing with "joint crimes" (*gong fanzui*): those who formulate the plans are considered principals, and other participants are accessories; punishments for accessories shall be reduced by one degree. There are several exceptions to this rule. One is for joint crimes by family members: if members of one family commit crimes jointly, only the most senior or eldest member (usually an adult male) shall be punished. If such a member is 80 years of age or older or incapacitated, the punishment shall devolve upon the next eldest member. Another exception is that if a specific article speaks of "all" (*jie*), then the offenders in joint crimes shall not be differentiated into principals and accessories. A third exception is concerned with some special types of crimes such as entering imperial palaces without authorization or committing fornication, in which all offenders shall be punished as principals (Art. 29).

To punish criminals of joint crimes who flee, the *Code* stresses evidence in differentiating between principals and accessories. Suppose that two persons jointly commit a crime and one is captured and another escapes. If the captured one claims that the one who fled is a principal and there is no other witness, then the captured one shall be considered an accessory. Later, if the one who escapes is also captured and claims that the one who was first captured is the principal and the interrogation confirms it, then the criminal who was first captured shall be repunished as the principal. On the other hand, if criminals in joint crimes flee and there are three or more witnesses who can confirm the criminal facts, the criminal liability of principal and accessory shall be decided immediately, and no confrontational interrogation is necessary (Art. 30).

Public and Private Crimes

Public and private crimes are legislated to differentiate offenses by government officials and functionaries. The distinction between the two lies in the wrongdoers' motives—whether or not they acted for public or private interests. According to the *Code*, "public crimes" (*gongzui*) refer to cases where officials and functionaries commit offenses in public matters or without private motives (Arts. 27–28). "Private crimes" (*sizui*), on the contrary, denote offenses committed to seek private interests. In terms of mental states, public crimes are generally negligent or mistaken offenses, and private crimes are deliberate ones.

The general treatment of public crimes is more lenient than that of private crimes. For the former, if the crimes are punishable by beating with the light stick, officials may redeem the penalties, and functionaries may have the penalties meted out every season. If the crimes are punishable by heavier penalties, for both officials and functionaries, the crimes should be recorded in government files, which should be examined every nine years to determine the demotion or promotion of the offenders according to the number of times and degree of seriousness of their crimes (Art. 7). For private crimes, on the other hand, the offenders shall not only be punished by regular penalties but also either have their offenses recorded or be transferred, demoted, or dismissed from office (Art. 8).

In handling public crimes, the *Code* prescribes different rules for the different levels of the administrative hierarchy. Within each office, official personnel are divided into four categories: functionaries, staff supervisors, associate officials, and senior officials. If a person in any of these categories commits a public crime, such as making errors in preparing government documents, the officials or functionaries above and below him in the hierarchy will also be punished, with the penalties determined by their level in the hierarchy. If one official commits a private crime of deliberately exonerating or implicating others, the rest of the officials shall still be punished as negligently committing the crime even though they do not know the circumstances (Art. 27). Concern for official responsibilities can also be found in provisions regarding local officials. District magistrates, for example, shall be punished if households are unregistered (Art. 81) or if land is allowed to go uncultivated in communities (Art. 103).

To encourage offenders of public crimes to confess voluntarily, the *Code* grants favorable treatment for the officials or functionaries who make errors in public matters but themselves discover and report the errors. If they do so, not only they themselves but also their colleagues in the same office who would have been prosecuted with them shall all be exempted from punishment. This principle, however, excludes the cases where, after officials have judged law cases, the wrongly sentenced punishments have already been carried out (Art. 28).

Collective Prosecution

Collective prosecution, a principle that incriminates the persons who have certain relationships with the criminals, pertains to two groups of people. The primary group is made up of relatives. For the most serious crimes, such as plotting rebellion, great sedition, or treason, making or keeping insect poisons, mutilating living persons, or killing three persons of one family, the criminals' close relatives shall either be executed, exiled, or enslaved. Those who are exiled because of these crimes shall not return to their hometowns even when amnesties are issued. And when the criminals are sentenced to life exile or banishment, their wives and concubines shall follow them to their new destinations (Arts. 15, 277–78, 310–12). Other crimes that entail "collective prosecution" of relatives include forming treacherous cliques,

Introduction: The Making of The Great Ming Code

associating with court attendants, and memorializing in praise of the virtues and achievements of high officials (Arts. 60–62).

Collective prosecution is also applied to officials and functionaries who either work in the same office or belong to the same chain of command. For the above-noted "public crimes," for example, if officials and functionaries in the same office make mistakes in signing documents together, the penalties for the four classes of personnel shall be decreased progressively. The functionaries who carry out the actual transactions shall be punished as principals; the penalty for staff supervisors shall be reduced by one degree; for the associate officials, two degrees; for head officials, three degrees (Art. 27). Similarly, if officials in superior offices fail to prevent the commission of crimes by their subordinates in lower offices, they shall also be punished for dereliction of duties (e.g., Arts. 127, 433).

PENAL SYSTEM

The basic penal system, the "five punishments" (*wuxing*), is laid out in the very first article of the *Code*:

1. Beating with the light stick (*chi*),[194] five degrees: 10, 20, 30, 40, 50 strokes
2. Beating with the heavy stick (*zhang*),[195] five degrees: 60, 70, 80, 90, 100 strokes
3. Penal servitude (*tu*),[196] five degrees:
    One year plus 60 strokes of beating with the heavy stick
    One and one-half years plus 70 strokes of beating with the heavy stick
    Two years plus 80 strokes of beating with the heavy stick
    Two and one-half years plus 90 strokes of beating with the heavy stick
    Three years plus 100 strokes of beating with the heavy stick
4. Life exile (*liu*),[197] three degrees:
    2,000 *li* plus 100 strokes of beating with the heavy stick
    2,500 *li* plus 100 strokes of beating with the heavy stick
    3,000 *li* plus 100 strokes of beating with the heavy stick
5. Death (*si*),[198] two degrees: strangulation and decapitation

In addition, many other sorts of penalties, which might be called "supplemental punishments," are employed in the articles dealing with specific crimes. The heaviest penalty is sentencing to death by slicing (*lingchi chusi*). This penalty serves to punish the most heinous crimes such as plotting rebellion and great sedition or killing parents (by children), husband (by wife or concubine), household head (by slave or hired laborer), and ordinary persons (with extreme method of dismemberment).[199] To supplement life exile, the *Code* stipulates military exile (*chongjun*) and banishment (*qianxi*). Military exile is primarily used for guilty military personnel, who were sent to frontier regions to perform military services.[200] Banishment is a minor type of exile, which sent criminals at least 1,000 *li* away to resettle.[201]

The *Code* also punishes guilty officials with fines on their salaries (*fafeng*), making a record of their transgression (*jiguo*), demotion (*jiangji*), revocation of official certificate (*zhuiduo*), disenrollment from official register (*chuming*), and dismissal from office (*bazhi*).[202] In order to accomplish restitution of property, it demands the return of illicit goods to private owners (*huanzhu*) or the government (*huangguan*) and the confiscation of the criminal's property by the government (*jimo*).[203] When crimes involve changes of personal status, the *Code* requires the correction (*gaizheng*) of the illegal status, such as making Buddhist and Daoist priests return to lay status, dissolving marital and adoptive relationships, and separating illegally combined households.[204] When certain types of robbery are committed, the law inflicts tattooing (*cizi*).[205] For the most heinous crimes, the *Code* enslaves the criminals' female and young male relatives to either the government or meritorious officials' households (Arts. 60, 277–78). While some of the abovementioned remedies are no longer prescribed as penalties in present-day law codes, the Ming law compilers did not perceive any distinction between them and the five punishments—they are all means to "punish" evildoing.

Increasing or Reducing Punishments

The *Code* specifies a general rule on how punishments shall be increased or reduced (Art. 38). In increasing punishment, the severity of the penalty is increased from the "basic punishment" (*benzui*). Thus, if one commits a crime for which the basic punishment is 100 strokes with the heavy stick and the punishment is increased one degree, then the criminal shall be punished by 60 strokes with the heavy stick and penal servitude for one year. Similarly, in reducing punishment, the penalty is reduced from the "basic punishment" (Art. 38).

However, when penalties are reduced from either the two degrees of death penalty or the three degrees of life exile, each category of punishment is counted as one degree. If, for instance, one commits a crime punishable by the death penalty, and it is reduced by one degree, the criminal is punished by life exile to 3,000 *li*; if it is reduced by two degrees, however, he is punished by penal servitude for three years (skipping the category of life exile) (Art. 38).

In increasing punishments, if the crimes involve illicit goods, it is essential that the punishments only be increased when the "amount is complete" (*shuman*). For instance, if the law requires that a penalty be increased by

Introduction: The Making of The Great Ming Code lxxi

one degree for every 100 *guan* of illicit goods, it shall not be increased even though the value of the goods amounts to 90 *guan*. Moreover, when punishments are increased, they shall be limited to 100 strokes with the heavy stick and life exile to 3,000 *li*, unless the specific articles stipulate the death penalty (Art. 38).

In addition, the *Code* allows "cumulative reduction" (*leijian*) of punishments. If one person, for example, commits a crime for which the punishment may be reduced on several grounds such as "accessory," "voluntary confession," "negligence," and "public crime," the punishment may be cumulatively reduced (Art. 11).

Redemption

Redemption provides offenders with opportunities for performing labor service or paying a sum of money in lieu of physical punishment. In the Ming period, the redemption system was regulated both by *The Great Ming Code* (*lüshu*) and regulations (*lishu*).[206]

The first article of the *Code* prescribes the basic redemption fines, which match the system of five punishments. A crime rating 10 strokes with the light stick might be redeemed by paying 600 *wen* of copper cash, while a capital crime could be redeemed with 42 *guan* of copper cash (Art. 1).

Crimes that are entitled to redemption include the following nine categories:

1. "Public crimes" punishable by beating with the light stick committed by all categories of officials and functionaries (Art. 7).

2. "Private crimes" punishable by beating with the light stick committed by military officers (Art. 8).

3. "Public crimes" committed by those who have not yet become officials and are discovered when the offenders have become officials (Art. 13).

4. Crimes punishable by life exile or penal servitude while the offenders' paternal grandparents or parents are aged or disabled and thus require service but the family has no other able-bodied adult males. The crimes may be redeemed after the offenders are subjected to 100 strokes of beating with the heavy stick (Art. 18).

5. Crimes punishable by life exile or penal servitude committed by students of astronomy in the Directorate of Astronomy who have already learned a skill and can specialize in a particular duty. The crimes may be redeemed after the offenders are punished by 100 strokes of beating with the heavy stick (Art. 19).

6. Crimes punishable by penal servitude or life exile committed by women. The crimes may be redeemed after the female offenders are punished by 100 strokes of beating with the heavy stick. Unlike male

offenders, women were allowed to wear undergarments during the beating. However, for crimes of fornication, female offenders were, like male offenders, stripped of their clothing to receive the punishment (Art. 19).

7. Crimes rating life exile or lighter committed by those who are 70 years of age or older or 15 years of age or younger or disabled and crimes of robbery or injury committed by those who are 80 years of age or older or 10 years of age or younger or incapacitated (Art. 21).

8. Crimes of negligent killing or injury. In this case, however, the money paid will go to the victims' families instead of to the government (Art. 315).

9. Crimes of accusing someone of two or more crimes among which only the more serious one is true, or of accusing someone of a crime that is claimed to be more serious than the actual act, and, in both situations, the punishments for the falsely accused crimes have not been carried out. In this case, the punishments of beating with the light and heavy sticks may be directly redeemed; those of penal servitude and life exile shall be converted to 100 strokes of beating with the heavy stick, and the remaining penalties can be redeemed (Art. 359).[207]

Mourning Degrees

Mourning degree between relatives is one of the most important principles that decide the severity of punishments.[208] The *Code* stipulates the five degrees and eight grades of mourning relationship:

1. *Zhancui* (garment of unhemmed sackcloth), three years (e.g., for parents or husband).
2. *Zicui* (garment of hemmed sackcloth), one year, with staff (e.g., for sons or wife); one year, without staff (e.g., for paternal grandparents); five months (e.g., for paternal great-grandparents); and 3 months (e.g., for paternal great-great-grandparents).
3. *Dagong* (garment of greater coarseness), nine months (e.g., for married daughter).
4. *Xiaogong* (garment of lesser coarseness), five months (e.g., for brother's sons' son).
5. *Sima* (garment of slightly finer woven cloth), three months (e.g., for daughter's son).

This system not only defines the time period and dress required in mourning the death of relatives but also governs the severity of punishments for crimes between relatives according to the closeness of their mourning degree. Generally speaking, for crimes of homicide, injury, or assault, the closer the relationship, the heavier the penalty.[209] For crimes of theft, on the contrary,

Introduction: The Making of The Great Ming Code   lxxiii

the closer the relationship, the lighter the penalty (Art. 295). The mourning degree for proper mother (*dimu*), adoptive mother (*yangmu*), stepmother (*jimu*), and carrying mother (*cimu*) is three years with unhemmed sackcloth. The penalty for harming them will be the same as for one's natural mother (Art. 40).[210]

Based on mourning relationships, the *Code* allows criminals to stay home to support their old or disabled parents. Suppose that someone commits a crime punishable by the death penalty, life exile, or penal servitude, and, at the same time, his paternal grandparents or parents are at least 80 years of age or are maimed or incapacitated and require someone to take care of them but do not have any other able-bodied adult males to perform the service. The *Code* provides that cases of capital crimes shall be memorialized petitioning imperial decisions, as long as the crimes are not of the type that cannot be pardoned even when general amnesties are issued. For crimes punishable by penal servitude or life exile, the offenders shall only be punished by 100 strokes with the heavy stick, and the remaining penalties may be redeemed. Then the offenders may stay home to support their elderly or disabled parents (Art. 18).

Because of their close mourning relationship, family members are also allowed to conceal crimes among themselves, as long as the crime is not plotting rebellion, great sedition, or treason. The *Code* distinguishes two categories of relatives and treats them differently in regard to concealing crimes. The first group of people will not be punished at all for their acts if close relatives conceal one another's crimes, slaves or hired laborers conceal the household head's crimes, or relatives, slaves, or hired laborers inform the criminal when the authorities come to arrest them so that the criminals can be concealed or flee. The relatives in this category include those who live together (*tongju*), relatives of the third degree of mourning or closer, maternal grandparents, grandsons in the female line (*waisun*), wife's parents, sons-in-law, wives of maternal grandfathers, husband's brothers, and brothers' wives. The second category of people will be punished but will have the penalties reduced: relatives of the fourth degree or more distant who conceal each other's crimes or divulge the matter shall have their punishment reduced three degrees below that for ordinary persons, and relatives who have no mourning relationship with the criminal shall have their punishment reduced one degree (Art. 31).

Eight Deliberations and Petitions

The principles of the Eight Deliberations (Bayi) and petitions (*qing*) grant judicial procedural privileges to the ruling elite. The Eight Deliberations require that when crimes other than the Ten Abominations are committed by imperial relatives,[211] old imperial retainers, meritorious officials, worthies, talents, diligent subjects, high officials, or descendants of preceding dynasties (eight categories in all), the facts of the crimes must be reported to the throne in sealed memorials petitioning imperial decisions on whether or not the offenders will be interrogated. Regular judicial officials have no authority to initiate interrogation of these eight categories of people. When the emperor decides that the case should be tried, high officials have to memorialize again petition for a number of officials to deliberate the case. When the deliberation is permitted, the results must be memorialized to the throne for final decision (Arts. 3–4).

"Petition" refers to the rule that when crimes are committed by officials (including all those in the capital and those of the fifth rank or higher in the provinces), memorialized petition for an imperial decision to carry out the interrogation must be made (Arts. 5–6, 9). The major difference between the Eight Deliberations and petition is that, for the latter, the memorial has proposed the interrogation and petitioned directly to carry it out. The crimes by civilian officials of the sixth rank or lower may be interrogated by regular judicial officials, but the final decision shall still be approved by the throne. If officials of prefectures, subprefectures, or districts commit crimes, their superior government offices shall only memorialize to petition for the permission to conduct the interrogation. After receiving the permission, they may deliberate the cases and memorialize again. The court will send responsible officials to investigate the cases and verify the facts. Only then can the judgment be made (Art. 5).

Voluntary Confession

The *Code* prescribes lenient treatment for those who voluntarily confess crimes. As long as the confessions are truthful and complete before the matters are discovered by government authorities, criminals may be exempted from punishment. The *Code* not only encourages criminals to give themselves up in person but also allows them to send others to make the confession for them. Also, based on the aforementioned rule on mutual concealment of crimes among close relatives (Art. 31), the accusation of crimes to the authorities by those who are allowed mutual concealment is considered the same as voluntary confession in person. Furthermore, the *Code* permits criminals to make retribution to the victims, which will have the same effect as voluntary confession to the government. For instance, if someone takes another's property by forcible robbery, theft, or fraud and makes voluntary confession to the owners of the property, or if he accepts illicit goods from others and repents his transgression and returns the goods to the owner, he shall be judged the same as if he made voluntary confession to the authorities and shall be exempted from punishment. In crimes of forcible robbery or theft, if criminals can capture their companions and send them to the authorities, they may also be exempt from punishment (Art. 24).

Not all voluntary confessions are exempted from punishment. Two exceptions are made by the *Code*. One is that, under certain circumstances, criminals shall still be punished even though they confess to the government, but the penalties shall be reduced. For example, if criminals make untruthful and incomplete confessions, they shall be punished only for crimes that have not yet been confessed truthfully or completely; if the punishment extends to death, it may be reduced by one degree. If criminals know that others intend to accuse them, or they have fled or engaged in treason, and they make confession, their punishment shall be reduced by two degrees. If those who have fled or engaged in treason return to their original places, they may have their penalties reduced by two degrees without making the voluntary confession (Art. 24).

A second exception concerns crimes that have already caused harmful results. These crimes include killing or injuring others, destroying or losing articles such as official seals that cannot be restored, fleeing after the crimes are discovered, passing checkpoints without authorization (*sidu*) or by circumvention (*yuedu*), committing fornication, and studying astronomy without authorization. In all these cases, the law on voluntary confession does not apply (Art. 24).

Military Personnel

Military personnel are treated differently from civilians in certain respects. When military officers at all levels (as opposed to civil officials of the fifth rank or higher) commit crimes, their cases shall be submitted to the throne to seek permission to interrogate; no offices shall conduct the trials without authorization (Art. 6). The punishments for military officers or soldiers who commit crimes punishable by penal servitude or life exile shall be converted to military exile (Art. 10). Since military personnel in fortified cities of distant frontiers occupy important positions, if they plot treason, they may be executed (if "there is no injustice") before the cases are reported to the central government (Art. 33).

Recidivists

For recidivists, *The Great Ming Code* stipulates a general principle and some special punishments. The general principle, based on whether or not the criminals have already been punished by the government, specifies two situations. The first concerns those who commit more than one crime before they are punished. The *Code* states that no matter how many crimes are discovered at the time of judgment, the criminals shall be punished only by the penalty for the most serious crimes (Arts. 20, 25). That is, the punishment is not increased because of the repeated commission of crimes. If crimes are of equal severity, only punishment for one crime shall be meted out. This ensures that punishment for several crimes shall not be more severe than any punishment for a single crime. This principle also applies to cases in which one crime is discovered and judged and punishment carried out, then other crimes are discovered later. Under such a circumstance, if the later-discovered crimes are less or equally serious than the previous one, the criminals shall not be punished again; if they are more serious than the previous one, the punishment for the previous crime shall be subtracted from the punishment for the more serious one and only the remaining punishment shall be meted out (Art. 25).

Nevertheless, if the criminals commit crimes again after they have once been punished by the government, they shall be punished again for the later crimes. The total punishment, however, shall not exceed 100 strokes with the heavy stick and penal servitude for four years at the place of life exile. For example, if the criminals punished by penal servitude or life exile have already been sent to places of servitude or exile and again commit crimes punishable by life exile, the punishment for the later crimes shall be converted into 100 strokes with the heavy stick and four years of labor at their places of exile. If the later crimes are punishable by penal servitude, the required labor shall not exceed four years (Art. 20).

In addition to the above principle, some special punishments are inflicted on recidivists who are meritorious officials (Arts. 237, 375), military personnel (Arts. 230, 238), and thieves (Art. 292). For these people, their repeated crimes will entail increased penalties, amounting to strangulation.

Conversion of Punishments

For certain criminals of special status, the *Code* provides a system to convert their punishment. The first special group of people comprises government artisans, musicians, astronomy students, and women. Basically, the punishment of life exile for government artisans and musicians shall be converted into 100 strokes of beating with the heavy stick and four years of labor. If astronomy students have learned skills and can perform specialized duties and they commit crimes punishable by life exile or penal servitude, their punishments shall be converted into 100 strokes with the heavy stick, and the remaining punishments may be redeemed. If women commit crimes punishable by penal servitude or life exile, their punishments shall be converted into 100 strokes with the heavy stick and they may redeem the remaining punishments (Art. 19).

Another group of people whose punishments could be converted com-

Introduction: The Making of The Great Ming Code lxxvii

prises those who were allowed to remain at home to take care of their old or disabled paternal grandparents or parents. If they committed crimes punishable by penal servitude or life exile, they could be punished by 100 strokes of beating with the heavy stick, and the remaining punishment could be redeemed (Art. 18).

In sum, the *Code* attests to the mature legislative status of criminal justice in late imperial China. Its organization into chapters, sections, and articles is coherent and rational. Its general principles differentiate specific circumstances and assign different criminal liabilities to people with different intentions and motives, different statuses, and different physical abilities. A variety of punishments are employed to deal with different crimes. From the point of view of criminal justice, *The Great Ming Code* marked another major legislative development since *The Tang Code* (653) in Chinese and East Asian legal history.

The Great Ming Code as Fundamental Dynastic Law: Its Place in the Early Ming Legal System

The Hongwu reign was one of the most productive periods in Chinese legislative history. Many legal regulations were enacted and promulgated. Nevertheless, it was *The Great Ming Code* that served as the basic law of the Ming dynasty. Zhu Yuanzhang regarded the *Code* as an "ancestral institution [*zuzhi*]."[212] The *Code* compilers called it "the yardstick for one hundred generations [*baidai zhi zhunsheng*]."[213] The judicial officials looked upon it as "the permanent law of ten thousand generations [*wanshi zhi changfa*]."[214] As "the law of the whole dynasty [*yidai fa*],"[215] the *Code* provided fundamental principles and extensive remedies in dealing with the legal problems of the land. It was decided that judicial activities in and outside the capital "should all be based on [the *Code*] that was promulgated in the thirtieth year [of the Hongwu reign]."[216] The status of the *Code* as the basic law of the dynasty is demonstrated by its holistic character and its place in the legal system of the Hongwu reign.

Holism of *The Great Ming Code*

The Great Ming Code comprehensively regulates social relations by dividing crimes into six broad categories according to the six major branches of the central government: personnel, revenue, rites, wars, justice, and public works. This signified a major change in Chinese legislative history. As noted in the second section, although the early Ming law compilers initially intended to follow the legal system of the Tang dynasty, they eventually adopted a code structure that was based on the Six Ministries and that was considerably different from *The Tang Code*.[217] Why did they resolve on the particular structure of *The Great Ming Code?* One explanation cites possible influence by *The Institutes of the Yuan Dynasty* (1320–22).[218] This explanation might apply to the *Code* of 1368 but seems insufficient for the document compiled in 1389, which, after the Tang model was adopted in 1374, changed back to the six-ministry structure. Why did this change take place? In particular, the said Yuan institutional text consists of more than six chapters. It structures the contents into 10 categories, including the important Censorate as well as the Six Ministries. If the Ming intended to follow the Yuan example, which was based on government branches, why did they leave out the Censorate? Indeed, when the founding emperor abolished the Secretariat, he did not plan to promote the status of the Six Ministries by degrading other branches. Instead, he lost no time in strengthening the military and censorial hierarchical systems.[219] On many occasions, Zhu Yuanzhang pointed out the importance of all the top-echelon agencies of the central government in transforming the empire. In *August Ming Ancestral Instruction* (Huang Ming zuxun), for instance, he announced to his descendants: "Now our dynasty has abolished the prime minister and established such offices as the Five Chief [Military] Commissions, the Six Ministries, the Censorate, the Office of Transmission, and the Grand Court of Revision to manage the affairs of the realm. They parallel one another and dare not seek to dominate each other. It is the court which provides overall control of government affairs. That is why there is stability."[220] If the listed offices paralleled each other and all reported to the throne independently, why did the law compilers choose to organize the *Code* only by the Six Ministries?

It is my speculation that the early Ming ruling elite restructured the *Code* because they believed that the Six Ministries symbolized the comprehensiveness of the social relations regulated by the imperial government. Zhu Yuanzhang claimed that he eliminated the office of prime minister in order to "follow the ancient system of six ministers [*liuqing*]."[221] This "ancient system" refers to an idealized institution of six major officials suggested in *The Institutes of Zhou* (Zhouli). According to this Confucian classic, all government personnel are grouped under the six ministers of Heaven, Earth, Spring, Summer, Autumn, and Winter, who are in charge of the same sorts of government affairs as the Six Ministries in Ming times.[222] This system not only gathers all government affairs into the hands of the six ministers but also symbolizes the comprehensiveness of cosmic space (Heaven and Earth) and cosmic time (four seasons). The duties of these six offices, therefore, are all-inclusive; they cover every foreseeable matter in "all under Heaven [*tianxia*]."[223]

It is possible that when Zhu Yuanzhang and his officials chose the Six Ministries as the structural principle for the *Code*, they envisioned a dynas-

Introduction: The Making of The Great Ming Code lxxix

tic law of an all-encompassing nature. The legal problems stipulated under governmental categories and terminology in the *Code* are by no means limited to government matters. Although many of the articles are concerned with officials and their minions, the *Code* regulates all sorts of crimes by people in all sorts of occupations. Dynastic matters such as dynastic security and family harmony, official administration and economic regulation, sacrificial ceremony and military operation, judicial rules and public order, and human lives and dignity are all regulated in this single document. Indeed, in imperial China, the ruling elite recognized no limits to the responsibility of the government and the exercise of power by the government. Romeyn Taylor comments on the undifferentiated character of the cosmically ordained Chinese "empire-society"[224] and contends that "no autonomous political domain, no body politic, no state was acknowledged to exist in contradiction to society."[225] In serving the dynasty, therefore, government was considered to have the obligation as well as the authority to manage every aspect of dynastic matters.

The holistic nature of the *Code* is most clearly indicated in Article 410, "Doing What Ought Not to Be Done." The legal note in the article interprets such an act as one for which "neither the *Code* nor the *Commandment* has an article dealing with the act, but which shall not be done according to reason [*li*]." Evidently this article served to handle any omissions in the written legal regulations. Early Ming lawmakers knew that law codes could not specify every single social problem, and thus they intended to use this provision to punish all sorts of crimes:[226] minor matters would be punished by 40 strokes with the light stick; serious ones, 80 strokes with the heavy stick. With this provision, the scope of the *Code*'s binding force becomes unlimited. It is also worth noting that the most severe penalty prescribed in this article is 80 strokes with the heavy stick, which is relatively light. According to *The Great Ming Commandment*, such a penalty can be decided and carried out at the subprefecture level.[227] The lightness of the penalty might suggest, I again speculate, that the early Ming lawmakers assumed that in the rest of the articles they had already listed all problems that would entail penalties harsher than 80 strokes with the heavy stick. At any rate, this article reveals that the *Code* punished any act that endangered the social relations that were prescribed to protect the dynasty. The all-encompassing nature of the *Code* is manifested in the Ming legal system.

THE GREAT MING CODE AND THE GREAT MING COMMANDMENT

These two law codes were promulgated at the same time in 1367. The founding emperor, Zhu Yuanzhang, clarified their relationship in his edict proclaiming the two laws in the first month of 1368. He declared that the

Commandment was enacted to educate people before wrongful acts were committed, whereas the *Code* was intended to punish people after they committed crimes. He hoped that people would observe the *Commandment* so that they would not fall into the realm of the *Code* and be punished.[228] To be sure, the distinction drawn by the emperor was not abundantly clear. But one point was made certain: the binding force of the *Commandment* was to be realized by the *Code*.

Indeed, the *Commandment* provides the empire with rules. The document, however, prescribes no coercive remedies to guarantee the enforcement of the rules. Examining the text closely we find several ways in which its articles are structured. (1) Some articles state what one ought to do but have no punishments attached (e.g., Art. 4). (2) Others set up rules and further stipulate that "violations will be punished" but do not provide any specific sanctions either (e.g., Arts. 15, 26, 74). (3) Still others do entail punishments; but all of these stipulations are citations from the *Code*. For instance, some generally state: "They shall be punished in accordance with the *Code*" (e.g., Arts. 11, 37). And some cite more specific sources from the *Code*: "They shall be punished in accordance with the article 'Doing What Ought Not to Be Done'" (Arts. 10, 38, 44, 68); "They shall be punished the same as 'desertion'" (Art. 71); "They shall be punished as 'treacherous officials' [*jianchen*]: The minor criminals shall be exiled to malarial regions; the serious criminals shall be sentenced to capital punishment" (Art. 67).[229] In any case, we cannot find any specific sanctions provided by the *Commandment*. It was promulgated as a separate legal document, yet it could not be applied to any concrete law case independently but had to be utilized together with the *Code* in order to have a legal function.

That the *Commandment* relies on the *Code* for enforcement is also illustrated in their overlapping contents. A separate legal document, the *Commandment* evidently contains some rules that are not specified in the *Code*. These rules include "seven grounds for repudiation of wives [*qichu*]" and "three restrictions on divorce [*sanbuqu*]" in family relations (Art. 28) and sumptuary regulations on styles of clothing, residences, and other things (Arts. 47, 51). On the other hand, however, quite a few articles in the *Commandment* overlap those in the *Code*. To be sure, those articles that cite punishments from the *Code* as mentioned above indicate that the *Code* contains similar contents. In addition, many other articles do not indicate their connections with the *Code* but can be found in the latter document.[230]

Even those articles with rules that are not specified in the *Code* are enforced by the *Code*. Let us take the rules mentioned above as examples. The "seven grounds for repudiation of wives" and "three restrictions on divorce" are mentioned in the *Code* in Article 123, "Repudiating Wives." The sumptuary regulations are regulated by Article 194, "Violating Sumptuary Regulations on Clothing and Houses." Finally, for those articles that can-

Introduction: The Making of The Great Ming Code   lxxxi

not be found in the *Code*, the *Code* provides a special article, "Violating the *Commandment*": if the *Commandment* stipulates prohibitions but the *Code* does not specify punishments, the violation of the former shall be punished by 50 strokes of beating with the light stick (Art. 409). The "incorporated commentary" to the *Code* explains that if both the legal texts carry the same kinds of rules, the violations shall be punished in accordance with the *Code*; if the *Commandment* sets up some rules but the *Code* does not fix punishments for violating them, then this article shall be applied.[231] This article not only ensures that the *Code* covers a substantial portion of the contents in the *Commandment* but also reveals that the former regulates all the important issues articulated in the latter—because the light penalty of "50 strokes of beating with the light stick" will punish only the minor crimes that are stipulated by the *Commandment* and that are left out by the *Code*.

It seems apparent that the enforcement of the *Commandment* is dependent on the sanctions in the *Code*. Likewise, some of the regulations in the *Code* would not have been applied to society without the rules established in the *Commandment*; that is, the former punishes the violation of the social norms specified in the latter. In fact, if we view the two law codes in terms of the three basic elements required for a criminal legal norm (as discussed in the preceding section), the provisions in the *Commandment* formulate some of the "rules" for the *Code*, and the *Code* defines the "conditions" and proposes "sanctions" to enforce those rules. These two law codes thus can be understood as one unit, with the *Code* playing a leading role.

THE GREAT MING CODE AND THE GRAND PRONOUNCEMENTS

The Grand Pronouncements is a special "case law code" written by the founding emperor personally in colloquial language.[232] It consists of four parts: three "compilations" (*bian*) aimed at the emperor's subjects in general and one volume addressed to military officers. It took the Hongwu emperor merely two years, from 1385 through early 1388,[233] to compile and promulgate the 236-article document. The relatively short time span and the extraordinarily harsh penalties employed reveal the founding emperor's skepticism regarding regular legal methods and his anxiety to eliminate "evil" social elements. When the first compilation of the text was promulgated to the realm, Zhu Yuanzhang ordered that every household possess one copy of this law. Those who committed crimes punishable by beating with the light or heavy stick, penal servitude, or life exile could have their penalties reduced by one degree if they had a copy of the legal text, and their punishments would be increased by one degree if they did not have a copy.[234] When the second and third compilations were finished, Zhu declared that those who did not respect and did not receive copies of the text were not his "transformed" subjects and thus should be banished from the Chinese empire.[235] Zhu further made it clear that the text had to be studied in government schools and be used in civil service examinations.[236] It is said that in 1392 more than 190,000 teachers and students who taught and studied the text visited the court and were rewarded by the emperor.[237] Yang Yifan finds a number of articles in *The Grand Pronouncements* which show how the law was implemented, and he concludes that *The Grand Pronouncements* took effect with legally binding force on the very day when it was issued.[238]

Yang Yifan has done a comparative study of the *Code* and *The Grand Pronouncements* and comes to the following conclusions. First, Zhu Yuanzhang employed a number of brutal punishments in *The Grand Pronouncements*, which included exterminating criminals' clans, executing by slow slicing, pulling out sinew and severing fingers, removing the kneecap, sentencing to military exile, castration, amputating legs, and imposing the wooden cangue.[239] These punishments are either not prescribed in the *Code* or applied to crimes far more widely than they are in the *Code*. Second, for some crimes that are specified in both documents, the penalties employed in *The Grand Pronouncements* are much more severe than those in the *Code*.[240] Assigning tax duties or corveé services unequally, for example, is punishable by 100 strokes of beating with the heavy stick in the *Code* but entails extermination of one's clan in *The Grand Pronouncements*.[241] Third, *The Grand Pronouncements* specifies a number of crimes that are not defined in the *Code*, such as "hiding others' *Grand Pronouncements*" and "obstructing others from capturing harmful officials."[242] Apparently, *The Grand Pronouncements* has certain overruling force against the *Code*.

Nevertheless, important as the law was, on many occasions Zhu Yuanzhang admitted that many of the sanctions he employed in the *Pronouncements* were "extralegal" (*fawai*) punishments. In 1395, when *The August Ming Ancestral Instruction* (Huang Ming zuxun) was finished, Zhu informed his officials why he stipulated such extralegal measures to deal with crimes:

> It has been more than forty years since I first took up arms. I have personally ordered the affairs of the realm. The good and bad, true and false, of human nature have all been experienced by me. Those who were wicked and crafty by nature and committed serious crimes obvious beyond doubt have been specifically ordered to be punished by extralegal penalties with the intention of making people take heed and thus not lightly dare to break the law. Nevertheless, this is just an expedient measure to punish the wicked; it is not the permanent law [*changfa*] of the ruler who preserves the accomplishments. From now on, when my descendants become emperors they shall only enforce the *Code* and *The Grand Pronouncements*. They certainly shall not employ any punishments like tat-

tooing, cutting off the feet, cutting off the nose, and castration. Because the succeeding rulers will be born and raised in the palace, they cannot have a complete knowledge of human nature's good and evil. I fear that in time something untoward will transpire, harming the innocent by mistake. If there are officials who dare to memorialize requesting the use of these punishments, civil and military officials shall immediately submit accusations. The criminals shall be executed.[243]

This "imperial instruction" clearly justifies the emperor's usage of extralegal punishments. What interests us more, however, is the description of the nature of *The Grand Pronouncements*. The emperor first admits that the extralegal punishments should not be considered "permanent law." At this point, it is not clear whether or not he includes the extralegal punishments in *The Grand Pronouncements*. Yet after he requires succeeding emperors to uphold both the *Code* and *The Grand Pronouncements*, he prohibits them from employing four sorts of brutal punishments. Those four punishments are precisely the ones often meted out in *The Grand Pronouncements*. If we read the passage as a whole, it seems that Zhu Yuanzhang also denied some extralegal punishments in *The Grand Pronouncements* to be considered "permanent law." So I speculate that, possibly after several years' practice, Zhu realized the limited role of cruel punishments in achieving great government and began to revise the contents of *The Grand Pronouncements* and to reconsider its position in the legal system. In any case, as Zhu himself implied, the extralegal punishments employed in *The Grand Pronouncements* as "an expedient measure" did not challenge the *Code*'s nature as the fundamental law of the dynasty.

The relationship between the *Code* and *The Grand Pronouncements* became clearer when *The Code with Pronouncements* (Lü gao; later referred to as *The Great Ming Code with Pronouncements* [Da Ming lü gao]) was established and promulgated in 1397. On this occasion, Zhu Yuanzhang once again explained to his officials why he utilized the harsh *Grand Pronouncements*. The regular rituals and the *Code*, according to him, could not effectively prevent the wayward from doing evil things; therefore, he compiled the special law in his spare time after handling governmental affairs. In order to make it known to all his subjects, he specifically had judicial officials select the essential articles from *The Grand Pronouncements* and "attach" (*fuzai*) them to the *Code*. All other interdicts should be abandoned. Except for crimes such as plotting rebellion and those capital crimes specified in *The Code with Pronouncements*, all miscellaneous crimes should be judged in accordance with *The Regulation on Redemption of Crimes* (Shuzui tiaoli).[244]

The Code with Pronouncements[245] is a special "regulation," which is also entitled *Imperially Approved Regulation of the Code with Pronouncements* (Qinding lü gao tiaoli).[246] It is composed of 111 articles selected from the

Code and 36 articles from *The Grand Pronouncements*. Among the 147 articles, 102 from the *Code* and 12 from *The Grand Pronouncements* are categorized as "unredeemable capital crimes" (*buzhunshu sizui*), and 9 from the *Code* and 24 from *The Grand Pronouncements* are categorized as "redeemable capital crimes" (*zhunshu sizui*). Thus, this list of article titles (rather than a full quotation of their contents) distinguishes whether or not a capital crime stipulated in the two law codes can be redeemed with money or be pardoned by amnesty. This regulation transformed both the original *Great Ming Code* and *The Grand Pronouncements*. For the *Code*, it confirmed the principle of distinguishing between "true capital crimes" (*zhenfan sizui*) and "miscellaneous capital crimes" (*zafan sizui*) that had been practiced since the early Hongwu reign[247] and that softens the provisions in the *Code* by making a number of capital crimes redeemable. The regulation also makes *The Grand Pronouncements* less severe by categorizing a substantial number of capital crimes as redeemable.

Yang Yifan claims that *The Code with Pronouncements* is an integral part of *The Great Ming Code*, just like *The Great Ming Code with Regulations* (Da Ming lü fuli) in later times. Therefore, according to Yang, *The Great Ming Code* exists in two versions: one contains only the 460 articles, whereas the other also includes *The Code with Pronouncements*.[248] This argument is problematic. The imperial proclamation makes it clear that *The Code with Pronouncements* served only as an appendix attached to the main body of *The Great Ming Code*, while the latter still stood as the basic law of the dynasty and was to be observed in dealing with legal cases. In this way, not only were the contents of *The Code with Pronouncements* altered from 236 articles to 36 articles with the emphasis on capital crimes, but more important, the status of *The Code with Pronouncements* was dramatically changed from a once-independent law code to a dependent regulation. Among the 36 articles listed in *The Code with Pronouncements*, 12 are not stipulated by the *Code* at all; 14 have similar provisions in the *Code* but they are not exactly the same; and only 10 have the exact same crimes as defined in the *Code*.[249] To me, *The Imperially Approved Regulation of the Code with Pronouncements* can be read more as a supplement to *The Great Ming Code* instead of an integral part, just like *The Regulation on Redemption of Crimes*, which was issued on the same day that *The Imperially Approved Regulation of the Code with Pronouncements* was established.[250] In other words, *The Grand Pronouncements* had not become the fundamental law of the dynasty.

In reality, "since *The Code with Pronouncements* was issued, the great variety of harsh punishments prescribed in *The Grand Pronouncements* were not randomly used."[251] Huang Chang-chien's intensive study of the legal practices of the Ming suggests that right after Zhu Yuanzhang's death, the legitimacy and effectiveness of *The Grand Pronouncements* began to be ques-

Introduction: The Making of The Great Ming Code   lxxxv

tioned.²⁵² In order not to violate the rule on "altering the established laws," succeeding emperors simply emphasized *The Great Ming Code* but kept silent about *The Grand Pronouncements*. By the middle of the Ming dynasty, *The Grand Pronouncements* was rarely seen among the people. Its legal relevance lay only in the convention by which criminals would have their penalties reduced one degree if, as Zhu Yuanzhang had ordered, they possessed a copy of the legal text.²⁵³

THE GREAT MING CODE AND SPECIAL STATUTES, PLACARDS, AND REGULATIONS

The Imperially Approved Regulation of the Code with Pronouncements was only one of the regulations that were promulgated in the founding emperor's reign. Indeed, the Hongwu era witnessed the issuance of a great number of special regulations (*li*),²⁵⁴ decrees (*zhao*), commands (*ling*), and placards (*bangwen*), which closely interacted with the making of *The Great Ming Code*.²⁵⁵

Zhu Yuanzhang saw it as his sacred mission to save the realm after nearly one hundred years of Mongol rule. To achieve this end, he mobilized all the resources he could to create a new social and legal order. In the field of law, he organized officials to enact and revise *The Great Ming Code* as a fundamental law for the founding and maintaining of a long-lasting dynasty; he also felt urgency to employ other legal means to consolidate the new regime and to further transform the empire. The basic characteristic of these numerous special laws is that, unlike *The Great Ming Commandment*, they were "complete" criminal norms; that is, they included all three elements—rule, conditions, and sanction—that legal norms should contain. They were related to the *Code* in the following aspects.

First, some of the special laws were incorporated into the *Code*. As noted above, the making of the *Code* was a long-term process. Zhu Yuanzhang and his officials kept revising the legal document in the hope that they could provide a permanent law code for generations to come. In this process, lawmakers adopted one after another contemporary separate regulation as specific articles in the *Code*. A well-known example took place in 1372, when Zhu publicized the so-called iron placard (*tiebang*) to admonish meritorious officials.²⁵⁶ With nine items, the placard prohibited dukes and marquises from bullying common people and from associating with military personnel. Most of the nine articles were later made part of the *Code* (Arts. 90, 98–99, 237, 373).²⁵⁷ As another example, in 1381, the emperor issued a new command which stated that those who arranged bribes for officials should be punished together with those who received the bribes, and their families should be banished (*qianxi*) to the frontier.²⁵⁸ This provision with the penalty of banishment was also added to the *Code* (Art. 367).²⁵⁹ Although the stipulation in the *Code* was slightly modified from that of the statute, the main idea remained.

Other special laws were made to supplement the *Code*. A single written document, the *Code* could by no means meet the demands of the time. It therefore became imperative for the government to create flexible regulations to supplement the basic law. Yang Yifan has collected 22 "harsh statutes" (*junling*) of the Hongwu period, 10 of them punishing acts that are not specified in the *Code*.²⁶⁰ He finds that many placards either supplement the *Code* or make the provisions of the *Code* more specific.²⁶¹ During the Hongwu emperor's final days of rule, he promulgated *The Placard of Instructions for the People* (Jiaomin bangwen).²⁶² This document also provides supplemental prescriptions on criminal acts and judicial procedure.

Finally, many special laws were made to carry out the founding emperor's "harsh-law" policy, which, although punishing the same crimes, contradicted the stipulations in the *Code*. For instance, according to the *Code*, the act of false accusation was not to be punished by the death penalty unless those who were falsely accused were executed (Art. 359), whereas a placard in 1389 stipulated death by slow slicing for such a crime.²⁶³ A few compiled regulations also altered the contents of the *Code*, among which the *Regulations concerning Military Exile* (Chongjun tiaoli), *Regulation concerning True and Miscellaneous Capital Crimes* (Zhenfan zafan sizui tiaoli), *Regulation of Hongwu 30* (Sanshi nian tiaoli), as well as the above-mentioned *Imperially Approved Regulation of the Code with Pronouncements* were well-known examples. Many crimes punishable by beating with the heavy stick or penal servitude in the *Code* are punishable by exile or death in these regulations.²⁶⁴

Nevertheless, the contradiction between the special laws and the *Code* during the Hongwu period should not be exaggerated. After all, *The Great Ming Code* underwent constant revisions throughout the first 30 years of the dynasty. Most of the comparisons we have reviewed above are between early special laws and the final version of the *Code*, but we are unable to figure out exactly when the articles in the *Code* were enacted. It might be possible that some of the stipulations in the *Code* were not contrary to the special laws but were changed later when the text assumed its final form in 1397.

More important, the Hongwu emperor and his court officials were on the alert against the permanent *Code* being overruled by temporary special laws. In 1391, the assistant prefect from Jiaxing, Pang An, reported that someone who smuggled salt was captured and the salt was given to the person who seized the smuggler as a reward. Officials from the Ministry of Revenue opposed this decision and requested that the salt be forfeit to the government in accordance with the "regulation" (*li*). Pang An argued that "the *Code* is the permanent law for ten thousand generations, whereas the reg-

Introduction: The Making of The Great Ming Code lxxxvii

ulations are decrees for temporary purpose." If the salt was forfeit to the government according to the regulation, he asserted, it would contradict the stipulation in the *Code* that required that the salt be given to the capturer as a reward. This would result in a loss of faith in the *Code* throughout the realm. Zhu Yuanzhang was convinced by Pang An's argument and ordered that the *Code* should be followed.[265]

On another occasion, in the second month of 1395, an official at the Ministry of Justice memorialized requesting the revision of the provisions in the *Code* that contradicted special regulations, so that the *Code* could be effectively practiced by various government offices. Zhu Yuanzhang refused this suggestion on the ground that only the *Code*, the standard law, should be constantly followed:

> The laws and commands are the implements for guarding the people and the methods for assisting government. In these are the standard provisions [*jing*] and the expedient provisions [*quan*]. The *Code* is the permanent standard provision, while the special regulations are the momentary measures taken to meet expediencies. I have ruled the realm for nearly thirty years and have commanded the responsible offices to establish the *Code* for a long time. What use is there in revising it?[266]

The emperor was aware of the relationship between the *Code* and ad hoc regulations and defended the former's status as the fundamental law of the dynasty. Eventually, this stance was to become a provision in Article 439 of the permanent law code:

> The imperial decrees that decide penalties for individual cases as temporary expediencies and that are not promulgated as [a part of] the established *Code* shall not be cited by analogy as [articles of] the *Code*. If they are cited analogically without authorization so that penalties are decreased or increased, [the officials] shall be punished on the basis of deliberately or negligently [exonerating the guilty or implicating the innocent] [Art. 433].

In short, the nature of *The Great Ming Code* as the fundamental law of the dynasty is evinced in its comprehensiveness and its intricate relationship with other legal systems of the Hongwu reign. By restructuring the *Code* under the six major categories of cosmological significance, the early Ming ruling elite envisioned a legal text that regulated all important areas of social relations. Practically, the *Code* incorporated a number of legal documents such as the *Commandment* into its judicial network and enforced them by means of punishments. Most of the special laws with their own sentencing directives primarily functioned as minor supplements to the *Code*. The single major piece of legislation that challenged the supreme authority of the

Code—*The Grand Pronouncements*—was basically employed by the emperor himself as an educational handbook. Because of its expedient nature, the legal authority of *The Grand Pronouncements* focused only on the application of the death penalty by the end of the Hongwu reign and faded away from the Ming legal system soon after the death of its author, the founding emperor. To be sure, since the mid-Ming, "regulations" (*li*) had become more and more important in the Ming legal system.[267] *The Great Ming Code*, however, continued to function as the fundamental law of the dynasty and was revered by succeeding emperors[268] and enforced by judicial officials of the empire.[269] The emperors and court officials of later generations complied with what Zhu Yuanzhang had ruled: the established *Code* should not be changed; whoever dared to propose such a change would be punished for "changing the ancestral institutions."[270] That *The Great Ming Code* was stable and effective throughout the entire Ming period was probably not only the result of the founding emperor's warning but also because, to a great extent, the law found the "happy medium" of the time.

NOTES (see abbreviations list on page 293)

1. The making of *The Great Ming Code* has been briefly mentioned in Hucker, *The Ming Dynasty*, 44–45; in Langlois, "Ming Law"; and in several of Farmer's works, such as "*The Great Ming Commandment (Ta Ming Ling)*," 181–87, and *Zhu Yuanzhang and Early Ming Legislation*. In "Lüjie bianyi, Da Ming lü zhijie ji Ming lü jijie fuli sanshu suozai Ming lü zhi bijiao yanjiu," Huang Chang-chien compares and contrasts three versions of *The Great Ming Code*. Yang Yifan offers a more comprehensive textual analysis of the *Code* in his *Hongwu falü dianji kaozheng*. My Ph.D. dissertation "*The Great Ming Code*: A Cosmological Instrument for Transforming 'All under Heaven'" studies the cosmological foundation of this Ming legal enactment.

2. For a general treatment of Ming history in English, see Mote and Twitchett, *Cambridge History of China*, vols. 7 and 8, *The Ming Dynasty, 1368–1644*. For accounts of the Ming founding, see Farmer, *Early Ming Government*; Dreyer, *Early Ming China*; and Dardess, *Confucianism and Autocracy*.

3. Zhu Yuanzhang was posthumously known as Ming Taizu (Grand Progenitor of the Ming). A comprehensive treatment of him in Chinese is Wu Han's *Zhu Yuanzhang zhuan*. For English accounts of this emperor, see the biography by Teng Ssu-yü in *DMB*, 381–92; Taylor, *Basic Annals of Ming T'ai-tsu*; and Hok-lam Chan, "The Rise of Ming T'ai-tsu."

4. Farmer, *Zhu Yuanzhang and Early Ming Legislation*, 1–4.

5. For brief treatments of the late Yuan political and social problems, see Mote, "Rise of the Ming Dynasty," and Dreyer, *Early Ming China*, 12–19.

6. Dardess, *Conquerors and Confucians*.

7. See Romeyn Taylor's entry in *DMB*, 600–602.

8. See Romeyn Taylor's entry in *DMB*, 185–88.

9. See John Dardess's entry in *DMB*, 485–88.

10. See Romeyn Taylor's entry in *DMB*, 777–80.
11. See John Dardess's entry in *DMB*, 99–103.
12. See Romeyn Taylor's entry in *DMB*, 435–38.
13. Huang Miantang and Liu Feng, *Zhu Yuanzhang pingzhuan*, 11–13; Farmer, *Early Ming Government*, 28–30; Mote, "Rise of the Ming Dynasty," 18–43; Dreyer, *Early Ming China*, 18–25.
14. *TS*, 65.1225.
15. Wu Han, *Zhu Yuanzhang zhuan*, 11–49; Farmer, *Early Ming Government*, 30, 32; Mote, "Rise of the Ming Dynasty," 44–46.
16. See Chou Tao-chi's entry in *DMB*, 1023–26.
17. See Edward Farmer's entry in *DMB*, 602–8.
18. See Edward Dreyer and Hok-lam Chan's entry in *DMB*, 1277–80.
19. See F. W. Mote's entry in *DMB*, 115–20.
20. See Romeyn Taylor's entry in *DMB*, 850–54.
21. See F. W. Mote's entry in *DMB*, 1225–31.
22. See Hok-lam Chan's entry in *DMB*, 932–38.
23. Mote, "Rise of the Ming Dynasty," 47–57; Farmer, *Early Ming Government*, 32–38; Dreyer, *Early Ming China*, 25–64.
24. Wu Han, *Zhu Yuanzhang zhuan*, 141–43; Farmer, *Early Ming Government*, 38; Dreyer, *Early Ming China*, 69–70; *DMB*, 384–85.
25. See John Dardess's entry in *DMB*, 1069–73.
26. Wu Han, *Zhu Yuanzhang zhuan*, 126–38; Dreyer, "Military Origins of Ming China," 96–101.
27. Langlois, "The Hung-wu Reign," 143–46; Dreyer, *Early Ming China*, 109–14.
28. Langlois, "The Hung-wu Reign," 157–58; Dreyer, *Early Ming China*, 140–44.
29. Hucker, "Ming Government," 10; Dreyer, *Early Ming China*, 114–22.
30. Wu Han, *Zhu Yuanzhang zhuan*, 198–200; Taylor, "Yüan Origins of the Wei-so System"; Dreyer, *Early Ming China*, 76–87.
31. See Hok-lan Chan's entry in *DMB*, 638–41.
32. Wu Han, *Zhu Yuanzhang zhuan*, 251–52; Farmer, *Early Ming Government*, 71–86; Langlois, "The Hung-wu Reign," 139–42; Dreyer, *Early Ming China*, 91–106; Mote, "The Growth of Chinese Despotism."
33. Wu Han, *Zhu Yuanzhang zhuan*, 163–65; Dreyer, *Early Ming China*, 87–90, 125–28.
34. Farmer, *Zhu Yuanzhang and Early Ming Legislation*, 74–75, 195–209; George Jer-lang Chang, "The Village Elder System of the Early Ming Dynasty," 53–62.
35. Andrew, "Zhu Yuanzhang and the *Great Warnings* (*Yuzhi dagao*)."
36. Wu Han, *Zhu Yuanzhang zhuan*, 187–93; Dreyer, *Early Ming China*, 97–99, 131–40; Elman, *A Cultural History of Civil Examinations in Late Imperial China*.
37. Ray Huang, "The Ming Fiscal Administration," 107.
38. Wu Han, *Zhu Yuanzhang zhuan*, 183–85, 212–43; Ray Huang, "The Ming Fiscal Administration," 126–38; Langlois, "The Hung-wu Reign," 123; Brook, *The Confusions of Pleasure*, 66–70; Farmer, *Zhu Yuanzhang and Early Ming Legislation*, 105–7; Dreyer, *Early Ming China*, 122–31.
39. Farmer, *Zhu Yuanzhang and Early Ming Legislation*, 18–32.
40. Langlois and Sun, "Three Teachings Syncretism," 97.
41. Farmer, *Early Ming Government*, 40–41; Dreyer, *Early Ming China*, 1–11, 155–56.

42. Dardess, *Confucianism and Autocracy*, 24–32; Farmer, *Zhu Yuanzhang and Early Ming Legislation*, 24–29; Wing-tsit Chan, "The Ch'eng-Chu School of Early Ming," 44.

43. *TS*, 6.74–75; Zhu Yuanzhang, *Taizu baoxun*, 1.415.

44. Dreyer, *Early Ming China*, 66–69.

45. Wu Han, *Zhu Yuanzhang zhuan*, 188–89; Hok-lam Chan's entry "Liu San-wu" in *DMB*, 956–58.

46. Frederick Mote's entry in *DMB*, 1225–31.

47. Romeyn Taylor's entry in *DMB*, 1263–66; *MS*, 136.3925–27.

48. *MS*, 136.3930–31.

49. *The Collected Rituals of the Great Ming* lists five major categories of rituals: "auspicious rituals" (*jili*), "felicitation rituals" (*jiali*), "rituals for guests" (*binli*), "military rituals" (*junli*), and "rituals at the time of ill omen" (*xiongli*). They cover a broad range of matters such as sacrifice to spirits, court audience, capping, marriage, foreign tribute, military operations, mortuary procedure, regalia, and music.

50. *TS*, 131.2078–79; *MS*, 137.3954.

51. *TS*, 152.2386–87; *MS*, 137.3947–48.

52. Wu Han, *Zhu Yuanzhang zhuan*, 188, 286–89.

53. Orthodox Confucianism is expressed in two important works that were completed in 1415: *The Great Compendium of the Four Books and Five Classics* (Sishu Wujing daquan) and *The Great Compendium of the Philosophy of Human Nature* (Xingli daquan). See Hok-lam Chan, "The Chien-wen, Yung-lo, Hung-hsi, and Hsüan-te Reigns," 218–20.

54. Langlois, "Ming Law"; Farmer, *Zhu Yuanzhang and Early Ming Legislation*. For a list of the legal enactments during the Hongwu reign, see Yang, *Hongwu falü dianji kaozheng*.

55. See Edward Dreyer and Hok-lam Chan's entry in *DMB*, 788–91.

56. Wu Han, *Zhu Yuanzhang zhuan*, 244–75; Langlois, "The Hung-wu Reign"; and Dreyer, *Early Ming China*, 100–106, 140–48.

57. Farmer, *Zhu Yuanzhang and Early Ming Legislation*, 15–17.

58. The Han regime that was centered at Wuchang was founded by Chen Youliang (1320–63), one of the leading rebels at the end of the Yuan dynasty. For a brief account of Chen Youliang and his regime, see the entry "Ch'en Yu-liang" by Romeyn Taylor in *DMB*, 185–88. For the conquest of the Han, see Taylor, *Basic Annals of Ming T'ai-tsu*, 48.

59. *MS*, 93.2280.

60. *MS*, 1.12. Zhu's remarks are translated by Taylor in *Basic Annals of Ming T'ai-tsu*, 48; however, according to Taylor's suggestion, I have substituted the word "dynasty" for "state" in the original translation.

61. For a brief account of Zhang Shicheng, see the entry "Chang Shih-ch'eng" by John Dardess in *DMB*, 99–103.

62. *MS*, 1.16. According to *The Veritable Records of the Ming*, the compilation of this code began on the Jiayin day in the tenth month of Wu 1 (November 3, 1367) and was finished and ordered to be promulgated on the Jiachen day in the twelfth month of the same year (December 23, 1367). On the Wuwu day of the same month (January 6, 1368), only 14 days after its promulgation, a simplified version of the *Code* and the *Commandment* called *Lü ling zhijie* (Code and commandment directly explained) was completed and ordered to be promulgated to the realm (*TS*, 26.388–89; 28a.422–23, 431–32). "The Imperial Preface" to *The Great*

Introduction: The Making of The Great Ming Code

Ming Commandment, however, dates the promulgation to the eighteenth day in the first month of Hongwu 1 (February 6, 1368) (*HMZS*, 1.7). For this reason, Yang Yifan calls *The Ming Code* "the *Code* of Hongwu 1" (*Hongwu falü dianji kaozheng*, 2–3). But since "The Imperial Preface" is written for the *Commandment*, it is not entirely clear that the *Code* was promulgated at the same time. Therefore, I would rather follow the records in *The Veritable Records of the Ming* and call *The Ming Code* the "*Code* of Wu 1."

63. *TS*, 8.111–12.
64. *TS*, 14.193; 18.244.
65. *TS*, 14.176, 182; 26.389–90.
66. *TS*, 6.64; 7.81–82; 24.347.
67. For a brief account of Li Shanchang, see the entry "Li Shan-ch'ang" by Romeyn Taylor in *DMB*, 850–54.
68. *TS*, 27.419–20.
69. *TS*, 26.388–89.
70. *TS*, 28a.422.
71. *TS*, 25.362.
72. They are in Articles 256–57, 306, 336, 338–39 of the *Tang Code*; see *Tang lü shuyi*, 329–30, 387, 422, 425–26.
73. *TS*, 27.419–20. Zhu Yuanzhang did not specifically talk about killing while forcibly taking away prisoners, so we do not know how he would categorize this crime.
74. *TS*, 26.388–89. Romeyn Taylor says that Li Shanchang was appointed head of the drafting commission in "December" (*DMB*, 851). This is different from what *The Veritable Records of the Ming* tells us: November 3 was the eleventh day of the tenth month.
75. *The History of the Ming Dynasty* lists the number of "code councilors" as 20 (*MS*, 93.2280). This has been accepted by many Chinese legal historians, including some Ming law experts such as Yang Yifan and Huai Xiaofeng; see Yang, *Hongwu falü dianji kaozheng*, 2; Huai, *Da Ming lü*, "Collation Explanation," 1; Zhang Jinfan, *Zhongguo fazhi shi*, 273. Huang Yunmei has pointed out, however, that *The Veritable Records of the Ming* and *Guoque* list 28 persons (*TS*, 26.388–89; Tan Qian, *Guoque*, 2.344). Huang Yunmei considers the record in *The History of the Ming Dynasty* to be mistaken (*Ming shi kaozheng*, 3.859). Yang Yifan, Huai Xiaofeng, and many other historians have not discussed this difference in their recently published works. It is not clear to me whether they do not agree with what *The Veritable Records of the Ming* says or they are not yet aware of the discrepancy. In his 1963 work "Dai Min ryō kaisetsu," 92–96, Japanese historian Naito Kenkichi gives 29 code councilors. My study follows Naito's argument.
76. A native of Taiyuan, Yang Xian was actively involved in the Ming founding. He joined Zhu Yuanzhang in 1356 (*MS*, 1.5) and soon was sent as an emissary to Zhang Shicheng to foster friendly relations (*MS*, 123.3693). In Zhu Yuanzhang's struggle for the new dynasty, Yang served successively as chief minister of the Court of the Government Granaries (*MS*, 78.1896), assistant administrator of the Secretariat (*MS*, 93.2280), assistant director of the Household of the Heir Apparent (*MS*, 115.3548), right grand councilor, and left grand councilor (*MS*, 109.3307). He was once criticized by Zhu Yuanzhang for advocating harsh law (*MS*, 94.2319; *TS*, 25.362). In the early Ming power struggles, he falsely accused Li Wenzhong

(*MS*, 113.3506) and Wang Guangyang (*MS*, 127.3774) and was executed in 1370 for monopolizing court affairs (*TS*, 54.1069–71).

77. Although we know little about Fu Huan, he might have taken an active part in the early Ming codification work. He was one of the officials to whom Zhu Yuanzhang addressed his concern to eliminate collective persecution in the law code (*TS*, 25.362). He was given the responsibility not only for drafting the law code but also for compiling the ritual regulations (*MS*, 47.1224). In the eighth month of Hongwu 1, he was dismissed from his position as assistant administrator in the Secretariat.

78. In *TS*, the name "Xu Ben" appears several times. In addition to the reference on lawmaking, Xu served as provincial administration commissioner for Guangdong from Hongwu 13 (1380) on (*TS*, 133.2112). In Hongwu 18 (1385), he was appointed to be minister of public works but was dismissed in the next year (*TS*, 170.2581; *MS*, 111.3398, 3399).

79. A statesmen, thinker, and astrologer, Liu Ji played an important role in the construction of early Ming institutions in general and in the establishment of the law codes in particular. For a general account of his life, see the entry "Liu Ji" by Hok-lam Chan in *DMB*, 932–38.

80. A high-ranking executive official of the Censorate, Wen Yuanji was responsible for admonishing the throne. He was once criticized by Zhu Yuanzhang for not presenting remonstrances to the new regime (*TS*, 30.529–30). In 1368, he concurrently held the position of advisor to the heir apparent (*MS*, 115.3548). In the winter of that year, he and some other court officials were sent to the provinces to look for talented persons, and most of those who were recommended by them were employed by the government (*TS*, 36.659–60; *MS*, 71.1712).

81. Fan Xianzu concurrently held the position of advisor to the heir apparent (*MS*, 72.1731, 12.3548).

82. A native of Guangde Subprefecture, Qian Yongren once served in the Yuan government. Later, he joined Zhu Yuanzhang. Soon after he finished drafting the law codes, he helped formulate ritual regulations. In 1368, when the Six Ministries were established, he became the first minister of rites in the new government. At the end of that year, he retired because of old age and lived with his family in Huzhou Subprefecture near Lake Tai (*MS*, 49.1271, 13.3927; *TS*, 37.707).

83. When the Six Ministries were established in the eighth month of 1368, Sheng Yuanfu became one of the two vice ministers of justice, assisting Minister Zhou Zhen. A month later, he replaced Teng Yi as minister of personnel. Soon after, he was appointed administration vice commissioner of Shandong Branch Secretariat. In Hongwu 2 (1369), he was transferred to be administration vice commissioner of Beiping Branch Secretariat (*TS*, 34.610; 35.632; 40.811–12).

84. An early supporter of Zhu Yuanzhang, Tao An became the first Hanlin academician in the new government in 1367. Besides the law code drafting, he was also involved in making ritual regulations as the director-general. For a general account of Tao An's life, see the entry "Tao An" by Romeyn Taylor in *DMB*, 1263–66.

85. A native of Jiangning near Nanjing, Zhou Zhen had expertise in legal affairs. He became the assistant surveillance commissioner of Jiangxi Branch Secretariat in 1364. In 1368, he was appointed the first minister of justice. Before long, he was transferred to be a secretarial censor. In the next year, he went out to serve as the administration vice commissioner in Guangdong Branch Secretariat, where he

Introduction: The Making of The Great Ming Code　　　　　　　　xciii

reportedly won the affection of the local people by his benevolent rule. In 1370, he came back to the central government to be the vice censor-in-chief. In the same year, he retired because of illness (*MS*, 138.3967).

86. After the founding of the dynasty, Liu Weijing became the assistant administrator of the Secretariat in the twelfth month of 1368. In the next year, when the Guangxi Branch Secretariat was created, he was transferred as its administration vice commissioner (*MS*, 109.3306, 3307; *TS*, 40.811–12). In the "Biography of Zhou Zhen" in *The History of the Ming*, "Liu Weijing" was mistakenly written as "Liu Weiqian" (*MS*, 138.3967), who in 1372 was in charge of revising *The Great Ming Code* as the minister of justice (*MS*, 138.3968; *TS*, 86.1534–35).

87. A native of Poyang, Jiangxi, Zhou Zhen eventually became the minister of justice (*MS*, 138.3968).

88. I have not been able to find any other information about Chen Min. Li Yumin's *Ming shi renming suoyin* (2.1024) says that, according to the "Chronological Tables of Seven Ministers" in *The History of the Ming*, Chen was the minister of personnel in 1383. When I referred to the said source in *The History of the Ming Dynasty*, however, I found that the minister of personnel was Chen Jing rather than Chen Min (*MS*, 111.3397).

89. Pan Fu, a native of Dangtu, Nanjing, died soon after the drafting of the law codes was completed. His father, Pan Tingjian, supported Zhu Yuanzhang in Zhu's early years and, together with Tao An, became an academician of Hanlin Academy in 1367 (*MS*, 135.3918).

90. A native of Zhenjiang, Teng Yi participated in drafting the law codes as a local government official. When the Six Ministries were first established in the eighth month of 1368, Teng was appointed minister of personnel. A month later, he was transferred to be the administration vice commissioner of Jiangxi Branch Secretariat, in which position he soon died (*MS*, 138.3963, 3964; *TS*, 34.609; 35.632).

91. Liu Chengzhi (a) is written as Liu Chengzhi (b) in *The History of the Ming Dynasty*. He is the *Code* councilor whose name is left out of *The Veritable Records of the Ming*. A native of Ganxian, Jiangxi, Liu Chengzhi served as the director of studies in the Directorate of Education before the founding of the new dynasty (*MS*, 137.3953).

92. I have not been able to find more information about Cheng Kongzhao except that, during his service as an assistant surveillance commissioner, he exposed the well-known Confucian scholar Xu Cunren's secret affairs to Zhu Yuanzhang, which resulted in Xu's death in prison (*MS*, 137.3954).

93. A native of Linchuan, Jiangxi, Wu Tong first served as "erudite" of the Directorate of Education. Besides helping formulate the law codes, he also participated in discussions on the ceremonies for ascending the throne and performing sacrifices to spirits (Zang Lihe et al., *Zhongguo renming da cidian*, 313).

94. *MS*, 127.3770.
95. *MS*, 93.2279.
96. *TS*, 86.1534–35.
97. *TS*, 28a.422.
98. *MS*, 128.3777–82; *DMB*, 932–38.
99. For a brief account of Liu Ji's theories on government, see Dardess, *Confucianism and Autocracy*, 133–47.
100. *MS*, 128.3779.

101. *MS*, 138.3967.
102. *TS*, 28a.431–32.
103. *TS*, 28a.422–23.
104. Johnson, *The T'ang Code*, vol. 1.
105. Yang, *Hongwu falü dianji kaozheng*, 3–4. This structural change is ignored by Shen Jiaben (1840–1913), a prominent late Qing court official and jurist. Shen asserts that the *Code* was not organized by the names of the Six Ministries until 1389, after the Secretariat had been abolished and the Six Ministries had taken charge of central-government affairs. See his "*Ming lü* mujian," 1783.
106. Hucker, *The Ming Dynasty*, 44. This argument is also made in Romeyn Taylor's entry "Li Shanchang" in *DMB*, 851.
107. *HMZS*, 1.7.
108. The relationship between the *Code* and the *Commandment* will be discussed later in the Introduction.
109. *TS*, 28a.422–23. Also see *MS*, 93.2280.
110. Some Chinese scholars also maintain that, in 1368, only *The Great Ming Commandment* had been compiled and promulgated. This view has been criticized by Yang Yifan in *Hongwu falü dianji kaozheng*, 2–3.
111. *TS*, 28a.431–32.
112. *The Veritable Records of the Ming* tells us that the law codes were "re-promulgated" (*TS*, 81.1464). The *Ming History*, however, states that the law codes were "promulgated," which gives its readers the impression that the codes were promulgated for the first time in 1373 (*MS*, 93.2281). I suspect that the record in *The History of the Ming Dynasty* is mistaken.
113. *TS*, 34.616.
114. *TS*, 73.1338–39.
115. *TS*, 84.1499–500.
116. *TS*, 86.1534–35.
117. Ibid.
118. *TS*, 86.1534.
119. Jones, *The Great Qing Code*; Wu Tan, *Da Qing lü li tongkao jiaozhu*.
120. *The Ming Code* of 1367 was composed of 285 articles. It is possible that the articles were increased in its re-promulgation in 1368, which would imply that the new *Code* adopted most of the contents of the 1367 version.
121. *TS*, 86.1534–35.
122. Ibid. Also see Johnson, *The T'ang Code*.
123. *TS*, 86.1534–35.
124. Huang Chang-chien points out that Hu became the left grand councilor in 1377; see Huang Chang-chien, *Ming Taizu shilu jiaokan ji*, 2.419.
125. See Romeyn Taylor's entry in *DMB*, 1389–92.
126. *The Veritable Records of the Ming* edited by Huang Chang-chien and reprinted by the Academia Sinica in Taibei, *The History of the Ming Dynasty*, and the *Guoque* all state that "altogether 13 articles" (*fan shisan tiao*) were changed. Nevertheless, another edition of *Veritable Records of the Ming* with the seal of "Bao-jing lou" (The building which embraces the classics) records that 93 articles were revised. This difference has been collated by Huang Chang-chien (see Huang Chang-chien, *Ming Taizu shilu jiaokan ji*, 2.419), but he does not discuss this discrepancy in his works. Another Chinese Ming specialist, Huang Yunmei, in researching *The History of the Ming Dynasty*, points out that the number 13 in

Introduction: The Making of The Great Ming Code xcv

the dynastic history is different from the 93 in *The Veritable Records of the Ming*. He suspects that the former is mistaken and that the character 9 was omitted. He does not specify which edition of *The Veritable Records of the Ming* he is referring to, however. See his *Mingshi kaozheng*, 3.860.

127. *TS*, 110.1821–22; Huang Chang-chien, *Ming Taizu shilu jiaokan ji*, 2.419. *The Veritable Records of the Ming* does not explicitly record that the newly revised law document was promulgated.

128. *TS*, 156.2427. This became Article 220 in *The Great Ming Code* of 1397.

129. Huang Chang-chien, "Ming Hongwu Yongle chao de bangwen junling," 238. Also see Yang Yifan, *Hongwu falü dianji kaozheng*, 6–7.

130. *TS*, 117.1920.

131. *TS*, 141.2222–23.

132. Article 135 of *The Great Ming Code* of 1397.

133. Huang Chang-chien, "Lüjie bianyi, Da Ming lü zhijie ji Ming lü jijie fuli sanshu suozai Ming lü zhi bijiao yanjiu," 236.

134. According to the *Shanghai Gazetteer*, *Gazetteer of Songjiang Prefecture*, and *The Veritable Records of the Ming*, He Guang was appointed a district magistrate in Jiangxi through civil service examination in the Hongwu era. In 1404 (Yongle 2), he first became a censor and then was promoted to be the surveillance vice commissioner of Shaanxi (Huang Chang-chien, "Lüjie bianyi, Da Ming lü zhijie ji Ming lü jijie fuli sanshu suozai Ming lü zhi bijiao yanjiu," 210–11).

135. Liu Hainian and Yang Yifan, *Zhongguo zhenxi falü dianji jicheng*, ser. 2, 1.6–17.

136. Huang Chang-chien, "Ming Hongwu Yongle chao de bangwen junling," 238. This argument is accepted by Yang Yifan in *Hongwu falü dianji kaozheng*, 7, 39, but I am not completely convinced that the *Code* quoted in the book was the one promulgated in 1376. Its chapter numbers and titles, article numbers and titles, and even sequence are all identical to the law code's final version of 1397, and it seems unlikely that the *Code* took this form as early as 1376 because many institutional changes took place after 1376, including the well-known abolition of the Secretariat in 1380, many of which affected the contents of the *Code*. It might be safer to guess that between 1376 and 1389, *The Great Ming Code* was substantially revised but that the revisions were not recorded in surviving historical materials.

137. Liu Hainian and Yang Yifan, *Zhongguo zhenxi falü dianji jicheng*, ser. 2, 1.377.

138. *TS*, 197.2955–56.

139. In the *Code*, "Minglilü" (Laws on punishments and general principles) has 47 articles; "Lilü" (Laws on personnel), 33; "Hulü" (Laws on revenue), 95; "Lilü" (Laws on rituals), 26; "Binglü" (Laws on military affairs), 75; "Xinglü" (Laws on penal affairs), 171; and "Gonglü" (Laws on public works), 13. See *MS*, 93.2281–82; *TS*, 197.2955–56.

140. *TS*, 197.2955.

141. Both Huang Chang-chien and Yang Yifan believe that the record is mistaken (Huang, "Ming Hongwu Yongle chao de bangwen junling," 239; Yang, *Hongwu falü dianji kaozheng*, 9–10). It seems arbitrary, however, to eliminate any possibility that the structure of the *Code* might have been changed again sometime after 1374.

142. *MS*, 93.2282–83.

143. In *The Great Ming Code* of 1397, the eight diagrams are "General Mourning Degrees"; "Formal Mourning Degrees for the Relatives of Nine Generations and Five Mourning Degrees within One's Own Lineage"; "Wife's Mourning Degrees for Husband's Relatives"; "Concubine's Mourning Degrees for Household Head's Relatives"; "Married Daughter's Reduced Mourning Degrees for Her Own Lineage"; "Mourning Degrees for External Relatives"; "Mourning Degrees for Wife's Relatives"; and "Mourning Degrees for Three Fathers and Eight Mothers." See *HMZS*, 4.1627–36.

144. See Peter H. Lee's entry on Yi Song-gye in *DMB*, 1598–1603.

145. Huang Chang-chien renders his name as "Jin Qi" in Chinese, but Yang Yifan says it is "Jin Zhi" (Huang, "*Lü jie bianyi, Da Ming lü zhijie* ji *Ming lü jijie fuli* sanshu suo zai *Ming lü* zhi bijiao," 208; Yang, *Hongwu falü dianji kaozheng*, 8, 224–25). Wolfgang Franke also considers "Kim Chi" ("Jin Zhi" in Chinese) as one of the compilers (*An Introduction to the Sources of Ming History*, 185).

146. For a brief introduction to the different editions of *Taemyong yul chehae*, see Huang Chang-chien, "*Lü jie bianyi, Da Ming lü zhijie* ji *Ming lü jijie fuli* sanshu suo zai *Ming lü* zhi bijiao," 208; Yang, *Hongwu falü dianji kaozheng*, 225; and Franke, *An Introduction to the Sources of Ming History*, 185. Its text is reprinted in Liu Hainian and Yang Yifan, *Zhongguo zhenxi falü dianji jicheng*, ser. 2, 1.397–632.

147. Huang Chang-chien, "*Lü jie bianyi, Da Ming lü zhijie* ji *Ming lü jijie fuli* suo zai *Ming lü* zhi bijiao"; Yang, *Hongwu falü dianji kaozheng*, esp. 225–47.

148. Liu Hainian and Yang Yifan, *Zhongguo zhenxi falü dianji jicheng*, ser. 2, 1.548.

149. Yang, *Hongwu falü dianji kaozheng*, 8–9.

150. Huang Chang-chien, "*Lü jie bianyi, Da Ming lü zhijie* ji *Ming lü jijie fuli* sanshu suo zai *Ming lü* zhi bijiao," 217–29.

151. *MS*, 4.59; 93.2283.

152. First compiled in 1402, the currently preserved *Ming Taizu shilu* was revised in 1412, nine years after Zhu Di defeated his nephew Zhu Yunwen and took the throne. It is not a surprise that some events regarding the deposed emperor were left out of the historical materials. For a brief discussion of *Ming shilu*, see Franke, *An Introduction of the Sources of Ming History*, 8–23, 29–33.

153. *MS*, 93.2283.

154. *TS*, 221.3233.

155. *TS*, 253.3647–48. In one of his early works, Yang Yifan points out the time problem with revisions to the "Treatise on Punishments." But he interprets the "twenty-ninth year" of Hongwu in the "Basic Annals of Gongmin di" as the time when the revisions took place (*Ming chu zhongdian kao*, 7–8). Actually, what is explicitly said in the "Basic Annals" is that Hongwu 29 was the year when the ritual for "princes seeing the Eastern Palace" was reestablished. No specific time is indicated for the code revision, which is used as an example to support the general statement that the imperial grandson-heir, like his father, was interested in the policy of leniency. The sentence starts with the word "*chang*" (once), which only indicates an uncertain date in the past. Yang does not discuss this revision in his *Hongwu falü dianji kaozheng*.

156. As we will see in the following paragraphs, the two versions of *The Great Ming Code* have different penalty stipulations in only several articles. I am not able to reconcile these discrepancies.

Introduction: The Making of The Great Ming Code

157. The emperor is emphasizing the cosmic harmony of Heaven, Earth, and human beings here.

158. *TS*, 253.3647–48. A similar version of the decree can also be seen in *MS*, 93.2284. This decree was modified and became "The Imperial Preface" to *The Great Ming Code* (*HMZS*, 4.1607–8).

159. Zhang Weiren has collected 27 editions of *The Great Ming Code* (Zhang Weiren, *Zhongguo fazhi shi shumu*, 14–29). Thirteen editions appear in Franke's *An Introduction to the Sources of Ming History*, 184–87.

160. The arrangement of articles in the new *Code* is identical to that of *The Great Ming Code* collected in He Guang's *Code with Commentaries and Explication of Questions*. Huang Chang-chien argues that the article sequence of the *Code* of 1376 was changed in the 1389 revision but was restored in the final version of 1397 ("Lü jie bianyi, Da Ming lü zhijie ji Ming lü jijie fuli sanshu suozai *Ming lü* zhi bijiao yanjiu," 235).

161. My study of *The Imperially Approved Code and Pronouncements* is based on the text in Huang Chang-chien's "*Da Ming lü gao* kao" and Yang Yifan's *Hongwu falü dianji kaozheng*, 13–22.

162. See *TS*, 253.3647; *MS*, 93.2284. In "The Imperial Preface" to the *Code*, however, the code is still entitled *The Great Ming Code*. See *HMZS*, 4.1067.

163. Yang Yifan asserts that *The Imperially Approved Code and Pronouncements* is part of *The Great Ming Code*. *The Great Ming Code* in a broader sense, he argues, includes both the whole text of the *Code* and the new regulation (*Hongwu falü dianji kaozheng*, 16–17). It seems to me, however, that though the new regulation has a legal effect on the *Code*, it should not be considered part of the *Code*. First, all the surviving sources (including "The Imperial Preface" to the *Code* and *The Veritable Records of the Ming*) explicitly tell us that the new regulation was attached to the *Code* (*lü*), which indicates that the *Code* is a separate and independent document. Second, regulations on how to deal with "true" and "miscellaneous" capital crimes had been made much earlier in the Hongwu reign. According to *The Veritable Records of the Ming*, as early as 1372 the "miscellaneous" capital crimes were ordered by the emperor to be redeemed by labor services in the Linhao area (*TS*, 76.1399). Huang Chang-chien has collected 14 events from *The Veritable Records of the Ming* and two records from *Da Ming huidian* (The collected institutes of the great Ming) where the true capital crimes are ordered to be punished but the miscellaneous ones could be redeemed (Huang, "*Da Ming lü gao* kao," 168–80). In fact, *The Imperially Approved Code and Pronouncements* belongs to a legislative tradition in imperial China in which specific regulations were issued to modify the basic law. Strong as its effect on the basic law code, the regulation is better understood as not part of the *Code*. *The Great Ming Code* bases many of its stipulations on *The Great Ming Commandment*; in the *Code* (Art. 409) there is even an article entitled "Violating the *Commandment*," but the latter has not been considered a part of the former by most historians.

164. This is reflected in the nine articles compiled in 1497 concerning "miscellaneous capital crimes" that can be redeemed. See *JF*, 118–21.

165. For example, monopolizing the payment of taxes in the *Code* (Art. 130) is punished by 60 strokes of beating with the heavy stick; in the new regulation, it is punished by death, which can be redeemed (Yang, *Hongwu falü dianji kaozheng*, 21).

166. The following capital crimes, for instance, are added to the law code: "cul-

tivated talents [*xiucai*] severing their fingers and slandering," "scholars in the realm not willing to be employed by the ruler," and "hindering the elderly from coming to the capital" (Yang, *Hongwu falü dianji kaozheng*, 20).

167. Huang Chang-chien, "Da Ming lü gao kao," 187–203.

168. There are a number of literary differences that do not affect the basic contents of the *Code*. For those differences, see Yang's collation chart in his *Hongwu falü dianji kaozheng*, 227–47.

169. For the above comparative study of the 1389 and 1397 versions of the *Code*, see Huang Chang-chien, "Lü jie bianyi, Da Ming lü zhijie ji Ming lü jijie fuli sanshu suozai Ming lü zhi bijiao yanjiu," 211–29.

170. *MS*, 93.2284.

171. *TS*, 177.2679.

172. Eisenstadt, "Study of Oriental Despotisms as Systems of Total Power," 445.

173. *TS*, 177.2679.

174. *MS*, 93.2279.

175. *HMZS*, 4.1607–8.

176. Wu Zumou, *Faxue gailun*, 47–48.

177. *The Great Ming Commandment*, Art. 51. See Farmer, *Zhu Yuanzhang and Early Ming Legislation*, 171–74.

178. *MS*, 56.1419–21.

179. Although the four articles do not list specific crimes and punishments, they serve as an integral part of the criminal law. As "subprinciples," they define the meaning of crimes and provide rules on how crimes should be treated. Article 124 decides how marriage-overseers and matchmakers should be punished. Article 303 defines what "robbery" means. Article 326 delimits the period of criminal responsibility in cases of injury. And Article 441 regulates how penalties should be adjusted when an amnesty is issued.

180. "The Meanings of Eight Characters as Used in the General Principles." In *HMZS*, 4.1637.

181. *HMZS*, 4.1621–38. During Ming Shenzong's Wanli reign (1573–1620), three diagrams on penalty redemption were added to the list. See *HMZS*, 4.1639–51; Zhang Jinfan and Huai Xiaofeng, *Zhongguo fazhi tongshi*, 7.31.

182. *MS*, 93.2283.

183. Local magistrates, for example, should bear criminal liability if they fail to inspect fields damaged by natural calamities such as flood, drought, frost, hail, or locusts (Art. 97).

184. A person commits a crime if he knows his companions plot to harm others but fails to stop them immediately (Art. 324).

185. Langlois, "Ming Law," 178.

186. This article might have been written in Hongwu 1, when the *Code* was first promulgated.

187. This article might have been added to the *Code* in Hongwu 7, when the second edition of the law was proclaimed.

188. *Tang lü shuyi*, Art. 48, p. 133.

189. Ibid.; Johnson, *T'ang Code*, 1.252.

190. *JF*, 1.344.

191. *JF*, 1.284. For a general discussion of punishment of the mentally disordered, see Bünger, "The Punishment of Lunatics and Negligence according to Classical Chinese Law."

192. *JF*, 1.284.

193. Specific regulations on "instigators" are stipulated in Arts. 312, 363, 389, 427.

194. Beating with a stick on a criminal's back, buttocks, or thighs first became a formal punishment when Emperor Wen of Han (r. 179–157 B.C.E.) reformed the penal system by abolishing the "corporal punishments" ("corporal punishments" here refer to cutting off parts of the body and tattooing but not beating or whipping). In the Northern Qi dynasty, beating with a heavy stick was called *zhang*. In the Sui dynasty, the punishment of *chi* (beating with the light stick) was added. In the Ming dynasty, the light stick was made of *Vitex negundo* (*jingtiao*) and was 3 *chi* and 5 *cun* long, with its large end 2 *fen* and 7 *li* in diameter and its small end 1 *fen* and 7 *li* in diameter. The criminal was beaten on the buttocks. See *MS*, 93.2282; *The Great Ming Commandment*, Art. 85.

195. A heavy stick was used to beat a criminal's back, buttocks, or thighs. It had the same origin as beating with the light stick and was first called *zhang* in the Eastern Han Dynasty (25–220). In the period of the Northern dynasties (386–581), it became one of the five basic punishments. The Sui dynasty (581–617) substituted it for "whipping." In the Ming dynasty, the heavy stick was also made of *Vitex negundo* and was 3 *chi* and 5 *cun* long, with the large end 3 *fen* and 2 *li* in diameter and the small end 2 *fen* 2 *li* in diameter. See *MS*, 93.2282.

196. Penal servitude is a penalty that sends criminals away to perform labor service for a given time. Before it was incorporated into the five basic punishments with the name of *tuxing* in the Northern Zhou dynasty (557–81), it had a variety of names, such as *kunxing, zuoxing,* and *naixing*. In the Song dynasty (960–1279), penal servitude began to be accompanied by beating with the heavy stick. Article 47 of *The Great Ming Code* specifies the places where the criminals given such a penalty were to be sent to perform labor (*HMZS*, 4.1745–53), but most of the regulation was changed in later times.

197. Life exile is a penalty that sends criminals to distant places to perform a fixed term of labor service and registers them at their places of exile after their term of labor services is completed. *The Book of Documents* states, "Exile can be used to pardon those who are punished by one of the five punishments" (*liu you wuxing*). The penalty of banishment (*qianxi*) in the Qin and Han dynasties was similar to this penalty. Exile first became a penalty, called *liu*, in the Southern Liang dynasty (502–57), and it became one of the five basic punishments in the Northern Qi (550–77) and Northern Zhou dynasties. Article 47 of *The Great Ming Code* specifies the places of exile, but the regulation was largely changed in later times. Other punishments in the *Code* are resettlement (*anzhi*), banishment (*qianxi*), relocation (*yixiang*), and military exile (*chongjun*), which are similar to life exile. See Wu Yanhong, "Mingdai liuxing kao."

198. The death penalty was called *dapi* in the pre-Qin period. Sometimes the decapitated head was displayed in public (*xiaoshou*), and sometimes the body was displayed in the market (*qishi*). Sometimes a person was killed by having five horse-drawn carts tear the body into five pieces (*chelie*). The Sui law reduced the methods of execution to two: strangulation and decapitation. In *The Great Ming Code*, in addition to the regular methods, the most severe penalty—death by slow slicing (*lingchi*)—was used to deal with the most heinous crimes. For death penalties, see, e.g., Arts. 277–78, 307, 342.

199. "Sentencing to death by slicing" began to be used at the latest during the

period of Five Dynasties (907–60). It became one of the formal death penalties in the Khitan Liao dynasty (907–1125), but was used only as an extralegal method in the Song dynasty. In *The Great Ming Code,* this penalty punishes 13 offenses in nine articles. See Arts. 277, 307–8, 310–11, 337–38, 341–42.

200. See, e.g., Arts. 8, 10, 35. The *Code* punished nearly 50 major offenses with military exile. This penalty seems to have started in the Qin dynasty (221–207 B.C.E.), when criminals sentenced to life exile were sent to frontiers as soldiers. It became widely used in the Song and often served as a substitute for the death penalty in the Yuan. During the Ming, it developed into various degrees, including farthest frontier, malarial region, distant frontier, and distant military guards. See Wu Yanhong, *Mingdai chongjun yanjiu,* esp. 2–16.

201. See, e.g., Arts. 17, 47, 52, 127, and 367.

202. See, e.g., Arts. 8, 14, 48, and 63.

203. See, e.g., Arts. 23 and 170.

204. See, e.g., Arts. 81, 83–84, 117, and 298.

205. See, e.g., Arts. 287–88, 291–92, and 304.

206. For a general account of the Ming redemption system in Chinese, see *MS,* 93.2293–2301. General studies of the topic in English can be found in Langlois, "The Code and *ad hoc* Legislation in Ming Law," 102–11; MacCormack, *Traditional Chinese Penal Law,* 105–8, 113, 192.

207. John Langlois also mentions these provisions except that he omits the provision for women and does not specify the rules in most of these provisions. See his "The Code and *ad hoc* Legislation in Ming Law," 105–6.

208. For a brief account of the system of mourning degrees, see Bodde and Morris, *Law in Imperial China,* 35–38. The Ming mourning-degree system was first enacted in *The Great Ming Commandment.* See *The Great Ming Commandment,* Art. 50; Farmer, *Zhu Yuanzhang and Early Ming Legislation,* 164–71.

209. See, e.g., Arts. 307, 342, 392.

210. For a detailed discussion of the relationship between mourning degrees and punishments, also see Ch'u T'ung-tsu, *Law and Society in Traditional China,* 15–90.

211. "Imperial relatives" are defined as the families of the empress, imperial consorts, heir apparent, princes' consorts, commandery princes' consorts, imperial princesses' consorts, ceremonial companions, the dukes Xu Da (1332–85), Li Wenzhong (1339–84), and Tang He (1326–95), and the marquises Mu Ying (1345–95) and Guo Ying (1335–1403). See Zhu Yuanzhang, *Huang Ming zuxun,* 389–90; Farmer, *Zhu Yuanzhang and Early Ming Legislation,* 119.

212. *MS,* 93.2279.

213. Song Lian, "Memorial to Present the *Great Ming Code,*" in *HMZS,* 4.1616.

214. *MS,* 93.2288.

215. *MS,* 93.2284.

216. Ibid.

217. *The Tang Code* classifies crimes into 11 chapters: "Imperial Guard and Prohibitions," "Administrative Regulations," "Household and Marriage," "Public Stables and Warehouses," "Unauthorized Levies," "Violence and Robbery," "Assaults and Accusations," "Fraud and Counterfeit," "Miscellaneous Articles," "Arrest and Flight," and "Judgment and Prison." See Johnson, *The T'ang Code,* vol. 2. A major difference between the structures of *The Tang Code* and *The Great Ming Code* is that the former uses two classification criteria: social relations damaged by

Introduction: The Making of The Great Ming Code

crimes and the criminal acts themselves. The latter unifies the classification standard: damaged social relations.

218. Yang, *Hongwu falü dianji kaozheng*, 3–4.

219. For the three hierarchies of the Ming government, see Hucker, "Ming Government," 72–103.

220. Zhu Yuanzhang, *Huang Ming zuxun*, 389. This passage is translated in Farmer, *Zhu Yuanzhang and Early Ming Legislation*, 118–19.

221. *TS*, 129.2049.

222. For *The Institutes of Zhou*, see Ruan, *Shisan jing zhushu*, 1.631–939.

223. It is noteworthy that in the "Treatise on Personnel" of *The History of the Ming Dynasty*, only the Six Ministries are defined as government offices in charge of affairs of "all under Heaven." See *MS*, 72.1734–63. Moreover, of all the government offices Zhu Yuanzhang listed in the *Huang Ming zuxun*, only the Six Ministries deal with matters among the people through their corresponding "six offices" at the district level. See Bo, "Mingdai zhouxian," 354.

224. Taylor, "Chinese Hierarchy in Comparative Perspective," 500.

225. Ibid., 493.

226. The "incorporated commentary" to the *Code* explains that violating principles "is also a crime" and therefore should be punished even though it is specified in neither the *Code* nor the *Commandment*. See *JF*, 5.1891.

227. *HMZS*, 1.86.

228. Zhu Yuanzhang, *Huang Ming zhaoling*, 11.

229. Note that the penalties prescribed in Article 60 of the *Code* include only "decapitation" and "enslavement of wives and children." It is possible that after Hu Weiyong and his alleged associates were executed in Hongwu 13 (1380), the *Code* was revised and thus became harsher on this issue. This also brings up the question regarding when the concept of "treacherous cliques" was introduced and when stipulation on this crime was created. This will be discussed later.

230. In the *Commandment*, nearly half of the 145 articles can also be found in the *Code*. It should be pointed out that after their promulgation, the *Commandment* remained unchanged, whereas the *Code* underwent a number of revisions. The *Code* of 1367, which became effective at the same time as the *Commandment*, was lost. While this makes it difficult to argue exactly what articles were enacted in the *Code*, I still assume that the stipulations such as the "five punishments," "Ten Abominations," "Eight Deliberations," "voluntary confessions," and "methods of reducing punishments," which had become core principles in the law codes since the Sui dynasty (581–617), must have also appeared in the initial version of *The Ming Code*.

231. *JF*, 5.1891.

232. For studies of *The Grand Pronouncements*, the followings are noteworthy. Shen Jiaben ("*Ming lü* mujian") lists the severe penalties prescribed in the document. Teng Ssu-yu ("Ming *Dagao* yu Mingchu zhengzhi shehui") analyzes early Ming political history based on the text. Huang Chang-chien ("*Da Ming lü gao* kao") specifically discusses *The Great Ming Code with Pronouncements*. Anita Andrew ("Zhu Yuanzhang and the *Great Warning*") studies the early Ming autocracy and rural reform as seen in the text. Yang Yifan (*Ming Dagao yanjiu*) provides textual research on the document. The text of *The Grand Pronouncements* can be found in Yang Yifan, *Ming Dagao yanjiu*, 195–452; Zhang Dexin and Mao Peiqi, *Hongwu yuzhi quanshu*, 745–951.

233. For a study of the dates when the four parts of *The Grand Pronouncements* were issued, see Yang, *Ming Dagao yanjiu*, 6–8.
234. Zhu Yuanzhang, *Yuzhi dagao*, 252.
235. Zhu Yuanzhang, *Yuzhi Dagao xubian*, 337; Zhu Yuanzhang, *Yuzhi Dagao sanbian*, 419.
236. *TS*, 177.2676, 212.3141; Tan Qian, *Guoque*, 9.724.
237. *MS*, 93.2284; *Guoque*, 9.724.
238. Yang, *Ming Dagao yanjiu*, 45–57.
239. Ibid., 61.
240. Ibid., 64–76.
241. Ibid., 65.
242. Zhu Yuanzhang, *Yuzhi Dagao sanbian*, 403–4, 408–9.
243. *TS*, 239.3477–78. This passage also appears in Zhu Yuanzhang, *Huang Ming zuxun* (389), which specifies the punishment for the officials as "sentencing to death by slow slicing and executing his whole family." This passage is translated in Farmer, *Zhu Yuanzhang and Early Ming Legislation*, 118. I have slightly modified it in this quotation.
244. See "The Imperial Preface to *The Great Ming Code*," *HMZS*, 4.1607–8. This passage also appears in *The Veritable Records of the Ming* and *The History of the Ming Dynasty*; see *TS*, 252.3647–48; *MS*, 93.2284. The title of the law code in the latter two documents, however, is *Da Ming lü gao* (The great Ming code and pronouncements) instead of *Lü gao*. *The Regulations on Redemption of Crimes* was established on the same day as *The Code with Pronouncements* was promulgated; see *TS*, 253.3647.
245. Huang, "*Da Ming lü gao kao*," 156–66. *The Code with Pronouncements* has also been studied by Yang Yifan (*Hongwu falü dianji kaozheng*, 13–22).
246. We will discuss the relationship between *The Great Ming Code* and "regulations" below.
247. Article 16 of the *Code* defines a number of acts as "true crimes" (*zhenfan*), which can never be pardoned despite the announcement of an amnesty. Crimes committed negligently, mistakenly, or by implication of others or public crimes committed by officials or functionaries may be pardoned under an amnesty. We are unable to identify when this article was written, however. *The Veritable Records of the Ming* starts to give an account of "miscellaneous capital crimes" in the fifth month of 1372. See Huang Chang-chien, "*Da Ming lü gao kao*," 179–80.
248. Yang, *Hongwu falü dianji kaozheng*, 14, 16.
249. See the list and comparison in ibid., 131–34.
250. By the same token, the "regulations" in *The Great Ming Code with Regulations*, which was compiled after the mid-Ming period, should not be viewed as an integral part of *The Great Ming Code* either.
251. *MS*, 93.2284.
252. Huang Chang-chien, "*Da Ming lü gao kao*," 187–99. This issue has also been studied by Yang Yifan (*Ming Dagao yanjiu*, 138–43).
253. Ying Jia's *Yanyu gao* records how the author applied the principle of "reduction of penalty due to the possession of *The Grand Pronouncements*" to his case judgments during the Jiajing reign (1522–66). Wu Yanhong argues that, in judicial practice since the mid-Ming, criminals often had their penalties reduced under this imperial principle regardless of whether or not they possessed a copy of *The Grand Pronouncements*. See Wu, "Mingdai liuxing kao."

Introduction: The Making of The Great Ming Code ciii

254. This *li* is sometimes translated by other scholars as "precedent" or "substatute."

255. Huang Chang-chien's "Ming Hongwu Yongle chao de bangwen junling" and Yang Yifan's *Hongwu falü dianji kaozheng* (149–63) offer general studies of the placards and harsh statutes promulgated in the Hongwu and Yongle reigns. John Langlois ("The Code and *ad hoc* Legislation in Ming Law") examines the contradiction between *The Great Ming Code* and ad hoc legislation in Ming law.

256. *TS*, 74.1377–81.

257. Arts. 90, 98–99, 237, and 375.

258. *TS*, 136.2155.

259. Art. 367.

260. Yang Yifan, *Hongwu falü dianji kaozheng*, 150–52.

261. Ibid., 157–59. For a complete quotation of the placards, see Huang Chang-chien, "*Minglü* zhi bijiao yanjiu," 263–86.

262. The *Jiaomin bangwen* can be found in the Taibei edition of *HMZS*, 3.1405–44. It also appears in the Tokyo edition of *HMZS*, 1.467–76. For an English translation of the text, see Farmer, *Zhu Yuanzhang and Early Ming Legislation*, 195–209.

263. Huang Chang-chien, "*Minglü* zhi bijiao yanjiu," 264.

264. Yang, *Hongwu falü dianji kaozheng*, 153–54. Contradicting regulations indeed became a serious problem during the mid-Ming period. Since the founding emperor forbade succeeding rulers to change a single word in the established *Great Ming Code* (Art. 63), making new regulations was a legitimate and effective method to meet changing circumstances (*MS*, 93.2287). Beginning in the Hongzhi emperor's reign (14—[last two digits of the first year of his reign are missing]–1505), the imperial court compiled several versions of regulations which were entitled *Wen xing tiaoli* (Regulations for trying penal cases). Eventually, the compiled regulations were attached to *The Great Ming Code* under specific articles, becoming a substantial part of the Ming legal system. See Langlois, "The Code and *ad hoc* Legislation in Ming Law," 92–112. Huang Chang-chien's *Mingdai lü li huibian* systematically edits the regulations compiled since the Hongzhi emperor.

265. *MS*, 93.2288. For the provision in the *Code*, see Art. 149.

266. *TS*, 236.3456. The translation is offered in Langlois, "The Code and *ad hoc* Legislation in Ming Law," 90, with my slight modification.

267. In his *Yanyu gao*, for instance, the judicial official and jurist Ying Jia emphasizes the equal importance of the *Code* and *Wen xing tiaoli* (Regulations for trying penal cases), compiled during Xiaozong's Hongzhi reign. Although the regulations were enacted to "assist" (*fu*) the *Code*, Ying asserts that both were "levels, plumb lines, compasses, and squares [i.e., rules and criteria] for judging law cases" (*zhiyu zhi zhunsheng guiju*) (*Yanyu gao*, 7.2a). The late Ming official Mao Yilu's *Yunjian yanlüe* reveals that in law enforcement, judicial officials would first decide the punishments according to the *Code* and then apply the regulations to have the punishments redeemed by either money or labor services. In other words, in each law case, both the *Code* and regulations were employed to decide the final legal sanctions (Wu Yanhong and Jiang Yonglin, "'Satisfying Both Sentiment and Law'"). For a collection of various editions of the regulations, see Huang Chang-chien, *Mingdai lüli huibian*.

268. *MS*, 93.2286.

269. In studying the late Ming magistrate Zhang Kentang's law enforcement

in north China (as seen in his casebook *Xunci*), I find that *The Great Ming Code* was used by the magistrate as the basic legal criterion in judging law cases. See my article "Defending Dynastic Order at the Local Level." In addition, other extant Ming casebooks such as Ying Jia's *Yanyu gao* (Jiangnan area), Mao Yilu's *Yunjian yanlüe* (Songjiang Prefecture), Qi Biaojia's *Puyang yandu* (Xinghua Prefecture, Fujian), Yan Junyan's *Mengshuizhai cundu* (Guangzhou Prefecture), and Li Qing's *Zheyu xinyu* (Ningbo Prefecture) all indicate that *The Great Ming Code* was carefully applied by these officials in their legal practice.

270. *MS*, 93.2279.

The Great Ming Code / Da Ming lü

The Imperial Preface to *The Great Ming Code*

I have the realm and govern it by imitating antiquity. Rituals are manifested to guide the people; law codes are established to restrain the wayward. They were promulgated in statutes and carried out for a long time. Nevertheless, there were still many who violated them one after another. I therefore went beyond the "five punishments" [*wuxing*] and used harsh laws to govern them, hoping that the people would be afraid and thus not violate [the laws]. Long ago, I made *The Grand Pronouncements* [*Dagao*] and clearly displayed it among the people to let them know the way to pursue good fortune and avoid bad luck. But since law is kept in government offices, people cannot know all the stipulations. So I specifically ordered officials at the Six Ministries and the Censorate to look up the articles in *The Grand Pronouncements* and select the most important ones to attach to the *Code*. All placards and interdicts issued in the past years shall be eliminated. From now on, judicial offices shall follow only the *Code* and *Pronouncements* to deliberate on punishments. With regard to the penalty of tattooing, except for the dependents of those guilty of "treacherous cliques" and "rebellions" and those who should be punished in accordance with the *Code,* all other criminals shall not be sentenced to tattooing. The miscellaneous capital crimes and the crimes punishable with the penalties such as penal servitude, life exile, banishment, beating with the light stick, and beating with the heavy stick shall all be judged in accordance with *The Regulation on Redemption of Crimes* that was issued today. Now the law is codified and promulgated to the realm, so that the people will know what to observe.

On the —— day of the fifth month of the thirtieth year of the Hongwu reign.

Diagrams

The following abbreviations are used in the mourning-degree diagrams.

DG	*dagong*
M	married
N	no mourning relationship
SM	*sima*
UM	unmarried
XG	*xiaogong*
ZC	*zicui*
ZhC	*zhancui*
b	brother, brother's
d	daughter, daughter's
e	eldest
f	father, father's
h	husband, husband's
m	mother, mother's
o	other
s	sister, sister's
S	son, son's
w	wife, wife's

The diagram "Formal Mourning Degrees for the Relatives of Nine Generations and Five Mourning Degrees within One's Own Lineage" was drawn by referring to Farmer, *Zhu Yuanzhang and Early Ming Legislation*, 164–71; McKnight, *Law and Order in Sung China*, 54; and Feng, *Chinese Kinship System*, 2–3, 8–13, 22, 26.

The Five Punishments

Beating with the Light Stick: Five Degrees

10	Beating with the light stick means that someone commits
20	a minor crime and is beaten with a small *Vitex negundo*
30	branch. There are five degrees of severity: From 10 to 50
40	strokes. Each 10 strokes shall be considered one degree of
50	punishment.

Beating with the Heavy Stick: Five Degrees

60	Beating with the heavy stick means that someone commits
70	a crime and is beaten with a large *Vitex negundo* branch.
80	There are five degrees of severity: from 60 to 100 strokes.
90	Each 10 strokes shall be considered one degree of
100	punishment.

Penal Servitude: Five Degrees

1 year, 60 strokes	Penal servitude means that someone commits a fairly
1.5 years, 70 strokes	serious crime and is taken into custody by the govern-
2 years, 80 strokes	ment to perform hard labor such as making salt and
2.5 years, 90 strokes	smelting iron. There are five degrees of severity: from
3 years, 100 strokes	1 to 3 years; each 10 strokes and one-half year shall be
	considered one degree.

Life Exile: Three Degrees

2,000 *li*, 100 strokes	Life exile means that someone commits a serious crime.
2,500 *li*, 100 strokes	Cannot bear to execute him; [instead] exile him to a
3,000 *li*, 100 strokes	distant place and do not allow him to return to his native
	place. There are three degrees of severity: from 2,000 to
	3,000 *li*; each 500 *li* shall be considered one degree.

Death: Two Degrees

These are extreme penalties.
Strangulation: Retain
the whole body.
Decapitation: Separate
the head and body.

Banishment

This entails moving at least 1,000 *li* from one's native place.

The Penal Instruments

Light Stick
Large end: 2 *fen* 7 *li* in diameter
Small end: 1 *fen* 7 *li* in diameter
Length: 3 *chi* 5 *cun*

To be made from a small *Vitex negundo* branch. Must remove knots or nodes. Use official measuring stick to bring it in line with the regulations. Shall not use resin or other materials to bind it. When imposing punishments use the small end. Apply to the buttocks.

Heavy Stick
Large end: 3 *fen* 2 *li* in diameter
Small end: 2 *fen* 2 *li* in diameter
Length: 3 *chi* 5 *cun*

To be made from a large *Vitex negundo* branch. Must also remove knots or nodes. Use official measuring stick to bring it in line with the regulations. Shall not use resin or other materials to bind it. When imposing punishments use the small end. Apply to the buttocks.

Interrogating Stick
Large end: 4 *fen* 5 *li* in diameter
Small end: 3 *fen* 5 *li* in diameter
Length: 3 *chi* 5 *cun*

To be made from a *Vitex negundo* branch. For those who commit serious crimes, if the illicit goods and evidence are clear but they refuse to admit and confess the crimes, establish clear files, and they shall be interrogated with torture according to the law. Apply to the buttocks and legs.

Cangue
Length: 5 *chi* 5 *cun*
Width of each end: 1 *chi* 5 *cun*

To be made of seasoned wood. For capital crimes, it shall weigh 25 *jin*; for life exile and penal servitude, 20 *jin*; for the heavy stick, 15 *jin*. Carve the length and weight upon it.

Manacle
Length: 1 *chi* 6 *cun*
Thickness: 1 *cun*

To be made of seasoned wood. Apply to men who commit capital crimes. For men who commit crimes punishable with life exile or less and women who commit capital crimes, this shall not be applied.

Iron Fetter
Length: 1 *zhang*

To be made of iron. Apply to those who commit minor crimes.

Chain
Rings weigh 3 *jin* in total

To be made of iron. Those who commit crimes punishable with penal servitude wear chains to perform labor services.

General Mourning Degrees

Zhancui
(Unhemmed sackcloth)
[First degree]

3 years
To be made of the coarsest hemp cloth without a hem.

Zicui
(Hemmed sackcloth)
[Second degree]

3 years
Staff for a year (i.e., 1 yr)
One year without staff (also 1 yr)
5 months
3 months
To be made of slightly finer hemp cloth with a hem on the lower border.

Dagong
(Greater coarseness)
[Third degree]

9 months
To be made of coarse woven cloth.

Xiaogong
(Lesser coarseness)
[Fourth degree]

5 months
To be made of slightly coarse woven cloth.

Sima
(Coarse hemp)
[Fifth degree]

3 months
To be made of slightly finer woven cloth.

Formal Mourning Degrees for the Relatives of Nine Generations and Five Mourning Degrees within One's Own Lineage*

			gao zu fu mu (ffff, fffm; ZC, 3 mos)				
			zeng zufumu (fff, ffm; ZC, 3 mos)	zu zeng zufumu (fffb, fffbw; SM)			
			zufumu (ff, fm; ZC, 1 yr without staff)	zu zufumu (ffb, ffbw; XG)	zu boshu zufumu (ffb, ffbw; XG)		
		gu (fs; UM, 1 yr with staff; M, DG)	fumu (ZhC, 3 yrs)	boshu fumu (fb, fbw; 1 yr with staff)	tang boshu fumu (ffbS, ffbSw; XG)	zu boshu fumu (fffbSS, fffbSSw; SM)	
	tanggu (ffbd; UM, XG; M, SM)	zimei (s; UM, 1 yr with staff; M, DG)	JISHEN (EGO)	xiongdi (b; 1 yr with staff) xiongdiqi (bw; XG)	tang xiongdi (fbS; DG) tang xiongdi qi (fbSw; SM)	zaicong xiongdi (ffbSS; XG) zai- zaicong xiongdi qi (ffbSSw; N)	zu xiongdi (fffbSSS; SM) zu xiongdi w (fffbSSSw; N)
zugu (fffbd; UM, SM; M, N)	tang zimei (fbd; UM, DG; M, XG)	zhinü (bd; UM, 1 yr with staff; M, DG)	zhangzi zhangzi fu (eS, eSw; 1 yr with staff) zhongzi zhongzi fu (oS; 1 yr with staff; M, DG)	zhi (bS; 1 yr with staff) zhi fu (bSw; DG)	tang zhi (fbSS; XG) tangzi fu (fbSSw; SM)	zaicong zhi (ffbSSS; SM) zaicong zhi fu (ffbSSSw; N)	
zu zugu (fffbd; UM, SM; M, N)	zaicong zimei (ffbSd; UM, XG; M, SM)	tang zhinü (fbSd; UM, XG; M, SM)	disun (wSwS; 1 yr with staff) disun fu (wSwSw; XG) zhongsun (SoS; DG) disun fu (SoSw; SM)	zhisun (bSS; XG) zhisun fu (bSSw; SM)	tang zhisun (fbSSS; SM) tang zhisun fu (fbSSSw; N)		
	zaicong zhinü (ffbSSd; UM, SM; M, N)	zhi sunnü (bSd; UM, XG; M, SM)	zengsun (SSS; SM) zengsun fu (SSSw; N)	zeng zhisun (bSSS; SM) zeng zhisun fu (bSSSw; N)			
zu zimei (fffbSSd; UM, SM; M, N)		tang zhi sunnü (fbSSd; UM, SM; M, N)	xunsun (SSSS; SM) xunsun fu (SSSSw; N)				
		zhi zeng sunnü (bSSd; UM, SM; M, N)					
			congzu zugu (ffs; UM, XG; M, SM)				
			zu zeng zugu (fffs; UM, SM; M, N)				

Notes to Formal Mourning Degrees:

The wife's son's son who, after his father dies, becomes the heir to the grandparents shall wear unhemmed sackcloth for three years. If he becomes the heir of great-grandparents or great-great-grandparents, the mourning degree shall be the same. If the grandfather is alive, the mourning degree for the grandmother shall only be one year with staff.

The male who is adopted to be others' heir shall have all the mourning degrees for his natural relatives reduced one degree. For his natural parents, reduce the mourning degree to one year without staff. Parents' reciprocal mourning degree shall be the same.

If the daughter of father's sister or one's own sister or one's own son is unmarried, or already married but repudiated and returned home, her mourning degree shall be the same as the male. If she is married but left without husband and son, her mourning degree for all her brothers, sisters, and brothers' sons shall be one year without staff.

All the relatives of the same ancestor within the five generations but beyond the coarse-hemp [*sima*] degree are relatives of the sixth degree of mourning [*tanwen*]. For their funerals, a white garment shall be worn and the head shall be bound with a piece of one-*chi*-long cloth.

Wife's Mourning Degrees for Husband's Relatives

				fu gao zu fu mu (hfff, hfffm; SM)			
			fu zeng zugu (hfffs; N)	fu zeng zufumu (hfff, hfffm; SM)	fu zu zeng zufumu (hfffb, hfffbw; N)		
		fu tang zugu (hfffbd; N)	fu zugu (hffs; UM, SM; M, N)	fu zufumu (hff, hfm; DG)	fu boshu zufumu (hffb, hffbw; SM)	fu zu boshu zufumu (hfffbS, hfffbSw; N)	
	fu zugu (hfffbSd; N)	fu tanggu (hffbd; UM, SM; M, N)	fu xingu (hfs; XG)	jiugu (hf, hm; ZhC, 3 yrs)	fu boshu fumu (hfb, hfbw; DG)	fu tang boshu fumu (hffbS, hfbSw; SM)	fu zu boshu fumu (hfffbSS, fffbbSw; N)
fu zu zimei (hfffbSSd; N)	fu zaicong zimei (hffbSSd; N)	fu tang zimei (hfbd; SM)	fu zimei (hs; XG)	w for h (ZhC, 3 yrs) h for w (ZC, 1 yr with staff; when parents are alive, 1 yr without staff)	fu xiongdi ji qi (hb, hbw; XG)	fu tang xiongdi ji qi (hfbS, hfbSw; SM)	fu zaicong xiongdi (hffbSS; N); (hfffbSSS; N)
	fu zaicong zhinü (hffbSSd; UM, SM; M, N)	fu tang zhinü (hfbSd; UM, XG; M, SM)	fu zhinü (hbd; UM, 1 yr with staff; M, DG)	zhangzi zhangzi fu (eS, eSw; 1 yr with staff) zhongzi (oS; 1 yr with staff) zhongzi fu (oSw; DG)	fu zhi (hbS; 1 yr with staff) fu zhi fu (hbSw; DG)	fu tangzhi (hfbSS; XG) fu tangzi fu (hfbSSw; SM)	fu zaicong zhi (hffbSSS; SM)
		fu tang zhi sunnü (hfbSSd; SM)	fu zhi sunnü (hbSd; UM, XG; M, SM)	sun (DG) sun fu (SM)	fu zhisun (hbSS; XG) fu zhisun fu (hbSSw; SM)	fu tang zhisun (hfbSSS; SM)	
			fu zeng zhi sunnü (hbSSd; SM)	zengsun (SSS; SM)	fu zeng zhisun (hbSSS; SM)		
				xuansun (SSSS; SM)			

When the husband becomes the heir of his paternal grandparents, great-grandparents, or great-great-grandparents, [the wife] shall follow all her husband's mourning degrees.

When the husband is an adopted heir, the wife's mourning degree for his natural parents shall be "greater coarseness" [*dagong*].

Concubine's Mourning Degrees for Household Head's Relatives

	jiazhang fumu (household head's parents) 1 year	
zhengqi (wife) 1 year		*jiazhang* (household head) *zhancui*: 3 years
wei qi zi (for her own son) 1 year	*jiazhang zhangzi* (household head's eldest son) 1 year	*jiazhang zhongzi* (household head's other son) 1 year

Married Daughter's Reduced Mourning Degrees for Her Own Lineage

		gao zufumu (ffff, fffm; ZC, 3 mos)		
		zeng zufumu (fff, ffm; ZC, 3 mos)		
	zuzimei (ffs; UM, SM; M, N)	*zufumu* (ff, fm; ZC, 1 yr without staff)	*zuxiongdi* (ffb; SM)	
fu tang zimei (ffbd; UM, SM; M, N)	*fu zimei* (fs; DG)	*fumu* (1 yr without staff)	*bo shu fumu* (fb, fbw; DG)	*fu tang xiongdi* (ffbS; SM)
tang zimei (fbd; UM, XG; M, SM)	*zimei* (s; DG)	**JISHEN** (EGO)	*xiongdi* (b; DG)	*tang xiongdi* (fbS; XG)
tang zhinü (fbSd; SM)	*xiongdi nü* (bd; DG)	*xiongdi zi* (bS; DG)	*tangzhi* (fbSS; SM)	

Mourning Degrees for External Relatives

		mu zufumu (mff, mfm; N)		
	mu zhi zimei (ms; XG)	*wai zufumu* (mf, mm; XG)	*mu zhi xiongdi* (mb; XG)	
tangyi zhi zi (mfbdS; N)	*liangyi zhi zi* (msS; SM)	**JISHEN** (EGO)	*jiu zhi zi* (mbS; SM)	*tangjiu zhi zi* (mfbSS; N)
	yi zhi sun (msSS; N)	*gu zhi zi* (fsS; SM)	*jiu zhi sun* (mbSS; N)	
		gu zhi sun (fsSS; N)		

Mourning Degrees for Wife's Relatives

	qi zu fu mu (wff, wfm; N)		
qi zhi gu (wfs; N)	*qi fu mu* (wf, wm; SM)	*qi bo shu* (wfb; N)	
qi zhi zimei (ws; N)	**JISHEN** (EGO)	*qi xiongdi ji fu* (wb, wbw; N)	*qi wai zufumu* (wmf, wmm; N)
qi zimei zi (wsS; N)	*nü zhi zi* (dS; SM)		
	nü zhi sun (dSS; N)		

Mourning Degrees for Three Fathers and Eight Mothers

tongju jifu (stepfather who lives [with stepson])	If neither has [relatives], i.e., if the stepfather does not have a son and [the stepson] himself does not have a father's brother or his own brother, 1 yr; if both have [relatives], i.e., the stepfather has a son or son's son, and [the stepson] himself has a father's brother or his own brother, *zicui*, 3 mo.
cong jimu jia	Following the stepmother who remarries [i.e., marries a stepfather] after the father dies, ZC, 1 yr with staff.
bu tongju jifu (stepfather who does not live [with stepson])	If [the stepson] used to live with the stepfather but does not live with him now, ZC, 3 mo; if [the stepson] has never followed his mother to live with the stepfather, N.
cimu (carrying mother)	After one's natural mother dies, father makes another concubine raise him, ZhC, 3 yr.
jimu (stepmother)	Father marries another wife, ZhC, 3 yr.
dimu (proper mother)	This is what a concubine's son calls his father's wife, ZhC, 3 yr.
yangmu (adoptive mother)	One has been an adopted member of another family since childhood, Zhc, 3 yr.
chumu (repudiated mother)	Natural mother who is repudiated by father, ZC, 1 yr with staff.
jiamu (remarried mother)	After father's death, natural mother remarries another person, ZC, 1 yr with staff.
rumu (wet nurse)	Father's concubine who nurses father's child [who is not her own child], SM.
shumu (secondary mother)	Father's concubine who has borne a child. Wife's sons and other sons, ZC, 1 yr with staff; natural sons, ZhC, 3 yr.

Six Types of Illicit Goods

	[Penalties]	Supervisors and Custodians Stealing	Ordinary Persons Stealing; Subverting the Law	Theft; Not Subverting the Law	Illicit Goods Obtained through Malfeasance
Beating with the Light Stick	20				Below 1
	30				1–10 guan
	40				20 guan
	50				30 guan
Beating with the Heavy Stick	60			Less than 1 guan	40 guan
	70		Less than 1 guan		50 guan
	80	Less than 1 guan	1–5 guan	20 guan	60 guan
	90	1–2.5 guan	10 guan	30 guan	70 guan
	100	5 guan	15 guan	40 guan	80 guan
Penal Servitude	1 year/60 strokes of beating with the heavy stick	7.5 guan	20 guan	50 guan	100 guan
	1.5 years/70 strokes of beating with the heavy stick	10 guan	25 guan	60 guan	200 guan
	2 years/80 strokes of beating with the heavy stick	12.5 guan	30 guan	70 guan	300 guan
	2.5 years/90 strokes of beating with the heavy stick	15 guan	35 guan	80 guan	400 guan
	3 years/100 strokes of beating with the heavy stick	17.5 guan	40 guan	90 guan	500 guan
Life Exile	2,000 li/100 strokes of beating with the heavy stick	20 guan	45 guan	100 guan	
	2,500 li/100 strokes of beating with the heavy stick	22.5 guan	50 guan	110 guan	
	3,000 li/100 strokes of beating with the heavy stick	25 guan	55 guan	220 guan	
Death (Miscellaneous Offenses)	Strangulation		80 guan		
	Decapitation	40 guan			

The Meanings of Eight Characters as Used in the General Principles

yi (on the basis of)	An act that is to be punished "on the basis of" a specified crime is considered the same as a true crime. For instance, if supervisors or custodians trade with government property, that does not differ from true robbery. Therefore, they shall be punished "on the basis of" subverting the law or "on the basis of" robbery. Moreover, they shall be disenrolled from their official registers; they shall be sentenced to tattooing; and their punishment may amount to decapitation or strangulation. Any of the penalties in the *Code* may be applied to them.
zhun (as comparable to)	An act that is considered "as comparable to" a specified crime differs from a true crime. For instance, if [the law states] "as comparable to subverting the law" or "as comparable to robbery," the punishments are only comparable. Disenrollment from official registers and tattooing shall not be inflicted. The maximum punishment shall be limited to 100 strokes of beating with the heavy stick and life exile to 3,000 *li*.
jie (all)	"All" does not distinguish principals and accessories but punishes [the criminals] with the same penalties. For instance, if the supervisory and custodial officials and functionaries collaborate to commit robbery of government property that has been put under their jurisdiction or custody, and if the illicit goods taken together amount to the value of [40] *guan*, they shall "all" be punished by decapitation.
ge (each)	"Each" punishes different criminals with the same penalty. For instance, if various sorts of craftsmen who are sent to the Palace Treasury to work do not personally work but privately hire others to use false names to substitute the services, they and those who substitute for them shall "each" be punished by 100 strokes of beating with the heavy stick.
qi (but)	"But" changes the preceding provisions. For instance, in deciding punishments for those entitled to the Eight Deliberations, first memorialize petitioning permission to deliberate; "but" this provision is not applicable to cases involving violation of any of the Ten Abominations.
ji (and/or)	"And/or" connects different matters. For instance, the illicit goods that criminate both parties "and/or" forbidden articles shall be confiscated by the government.
ji (then)	"Then" clarifies the meaning at the end of a provision. For instance, if a crime is discovered and the criminals are in flight, as long as three or more witnesses confirm the fact, "then" the case shall be considered established.
ruo (if)	"If" is used to apply the preceding provision to a different context. For instance, in cases where those who commit crimes before becoming aged or maimed have become aged or maimed when the affairs are discovered, they shall be judged according to the provision on those who are aged or maimed; "if," within their term of years of penal servitude, the criminals become aged or maimed, they shall also be governed by this provision.

Chapter 1

Laws on Punishments and General Principles [Mingli(lü)]

Article 1   The Five Punishments [Wuxing]
  [1] The punishment of beating with the light stick [*chi*], five degrees:
    10 strokes (redemption by copper currency of 600 *wen*);
    20 strokes (redemption by copper currency of 1 *guan* and 200 *wen*);
    30 strokes (redemption by copper currency of 1 *guan* and 800 *wen*);
    40 strokes (redemption by copper currency of 2 *guan* and 400 *wen*);
    50 strokes (redemption by copper currency of 3 *guan*).
  [2] The punishment of beating with the heavy stick [*zhang*], five degrees:
    60 strokes (redemption by copper currency of 3 *guan* and 600 *wen*);
    70 strokes (redemption by copper currency of 4 *guan* and 200 *wen*);
    80 strokes (redemption by copper currency of 4 *guan* and 800 *wen*);
    90 strokes (redemption by copper currency of 5 *guan* and 400 *wen*);
    100 strokes (redemption by copper currency of 6 *guan*).
  [3] Penal servitude [*tu*], five degrees:
    One year plus 60 strokes of beating with the heavy stick (redemption by copper currency of 12 *guan*);
    One and one-half years plus 70 strokes of beating with the heavy stick (redemption by copper currency of 15 *guan*);
    Two years plus 80 strokes of beating with the heavy stick (redemption by copper currency of 18 *guan*);
    Two and one-half years plus 90 strokes of beating with the heavy stick (redemption by copper currency of 21 *guan*);
    Three years plus 100 strokes of beating with the heavy stick (redemption by copper currency of 24 *guan*).
  [4] The punishment of life exile [*liu*], three degrees:
    2,000 *li* plus 100 strokes of beating with the heavy stick (redemption by copper currency of 30 *guan*);
    2,500 *li* plus 100 strokes of beating with the heavy stick (redemption by copper currency of 33 *guan*);
    3,000 *li* plus 100 strokes of beating with the heavy stick (redemption by copper currency of 36 *guan*).
  [5] The death penalty [*si*], two degrees:

Strangulation [*jiao*] and decapitation [*zhan*] (redemption by copper currency of 42 *guan*).

Article 2   The Ten Abominations [Shie]

The first is plotting rebellion [*moufan*]. (This means to plot to endanger the Altars of Soil and Grain [*she ji*] [Art. 277].)

The second is plotting great sedition [*moudani*]. (This means to plot to destroy imperial ancestral temples, mausoleums, or palaces [Art. 277].)

The third is plotting treason [*moupan*]. (This means to plot to betray one's own country or to go over to another country [Art. 278].)

The fourth is contumacy [*eni*]. (This means to strike [Art. 342] or to plot to kill [Art. 307] paternal grandparents, parents, or husband's paternal grandparents or parents; or to kill paternal uncles or their wives, paternal aunts, older brothers or sisters, maternal grandparents [Art. 341], or husband [Art. 338].)

The fifth is depravity [*budao*]. (This means to kill three persons of one family who have not committed a crime punishable by the death penalty, to dismember persons [*zhijie ren*] [Art. 310], to mutilate living persons [*caisheng*] [Art. 311], to make or keep insect poisons [*zaoxu gudu*], or to practice sorcery [*yanmei*] [Art. 312].)

The sixth is great irreverence [*da bujing*]. (This means to steal the objects for the Great Sacrifices [Dasi] to the spirits [Art. 280] or the clothing or personal effects of the Carriage [*chengyu*, i.e., the emperor] [Art. 283]; to steal [Art. 283] or counterfeit imperial seals; mistakenly not to follow the correct prescriptions when preparing imperial medicine or to make a mistake in writing or attaching the label [Art. 182]; mistakenly to violate the dietary proscriptions when preparing the imperial food [Art. 182]; or mistakenly to fail to make the imperial touring boats sturdy [Art. 183].)

The seventh is lack of filial piety [*buxiao*]. (This means to accuse to the court [Art. 360], to cast a spell on [*zhou*] [Art. 312], or to curse with bad language [*ma*] [Art. 352] paternal grandparents, parents, husband's paternal grandparents or parents; while paternal grandparents or parents are still alive, to establish a separate family registration [*bieji*] or separate property [*yicai*] [Art. 93] or to fail to provide sufficiently for them [Art. 361]; during the period of mourning for parents, to arrange for one's own marriage [Art. 111], to make music [Art. 198], or to take off mourning garments and put on ordinary clothing [Art. 198]; on hearing of the death of paternal grandparents or parents, to conceal and not to mourn the death [Art. 198]; or to state falsely that paternal grandparents or parents have died [Art. 198].)

The eighth is discord [*bumu*]. (This means to plot to kill [Art. 307] or to sell [Art. 298] relatives of the fifth degree of mourning [*sima*] or closer; or to strike [Arts. 338, 343] or accuse to the court [Art. 360] one's husband, senior [*zun*] or older [*zhang*] relatives of the third degree of mourning [*dagong*] or closer, or senior relatives [*zunshu*] of the fourth degree of mourning [*xiaogong*] or closer.)

The ninth is unrighteousness [*buyi*]. (This means for commoners to kill their own prefect [*zhifu*], subprefect [*zhizhou*], or magistrate [*zhixian*] [Art. 306]; for soldiers to kill their own guard commander [*zhihui*], battalion commander [*qianhu*], or company commander [*baihu*] [Art. 306]; for functionaries [*lizu*] to kill their own department head of the fifth rank or above [Art. 306]; to kill the teacher from whom one has received one's education [*shouyeshi*] [Art. 334]; or on hearing of one's husband's death, to conceal and not to mourn the death [Art. 198], to make music [Art. 198], to take off the mourning garments and put on ordinary clothing [Art. 198], or to remarry [Art. 111].)

The tenth is incest [*neiluan*]. (This means to commit fornication with relatives of the fourth degree of mourning or closer [Art. 392] or with one's father's or paternal grandfather's concubines [Art. 392], or [for those women] to give their consent [Arts. 392, 390].)

Article 3 The Eight Deliberations [Bayi]

The first is deliberation for relatives [*yiqin*]. (This refers to relatives of the emperor of the sixth degree of mourning [*tanwen*] or closer, the relatives of the grand empress dowager [*tai huang taihou*] and the empress dowager [*huang taihou*] of the fifth degree of mourning or closer, the empress's relatives of the fourth degree of mourning or closer, or relatives of the wife of the heir apparent [*huang taizi*] of the third degree of mourning or closer.)

The second is deliberation for old retainers [*yigu*]. (This refers to the old retainers of the imperial family who have been in the service of the emperor and received special favors from the emperor for a long period of time.)

The third is deliberation for meritorious subjects [*yigong*]. (This refers to those who can kill enemy generals, carry off their flags, or destroy enemy troops in an area of 10,000 *li*; who can cause troops to surrender and obtain peace for a time; or who can extend the boundaries of the country and accomplish extraordinary meritorious deeds, whose heroic achievements are recorded on the grand banner [*taichang*].)

The fourth is deliberation for worthies [*yixian*]. (This refers to those greatly virtuous worthy men [*xianren*] and gentlemen [*junzi*] whose speech and conduct can be regarded as models.)

The fifth is deliberation for talents [*yineng*]. (This refers to those of great ability who can lead armies, manage governmental affairs, assist the ruler, and serve as models on how to conduct human relationships.)

The sixth is deliberation for diligent subjects [*yiqin*]. (This refers to high military and civil officials of extraordinary diligence who reverently hold office and work on public affairs day and night or who are sent on a mission to distant areas and experience dangers and difficulties.)

The seventh is deliberation for subjects of high position [*yigui*]. (This refers to those with noble titles [*jue*] of the first rank, civil and military active-duty officials [*zhishiguan*] of the third rank or above, and titular officials [*sanguan*] of the second rank or above.)

The eighth is deliberation for guests [*yibin*]. (This refers to descendants of preceding dynasties who have been received as guests of the state.)

Article 4 Committing Crimes by Those Entitled to the Eight Deliberations [Yingyizhe fanzui]

[1] In all cases where those entitled to the Eight Deliberations commit crimes, the facts shall be reported to the throne in a sealed memorial petitioning an imperial rescript. Their cases shall not be tried without authorization. If an imperial rescript is received to conduct the interrogation, set forth the crimes that are committed and the circumstances that shall be deliberated, and first memorialize petitioning permission to deliberate. After deliberation, memorialize petitioning the decision by the throne. ("Deliberation" means to investigate the original circumstances of the crime and try the case. In the memorial set forth the facts of the crime committed by those who are "relatives," "old retainers," "meritorious subjects," "worthies," "talents," "diligent subjects," "subjects of high position," or "guests." The memorial shall be sealed and sent to the throne to petition an imperial rescript. Once an imperial rescript is received to conduct the trial, only then may the case be tried. Take clear confessions, set forth the culpable punishments, and memorialize petitioning the Five Chief Military Commissions [Wujun Dudu Fu], Four Supports [Sifu], Remonstrance Bureau [Jianyuan], Ministry of Justice [Xingbu], investigating censors [*jiancha yushi*], and judges [*duanshiguan*] to deliberate collectively. After deliberation, they shall memorialize the throne. In cases of capital punishment, state only that the crime shall be punished by the death penalty according to the *Code*. They shall not specify the judgment of strangulation or decapitation. Memorialize petitioning the decision by the throne.)

[2] This provision is not applicable to cases involving commission of any of the Ten Abominations.

Article 5 Committing Crimes by Officials [Zhiguan youfan]

[1] In all cases where officials in the capital or officials of the fifth rank or higher in the provinces commit crimes, memorialize petitioning an imperial rescript. Their cases shall not be tried without authorization. Crimes by officials of the sixth rank or lower shall be interrogated by regional inspectors [*fenxun yushi*], Provincial Surveillance Commissions [Ancha Si], or their branch offices [*fensi*] until the cases are well understood. Consider the matter and propose a provisional sentence, then memorialize for disposition.

Laws on Punishments and General Principles 21

[2] If officials of prefectures [*fu*], subprefectures [*zhou*], or districts [*xian*] commit crimes, their superior government offices that have jurisdiction over them shall not interrogate the cases without authorization. They shall only set forth the crimes that are committed and report them to the throne in a sealed memorial. If it is permitted to conduct the interrogation, they shall consider the matter and propose a provisional sentence according to the *Code* and memorialize again. They shall not make the judgment and carry out the punishment until the court sends responsible officials to investigate the case and verify the facts.

[3] For those who commit crimes punishable by beating with the light stick [*chijue*], fining a salary [*fafeng*], redemption [*shoushu*], or making a record of the transgression [*jilu*], the provision on memorializing and petitioning shall not apply.

[4] If subordinate officials are mistreated by their superior officials in an unreasonable manner, they may also set forth the facts and report directly to the throne in a sealed memorial. (*The Commandment* [*ling*] says: "A fine of one month's salary is a fine of copper currency of 100 *wen*.")

Article 6 Committing Crimes by Military Officers [Junguan youfan]

[1] In all cases where military officers commit crimes, their own offices [*benguan yamen*] shall set forth the affairs and submit a report to the Five Chief Military Commissions. Then memorialize petitioning an imperial rescript to permit the interrogation.

[2] When the Six Ministries, Investigation Bureau [*chayuan*], Provincial Surveillance Commissions or their branch offices, or local government offices at different levels handle public affairs, and there are matters involving only military officers or if they intend to report unfair or illegal practices by military officers, it is essential that they keep the cases confidential and report them to the throne in a sealed memorial. They shall not interrogate the cases without authorization.

[3] If an imperial rescript is received to conduct the interrogation, with the exception of crimes punishable by beating with the light stick or redemption that shall be clearly memorialized again, for crimes punishable by beating with the heavy stick or heavier penalties, it is essential to estimate the merits and deliberate the cases, then memorialize for disposition.

[4] If staff supervisors [*shouling guan*] of offices that command troops [*guanjun yamen*] commit crimes, this provision shall not apply.

Article 7 Committing Public Crimes by Civil or Military Officials [Wenwuguan fan gongzui]

In all cases where high or low officials or functionaries of military or civil offices in the capital or in the provinces commit public crimes [*gongzui*], for crimes punishable by beating with the light stick, the punishment for officials may be redeemed; the punishment for functionaries shall be executed in different categories every season [*meiji leijue*]; their transgressions may not be recorded. For crimes punishable by beating with the heavy stick or heavier penalties, establish clear files, make an examination every year, and record the crimes; make a general examination every nine years and demote or promote the officials according to the number of times and degree of seriousness of their crimes.

Article 8   Committing Private Crimes by Civil or Military Officials [Wenwuguan fan sizui]

[1] In all cases where civil officials commit private crimes punishable by 40 strokes of beating with the light stick or lighter penalties, they shall have their transgressions recorded and return to their appointments [*fuguo huanzhi*]. For crimes punishable by 50 strokes of beating with the light stick, they shall be removed from their current appointments [*jie xianren*] and be reassigned to other posts [*biexu*]. For crimes punishable by 60 strokes of beating with the heavy stick, they shall be demoted one grade; 70 strokes, two grades; 80 strokes, three grades; 90 strokes, four grades. They shall all be removed from their current appointments; the ranked officials [*liuguan*] shall be reassigned to the miscellaneous offices [*zazhi*]; the miscellaneous officials shall be reassigned to the distant frontiers [*bianyuan*]. For crimes punishable by 100 strokes of beating with the heavy stick, they shall be dismissed from their appointments and not be reassigned [*bazhi buxu*].

[2] If military officers commit private crimes punishable by beating with the light stick, they shall have their transgressions recorded and may redeem their punishment. For crimes punishable by beating with the heavy stick, they shall be removed from their current appointments and be reassigned with their grades demoted. For those who shall be dismissed from their appointments and not be reassigned, they shall be demoted to platoon commanders [*zongqi*]. For those who shall be punished by penal servitude or life exile, they shall be sent into military exile [*chongjun*] to military guards according to the distance of the places. If they can achieve meritorious deeds, they will be promoted without reference to regular rules.

[3] If unranked officials [*weiru liupinguan*] or functionaries [*lizu*] commit crimes punishable by 40 strokes of beating with the light stick, they shall have their transgressions recorded and return to their appointments [*zhi*] or employment [*yi*], respectively. For crimes punishable by 50 strokes of beating with the light stick, they shall be removed from their current employment and reassigned to other posts. For crimes punishable by beating with the heavy stick, they shall all be dismissed from their appointments or employment and not be reassigned.

Article 9   Committing Crimes by the Parents or Paternal Grandparents of Those Entitled to the Eight Deliberations [Yingyizhe zhi fuzu youfan]

[1] In all cases where the paternal grandparents, parents, wives, sons, or sons' sons of those entitled to the Eight Deliberations commit crimes, the facts shall be reported to the throne in a sealed memorial petitioning an imperial rescript. Their cases shall not be interrogated without authorization. If an imperial rescript is received to conduct the interrogation, set forth the crimes that are committed and the circumstances that shall be deliberated and memorialize petitioning permission to deliberate. After deliberation, memorialize petitioning the decision by the throne.

[2] If the maternal grandparents, paternal uncles or their wives, paternal aunts, brothers, sisters, sons-in-law, or sons of brothers of the relatives of the emperor, of the imperial relatives by marriage, or of meritorious officials [commit crimes], or [if] the parents, wives, sons, or sons' sons who have the inheritance privilege [xi] or protection privilege [yin] of officials of the fourth or fifth rank commit crimes, their cases shall be interrogated by the authorities according to the *Code*. Consider the matter and propose a provisional sentence, then memorialize petitioning the decision by the throne.

[3] This provision is not applicable to cases involving violation of any of the Ten Abominations, collective prosecution for rebellion or sedition [*fanni yuanzuo*], fornication [*jian*], robbery [*dao*], homicide, or acceptance of property with subversion of the law [*shoucai wangfa*].

[4] If other relatives, bond servants [*nupu*], bailiffs [*guanzhuang*], or chief tenant farmers [*dianjia*] presume upon their powerful connections to bully respectable people or offend government offices, the penalties for them shall be increased one degree over those for ordinary persons. Only punish the criminals. This is not governed by the provision of petitioning the throne. ("Other relatives" refers to relatives such as paternal male third cousins [*fangzu xiongdi*], father's male second cousins [*fangzu boshu*], maternal uncles [*mujiu*], maternal aunts' husbands [*muyifu*], paternal aunts' husbands [*gufu*], wife's brothers, wife's sisters' husbands, sisters' sons, and wife's nephews. If these persons or domestic bond servants, bailiffs, or chief tenant farmers use their power and influence to bully respectable people or offend government offices, when the affairs come to light, they may not be memorialized. The penalties shall be increased one degree over those for ordinary persons. Only punish the criminals themselves.)

[5] If, while government offices are conducting interrogations, the criminals are protected and not surrendered, the responsible offices may send a sealed memorial petitioning the decision by the throne. (This means that if, after someone reports the case to the responsible government office, public runners are sent to seize the accused for trial, and the relatives of the

emperor, the relatives of the imperial relatives by marriage, or meritorious officials protect them and do not surrender them, the responsible offices may send a sealed memorial petitioning the decision by the throne.)

Article 10   Committing Crimes by Military Officers or Soldiers Who Shall Be Exempted from Penal Servitude or Life Exile
[Junguan junren fanzui mian tuliu]

[1] In all cases where military officers or soldiers commit crimes punishable by penal servitude or life exile, in each case they shall be punished by 100 strokes of beating with the heavy stick. For crimes punishable by the five degrees of penal servitude, they shall all be sent into military exile to military guards within 2,000 *li*. For crimes punishable by the three degrees of life exile, they shall be sent into military exile to military guards according to the distance of places. For those who shall be sent into military exile to distant frontiers, they shall be sent according to the *Code*. They shall all be exempted from tattooing.

[2] If military servants [*junding*], military functionaries [*junli*], or commandants [*xiaowei*] commit crimes, their cases shall all be judged the same as those of soldiers, and they shall also be exempted from penal servitude, life exile, or tattooing. ("Military servants" refers to persons other than military officers or soldiers. "Military functionaries" refers to those soldiers who join the army requesting rations [*ruwu qingliang*] and who are literate and selected as military functionaries. If they commit crimes, their cases shall be judged the same as those of soldiers. If functionaries of all localities who are sent to serve as salary-requesting staff foremen [*qingfeng sili*] commit crimes, their cases shall be judged the same as cases concerning staff foremen in prefectures, subprefectures, or districts.

Article 11   Committing Crimes for Which Penalties May Be Cumulatively Reduced [Fanzui de leijian]

In all cases where one person commits a crime for which the penalties shall be reduced, such as reduction of penalty for accessories [*weicong*] [Art. 29] (This refers to cases of joint crimes where those who formulate the plan [*zaoyi*] are principals. The penalty for accessories shall be reduced two degrees.), reduction of penalty for voluntary confessions [*zishou*] [Art. 24] (This refers to cases where the person who violates the law knows that someone else intends to accuse him to the court and thus makes the voluntary confession. The penalty for him shall be reduced two degrees.), reduction of penalty according to whether the crime is deliberate or negligent (This refers to cases where a functionary deliberately exonerates a guilty person from punishment, and after he releases the criminal, he arrests him again. The penalty for the functionary shall be reduced only one degree. If the staff supervisor [*shouling guan*] does not know the circumstances, he shall be punished on the basis of negligence. The penalty for his negligent exoneration shall be reduced five degrees. Furthermore, the penalty for a staff supervisor shall be reduced one degree from that for a functionary, so in this case the penalty for the staff supervisor shall be reduced a total of seven degrees.), or the progressive reduction of penalty for public crimes (This refers to cases where members of the same office [*tongliao*] commit public crimes [Arts. 27–28] by negligently implicating the innocent [Art. 433]. The penalty for the functionary shall be reduced three degrees; if the penalty for the criminal has not yet been executed or the criminal has not yet been released, the penalty for the functionary shall be reduced one more degree: it shall be reduced a total of four degrees. The penalty for the staff supervisor shall be reduced five degrees; for the associate official [*zuoer guan*], six degrees; for the head official [*zhangguan*], seven degrees.), it may be cumulatively reduced. (The penalty for cases such as these may all be cumulatively reduced.)

Article 12 Leaving Offices for Legitimate Reasons [Yili quguan]

In all cases where officials leave offices because of reasons such as completion of service terms [*renman*], replacement [*dedai*], transferal [*gaichu*], or retirement [*zhishi*], they shall be treated the same as incumbent officials [*xianren*]. (This means that the dismissal [*jieren*] is not due to the commission of crimes but to such reasons as elimination of redundant personnel or dissolution of yamen. Although officials are dismissed or demoted because of certain acts, as long as their certificates of appointment [*gaoming*] are not revoked, they shall be treated the same as incumbent officials.) Those who hold enfeoffed official titles during their lifetime [*feng*] or who are posthumously awarded official titles [*zeng*] shall be treated the same as regular officials [*zhengguan*]. If a wife commits a crime against her husband or breaks the bond of righteousness [*yi*], she may receive the same official rank as that of her son. (This means that although a wife breaks the bond of righteousness with her husband's family, or while her husband is living she is repudiated by him, if her son obtains an official title, she may receive the same official rank as that of her son. This is because the relationship between mother and son cannot be extinguished.) If these types of persons commit crimes, they shall be judged according to the law on crimes committed by officials [Art. 5].

Article 13 Committing Crimes by Those Who Have Not Yet Become Officials [Wuguan fanzui]

[1] In all cases where those who have not yet become officials commit crimes, and the affairs are discovered after they have become officials, for public crimes, they may also redeem their punishment and have their transgressions recorded.

[2] If officials of lower rank commit crimes and by the time the affairs are discovered they have been reassigned to other posts [*qianguan*], or if officials commit crimes while they are holding offices and by the time the affairs are discovered they have left government service, for public crimes punishable by beating with the light stick or a lighter penalty, they shall not be punished; for crimes punishable by beating with the heavy stick or heavier penalties, they shall have their transgressions recorded for the general evaluation. If they have already been dismissed from appointments because of the affairs, they shall not be punished for any crimes punishable by beating with the light or heavy stick or heavier penalties. For cases involving concealing money or grain or losing government property, although they may have their transgressions recorded and be exempted from punishment, the affairs shall be thoroughly investigated and clearly settled. Only if they commit private crimes shall they be punished according to the *Code*. ("Those who have been reassigned to other posts" refers to officials who have been transferred, appointed to hold neighboring offices temporarily, or replaced. "Those who have left government service" refers to officials such as those who have completed their service terms, been in mourning for parents [*dingyou*], or been retired.) If functionaries commit public or private crimes, they shall also be judged according to the above provision.

Article 14   Disenrollment and Labor Service [Chuming dangchai]

In all cases where officials commit crimes for which they shall be dismissed from their appointments and not be reassigned, shall have their certificates of appointment revoked [*zhuiduo*], and shall have their official registers disenrolled [*chuming*], they shall be deprived of both official and noble titles. If Buddhist or Daoist priests commit crimes and they have been punished, they shall return to lay status. They shall return respectively to their original status of military persons, civilians, artisans, or salt makers and be sent to their native places of registration to perform appropriate services.

Article 15   Families of Those Punished by Life Exile [Liuqiu jiashu]

In all cases of committing crimes punishable by life exile, the offender's wife and concubines shall accompany him. If his father, paternal grandfather, sons, or sons' sons wish to accompany him, they may do so. Families of those who are banished to settle in remote regions [*qianxi anzhi*] also follow this provision. If those who are exiled or banished die, although the register of their families has already been attached to the place of exile, their families may return to their original homes if they wish. The punishment of life exile for plotting rebellion, sedition, or treason, for making or keeping insect poisons, for mutilating living persons, or for killing three persons of one family shall still be enforced even though an amnesty is proclaimed

Laws on Punishments and General Principles 27

[*huishe youliu*]; their families shall not be governed by the provision of being permitted to return.

Article 16   Crimes That Shall Not Be Pardoned under the General Amnesty [Changshe suo buyuan]

[1] In all cases of committing "true crimes" [*zhenfan*] such as any of the Ten Abominations [Art. 2], homicide [Art. 305], robbery of government property [Arts. 287–88], forcible robbery [*qiangdao*] [Art. 289], theft [*qiedao*] [Art. 292], arson [Art. 407], excavation of graves [Art. 299], acceptance of illicit goods [*zang*] with or without subversion of law [Art. 367], fraud and counterfeiting [Arts. 378–89], fornication [Arts. 390–99], kidnapping or kidnapping and selling or seducing persons [*lüeren lüemai heyou renkou*] [Art. 298], formation of treacherous cliques [*jiandang*], causing others to be executed by putting forward malicious whispers to the throne [Art. 60], deliberately exonerating the guilty or incriminating the innocent [*gu churu renzui*] [Art. 433], knowing the circumstances and deliberately releasing, conniving with, hiding, or guiding [to escape] criminals [Art. 417], or urging the authorities by offering bribes [Art. 367], the offenders shall not be pardoned despite the amnesty. (This means that those who are punished because of deliberate crimes shall not be pardoned despite an amnesty.) For those who negligently or mistakenly commit crimes (This refers to crimes such as negligently killing or injuring persons [Art. 315], negligently causing fire [Art. 406], or negligently destroying or losing government property [Art. 104].), who get punished by implication of others (This means that people are punished for crimes committed by others by implication, such as failing to discover, guard against, or restrain others' crimes [e.g., Arts. 138–39] or getting involved in or allowing others' crimes.), or officials or functionaries who commit public crimes (This refers to cases where officials or functionaries are punished because of public affairs, of negligently exonerating the guilty or implicating the innocent [Art. 433], or of delaying or making mistakes in official documents [Arts. 71, 67], etc.), in all these cases they shall be pardoned under the amnesty. (This means that in all these cases the criminals shall be exempted from punishment under the amnesty.) If a decree of amnesty temporarily specifies some crimes and specially pardons them (This means that the decree of amnesty does not speak of "crimes that shall not be pardoned under the general amnesty" but temporarily specifies some crimes and pardons them. These crimes shall be specially pardoned according to the amnesty.) or reduces the penalty to a lighter one (This refers to cases where the death penalty is reduced to life exile, life exile is reduced to penal servitude, or penal servitude is reduced to beating with the heavy stick, etc.), this provision shall not apply. (This means that the provision of "crimes that shall not be pardoned by the general amnesty" shall not apply to all these special cases.)

[2] (The *Commandment* says: "From now on, in case there is an amnesty proclaimed by the reigning dynasty [*guojia*], with the exception that those prisoners presently in confinement whose cases have not yet been decided and those who ought to be pardoned shall all be released, the cases where the prisoners have already been punished by penal servitude or life exile or banished to malarial regions to settle shall be considered closed. Except for those who should be released from penal servitude when their terms end, the criminals who have been exiled or banished to settle shall return" [Art. 109].)

Article 17   *Those Punished by Penal Servitude or Life Exile Are En Route When the Amnesty Is Proclaimed* [Tuliuren zaidao huishe]

[1] In all cases where those punished by penal servitude or life exile are en route when an amnesty is proclaimed, if it is calculated that they exceed the time limits of their journey, they shall not be released under the amnesty. (This means, for example, that in the case of life exile of 3,000 *li*, if one day's travel is 50 *li*, then altogether the time limit shall be 60 days. If an amnesty is proclaimed before the 60-day limit is reached, irrespective of the distance already covered, the criminals shall be released under the amnesty. If the time limit has been exceeded, the criminals shall not be pardoned.) If there is a reason, this provision is not applicable. ("There is a reason" means, for example, that en route the criminals become ill, are stopped by wind, or are robbed. If there are certificates issued by local government offices guaranteeing the facts after investigation, in all these cases the number of days delayed by these causes may be excluded from the time limit. Therefore, it is stated: "This provision is not applicable.") For those who escape, even though an amnesty is proclaimed within the time limit for the journey, they shall not be released and shall not be exempted from punishment. If those who escape die, and the families who accompany them wish to return to their original homes, they may return. Those who are banished to settle in remote regions shall follow this provision.

[2] For those punished by penal servitude, life exile, or banishment and settlement who arrive at where they are sent, those punished by life exile for collective prosecution for plotting rebellion, sedition, or treason, or those punished by life exile for making or keeping insect poisons, mutilating living persons, or killing three persons in a family, that [punishment] shall still be enforced even though an amnesty is proclaimed; they shall not be pardoned and shall not be released.

Article 18   *Committing Crimes and Remaining at Home to Care for Relatives* [Fanzui cunliu yangqin]

In all cases of committing crimes punishable by the death penalty other than any of those that shall not be pardoned under a general amnesty [Art.

16], if the offenders' paternal grandparents or parents are aged or maimed and require care but the family has no other adult male, set forth the crimes that are committed and memorialize petitioning the decision by the throne. For crimes punishable by penal servitude or life exile, they shall be punished only by 100 strokes of beating with the heavy stick. The remaining punishment may be redeemed. The offenders may remain at home to care for their relatives.

Article 19 Committing Crimes by Government Artisans, Musicians, and Women [Gongyuehu ji furen fanzui]

In all cases where government artisans or musicians commit crimes punishable by life exile, all three degrees of life exile shall be converted into 100 strokes of beating with the heavy stick and four years of labor in their original places of service. If astronomy students from the Directorate of Astronomy have already learned a skill and can specialize in a particular duty, the penalty for their crimes punishable by life exile or penal servitude shall each be converted into 100 strokes of beating with the heavy stick; the remaining penalty may be redeemed. (For those who commit crimes punishable by life exile for collective prosecution for plotting rebellion, sedition, or treason or by life exile for making or keeping insect poisons, mutilating living persons, killing three persons of one family, that [punishment] shall still be enforced even though an amnesty is proclaimed. For those who commit theft, the provision of remaining "in their original places of service" is not applicable. "The remaining penalty may be redeemed" means that the penalty for the crime punishable by 100 strokes of beating with the heavy stick and life exile to 3,000 *li* shall be converted into 100 strokes of beating with the heavy stick and redemption by 30 *guan* of copper currency. The penalty of 100 strokes of beating with the heavy stick and penal servitude for three years shall be converted into 100 strokes of beating with the heavy stick and redemption by 18 *guan* of copper currency. Other articles shall follow this principle.) If women commit crimes punishable by beating with the heavy stick, for fornication they shall be stripped of their clothing to receive punishment. For other crimes they may wear unlined garments to receive punishment. They shall all be exempted from tattooing [*cizi*]. For crimes punishable by penal servitude or life exile, the punishment shall be converted into 100 strokes of the heavy stick; the remaining punishment may be redeemed.

Article 20 Committing Crimes Again by Those Punished by Penal Servitude or Life Exile [Tuliuren you fanzui]

In all cases where crimes have already been discovered and the criminals again commit crimes, they shall be punished by the penalty for the more serious crime. If the criminals punished by penal servitude or life exile have already been sent to places of servitude or exile, and they again commit crimes, they shall be punished again for the later crimes according to the *Code*. If they again commit crimes punishable by life exile, they shall be punished according to the law on remaining in original places [*liuzhu fa*] [Art. 19]: all three degrees of life exile shall be converted into 100 strokes of beating with the heavy stick and four years of labor at their places of exile. If they again commit crimes punishable by penal servitude, they shall be punished according to the number of strokes of the heavy stick and the number of years of penal servitude that are fixed for the later crime; the required labor shall not exceed four years either. (This refers to cases such as those where the criminals commit crimes punishable by penal servitude for three years and after they have performed one year's labor, then they again commit crimes punishable by penal servitude for three years: they shall be punished only by an additional 100 strokes of beating with the heavy stick and penal servitude for one year. Therefore, in total the term of penal servitude shall not exceed four years. For crimes punishable by the three degrees of life exile, although they shall all be converted into 100 strokes of beating with the heavy stick and four years of labor, if the terms of penal servitude for first crimes have not yet been completed, then the criminals shall also perform only four years of labor in total.) If the criminals commit crimes punishable by beating with the heavy stick or a lighter penalty, they shall each be punished according to the number of strokes for the later crimes. For cases where the punishment shall be converted into additional strokes of beating with the heavy stick, they shall also follow this provision. (This means that if government artisans, musicians, or women commit crimes, they shall also be punished according to this provision.)

Article 21   Redeeming Punishment by Those Who Are Aged, Juvenile, or Disabled [Laoxiao feiji shoushu]

In all cases where those who are 70 years of age or older or 15 years of age or younger or disabled [*feiji*] commit crimes punishable by life exile or lighter, they may redeem their punishment. (For those punished by the death penalty, by life exile for collective prosecution for plotting rebellion, sedition, or treason [Arts. 277–78], or life exile for making or keeping insect poisons [Art. 312], mutilating living persons [Art. 311], killing three persons of one family [Art. 310], that [punishment] shall still be enforced even though an amnesty is proclaimed; this provision shall not apply. For all other crimes involving encroachment upon or harm to people, they may redeem their punishment.) If those who are 80 years of age or older or 10 years of age or younger or incapacitated [*duji*] commit crimes involving homicide or other actions punishable by the death penalty, deliberate the matter and propose a provisional sentence, memorialize petitioning the decision by the throne. If they rob or injure people, they shall also redeem their punish-

Laws on Punishments and General Principles 31

ment. (This means that since they have encroached upon or harmed people, they shall not be completely exempted from punishment: they are also ordered to redeem their punishment.) For all other crimes, they shall not be punished. (This means that with exception of crimes involving homicide or other actions punishable by the death penalty that shall be petitioned to the throne, or crimes involving robbery or injury that shall be redeemed, all other crimes shall not be punished.) As for those who are 90 years of age or older or 7 years of age or younger, even though they commit crimes punishable by the death penalty, they shall not be punished. (For those who are 90 years of age or older and who commit rebellion or sedition, this provision shall not apply.) If there are persons who instigate them to commit crimes, then the instigators shall be punished. If there are illicit goods requiring repayment, those who receive the illicit goods shall make the repayment. (This means that those who are 90 years of age or older or 7 years of age or younger all have little intelligence or strength. If some persons instigate them to commit crimes, only the instigators shall be punished. If goods that have been robbed are taken and used by others, those who take and use the goods shall make the repayment. If the aged or juvenile themselves use the goods, then repayment shall fall upon the aged or juvenile.)

Article 22   Committing Crimes before Becoming Aged or Maimed
[Fanzui shi wei laoji]

In all cases where those who commit crimes before becoming aged or maimed [*ji*] have become aged or maimed when the affairs are discovered, they shall be judged according to the provision on those who are aged or maimed [Art. 21]. (This refers to cases such as those where the criminals commit crimes at 69 years of age or younger, and when the affairs are discovered they have reached 70 years of age, or the criminals commit crimes before they are disabled, and when the affairs are discovered they have become disabled; they may redeem their punishment as the aged or maimed. If the criminals at 79 years of age or younger commit crimes punishable by the death penalty, and when the affairs are discovered they have reached 80 years of age, or if the criminals commit crimes when they are disabled, and when the affairs are discovered they have become incapacitated, they may be governed by the provision on petitioning the throne. If the criminals commit crimes punishable by the death penalty at 89 years of age, and when the affairs are discovered they have reached 90 years of age, they may be governed by the provision that there shall be no punishment.) If within their term of years of penal servitude, the criminals become aged or maimed, they shall also be governed by this provision. (This refers to cases such as those where criminals of 69 years of age or younger commit crimes punishable by penal servitude for three years, and before the term of labor is completed they reach 70 years of age, or when they are sent into labor they are not ill, but within the term of years of penal servitude they become disabled; in both cases they may redeem their punishment as the aged or maimed. Take one year of penal servitude at the rate of 360 days and convert the labor into redemption in accordance with the amount of copper currency that shall be paid for redemption. For example, if the criminals commit crimes punishable by 60 strokes of beating with the heavy stick and penal servitude for one year, after the punishment has been carried out and the criminals have performed labor for five months, they become aged or maimed. In this case, 60 strokes of beating with the heavy stick and penal servitude shall in total be redeemed by copper currency of 12 *guan*. Excluding copper currency of 3 *guan* and 600 *wen* for the beating with the heavy stick that has already been received, the remaining penal servitude for one year shall be redeemed by copper currency of 8 *guan* and 400 *wen*; then the amount of copper currency for redemption of penal servitude for each month shall be calculated as 700 *wen*. Excluding copper currency of 3 *guan* and 500 *wen* for five months of labor that have already been performed, the remaining seven months of labor that have not yet been performed shall be redeemed by copper currency of 4 *guan* and 900 *wen*. For other degrees of penal servitude, their term of years and the amount of copper currency that shall be paid for redemption are different; in each case, the term of years shall be redeemed by the specified amount of copper currency.) If some persons commit crimes when they are juvenile, and when the affairs are discovered they have grown up, they shall be judged in accordance with the provision on those who are juvenile. (This refers to cases where those of 7 years of age commit crimes punishable by the death penalty, and when the affairs are discovered they have reached 8 years of age; they shall not be punished. For those of 10 years of age who kill others, and when the affairs are discovered they have reached 11 years of age, their cases shall still be petitioned to the throne. For those of 15 years of age who act as robbers, and when the affairs are discovered they have reached 16 years of age, they may still be allowed to redeem their punishment.)

Article 23   Restitution and Confiscation of Illicit Goods [Jimo zangwu]

[1] In all cases involving illicit goods that criminate both parties [*bici juzui zhi zang*] (this refers to cases where the punishment shall be determined in accordance with the value of the illicit goods, such as taking bribes with or without subversion of law) or forbidden articles (this refers to things such as forbidden weapons or proscribed books), such goods or articles shall be confiscated by the government. If the illicit goods are taken or given without consent [*quyu buhe*], obtained by using force and making trouble [*yongqiang shengshi*], or solicited through extortion [*biqu qiusuo*], such goods shall all be returned to the owner. (This refers to cases such as those where goods are obtained by threats [*konghe*] [Art. 296], fraud [*qizha*] [Art. 297],

Laws on Punishments and General Principles   33

gaining excessive profits through forcing purchase or sale [*qiang maimai you yuli*] [Art. 173], levying tax excessively [*kelian*] [Art. 374], or solicitation [*qiusuo*] [Arts. 371–72].) In cases involving illicit goods that shall be confiscated because of crimes, upon the declaration of an amnesty, even though punishment has been carried out, if the goods have not yet been seized by the government, such goods shall be exempted from confiscation in accordance with the amnesty. If the goods have already been seized by and been in the custody of the government, or if the goods involved the commission of plotting rebellion, sedition, or treason [Arts. 277, 278], such goods shall not be released and exempted from confiscation. If the punishment has not yet been carried put, and the goods have not yet been disposed of for custody even though they have been sent to the government, they shall still be considered as not yet being seized by the government. For family members who shall be collectively prosecuted, even though they have already been seized by the government, if the criminals may be exempted from punishment, they shall also be exempted from punishment and released.

[2] If criminals are punished on the basis of illicit goods, and the original illicit goods still exist, such goods shall be returned to the government or owners. (This means that government goods return to the government, and private goods return to the owners. If the original goods are donkeys and they have been exchanged for horses, or if domestic animals produce young, such as mares giving birth to colts, or sheep giving birth to lambs, they are all considered to be in existence [at the time of the crime].) If the goods have already been expended, or the criminals themselves die, the goods shall not be repaid. (If the criminals are punished for other crimes and die, the cases shall be considered the same.) All other illicit goods shall be repaid. If the illicit goods are calculated from the value of wages for hired laborers or the rent, such goods shall not be repaid either.

[3] In assessing the value of illicit goods, it shall be assessed in accordance with the average price of goods at the time and place of the crimes, and the punishment be decided accordingly. In assessing the wages of hired laborers, one man for one day shall be the equivalent of 60 *wen* of copper currency. In assessing the value of things such as cattle, horses, camels, mules, donkeys, carts, boats, stone rollers [for grinding grain], shops, or inns, it shall be assessed in accordance with the value of the rent at the time of crimes. Even though the amount of the rent is large, it shall not exceed the basic value of the things. (This refers to cases such as those where a boat is worth 10 *guan* of copper currency, so the value of the rent that shall be returned shall not be 11 *guan*.)

[4] If the illicit goods are gold or silver, they shall be repaid to the government or be returned to the owner in accordance with the purity that is originally confessed by the criminals. If they have already been expended

and do not exist, the restitution shall be in fine metal. (This means that if the original illicit goods that are stolen or obtained are gold or silver, and they have been expended and no longer exist, they shall all be repaid in fine metal.)

Article 24   *Voluntary Confession of Crimes* [Fanzui zishou]

[1] In all cases of voluntarily confessing crimes that have not yet been discovered, the criminals shall be exempted from punishment; the original illicit goods shall still be repaid. (This means, for example, that the illicit goods taken with or without subversion of the law [Art. 367] shall be seized by the government; the illicit goods taken by means such as using force and making trouble, extortion [Art. 298], fraud [Art. 297], excessive collection [Art. 374], or solicitation [Arts. 371, 372], or taken in forcible robbery [Art. 289] or theft [Art. 292], shall be returned to the owner.) If lesser crimes have been discovered but more serious crimes are voluntarily confessed, the criminals shall be exempted from the punishment for the more serious crimes. (This means, for example, that if theft has been discovered and illegitimately minting copper currency [*si juqian*] [Art. 383] is voluntarily confessed, the criminal shall be exempted from the punishment for minting coinage and only be punished for theft.) If, while matters that are reported are under interrogation, the criminals speak of other crimes, the cases shall also be judged in accordance with this provision. (This refers to cases such as those where smuggling salt [*siyan*] [Arts. 149–60] is discovered and interrogated, and without torture, the criminal himself speaks of other crimes of stealing a cow and taking other's property by fraud; he shall be punished only for smuggling salt and be exempted from the punishment for the other crimes.)

[2] If the criminals send others to make the confession for them, or those who are allowed mutual concealment by the law [Art. 31] make the confession for them, or [those who are allowed mutual concealment by the law] accuse each other to the court, in each case it shall be judged the same as under the law on the criminals' voluntary confession in person. ("Sending others to make the confession for them" means, for example, that A commits a crime and sends B to make the voluntary confession for him, irrespective of whether the latter is a relative or a nonrelative; A shall be exempted from punishment as for the voluntary confession. "Those who are allowed mutual concealment by the law make the confession for them" and "[those who are allowed mutual concealment] accuse each other to the court" mean that those who live together [*tongju*] or relatives of the third degree of mourning or closer or hired laborers make the confession for the household head. The criminals in these cases shall all be exempted from the punishment as if they made the voluntary confession themselves. If relatives of the fourth or fifth degree of mourning make the confession or accuse to the

Laws on Punishments and General Principles 35

court, the penalty for the criminals shall be reduced three degrees from that for ordinary persons. If relatives beyond the mourning system [*wufu zhi qin*] make the confession or accuse to the court, the penalty for the criminals shall still be reduced one degree from that for ordinary persons. In cases where plotting rebellion, sedition, or treason has not been carried out, and relatives make the confession for the criminals or accuse them to the court, or capture them and send them to the authorities, in both of these cases the responsible criminals [*zhengfan*] shall be judged the same as under the law of voluntary confession and be exempted from punishment. If those plots have been carried out, the responsible criminals shall not be exempted from punishment, but those who would be collectively prosecuted shall be judged the same as under the law on voluntary confession and be exempted from punishment.) If criminals make the voluntary confession untruthfully or incompletely, they shall be punished for crimes that have not yet been confessed truthfully or completely; if the punishment extends to death, it may be reduced one degree. (If the voluntary confession of the amount of the illicit goods is incomplete, criminals shall be punished only in accordance with the value of the incomplete amount.) If criminals know that someone intends to accuse them to the court, or they have fled or engaged in treason, and they make the voluntary confession, then they shall have their penalty reduced two degrees. If those who have fled or engaged in treason return to their original places, even though they do not make voluntary confession, they shall have their penalty reduced two degrees.

[3] If criminals harm or injure people (If they kill or injure people because of committing crimes and make voluntary confession, they shall be exempted from punishment for the crimes that are the causes of the killing or injuring; they shall still be punished in accordance with the law on deliberately killing or injuring. If the crimes are negligent, they shall be judged in accordance with the relevant law.) or [destroy or lose] articles that cannot be compensated (This refers to articles such as seals, official documents, forbidden military weapons, or proscribed books. These are articles that private households shall not possess and that cannot be compensated. Therefore, the criminals cannot make the voluntary confession. If the original articles exist, criminals may be judged the same as under the law on voluntary confession and be exempted from punishment.) or flee after the matters are discovered (Even though criminals shall not make the voluntary confession for crimes that have been committed, they shall have their penalty for flight reduced two degrees.) or pass checkpoints without authorization [*sidu*] or by circumvention [*yuedu*], commit fornication, or study astronomy without authorization, in all theses cases the law on voluntary confession shall not apply.

[4] For those who take others' property by forcible robbery, theft, or fraud and make voluntary confession to the owners of the property, or who accept

illicit goods from others either with or without subversion of law and repent their transgressions and return the goods to the owners, they shall all be judged the same as if they had made voluntary confession to the authorities and be exempted from punishment. If they know others intend to accuse them to the court and make the confession and return the property to the owners, they shall also have their penalty reduced two degrees. If those who have committed forcible robbery or theft can capture their companions and send them to the authorities, they shall also be exempted from punishment and be rewarded as ordinary persons.

Article 25   Sentencing on the Basis of the Punishment for the More Serious Crime When Two Crimes Are Discovered Together [Erzui jufa yi zhong lun]

In all cases where two or more crimes are discovered together, the criminals shall be punished on the basis of the punishment for the most serious crime. If the crimes are of equal severity, the criminals shall be punished in accordance with one of them. If one crime is discovered first and has already been judged and punishment carried out and then other crimes are discovered later, if they are less or equally serious, the criminals shall not be punished. If they are more serious, the criminals shall be punished again. Calculate the previous punishment and subtract it from the subsequent one. (This refers to cases such as those where two cases of theft are committed. One of them is discovered first, the illicit goods amount to 10 *guan*, and accordingly a beating with 70 strokes of the heavy stick is carried out. The other case is discovered later, and the illicit goods amount to 40 *guan*, for which the criminals shall be punished by 100 strokes of beating with the heavy stick. Therefore, the criminals shall subsequently be punished by 30 more strokes of beating with the heavy stick. However, if officials who have salaries [*youlu ren*] receive successively from others illicit goods worth 80 *guan* with subversion of the law, and goods worth 40 *guan* are discovered first and the criminals are judged and punished by 100 strokes of beating with the heavy stick and three years of penal servitude, and then other goods worth 40 *guan* are discovered later, this is not the same as the principle that only the illicit goods presently discovered shall be combined. The illicit goods that are discovered later shall be combined with the goods that are discovered first: they amount to 80 *guan* in total. Therefore, the punishment shall be changed, and the criminals shall be strangled for the whole crime.) If provisions such as confiscation by the government [*ruguan*], repayment [*peishang*], tattooing, dismissal from appointments, maximum punishment [*zuizhi*] are involved, in each case such a provision shall be applied. (This means that if, for example, one person commits several crimes, in each case the criminal shall be punished in accordance with the original provision: for accepting illicit goods with or without subversion of the law, the illicit goods shall be confiscated by the government; for destroying articles, the articles shall be repaid; for committing theft, there shall be tattooing; for committing private crimes punishable by 100 strokes of beating with the heavy stick or more by officials, there shall be dismissal from appointments; for accepting illicit goods worth 120 *guan* without subversion of the law, the maximum punishment shall be 100 strokes of beating with the heavy stick and life exile to 3,000 *li*.)

Article 26   Fleeing Together after Committing Crimes [Fanzui gongtao]

   In all cases where those who commit crimes flee together, if those whose crimes are less serious can seize those whose crimes are more serious and turn them over to the authorities, or if the crimes are equally serious, they can seize one-half or more of their fellows and turn them over to the authorities, they shall all [i.e., those who turned their fellow criminals in] be exempted from punishment. (This refers to cases where after joint crimes are discovered, the criminals flee together. If those who shall be punished by life exile can seize those who shall be punished by the death penalty or if those who shall be punished by penal servitude can seize those who shall be punished by life exile and turn them over to the authorities, or if five persons commit a joint crime and flee, one of them can seize two of the others and turn them over to the authorities, for such cases, the criminals shall all be exempted from punishment. For cases involving harming or injuring people or fornication, the criminals shall not be exempted from punishment and shall be punished in accordance with the regular rule.) As for those who shall be punished by implication of others, if the principal criminals themselves die, their penalty for original crimes may be reduced two degrees. (This refers to cases where one gets punished by implication for crimes committed by others, such as concealing, guiding, or aiding criminals, or failing as a guarantor, or giving false evidence, or failing to discover, guard against, or restrain others' crimes, or allowing others' crimes. If the principal criminals die themselves rather than being executed, then the penalty may be reduced two degrees.) If the principal criminals make voluntary confessions, are included in an amnesty so that they shall be pardoned and exempted from punishment, or are granted a special imperial grace so that their punishment shall be reduced or redeemed, those who are implicated shall also be judged in accordance with the law by which the principal criminals shall be pardoned and exempted from punishment or have their punishment reduced or redeemed. (This refers to cases where one gets punished by implication of other criminals. If the principal criminals later make voluntary confession, are included in an amnesty so that they shall be completely exempted from punishment, or are granted a special imperial grace so that they shall have their punishment reduced one or two degrees or redeemed, those who are implicated shall all be judged in accordance with the law by which the principal criminals shall be completely exempted from punishment or have their punishment reduced or redeemed.)

Article 27   Committing Public Crimes by Those in the Same Office
[Tongliao fan gongzui]

[1] In all cases where those in the same office commit public crimes (this refers to cases where officials and functionaries in the same office make mistakes in signing documents together or in deciding public matters and show no private motives), the functionaries [*lidian*] shall be punished as principals [*shou*]; the staff supervisors shall have their penalty reduced one degree from that for the functionaries; the associate officials shall have their penalty reduced one degree from that for the staff supervisors; the head officials shall have their penalty reduced one degree from that for associate officials. (If, within the four classes of officials, there are posts that have not been filled, the punishment shall still be progressively reduced [*dijian*] in accordance with the four classes of officials. If the four classes of officials are not established in some government offices, the punishment shall be successively reduced only in accordance with the numbers that are presently established.)

[2] If one of the officials in the same office has private interests, he himself shall be punished in accordance with the law on deliberately exonerating the guilty or implicating the innocent [Art. 433]. The others who do not know the circumstances shall be punished only in accordance with the law on negligently exonerating the guilty or implicating the innocent [Art. 433]. (This means, for example, that there are five officials and functionaries in the same office who sign documents together. If one of them has private interests, he shall be punished in accordance with the law on deliberately exonerating the guilty or implicating the innocent. If the other four do not know there are private interests involved, even though they sign the documents together, they shall be punished only in accordance with the law on negligently exonerating the guilty or implicating the innocent and shall still have their punishment reduced in accordance with the four classes of officials.)

[3] If lower offices send up reports to higher offices, and the higher offices do not discover the mistakes or errors in them and allow them to be carried out, then the officials and functionaries in the higher offices shall have their punishment successively reduced two degrees from that for the officials and functionaries in the lower offices. (This refers to cases such as those where districts send up reports to subprefectures, subprefectures send up reports to prefectures, or prefectures send up reports to Provincial Administration Commissions [Buzheng Si].) If higher offices send down documents to lower offices, and the lower offices carry them out even though there are errors in them, then in each case the officials and functionaries shall have their

Laws on Punishments and General Principles 39

punishment reduced three degrees from that for officials and functionaries in the higher offices. (This refers to cases such as those where Provincial Administration Commissions send down documents to prefectures, prefectures send down documents to subprefectures, or subprefectures send down documents to districts.) In each case the functionaries shall also be principals.

Article 28   Making Errors in Public Matters [Gongshi shicuo]

[1] In all cases where officials or functionaries make errors in public matters, and they themselves discover and report the errors [*zi jueju*], they shall be exempted from punishment. For officials and functionaries in the same office who shall be implicated together [*lianzuo*], if one of them discovers and reports the error, the others shall all be exempted from punishment. (This refers to cases where punishments result from public matters and there are no private motives involved. If the matters have not been discovered, and one of the officials or functionaries in the same office who sign the documents together can report or correct the error, they shall all be exempted from punishment.)

[2] If errors are made in judging crimes and the punishment has already been carried out, this provision shall not be applicable. (This refers to cases where the death penalty or beating with the light or heavy stick has been carried out, those punished by life exile have already arrived at places of exile, or those punished by penal servitude have already finished their labor. Such cases are all considered as "the punishment has already been carried out." Even though the officials themselves report the matters, they shall all not be exempted from punishment. Each shall be punished in accordance with the law on having the punishment for negligently implicating the innocent reduced three degrees [Art. 433] and on officials and functionaries having their punishment successively reduced [Art. 27]. Therefore, it is stated: "This provision shall not be applicable." As for negligently exonerating the guilty, although the punishment has already been carried out or the criminals have already been released, if the matters have not yet been discovered and the responsible officials or functionaries can themselves report the matter and correct the error, they shall all be exempted from punishment for the error.)

[3] If official documents are delayed and if among those who shall be implicated together one person discovers and reports the matter, the others shall be exempted from punishment. But the responsible functionary shall not be exempted from punishment. (This means that in dealing with official cases, matters of least importance have a five-day time limit; matters of medium importance have a ten-day time limit; and matters of greatest importance have a twenty-day time limit. If the cases have not yet been finished within these limits, it is called "delay." If officials themselves report

the matter, they shall all be exempted from punishment; only the responsible functionary shall not be exempted from punishment.) If the responsible functionary himself reports the matter, [the punishment for all officials and functionaries] shall be reduced two degrees. (This means that if the responsible functionary himself reports the matter, those who shall be implicated together shall have their punishment reduced two degrees.)

Article 29   Distinguishing Principals and Accessories in Joint Crimes [Gong fanzui fen shoucong]

[1] In all cases where crimes are committed jointly the person who formulates the plan shall be the principal. The penalty for accessories shall be reduced one degree.

[2] If the members of one family commit crimes jointly, only the senior or older member shall be punished. If the most senior or eldest member is 80 years of age or older or incapacitated, the punishment shall devolve upon the next senior or oldest member in the joint crime. (This means that if senior or older members and junior or younger members [*biyou*] commit crimes jointly, only the senior or older members shall be punished; the junior or younger members shall be exempted from punishment. If the most senior or eldest member is 80 years of age or older or incapacitated, and shall not be punished in accordance with the principle [Art. 21], then the punishment shall devolve upon the next eldest member in the joint crime. If female senior or older members and male junior or younger members commit crimes jointly, although the women are principals, still only punish the men.) If the members of one family encroach upon [*qin*] or harm [*sun*] people, then they shall be punished in accordance with the law on ordinary principals and accessories. ("Encroaching upon" refers to cases such as robbery of property; "harming" refers to cases such as affray, striking, killing, or injuring. If the father and sons together with other members of the family commit such crimes jointly, then they shall be punished in accordance with the law on ordinary principals and accessories. Since they have encroached upon or harmed people, the punishment shall not be limited to the senior or older members.) If crimes are committed jointly and the basic punishments for the principal and accessories are different, they shall each be punished in accordance with the specific provisions on the principal and accessories. (This refers to cases, for example, where A induces outsiders and strikes his older brother jointly; A shall be punished by 90 strokes of beating with the heavy stick and penal servitude for two and one-half years in accordance with the law on younger brothers striking older brothers [Art. 341]. The outsiders shall be punished by 20 strokes of beating with the light stick in accordance with the law on ordinary affrays and strikes [Art. 325]. For another example, if a junior or younger family member induces outsiders to steal his own family's property worth 20 *guan*, the junior or younger family member shall

be punished by 40 strokes of beating with the light stick on the basis of "unauthorized use of property" [*sishan yongcai*] [Art. 94], with the punishment being increased two degrees. The outsiders shall be punished by 70 strokes of beating with the heavy stick in accordance with the law on accessories to ordinary theft [Art. 292].)

[3] If a specific article refers to "all" [*jie*], then the punishment does not distinguish between principals and accessories. If it does not refer to "all," the law on principals and accessories shall be applied.

[4] For crimes of unauthorized entry into the gates of the imperial city [*huangcheng*] or of palaces [*gongdian*] [Art. 203], passing checkpoints without authorization or by circumvention [Art. 241], taking flight in order to evade labor service [Art. 90], or committing fornication [e.g., Art. 390], there shall also be no distinction between principals and accessories. (This means that in each case the criminals personally commit the crimes; therefore, there shall be no distinction between principals and accessories; they shall all be punished as responsible criminals.)

Article 30 Fleeing When Crimes Are Discovered [Fanzui shifa zaitao]

[1] In all cases where two persons jointly commit a crime and one of them takes flight, if the one who has been seized claims that the one who is in flight is the principal and there are no other witnesses, then he shall be punished as an accessory. If the one who is in flight [the putative principal] is seized thereafter and claims that the one who was first seized is the principal, and the interrogation confirms it, then the criminal who was first seized shall be repunished as the principal. Calculate the previous punishment and subtract it from the subsequent one.

[2] If the crime is discovered and the criminals are in flight, as long as three or more witnesses [*zhongzheng*] confirm the fact [i.e., confirm who is the principal and who is the accessory], then the case shall be considered established [*yucheng*]; it is not necessary that there be a confrontational interrogation [*duiwen*] [cf. Arts. 428–29].

Article 31 Mutual Concealment by Relatives [Qinshu xiangwei rongyin]

[1] In all cases where those who live together [*tongju*] ("Living together" refers to the situation in which relatives have common property [*tongcai*] and dwell together [*gongju*]. It is not limited by differences in household registration. Even those who are outside the mourning relationship are also included.), or relatives of the third degree of mourning or closer (this refers to relatives of the third degree of mourning or closer who live separately), or maternal grandparents, grandsons in the female line, wife's parents, sons-in-law, wives of grandsons in the male line, husband's brothers, or brothers' wives are guilty and mutually conceal each other's crime, or slaves or hired laborers conceal the household head's crime, they shall all not be punished.

[2] If they divulge the matter and inform the criminal, so that the criminal can be concealed or flee, they shall not be punished either. (This means that if one of the relatives who are allowed mutual concealment commits a crime, the authorities are searching for him, and his relatives divulge the matter and secretly deliver the information to the criminal so that he can be concealed or flee, they shall not be punished either.)

[3] If the relatives of the fourth degree or farther conceal each other's crime or divulge the matter, they shall have their punishment reduced three degrees below that for ordinary persons; relatives outside the mourning relationship shall have their punishment reduced one degree. (This refers to relatives of the fourth degree or farther who live separately.)

[4] If the crime is plotting treason or more serious, this article shall not be applicable. (This means that although they are relatives within the mourning relationship, if the crime is plotting rebellion, plotting great sedition, or plotting treason, and they conceal the crime and do not report to the authorities, they shall be punished in accordance with the law. Therefore, it is stated: "This article shall not be applicable.")

Article 32   Committing Capital Crimes by Functionaries [Lizu fan sizui]

In all cases where functionaries [*lidian*], ushers [*zhihou*], or jailers [*jinzi*] in a yamen outside the capital commit capital crimes, the head official of that yamen shall make the case clear through interrogation. Then he may execute the criminal in accordance with the law without reporting [to the superior offices]. Afterward, he shall report the case to the directly superior office, which shall report it to the Ministry of Justice, then memorializing to the throne.

Article 33   Executing Military Personnel Guilty of Treason [Chujue panjun]

In all cases where military personnel [*junren*] in fortified cities of distant frontiers plot treason and the commandant [*shouyu guan*] seizes them and brings them to the authorities, if there is good evidence that proves the matter clearly, and the criminals make confessions upon interrogation, then hand over the matter to the Regional Military Commission [Du Zhihui Shi Si], which shall assign officials to conduct the interrogation. If there is no injustice [in executing them], the criminals shall be executed immediately in accordance with the law. Then report the matter with the reasons for judgment [*juyou*] to the Five Chief Military Commissions, which shall memorialize the throne. At places where Provincial Administration Commissions and Surveillance Commissions are located, the matter shall be interrogated and settled jointly. If the criminals are seized and executed before the troops as the troops go into battle, this provision is not applicable.

Laws on Punishments and General Principles 43

Article 34   Killing Military Personnel [Shahai junren]

In all cases of killing military personnel, the criminals shall be executed in accordance with the law; besides, take other adult males of the criminals' families into military service to fill up the vacancies.

Article 35   Military Personnel and Civilians Residing in the Capital Who Commit Crimes [Zaijing fanzui junmin]

In all cases where military personnel or civilians residing in the capital commit crimes punishable by 80 strokes of beating with the heavy stick or more, the military personnel shall be sent into military exile to military guards in the provinces; the civilians shall be sent to other prefectures as local residents.

Article 36   Committing Crimes by Persons beyond the Pale of Civilization [Huawairen youfan]

In all cases where persons beyond the pale of civilization commit crimes, they shall all be judged in accordance with the *Code*.

Article 37   Specific Articles Having Different Regulations for Punishment [Bentiao bieyou zuiming]

[1] In all cases where specific articles have specified regulations for punishment that are different from those in the "Laws on Punishments and Principles," the matters shall be judged in accordance with the specific articles.

[2] Although the specific articles have specified regulations for punishment, if the criminals [use those articles] to circumvent the law [*guibi*], and the crimes result in heavier penalties, they shall be punished in accordance with the heavier penalties.

[3] If the law provides for heavier penalties, but the criminals do not know the circumstances when they commit the crimes, they shall be punished as ordinary persons. (This refers to cases such as those where a paternal uncle and his nephew in the male line have grown up in different places and they do not know each other at all. If the nephew strikes and injures the uncle, and he does not know that the victim is his uncle until the authorities interrogate the matter, he shall only be punished in accordance with the law on affrays between ordinary persons [Art. 325]. Or someone commits theft at another place [rather than the one for sacrificing to the spirits] and steals the objects for the Great Sacrifices to the spirits. Cases such as these are examples in which the criminals "do not know the circumstances when they commit the crimes," and the criminals shall be judged as ordinary persons and punished in accordance with the law on ordinary robbery.) If the law provides for lighter penalties, the criminals shall be punished in accordance with those specific provisions. (This refers to cases such as those where a father

does not recognize his son and does not know the circumstance until after he strikes the son. He shall be punished only in accordance with the law on striking the son and shall not be punished on the basis of ordinary striking.)

Article 38   Principles for Increasing and Reducing Punishments
[Jiajian zuili]

In all cases where "increase" [*jia*] is referred to, the basic punishment [*benzui*] shall be increased in severity. (This refers to cases such as those where someone commits a crime punishable by 40 strokes of beating with the light stick, and it is increased by one degree; then the criminal shall be punished by 50 strokes of beating with the light stick. If he commits a crime punishable by 100 strokes of beating with the heavy stick, and it is increased by one degree, then penal servitude shall be added and the beating with the heavy stick shall be reduced; namely, he shall be punished by 60 strokes of beating with the heavy stick and penal servitude for one year. If he commits a crime punishable by 60 strokes of beating with the heavy stick and penal servitude for one year, and it is increased by one degree, then he shall be punished by 70 strokes of beating with the heavy stick and penal servitude for one and one-half years. If he commits a crime punishable by 100 strokes of beating with the heavy stick and penal servitude for three years, and it is increased by one degree, then he shall be punished by 100 strokes of beating with the heavy stick and life exile to 2,000 *li*. If he commits a crime punishable by 100 strokes of beating with the heavy stick and life exile to 2,000 *li*, and it is increased by one degree, then he shall be punished by 100 strokes of beating with the heavy stick and life exile to 2,500 *li*.) If "reduce" is referred to, the basic punishment shall be reduced in severity. (This refers to cases such as those where someone commits a crime punishable by 50 strokes of beating with the light stick, and it is reduced by one degree; then the criminal shall be punished by 40 strokes of beating with the light stick. If he commits a crime punishable by 60 strokes of beating with the heavy stick and penal servitude for one year, and it is reduced by one degree, then he shall be punished by 100 strokes of beating with the heavy stick. If he commits a crime punishable by 100 strokes of beating with the heavy stick and penal servitude for three years, and it is reduced by one degree, then he shall be punished by 90 strokes of beating with the heavy stick and penal servitude for two and one-half years.) However, for the two degrees of death penalty and the three degrees of life exile, each shall be considered as one degree of reduction of punishment. ("Two degrees of death penalty" refers to strangulation and decapitation. "Three degrees of life exile" refers to life exile to 2,000 *li*, 2,500 *li*, and 3,000 *li*. "Each shall be considered as one degree of reduction of punishment" means, for example, that someone commits a crime punishable by the death penalty, and it is reduced by one degree, then the criminal shall be punished by life exile to 3,000 *li*. If it is reduced by two degrees, then he shall be punished by penal servitude for three years. If he commits a crime punishable by life exile to 3,000 *li*, and it is reduced by one degree, then he shall also be punished by penal servitude for three years.) In the case of increasing punishment, it shall be imposed only when the amount is complete. (This means, for example, that if the punishment shall be increased for 40 *guan* of illicit goods, even though the illicit goods amount to 39 *guan* 990 *wen*, with only 10 *wen* lacking, the punishment for 40 *guan* shall still not be imposed.) Moreover, increasing punishment shall be limited to 100 strokes of beating with the heavy stick and life exile to 3,000 *li*; it shall not be increased to death. If a specific article increases the punishment to death, follow that article. (If the punishment shall be increased to strangulation, then it shall not be increased to decapitation.)

Article 39   The Terms "Sedan Chair" and "Carriage"
[Cheng chengyu chejia]

In all cases where the term "sedan chair" [*chengyu*], "carriage" [*chejia*], or "imperial" [*yu*] is referred to, the grand empress dowager [*taihuang taihou*], empress dowager [*huang taihou*], and empress [*huanghou*] shall all be considered the same. In reference to "imperial decree" [*zhi*], the orders [*ling*] of the grand empress dowager, empress dowager, and heir apparent shall all be considered the same.

*Article 40   The Terms "Relatives of Mourning for One Year"
and "Paternal Grandparents"* [Cheng jiqin zufumu]

In all cases where the term "relatives of mourning for one year" [*jiqin*] or "paternal grandparents" [*zufumu*] is referred to, the paternal great-grandparents and great-great-grandparents [*zeng gao*] shall be considered the same. In reference to "son's son" [*sun*], the great-grandsons and great-great-grandsons in the male line [*zeng xuan*] shall be considered the same. If the son's son by the proper wife [*disun*] becomes the heir of his paternal grandparents [*chengzu*], they shall be considered the same as his parents. (In case of collective prosecution, the specific law on paternal grandparents and sons' sons shall be applied.) The "proper mother" [*dimu*], "stepmother" [*jimu*], "carrying mother" [*cimu*], and "adoptive mother" [*yangmu*] shall be considered the same as the natural mother [*qinmu*]. In reference to "children" [*zi*], both males and females shall be included. (In case of collective prosecution, females shall not be included.)

Article 41   The Term "Shall Be Punished by the Same Penalty"
[Cheng yu tongzui]

[1] In all cases where the term "shall be punished by the same penalty" [*yu tomhzui*] is referred to, the criminals shall be punished only by that pun-

ishment. If the punishment reaches death, it shall be reduced by one degree. The punishment shall be limited to 100 strokes of beating with the heavy stick and life exile to 3,000 li, and the law on tattooing, strangulation, and decapitation shall not be applied. However, for those who receive property and deliberately connive at the actions and [are required by the law] to be punished by the same penalty, they shall be punished by the whole penalty [quanke]. (The death penalty shall be limited to strangulation.) For those who deliberately release criminals guilty of plotting rebellion, sedition, or treason, they shall all be punished in accordance with the basic law [benlü].

[2] When terms such as "shall be punished as comparable to subversion of law" [zhun wangfa lun] or "shall be punished as comparable to robbery" [zhun dao lun] are referred to, the punishment shall only be comparably applied: it shall also be limited to 100 strokes of beating with the heavy stick and life exile to 3,000 li, and tattooing shall be exempted.

[3] When terms such as "shall be punished on the basis of subversion of law" [yi wangfa lun] or "shall be punished on the basis of robbery" [yi dao lun] are referred to, the punishment shall be the same as for the actual crimes: the tattooing, strangulation, or decapitation shall all be applied in accordance with the basic law.

Article 42   The Terms "Supervisors" and "Custodians"
[Cheng jianlin zhushou]

[1] In all cases where the term "supervisors" [jianlin] is referred to, it means those who are in charge of subordinates [tongshe suoshu] in offices both in the capital and in the provinces, those who are involved in dealing with official documents [you wenan xiang guanshe], and those who, although they are not in charge of the people, are in charge of some matters; these are supervisors. When the term "custodians" [zhushou] is referred to, it means functionaries [lidian] who have control over documents and are solely in charge of some matters, and those officials, functionaries, storehousemen [kuzi], granary keepers [douji], account keepers [zuan], checkers [lan], and jailers [jinzi] who guard granaries, jails, or miscellaneous articles; these are all custodians.

[2] For those who are temporarily sent to control and direct some matters, although their official duties are not to control and direct such matters, they shall also be considered either "supervisors" or "custodians."

Article 43   The Term "Day" as Being One Hundred Units
[Cheng rizhe yi baike]

In all cases where the term "one day" is referred to, it means 100 units [ke]. In calculating labor, it shall be calculated from dawn to dusk. When the term "one year" is referred to, it means 360 days. When the term "person's age" is referred to, it shall be based upon the household register [ji].

(This means that if a person's age is referred to, the age that is registered will be taken as a standard.) When the term "group" [*zhong*] is referred to, it means three or more persons. When the term "plot" [*mou*] is referred to, it means two or more persons. (If the circumstances of the plot are clear and evident, it shall be considered the same as two persons although there is only one person.)

Article 44   The Terms "Daoist Priests" and "Daoist Nuns"
[Cheng daoshi nüguan]

In all cases where the term "Daoist priests" [*daoshi*] or "Daoist nuns" [*nuguan*] is referred to, the Buddhist priests [*seng*] or Buddhist nuns [*ni*] shall be included. Their relationship to the masters from whom they have received their education shall be considered the same as that to paternal uncles and their wives. ("The masters from whom they have received their education" refers to those from whom they have personally received canonical instructions in Buddhist temples [*si*] and Daoist monasteries [*guan*] and who ought to be treated as masters.) The relationship to disciples shall be considered the same as that to children of older or younger brothers.

Article 45   Deciding Penalties in Accordance with the Newly Promulgated Code [Duanzui yi xinban *Lü*]

The *Code* [Lü] shall take effect from the day it is promulgated. If crimes are committed before then, they shall all be judged in accordance with the new *Code*.

Article 46   Deciding Penalties without Specific Articles
[Duanzui wu zhengtiao]

The provisions in the *Code* and *Commandment* [Ling] will not cover all matters. When there is no specific article [*wu zhengtiao*] in deciding a penalty, cite [a closely analogous article in] the *Code* and decide the case by analogy [*yinlü bifu*]. Propose whether the penalty shall be increased or reduced and submit it to the Ministry of Justice. After deliberation, it shall be memorialized to the throne. If someone decides the penalty without authorization and causes it to be wrongly reduced or increased, he shall be punished on the basis of deliberately or negligently [reducing or increasing the punishment].

Article 47   Places for Penal Servitude, Life Exile, and Banishment
[Tuliu qianxi difang]

[PENAL SERVITUDE]

Penal servitude for labor service shall, in accordance with the number of years set for the servitude, begin from the day the criminals arrive at the places for performing the penal servitude. Those who are sent to the salt farms [*yanchang*] shall make three *jin* of salt each day; those who are sent to the iron smelters [*tieye*] shall smelt three *jin* of iron each day. Their products shall be kept in separate accounts.

For those from prefectures and subprefectures directly under the central government [*zhili fuzhou*]:

> Those from south of the Yangzi shall be sent to salt farms in Shandong.
> Those from north of the Yangzi shall be sent to salt farms in Hejian.
> Those from prefectures of the Fujian Administration Commission shall be respectively sent to salt farms in Lianghuai.
> Those from prefectures of the Zhejiang Administration Commission shall be respectively sent to salt farms in Shandong.
> Those from prefectures of the Jiangxi Administration Commission shall be respectively sent to iron smelters in places such as Taian and Laiwu.
> Those from prefectures of the Huguang Administration Commission shall be respectively sent to salt farms in Haibei in Guangdong.
> Those from prefectures of the Henan Administration Commission shall be respectively sent to salt farms in Zhedong.
> Those from prefectures of the Shandong Administration Commission shall be respectively sent to salt farms in Zhedong.
> Those from prefectures of the Shanxi Administration Commission shall be respectively sent to iron smelters in Gongchang.
> Those from prefectures of the Beiping Administration Commission shall be respectively sent to iron smelters in Pingyang.
> Those from prefectures of the Shaanxi Administration Commission shall be respectively sent to salt wells [*yanjing*] in Daning and Mianzhou.
> Those from prefectures of the Guangxi Administration Commission shall be respectively sent to salt farms in Lianghuai.
> Those from prefectures of the Guangdong Administration Commission shall be respectively sent to salt farms in Zhexi.
> Those from prefectures of Haibei and Hainan shall be sent to iron smelters in Jinxian and Xinyu, respectively.
> Those from prefectures of the Sichuan Administration Commission shall be respectively sent to iron smelters in Huangmei and Xingguo.

[Life Exile]

Those punished by the three degrees of life exile shall, in accordance with the distance of places of exile, be sent to settle in desolate or coastal subprefectures or districts.

> Those from prefectures and subprefectures directly under the central government shall be exiled to Shaanxi.
> Those from prefectures of the Fujian Administration Commission shall be respectively exiled to Shandong and Beiping.
> Those from prefectures of the Zhejiang Administration Commission shall be respectively exiled to Shandong and Beiping.
> Those from prefectures of the Jiangxi Administration Commission shall be respectively exiled to Guangxi.
> Those from prefectures of the Huguang Administration Commission shall be respectively exiled to Shandong.
> Those from prefectures of the Henan Administration Commission shall be respectively exiled to Fujian.
> Those from prefectures of the Shandong Administration Commission shall be respectively exiled to Fujian.
> Those from prefectures of the Shanxi Administration Commission shall be respectively exiled to Fujian.
> Those from prefectures of the Beiping Administration Commission shall be respectively exiled to Fujian.
> Those from prefectures of the Shaanxi Administration Commission shall be respectively exiled to Fujian.
> Those from prefectures of the Guangxi Administration Commission shall be respectively exiled to Guangdong.
> Those from prefectures of the Guangdong Administration Commission shall be respectively exiled to Fujian.
> Those from prefectures of the Sichuan Administration commission shall be respectively exiled to Guangxi.

[Military Exile]

Military exile to distant frontiers [*bianyuan chongjun*]
  For those from prefectures and subprefectures directly under the central government:

> Those from south of the Yangzi shall be sent to
>   the Regional Military Commission of Dingyuan;
>   the Yongning Guard [*wei*] under the jurisdiction of the Regional Military Commission of Beiping;

the Regional Military Commission of Shanxi;

the Lanzhou Guard and Hezhou Guard under the jurisdiction of the Regional Military Commission of Shaanxi.

Those from north of the Yangzi shall be sent to

the Hainan Guard under the jurisdiction of the Regional Military Commission of Guangdong;

the Yazhou Battalion [*qianhu suo*] of the Guizhou Guard under the jurisdiction of the Regional Military Commission of Sichuan.

Those from prefectures of the Fujian Administration Commission shall be respectively sent to the Yongping Guard under the jurisdiction of the Regional Military Commission of Beiping.

Those from prefectures of the Zhejiang Administration Commission shall be respectively sent to the Regional Military Commission of Dingliao.

Those from prefectures of the Jiangxi Administration Commission shall be respectively sent to the Regional Military Commission of Shanxi.

Those from prefectures of the Huguang Administration Commission shall be respectively sent to the Regional Military Commission of Shanxi.

Those from prefectures of the Henan Administration Commission shall be respectively sent to the Taiping Battalion of the Nanning Guard under the jurisdiction of the Regional Military Commission of Guangxi.

Those from prefectures of the Shandong Administration Commission shall be respectively sent to the Hainan Guard under the jurisdiction of the Regional Military Commission of Guangdong.

Those from prefectures of the Shanxi Administration Commission shall be respectively sent to the Hainan Guard under the jurisdiction of the Regional Military Commission of Guangdong.

Those from prefectures of the Beiping Administration Commission shall be respectively sent to the Taiping Battalion of the Nanning Guard under the jurisdiction of the Regional Military Commission of Guangxi.

Those from prefectures of the Shaanxi Administration Commission shall be respectively sent to the Taiping Battalion of the Nanning Guard under the jurisdiction of the Regional Military Commission of Guangxi.

Those from prefectures of the Guangxi Administration Commission shall be respectively sent to the Lanzhou Guard and Hezhou Guard under the jurisdiction of the Regional Military Commission of Shaanxi.

Those from prefectures of the Guangdong Administration Commission shall be respectively sent to the Regional Military Commission of Shanxi.

Those from prefectures of the Sichuan Administration Commission shall be respectively sent to the Taiping Battalion of the Nanning Guard under the jurisdiction of the Regional Military Commission of Guangxi.

CHAPTER 2

Laws on Personnel [Lilü]

Section 1 Administrative Institutions [*Zhizhi*] [Fifteen Articles]

Article 48 Selecting Military Posts [Xuanyong junzhi]

In all cases where guards lack battalion commanders, company commanders, or judges [*zhenfu*], one copy of the document concerning the vacancies [*queben*] shall be sealed and sent to the throne to open; another copy shall be sent to Regional Military Commissions and then transferred to the Five Chief Military Commissions to memorialize petitioning the decision of selection by the throne. If the responsible officials or functionaries in advance ask somebody to take charge of the matters and hope that the posts can be actually conferred, they shall each be punished by 100 strokes of beating with the heavy stick, and they shall be dismissed from their appointments or employments and sentenced to military exile. When selecting platoon commanders, they shall be appointed from those who have used iron spears. As for squad commanders [*xiaoqi*], they can be selected at convenience; this article shall not be applicable.

Article 49 Selecting Officials by High Officials without Authorization [Dachen zhuanshan xuanguan]

[1] In all cases of appointing officials, the selections shall be made by the court. If high officials make the selections without authorization, they shall be punished by decapitation.

[2] No relatives of high officials shall be appointed officials unless special imperial decrees are received. Violators shall be punished by the same penalty.

[3] If incumbent court officials are sent on missions or transferred by the throne in person but they, regardless of whether it is far or near, make pretexts and do not go, they shall be punished by 100 strokes of beating with the heavy stick and be removed from their appointments without reassignment.

Article 50 Civil Officials Shall Not Be Designated as Dukes or Marquises [Wenguan buxu feng gonghou]

In all cases where civil officials have not accomplished extraordinary meritorious deeds for the dynasty but the authorities misleadingly petition the throne and confer upon them the noble titles of dukes or marquises, the responsible officials and those who have been so designated shall all be punished by decapitation. For those who, during their lifetime, become grand councilors from generals, eliminate great calamities, and are thoroughly loyal to the dynasty and thereby are designated by the titles of marquises or dukes, this article shall not be applicable.

Article 51 Officials' Protection Privilege [Guanyuan xiyin]

[1] In all cases where civil or military officers have inheritable titles, their wives' eldest sons or sons' sons [di zhang zisun] shall be designated to inherit them. If such eldest sons or sons' sons have a reason [so that they may not inherit], then the subsequent sons or sons' sons of the officials' wives [di ci zisun] shall inherit the titles. Only when there are no subsequent sons or sons' sons by the officials' wives shall concubines' eldest sons or sons' sons [shu zhang zisun] be allowed to inherit the titles. If there are no sons or sons' sons by concubines, younger brothers or brothers' sons who are entitled to succeed may inherit the titles. If the sons or sons' sons by concubines or younger brothers or brothers' sons do not follow the order and inherit the titles by confusing the positions, they shall be punished by 100 strokes of beating with the heavy stick and penal servitude for three years.

[2] If military officers' sons or sons' sons are young and cannot inherit [the titles], report to the court, record their names, petition for their emoluments, and adequately support their families. They shall not inherit the positions and take charge of military affairs until they reach 16 years of age. If the line is indeed extinct, and there is no one capable of inheriting, the officers' widows and children may also petition for their emoluments in accordance with regulations, and they shall be supported during their lives. If the officials' families adopt persons of different surnames outside the families as sons and deceive the government and fraudulently inherit the titles, the adopted sons shall be punished by 100 strokes of beating with the heavy stick and be sent to the distant frontier in military exile. The emoluments received by the officials' families shall cease [from the date when the matter is discovered]. Other persons who instigate the offenders shall be punished by the same penalty as that for the offenders.

[3] If the responsible authorities know the circumstances and allow the action to take place, they shall be punished the same. If they do not know, they shall not be punished.

Article 52   Appointing Too Many Officials or Functionaries [Lanshe guanli]

[1] In all cases where every yamen in the capital or outside has an established number of officials but too many [officials] are appointed, for each supernumerary the responsible officials or functionaries shall be punished by 100 strokes of beating with the heavy stick. For each additional three supernumeraries the penalty shall be increased one degree; the punishment shall be limited to 100 strokes of beating with the heavy stick and penal servitude of three years.

[2] If persons such as functionaries, seal keepers [*zhiyin*], runners [*chengchai*], ushers, jailers, or archers [*gongbing*] fill these posts beyond the established number, they shall be punished by 100 strokes of beating with the heavy stick and banishment. For knowingly permitting one such supernumerary, the principal officials [*zhengguan*] shall be punished by 20 strokes of beating with the light stick; staff supervisors, 30 strokes of beating with the light stick; functionaries, 40 strokes of beating with the light stick. For each additional three supernumeraries the penalty shall be increased one degree. The punishment shall be limited to 100 strokes of beating with the heavy stick. The punishment shall be inflicted only on those who are responsible.

[3] If discharged officials or functionaries, outside the government, interfere with government affairs, associate [with officials] and grasp [authority], write and distribute documents, control government agencies, corrupt the administration and harm the people, they shall all be punished by 80 strokes of beating with the heavy stick; 20 *liang* of silver shall be levied from the offenders to pay as recompense to those who report the cases. Moreover, their transgressions shall be written on the top of their household doors. If they do not commit any crimes for three years, the government will remove [the records]; if they commit crimes again, the penalty shall be increased two degrees and they shall be banished. If the crimes are committed to circumvent the law, they shall be punished according to the heavier penalties.

[4] If government agencies hire persons to write tax account books and household registers, there shall be no punishment.

Article 53   Recommending Inappropriate Persons [Gongju fei qiren]

[1] In all cases where inappropriate persons are recommended [for civil service degrees or government offices], or talented persons who can benefit the times and who shall be recommended are not recommended, for one such person, [the responsible persons] shall be punished by 80 strokes of beating with the heavy stick. For each additional two persons, the penalty shall be increased one degree. The punishment shall be limited to 100 strokes of beating with the heavy stick. If the persons recommended know the circumstances, they shall be punished the same. If they do not know, they shall not be punished.

Laws on Personnel

[2] If examiners, in testing skills and abilities, do not make their judgments in accordance with the facts [bu yishi], the penalty shall be reduced two degrees.

[3] In case of negligence, the penalty in each case shall be reduced three degrees.

Article 54   Recommending Officials or Functionaries Who Have Transgressed [Juyong youguo guanli]

In all cases where officials or functionaries have been tried for crimes and have been dismissed from their appointments or employments and shall not be reassigned, no yamen shall misleadingly recommend them [menglong baoju]. In case of violation, the officials who recommend and the persons who conceal the transgressions shall each be punished by 100 strokes of beating with the heavy stick; and they shall be dismissed from their appointments or employments and shall not be reassigned.

Article 55   Leaving Official Appointments or Employments without Authorization [Shanli zhiyi]

[1] In all cases where officials or functionaries, without reason, leave their appointments or employments without authorization, they shall be punished by 40 strokes of beating with the light stick. If they take flight to avoid difficult affairs, they shall be punished by 100 strokes of beating with the heavy stick; and they shall be dismissed from their appointments or employments and shall not be reassigned. If the affairs that are avoided are more serious, in each case they shall be punished according to the heavier penalties.

[2] If those who serve in government agencies should be on duty [by day] but they are not, or should be on watch [by night] but they are not, in each case they shall be punished by 20 strokes of beating with the light stick. If those who guard granaries and storehouses, workplaces, prisons, miscellaneous property, or other matters should be on duty but they are not, or should be on watch but they are not, in each case they shall be punished by 40 strokes of beating with the light stick.

Article 56   Exceeding the Time Limit by Officials When Going to Their Posts [Guanyuan furen guoxian]

[1] In all cases where officials who have been appointed shall each go to their posts in accordance with the established time limit, for those in the capital, the time shall be calculated from the day when orders of appointments are given; for those outside the capital, the time shall be calculated from the day when notices of appointments are received. If they exceed the time limit without reason, for 1 day [over the time limit] they shall be punished by 10 strokes of beating with the light stick. For each additional 10

days, the penalty shall be increased one degree. The punishment shall be limited to 80 strokes of beating with the heavy stick; they shall have their transgressions recorded and retain their appointments.

[2] When successors arrive, if the old officials in each case have, in accordance with the established time limit, handed over [all of the records] of such matters as household registration, tax in money and grain, and legal cases and all of the required documents and records but they, without reason, do not leave their offices after more than 10 days, they shall be punished two degrees less than "exceeding time limit when going to posts."

[3] If they, while en route, are detained by winds, are plundered by thieves, fall sick, or go into mourning, so that they cannot proceed, they may obtain statements from local authorities for examination. If there is any circumvention of law, deceit, or false pretenses, they shall be punished by the heavier penalties. If the said authorities collude and serve as guarantors, the punishment shall be the same.

Article 57 Failing to Attend Audiences at the Court or to Fill Official Posts without Reason [Wugu bu chaocan gongzuo]

In all cases where officials of higher or lower ranks, without reason, in the capital fail to attend audiences at the court, or outside the capital fail to fill official posts to take care of their duties, or where officials or functionaries who are on leave which expires fail to return to their appointments or employments without reason, for one day [of delay] they shall be punished by 10 strokes of beating with the light stick. For each additional three days, the penalty shall be increased one degree. In each case the punishment shall be limited to 80 strokes of beating with the heavy stick; and the offenders shall have their transgressions recorded and remain in their appointments.

Article 58 Summoning Subordinate Officials without Authorization [Shangou shuguan]

In all cases where superior offices urge [subordinate offices] to manage public affairs, they shall establish records and fix time limits and issue wooden warrants or dispatch messengers to subordinate yamens to supervise and manage. If there are any delays or errors, they shall be punished in accordance with the *Code* [e.g., Arts. 71, 75, 77]. If they, without authorization, summon subordinate officials or call functionaries to come to attend on them or assign judges, prison warders, or staff supervisors of subprefectures or districts, and thereupon public affairs are interfered with or abandoned, they shall be punished by 40 strokes of beating with the light stick. If subordinate officials receive commands and go along with them, or send functionaries to superior offices to attend on them, the punishment shall be the same. Only if there are important matters such as criminal cases that must be investigated or verified or money or grain that must be surveyed or con-

Laws on Personnel

struction work that must be supervised may they summon [help] and investigate. As soon as the matters are finished, they shall release [the summoned persons]. If they detain them without reason for three days, they shall be punished by 20 strokes of beating with the light stick. For each additional three days, the penalty shall be increased one degree. The punishment shall be limited to 50 strokes of beating with the light stick.

Article 59   Career Records of Officials or Functionaries [Guanli jiyou]

[1] In all cases where each yamen submits career records of officials and functionaries [after the time due for scrutiny] to the Ministry of Personnel, [the Bureau of Evaluations] shall, within the time limit of five days, transfer [the records to each office for] verification and make them complete, according to which [officials and functionaries will be] selected in different categories and appointed [leixuan quanzhu]. If [the said bureau] does not transfer [the records for] verification and make them complete, for one day of delay functionaries shall be punished by 10 strokes of beating with the light stick. For each additional day, the penalty shall be increased one degree. The punishment shall be limited to 40 strokes of beating with the light stick. The penalty for staff supervisors shall be reduced one degree.

[2] If [the officials or functionaries who shall have their career records submitted] conceal or omit their public or private transgressions and do not report, they shall be punished in accordance with the crimes that are concealed. If the crimes are punishable by redemption or the recording of the transgression, in each case they shall also be punished in accordance with the crimes punishable by redemption or the recording of the transgression. If they report their major crimes as minor crimes, they shall be punished in accordance with the crimes that are concealed. If the offices [which the officials or functionaries belong to] collude [with the officials or functionaries] and conceal or omit [the transgressions], they shall be punished the same. If they make errors or omissions in transferring [the reports of the officials or functionaries], or superior offices fail to verify [the reports], they shall be punished in accordance with "making errors or failing to report archives" [Art. 72].

[3] If [the Ministry of Personnel] fails to attach records of conduct, for one through three persons, the functionaries shall be punished by 10 strokes of beating with the light stick. For each additional three persons, the penalty shall be increased one degree. The punishment shall be limited to 40 strokes of beating with the light stick.

[4] If [the officials or functionaries who shall have their career records submitted, their offices, and the Ministry of Personnel jointly] change dates, places, or backgrounds or conceal transgressions, they shall all be punished by 100 strokes of beating with the heavy stick; and they shall be dismissed from their appointments or employments and shall not be reassigned.

[5] If the crimes are committed to circumvent the law, or the acceptance of illicit goods is involved, in each case they shall be punished in accordance with the heavier penalties.

Article 60   Treacherous Cliques [Jiandang]

[1] In all cases where treacherous or evil persons put forward calumnious whispers and in tricky words cause the throne to execute others, they shall be punished by decapitation.

[2] If someone commits a crime punishable by the death penalty according to the *Code*, and high ministers or low officials put forward cunning words [to the throne] to petition for the exemption of the punishment in order to court popularity in secret, they shall also be punished by decapitation.

[3] If officials at the court form cliques to disorder the government of the court, they shall all be punished by decapitation. Their wives and children shall be enslaved, and their property confiscated by the government.

[4] If officials or functionaries in the Ministry of Justice or all other government offices do not enforce the law but obey superiors' instructions to exonerate the guilty or implicate the innocent, the punishment shall also be the same. If they do not yield to the power, clearly show the real facts, and personally go to the throne to report in accordance with the law, the punishment shall be imposed only on the treacherous officials. The reporters shall be exempted from the punishment and, moreover, shall be awarded equally with the offenders' property. Those who are officials shall be promoted two ranks; those who are not officials may be awarded with an official position or two thousand *liang* of silver.

Article 61   Associating with Court Attendant Officials
[Jiaojie jinshi guanyuan]

In all cases where officials or functionaries in any yamen and eunuch officials or court attendant personnel associate with each other, leak information on court affairs, practice fraud through intrigue, and collude to memorialize the throne, they shall all be punished by decapitation. Their wives and children shall be punished by life exile to 2,000 *li* to settle there.

Article 62   Memorializing in Praise of the Virtues and Achievements of High Officials [Shangyan dachen dezheng]

In all cases where officials or functionaries in any yamen, scholars, or common people memorialize in praise of the admirable achievements, talents, or virtues of high officials in charge of government affairs, they are precisely treacherous cliques. It is essential that they be interrogated and their backgrounds be made clear. The offenders shall be punished by decapitation. Their wives and children shall be enslaved, and their property confiscated by the government. If the high officials in charge of government affairs know the circumstances, they shall be punished the same. If they do not know, they shall not be punished.

Section 2 Official Documents [*Gongshi*] [Eighteen Articles]

Article 63 Explaining and Reading the Code *and* Commandment [Jiangdu lüling]

[1] In all cases where the dynasty's *Code* and *Commandment* analyze and deliberate the seriousness of the circumstances, determine the crimes, and are promulgated to the realm, they shall be eternally observed. It is essential that officials and functionaries in all the government offices thoroughly read them and be able to explain clearly the meaning of the *Code* so that they can analyze and decide matters. At the end of every year, they shall be examined: in the capital, by the Investigation Bureau, and outside the capital, by investigating censors and officials of Provincial Surveillance Commissions within their jurisdictions. If there are officials or functionaries who cannot explain or do not understand the meaning of the *Code*, for the first offense, they shall be fined one month's cash salary. For the second offense, they shall be punished by 40 strokes of beating with the light stick and have their transgressions recorded. For the third offense, they shall be demoted and employed in their original yamen.

[2] If persons such as laborers or artisans of all sorts can thoroughly read, explain, or understand the meaning of the *Code*, and if they commit negligent offenses or they are found guilty as accessories to crime, they shall all be exempted from the punishment for one time, regardless of the seriousness of the offenses. If the matters involve plotting rebellion, great sedition, or treason, this law shall not be applicable.

[3] If officials, functionaries, or other persons fraudulently deceive the government, absurdly produce different opinions, make changes without authorization, and cause confusion in the established law, they shall be punished by decapitation.

Article 64 Violating Imperial Edicts [Zhishu youwei]

[1] In all cases where imperial edicts are received and should be carried out but are violated, the violators shall be punished by 100 strokes of beating with the heavy stick. For those who violate orders of the heir apparent, the punishment shall be the same. For those who violate orders of princes, they shall be punished by 90 strokes of beating with the heavy stick. If they make errors concerning the meanings of the edicts or orders, in each case the penalty shall be reduced three degrees.

[2] If imperial edicts or orders of the heir apparent are delayed for one

day, the offenders shall be punished by 50 strokes of beating with the light stick. For each additional day, the penalty shall be increased one degree. The punishment shall be limited to 100 strokes of beating with the heavy stick. For delaying orders of princes, in each case the penalty shall be reduced one degree.

Article 65   Discarding or Destroying Imperial Edicts or Official Seals [Qihui zhishu yinxin]

In all cases where people discard or destroy imperial edicts, imperial decrees stamped with imperial seals for using post horses [*qima yubao shengzhi*], authorization tallies for using post boats [*qichuan fuyan*], official seals of each yamen, or bronze warrants for night patrol [*yexun tongpai*], they shall be punished by decapitation. If they discard or destroy official documents, they shall be punished by 100 strokes of beating with the heavy stick. Those who circumvent the law shall be punished according to the heavier penalties. If the matters involve military operations and provisions, the penalty shall be strangulation. If relevant officials or functionaries know the circumstances but do not report, they shall be punished by the same penalty as that for the offenders. If they do not know, they shall not be punished. For mistaken destruction, in each case the penalty shall be reduced three degrees. If the destruction or loss is due to water, fire, or theft and there is clear proof, there shall be no punishment.

Article 66   [*Losing Imperial Edicts*] [Yishi zhishu][1]

[1] In all cases where people lose imperial edicts, imperial decrees, authority tallies [*fuyan*], seals or bronze warrants [*tongpai*], they shall be punished by 90 strokes of beating with the heavy stick and penal servitude for two and one-half years. For official documents, they shall be punished by 70 strokes of beating with the heavy stick. If matters involve military operations and provisions, they shall be punished by 90 strokes of beating with the heavy stick and penal servitude for two and one-half years. In all cases they shall have their salaries withheld and they shall be ordered to search [for the missing items]. If they find them within 30 days, they shall be exempted from punishment.

[2] If those who guard government property lose registers and thus cause errors and confusion in the quantities of money and grain, they shall be punished by 80 strokes of beating with the heavy stick. If they find them within the time limit, they may also be exempted from punishment.

[3] When functionaries of any yamen reach the time due for scrutiny [*kaoman*] and shall be replaced, they shall prepare clear reports and transfer all the documents of which they were originally in charge to their successors. For any violations, they shall be punished by 80 strokes of beating with the heavy stick. If staff supervisors or functionaries in charge do not

Laws on Personnel

wait for the transference and collude to issue career records, the punishment shall be the same.

Article 67   Mistakenly Violating Name Taboos in Memorials or Statements to the Throne [Shangshu zoushi fanhui]

[1] In all cases where people violate imperial names or imperial ancestral temple title taboos in memorials or statements to the throne, they shall be punished by 80 strokes of beating with the heavy stick. If they mistakenly violate the taboos in other documents, they shall be punished by 40 strokes of beating with the light stick. If they use [these characters] as personal names and thus violate [the taboos], they shall be punished by 100 strokes of beating with the heavy stick. However, if [the characters by which they violate the taboos] have similar sounds but different forms from the imperial names or imperial ancestral temple title taboos, or there are two characters but only one is used, in all cases there shall be no punishment.

[2] If they commit errors in memorials or statements to the throne—for instance, when they ought to say "pardon" but say "do not pardon," or when they ought to say "thousand *shi*" but say "ten *shi*"—that cause harm, they shall be punished by 60 strokes of beating with the heavy stick. If they make errors in documents submitted to the Six Ministries that cause harm, they shall be punished by 40 strokes of beating with the light stick. For errors in documents to other yamens, they shall be punished by 20 strokes of beating with the light stick. If, although they make errors in the documents they submit, the documents can still be carried out and do not cause harm, they shall not be punished.

Article 68   Not Memorializing Matters That Ought to Be Memorialized [Shi yingzou buzou]

[1] In all cases where military officers commit crimes, if relevant officials or functionaries ought to petition for the imperial decree but they do not petition for the imperial decree, or if they ought to view their [the cases'] merits and refer [the cases] to higher authorities for deliberation but do not refer [them] for deliberation, they shall be punished by strangulation.

[2] When civil officials commit crimes, if [relevant officials or functionaries] ought to petition the throne but do not petition, they shall be punished by 100 strokes of beating with the heavy stick. If they circumvent the law, they shall be punished according to the heavier penalties.

[3] If [the relevant officials or functionaries] do not memorialize other matters that ought to be memorialized, such as military operations, money and grain, selection of personnel, institutions, criminal cases, death penalties, disasters, and anomalies, they shall be punished by 80 strokes of beating with the heavy stick. If they do not report what ought to be reported to

the superior offices, they shall be punished by 40 strokes of beating with the light stick.

[4] If they have already memorialized or reported but do not wait for reply and act without authorization, the punishment shall be the same as that for not memorializing or not reporting.

[5] If there are public matters that ought to be memorialized, it is essential to propose decisions and to write memorials in accordance with the law. The memorial presenters and relevant officials and functionaries shall sign their names and memorialize clearly. If, in order to circumvent the law, they add or exclude key circumstances and misleadingly memorialize and the matters are allowed to be carried out, and if this is discovered later, although many years have passed, they shall be interrogated clearly and be punished by decapitation.

[6] When [officials or functionaries] report public matters to their immediately superior office, they shall first, according to the facts, set out whether or not the matters should be carried out and propose decisions. If the proposals are approved, the superior offices shall establish sealed files, write down brief circumstances and reasons, and order the staff supervisors and functionaries to sign their names for inspection. If [officials or functionaries], concerning the matters that ought not to be carried out, falsely claim that reports are made and permissions are obtained, or if they spy on [superior offices that are] occupied with public matters and take advantage of this to make misleading reports and have the matters allowed to be carried out, they shall be punished in accordance with the article on falsely transmitting the words of officials in each yamen [Art. 379]. If they circumvent the law, they shall be punished in accordance with the heavier penalty.

Article 69   Not Returning after Being Sent on Missions with Imperial Edicts [Chushi bu fuming]

[1] In all cases where emissaries receive imperial edicts and go on missions and do not return to make reports but interfere with other matters, they shall be punished by 100 strokes of beating with the heavy stick. If emissaries of any yamen go on missions and do not return to make reports but interfere with other matters, for ordinary matters, they shall be punished by 70 strokes of beating with the heavy stick; for military or other important matters, they shall be punished by 100 strokes of beating with the heavy stick. If they act without reason or exceed their duties and encroach upon others' authorities, they shall be punished by 50 strokes of beating with the light stick.

[2] If, after they return, they do not return imperial decrees within three days, they shall be punished by 60 strokes of beating with the heavy stick. For each additional two days, the penalty shall be increased one degree. The punishment shall be limited to 100 strokes of beating with the heavy stick.

Laws on Personnel

If they do not return authorization tallies, they shall be punished by 40 strokes of beating with the light stick. For each additional three days, the penalty shall be increased one degree. The punishment shall be limited to 80 strokes of beating with the heavy stick.

[3] If they circumvent the law, they shall be punished by the heavier penalty.

Article 70   Divulging Important Military Information
[Louxie junqing dashi]

[1] In all cases where those who know of the secret important matters concerning the transferal of troops by the court or generals of regional commands [zongbing jiangjun] to attack foreign countries or to apprehend rebels in rebellion or great sedition, and who then divulge them to enemies, they shall be punished by decapitation. If they divulge the important military information that is reported by frontier generals, they shall be punished by 100 strokes of beating with the heavy stick and penal servitude for three years. Those who first transmit the information shall be considered principals; those who retransmit it to enemies shall be considered accessories, [whose penalty] shall be reduced one degree.

[2] Those who, without authorization, open sealed official documents and read them shall be punished by 60 strokes of beating with the heavy stick. If the matters involve important military affairs, they shall be punished according to "divulging."

[3] If court attendant officials divulge information concerning secret important matters to others, they shall be punished by decapitation. For ordinary matters, they shall be punished by 100 strokes of beating with the heavy stick, and they shall be dismissed from their appointments and shall not be reassigned.

Article 71   Delaying Transmitting Official Documents
[Guanwenshu jicheng]

[1] In all cases of delaying transmitting official documents for one day, functionaries shall be punished by 10 strokes of beating with the light stick. For each additional three days, the penalty shall be increased one degree. The punishment shall be limited to 40 strokes of beating with the light stick. In each case the penalty for staff supervisors shall be reduced one degree.

[2] When [officials or functionaries in] any yamen receive reports concerning public matters from subordinate offices, they shall promptly deliberate whether or not the matters shall be carried out and clearly decide and make replies. If relevant officials or functionaries do not decide matters resolutely but confusedly transfer them or shift them to each other, so that the handling of public matters is delayed, they shall be punished by 80 strokes of beating with the heavy stick. If subordinate officials or functionaries do

not take care of practicable matters but create doubts and report them, the punishment shall be the same. If matters for which they are responsible are already resolutely decided and carried out or transferred, but some of them have not been finished or accomplished, they shall be punished according to "delaying transmitting official documents."

Article 72   Inspecting Documentary Files [Zhaoshua wenjuan]

[1] In all cases where sealed official documentary files of each yamen are arranged, if one or two rolls are delayed, functionaries shall be punished by 10 strokes of beating with the light stick. For three to five rolls, they shall be punished by 20 strokes of beating with the light stick. For each additional five rolls, the penalty shall be increased one degree. The punishment shall be limited to 40 strokes of beating with the light stick. For staff supervisors of prefectures, subprefectures, or districts and officials of granaries, treasuries, agencies [wu], works [chang], services [ju], offices [suo], rivers, or lakes, in each case the penalty shall be reduced one degree.

[2] If there are errors or omissions in making reports, for one roll functionaries shall be punished by 20 strokes of beating with the light stick. For two or three rolls, they shall be punished by 30 strokes of beating with the light stick. For each additional three rolls, the penalty shall be increased one degree. The punishment shall be limited to 50 strokes of beating with the light stick. For staff supervisors of prefectures, subprefectures, and districts and officials of granaries and treasuries, agencies and works, services and offices, and rivers and lakes, in each case the penalty shall be reduced one degree. As for principal officials or police chiefs [xunjian] of prefectures, subprefectures, or districts, for one to five rolls they shall be fined ten days' cash emolument. For each additional five rolls, the penalty shall be increased one degree. The punishment shall be limited to a fine of one month's cash emolument.

[3] If they circumvent the law and commit crimes such as concealing money or grain and illegally judging criminal cases, in each case they shall be punished according to the heavier penalty.

Article 73   Reviewing Documentary Files [Mokan juanzong]

[1] In all cases where [records offices] have reviewed and discovered incomplete documentary files of any yamen, in which inspections by investigating censors or Provincial Surveillance Commissions have found delays and errors, if, after one season has passed, insufficient money or grain has not been levied and the deficiencies have not been completely made up, take the deficiency as 10 portions, then for 1 portion, the proctorial officials or functionaries [tidiao guanli] shall be punished by 50 strokes of beating with the light stick. For each additional portion, the penalty shall be increased one degree. The punishment shall be limited to 100 strokes of beating with

Laws on Personnel

the heavy stick. For matters concerning criminal cases or building projects that can be finished but are not finished or that should be corrected but are not corrected, they shall be punished by 40 strokes of beating with the light stick. For each additional month, the penalty shall be increased one degree. The punishment shall be limited to 80 strokes of beating with the heavy stick. If illicit goods are received, calculate the amount of the goods, and they shall be punished on the basis of subverting the law [Art. 367] according to the heavier penalty.

[2] If [the documentary files] are concealed and omitted and are not reported for reviewing, for one roll [the officials or functionaries in charge] shall be punished by 40 strokes of beating with the light stick. For each additional roll, the penalty shall be increased one degree. The punishment shall be limited to 80 strokes of beating with the heavy stick. If matters involve money or grain, for one roll they shall be punished by 80 strokes of beating with the heavy stick. For each additional roll, the penalty shall be increased one degree. The punishment shall be limited to 100 strokes of beating with the heavy stick. If they circumvent the law, they shall be punished according to the heavier penalty.

[3] If the officials or functionaries hear that the matters have been discovered and immediately make up the documentary files in order to avoid [the punishment for] delays and errors, for money or grain calculate the amount of the increase, and they shall be punished on the basis of falsely issuing tax receipts [Art. 131]. For matters concerning criminal cases, they shall be punished on the basis of adding to or subtracting from official documents [Art. 75]. If colleagues or superior officials know the circumstances and do not report them, or they collude with [the criminals] to practice fraud, their punishment shall be the same. If they do not know the circumstances or do not sign their names to the documents, they shall not be punished.

Article 74   Colleagues Affixing Dates or Signatures to Documentary Files on Others' Behalf [Tongliao dai panshu wenan]

In all cases where colleagues, on others' behalf, affix dates or signatures to official documents that need to be transmitted, they shall be punished by 80 strokes of beating with the heavy stick. If they act on others' behalf because the documentary files are lost, the penalty shall be increased one degree. If they add to or subtract from the facts so that they exonerate the guilty or incriminate the innocent [Art. 433], their punishment should be heavier, and they shall be punished according to the heavier penalty.

Article 75   Adding to or Subtracting from Official Documents [Zengjian guanwenshu]

[1] In all cases of adding to or subtracting from official documents, [the criminals] shall be punished by 60 strokes of beating with the heavy stick.

If they circumvent the law, and if the punishment is beating with the heavy stick or more severe, then the original punishments [for the law that is circumvented] shall be increased two degrees. The punishment shall be limited to 100 strokes of beating with the heavy stick and life exile to 3,000 *li*. If the documents have not been carried out, in each case the penalty shall be reduced one degree [from the penalty that is increased]. If they circumvent the law to avoid the death penalty, they shall be punished according to the regular law. If relevant officials or functionaries, in order to circumvent the law, add to or subtract from documentary files, the punishment shall be the same. If they add to or subtract from [the documents] in order to avoid [the punishment for] delays or errors, they shall be punished by 40 strokes of beating with the light stick.

[2] If, in transmitting documents, errors are mistakenly made in copying crucial characters concerning important matters such as troops, money, grain, and criminal cases, and then [the characters] are erased, added, or altered, functionaries shall be punished by 30 strokes of beating with the light stick. The penalty for staff supervisors who are negligent in reviewing shall be reduced one degree. If matters of transferring troops or supplying military requirements of funds and provisions on frontiers are hindered, both the staff supervisors and the functionaries shall be punished by 80 strokes of beating with the heavy stick. If they circumvent the law and deliberately alter and add [the characters], they shall be punished on the basis of adding to or subtracting from official documents. If [official documents] are not carried out yet, in each case the penalty shall be reduced one degree. If military operations are bungled [because of such errors], regardless of whether they were deliberate or due to negligence, they shall all be punished by decapitation. If no law is circumvented, or ordinary characters happen to be written by mistake, they shall all not be punished.

Article 76   Covering Up and Keeping Seals [Fengzhang yinxin]

In all cases concerning seals of each yamen in the capital or outside, head officials shall keep them; associate officials in the same offices shall cover the seal surfaces up with paper. Both [i.e., the senior and the associate officials] shall sign their names on the paper. If associate officials in the same offices are out on errands or there are accidents, staff supervisors may cover the seals up. Any violations shall be punished by 100 strokes of beating with the heavy stick.

Article 77   Omitting to Affix Seals [Loushi yinxin]

[1] In all cases where any yamen transmits outgoing documents but omits to affix seals, relevant functionaries, reviewing staff supervisors, and com-

munications functionaries each shall be punished by 60 strokes of beating with the heavy stick.

[2] If seals are not employed at all, each shall be punished by 80 strokes of beating with the heavy stick.

[3] If matters of transferring troops or supplying military requirements of funds and provisions on the frontiers are hindered, each shall be punished by 100 strokes of beating with the heavy stick. If military operations are bungled [because of such omissions], they shall be decapitated.

Article 78   Omitting to Employ Seals on Paper Currency [Louyong chaoyin]

In all cases where [the Directorate of Paper Currency] does not print paper money carefully, and thus omits to employ seals or employs seals upside down, for one sheet [the responsible persons] shall be punished by 10 strokes of beating with the light stick. For each additional three sheets, the penalty shall be increased one degree. The punishment shall be limited to 80 strokes of beating with the heavy stick. If the Treasury of Treasure Paper Currency [Baochao Ku] does not carefully check and misleadingly accepts them into the Treasury, the punishment shall be the same.

Article 79   Employing Seals of Transferring Troops without Authorization [Shanyong diaobing yinxin]

In all cases concerning seals of regional command generals or Regional Military Commissions of all localities—except for cases in which such seals ought to be employed, such as transferring troops, managing military affairs, or transmitting official documents—if they are employed without authorization, for issuing deeds or using public offices for private gain such as forwarding private goods in dispatches, staff supervisors and functionaries shall each be punished by 100 strokes of beating with the heavy stick, and they shall be dismissed from their appointments and employments and shall not be reassigned. The cases for principal officials shall be memorialized to the throne for the imperial decision.

Article 80   Warrants [Xinpai]

[1] In all cases where prefectures, subprefectures, and districts establish warrants, [the warrants] set the time limits for accomplishing the matters in accordance with the distances of the places, and they shall be handed in for cancellation after matters are accomplished. Any violations shall be punished by 10 strokes of beating with the light stick. For each additional day, the penalty shall be increased one degree. The punishment shall be limited to 40 strokes of beating with the light stick.

[2] If officials of prefectures, subprefectures, or districts, in urging [subordinate offices] to handle some matters, do not issue and send warrants in

accordance with the *Code* but directly go to their subordinate offices and stay there to urge, they shall be punished by 100 strokes of beating with the heavy stick. (This means, for example, that officials of prefectures shall not go to subprefectures' yamens, officials of subprefectures shall not go to districts' yamens, and officials of districts shall not go to rural communities.) However, this article shall not be applicable to matters such as examining bridges, dikes, postal relay stations, or express-delivery stations or inspecting the effects of calamities, inquests, pursuit of criminals, or confiscation of property.

Note

1. This article has no heading. In the *Da Ming lü jijie fuli* (*The great Ming code with commentaries attached by regulations*, 2:476–78), this article is combined with the preceding article (Art. 65). This is also the case in both *The Tang Code* and *The Great Qing Code*. However, according to both the numbering of this section and the entire *Code* and the starting character (*fan*, "in all cases"), this should be a separate article.

CHAPTER 3

Laws on Revenue [Hulü]

Section 1 Households and Corvée Services [*Huyi*] [Fifteen Articles]

Article 81 Omitting to Register Households or Household Members [Tuolou hukou]

[1] In all cases where a household is completely unregistered, if it should contribute to land taxes or corvée services, the household head [*jiazhang*] shall be punished by 100 strokes of beating with the heavy stick. If it should not contribute to land taxes or corvée services, [the household head] shall be punished by 80 strokes of beating with the heavy stick. It shall be registered and corvée services shall be performed.

[2] If [the household head] hides persons of other households in his own household and does not report [them], or fraudulently combines other households to register as one household, and if the households should contribute to land taxes or corvée services, [the household head] shall also be punished by 100 strokes of beating with the heavy stick. If the households should not contribute to land taxes or corvée services, [the household head] shall also be punished by 80 strokes of beating with the heavy stick. If he hides relatives of other households in his own household and does not report [them] or fraudulently combines other households of relatives to register as one household, in each case the penalty shall be reduced two degrees. Those who are hidden shall be punished by the same penalties. [The false registration] shall be corrected, independent households established, the registers separated, and the corvée services performed. However, this article shall not be applicable to older or younger uncles, younger brothers and nephews of the same lineage, or sons-in-law who have never lived separately.

[3] If those who currently perform services in the government completely omit to register their households, they shall be punished only according to the law on omitting to register household members.

[4] If the household head hides his own able-bodied adult male household members and does not register them or increases or decreases their ages or fraudulently claims them to be old, young, disabled, or sick so as to avoid corvée services, for 1 to 3 persons he shall be punished by 60 strokes of beat-

ing with the heavy stick. For each additional 3 persons, the penalty shall be increased one degree. The punishment shall be limited to 100 strokes of beating with the heavy stick. If those who are hidden are not able-bodied adult males, for 3 to 5 persons the household head shall be punished by 40 strokes of beating with the light stick. For each additional 5 persons, the penalty shall be increased one degree. The punishment shall be limited to 70 strokes of beating with the heavy stick. [Those who are hidden] shall be registered, and [those able-bodied adult males] shall perform corvée services.

[5] If the household head hides able-bodied adult males from other households in his own household and does not register them, the punishment shall be the same. Those who are hidden shall be punished by the same penalty, and they shall be sent back to their own households and be registered to perform corvée services.

[6] If community heads [*lizhang*] are negligent in investigating, and as a result, households are unregistered, for 1 to 5 households they shall be punished by 50 strokes of beating with the light stick. For each additional 5 households, the penalty shall be increased one degree. The punishment shall be limited to 100 strokes of beating with the heavy stick. If, [as a result,] individuals are unregistered, for 1 to 10 persons, [the community heads] shall be punished by 30 strokes of beating with the light stick. For each additional 10 persons, the penalty shall be increased one degree. The punishment shall be limited to 50 strokes of beating with the light stick. If the district principal officials in charge and staff supervisors [are negligent in investigating, and as a result,] households are unregistered, for 10 households they shall be punished by 40 strokes of beating with the light stick. For each additional 10 households, the penalty shall be increased one degree. The punishment shall be limited to 80 strokes of beating with the heavy stick. If individuals are unregistered, for 10 persons, they shall be punished by 20 strokes of beating with the light stick. For each additional 30 persons, the penalty shall be increased one degree. The punishment shall be limited to 40 strokes of beating with the light stick. If they know the circumstances, they shall all be punished according to the penalties for the criminals. If illicit goods are received, calculate the amount of the goods, and they shall be punished according to the heavier penalty on the basis of subverting the law [Art. 367]. If the officials and functionaries have already investigated and set up files three times to order community heads to write written reports and repeatedly instructed them to do so, and such matters arise, then only the community heads shall be punished.

Article 82   *Households Should Be Established according to the Registers* [Renhu yiji weiding]

[1] In all cases [of household registration,] the various households of military people, civilians, post couriers [*yi*], salt workers [*zao*], physicians [*yi*],

Laws on Revenue 71

diviners [*bu*], artisans [*gong*], and musicians [*yue*] shall be established according to their [original] registers. For those who deceitfully claim [*zha*] or falsely claim [*mao*] [to be another sort of household] so as to escape [from their own household registers] and to avoid their heavier obligation and assume [others'] lighter obligation, they shall be punished by 80 strokes of beating with the heavy stick. If authorities casually permit households to escape, or to alter registers, the punishment shall be the same.

[2] For those who deceitfully claim to be soldiers at the military guards and do not perform either military or civilian services, they shall be punished by 100 strokes of beating with the heavy stick and be sent to the distant frontier in military exile.

Article 83 Establishing Buddhist or Daoist Monasteries without Authorization and Ordaining Buddhist or Daoist Priests without Authorization [Sichuang anyuan ji sidu sengdao]

[1] In all cases where Buddhist or Daoist monasteries, except for the existing ones, are not allowed to be established or enlarged without authorization, any violations shall be punished by 100 strokes of beating with the heavy stick and returning to lay status [*huansu*]. Buddhist or Daoist priests shall be sent to the distant frontiers in military exile. Buddhist or Daoist nuns shall be enslaved to the government.

[2] If Buddhist or Daoist priests do not petition for ordainment certificates but they themselves shave their heads without authorization, they shall be punished by 80 strokes of beating with the heavy stick. If this is initiated by household heads, the household heads shall be punished. If abbots of Buddhist or Daoist monasteries or teachers ordain without authorization, the punishment shall be the same, and they shall all be returned to lay status.

Article 84 Illegally Designating Wives' Sons [as Heirs] [Li dizi weifa]

[1] In all cases of illegally designating wives' sons [as heirs], the offenders shall be punished by 80 strokes of beating with the heavy stick. If wives are over 50 years of age and have no sons, the eldest son of a concubine may be designated. If the eldest son is not designated, the punishment shall be the same.

[2] If persons of the same lineage are adopted as sons, and [the adopted sons] forsake [the adoptive parents] while the adoptive parents have no sons, they shall be punished by 100 strokes of beating with the heavy stick, and they shall be returned to the control of the adoptive parents. If [the adoptive parents] have their natural sons and [the adopted sons'] natural parents have no other son, [the adopted sons] may return [to their natural parents] if they wish to do so.

[3] If persons of different surnames are adopted and thereby lineage sys-

tems are disrupted, the penalty shall be 60 strokes of beating with the heavy stick. For those who give their sons to families with different surnames as heirs, the punishment shall be the same. Their sons shall be returned to their own lineages.

[4] Nevertheless, abandoned children of 3 years of age or younger, even though they are of different surnames, may still be adopted, and they shall immediately take the adopters' surnames.

[5] When heirs are designated, even though those who are designated are from the same lineages, if the senior or junior orders are violated [zunbei shixu], the punishment shall also be the same. The [adopted] sons shall also be returned to their lineages, and those who ought to succeed shall be designated.

[6] If commoners' families raise slaves, the penalty shall be 100 strokes of beating with the heavy stick. [The slaves] shall be immediately released and returned to the status of honorable people [liang].

Article 85   Taking Stray Children [Shouliu mishi zinü]

[1] In all cases where [persons] take stray children of other families and do not send them to the authorities but sell them as slaves, they shall be punished by 100 strokes of beating with the heavy stick and penal servitude for three years. If [they sell them] as wives, concubines, sons, or sons' sons, they shall be punished by 90 strokes of beating with the heavy stick and penal servitude for two and one-half years. If they get stray slaves and sell them, the penalty shall be reduced one degree from that for [selling] honorable people. Those who are sold shall not be punished and shall be returned to their relatives for reunion.

[2] If they take runaway children and sell them as slaves, they shall be punished by 90 strokes of beating with the heavy stick and penal servitude for two and one-half years. If [they sell them] as wives, concubines, sons, or sons' sons, they shall be punished by 80 strokes of beating with the heavy stick and penal servitude for two years. If they get runaway slaves and sell them, in each case the penalty shall be reduced one degree from that for [selling] honorable people. The penalty for those runaway persons who are sold shall be reduced one degree. If the penalties for the running away are heavier, then they shall be punished according to the heavier penalties.

[3] If they take [the stray persons] as their own slaves, wives, concubines, sons, or sons' sons, the punishment shall be the same. If they hide them in their homes, they shall all be punished by 80 strokes of beating with the heavy stick.

[4] If the buyers or brokers know the circumstances, the penalty for them shall be reduced one degree from that for offenders. The money paid shall be recovered by the government. If they do not know the circumstances,

Laws on Revenue

none of them shall be punished, and the money paid shall be recovered by the owners.

[5] For those who fraudulently claim honorable people to be slaves, they shall be punished by 100 strokes of beating with the heavy stick and penal servitude for three years. If [they fraudulently claim honorable people] as their wives, concubines, sons, or sons' sons, they shall be punished by 90 strokes of beating with the heavy stick and penal servitude for two and one-half years. If they fraudulently claim others' slaves [as their own], they shall be punished by 100 strokes of beating with the heavy stick.

Article 86   Unequally Levying Taxes and Corvée Services [Fuyi bujun]

In all cases where authorities levy grain taxes [*shuiliang*] and miscellaneous corvée services [*zafan chaiyi*], they shall investigate the number of households and individuals and field products within the registers and establish the [upper, middle, and lower] degrees and levy [the taxes and corvée services]. If they release the rich and levy the poor or shift the degrees and practice fraud, the aggrieved poor people may accuse them to, from bottom to top [from lower to higher authorities], their superior offices. The relevant officials and functionaries shall be punished by 100 strokes of beating with the heavy stick. If the superior offices do not accept and hear the cases, they shall be punished by 80 strokes of beating with the heavy stick. If illicit goods are accepted, calculate the amount of the goods, and they shall be punished by the heavier penalties on the basis of subverting the law [Art. 367].

Article 87   Unequally Assigning [Corvée Services to]
Able-Bodied Adult Males [Dingfu chaiqian buping]

[1] In all cases where, in assigning corvée services to able-bodied adult males or miscellaneous artisans, the assignments are unequal, for one person [those in authority] shall be punished by 20 strokes of beating with the light stick. For each additional five persons, the penalty shall be increased one degree. The punishment shall be limited to 60 strokes of beating with the heavy stick.

[2] If the able-bodied adult males or miscellaneous artisans, when assigned to corvée services, delay in performing the services, or if, when their services are fulfilled, the authorities do not release them, for one day the penalty shall be 10 strokes of beating with the light stick. For each additional three days, the penalty shall be increased one degree. The punishment shall be limited to 50 strokes of beating with the light stick.

Article 88   Hiding [Persons from] Corvée Services [Yinbi chaiyi]

[1] In all cases where influential individuals [*haomin*] have their sons, sons' sons, younger brothers, or nephews follow officials and thus hide them from

performing corvée services, the household heads shall be punished by 100 strokes of beating with the heavy stick. For officials who hide them from corvée services, the punishment shall be the same. If illicit goods are accepted, calculate the amount of the goods, and they shall be punished according to the heavier penalties on the basis of subverting the law [Art. 367]. Those who follow [the officials] shall be exempted from the punishment [of beating with the heavy stick] and shall be sent to frontiers in military exile.

[2] If meritorious officials hide [persons from corvée services], for the first time they shall be exempted from the punishment [of beating with the heavy stick] and shall have their transgressions recorded. For the second time, one-half of their emolument shall be stopped. For the third time, their whole emolument shall be stopped. For the fourth time, they shall be punished according to the *Code*.

Article 89   Prohibition [against Fraudulently Claiming to Be]
Security Group Chiefs or Community Heads [Jinge zhubao lizhang]
[1] In all cases where, among people of all localities, one community head and 10 tithing chiefs [*jiashou*] are selected from every 100 households by discussion, they shall serve in turn for one year to collect taxes and manage public affairs. For those who fraudulently claim to be security group chiefs [*zhubao*], deputy community heads [*xiao lizhang*], security group heads [*baozhang*], tithing chief managers [*zhushou*], or the like and create trouble and harass the people, they shall be punished by 100 strokes of beating with the heavy stick and banished [for life].

[2] If village elders [*qilao*] ought to be established, they shall be selected from those who are elderly and virtuous in villages and who are trusted by the villagers. Discharged functionaries or runners [*baxian lizu*] or persons who have transgressions shall not be selected as [village elders]. Any violations shall be punished by 60 strokes of beating with the heavy stick. Relevant officials and functionaries shall be punished by 40 strokes of beating with the light stick.

Article 90   Fleeing to Evade Corvée Services [Taobi chaiyi]
[1] In all cases where households flee to neighboring subprefectures or districts to evade corvée services, they shall be punished by 100 strokes of beating with the heavy stick, and they shall be returned to their original places of registration to perform services. If the community heads who have the jurisdiction or the proctorial officials or functionaries deliberately permit them, or the neighboring households hide them among themselves, in each case the punishment shall be the same. If the [neighboring] community heads know the circumstances but do not return them, or the original government offices do not send requests to procure their return, or the original government offices send requests to procure the return but the local

Laws on Revenue

government offices keep them and do not return them, in each case the penalty shall be 60 strokes of beating with the heavy stick. For those who moved to other prefectures before the tenth month of the seventh year of the Hongwu reign [1374] and registered themselves and performed the services, they shall not be punished. For those who fled after the time limit, they shall be punished according to the *Code*.

[2] If the able-bodied adult males and various sorts of artisans who are performing labor services or households of artisans or musicians or other miscellaneous households flee, for one day [of being absent from their original location], they shall be punished by 10 strokes of beating with the light stick. For each additional five days, the penalty shall be increased one degree. The punishment shall be limited to 50 strokes of beating with the light stick. If officials or functionaries in charge deliberately permit them, in each case the punishment shall be the same. If illicit goods are accepted, calculate the amount of the goods, and they shall be punished according to the heavier penalties on the basis of subverting the law [Art. 367]. If they fail to be aware of the flight, for five persons they shall be punished by 20 strokes of beating with the light stick. For each additional five persons, the penalty shall be increased one degree. The punishment shall be limited to 40 strokes of beating with the light stick. [If they fail to be aware of the flight] for fewer than five persons, they shall be exempted from punishment.

Article 91   Appointing Prison Guards [Dianchai yuzu]

In all cases of appointing prison guards in each locality, they shall be appointed from among those who are trustworthy and experienced. If [those who are appointed] ask others to be their substitutes for the service, they shall be punished by 40 strokes of beating with the light stick.

Article 92   Privately Employing Commoners or Government Artisans under One's Jurisdiction to Perform Services [Siyi bumin fujiang]

In all cases where officials of relevant authorities privately employ commoners under their jurisdiction or overseers of works privately employ government artisans to perform services beyond 100 *li*, or [the officials or overseers] keep them for a long time in [their] households to serve at their call, for 1 person [the officials or overseers] shall be punished by 40 strokes of beating with the light stick. For each additional 5 persons, the penalty shall be increased one degree. The punishment shall be limited to 80 strokes of beating with the heavy stick. For each person and each day, 60 *wen* of wages shall be restituted. In cases of festivity or mourning, or if [the commoners or government artisans] are employed in [the officials' or overseers'] households to perform miscellaneous services, there shall be no punishment. The number of persons so employed in service shall not exceed 50, and each person shall not be employed for more than three days. Any violations shall be punished as "privately employing [commoners or artisans] to perform services."

Article 93   Establishing Separate Household Registers or Dividing the Family Property [Bieji yicai]

In all cases where paternal grandparents or parents are living, and sons or sons' sons establish separate household registers or divide the family property, they shall be punished by 100 strokes of beating with the heavy stick. (They shall be punished only if the paternal grandparents or parents accuse them to the court in person.) If, during the mourning period for their parents, brothers establish separate household registers or divide the family property, they shall be punished by 80 strokes of beating with the heavy stick. (They shall be punished only if their superior or older relatives of the [mourning] degree of one year or closer accuse them to the court in person.)

Article 94   Inferior or Younger Family Members Making Use of Family Property without Authorization [Beiyou sishan yongcai]

In all cases where inferior or younger family members who are living in the same households make use of family property worth 20 *guan* without the authorization of the superior or older family members, they shall be punished by 20 strokes of beating with the light stick. For each additional 20 *guan*, the penalty shall be increased one degree. The punishment shall be limited to 100 strokes of beating with the heavy stick. If senior or older family members who are living in the same households should divide the family property but do not divide equitably, the penalty shall be the same.

Article 95   Supporting Orphans and Elderly Persons [Shouyang gulao]

In all cases where widowers, widows, orphans, childless elderly persons, or incapacitated persons are poor, have no relatives to rely on, and cannot survive by themselves, if officials having jurisdiction ought to support them but do not support them, they shall be punished by 60 strokes of beating with the heavy stick. If officials or functionaries deduct a portion from the food or clothing that should be distributed, they shall be punished on the basis of the law on "supervisors or custodians themselves stealing" [Art. 287].

Section 2   Fields and Houses [*Tianzhai*] [Eleven Articles]

Article 96   Fraudulently Concealing Fields and Their Produce [Qiyin tianliang]

[1] In all cases where people fraudulently conceal fields and their produce and thus avoid being recorded on the tax rolls, for 1 to 5 *mu* they shall be punished by 40 strokes of beating with the light stick. For each additional

Laws on Revenue   77

5 *mu*, the penalty shall be increased one degree. The punishment shall be limited to 100 strokes of beating with the heavy stick. The fields shall be forfeit to the government. The grain taxes that are concealed shall be levied according to the number [of *mu* and years].

[2] For those who change the location of all or some of the fields [on the registers], change the classification of the fields from the high tax category to the low, thus deceitfully reducing the amount of the grain tax, for those who fraudulently assign the fields and grain tax [to those who are exempted from taxes] and deceitfully avoid government labor services, and for those who accept the commendation, the punishment shall be the same.

[3] If the community heads know the circumstances but do not report to the authorities, they shall be punished by the same penalty as that for the offenders.

[4] In cases where people return to their villages and resume their occupations, and where the able-bodied adult males are few, and their former fields are many, they may do their utmost to cultivate and then shall report them [the number of fields and able-bodied adult males] to the authorities, pay taxes, and perform corvée services according to the quantity of their fields. If they occupy too many fields and cause some of them to go uncultivated, for 3 to 10 *mu* they shall be punished by 30 strokes of beating with the light stick. For each additional 10 *mu*, the penalty shall be increased one degree. The punishment shall be limited to 80 strokes of beating with the heavy stick. Their fields shall be forfeit to the government. If the able-bodied adult males are many and their former fields are few, they may report the situation to the authorities, who shall calculate the number of able-bodied adult males and distribute some nearby wasteland to them to cultivate.

Article 97 *Inspecting Fields and Their Produce Damaged by Natural Calamities* [Jianta zaishang tianliang]

[1] In all cases where natural calamities such as flood, drought, frost, hail, or locusts occur within any administrative unit and damage the fields and their produce, if officials or functionaries who should receive the reports do not immediately receive them, report them [to superior authorities], and inspect the fields by themselves, or if their superior officials do not send deputies to make further inspections, in each case they shall be punished by 80 strokes of beating with the heavy stick. If the officials or functionaries who are responsible for the initial or further inspections do not go to the fields in person, or, although they go, they do not diligently inspect the fields to ascertain the facts but merely rely on what the community heads and the tithing chiefs misleadingly report, and in the process, they reckon the cultivated fields as uncultivated land, reckon the uncultivated land as cultivated fields, increase or reduce the degree [of the calamities], or collaborate to practice fraud, and thus deceive the government and harm the

people, in each case they shall be punished by 100 strokes of beating with the heavy stick; and they shall be removed from their appointments or employments and shall not be reassigned. If taxes are wrongly collected or exempted, and upon calculation of the amount of illicit goods, the penalty for illicit goods of this amount is heavier, they shall be punished for illicit goods obtained through malfeasance [Art. 368]. The community heads and tithing chiefs, in each case, shall be punished by the same penalty. If they receive property, in all the cases they shall, upon calculation of the amount of illicit goods, be punished by the heavier penalties on the basis of [accepting property and] subverting the law [Art. 367].

[2] If inspecting officials, functionaries, community heads, or tithing chiefs fail to inspect carefully and thus make incorrect reports, the area of the fields [that are incorrectly characterized] shall be calculated. For less than 10 *mu*, they shall be exempted from punishment. For 10 to 20 *mu*, they shall be punished by 20 strokes of beating with the light stick. For each additional 20 *mu*, the penalty shall be increased one degree. The punishment shall be limited to 80 strokes of beating with the heavy stick.

[3] For those households who falsely report all or part of their cultivated fields as being damaged, for 1 to 5 *mu* they shall be punished by 40 strokes of beating with the light stick. For each additional 5 *mu*, the penalty shall be increased one degree. The punishment shall be limited to 100 strokes of beating with the heavy stick. The tax to be paid in grain shall be collected and paid to the government according to the amount of the tax.

Article 98   Meritorious Officials' Fields [Gongchen tiantu]

In all cases where meritorious officials' households have their own fields in addition to the public fields that are bestowed on them, the bailiffs shall report all the fields to the authorities so that they will be registered, and the taxes shall be paid and corvée services be performed. Any violations, for 1 to 3 *mu*, shall be punished by 60 strokes of beating with the heavy stick. For each additional 3 *mu*, the penalty shall be increased one degree. The punishment shall be limited to 100 strokes of beating with the heavy stick and penal servitude for three years. The bailiffs shall be punished. The fields shall be forfeit to the government. The unpaid tax in grain shall be levied in accordance with the number [of *mu* and years]. If the community heads, officials, or functionaries of relevant authorities make false field investigations, or they know the circumstances but do not report [them], they shall be punished by the same penalty. If they do not know, they shall not be punished.

Article 99   Fraudulently Selling Fields and Houses [Daomai tianzhai]

[1] In all cases of fraudulently selling or exchanging, falsely claiming, selling in written contracts of conditional sale [*dian*] without real money, or taking possession of others' fields or houses, the offenders shall, for 1 *mu* of

cultivated land or 1 room of a house or less, be punished by 50 strokes of beating with the light stick. For each additional 5 *mu* of cultivated land or 3 rooms of a house, the penalty shall be increased one degree. The punishment shall be limited to 80 strokes of beating with the heavy stick and penal servitude for two years. If [the fields or houses] belong to the government, in each case the penalty shall be increased two degrees.

[2] If they forcibly occupy government or other persons' mountains, plains, lakes, tea plantations, reed marshes, or smelters of gold, silver, copper, tin, or iron, they shall be punished by 100 strokes of beating with the heavy stick and life exile to 3,000 *li*.

[3] If they take land [the ownership of which] is in dispute or that belongs to others and recklessly declare it to be their property and misleadingly assign it to officials or powerful persons, the donor and the donee shall each be punished by 100 strokes of beating with the heavy stick and penal servitude for three years.

[4] The land, the price of land that is fraudulently sold, and the profits obtained in the relevant years shall, in each case, be returned to the government or owners.

[5] If meritorious officials commit such crimes, for the first time they shall be exempted from punishment but have the transgressions recorded. For the second time, one-half of their emoluments shall be stopped. For the third time, all of their emoluments shall be stopped. For the fourth time, they shall be punished the same as commoners.

Article 100 Purchasing Fields or Houses [by Officials or Functionaries] in the Locations of Their Service [Rensuo zhimai tianzhai]

In all cases where officials or functionaries of relevant authorities shall not purchase fields or houses in locations of their current service, these violations shall be punished by 50 strokes of beating with the light stick, they shall lose their appointments or employments, and the fields and houses shall be forfeit to the government.

Article 101 Purchasing Fields or Houses by Mortgage [Dianmai tianzhai]

[1] In all cases of purchasing fields or houses by mortgage and failing to pay deed taxes, the offenders shall be punished by 50 strokes of beating with the light stick, and one-half of the price of the fields or houses shall be forfeit to the government. If they do not transfer [the fields to their own registers], for 1 to 5 *mu* they shall be punished by 40 strokes of beating with the light stick. For each additional 5 *mu*, the penalty shall be increased one degree. The punishment shall be limited to 100 strokes of beating with the heavy stick. The fields shall be forfeit to the government.

[2] For those who fraudulently sell or mortgage to others fields or houses that are already sold or mortgaged, calculate the amount of the illicit goods

according to the price received, and the crime shall be punished as "theft" [Art. 292], but the tattooing shall be exempted. The price shall be levied on [the seller] and returned to the [second] purchaser; the fields or houses shall remain in the hands of the original purchaser by mortgage. If the subsequent purchasers by mortgage and their sureties know the circumstances, they shall be punished by the same penalty as that for the offenders, and the price shall be levied and paid to the government. If they do not know the circumstances, they shall not be punished.

[3] If the term of the mortgage of fields, houses, gardens, forests, mills, or other things expires, and the owners of these things come to pay the price and redeem the things, if the mortgagees make excuses and refuse to let the things be redeemed, they shall be punished by 40 strokes of beating with the light stick. The profits received for the years subsequent to the term shall be levied on [the mortgagees] and returned to the owners, and the things shall still be redeemed in accordance with the price. If the term expires but the owners are not able to redeem the things, this law shall not be applied.

Article 102   Fraudulently Cultivating Government or Private Land [Dao gengzhong guanmin tian]

In all cases of fraudulently cultivating others' land, the offenders shall, for 1 *mu* or less, be punished by 30 strokes of beating with the light stick. For each additional 5 *mu*, the penalty shall be increased one degree. The punishment shall be limited to 80 strokes of beating with the heavy stick. As for uncultivated land, the penalty shall be reduced one degree. If force is used, in each case the penalty shall be increased one degree. For government land, in each case the penalty shall be increased two degrees. The profits shall be levied on [the cultivators] and returned to the government or the owners.

Article 103   Allowing Land to Go Uncultivated [Huangwu tiandi]

In all cases where the land within the jurisdiction of community heads is registered for the payment of taxes and performance of services but left uncultivated without reason, or [the land that] is planned for planting mulberry or hemp is not sown [to those crops], divide all the land into 10 portions, for 1 portion the community heads shall be punished by 20 strokes of beating with the light stick. For each additional portion, the penalty shall be increased one degree. The punishment shall be limited to 80 strokes of beating with the heavy stick. In each case, the penalty for district officials shall be reduced two degrees. The head official shall be the principal; the assistant officials are accessories. As for private households, also calculate the amount of land that is uncultivated or not sown to such crops as mulberry or hemp, and then divide [all the land of each household] into 5 portions, for one portion the penalty shall be 20 strokes of beating with the light stick. For each additional portion, the penalty shall be increased one

Laws on Revenue

degree. The tax in grain that should be paid shall be levied on [the owners] and paid to the government. (The crops such as mulberries, jujubes, yellow hemp, ramie, cotton, indigo, or safflower that should be planted shall be planted in accordance with what is suitable to the soil conditions of each village.)

Article 104   Discarding or Destroying Things Such as Utensils or Crops
[Qihui qiwu jiase deng]

[1] In all cases of discarding or destroying others' utensils or destroying or cutting timber or crops, calculate the amount of the illicit goods; the offenders shall be punished for theft [Art. 292], but tattooing shall be exempted. For government property, the penalty shall be increased two degrees. If they lose or mistakenly destroy government property, in each case the penalty shall be reduced three degrees. Check the amount and levy for repayment. For private property, they shall compensate for the damage but shall not be punished.

[2] If they destroy stone tables or stone animals on others' tombs, they shall be punished by 80 strokes of beating with the heavy stick. For ancestral tablets, the penalty shall be 90 strokes of beating with the heavy stick. If they destroy others' things such as houses or walls, calculate the amount of money required to repair them; they shall be punished for illicit goods obtained through malfeasance [Art. 368]. In each case, they shall be ordered to repair them. For government houses, the penalty shall be increased two degrees. If they mistakenly destroy such things, they shall only be ordered to repair but not be punished.

Article 105   Eating Melons or Fruits of Gardens or Orchards without Authorization [Shanshi tianyuan guaguo]

In all cases of eating things such as melons or fruits in others' gardens or orchards without authorization, the offenders shall be punished for illicit goods obtained through malfeasance [Art. 368]. If they discard or destroy them, the penalty shall be the same. If they take them away without authorization or eat melons or fruits of government gardens or orchards or government-made liquor or foods, the penalty shall be increased two degrees. If the custodians give these things or know the circumstances but do not report, they shall be punished the same. If custodians take these things away without authorization, they shall be punished on the basis of supervisors or custodians themselves stealing [Art. 287].

Article 106   Borrowing Government Carriages or Boats without Authorization [Sijie guan chechuan]

In all cases where supervisors or custodians privately borrow government property such as carriages, boats, shops, inns, or mills for their own use or lend them to others, they as well as those who borrow them shall each be punished by 50 strokes of beating with the light stick, and rental shall be levied in accordance with the number of days and paid to the government. If, on calculation of the rental, the penalty shall be heavier, then in each case, they shall be punished for illicit goods obtained through malfeasance [Art. 268] with the penalty increased one degree.

Section 3 Marriages [*Hunyin*] [Eighteen Articles]

Article 107   Marriages of Men and Women [Nannü hunyin]

[1] In all cases where marriages are being arranged for men and women, if there are circumstances such as being disabled, sick, aged, young, or offspring of concubines, adopted sons, or foster sons, it is essential that the two families inform each other clearly, so that both families may, on the basis of their own wishes, write out marriage contracts and make engagements or arrange marriages in accordance with the rituals. If [those who are in charge of the women's marriages] agree to marry them off and have drawn up marriage contracts, or they have private agreements (that means they already know in advance of such matters as the husbands' disability, sickness, old or young age, or their status as offspring of concubines or foster sons), and they arbitrarily change their minds, they shall be punished by 50 strokes of beating with the light stick. Even if there are no marriage contracts, as long as betrothal gifts have been accepted, the case shall be the same.

[2] If they again marry the women to others, and if the marriages are not consummated, they shall be punished by 70 strokes of beating with the heavy stick. If the marriages are consummated, they shall be punished by 80 strokes of beating with the heavy stick. For the families to which the women are subsequently engaged or married, if they know the circumstances, their family heads shall be punished the same, and the betrothal gifts shall be forfeit to the government. If they do not know the circumstances, they shall not be punished, and the betrothal gifts shall be returned to them. The women shall return to their first husbands. If the first husbands do not want to marry them, they shall get two times the value of the betrothal gifts, and the women shall return to their subsequent husbands. If men's families change their minds, the penalty shall be the same, and the betrothal gifts shall not be returned.

[3] If the men and women whose marriages are not consummated commit crimes of fornication, theft, or robbery, this law shall not be applied.

[4] In marriages, if women's families practice fraud, they shall be punished by 80 strokes of beating with the heavy stick. (This means, for example, that if a woman is disabled, [the person who is in charge of the marriage] makes her older or younger sister fraudulently meet the man but subsequently marries the disabled woman off.) The betrothal gifts shall be

returned. If men's families practice fraud, the penalty shall be increased one degree. (This means, for example, that [a woman] is engaged to a man who is a member of his family by birth but [she] marries an adopted one; or, for another example, that a man is disabled, and [the person who is in charge of the marriage] makes his younger or older brother fraudulently meet the woman but subsequently lets the disabled man marry her.) The betrothal gifts shall not be returned. If the marriages are not consummated, [the men and women shall marry] in accordance with the original agreements. If the marriage is consummated, it shall be dissolved.

[5] For those who will get married, although betrothal gifts are already presented, if the agreed-upon time has not yet arrived but the men's families forcibly take the women in marriage, or if the agreed-upon time has already arrived but the women's families deliberately ignore the fact, in both cases they shall be punished by 50 strokes of beating with the light stick.

[6] If inferior or younger family members are away on government service or on business, and their paternal grandparents, parents, or fathers' brothers or their wives, fathers' sisters, or older brothers or sisters arrange their marriages, but the inferior or younger family members themselves have already married wives, if the marriages are consummated, the marital relationships shall be kept. If the marriages are not consummated, the superior or older family member's arrangements shall be followed. Any violations shall be punished by 80 strokes of beating with the heavy stick.

Article 108   Mortgaging or Renting Out Wives or Daughters
[Diangu qinü]

[1] In all cases of mortgaging or renting out wives or concubines to others as wives or concubines in order to acquire property, the offenders shall be punished by 80 strokes of beating with the heavy stick. For those who mortgage or rent out daughters, they shall be punished by 60 strokes of beating with the heavy stick. The women shall not be punished.

[2] For those who fraudulently claim that their wives or concubines are their older or younger sisters and marry them to others, they shall be punished by 100 strokes of beating with the heavy stick. Their wives or concubines shall be punished by 80 strokes of beating with the heavy stick.

[3] For those who know the circumstances and purchase the women or marry them, in each case they shall be punished the same. The marriages shall be dissolved, and the betrothal gifts shall be forfeit to the government. If they do not know the circumstances, they shall not be punished, and the betrothal gifts shall be returned to them.

Article 109   Disordering Wives and Concubines [Qiqie shixu]

[1] In all cases of making wives concubines, the offenders shall be punished by 100 strokes of beating with the heavy stick. If their wives are still liv-

ing and they make concubines their wives, they shall be punished by 90 strokes of beating with the heavy stick. Their [the women's] status shall be corrected.

[2] For those who have a wife but marry another wife, they shall also be punished by 90 strokes of beating with the heavy stick, and the marriages shall be dissolved. For commoners, only if they are 40 years of age or older and have no sons may they marry concubines. Any violations shall be punished by 40 strokes of beating with the light stick.

Article 110   Expelling Sons-in-Law and Marrying Off Daughters [Zhuxu jianü]

In all cases of expelling sons-in-law and marrying off daughters or taking in other sons-in-law, the offenders shall be punished by 100 strokes of beating with the heavy stick. Their daughters shall not be punished. If the men's families [in the subsequent marriages] know the circumstances and take in [the daughters] in marriage, the penalty shall be the same. If they do not know, they shall not be punished. The daughters shall be returned to their first husbands; and [the couples] shall be reunited and leave [the women's homes] and live apart from them.

Article 111   Marrying Off or Taking in Marriage during the Mourning Period [Jusang jiaqu]

[1] In all cases of marrying themselves off or taking in marriage by themselves during the mourning period for parents or husband, the offenders shall be punished by 100 strokes of beating with the heavy stick. If, during the mourning period, men marry concubines, or wives or daughters marry themselves off as concubines, in each case the penalty shall be reduced two degrees. For women with titles of honor whose husbands are dead and who remarry themselves off, the penalty shall be the same, and the imperial commissions shall be revoked. In all the cases, the marriages shall be dissolved. For those who know the circumstances and marry them, in each case the penalty shall be reduced five degrees. If they do not know the circumstances, they shall not be punished. For those who marry themselves off or take in marriage by themselves during the mourning period for paternal grandparents, father's older or younger brothers or their wives, father's sisters, or older brothers or sisters, they shall be punished 80 strokes of beating with the heavy stick. For concubines, they shall not be punished.

[2] If, during the mourning period for their parents, husbands' parents, or husbands, people take charge of marriages for those who should get married, they shall be punished by 80 strokes of beating with the heavy stick.

[3] If the mourning period for husbands expires and the women wish to preserve their chastity, those who are not their paternal grandparents or parents and who force them to remarry shall be punished by 80 strokes of beating with the heavy stick. If relatives of the mourning degree of one

Laws on Revenue

year force them to remarry, the penalty shall be reduced two degrees. The women shall not be punished, and they shall be returned to their former husbands' families and be permitted to preserve their chastity. The men who marry them shall not be punished either; and the betrothal gifts shall be returned.

Article 112   Marrying Off or Taking in Marriage While Parents Are Imprisoned [Fumu qiujin jiaqu]

In all cases where paternal grandparents or parents commit capital crimes and are imprisoned, but the children or paternal grandchildren marry themselves off or take in marriage by themselves, they shall be punished by 80 strokes of beating with the heavy stick. For concubines, the penalty shall be reduced two degrees. If they are following instructions from their paternal grandparents or parents and marry off women or take wives, they shall not be punished. No feast shall be given either.

Article 113   Marrying Persons with the Same Surname [Tongxing weihun]

In all cases of marrying persons with the same surname, both families shall be punished by 60 strokes of beating with the heavy stick, and the marriages shall be dissolved.

Article 114   Marrying Superior or Inferior Relatives [Zunbei weihun]

[1] In all cases where superior and inferior relatives within the degree of mourning in the external line by marriage marry each other, or men marry their older or younger sisters of the same mothers but different fathers or daughters of their wives by former husbands, they shall all be punished on the basis of "fornication" [Art. 392].

[2] Marriages with the following relatives are prohibited: daughters of parents' fathers' or mothers' sisters or brothers, parents' mothers' sisters, daughters of parents' mothers' fathers' sisters, mother's father's sisters, daughters of mother's father's father's brothers, daughters of mother's father's brothers, daughters of mother's father's father's brothers' sons, daughters of father's brothers' daughters, [sisters of] sons-in-law, and sisters of sons' or sons' sons' wives. Any violations, in each case, shall be punished by 100 strokes of beating with the heavy stick.

[3] In the case of marrying daughters of one's own father's sisters or daughters of one's mother's brothers or sisters, [both the man and the woman] shall be punished by 80 strokes of beating with the heavy stick.

[4] All the marriages shall be dissolved.

Article 115   Marrying Relatives' Wives or Concubines [Qu qinshu qiqie]

[1] In all cases of marrying female relatives outside the mourning degrees or wives of relatives outside the mourning degrees from the same lineage

[*zong*], each party shall be punished by 100 strokes of beating with the heavy stick. In the case of marrying wives of relatives of the fifth degree of mourning or wives of mother's brothers or of sisters' sons, each party shall be punished by 60 strokes of beating with the heavy stick and penal servitude for one year. If the female relatives are in the fourth degree of mourning or closer, in each case they shall be punished on the basis of "fornication" [Art. 392]. In the case of marrying those who are repudiated or who remarry as wives or concubines, each party shall be punished by 80 strokes of beating with the heavy stick.

[2] In the case of taking in [*shou*] father's or paternal grandfather's concubines or father's older or younger brothers' wives, each party shall be punished by decapitation. In the case of taking in older brothers' wives after older brothers die or taking in younger brothers' wives after younger brothers die, each party shall be punished by strangulation.

[3] For marrying relatives' concubines, in each case the penalty shall be reduced two degrees.

[4] For marrying paternal female relatives in the father's, sons', or one's own generation within the fifth degree of mourning or closer, each party shall also be punished on the basis of "fornication" [Art. 392].

[5] All the marriages shall be dissolved.

Article 116   Marrying Women or Daughters of Those under [the Officials'] Jurisdiction as Wives or Concubines [Qu bumin funü wei qiqie]

In all cases where officials who directly govern people in prefectures, subprefectures, or districts, during the terms of their offices, marry [married] women or [unmarried] daughters of those under their jurisdiction as wives or concubines, they shall be punished by 80 strokes of beating with the heavy stick. If supervisory officials marry wives, concubines, or daughters of those involved in the matters as wives or concubines, they shall be punished by 100 strokes of beating with the heavy stick. The women's families [the husbands or the fathers] shall be punished by the same penalty. The wives or concubines shall be taken away from both the families [the officials' and the original families]; the daughters shall be returned to their parents. The wedding gifts shall be forfeit to the government. If the marriages are forceful, in each case, the penalty shall be increased by two degrees; the women's families shall not be punished. The wedding gifts shall not be confiscated. If the marriages are arranged for sons, sons' sons, younger brothers, brothers' sons, or household servants, the punishment shall be the same; the men and the women [who get married] shall not be punished.

Article 117   Marrying Runaway Women [Qu taozou funü]

In all cases of marrying as wives or concubines women who commit crimes and who run away, if the men know the circumstances, they shall

Laws on Revenue

be punished by the same penalty. If the penalty amounts to death, it shall be reduced one degree. The marriages shall be dissolved. If they do not know the circumstances, they shall not be punished. If the women do not have husbands, and amnesties are issued that exempt them from penalties, the marriages shall not be dissolved.

Article 118   Forcibly Seizing Wives or Daughters of Honorable Families
[Qiangzhan liangjia qinü]

In all cases where overbearing or influential persons forcibly take wives or concubines of honorable families and vilely seize them as wives or concubines, they shall be punished by strangulation. The women shall be returned to their relatives. If [the overbearing or influential persons seize and] marry the women to their sons, sons' sons, younger brothers, brothers' sons, or household servants, the punishment shall be the same. The men and women [who get married] shall not be punished.

Article 119   Marrying Musicians as Wives or Concubines
[Qu yueren wei qiqie]

In all cases where officials or functionaries marry musicians as wives or concubines, they shall be punished by 60 strokes of beating with the heavy stick. The marriages shall be dissolved in both cases. If the officials' sons or sons' sons marry them, the punishment shall also be the same. A record of their transgression shall be made, and on the day when they inherit the title of honor, their rank shall be reduced one degree and they shall be appointed in distant places. Those who married before the first year of the Hongwu reign [1368] shall not be punished.

Article 120   Buddhist or Daoist Priests Taking Wives [Sengdao ququ]

[1] In all cases where Buddhist or Daoist priests take wives or concubines, they shall be punished by 80 strokes of beating with the heavy stick; and they shall return to lay status. The punishment for the women's families shall be the same. The marriages shall be dissolved. If the head priests of the Buddhist or Daoist temples know the circumstances, they shall be punished the same. If they do not know, they shall not be punished.

[2] If the Buddhist or Daoist priests deceitfully claim that they seek to marry the women to relatives or servants, but they themselves seize them, they shall be punished on the basis of "fornication" [Art. 396].

Article 121   Marriages between Honorable and Mean Persons
[Liangjian wei hunyin]

In all cases where household heads arrange for their slaves to marry daughters of honorable families as wives, they shall be punished by 80 strokes of beating with the heavy stick. For the women's families, the penalty shall be reduced one degree; if they do not know the circumstances, they shall not be punished. If the slaves marry on their own, the punishment shall be the same. If the household heads know the circumstances, the penalty shall be reduced two degrees. If, subsequently, [the honorable persons] are registered as female slaves, the responsible persons shall be punished by 100 strokes of beating with the heavy stick. If the male or female slaves are fraudulently claimed to be honorable persons and thus marry honorable persons as husbands or wives, they shall be punished by 90 strokes of beating with the heavy stick. In each case, the marriage shall be dissolved; the status shall be corrected.

Article 122   Marriages by Mongols and Semu People
[Menggu Semuren hunyin]

Mongols and Semu people shall marry with Chinese persons. (It is essential that both parties be willing.) They shall not marry within their own race. Any violations shall be punished by 80 strokes of beating with the heavy stick, and both the men and the women shall be enslaved by the government. If Chinese persons do not wish to marry Qincha Muslims, the latter may marry with each other among their own race; the above prohibition shall not be applied.

Article 123   Repudiating Wives [Chuqi]

[1] In all cases where [husbands] repudiate wives without any of the [seven] causes for repudiation or without circumstances that extinguish the duties [*yijue*], they shall be punished by 80 strokes of beating with the heavy stick. If they repudiate wives who commit one of the actions that constitute the seven causes for repudiation [*qichu*] but who meet one of the three restrictions on divorce [*sanbuqu*], the penalty shall be reduced two degrees. The wives shall be returned to the husbands for reunion.

[2] If husbands do not divorce wives who commit actions that extinguish the duties and who shall be divorced, they shall also be punished by 80 strokes of beating with the heavy stick. If husbands and wives do not get along together and they are both willing to divorce, they shall not be punished.

[3] If wives betray their husbands and run away, they shall be punished by 100 strokes of beating with the heavy stick and may, according to their husbands' will, be married off or sold. If they subsequently remarry, they shall be punished by strangulation. If, within three years after their husbands run away, they do not report to the authorities but run away [themselves], they shall be punished by 80 strokes of beating with the heavy stick. If they remarry, they shall be punished by 100 strokes of beating with the heavy stick. For concubines, in each case the penalty shall be reduced two degrees.

[4] If female slaves betray their household heads and run away, they shall be punished by 80 strokes of beating with the heavy stick. (If male slaves

Laws on Revenue

run away, the punishment shall also be the same.) If they subsequently remarry, they shall be punished by 100 strokes of beating with the heavy stick. They shall be returned to their household heads.

[5] For those who harbor the escaped women or who know the circumstances but marry them, in each case the punishment shall be the same. If the penalty amounts to death, it shall be reduced one degree. If they do not know the circumstances, in both cases they shall not be punished.

[6] If the remarriages are arranged by superior or older relatives of the mourning degree of one year or closer, those who arrange the remarriages shall be punished; the wives or concubines shall only be punished for the crime of "flight." In cases where other relatives arrange the remarriages ("other relatives" refers to inferior or younger relatives of the mourning degree of one year or to superior, older, inferior, or younger relatives of the third degree of mourning or more distant who arrange the remarriages), if the matters are initiated by those who arrange the remarriages, those who arrange the remarriages shall be punished as principals; the men and women shall be punished as accessories. If the matters are initiated by the men and women, the men and women shall be punished as principals; and those who arrange the remarriages shall be punished as accessories. If the penalty amounts to death, in all the cases it shall be reduced one degree for those who arrange the remarriages.

Article 124 Punishments for Matchmakers and Others Who Arrange Marriages That Violate the Code *[Jiaqu weilü zhuhun meiren zui]*

[1] In all cases of marriages that violate the *Code*, if they are arranged by paternal grandparents, parents, fathers' older or younger brothers or their wives, older brothers, older sisters, or maternal grandparents, only those who arrange the marriages shall be punished. If they are arranged by other relatives ("other relatives" refers to inferior or younger relatives of the mourning degree of one year or to superior, older, inferior, or younger relatives of the third mourning degree or more distant who arrange the marriages) and if the matters are initiated by those who arrange the marriages, those who arrange the marriages shall be punished as principals; the men and women shall be punished as accessories. If the matters are initiated by the men and women, the men and women shall be punished as principals; those who arrange the marriages shall be punished as accessories. If the penalty amounts to death, in all cases it shall be reduced one degree for those who arrange the remarriages.

[2] If the men or women are forced [to marry] by those who arrange the marriages and they cannot control the matters according to their own wills, or if the men are under 20 years of age or the women are still at home, only those who arrange the marriages shall be punished. In all cases, the men and women shall not be punished.

[3] If the marriages are not consummated, the penalty shall be reduced five degrees from that for the completed marriages.

[4] If matchmakers know the circumstances, in each case the penalty shall be reduced one degree from that for the offenders. If they do not know, they shall not be punished.

[5] For marriages that violate the *Code*, if each specific article stipulates "[the marriages shall be] dissolved" or "[the status shall be] corrected," [the marriages shall] still be dissolved and [the status shall] still be corrected although there are amnesties. In cases where [marriages are] dissolved, the women shall be returned to their own lineages.

[6] As to wedding gifts, if those who take in marriage know the circumstances, the gifts shall be forfeit to the government; if they do not know, the gifts shall be returned to the owners.

Section 4 Granaries and Treasuries [*Cangku*] [Twenty-four Articles]

Article 125 Rules of Paper Currency [Chaofa]

[1] In all cases where paper currencies are printed out, they shall be circulated together with Hongwu and Dazhong circulating coins and copper cashes of previous dynasties. In purchases or sales of various goods among the people, or in payment of various taxes such as those on tea, salt, or trade, they shall all be accepted. Any violations shall be punished by 100 strokes of beating with the heavy stick.

[2] When people bring paper currencies to granaries, markets, treasuries, or tax offices to pay various taxes in lieu of paying in grain or to purchase salt or other goods, or when any yamen delivers illicit goods or fines, it is essential that personal names or marks be recorded on the backs of the currencies for later examination. If those who handle the transactions do not diligently examine [currencies] and thus accept counterfeit currencies, currencies with characters cut out, or currencies that are pieced together, they shall be punished by 100 strokes of beating with the heavy stick; double the amount of the money paid shall be levied. (This means that if counterfeit currencies or currencies that are cut or pieced together are mistakenly accepted, for 1 *guan* they shall be levied a fine of 2 *guan*.) The counterfeit or damaged currencies shall be burned. During the transactions in the markets among the people, it shall also be permitted to use personal marks. Those who do not carefully examine and thus mistakenly circulate [the counterfeit or damaged currencies] shall be punished by 100 strokes of beating with the heavy stick; double the amount of the paper currencies shall be levied [as a fine]. Only those who use the currencies shall be punished. For those

who know the circumstances and who use the currencies, this article shall also be applied.

Article 126   Rules of Coinage [Qianfa]

[1] In all cases concerning the rules of coinage, the Metropolitan Coinage and other services are established to smelt and coin Hongwu circulating copper cashes. They shall be circulated together with Dazhong circulating copper cashes and copper cashes of previous dynasties. When they are coined as two, three, five, or ten [*qian*], they shall be weighed according to their denominations. The prices of various things such as gold, silver, rice, wheat, cotton, and silk of the people shall all be decided on the basis of their current value for the convenience of the people. Those who block [the process] and thus cause [the copper cashes] not to circulate shall be punished by 60 strokes of beating with the heavy stick.

[2] Except for mirrors and military weapons in military and civilian households, and bells, chimes, and cymbals of Buddhist and Daoist temples and nunneries, all other unnecessary copper objects shall be sold to the government. For every *jin* the government shall give 150 *wen* of copper cashes. For those who illegally purchase or sell [copper objects] or who collect and hide the objects in their houses and do not go to the government to sell the objects, in each case they shall be punished by 40 strokes of beating with the light stick.

Article 127   Violating the Time Limits in Collecting Grain Taxes [Shouliang weixian]

In all cases of collecting summer taxes, the granaries shall open on the fifteenth of the fifth month; the collections shall be completed by the end of the seventh month. For autumn taxes, the granaries shall open on the first of the tenth month; the collections shall be completed by the end of the twelfth month. In places where harvests take place early and thus collections are made ahead of this schedule, this article shall not be applied. If the payment of the summer taxes is delayed until the end of the eighth month, or the payment of the autumn taxes is delayed until the end of the first month of the following year, and the amount of the taxes is deficient, then take the total quantity [of the grain taxes] as the base, and for a shortage of one-tenth, the proctorial grain officials or functionaries, the collection-monitoring community heads, and the households that owe grain taxes shall each be punished by 60 strokes of beating with the heavy stick. For each additional one-tenth, the penalty shall be increased one degree. The punishment shall be limited to 100 strokes of beating with the heavy stick. If [the proctorial officials or functionaries or community heads] receive illicit goods, calculate the amount of the illicit goods, and they shall be punished by the heavier penalties on the basis of subverting the law [Art. 367]. If the time limits are violated for more than one year and the amount of the taxes is deficient, the households and the community heads shall be punished by 100 strokes of beating with the heavy stick and banishment. The proctorial grain officials and functionaries shall be punished by strangulation.

Article 128   Collecting Too Much Grain Tax above the Level of the Grain Measures [Duoshou shuiliang humian]

In all cases of collecting grain taxes in each granary, the taxpayers themselves shall be allowed to use rods to level off the measures in paying the taxes. [The government] shall receive [the grain in the measures] as the correct amount and make the records. [Furthermore,] the *Commandment* shall be followed in calculating the extra allowance [*zhehao*]. If the granary officials or measurers do not allow the taxpayers to use rods [to level off the measures] but kick the measures or pile grains up in cones, and thus collect too much grain above the level of the measures, they shall be punished by 60 strokes of beating with the heavy stick. If they shall be punished by heavier penalties upon the calculation of the amount of the excess grain as illicit goods, they shall be punished for illicit goods obtained through malfeasance [Art. 368]. The punishment shall be limited to 100 strokes of beating with the heavy stick. If the officials or functionaries in charge know the circumstances but do not report, they shall be punished the same. If they do not know, they shall not be punished.

Article 129   Concealing or Consuming Tax Paid in Grain or Other Taxable Materials [Yinni feiyong shuiliang kewu]

In all cases of transporting one's own household's tax grain, taxable materials, or objects that shall be forfeit to the government, if [the household members] conceal or consume them and thus do not turn them in, or deceitfully claim that the objects are damaged or lost and cheat the authorities, calculate the amount that they owe, and they shall be punished as comparable to having committed theft [Art. 292], but the tattooing shall be exempted. If the officials or functionaries in charge of transportation know the circumstances, they shall be punished the same. If they do not know, they shall not be punished.

Article 130   Monopolizing Payment of Tax Paid in Grain [Lanna shuiliang]

[1] In all cases of monopolizing payment of tax paid in grain, the offenders shall be punished by 60 strokes of beating with the heavy stick. They shall be ordered to go to the granaries to pay the full amount. Moreover, a fine of one-half of the amount of the tax shall be imposed on the offenders, which shall go to the government.

Laws on Revenue

[2] If supervisors or custodians monopolize the payment, the penalty shall be increased two degrees.

[3] In cases where small households that have only odd pieces of land or that have only single able-bodied adult males and, for convenience, pay taxes by adding their rice and wheat to that of other taxpayers, they shall not be punished.

Article 131 Fraudulently Issuing Invoices or Receipts
[Xuchu tongguan zhuchao]

[1] In all cases of accepting money, grain, or any other items that are paid to government granaries or treasuries, if the amount is not sufficient but the supervisors or custodians conspire with their superior officials or functionaries among the authorities and fraudulently issue invoices [*tongguan*], then calculate the amount that is fraudulently issued and add all quantities together as illicit goods; they shall all be punished on the basis of supervisors or custodians themselves stealing [Art. 287].

[2] If the officials who are designated to make inventories of money or grain, although the amount is not sufficient, report in collusion with [officials or functionaries in charge of the granaries or treasuries] that it is sufficient, the punishment shall be the same. If they receive property, calculate the illicit goods; they shall be punished by the heavier penalties on the basis of [accepting property and] subverting the law [Art. 367].

[3] If the supervisors or custodians do not receive taxes in kind but commute them to other types of property and fraudulently issue receipts [*zhuchao*], they shall also be punished on the basis of supervisors or custodians themselves stealing [Art. 287]. If the household [heads] who make the payment know the circumstances, the penalty shall be reduced two degrees, and the tattooing shall be exempted. The illicit goods that are already paid shall be forfeit to the government. If they do not know the circumstances, they shall not be punished, and the illicit goods shall be returned to the owners.

[4] If those in the same offices know the circumstances but do not report, they shall punished by the same penalty as that for the offenders. If they do not know or do not sign the documents, they shall not be punished.

Article 132 Secretly Using Excess Money or Grain to Make Up Deficits
[Fuyu qianliang sixia bushu]

[1] In all cases where any yamen, granary, or treasury has excess money or grains, it must be reported completely and accurately to the government and be clearly recorded in account books in the correct amount. If the supervisors or custodians secretly use the surplus money or grain to make up the deficits in other accounts, and thus cheat the government and practice fraud, then calculate the amount as illicit goods; they shall all be punished on the basis of supervisors or custodians themselves stealing [Art. 287].

[2] If the Palace Treasury receives gold or silk and does not complete the transaction on the same day, [the objects] may be registered and placed in the Treasury. If there are excess things, the Treasury shall clearly set up files, record them in account books, and report the correct amount to the Ministry of Revenue. Those who misleadingly take the gold or silk and other objects out without authorization shall be punished by decapitation. If the gatekeepers fail to question and search, they shall be punished by 100 strokes of beating with the heavy stick.

Article 133   Borrowing Money or Grain without Authorization
[Sijie qianliang]

[1] In all cases where supervisors or custodians, without authorization, borrow government money, grain, or other things to use or lend the things to others, even though there are written records, calculate the amount of the illicit goods; they shall be punished on the basis of supervisors or custodians themselves stealing [Art. 287]. If those who borrow the things are not supervisors or custodians, they shall be punished on the basis of ordinary persons stealing money or grain from granaries or treasuries [Art. 288].

[2] For those who exchange their own things for government objects, the punishment shall be the same.

Article 134   Borrowing Government Objects without Authorization
[Sijie guanwu]

In all cases where supervisors or custodians, without authorization, borrow government objects such as miscellaneous articles, clothes, rugs and bedding, tools, or utensils to use or lend the things to others, they, as well as those who borrow the objects, shall each be punished by 50 strokes of beating with the light stick. If the objects are kept for 10 days, in each case the penalty shall be reduced two degrees from that for illicit goods obtained through malfeasance [Art. 368]. If the objects are damaged or lost, they shall be punished according to the article concerning damaging or losing government property [Art. 104], and they shall be levied for compensation.

Article 135   Diverting [Items] in Expenditures or Receipts [Nuoyi chuna]

[1] In all cases where any yamen receives or expends money, grain, or other items, there should be established files and matching tallies. If supervisors or custodians do not receive or spend correctly but divert from government usage the items in expenditures or receipts, calculate the amount of illicit goods; they shall be punished as comparable to supervisors or custodians themselves stealing [Art. 287]. The punishment shall be limited to 100 strokes of beating with the heavy stick and life exile to 3,000 *li*. The tattooing shall be exempted.

[2] If yamen officials do not issue the half-sealed matching tallies but only

issue expedient notes without authorization, or although they issue the matching tallies but do not establish files, and then they make the payment, or if the granary or treasury officials or functionaries do not wait for the matching tallies, or although they have received the matching tallies but do not make records in the files, and then they make the payment, the punishment shall also be the same.

[3] In places where army troops proceed for attack or defense, the grain and fodder shall, after files are clearly established, be immediately delivered. The reports of the amounts shall be made to the superior authorities for recording the expenditures. Any violations shall be punished by 60 strokes of beating with the heavy stick.

Article 136 Deceitfully Embezzling by Weighers in Granaries and Employees [Kucheng guyi qinqi]

In all cases where collectors, weighers, measurers, or employees in granaries or treasuries, tax-collecting offices, storage sites, services, or courts deceitfully embezzle, borrow or lend, or transfer or exchange government money or grain, they shall all be punished on the basis of supervisors or custodians themselves stealing [Art. 287]. If hirers act together and share in the illicit goods, the penalty shall be the same. If they know the circumstances and do not share in the illicit goods, but they collaborate and make reports that thus deceive the government and do not accuse the offenders to the government, the penalty shall be reduced one degree. The punishment shall be limited to 100 strokes of beating with the heavy stick. If they do not know the circumstances, they shall not be punished.

Article 137 Fraudulently Issuing Government Grain [Maozhi guanliang]

In all cases where military officers, functionaries, platoon commanders, or squad commanders fraudulently issue military supplies to themselves, calculate the amount of the illicit goods; they shall be punished as comparable to having committed theft [Art. 292]; the tattooing shall be exempted.

Article 138 Watching Each Other for Money and Grain [Qianliang huxiang juecha]

[1] In all cases where officials, functionaries, bookkeepers [*cuan*], watchers [*lan*], collectors [*kuzi*], and measurers [*douji*] in granaries, treasures, tax-collecting offices, and storage sites watch each other, if they know government grain or money has been deceitfully embezzled, stolen, borrowed, or lent from granaries or treasures but conceal the matter and do not report to the government, or deliberately allow it to happen, they shall be punished by the same penalty as that for the offenders. If they fail to discover the matter, the penalty shall be reduced three degrees. The punishment shall be limited to 100 strokes of beating with the heavy stick.

[2] If officials or functionaries fraudulently establish files, divert items in expenditures or receipts, or fraudulently issue invoices or receipts, but the measurers, granary guardians, or chief watchers do not know the circumstances, they [the latter] shall not be punished.

Article 139   Failing to Discover Theft in Granaries and Treasuries
[Cangku bujue beidao]

In all cases where guardians do not search those who come out of granaries or treasuries, they shall be punished by 20 strokes of beating with the light stick. If, because they do not search, they fail to discover that goods are stolen out of granaries or treasuries, the penalty shall be reduced two degrees from that for theft [Art. 292]. If night watchmen fail to discover the theft, the penalty shall be reduced three degrees. If officials, bookkeepers, measurers, or collectors who are on duty at night in granaries or treasuries fail to discover the theft, the penalty shall be reduced five degrees. In all these cases, the punishment shall be limited to 100 strokes of beating with the heavy stick. For those who deliberately allow it to happen, in each case the penalty shall be the same as that for theft. In case of forcible robbery, they shall not be punished.

*Article 140   Waiting for Money and Grain to Be Expended
and Opening Official Seals without Authorization*
[Shouzhi qianliang ji shankai guanfeng]

[1] In all cases where officials, bookkeepers, measurers, or collectors in granaries or treasuries fulfill their required terms and should be replaced, they shall wait for the money, grain, and government goods to be completely expended. Career records shall be issued only if there are no shortages. If there are goods that should be handed over to successors, the proctorial officials or functionaries should investigate thoroughly by supervising physical inventories personally. They shall not hand the goods over by simply designating containers or granaries. Any violations shall be punished by 100 strokes of beating with the heavy stick.

[2] If government goods are sealed with stamps, and if the officials or functionaries in charge do not request the offices that seal the goods [for permission] and they open them without authorization, they shall be punished by 60 strokes of beating with the heavy stick.

Article 141   Violating [Rules] in Issuing or Receiving Government Goods
[Chuna guanwu youwei]

[1] In all cases where government goods are issued or received at granaries or treasuries, if old goods should be issued but new goods are issued, or goods of high quality should be received but goods of low quality are received, and so forth, or if, when responsible offices hire or buy with mutual

consent, prices are not paid immediately, or prices that are paid are either increased or reduced from the actual amount [of agreed prices], calculate the deficiency or excess in the prices; [the responsible officials] shall be punished for illicit goods obtained through malfeasance [Art. 368].

[2] In the case of salary payment, if they are not due yet but salaries are paid in advance, the penalty shall be the same.

[3] If supervisory officials or functionaries know the circumstances but do not report them, they shall be punished the same. If they do not know, they shall not be punished.

Article 142 Creating Obstructions in Receiving or Issuing [Government Goods] [Shouzhi liunan]

[1] In all cases where government goods are received or issued, if responsible officials or functionaries without good reason create obstructions and do not immediately receive or issue the goods, for one day [of obstruction] they shall be punished by 50 strokes of beating with the light stick. For each additional three days, the penalty shall be increased one degree. The punishment shall be limited to 60 strokes of beating with the heavy stick and penal servitude for one year.

[2] If doorkeepers create obstructions, the penalty shall be the same.

[3] If the persons who receive or deliver goods arrive one after another, and the responsible officials do not receive or issue goods in accordance with the [arriving] order, they shall be punished by 40 strokes of beating with the light stick.

Article 143 Delivering Gold or Silver in Standard Purity [Qijie jinyin zuse]

In all cases where all sorts of taxes are collected and goods are sold, the gold or silver that is delivered must be of standard purity. If the quality does not meet the standard, the proctorial officials and functionaries and the artisans shall each be punished by 40 strokes of beating with the light stick. They shall reimburse the government in equal shares.

Article 144 Damaging Goods in Granaries or Treasuries [Sunhuai cangku caiwu]

[1] In all cases where goods are deposited in granaries or treasuries or are stacked together, if the custodians do not arrange them properly or do not dry or air them on time and the goods are damaged, calculate the value of the damaged goods; the custodians shall be punished for illicit goods obtained through malfeasance [Art. 368]. They shall reimburse the government in equal shares.

[2] If there are matters that cannot be foreseen, such as unexpected rains cause floods, fires spread [to granaries or treasuries], or robbers plunder, and that cause damages, send officials to investigate the matters and report

the facts. If there is clear evidence, [the custodians] shall not be punished and shall not reimburse. If supervisors or custodians, in order to conceal the matters involving goods that are embezzled, borrowed, lent, or diverted, seize the opportunities of floods, fires, or robberies, set up false files, convert [the number of the goods], substitute records and registers, and make false reports to cheat the government, calculate the amount of illicit goods; they shall be punished on the basis of supervisors or custodians themselves stealing [Art. 287]. If those in the same office know the circumstances but do not report, they shall be punished the same. If they do not know, they shall not be punished.

Article 145   Transmitting Government Goods [Zhuanjie guanwu]

[1] In all localities where money or silk is collected, military supplies are purchased, or military implements or other things are manufactured, the items shall be delivered to and received at local subprefectures or districts. [The subprefectures or districts shall] send officials or functionaries continually to transmit the items in groups of their own kinds to local prefectures. If local prefectures do not immediately receive the items and assign people to transmit them but compel those [from the original subprefectures or districts] to transmit directly to the Provincial Administration Commissions, the responsible proctorial head officials, staff supervisors, and functionaries shall each be punished by 80 strokes of beating with the heavy stick. If Provincial Administration Commissions do not immediately receive and transmit [the items] but compel prefectures to transmit directly to the ministry, the staff supervisors and functionaries shall be punished by the same penalty.

[2] In transmitting government goods, if officials in charge of the convoy and the carriers do not arrange [the goods] properly and there are damages, calculate the value of the damaged goods; they shall be punished for illicit goods obtained through malfeasance [Art. 368], and they shall reimburse the government in equal shares. If there are matters that cannot be foreseen, such as wind and waves are encountered when sailing boats, fires spread to [the goods], or robbers plunder, and that cause damages, report the matters to the local government offices in charge. [The offices shall] send officials to investigate the matters and report the facts. If there is clear evidence, they shall not be punished and shall not reimburse the government. If there is embezzlement, calculate the value of the illicit goods; they shall be punished on the basis of supervisors or custodians themselves stealing [Art. 287].

[3] For those who, in transmitting government goods, do not deliver the original items but, without authorization, carry goods or money and purchase items at the place of delivery and deliver them to the government, also calculate the value of the illicit goods; they shall be punished on the basis of supervisors or custodians themselves stealing [Art. 287].

Article 146 Deciding the Seizure of Illicit Goods Improperly
[Niduan zangfa budang]

In all cases where the seizure of illicit goods is decided, if the goods should go to the government but are given to owners, or if the goods should be given to owners but go to the government, the offenders shall be punished for illicit goods obtained through malfeasance [Art. 368]. The punishment shall be limited to 100 strokes of beating with the heavy stick.

Article 147 Guarding Goods in the Hands of the Government
[Shouzhang zaiguan caiwu]

In all cases where government goods that should be given to individuals are taken out of granaries or treasuries but have not yet been given, or private goods that should be provided for government usage are sent to the government but have not yet entered granaries or treasuries, if those who guard the goods in the hands of the government embezzle, borrow, or lend the goods, calculate the value of the illicit goods; they shall be punished on the basis of supervisors or custodians themselves stealing [Art. 287].

Article 148 Concealing Household Goods That Go to the Government
[Yinman ruguan jiachan]

[1] In all cases where persons or goods are seized or confiscated, except for plotting rebellions, plotting treason, or treacherous cliques that are within the Ten Abominations [Art. 2] and where [persons or goods should be] seized or confiscated in accordance with the *Code,* in all other crimes where the *Code* does not stipulate [the seizure or confiscation], wives, children, or goods shall not be seized or confiscated by the government. Any violations shall be punished on the basis of deliberately increasing the penalty to life exile [Art. 433].

[2] For those who, in confiscating household goods that should go to the government, hide persons and do not report, calculate the number of the persons; they shall be punished on the basis of hiding able-bodied adult males [Art. 81]. If they hide fields, calculate the area of the fields; they shall be punished on the basis of fraudulently concealing fields and their produce [Art. 96]. If they hide goods, houses, or livestock, they shall be punished for illicit goods obtained through malfeasance [Art. 368]. In each case, the punishment shall be limited to 100 strokes of beating with the heavy stick. Persons and goods that are hidden shall go to the government. [Only] those who make the reports shall be punished.

[3] If community heads agree to the concealment or responsible officials or functionaries know the circumstances, they shall all be punished by the same penalty. Calculate the value of the goods that are hidden. [If it entails] heavier penalties, they shall be punished for illicit goods obtained through malfeasance [Art. 368] for the whole value [instead of half].

[4] For those who receive the goods, calculate the value of the illicit goods;

in each case they shall be punished on the basis of [accepting property and] subverting the law [Art. 367], with heavier penalties applied. For those who fail to discover and thus fail to report the matters, the penalty shall be reduced three degrees. The punishment shall be limited to 50 strokes of beating with the light stick.

Section 5 Taxes [*Kecheng*] [Nineteen Articles]

THE SALT RULES [*YANFA*] [TWELVE ARTICLES]

Article 149[1]

[1] In all cases where illegal transactions in salt are committed, the offenders shall be punished by 100 strokes of beating with the heavy stick and penal servitude for three years. If they carry military weapons, the penalty shall be increased one degree. If they falsely accuse innocent persons, the penalty shall be increased three degrees. If they resist arrest, they shall be decapitated. The salt, wagons, boats, and draft animals shall all be forfeit to the government. The guides, brokers, and those who hide [the salt smugglers] and who store [the smuggled salt] shall be punished by 90 strokes of beating with the heavy stick and penal servitude for two and one-half years. Those [who are hired to] carry the goods with poles or haul them in carts or on animals shall be punished by 80 strokes of beating with the heavy stick and penal servitude for two years. For those who are not bound [by law] to arrest [the perpetrators of the illegal salt transactions] but who can accuse and capture them, they shall be given the illegally transacted salt that is seized as a reward. If the perpetrators of the illegal salt transactions voluntarily confess their crimes, the penalty shall be exempted, and they shall be rewarded the same [as the accusers and capturers].

[2] If the matters are discovered, only the persons and salt that are captured at the time shall be dealt with. The responsible offices shall not [listen to] indirect accusations. Any violations shall be punished on the basis of deliberately incriminating others [Art. 433]. (This means that if offenders and salt are captured together, only the captured shall be dealt with. If the transacted salt is captured but no offenders are found, the salt shall be forfeit to the government, and it is not allowed to pursue and investigate further.)

Article 150

In all cases where salt workers and other employees in salt-working sites secretly carry surplus salt, other than the regular quota of salt [which they have to deliver to the government], away from the working sites or privately boil salt and sell it, they shall be punished the same as [if they were involved in] illegal transactions in salt [Art. 149]. If centurions [*baifu zhang*] know the circumstances and deliberately permit the action or collaborate [with the offenders] and sell the salt, they shall be punished by the same penalty as that for offenders.

Article 151

In all cases where married women commit illegal transactions in salt, if their husbands are at home or their sons know the circumstances, the penalty shall be inflicted upon the able-bodied adult males. If, although they have husbands, their husbands have gone to distant places, or their sons are young and weak, the penalty shall be inflicted upon the responsible women.

Article 152

In all cases where persons buy and consume illegally transacted salt, they shall be punished by 100 strokes of beating with the heavy stick. If they sell it, they shall be punished by 100 strokes of beating with the heavy stick and penal servitude for three years.

Article 153

In all cases where defending military offices, salt distribution commissions, or police offices patrol for and apprehend illegal salt transactors, they shall immediately transmit the transactors to local government offices with authority for investigation. No [apprehending] office shall interrogate without authorization. If officials or functionaries of local government offices with authority connive [with the apprehending offices] and release the transactors, they shall be punished by the same penalty as that for the offenders. For those who receive property, calculate the value of the illicit goods; they shall be punished on the basis of [accepting property and] subverting the law [Art. 367], with the heavier penalty applied.

Article 154

[1] In all cases where defending military offices, local government offices with authority, and police offices devise methods and assign persons constantly to patrol and prohibit illegal salt transactions in areas within their jurisdiction and in important places near the salt-working sites, if [the illegally transacted salt] slips through, the officials of the checkpoints and persons assigned to patrol against the illegal salt transaction shall, for the first time, be punished by 40 strokes of beating with the light stick. For the second time, they shall be punished by 50 strokes of beating with the light stick. For the third time, they shall be punished by 60 strokes of beating with the heavy stick. In all these cases they shall have their transgressions recorded and retain their appointments. If they know the circumstances and deliberately permit the actions or allow military soldiers to join [the illegal transactors] in selling salt, they shall be punished by the same penalty as that for

the offenders. If they receive property, calculate the value of the illicit goods; they shall be punished on the basis of [accepting property and] subverting the law [Art. 367], with the heavier penalty applied.

[2] If they appropriate the illegally transacted salt and do not deliver to the government, they shall be punished by 100 strokes of beating with the heavy stick and penal servitude for three years. If they falsely accuse innocent persons, the penalty shall be increased three degrees.

Article 155

In all cases where military soldiers commit illegal salt transactions, if their superior battalion or company commanders fail to control them, the company commanders shall, for the first time, be punished by 50 strokes of beating with the light stick. For the second time, they shall be punished by 60 strokes of beating with the heavy stick. For the third time, they shall be punished by 70 strokes of beating with the heavy stick. Their salaries shall be reduced by half. The battalion commanders shall, for the first time, be punished by 40 strokes of beating with the light stick. For the second time, they shall be punished by 50 strokes of beating with the light stick. For the third time, they shall be punished by 60 strokes of beating with the heavy stick. Their salaries shall be reduced by half. They shall all have their transgressions recorded and retain their appointments. If they know the circumstances and permit the actions or join [the illegal transactors] in selling salt, they shall be punished by the same penalty as that for the offenders.

Article 156

[1] In all cases where government salt is transported, each license shall be for 200 *jin* as one bag, plus 5 *jin* of permitted amount of waste. When passing salt control stations, the salt shall be pulled out to be weighed and inspected to verify the amount. For those who carry excess salt, they shall be punished according to the law on committing illegal transactions in salt [Art. 149].

[2] If salt merchants, when passing salt control stations, do not have their salt weighed and stamped, they shall be punished by 90 strokes of beating with the heavy stick and shall be taken back to have the salt weighed and inspected.

Article 157

[1] In all cases where salt merchants sell government salt, it is not permitted that the salt and the license be separated. Any violations shall be punished according to the law on committing illegal transactions in salt [Art. 149].

[2] After they sell the salt, if the merchants do not return and surrender

Laws on Revenue

their licenses within 10 days, they shall be punished by 40 strokes of beating with the light stick.

[3] If they use old licenses and fraudulently engage in salt transactions, they shall be punished according to the law on committing illegal transactions in salt [Art. 149].

Article 158

In all cases where persons transport government salt or salt makers deliver salt to warehouses, if they carry military weapons or do not use government boats to transport the salt, they shall be punished according to the law on committing illegal transactions in salt [Art. 149].

Article 159

In all cases where salt merchants sell government salt that is mixed with sand or dirt, they shall be punished by 80 strokes of beating with the heavy stick.

Article 160

In all cases where [salt merchants] sell licensed government salt, if they do not sell it in areas designated for the sale of salt but go to other areas and thus break the area limits to sell it, they shall be punished by 100 strokes of beating with the heavy stick. For those who know the circumstances and buy and consume the salt, they shall be punished by 60 strokes of beating with the heavy stick. If they do not know the circumstances, they shall not be punished. The salt shall be forfeit to the government.

Article 161 Supervisory [Officials or Functionaries] or Powerful Persons Engaging in Salt Transactions [Jianlin shiyao zhongyan]

In all cases where supervisory officials or functionaries use false names or powerful persons offer money or grain, and they petition to buy salt licenses and tallies and thus encroach upon the interests of the people, they shall be punished by 100 strokes of beating with the heavy stick and penal servitude for three years. The salt shall be forfeit to the government.

Article 162 Obstructing the Salt Laws [Zuhuai yanfa]

In all cases where merchants buy salt licenses and tallies, if they do not personally go to the working sites and obtain the salt but meantime sell [the licenses and tallies] by increasing the prices and thus obstruct the salt laws, the buyers and sellers shall each be punished by 80 strokes of beating with the heavy stick. The penalties for broker-guarantors shall be reduced one degree. The salt and money shall both be forfeit to the government. If retail shops purchase and sell the salt, this article shall not be applied.

Laws on Revenue

Article 163   Illegal Transactions in Tea [Sicha]

In all cases where illegal transactions in tea are committed, the penalty shall be the same as that for illegal transactions in salt. For those who take expired licenses that have been examined, clipped, and returned [by the tea control stations] and who enter the mountains and obtain tea, they shall be punished on the basis of illegal transactions in tea.

Article 164   Illegal Transactions in Alum [Sifan]

In all cases where alum is illegally processed and sold, the penalty shall be the same as that for illegal transactions in salt [Art. 149].

Article 165   Evading Taxes [Nishui]

[1] In all cases where merchants evade taxes or owners of wine or vinegar shops do not pay taxes, they shall be punished by 50 strokes of beating with the light stick. Half of the goods, wine, or vinegar shall be forfeit to the government. Divide the amount of the property that is forfeit to the government into 10 portions; 3 portions shall be given to the accusers as reward. If officials, bookkeepers, or guardians of the tax offices themselves seize the offenders, there shall be no reward. For those who enter the [city] gates but do not present certificates, they shall be punished the same as for evading taxes. For those who make wine or vinegar for their own consumption, this provision is not applicable.

[2] For those who buy animals but do not pay the sales taxes on the contracts, the penalty shall be the same. Moreover, levy one-half of the price from the buyers, and confiscate it for the government.

Article 166   Maritime Merchants Hiding Goods [Boshang nihuo]

In all cases where maritime merchants land at ports in ships, they shall immediately make accurate reports to the government concerning all the goods on which taxes will be levied in certain portions. If they go to and stay at the houses of local merchants or brokers and do not report, they shall be punished by 100 strokes of beating with the heavy stick. Although they report, if they do not report completely, the penalty shall be the same. The goods shall all be forfeit to the government. Those who let [the merchants] stay and who hide the goods shall be punished the same. For those who report the matters and who catch the offenders, the government shall give them 20 *liang* of silver as reward.

Article 167   Households Failing to Pay Taxes [Renhu kuidui kecheng]

[1] In all cases where the annual tax quotas among the people, such as taxes for tea, salt, or commerce, are not paid in full at the end of the year, calculate the deficiency, divide the taxes into 10 portions, and for 1 portion, [the responsible persons] shall be punished by 40 strokes of beating with

the light stick. For each additional portion, the penalty shall be increased one degree. The punishment shall be limited to 80 strokes of beating with the heavy stick. The taxes shall be levied and paid to the government.

[2] If officials of the tea and salt transportation commissions, salt-working sites, tea offices, tax offices, fishing tax offices, or other offices do not diligently levy taxes, and at the end of the year there is a shortage in payments in comparison with the preceding year's tax amount, also divide [the taxes] into 10 portions; for one portion [of deficiency], they shall be punished by 50 strokes of beating with the light stick. For each additional portion, the penalty shall be increased one degree. The punishment shall be limited to 100 strokes of beating with the heavy stick. The deficient amount of taxes shall be levied and paid to the government.

[3] If they conceal, embezzle, or borrow [the payments], in all the cases calculate the amount of the illicit goods; they shall be punished on the basis of supervisors or custodians themselves stealing [Art. 287].

Section 6 Monetary Obligations [Qianzhai] [Three Articles]

Article 168   Taking Interest in Violation of Prohibitions [Weijin quli]

[1] In all cases where money is loaned or property is pawned privately, the monthly interest shall not exceed 3 percent [sanfen]. Even though the months and years are many, the interest shall not exceed the principal. Any violations shall be punished by 40 strokes of beating with the light stick. Calculate the amount of excess interest as illicit goods, and if it results in a heavier penalty, [the responsible persons] shall be punished for illicit goods obtained through malfeasance [Art. 368]. The punishment shall be limited to 100 strokes of beating with the heavy stick.

[2] If supervisory officials or functionaries, within areas of their jurisdiction, loan money or pawn property, they shall be punished by 80 strokes of beating with the heavy stick. If they take interest in violation of prohibitions, and the amount of the excess interest, when calculated as illicit goods, results in heavier penalties, they shall be punished on the basis of [accepting property but] not subverting the law [Art. 367].

[3] In all the cases, the excess interest shall be levied and returned to the owners.

[4] For those who owe personal debts and who violate agreements and do not pay the debts, for 5 *guan* or more, if the delay is three months, they shall be punished by 10 strokes of beating with the light stick. For each additional month, the penalty shall be increased one degree. The punishment shall be limited to 40 strokes of beating with the light stick. For 50 *guan* or more, if the delay is three months, they shall be punished by 20 strokes of

beating with the light stick. For each additional month, the penalty shall be increased one degree. The punishment shall be limited to 50 strokes of beating with the light stick. For 250 *guan* or more, if the delay is three months, they shall be punished by 30 strokes of beating with the light stick. For each additional month, the penalty shall be increased one degree. The punishment shall be limited to 60 strokes of beating with the heavy stick. In all the cases, the principal and interest shall be levied and returned to the owners.

[5] If powerful or influential persons do not report to the government but, because of their private debts, take others' domestic animals or property away by force, they shall be punished by 80 strokes of beating with the heavy stick. If prices are assessed more than the principal and interest, calculate the excess property; they shall be punished for illicit goods obtained through malfeasance [Art. 368]. The excess quantity shall be levied and returned [to the obligors].

[6] If wives, concubines, sons, or daughters [of obligors] are taken in satisfaction of debts, [the responsible persons] shall be punished by 100 strokes of beating with the heavy stick. For those who take by force, the penalty shall be increased two degrees. If they forcibly seize and have sexual relations with others' women or girls, they shall be strangled. The persons who were seized shall be returned to their families. The private debts shall not be recovered.

Article 169   Consuming Property Received in Deposit
[Feiyong shouji caichan]

In all cases of receiving in deposit the property or domestic animals from others and of consuming them without authorization, the offenders shall be punished for illicit goods obtained through malfeasance [Art. 368], with the penalty reduced by one degree. If they deceitfully claim that [the deposited property or domestic animals] are dead or lost, they shall be punished as comparable to having committed theft [Art. 292], with the penalty reduced one degree. In both the cases the property shall be levied and returned to the owners. If [the deposited property] is consumed or lost because of floods, fire, or robbery or the domestic animals die of illness, and there is clear evidence, there shall be no punishment.

Article 170   Finding Lost Objects [De yishi wu]

[1] In all cases of finding lost objects, the objects shall be delivered to the government within five days. If they are government property, they shall be returned to the government. If they are private property, then ask people to claim them. [If they are claimed,] give half of the property to the finders as reward and return the other half to the owners. If, within 30 days, no one claims the objects, then give them all to the finders. If the finders

do not deliver the objects to the government within the time limit, for government property they shall be punished for illicit goods obtained through malfeasance [Art. 368]. For private property, the penalty shall be reduced two degrees, and half of the property shall be given to the government and half shall be returned to the owners.

[2] Those who dig up buried objects on government or private land may keep and use them. If they dig up ancient objects, bells, tripods, tallies, seals, or any rare objects, they shall deliver them to the government within 30 days. Any violations shall be punished by 80 strokes of beating with the heavy stick. The objects shall be forfeit to the government.

Section 7 Markets [*Shichan*] [Five Articles]

Article 171 Filling Positions of Commission Agents or Port Masters without Authorization [Sichong yahang butou]

In all cases where various commission agents or port masters for ships in cities or villages [are selected], they shall be selected from households that have substantial property to fill the positions. The government will give them sealed registers to record merchants and boatmen's places of registration, names, travel permits, identifications, goods lists, and quantities. Every month they shall go to the government [and present these registers] for examination. Those who fill the positions without authorization shall be punished by 60 strokes of beating with the heavy stick. The commission money obtained shall be forfeit to the government. If official commission agents or port masters permit the actions and conceal the matters, they shall be punished by 50 strokes of beating with the light stick. [Their titles and businesses] shall be terminated.

Article 172 Assessing Prices of Merchandise by Market Authorities [Shisi ping wujia]

[1] In all cases where commission agents of various merchandise assess merchandise prices, if they set the prices too expensive or too cheap and thus make the prices unjust, calculate the amount of increase or reduction in the prices; they shall be punished for illicit goods obtained through malfeasance [Art. 368]. If they take them as their own, they shall be punished as comparable to having committed theft [Art. 292] but be exempted from tattooing.

[2] If they assess illicit goods for criminals incorrectly and thus make penalties too light or too heavy, they shall be punished on the basis of deliberately exonerating the guilty or incriminating the innocent [Art. 433]. If they receive property, calculate the amount of the illicit goods; they shall be punished on the basis of [accepting property and] subverting the law [Art. 367], with heavier penalties applied.

Article 173 Monopolizing Markets [Bachi hangshi]

[1] In all cases where various goods are purchased or sold, if persons monopolize the markets without mutual agreements and solely take the profits, or if traders collude with commission agents and they jointly formulate crafty plots to make the sale prices of cheap goods expensive or of expensive goods cheap, they shall be punished by 80 strokes of beating with the heavy stick.

[2] For those who see others are engaged in purchase and sale and then aside claim high or low prices and compare prices in order to cause confusion and seek profits, they shall be punished by 40 strokes of beating with the light stick.

[3] [In the above cases,] if profits are already obtained, the amount of the illicit goods shall be calculated. If it results in a heavier penalty, the offenders shall be punished as comparable to having committed theft [Art. 292] but be exempted from tattooing.

Article 174 Manufacturing Volume Measures, Weights, or Linear Measures without Authorization [Sizao hu dou cheng chi]

[1] In all cases where volume measures, weights, or linear measures are manufactured without authorization and incorrectly and they are used in markets, or where government-issued volume measures, weights, or linear measures are deceitfully increased or reduced, the offenders shall be punished by 60 strokes of beating with the heavy stick. The government artisans shall be punished the same.

[2] If government-issued measures are not manufactured in accordance with the rules, the offenders shall be punished by 70 strokes of beating with the heavy stick. If officials in charge are negligent in inspections, the penalty shall be reduced one degree. If they know the circumstances, they shall be punished by the same penalty [as that for the offenders].

[3] Although the volume measures, weights, or linear measures that are used in markets are correct, if they are not inspected and stamped by the government, the offenders shall be punished by 40 strokes of beating with the light stick.

[4] If officials or functionaries in granaries or treasuries, without authorization, increase or decrease the government-issued volume measures, weights, or linear measures and use them to receive or pay out government property incorrectly, they shall be punished by 100 strokes of beating with the heavy stick. If the value of the property that is increased or decreased, when calculated as illicit goods, results in a heavier penalty, they shall be punished for illicit goods obtained through malfeasance [Art. 368]. If they take the goods as their own, they shall be punished on the basis of supervisors or custodians themselves stealing [Art. 287]. The artisans shall be punished by 80 strokes of beating with the heavy stick. If supervisory officials

know the circumstances but do not report, they shall be punished by the same penalty as that for the offenders. If they are negligent in inspections, the penalty shall be reduced three degrees. The punishment shall be limited to 100 strokes of beating with the heavy stick.

Article 175 Failing to Manufacture Utensils and Textiles in Accordance with the Rules [Qiyong bujuan bu rufa]

In all cases where utensils are not manufactured durably and correctly, or where textiles are spoilt, thin, short, or narrow, and [the utensils and textiles] are sold, in each case the offenders shall be punished by 50 strokes of beating with the light stick. The objects shall be forfeit to the government.

Note

1. None of the 12 articles under "The Salt Rules" has a title.

CHAPTER 4

Laws on Rituals [Lilü]

Section 1 Sacrifices [*Jisi*] [Six Articles]

Article 176   Sacrifices and Imperial Ancestor Worship [Jixiang]

[1] In all cases where the responsible offices fail to announce in advance the dates of Great Sacrifices [Dasi] or of imperial ancestor worship ceremonies [*miaoxiang*] to each yamen, the officials shall be punished by 50 strokes of beating with the light stick. If mistakes occur during the sacrifices, they shall be punished by 100 strokes of beating with the heavy stick. If the responsible offices have already announced the dates and some mistakes occur, those who make the mistakes shall be punished.

[2] If officials, having started the abstinence period [*shou shijie*], condole the bereaved [*diaosang*], visit the sick [*wenji*], make judgments and sign documents concerning punishments or the death penalty [*panshu xingsha wenshu*], or attend feasts [*yu yanyan*], they shall all be punished by a fine of one month's salary. If the responsible offices know that some officials are in mourning for their relatives of the fifth mourning degree or closer or have ever been punished by beating with the heavy stick but still appoint them as officiators [*zhishi*] or let them serve as associates in the sacrifices, the officials in the offices shall be punished by the same penalty. If they do not know the circumstances, they shall not be punished. If those who are in mourning or have committed transgressions do not themselves mention the matters, they shall be punished by the same penalty. If the officials who have started the abstinence period do not sleep in purified houses [*jingshi*] during the period of partial abstinence [*sanzhai*], they shall be punished by a fine of one-half month's salary. If they do not sleep in their own offices during the period of full abstinence [*zhizhai*], they shall be punished by a fine of one month's salary.

[3] If the offerings such as sacrificial beasts [*shenglao*], jade, silk, or grain for the Great Sacrifices are not prepared in accordance with the rules, the responsible officials shall be punished by 50 strokes of beating with the light stick. If one of the offerings is lacking, they shall be punished by 80

Laws on Rituals

strokes of beating with the heavy stick. If the whole altar of offerings is lacking, they shall be punished by 100 strokes of beating with the heavy stick.

[4] If the responsible offices do not feed the beasts for Great Sacrifices in accordance with the rules, so that they become thin or harmed, for one beast, the responsible officials shall be punished by 40 strokes of beating with the light stick. For each additional beast, the penalty shall be increased one degree. The punishment shall be limited to 80 strokes of beating with the heavy stick. If death results, the penalty shall be increased one degree.

[5] For offenses concerning the medium sacrifices [zhongsi], the punishment shall be the same. (Other articles shall follow this provision.)

Article 177 Destroying Mounds or Altars for Great Sacrifices
[Hui Dasi qiutan]

[1] In all cases where the mounds or altars [qiutan] for Great Sacrifices are destroyed or harmed, the offenders shall be punished by 100 strokes of beating with the heavy stick and life exile to 2,000 li. If outer gates are destroyed or harmed, the penalty shall be reduced two degrees.

[2] If the objects for Great Sacrifices to spirits are discarded or destroyed, the offenders shall be punished by 100 strokes of beating with the heavy stick and penal servitude for three years. If they are lost or mistakenly destroyed, in each case the penalty shall be reduced three degrees.

Article 178 Performing Sacrifices to Spirits Recorded in The Sacrificial Canon [Zhiji Sidian shenqi]

In all cases where the spirits who are recorded in *The Sacrificial Canon* [Sidian], such as those of soil and grain, mountains, rivers, wind, clouds, thunder, or rain, as well as [of] sage sovereigns, wise kings, loyal subjects, and martyrs, should be sacrificed to, the local government offices shall establish tablets on which shall be written the names of the spirits and the dates of their sacrifices. They shall uninterruptedly hang the tablets in clean places and perform sacrifices in accordance with the schedules. If they fail to perform sacrifice to the spirits at the scheduled time, they shall be punished by 100 strokes of beating with the heavy stick. If they perform sacrifice to spirits that shall not be sacrificed to, they shall be punished by 80 strokes of beating with the heavy stick.

Article 179 The Mausoleums of Rulers of Previous Dynasties
[Lidai diwang lingqin]

No person shall be allowed to collect firewood, till the land, or pasture domestic animals such as cattle or sheep on the mausoleums of rulers or on the tombs of loyal subjects, martyrs, past sages, or worthies of previous dynasties. Any violations shall be punished by 80 strokes of beating with the heavy stick.

Article 180   Profaning the Spirits [Xiedu shenming]

[1] In all cases where private families pray to Heaven [gaotian], worship the Dipper [baidou], burn incense at night, or light the celestial lamp [tiandeng] or the seven lamps [qideng], thus profaning the spirits, they shall be punished by 80 strokes of beating with the heavy stick. If women commit such crimes, the household heads shall be punished. If Buddhist or Daoist priests establish [Buddhist] fasting altars [xiuzhai] or [Daoist] sacrificial altars [shejiao], worship [Heaven] by presenting black-paper charms [qingci] or yellow-paper prayers [biaowen], or [use them to] pray to avert fire calamities, the punishment shall be the same; and they shall return to lay status.

[2] If official, military, or civilian families allow their wives or daughters to burn incense in the Buddhist temples or Daoist monasteries, they shall be punished by 40 strokes of beating with the light stick. Only the adult males shall be punished. If there are no adult males, the responsible women shall be punished. If the abbots [zhuchi] or gatekeepers do not forbid them, the punishment shall be the same [for them].

Article 181   Prohibiting Sorcery of Wizards and Witches [Jinzhi shiwu xieshu]

[1] In all cases where wizards or witches [shiwu] pretend to be mediums of heretical spirits [jiajiang xieshen]; draw magical signs or recite incantations over water [shufu zhoushui]; invoke spirits by sand-writing séance [fuluan daosheng]; call themselves "proper lord" [duangong], "grand guardian" [taibao], or "grand instructress" [shipo]; recklessly claim to be [members of] societies such as the Buddha Maitreya [Mile Fu], the White Lotus Society [Bailian She], the Light-Honoring Sect [Mingzun Jiao], or the White Cloud School [Baiyun Zong], all of which are heterodox teachings that create disturbances [zuodao luanzheng zhi shu]; conceal images [of heretical gods]; burn incense and gather crowds; gather at night and disperse at dawn; or pretend to practice virtuous deeds but actually incite and mislead people, the principals shall be punished by strangulation; the accessories in each case shall be punished by 100 strokes of beating with the heavy stick and life exile to 3,000 li.

[2] If military personnel or civilians dress themselves up as divine images and clang the gongs and beat the drums to welcome spirits in idolatrous processions and fairs, they shall be punished by 100 strokes of beating with the heavy stick. Only the principals shall be punished.

[3] If community heads know the circumstances but do not report to the authorities, in each case they shall be punished by 40 strokes of beating with the light stick.

Laws on Rituals

[4] The spring and autumn sacrificial societies [*chunqiu yishe*] among the people shall not be prohibited.

Section 2 Ceremonial Regulations [*Yizhi*]
[Twenty Articles]

Article 182   Preparing Imperial Medicine [Hehe yuyao]

[1] In all cases where physicians, in preparing imperial medicine, mistakenly do not follow the correct prescriptions or make mistakes in writing or attaching labels, they shall be punished by 100 strokes of beating with the heavy stick. If they do not prepare or select ingredients carefully, they shall be punished by 60 strokes of beating with the heavy stick. If cooks, in preparing imperial meals, mistakenly violate the dietary proscriptions, they shall be punished by 100 strokes of beating with the heavy stick. If the food and drink are not clean, they shall be punished by 80 strokes of beating with the heavy stick. If they do not select good materials, they shall be punished by 60 strokes of beating with the heavy stick. If they do not taste the meals, they shall be punished by 50 strokes of beating with the light stick. The penalty for supervisory or proctorial officials in each case shall be reduced two degrees from that for physicians and cooks.

[2] If supervisory or proctorial officials, cooks, or other persons mistakenly bring any kind of drug to the place where the imperial meals are prepared, they shall be punished by 100 strokes of beating with the heavy stick; and they shall immediately eat the drug they have brought. If the officials in charge of the door or the guards are negligent in searching, they shall be punished by the same penalty as that for the offenders.

[3] All of these crimes shall be immediately memorialized petitioning the decision by the throne.

Article 183   Clothing or Personal Objects of the "Sedan Chair" [Chengyu fuyu wu]

[1] In all cases where the clothing or personal objects of the Sedan Chair [i.e., the emperor] are not stored, repaired, or maintained in accordance with the rules, [the responsible custodians] shall be punished by 60 strokes of beating with the heavy stick. If there is a mistake in presenting these objects, they shall be punished by 40 strokes of beating with the light stick. If the carriages or horses are not properly exercised or trained, or if the harness or equipage is not sturdy or complete, they shall be punished by 80 strokes of beating with the heavy stick.

[2] If the custodians borrow the clothing or personal objects of the Sedan Chair for their own use, or they lend them to other persons, they, together with those who borrow the objects [from the custodians], shall each be pun-

ished by 100 strokes of beating with the heavy stick and penal servitude for three years. If they discard or destroy the objects, the penalty shall be the same. If they lose or mistakenly destroy the objects, in each case the penalty shall be reduced three degrees.

[3] If imperial boats are mistakenly not sturdily constructed, the government artisans shall be punished by 100 strokes of beating with the heavy stick. If the boats are not properly maintained or decorated, or poles or oars for the boats are lacking, the penalty shall be 60 strokes of beating with the heavy stick, and only those who are responsible shall be punished. The penalty for supervisory or proctorial officials in each case shall be reduced two degrees from that for the artisans.

[4] All these crimes shall be immediately memorialized petitioning the decision by the throne.

Article 184   Collecting and Keeping Proscribed Books and Practicing Astronomy without Authorization [Shoucang jinshu ji sixi tianwen]

In all cases where private households collect and keep celestial instruments [xuanxiang qiwu], proscribed books such as those written on astronomical prophecy [tianwen] or in pictorial signs or augural diagrams [tuchen], or rulers' images, golden tallies, or jade seals of previous dynasties, they shall be punished by 100 strokes of beating with the heavy stick. For those who practice astronomy without authorization, the penalty shall be the same. Moreover, levy 10 liang of silver on the offender and give it to the accuser as a reward.

Article 185   Clothing and Objects Bestowed by the Emperor [Yuci yiwu]

In all cases where the imperial messengers do not personally deliver the clothing and objects bestowed by the emperor to officials but transfer them to others to deliver, they shall be punished by 100 strokes of beating with the heavy stick; they shall be dismissed from their appointments and not be reassigned.

Article 186   Making Errors in Imperial Audiences or Congratulatory Ceremonies [Shiwu chaohe]

In all cases of imperial audiences or congratulatory ceremonies [chaohe] or greeting imperial edicts, if the officials of the responsible offices do not make an announcement in advance, they shall be punished by 40 strokes of beating with the light stick. For those who receive the announcement but make errors, the penalty shall be the same.

Article 187   Misbehaving during Ceremonies [Shiyi]

In all cases of sacrifices, worship at the imperial mausoleums, or court audiences, if the participants make mistakes in carrying out rituals or misbehave in ceremonies, they shall be punished by a fine of one-half month's salary. If the inspecting officials who shall prosecute do not prosecute, the punishment shall be the same.

Article 188 Failing to Observe the Proper Procedure in Making Responses to the Throne [Zoudui shixu]

In all cases where the attendant officials are specially asked for advice by the throne, the officials in higher ranks shall make responses first, and the officials in lower ranks shall make responses in their turn. If they fail to observe the proper procedure, whether they are too early or too late, they shall be punished by a fine of one-half month's salary.

Article 189 Obstructing Others from Attending Court Audiences [Chaojian liunan]

In all cases where officials of the Bureau of Ceremonies [Yizhi Si] use pretexts to obstruct officials or other persons who ought to attend court audiences from attending the audiences, and do not immediately present them to the throne, they shall be punished by decapitation. If high officials know the circumstances but do not prosecute them, the penalty shall be the same. If they do not know, they shall not be punished.

Article 190 Sending Memorials or Making Statements to the Throne [Shangshu chenyan]

[1] All gains or losses from dynastic policies or statutes, military or civilian advantages or disadvantages, and all activities that promote what is beneficial and abolish what is harmful shall be personally reported to the throne through the Five Chief Military Commissions or Six Ministries petitioning the imperial decision. The investigating censors and officials of Surveillance Commissions shall report their opinions straightforwardly without hiding the facts.

[2] High or low officials in the capital or in provinces, when there are inconvenient matters in their own yamen, shall set out the matters clearly and report them in sealed memorials petitioning the decision from the throne. If they know the circumstances but do not report and cause the matters to be delayed for years and months, the investigating censors in the capital or the Surveillance Commissions in the provinces shall prosecute them.

[3] If craftsmen and artisans of any sort have matters to report, they may also come directly before the throne to report. If their words are practicable, the information shall be immediately sent to the responsible offices to be acted upon. If any yamen obstructs it, the case shall be made clear through interrogation, and the offenders shall be punished by decapitation.

[4] In reporting matters, the words shall be straightforward, concise, and simple. Each case shall be set out with a heading. Empty ornamental words and superfluous phrases shall not be used.

[5] If persuasive persons [zongheng zhi tu], upon the pretext of memorializing the throne, give clever talks in an ingratiating manner [qiaoyan lingse] in hope of advancing themselves, they shall be punished by 100 strokes of beating with the heavy stick.

[6] If those who make appeals for grievances borrow sealed covers from military or civil offices and send them up to the throne, the borrowers and the lenders shall all be punished by decapitation.

Article 191   Incumbent Officials Erecting Stele without Authorization
[Xianrenguan zhezi libei]

In all cases where incumbent officials who have no governmental achievements erect stele or shrines without authorization, they shall be punished by 100 strokes of beating with the heavy stick. If they send other persons to praise their virtues fraudulently or to petition the throne [for erecting stele or shrines], they shall be punished by 80 strokes of beating with the heavy stick. For those who are sent by them, in each case the penalty shall be reduced one degree.

Article 192   Prohibition against Greeting and Bidding Farewell
[Jinzhi yingsong]

In all cases where superior officials or imperial emissaries pass through [local areas], or investigating censors or officials of Provincial Surveillance Commissions go to local areas to inspect or investigate, if the officials or functionaries of the local yamen go outside the walls of their cities to greet or bid farewell, they shall be punished by 90 strokes of beating with the heavy stick. For those who allow the greeting or bidding farewell and do not report it, the penalty shall be the same.

Article 193   Official Messengers Insulting Senior Officials
[Gongchai renyuan qiling zhangguan]

In all cases where official messengers who are sent to provinces do not comply with ritual rules but insult commanders, prefects, or subprefects, they shall be punished by 60 strokes of beating with the heavy stick. They shall have their transgressions recorded and return to their employment; the months during which they have worked and received salary shall not be counted [into the length of their service]. If commandants commit such an offense, they shall be punished by 70 strokes of beating with the heavy stick. If ushers or jailors commit such an offense, they shall be punished by 80 strokes of beating with the heavy stick.

Article 194   Violating Sumptuary Regulations on Clothing and Houses
[Fushe weishi]

[1] In all cases concerning the houses, carriages, clothes, and other objects of officials and commoners, each has its gradations. If the sumptu-

ary regulations are violated and the limitations are exceeded, for officials, they shall be punished by 100 strokes of beating with the heavy stick, and they shall be dismissed from their appointments and not be reassigned. For commoners, they shall be punished by 50 strokes of beating with the light stick; only the household heads shall be punished. In each case, artisans shall be punished by 50 strokes of beating with the light stick.

[2] If the use of the forbidden dragon or phoenix motif is usurped, both the officials and the commoners shall be punished by 100 strokes of beating with the heavy stick and penal servitude for three years. The artisans shall be punished by 100 strokes of beating with the heavy stick; they, together with their families, shall be sent to the capital to be registered as government artisans. The forbidden articles shall all be forfeit to the government.

[3] Those who report the cases [of usurping the use of the dragon or phoenix motifs to the authorities] shall be rewarded with 50 *liang* of silver by the government.

[4] If the artisans can make voluntary confessions, they shall be exempted from the punishment and be rewarded like ordinary people.

Article 195   Buddhist and Daoist Priests Honoring Parents
[Sengdao bai fumu]

[1] All Buddhist and Daoist priests and nuns shall honor their parents and conduct sacrifices to their ancestors; the mourning degrees shall all be the same as those for ordinary people. Any violations shall be punished by 100 strokes of beating with the heavy stick, and the offenders shall return to lay status.

[2] Buddhist and Daoist clothes shall use only silken or hempen cloth; they shall not use linen or silk gauze. Any violations shall be punished by 50 strokes of beating with the light stick, and the offenders shall return to lay status. The clothes shall be forfeit to the government. The Buddhist and Daoist robes are not within this prohibition.

Article 196   Failing to Prophesy Heavenly Portents [Shizhan tianxiang]

In all cases concerning the heavenly bodies or special phenomena, if officials at the Directorate of Astronomy fail to prophesy and memorialize, they shall be punished by 60 strokes of beating with the heavy stick.

Article 197   Soothsayers Recklessly Predicting Disaster or Good Fortune
[Shushi wangyan huofu]

No magicians or soothsayers shall predict disaster or good fortune [of the dynasty] in the homes of high or low civil or military officials. Any violations shall be punished by 100 strokes of beating with the heavy stick. Casting horoscopes [*tuisuan xingming*] in accordance with classics or divining [*buke*] shall not be prohibited.

Article 198 Concealing the Death of Parents or Husbands
[Ni fumu fu sang]

[1] In all cases where those who hear of their parents' or husband's death conceal and do not mourn it, they shall be punished by 60 strokes of beating with the heavy stick and penal servitude for one year. If, when the mourning period is not yet over, they take off mourning garments and put on ordinary clothing, forget grief and make music, or attend celebration banquets, they shall be punished by 80 strokes of beating with the heavy stick. If, on hearing of the death of superior or older relatives of the degree of mourning for one year, they conceal and do not mourn it, they shall also be punished by 80 strokes of beating with the heavy stick. If, when the mourning period is not yet over, they take off mourning garments and put on ordinary clothing, they shall be punished by 60 strokes of beating with the heavy stick.

[2] If the parents of officials or functionaries die and the officials or functionaries should take leave to observe mourning for the death, but they fraudulently claim that their paternal grandparents, paternal uncles, paternal aunts, or older brothers or sisters have died [rather than their parents] and do not take leave to observe the mourning, they shall be punished by 100 strokes of beating with the heavy stick, and they shall be dismissed from their appointments or employments and not be reassigned. If [their parents] are not dead but they fraudulently claim that they died, or they fraudulently claim an old death to be a new death, the penalty shall be the same. If they [take the action to] circumvent the law, they shall be punished according to the heavier penalty.

[3] If the mourning period is not yet over but they conceal the mourning [maoai] and carry on government services, they shall be punished by 80 strokes of beating with the heavy stick.

[4] If responsible officials know the circumstances and permit the action, in each case they shall be punished the same. If they do not know the circumstances, they shall not be punished.

[5] For those who perform government services in distant places and who shall take leave to observe mourning for their parents' death, the term of leave shall be calculated from the month and day when they learn of the death. For those who shall return to government service by curtailing sentiment [duoqing qifu], this article shall not be applicable.

Article 199 Abandoning Relatives to Take Government Offices
[Qiqin zhiren]

[1] In all cases where those whose paternal grandparents or parents are 80 years of age or older or incapacitated and there are no adult males in line to take care of them abandon their relatives to take government offices or fraudulently claim that their paternal grandparents or parents are aged or

infirm and petition to return to take care of them, in both cases they shall be punished by 80 strokes of beating with the heavy stick.

[2] For those who attend celebration banquets or make music while their paternal grandparents or parents or husbands are imprisoned for committing crimes punishable by the death penalty, the penalty shall be the same.

Article 200 Funerals [Sangzang]

[1] In all cases where there is a death in a household, it is essential that the dead be buried in accordance with the *Rituals*. If, because of fear aroused by geomancy [*fengshui*] or for some other reason, the coffin with the remains is kept in the house, and if for more than a year it is still exposed and the burial has not taken place, [the responsible persons] shall be punished by 80 strokes of beating with the heavy stick.

[2] Those who, in following their superior or older relatives' wishes, cremate the corpses or throw them into the midst of the water shall be punished by 100 strokes of beating with the heavy stick. [For cremating or throwing the corpses of] inferior or younger relatives, in both cases the penalty shall be reduced two degrees. If the death takes place in a distant place, and the son or son's son cannot bring the corpse back for burial and so cremates it, he may do so at his convenience.

[3] If the families of the dead observe fasts and set up altars, or if men and women indiscriminately gather together or drink wine and eat meat, the household heads shall be punished by 80 strokes of beating with the heavy stick. The penalty for Buddhist or Daoist priests shall be the same, and they shall return to lay status.

Article 201 Community Wine-Drinking Ceremonies [Xiang yinjiu li]

In all cases concerning community meetings in order of seniority or community wine-drinking ceremonies, there have been established rules. Any violations shall be punished by 50 strokes of beating with the light stick.

Chapter 5

Laws on Military Affairs [Binglü]

Section 1 Guarding Palaces [Gongwei] [Nineteen Articles]

Article 202   Entering the Gates of the Imperial Ancestral Temple without Authorization [Taimiao men shanru]

In all cases of entering the gates of the Imperial Ancestral Temple or of the imperial mausoleums without authorization, the offenders shall be punished by 100 strokes of beating with the heavy stick. If they enter the gates of the Altar of the Soil [Taishe], they shall be punished by 90 strokes of beating with the heavy stick. If they do not cross the portals, in each case the penalty shall be reduced one degree. If guarding officers deliberately connive at the actions, they shall be punished by the same penalty as that for the offenders. If they are negligent in discovering the matters, the penalty shall be reduced three degrees.

Article 203   Entering the Gates of Palaces and Halls without Authorization [Gongdian men shanru]

[1] In all cases of entering the Meridian Gate, Donghua Gate, Xihua Gate, or Xuanwu Gate of the Imperial City or the Forbidden Garden without authorization, in each case the offenders shall be punished by 100 strokes of beating with the heavy stick. If they enter the gates of palaces or halls without authorization, they shall be punished by 60 strokes of beating with the heavy stick and penal servitude for one year. If they enter the imperial kitchen or the place where the emperor is without authorization, they shall be punished by strangulation. If they do not cross the portals, in each case the penalty shall be reduced one degree.

[2] For those who are not registered for entering [the palaces or halls] but who fraudulently use others' names and enter, the penalty shall be the same.

[3] For those who should enter the palaces or halls but who enter without being registered, or those who should leave their posts of duty but who enter again without authorization, or those whose turn of duty does not arrive but who come on duty without authorization, in each case they shall be punished by 40 strokes of beating with the light stick.

Laws on Military Affairs

[4] For those who are not members of the Imperial Bodyguard on duty and who [as members of the Imperial Bodyguard] should carry military arms, if they carry knives of one *cun* and enter the gates of palaces or halls, they shall be punished by strangulation. If they enter the gates of the Imperial City, they shall be punished by 100 strokes of beating with the heavy stick and sent into military exile to distant frontiers.

[5] If gate officials or guard officers or soldiers deliberately connive at the actions, in each case they shall be punished by the same penalty as that for the offenders. If [the officials or officers are] negligent in discovering the matters, the penalty shall be reduced three degrees. The punishment shall be limited to 100 strokes of beating with the heavy stick. For soldiers, the penalty shall be reduced one more degree. In all the cases [i.e., in paragraph 5], only those who are on duty shall be punished. (Other articles shall follow this.)

Article 204 Substituting Imperial Bodyguards or Palace Guards without Authorization [Suwei shouwei ren sizi daiti]

[1] In all cases where members of the Imperial Bodyguard or Imperial City gate guards who should come on duty do not come on duty, they shall be punished by 40 strokes of beating with the light stick. For those who [should come on duty but do not come on duty and] privately arrange to substitute members of the Imperial Bodyguard or Imperial City gate guards who should come on duty, they as well as those who substitute shall each be punished by 60 strokes of beating with the heavy stick. If they use those who are not members of the Imperial Bodyguard or Imperial City gate guards and who are from other military guards to take false names and to substitute privately, they as well as those who substitute shall each be punished by 100 strokes of beating with the heavy stick. For officers who are company commanders and higher [ranks], in each case the penalty shall be increased one degree.

[2] For those who are on duty and who flee, the penalty shall be the same.

[3] For those who guard the gates of the capital city, the penalty shall be reduced one degree. For those who guard the gates of other cities, the penalty shall be reduced one more degree. If officers who are personally in charge know the circumstances and deliberately connive at the actions, they shall be punished by the same penalty as that for the offenders. If they are negligent in discovering the matters, the penalty shall be reduced three degrees. Those who have good reasons [for not going on duty] and go to their commanding officers and notify them shall not be punished.

Article 205 Delaying in Escorting the "Carriage" [Congjia jiwei]

[1] In all cases where those who shall escort the Carriage [i.e., the emperor] violate the time limits and do not arrive, or those who escort return

ahead of time, for one day, they shall be punished by 40 strokes of beating with the light stick. For each additional three days, the penalty shall be increased one degree. The punishment shall be limited to 100 strokes of beating with the heavy stick. For company commanders or above, in each case the penalty shall be increased one degree.

[2] If those who escort the Carriage flee, they shall be punished by 100 strokes of beating with the heavy stick and sent into military exile to distant frontiers. For company commanders or above, they shall be punished by strangulation.

[3] If officers who are personally in charge deliberately connive at the actions, in each case they shall be punished by the same penalty as that for the offenders. If they are negligent in discovering the matters, the penalty shall be reduced three degrees. The punishment shall be limited to 100 strokes of beating with the heavy stick.

Article 206   Walking on the Imperial Pathway [Zhixing yudao]

In all cases concerning the imperial pathway that goes out from the Meridian Gate to the imperial bridge, only the officers or soldiers on guard who shall guide or follow the imperial carriage may proceed on the east and west sideways. If all other civil or military officials, soldiers, or commoners walk on the pathway without good reason or pass over the imperial bridge without authorization, they shall be punished by 80 strokes of beating with the heavy stick. If they walk on the imperial pathway within palaces or halls, they shall be punished by 100 strokes of beating with the heavy stick. If officers on guard deliberately connive at the actions, in each case they shall be punished by the same penalty as that for the offenders. If they are negligent in discovering the matters, the penalty shall be reduced three degrees. If crossing the imperial pathway is merely walking across it for a moment, this prohibition shall not be applicable.

Article 207   Substituting Services by Craftsmen Working in the Palace Treasury [Neifu gongzuo renjiang tiyi]

In all cases where various sorts of craftsmen who are sent to the Palace Treasury or Imperial Storehouse to work do not personally wear the passes and enter the inner palaces to work but privately hire others to use false names and act as substitutes to perform the services, they and those who substitute shall each be punished by 100 strokes of beating with the heavy stick. The money used to hire persons shall be forfeit to the government.

Article 208   Failing to Leave Palaces or Halls after the Constructions or Manufactures Are Completed [Gongdian zaozuo ba buchu]

In all cases where constructions or manufactures are needed in the palaces, the officials in charge shall prepare [a list of] the names of laborers and artisans and send it to the gate officials and guarding officers. At the gate, [the gate officials and guarding officers] shall count them one by one and inspect [their features] before they enter for work. When it gets to be the hour of *shen* [4:00–6:00 P.M.], [the gate officials and guarding officers] shall still inspect their features, count them according to the registered number, and let them leave. Those who do not leave shall be punished by strangulation. If the overeers, proctorial or supervisory eunuchs, gate officials, and guarding officers and soldiers, in counting [the laborers and artisans] and inspecting [their features], discover that someone from the registered name list is missing, they shall search for him on the spot and immediately memorialize [to the throne]. If they know the circumstances but do not report, they shall be punished by the same penalty as that for the offenders. If they fail to discover the matters, the penalty shall be reduced three degrees; the punishment shall be limited to 100 strokes of beating with the heavy stick.

Article 209   Leaving or Entering Palace or Hall Gates without Authorization [Zhe churu gongdian men]

[1] In all cases where those who are required to leave palaces or halls and whose names are struck off the gate register remain and, without authorization, do not leave or where those who are accused or impeached [of offenses] and who are prohibited by government documents from [entering palaces or halls] enter palaces or halls without authorization even though their names are not struck off the gate register, in each case they shall be punished by 100 strokes of beating with the heavy stick.

[2] If Imperial Bodyguards are impeached [of offenses] in memorials to the throne, their supervisory officers shall first take away their arms. Any violations shall be punished by the same penalty.

[3] No people shall be allowed to leave or enter the palace or hall at night even though their names are recorded in the palace or hall gate register. If they enter, they shall be punished by 100 strokes of beating with the heavy stick. If they leave, they shall be punished by 80 strokes of beating with the heavy stick. For those who enter without their names being registered, the penalty shall be increased two degrees. For those who bear arms and enter gates of halls [or palaces], they shall be punished by strangulation.

Article 210   Controlling Identification Passes of Palace Eunuchs Who Enter or Leave [Guanfang neishi churu]

In all cases where palace eunuch officials of various directorates or palace grooms go out, officials at each gate shall obtain and keep their personal identification passes, clearly record their names and the numbers [of the passes] on the gate register, and write down the places where they will go and what business they are to do. The gate officials and guarding officers and soldiers shall search their bodies and permit them to go only if they do not carry [anything that shall not be carried]. When they return, they shall be searched the same way and given back the identification passes to enter. [In this way,] each month it will be possible to check the number of times they go out. If a miscellaneous drug is found, immediately require [those who carry it to] take it themselves. For those who do not submit to the search, they shall be punished by 100 strokes of beating with the heavy stick and be sent into military exile. For those who, without receiving imperial rescripts, carry arms and enter the gates of the Imperial City without authorization, they shall be punished by 100 strokes of beating with the heavy stick and be sent into military exile to the distant frontiers. For those who enter the gates of palaces or halls, they shall be punished by strangulation. If the gate officials or guarding officers are negligent in searching, they shall be punished by the same penalty as that for the offenders.

Article 211   Shooting Arrows at Palaces or Halls [Xiang gongdian shejian]

In all cases of shooting arrows or bullets or throwing tiles or stones at the Imperial Ancestral Temple or at imperial palaces or halls, the offenders shall be punished by strangulation. If they shoot at the Altars of Soil and Grain, they shall be punished by 100 strokes of beating with the heavy stick and life exile to 3,000 *li*. Only if they injure others, shall they be punished by decapitation.

Article 212   Arms of Imperial Guards [Suwei ren bingzhang]

In all cases where imperial guards should not be separated from their arms, any violations shall be punished by 40 strokes of beating with the light stick. If they leave their duty stations without authorization, they shall be punished by 50 strokes of beating with the light stick. If they stay overnight at other places, they shall be punished by 60 strokes of beating with the heavy stick. For company commanders or above, in each case the penalty shall be increased one degree. If the commanding officers know the circumstances but do not report, they shall be punished by the same penalty as that for the offenders. If they are negligent in discovering the matters, the penalty shall be reduced three degrees.

Article 213   Prohibiting Those Who Have Been Convicted from Serving as Imperial Guards [Jin jingduanren chong suwei]

[1] In all cases where persons in the capital commit crimes and are punished by the extreme penalty, their household members who live together with them shall be immediately sent to other prefectures to settle. Their relatives as well as those who have ever been convicted shall serve as neither [the emperor's] close attendants in inner palaces nor imperial guards to guard the gates of the Imperial City or of the capital city. Those who deceitfully

serve shall be punished by decapitation. If officials in charge do not use diligence to investigate carefully or if they listen to others' requests or receive payment and permit them to serve, the penalty shall be the same.

[2] If they are selected to serve by special rescripts from the throne, and memorials are replied to and clear files are established, this prohibition shall not be applicable.

Article 214   Intruding into the Imperial Procession [Chongtu yizhang]:
[Failing to Avoid the Imperial Procession][1]

In all places where the Carriage [i.e., the emperor] proceeds, except for close imperial attendants, imperial guards, and escorting officers and soldiers, all other military and civilian personnel shall withdraw. Those who intrude into the procession shall be punished by strangulation. If, in the open country, it is impossible to withdraw at the moment, they may prostrate themselves and wait. If civilian and military officers, without receiving a summons from the throne and without reason, intrude into the imperial procession, they shall be punished by 100 strokes of beating with the heavy stick. If the managers of ceremonial regalia or escorting officers or soldiers deliberately allow them to intrude, they shall be punished by the same penalty as that for the offenders. If they fail to discover [the intrusion], the penalty shall be reduced three degrees.

Article 215   Intruding into the Imperial Procession:
[Appealing for Redress of Wrongs That Are Not True]

In all cases of appealing for redress of wrongs, petitioners are allowed only to prostrate themselves outside the area of procession and wait [for the imperial decision]. If they intrude into the procession and the information they give is not true, they shall be punished by strangulation. If the information they give is true, the penalty shall be exempted.

Article 216   Intruding into the Imperial Procession:
[Failing to Guard against Domestic Animals]

In all cases where domestic animals of military or civilian households run loose, if the guards are not prepared and thus the animals intrude into the imperial procession, the guards shall be punished by 80 strokes of beating with the heavy stick. If the animals intrude into the Imperial City, the guards shall be punished by 100 strokes of beating with the heavy stick.

Article 217   The Camp Gates of the Imperial Traveling Palaces
[Xinggong yingmen]

In all cases concerning the outer or inner camp gates of the imperial traveling palaces, they shall be treated the same as those of the Imperial City. Those who enter without authorization shall be punished by 100 strokes of beating with the heavy stick. The gate of the imperial residence of the inner camp is the same as those of the imperial palaces and halls. Those who enter without authorization shall be punished by 60 strokes of beating with the heavy stick and penal servitude for one year.

Article 218 Climbing over City Walls [Yuecheng]

In all cases of climbing over the walls of the Imperial City, the offenders shall be punished by strangulation. For walls of the capital city, the penalty shall be 100 strokes of beating with the heavy stick and life exile to 3,000 *li*. For city walls of [the seats of] prefectures, subprefectures, districts, or towns, the penalty shall be 100 strokes of beating with the heavy stick. For walls of government buildings, the penalty shall be 80 strokes of beating with the heavy stick. For those who climb the walls but do not go over them, in each case the penalty shall be reduced one degree. For those who climb in order to circumvent the law[, the breaking of which would result in a heavier penalty], in each case they shall be punished according to the heavier penalty.

Article 219 Locking Gates through Which Passing Is Prohibited [Menjin suoyao]

[1] In all cases where the city gates shall be closed but mistakenly they are not locked, the offenders shall be punished by 80 strokes of beating with the heavy stick. If the gates are opened at nonprescribed times without authorization, the penalty shall be 100 strokes of beating with the heavy stick. For the gates of the capital city, in each case the penalty shall be increased one degree. If, because of urgent government affairs, the gates are opened or closed at nonprescribed times, this prohibition shall not be applicable.

[2] If the gates of the Imperial City should be closed but mistakenly are not locked, the offenders shall be punished by 100 strokes of beating with the heavy stick and sent into military exile to distant frontiers. If the gates are opened at nonprescribed times without authorization, the penalty shall be strangulation. If they are opened or closed in accordance with imperial rescripts, there shall be no punishment.

Article 220 Carrying Identification Tablets [Xuandai guanfang paimian]

In all cases where civilian and military officers who attend audiences at the court and palace eunuchs should carry ivory or iron tablets, and cooks and commandants who enter palace treasuries should carry bronze or wooden tablets, if they lose the tablets, the officials shall be fined 20 *guan* of paper currency, and the cooks and commandants shall be fined 10 *guan* of paper currency. If others find the tablets and immediately report to the authorities, they shall be rewarded with the money forfeited from those who lose them. For those who have the tablets but do not carry them, or those who do not have the tablets but enter without authorization, they shall be punished by 80 strokes of beating with the heavy stick. For those who borrow and who lend the tablets, the penalty shall be 100 strokes of beating with the heavy stick. If the crimes are committed in order to circumvent the law[, the breaking of which would result in a heavier penalty], the offenders shall be punished according to the heavier penalty. For those who find the lost tablets and [do not report to the authorities but] hide them, they shall be punished by 100 strokes of beating with the heavy stick and penal servitude for three years. For those who [know others hide the tablets and] accuse them to the authorities, they shall be rewarded with 50 *guan* of paper currency, which shall be forfeited by the offenders. For those who deceitfully carry [others'] tablets to attend a court audience or who, outside [the palaces], deceitfully use officials' names and their tablet numbers and claim to be the said officials and seek things from or do things to others, they shall be punished by strangulation. For those who forge the tablets, they shall be punished by decapitation. Those who accuse the offenders shall be rewarded with 100 *guan* of paper currency, which shall be forfeited from the offenders.

Section 2 Military Administration [*Junzheng*] [Twenty Articles]

Article 221 Moving Government Troops without Authorization [Shandiao guanjun]

[1] In all cases where generals command foot or cavalry troops that guard cities or station troops in frontier towns, if bandits are reported within areas under their control, they shall immediately send persons to make inquiries about the situation and its urgency. They shall first report the matters to their immediately superior officers, who shall transmit the information to the court and petition in memorials for issuing imperial rescripts to move government troops and quell the insurrections. If there is no urgent necessity and they do not first report to their superior officers, or if they report to the superior officers but do not await replies and, without authorization, move foot or cavalry troops under their command, or if their subordinate officers dispatch the troops without authorization, in each case they shall be punished by 100 strokes of beating with the heavy stick and sent into military exile to distant frontiers.

[2] If rebel forces suddenly arrive for a surprise attack, or within cities or towns where foot or cavalry troops are stationed there are people who engage in rebellion or treason, or rebels have persons cooperating from within, so the matters are urgent, or the distance is great, then they may, at their disgression, swiftly move foot or cavalry troops to take advantage of opportunities to suppress and apprehend [the enemy forces]. If the enemy

forces increase and spread and must be suppressed by different units jointly, although the neighboring military guards and battalions are not under [the generals'] command, they may also be moved [by the generals] to act in concert. [The commanding officers and supporting officers shall] both immediately report to their directly superior officers, who shall inform the court. If they do not immediately assemble troops or do not report to their superior officers, or the [commanders of the] neighboring military guards or battalions do not immediately dispatch troops to act in concert, they both shall be punished the same as for moving troops without authorization.

[3] With regard to moving troops within princely establishments in urgent situations, institutions have already been established. Within other areas, if superior officers or high officials use documents to move troops and transfer horses but the documents do not indicate the receipt of imperial rescripts, then those [who are requested to move] shall not leave the places where they are stationed without authorization. If military officers are transferred to other positions or they commit crimes and thus are recalled [for investigation], and if there are no [characters of] "memorializing and receiving imperial rescripts" [in the documents], they are also not permitted to move without authorization. Any violations shall be punished the same.

Article 222   *Reporting Military Matters* [Shenbao junwu]

[1] In all cases where generals participate in military campaigns under regional commanders, if they are ordered by regional commanders to attack and seize cities or fortified sites, after they capture [the targeted places], they shall immediately send messengers at full speed to report on the victory to regional commanders, the Five Chief Military Commissions, and the Ministry of War. They shall also prepare a separate memorial and send it under seal to the throne.

[2] If the number of enemy troops is large and they appear and disappear unexpectedly, and if the forces led [by the generals] are insufficient, [the generals] shall immediately petition the regional commanders to supply additional troops and make plans to suppress and apprehend [the enemy]. If they do not immediately petition at full speed, the regional commanders may consider the seriousness of the matters and punish them accordingly.

[3] If enemy troops come to surrender themselves, [the generals] shall immediately have them sent to the regional commanders, who shall report to the court petitioning for decisions on dealing with them. Those who are greedy to seize the property of those who surrender themselves and thus kill or injure them, or who, on the road, extort [property from them] by force and [cause them to] flee, shall be punished by decapitation.

Article 223   Reporting Military Information at Full Speed
[Feibao junqing]

In all cases of reporting military information at full speed, prefectures and subprefectures outside the capital shall send persons to report to the Provincial Administration Commissions and Regional Military Commissions. In addition, they shall inform the Surveillance Commissions within the said circuits. The military commanders shall send persons to inform the Regional Military Commissions. The Regional Military Commissions shall send persons to inform their immediately superior Chief Military Commission and to report to the throne in sealed memorials. The Provincial Administration Commissions shall send persons to inform the Ministry of War and to report to the throne in sealed memorials. Both the sealed memorials shall be opened before the throne. The Provincial Surveillance Commissions shall send persons to report directly to the throne. Inside the capital, the directly attached military and civilian offices shall send persons to report to their immediately superior Chief Military Commission and the Ministry of War, respectively. In addition, they shall prepare sealed memorials and report to the throne. If they communicate among each other but hide the information and do not immediately memorialize the throne, they shall be punished by 100 strokes of beating with the heavy stick and be dismissed from office without reappointment. If losses or mistakes in military operations result [*shiwu junji*], they shall be punished by decapitation.

Article 224   Requesting Military Supplies at the Frontiers
[Bianjing shensuo junxu]

In all cases where generals who guard frontiers request supplies such as military equipment, money, or provisions, they shall send persons to notify Provincial Administration Commissions and Regional Military Commissions. They shall also send persons to inform the Five Chief Military Commissions and other relevant ministries. In addition, they shall send sealed memorials to the throne. When the official documents arrive at the relevant ministries, they shall be immediately memorialized to have them dealt with, and the messengers shall be sent back. If there is a delay and matters are not immediately memorialized, or relevant government offices do not make reports in the prescribed manner, the offenders shall be punished by 100 strokes of beating with the heavy stick and be dismissed from office without reappointment. If losses or mistakes in military operations result, they shall be punished by decapitation.

Article 225   Losses or Mistakes in Military Operations [Shiwu junshi]

[1] In all cases where armies are engaged in campaigns, if military equipment, provisions, and forage that should be supplied are not prepared within

the prescribed time limit, the responsible officials and functionaries shall each be punished by 100 strokes of beating with the heavy stick. The punishment shall be inflicted on those who are responsible.

[2] If, in contact with the enemy, [the materials] are not sufficient, or military commanders are ordered to move the troops but do not advance the troops on time to act in concert, or assignees are ordered to report the dates [of operations] but violate the prescribed time limit [for doing so], and consequently losses or mistakes result, the offenders shall be punished by decapitation.

Article 226   Violating the Time Limit in Following [Orders] to Go on Campaigns [Congzheng weiqi]

[1] In all cases where military officers or soldiers are engaged in campaigns, if there are fixed dates for departure but they delay and do not proceed, for a delay of one day they shall be punished by 70 strokes of beating with the heavy stick. For each additional three days, the penalty shall be increased one degree. For those who, in order to avoid the campaigns, do things such as deliberately injuring or disabling themselves or falsely claiming to be ill, in each case the penalty shall be increased one degree. In all the [above-mentioned] cases, the punishment shall be limited to 100 strokes of beating with the heavy stick, and [the offenders shall be] sent on the campaigns.

[2] When armies reach enemy territories, if [military officers or soldiers] invent pretexts and violate the time limit, for a delay of one day they shall be punished by 100 strokes of beating with the heavy stick. For a delay of three days, they shall be punished by decapitation. For those who can accrue merit and thus redeem their crimes, the regional commanders may deal with the matters.

Article 227   Arranging for Substitutes in Service by Military Soldiers [Junren tiyi]

[1] In all cases where military soldiers do not personally go on campaign but hire others to substitute for them under their names, the substitutes shall be punished by 80 strokes of beating with the heavy stick, their household registers shall be changed into [military households], and they themselves shall be sent into military service. The soldiers [who hired the substitutes] shall be punished by 100 strokes of beating with the heavy stick and still be sent to military service. If soldiers who defend [fortified cities] hire others to serve under their names, in each case the penalty shall be reduced two degrees. If their sons, sons' sons, younger brothers, brothers' sons, or young and strong relatives who live in the same households voluntarily substitute for them, this is permitted. If the soldiers [who go on campaign or who defend fortified cities] are indeed old, feeble, and disabled, they may report

to their immediately superior offices. When the facts are verified to be true, they shall be relieved of their military status.

[2] If physicians are assigned to receive government medicine and follow the troops on campaign and if they hire unskilled physicians to substitute for them under their names, each shall be punished by 80 strokes of beating with the heavy stick. The money used for hiring shall be forfeit to the government.

Article 228   Commanding Officers Failing to Defend [Their Positions] Tenaciously [Zhujiang bu gushou]

[1] In all cases where generals who guard the frontiers are attacked and surrounded by the enemy in fortified places, if they do not defend the places tenaciously but abandon them without authorization or do not set up defenses and suffer a surprise attack by the enemy, and, as a result, the fortified positions are lost, they shall be punished by decapitation. When [the troops] are confronting the enemy, if those who are on watch on the heights or on patrol fail to give notice at full speed and thus cause the cities to be lost or troops to suffer casualties, they shall also be punished by decapitation. If [their behavior does not result in the loss of cities or troops but in] the enemy crossing the frontiers and capturing people or pillaging, they shall be punished by 100 strokes of beating with the heavy stick and sent into military exile to distant frontiers.

[2] If government troops retreat first when they confront the enemy, or they flee when they besiege enemy cities, they shall be punished by decapitation.

Article 229   Allowing Troops to Pillage [Zongjun lulüe]

[1] In all cases where generals who guard the frontiers, without receiving commands, privately order troops to capture people and seize property beyond the borders, they shall be punished by 100 strokes of beating with the heavy stick and be dismissed from office and sent into military exile. If their subordinates listen to and obey their orders, for military officers and platoon commanders the penalty shall be reduced proportionately by one degree, and only those who cause the action shall be punished. Squad commanders and soldiers shall not be punished.

[2] If soldiers, without receiving orders from their immediately superior officers, privately engage in pillage beyond the borders, the principals shall be punished by 100 strokes of beating with the heavy stick, and the accessories shall be punished by 90 strokes of beating with the heavy stick. If, [as the result of the pillage, foreign] persons are injured, the principals shall be punished by decapitation, and the accessories shall be punished by 100 strokes of beating with the heavy stick. [The accessories in the pillage in which foreign persons are injured and the principals and accessories who do not injure

foreign persons shall] all be sent into military exile. If the immediately superior officers do not control their troops strictly, they shall be punished by 60 strokes of beating with the heavy stick and be returned to their service with their transgressions recorded.

[3] If, in frontier cities, there are rebels who appear and disappear and if [the generals] take advantage of the situation to lead troops to attack and seize them, this prohibition shall not be applicable.

[4] For those who engage in pillage within territories that are already attached to the realm, they shall all be punished by decapitation without distinction of principals and accessories. If the immediately superior officers do not control [their troops] strictly, each shall be punished by 80 strokes of beating with the heavy stick and be returned to their service with their transgressions recorded.

[5] If [the generals] know the circumstances but deliberately connive at the actions, in each case they shall be punished by the same penalty as that for the offenders.

Article 230   Failing to Train Soldiers [Bu caolian junshi]

[1] In all cases where military officers who guard various places do not maintain discipline and do not train [their] soldiers or the fortifications of the cities [under their command] are not whole or armor and weapons are not in proper order and condition, they shall, for the first offense, be punished by 80 strokes of beating with the heavy stick and be returned to their service with their transgressions recorded. For the second offense, the penalty shall be 100 strokes of beating with the heavy stick. Commanders shall be demoted to associate commanders [*tongzhi*]; associate commanders to assistant commanders [*qianshi*]; assistant commanders to battalion commanders; battalion commanders to company commanders; company commanders to platoon commanders; platoon commanders to squad commanders; squad commanders to soldiers. They shall all be sent to guard distant frontiers.

[2] If officers do not control troops strictly or do not care for them properly and thus cause their subordinates to rebel, the immediately superior commanders, battalion commanders, company commanders, and judges shall each be punished by 100 strokes of beating with the heavy stick. Their [commissions] shall be revoked, and they shall be sent into military exile to distant frontiers. If [officers, because of the rebellion by the soldiers,] abandon the cities and flee, they shall be punished by decapitation.

Article 231   Provoking Honorable Persons to Revolt [Jibian liangmin]

In all cases where officials who shepherd the people fail to nourish and care for [the people] but act contrary to the law and provoke honorable persons to revolt so that crowds are gathered to rebel and cities are lost, they shall be punished by decapitation.

Laws on Military Affairs

Article 232   Selling Military Horses without Authorization [Simai zhanma]

In all cases where military soldiers who go on campaigns seize horses, they shall report the full number to the government. If they sell [the horses] without authorization, they shall be punished by 100 strokes of beating with the heavy stick. If military officers sell [the horses], they shall be punished the same and be dismissed from office and sent into military exile. Those who buy [the horses] shall be punished by 40 strokes of beating with the light stick. The horses and the price received shall be forfeit to the government. If military officers or soldiers buy [the horses], they shall not be punished.

Article 233   Selling Military Equipment without Authorization [Simai junqi]

In all cases where military soldiers sell any necessary military equipment that they are given, such as clothing, armor, lances, swords, flags, and banners, they shall be punished by 100 strokes of beating with the heavy stick and be sent into military exile to distant frontiers. If military officers sell them, they shall be punished the same and be dismissed from office and sent into military exile. Those who buy them shall be punished by 40 strokes of beating with the light stick. [Those who sell the items of equipment that] should be forbidden shall be punished on the basis of privately possessing [military weapons and equipment] [Art. 235]. The items of military equipment and the price that is received shall all be forfeit to the government. If military officers or soldiers buy them, they shall not be punished.

Article 234   Destroying or Discarding Military Equipment [Huiqi junqi]

[1] In all cases where generals are issued military equipment, if, after the [tasks of] campaigning or defense are over, they retain [the items of equipment] and do not return them to the government, for [a delay of] 10 days they shall be punished by 60 strokes of beating with the heavy stick. For each additional 10 days, the penalty shall be increased one degree. The punishment shall be limited to 100 strokes of beating with the heavy stick.

[2] If they discard them without authorization, for one item, they shall be punished by 80 strokes of beating with the heavy stick. For each additional item, the penalty shall be increased one degree. For over 20 items, they shall be punished by decapitation. If they lose or mistakenly destroy [the items], in each case the penalty shall be reduced three degrees. For military soldiers, in each case the penalty shall be reduced one more degree. Moreover, investigate the number and levy for repayment. If the damages or losses occur in battles, there shall be no punishment and no compensation.

Article 235   Possessing Prohibited Military Equipment without Authorization [Sicang yingjin junqi]

In all cases where some persons among the people possess, without authorization, prohibited military equipment such as armor for horses or men, shields, tubes of fire, catapults for throwing fire, banners, and signaling devices, for one such item, they shall be punished by 80 strokes of beating with the heavy stick. For each additional item, the penalty shall be increased one degree. For those who manufacture them without authorization, the penalty shall be increased one degree more than that for possessing them without authorization. In each case the punishment shall be limited to 100 strokes of beating with the heavy stick and life exile to 3,000 *li*. If the items are not complete, they shall not be punished. They may be ordered to deliver [the incomplete items] to the government. [The possession or manufacture of] bows and arrows, lances, swords, crossbows, fishing forks, and pitchforks is not prohibited.

Article 236   *Allowing Military Soldiers to Abandon Service*
[Zongfang junren xieyi]

[1] In all cases where supervisory company commanders, platoon commanders, squad commanders, or military functionaries allow military soldiers to go more than 100 *li* away to engage in business or in private farming or [the military leaders] hide the soldiers in their own places and employ them and thus make them abandon military service, for one person, they shall be punished by 80 strokes of beating with the heavy stick. For each additional three persons, the penalty shall be increased one degree. The punishment shall be limited to 100 strokes of beating with the heavy stick, and they shall be dismissed from office and be sent into military exile [to nearby military guards]. If they receive property and release them [the soldiers], they shall be punished on the basis of [accepting property and] subverting the law [Art. 367] according to the heavier penalty. The hidden military soldiers shall all be punished by 80 strokes of beating with the heavy stick. If [soldiers are] privately sent beyond the borders and they die or are captured by the enemy, [the officers] shall be punished by 100 strokes of beating with the heavy stick, and they shall be dismissed from office and sent into military exile to distant frontiers. If the number of people amounts to three, they shall be punished by strangulation. If the immediately superior officers or functionaries know the circumstances but conceal the matters and do not report and investigate, or they falsely claim that [those who disappear] desert and, in collaboration with the offenders, make such a report to the government, they shall be punished by the same penalty as that for the offenders. When squad commanders, platoon commanders, or company commanders allow military soldiers [to abandon service], if their immediately superior commanders, battalion commanders, judges, or supervisory officials or functionaries know the circumstances but deliberately connive at the actions or conceal the matters and do not report and investigate, or if commanders, battalion commanders, or judges

deliberately allow military soldiers [to abandon service], their subordinate company commanders, platoon commanders, or squad commanders know the circumstances but do not report, the penalty shall also be the same.

[2] If they do not control strictly so that such crimes are committed, or they are negligent in discovering and reporting such crimes, for 1 person under squad commanders, 5 persons under platoon commanders, 10 persons under company commanders, 50 persons under battalion commanders, in each case they shall be punished by 40 strokes of beating with the light stick. For 2 persons under squad commanders, 10 persons under platoon commanders, 20 persons under company commanders, 100 persons under battalion commanders, in each case they shall be punished by 50 strokes of beating with the light stick. They shall be returned to service with their transgressions recorded. If the number does not reach these amounts, they shall not be punished.

[3] If military officers employ military soldiers in their own houses but do not hide them or allow them to abandon service, for 1 person, they shall be punished by 40 strokes of beating with the light stick. For each additional 5 persons, the penalty shall be increased one degree. The punishment shall be limited to 80 strokes of beating with the heavy stick.

[4] In all these cases, for each person and each day, 60 *wen* of labor fee shall be levied and be forfeit to the government.

Article 237   *Employing Military Officers or Soldiers by Dukes or Marquises without Authorization* [Gonghou siyi guanjun]

In all cases where dukes or marquises do not receive special imperial rescripts, they shall not privately order military officers or soldiers of various military guards to perform services for them. If there is a violation, for the first and second offenses, they shall be exempted from punishment but have their transgressions recorded. For the third offense, they may be allowed to have the death penalty exempted once. If military officers or soldiers obey the orders, or, when the troops do not go on campaign, they place themselves at the doors of dukes or marquises to serve without authorization, in each case the military officers shall be punished by 100 strokes of beating with the heavy stick, and they shall be dismissed from office and be sent into military exile to distant frontiers. For military soldiers, the punishment shall be the same.

Article 238   *Officers or Soldiers Fleeing from Campaigns or Defense* [Congzheng shouyu guanjun tao]

[1] In all cases where military officers or soldiers engage in campaigns, if they privately flee and return home or flee to other places, for the first

time they shall be punished by 100 strokes of beating with the heavy stick and still be sent on campaign. For the second time, they shall be punished by strangulation. Those who know the circumstances and hide them shall be punished by 100 strokes of beating with the heavy stick and be sent into military exile. If community heads know the circumstances but do not report, they shall be punished by 100 strokes of beating with the heavy stick. When troops return [from campaign], if [officers or soldiers] return first, the penalty shall be reduced five degrees. If they consequently flee, they shall be punished by 80 strokes of beating with the heavy stick. If soldiers of various military guards in the capital flee, for the first time they shall be punished by 90 strokes of beating with the heavy stick and be sent into military exile to nearby military guards. If soldiers who defend fortified cities at various places flee, for the first time they shall be punished by 80 strokes of beating with the heavy stick and still be sent into military exile to their original military guards. For the second time, soldiers both [in and outside the capital] shall be punished by 100 strokes of beating with the heavy stick and be sent into military exile to distant frontiers. For the third time, they shall be punished by strangulation. Those who know the circumstances and hide them shall be punished by the same penalty as that for the offenders; the punishment shall be limited to 100 strokes of beating with the heavy stick and being sent into military exile. If community heads know the circumstances but do not report, in each case the penalty shall be reduced two degrees. If the immediately superior officers know the circumstances and deliberately connive at the actions, in each case they shall be punished the same [as the offenders]. The punishment shall be limited to 100 strokes of beating with the heavy stick, and the offenders shall be dismissed from office and sent into military exile. If military officers or soldiers who flee voluntarily surrender themselves to the government within 100 days, they shall be exempted from punishment. If they voluntarily surrender themselves beyond the time limit, the penalty shall be reduced two degrees. No matter which government offices they surrender themselves to, their cases may be decided [in accordance with this provision].

[2] If soldiers of any military guards go to other guards to serve, they shall be punished the same as for fleeing.

[3] If the immediately superior officers do not diligently control [their soldiers] and thus their soldiers flee, if 5 persons flee under squad commanders, the squad commanders shall be demoted to soldiers. If 25 persons flee under platoon commanders, the platoon commanders shall be demoted to squad commanders. If 10 persons flee under company commanders, one *shi* [of grain] shall be reduced from the commanders' salaries. If 20 persons flee, two *shi* shall be reduced from their salaries. If 30 persons flee, three *shi* shall be reduced from their salaries. If 40 persons flee, four

shi shall be reduced from their salaries. If the number of persons who flee amounts to 50, [their commissions] shall be revoked and they shall be demoted to platoon commanders. If 100 persons flee under battalion commanders, one *shi* [of grain] shall be reduced from the commanders' salaries. If 200 persons flee, two *shi* shall be reduced from their salaries. If 300 persons flee, three *shi* shall be reduced from their salaries. If 400 persons flee, four *shi* shall be reduced from their salaries. If the number of persons who flee amounts to 500, they shall be demoted to company commanders. For those who supervise more soldiers, they shall be judged by calculating and converting the number, and [their salaries shall be] reduced and [their ranks shall be] demoted accordingly. If the number does not reach these amounts, there shall be no punishment. [If the number of soldiers in a military unit is insufficient because of] illness, death, disability, or transfer, this prohibition shall not be applicable.

Article 239   Treating Military Dependents Preferentially [Youxu junshu]
   In all cases where dependents of military officers or soldiers who die in battle or from illness return to their homes, if officials having jurisdiction do not immediately provide supplies and subsidies for the journey, for one day's delay they shall be punished by 20 strokes of beating with the light stick. For each additional three days, the penalty shall be increased one degree. The punishment shall be limited to 50 strokes of beating with the light stick.

Article 240   Curfews [Yejin]
   [1] In all cases where curfews are imposed in the capital city, the period shall be between the third round of the first watch when the bell ceases to sound and the third round of the fifth watch before the bell starts to ring. Any violations shall be punished by 30 strokes of beating with the light stick. Any violations during the second, third, or fourth watch shall be punished by 50 strokes of beating with the light stick. For any violations in cities other than the capital, in each case the penalty shall be reduced one degree. In the case of urgent official matters, illness, birth, or death, they are not subject to this prohibition.
   [2] When the evening bell has not yet ceased to sound or the morning bell has already started to ring, if the night watchmen deliberately detain passersby and falsely accuse them of violating the curfew, they [the night watchmen] shall be punished [for violating the curfew].
   [3] If those who violate the curfew resist arrest or strike or grab [the night watchmen], they shall be punished by 100 strokes of beating with the heavy stick. If they consequently strike people to the extent of fracture or worse, they shall be punished by strangulation. If death results, they shall be punished by decapitation.

Section 3 Guard Posts and Fords [*Guanjin*] [Seven Articles]

Article 241 Passing Guard Posts or Fords without Authorization, by Circumvention, or by Deception [Siyuemao du guanjin]

[1] In all cases where those who do not have written passes pass guard posts or fords without authorization, they shall be punished by 80 strokes of beating with the heavy stick. For those who pass, by circumvention, guard posts otherwise than through gates or [who pass] fords otherwise than by ferries, they shall be punished by 90 strokes of beating with the heavy stick. If they pass frontier posts by circumvention, they shall be punished by 100 strokes of beating with the heavy stick and penal servitude for three years. If they subsequently enter foreign territories, they shall be punished by strangulation. If the guards [in control of the posts or fords] know the circumstances and deliberately connive at the actions, they shall be punished the same. If they are negligent in questioning closely, in each case the penalty shall be reduced three degrees. The punishment shall be limited to 100 strokes of beating with the heavy stick. For military soldiers, the penalty shall be reduced one more degree. In these cases only those who are on duty shall be punished. (Other articles shall follow this.)

[2] For those who have others' written passes and who deceitfully pass the guard posts or fords under others' names, they shall be punished by 80 strokes of beating with the heavy stick. If household members deceitfully pass under other members' names, only household heads shall be punished. If the guards [in control of the posts or fords] know the circumstances, they shall be punished the same. If they do not know, they shall not be punished.

[3] For those who take horses or mules and who privately pass the guard posts or fords or [who pass them] by deception, they shall be punished by 60 strokes of beating with the heavy stick. Those who pass by circumvention shall be punished by 70 strokes of beating with the heavy stick. ("Privately passing" means that persons have written passes but there are no written passes for horses or mules. "Passing by deception" means using the hair color and age of the horses or mules on others' passes. "Passing by circumvention" means that persons pass the guard posts or fords but horses or mules pass by going around.)

Article 242 Deceitfully Issuing Travel Passes [Zhamao gei luyin]

[1] In all cases where travel passes are issued to those who should not receive them, or military personnel deceitfully claim to be civilians or civilians deceitfully claim to be military personnel, or some persons assume others' names and receive travel passes or transfer issued travel passes to others, the offenders shall be punished by 80 strokes of beating with the heavy stick.

If, at the government offices where they pass or at the stations where they stop, they fraudulently exchange [expired] passes, or if officials or powerful or influential persons ask military or civilian yamens to deliver to them without authorization written notes that allow them to go deceitfully through [the guard posts or fords], in each case they shall be punished by 100 strokes of beating with the heavy stick. If the officials or functionaries in charge listen to [the requests] and accede to them or know the circumstances and issue [passes] to them, in each case they shall be punished the same. If they do not accede to them or do not know the circumstances, they shall not be punished.

[2] If police officers exceed their authority and issue passes, the punishment shall also be the same.

[3] If [officials or functionaries in charge] do not establish files but simply take blank sealed passes and fill them out privately and give to others, they shall be punished by 100 strokes of beating with the heavy stick and penal servitude for three years.

[4] If the offenders receive property, calculate the value of the illicit goods; they shall be punished on the basis of [accepting property and] subverting the law [Art. 367]; if they commit the offenses to circumvent the law, in each case they shall be punished in accordance with the heavier penalty.

[5] If military personnel or civilians go beyond 100 *li* but cannot show travel passes, the military personnel shall be punished on the basis of fleeing from military campaigns [Art. 238], and the civilians shall be punished on the basis of privately passing guard posts or fords [Art. 241].

Article 243   Causing Difficulties at Checkpoints [Guanjin liunan]

[1] In all cases where boats pass checkpoints, if guards do not immediately verify and examine [the written passes] and permit the boats to proceed but prohibit them from proceeding without reason, for one day [of delay] they shall be punished by 20 strokes of beating with the light stick. For each additional one day, the penalty shall be increased one degree. The punishment shall be limited to 50 strokes of beating with the light stick.

[2] If officials or powerful or influential persons pass checkpoints in boats and do not submit to verification and examination, they shall be punished by 100 strokes of beating with the heavy stick.

[3] If the wind and waves come up to make it dangerous [to cross], ferrymen shall not take the ferry across. Any violations shall be punished by 40 strokes of beating with the light stick. If [the ferrymen] do not take account of the wind and waves and deliberately set sail, and when they arrive at the middle, they stop the boats and extort money for traveling on the boats, they shall be punished by 80 strokes of beating with the heavy stick. If they consequently kill or injure others, they shall be punished on the basis of deliberately killing or injuring others [Arts. 313, 325].

Article 244 Sending Wives or Daughters of Military Deserters out of Cities
[Disong taojun qinü chucheng]

[1] In all cases where military officers or soldiers who guard the capital city send wives or daughters of military deserters out of the capital city, they shall be punished by strangulation. If civilians commit such offenses, they shall be punished by 100 strokes of beating with the heavy stick. If military officers or soldiers who guard cities or who work on colony farms in various places send wives or daughters of military deserters out of cities, they shall be punished by 100 strokes of beating with the heavy stick and be sent into military exile to distant frontiers. If civilians commit such offenses, they shall be punished by 80 strokes of beating with the heavy stick. If they receive property, calculate the value of the illicit goods; they shall be punished on the basis of [accepting property and] subverting the law [Art. 367] according to the heavier penalty. If the military deserters purchase such actions, the penalty shall be the same. If those who guard the gates know the circumstances and deliberately connive at the actions, they shall be punished by the same penalty as that for the offenders. If they are negligent in questioning and verifying them, the penalty shall be reduced three degrees. The punishment shall be limited to 100 strokes of beating with the heavy stick. For military soldiers, the penalty shall be reduced one more degree.

[2] In the case of sending wives or daughters of persons who are not military deserters out of cities, the penalty shall be 80 strokes of beating with the heavy stick. If the offenders commit such offenses in order to circumvent the law, they shall be punished according to the heavier penalty.

Article 245 Interrogating Spies [Panjie jianxi]

In all cases where spies within the country, whether they are in frontier regions or in the interior of the country, leak information to foreigners, or foreign spies enter the country to make inquiries about things, they, after being questioned and seized by the government, shall be interrogated about those who guide them or those who make the plots. If the cases are found to be true, all the offenders shall be punished by decapitation. If those who guard the places where [the spies] pass through know the circumstances and deliberately connive at the actions or hide them and do not send them to the authorities, they shall be punished by the same penalty as that for the offenders. If they are negligent in questioning [the spies], [the officers] shall be punished by 100 strokes of beating with the heavy stick; and the soldiers, by 90 strokes of beating with the heavy stick.

Article 246 Crossing Frontiers without Authorization or Going to Sea in Violation of the Prohibitions [Sichu waijing ji weijin xiahai]

In all cases of taking horses, cattle, iron articles for military use, copper cash, satin, or silks and, without authorization, crossing frontiers or going to sea to sell [them], the offenders shall be punished by 100 strokes of beating with the heavy stick. For the bearers or carters, the penalty shall be reduced one degree. Goods, wagons, and ships shall all be forfeit to the government. Divide all the [confiscated] property into 10 portions; 3 portions shall be given to the accusers as a reward. For those who take persons or military equipment and cross frontiers or go to sea, they shall be punished by strangulation. If they consequently leak information, they shall be punished by decapitation. If officials in charge of detaining the offenders or those who guard [the checkpoints or fords] collude with the offenders and secretly carry the items, or know the circumstances and deliberately connive at the actions, they shall be punished by the same penalty as that for the offenders. If they are negligent in discovering the matters, the penalty shall be reduced three degrees. The punishment shall be limited to 100 strokes of beating with the heavy stick. For military soldiers, the penalty shall be reduced one more degree.

Article 247   Employing Constables without Authorization [Siyi gongbing]

In all cases where constables are employed without authorization, for one person the offenders shall be punished by 40 strokes of beating with the light stick. For each additional three persons, the penalty shall be increased one degree. The punishment shall be limited to 80 strokes of beating with the heavy stick. For each [constable] and each day, 60 *wen* of salary shall be levied to the government. If officials in charge send [the constables] upon request, they shall be punished by the same penalty as that for the offenders. The penalty shall be inflicted on those who initiate the acts.

Section 4   Stables and Herds [*Jiumu*] [Eleven Articles]

Article 248   Raising Livestock Contrary to Law [Muyang chuchan bu rufa]

In all cases of raising horses, cattle, camels, mules, asses, or sheep, take 100 head as the basis. If there is death, injury, or loss, in each case a report shall be made in accordance with the facts. For those that die, the hide, mane, and tail shall immediately be turned in to the government. The tendons, horns, and hide of cattle shall also be turned in to the government. For each head, the herd directors and deputy herd directors shall each be punished by 30 strokes of beating with the light stick. For each additional 3 head, the penalty shall be increased one degree. When the punishment exceeds 100 strokes of beating with the heavy stick, for every [additional] 10 head, the penalty shall be increased one degree. The punishment shall be limited to 100 strokes of beating with the heavy stick and penal servitude for three years. For sheep, the penalty shall be reduced three degrees from that for horses. For asses and mules, the penalty shall be reduced two degrees from that for horses, cattle, and camels. If the livestock die because they are born prematurely, preserve them in ashes. When the matter is investigated and clarified, there shall be no punishment. In case of loss where compensation needs to be made or injury that makes the livestock unable to be used, the penalty shall be reduced one degree from that for death. The number of those dead or injured shall not be excluded [in calculating the compensation].

Article 249   Breeding Horses [Zisheng mapi]

In all cases where herd directors take charge of mares, 100 head shall constitute a herd, and each year 100 foals shall be born. If only 80 foals are born within one year, the herd directors shall be punished by 50 strokes of beating with the light stick. If 70 foals are born, the penalty shall be 60 strokes of beating with the heavy stick. For officials of the Herd Office [Duqun So] who do not diligently supervise matters, in each case the penalty shall be reduced three degrees. For officials of the Court of the Imperial Stud, the penalty shall be reduced two more degrees from that for the officials of the Herd Office.

Article 250   Verifying Livestock Incorrectly [Yan chuchan bu yishi]

In all cases where government horses, cattle, camels, mules, or asses are not verified and categorized correctly, for one head the offenders shall be punished by 40 strokes of beating with the light stick. For each additional three head, the penalty shall be increased one degree. The punishment shall be limited to 100 strokes of beating with the heavy stick. If the verification of sheep is not correct, the penalty shall be reduced three degrees. If, as a result, the price is increased or reduced, calculate the increase or reduction of the price; they shall be punished for illicit goods obtained through malfeasance [Art. 368]. For those who take [the livestock] for themselves, they shall be punished on the basis of supervisors or custodians themselves stealing [Art. 287]. In both cases they shall be punished according to the heavier penalty.

Article 251   Raising or Treating Emaciated or Sick Livestock Contrary to Law [Yangliao shoubing chuchan bu rufa]

In all cases where emaciated or sick horses, cattle, camels, mules, or asses are raised or treated contrary to law, the offenders shall be punished by 30 strokes of beating with the light stick. If death results, for one head they shall be punished by 40 strokes of beating with the light stick. For each additional three head, the penalty shall be increased one degree. The punishment shall be limited to 100 strokes of beating with the heavy stick. In the case of sheep, the penalty shall be reduced three degrees.

Article 252   Injuring Government Livestock on Their Backs or Necks When Riding Them [Cheng guanchu jipo lingchuan]

In all cases of riding government horses, cattle, camels, mules, or asses contrary to law and thus injuring them on their backs or necks to the point that the wound reaches three *cun* in circumference, the offenders shall be punished by 20 strokes of beating with the light stick. For five *cun* or more, they shall be punished by 50 strokes of beating with the light stick. If [the livestock] are raised [contrary to law] and become emaciated, calculate 100 head as the basis, and for 10 head of emaciated livestock, the herdsmen and the herd director and deputy herd director shall each be punished by 20 strokes of beating with the light stick. For each additional 10 head, the penalty shall be increased one degree. The punishment shall be limited to 100 strokes of beating with the heavy stick. In the case of sheep, the penalty shall be reduced three degrees. Officials of the Herd Office shall be punished according to the number of herd directors they supervise. For officials of the Court of the Imperial Stud, in each case the penalty shall be reduced three degrees from that for the officials of the Herd Office.

Article 253 Failing to Break and Train Government Horses
[Guanma bu tiaoxi]

In all cases where officials who are in charge of raising horses and who are permitted to ride the government horses fail to break and train the horses, for one head they shall be punished by 20 strokes of beating with the light stick. For each additional five head, the penalty shall be increased one degree. The punishment shall be limited to 80 strokes of beating with the heavy stick.

Article 254 Slaughtering Horses and Cattle [Zaisha maniu]

[1] In all cases of privately slaughtering one's own horses or cattle, the offenders shall be punished by 100 strokes of beating with the heavy stick. For camels, mules, or asses, the penalty shall be 80 strokes of beating with the heavy stick. If they mistakenly kill [the livestock], they shall not be punished. If [the livestock] die of illness and they are laid open and skinned without being reported to the government, the offenders shall be punished by 40 strokes of beating with the light stick. The tendons, horns, and hide shall be forfeit to the government.

[2] For those who deliberately kill others' horses or cattle, they shall be punished by 70 strokes of beating with the heavy stick and penal servitude for one and one-half years. For camels, mules, or asses, the penalty shall be 100 strokes of beating with the heavy stick. If, in calculating the value of the illicit goods, the penalty shall be heavier than this one, they shall be punished as comparable to theft [Art. 292]. (This means that in cases where some people deliberately kill others' horses or cattle, if the price is assessed and in calculating the illicit goods the penalty shall be heavier than 70 strokes of beating with the heavy stick and penal servitude for one and one-half years, or in the case of camels, mules, or asses, if the price is assessed and in calculating the illicit goods the penalty shall be heavier than 100 strokes of beating with the heavy stick, in both cases the penalty shall be judged as

comparable to theft. If [the livestock] belong to the government, the offenders shall be punished as comparable to ordinary persons stealing government property [Art. 288]. In all the cases the offenders may be exempt from tattooing. The price shall be levied and returned to the owners.) If [the livestock] are injured but not dead and cannot be ridden or used, or if swine, sheep, or other animals are slaughtered, calculate the reduction in value, and the offenders shall also be punished as comparable to theft [Art. 292]. In each case the reduction in value shall be levied and returned [to the government or the owners]. If the value is not reduced, the penalty shall be 30 strokes of beating with the light stick. ("Reduction in value" refers, for example, to cases in which livestock, such as horses or cattle, worth 30 *guan* of cash are killed, and then they are worth only 10 *guan* of cash; their value is thus reduced by 20 *guan* of cash. If they are injured but not dead and thus worth 20 *guan* of cash, then their value is reduced by 10 *guan* of cash. So calculate the value of the illicit goods on the basis of the reduction in price and also punish the offenders as comparable to theft. If [the livestock] belong to the government, the offenders shall also be punished as comparable to ordinary persons stealing government property [Art. 288]. The reduction in value shall still be levied from the offenders for compensation. "If the value is not reduced" means that although livestock worth, for example, 10 *guan* of cash are killed or injured, their appraised value does not decrease and they are still worth 10 *guan* of cash. Then the penalty shall only be 30 strokes of beating with the light stick, and there shall be no compensation.) For mistakenly killing or injuring, there shall be no punishment; only levy the reduction in value.

[3] For accessories, in each case the penalty shall be reduced one degree.

[4] For those who deliberately slaughter the horses, cattle, camels, mules, or asses of relatives of the fifth degree or above, they shall be punished the same as the owners who privately slaughter their livestock. If they slaughter livestock such as swine and sheep, calculate the reduction in value; they shall be punished for illicit goods obtained through malfeasance [Art. 368]. The punishment shall be limited to 80 strokes of beating with the heavy stick. If they mistakenly slaughter or deliberately injure [the livestock], in both cases they shall not be punished. In each case only the reduction in value shall be levied.

[5] If government or private livestock damage or eat government or private property and consequently are killed or injured, in each case the penalty shall be reduced three degrees from that for deliberate slaughtering or injuring. The reduction in value shall be levied, and the owners of the livestock shall compensate for the property that is damaged or eaten.

[6] For those who deliberately allow government or private livestock to run loose so that they damage or eat government or private property, they shall be punished by 30 strokes of beating with the light stick. If the [value of] the illicit goods entails a heavier penalty, they shall be punished for illicit

goods obtained through malfeasance [Art. 368]. If [the offenses are committed] negligently, the penalty shall be reduced two degrees. In each case they shall compensate for the property that is damaged.

[7] If government livestock damage or eat government property, only penalties shall be inflicted. It shall not be subject to the regulation of compensation.

[8] If livestock are about to butt, ram, kick, or bite persons and they are immediately killed or injured, there shall be neither punishment nor compensation.

Article 255   Livestock Biting and Kicking People [Chuchan yaoti ren]

[1] In all cases where horses, cattle, or dogs are liable to butt, ram, kick, or bite people and they are not marked or tied according to law, or where mad dogs are not killed, the owners shall be punished by 40 strokes of beating with the light stick. If the animals kill or injure people, the owners shall be punished on the basis of negligently [killing or injuring others] [Art. 315]. If they deliberately release [the animals to] kill or injure others, the penalty shall be reduced one degree from that for killing or injuring others in affrays [Arts. 313, 325].

[2] If those who are hired to treat and cure the animals or those who bump the animals without good reason are killed or injured, there shall be no punishment.

[3] For those who deliberately release dogs to kill or injure others' livestock, in each case they shall be punished by 40 strokes of beating with the light stick. The reduction in value shall be levied for compensation.

Article 256   Hiding Newborn Government Livestock
[Yinni zisheng guan chuchan]

In all cases of raising government livestock such as horses, mules, and asses, the newborn livestock shall be reported to the government within 10 days. If the births are concealed and not reported within the time limit, calculate the value of the illicit goods; the offenders shall be punished as comparable to theft [Art. 292]. If they steal and sell the livestock or exchange them, they shall be punished on the basis of supervisors or custodians themselves stealing [Art. 287]. If officials of the Herd Office and the Court of the Imperial Stud know the circumstances but do not report, they shall be punished by the same penalty as that for the offenders. If they do not know the circumstances, none of them shall be punished.

*Article 257   Borrowing or Lending Government Livestock
without Authorization* [Sijie guan chuchan]

In all cases where, without authorization, supervisors or custodians borrow government horses, cattle, camels, mules, or asses for themselves or lend them to others, they and those who borrow them shall each be punished by 50 strokes of beating with the light stick. Verify the [number of] days, and levy the rental price to the government. If the rental price entails a heavier penalty, in each case the penalty shall be increased one degree from that for illicit goods obtained through malfeasance [Art. 368].

Article 258   Government Messengers Demanding to Borrow Horses
[Gongshi rendeng suojie mapi]

In all cases where government messengers are assigned to government missions, if they, at the places they pass through, demand to borrow government horses to ride, they shall be punished by 60 strokes of beating with the heavy stick. In cases of asses or mules, they shall be punished by 50 strokes of beating with the light stick. For officials or functionaries who give [the animals], in each case the penalty shall be reduced one degree. The punishment shall be inflicted on those who are responsible.

Section 5   Postal Relay Stations [*Youyi*]
[Eighteen Articles]

Article 259   Delivering Government Documents [Disong gongwen]: *[Speed of Delivery]*[2]

In all cases where postal relay station soldiers deliver government documents, they shall proceed at the rate of 300 *li* each day and night. For every three units' delay [3/100 of one day] [Art. 43], they shall be punished by 20 strokes of beating with the light stick. For each additional three units, the penalty shall be increased one degree. The punishment shall be limited to 50 strokes of beating with the light stick. As soon as government documents arrive at postal relay stations, regardless of the number of the documents, they shall be immediately delivered. It is not permitted to wait for subsequent documents. For any violations, the postal relay station officials shall be punished by 20 strokes of beating with the light stick.

Article 260   Delivering Government Documents: [Damaged Documents]

In all cases where postal relay station soldiers deliver government documents, if they rub or damage the covers but do not disturb the original seals, for each cover they shall be punished by 20 strokes of beating with the light stick. For each additional three covers, the penalty shall be increased one degree. The punishment shall be limited to 60 strokes of beating with the heavy stick. If they damage government documents, for one document they shall be punished by 40 strokes of beating with the light stick. For each additional two documents, the penalty shall be increased one degree. The punishment shall be limited to 80 strokes of beating with the heavy stick. If they hide the documents or open the original seals, for one document they shall be punished by 60 strokes of beating with the heavy stick. For each additional document, the penalty shall be increased one degree. The punishment shall be limited to 100 strokes of beating with the heavy stick. For secret documents relating to military affairs, regardless of the number of the documents, the offenders shall immediately be punished by 100 strokes of beating with the heavy stick. If they commit such offenses in order to circumvent the law, in each case they shall be punished according to the heavier penalty. If the postal relay station officials do not report the matters, they shall be punished by the same penalty as that for the offenders. If the matters are reported but the officials with authority do not immediately accept and handle them, in each case they shall be punished by the penalty reduced two degrees from that for the offenders.

Article 261 Delivering Government Documents: [Inspection of Postal Relay Stations]

In all cases where the postal relay station chiefs in each district are specifically in charge of making inspection tours of the postal relay stations under them, and where proctorial officials or functionaries personally investigate the postal relay stations once a month, if they are negligent in discovering and reporting offenses [Arts. 259–60], calculate the number of documents that are delayed and covers that are rubbed or damaged but the original seals are not opened, and for 10 documents or more, the postal relay station chiefs shall be punished by 40 strokes of beating with the light stick; the proctorial functionaries, by 30 strokes of beating with the light stick; the officials, by 20 strokes of beating with the light stick. If the government documents are damaged or hidden or the original seals are opened, the penalty for [the postal relay station chiefs] shall be the same as that for the offenders. The penalty for the proctorial functionaries shall be reduced one degree. For the officials, the penalty shall be reduced one more degree. If proctorial officials and functionaries of prefectures and subprefectures are negligent in discovering and reporting the matters, in each case the penalty shall be progressively reduced one degree.

Article 262 Intercepting Sealed Government Documents [Yaoqu shifeng gongwen]

[1] In all cases where officials in various yamens outside the capital transmit sealed documents to the throne, if the superior officials order others to intercept them at the express stations en route and bring them back, regardless of distance, the chiefs and soldiers of the said stations shall proceed to the officials with authority to report. The officials shall immediately petition their superior officials to forward the matter to the ministry concerned.

If the matter proves to be true after investigation, the offenders shall be punished by decapitation. If the chiefs or soldiers of the stations conceal the matter and do not report, each shall be punished by 100 strokes of beating with the heavy stick. If the reports are made but the officials with authority do not immediately accept and handle the cases, the penalty shall also be the same.

[2] For intercepting sealed documents that are addressed to the Five Chief Military Commissions, the Six Ministries, or the Censorate, in each case the penalty shall be reduced two degrees.

Article 263   Damaged Postal Relay Station Buildings [Pushe sunhuai]

In all cases where the express station buildings are damaged but not repaired or where the equipment is not complete or the number of station soldiers is below the complement but no action is taken to make it up, or where the old or infirm are ordered to perform service, the station chiefs shall be punished by 50 strokes of beating with the light stick. The proctorial officials and functionaries in superior offices shall each be punished by 40 strokes of beating with the light stick.

Article 264   Employing Postal Relay Station Soldiers without Authorization [Siyi pubing]

No persons sent on government missions by various yamens shall be permitted to employ postal relay station soldiers to transport government goods or private baggage. Any violations shall be punished by 40 strokes of beating with the light stick. For each man each day, 66 *wen* of compensation for the work performed shall be levied to the government.

Article 265   Government Messengers Delaying in Their Mission [Yishi jicheng]

[1] In all cases where government messengers who use the postal relay stations for ordinary matters violate the prescribed time limit, for one day, they shall be punished by 20 strokes of beating with the light stick. For each additional three days, the penalty shall be increased by one degree. The punishment shall be limited to 60 strokes of beating with the heavy stick. For important military affairs, the penalty shall be increased three degrees. If consequently there are losses or mistakes in military operations, the offenders shall be punished by decapitation. If the officials at various postal relay stations deliberately hide the good horses and make pretexts and do not deliver them [to the messengers] so that the prescribed time limit is violated, clarify the matter through interrogation, and then the station officials shall be punished. If there is flood en route and the road is obstructed and thus it is difficult to proceed, there shall be no punishment.

Laws on Military Affairs 149

[2] If government messengers receive official documents and mistakenly do not proceed to the destinations that are written on the labels but wrongly proceed to other places so that they violate the prescribed time limit, the penalty shall be reduced two degrees. If the matter involves military affairs, the penalty shall not be reduced. If the labels on the documents are written incorrectly, those who wrote the labels shall be punished. The government messengers shall not be punished.

Article 266   Excessively Using Postal Horses [Duocheng yima]

[1] In all cases where government messengers use postal boats or horses beyond the proscribed number, for excessive use of one boat or one horse, they shall be punished by 80 strokes of beating with the heavy stick. For each additional one boat or one horse, the penalty shall be increased one degree. If they should use asses but use horses or if they should use horses of middle or lower grade but demand horses of high grade, they shall be punished by 70 strokes of beating with the heavy stick. If they consequently strike and injure postal relay station officials, in each case the penalty shall be increased one degree. If the postal relay station officials comply with the demand and give [the boats or horses], the penalty shall be reduced one degree from that for the offenders. If horses of high grade should be used but the postal relay station officials give horses of middle or lower grade, the officials shall be punished. If there are no horses of high grade in the postal relay station concerned, there shall be no punishment.

[2] If [government messengers] use the wrong route to ride post, or if they do not change boats or horses when they pass postal relay stations, they shall be punished by 60 strokes of beating with the heavy stick. If, consequently, horses die because [government messengers] proceed [by the wrong route], the penalty shall be increased one degree. The value of the horses shall be levied to the government.

[3] If the matters are not urgent and [the government messengers] do not proceed by the wrong route but the postal horses die en route, compensation shall be made but no punishment shall be inflicted.

[4] If the matters involve urgent military affairs and there are no boats or horses to exchange at the next postal relay station, there shall be neither punishment nor compensation.

Article 267   Accepting Excessive Supplies [Duozhi linji]

In all cases where government messengers receive excessive supplies, calculate [the amount of excess as] illicit goods; they shall be punished on the basis of [accepting property but] not subverting the law [Art. 367]. For the said officials or functionaries who give [the supplies], the penalty shall be reduced one degree. If [the government messengers] forcibly take [the supplies], they shall be punished on the basis of [accepting property and] subverting the law [Art. 367]. The officials and functionaries shall not be punished.

Article 268   Documents That Should Be Provided with Postal Relay Station Services [for Delivery] but Are Not Provided [Wenshu ying jiyi er buji]

[1] In all cases where the court dispatches troops with documents or announces urgent military affairs to generals at the frontiers, or generals at the frontiers or various yamens send military information at full speed to the court, those who deliberately do not send messengers and provide [the messengers] with postal relay station services shall be punished by 100 strokes of beating with the heavy stick. If, consequently, there are losses or mistakes in military operations, they shall be punished by decapitation.

[2] For important matters such as presenting letters of felicitation to the throne, relieving famine, reporting portents, and requesting military supplies, those who deliberately do not send messengers and provide [them] with postal relay station services shall be punished by 80 strokes of beating with the heavy stick. For ordinary matters for which postal relay station services should not be provided but are deliberately provided, the penalty shall be 40 strokes of beating with the light stick.

Article 269   Delaying Government Affairs That Should Be Carried Out [Gongshi yingxing jicheng]

In all cases where those who are assigned to carry out government affairs such as transporting government property and conveying convicts or livestock delay without authorization or violate the time limit that is prescribed for carrying out those affairs, for one day [of delay] they shall be punished by 20 strokes of beating with the light stick. For each additional three days, the penalty shall be increased one degree. The punishment shall be limited to 50 strokes of beating with the light stick. If they violate the time limit in transporting military supplies or in delivering military provisions during military operations, in each case the penalty shall be increased two degrees. The punishment shall be limited to 100 strokes of beating with the heavy stick. If it results that the army is deprived [of supplies] in the presence of the enemy and there are losses or mistakes in military operations, they shall be punished by decapitation. If the messengers mistakenly do not proceed to the destinations that are written on the labels but wrongly proceed to other places so that they violate the prescribed time limit, the penalty shall be reduced two degrees. For matters involving military affairs, the penalty shall not be reduced. If [the violation of the time limit] is because the labels on the documents were written incorrectly, those who wrote the labels shall be punished; the messengers shall not be punished.

Article 270   Occupying the Best Rooms of Postal Relay Stations
[Zhansu yishe shangfang]

In all cases where government functionaries who are sent to manage government affairs outside the capital occupy the main chambers or the best rooms of postal relay stations, they shall be punished by 50 strokes of beating with the light stick.

Article 271   Carrying Private Articles While Riding on Post Horses
[Cheng yima chai siwu]

In all cases where emissaries should ride post horses, if they carry private articles, apart from their personal clothing, for 10 *jin* they shall be punished by 60 strokes of beating with the heavy stick. For each additional 10 *jin*, the penalty shall be increased one degree. The punishment shall be limited to 100 strokes of beating with the heavy stick. For post asses, the penalty shall be reduced one degree. The private articles shall be forfeit to the government.

Article 272   Making Commoners Carry Sedan Chairs without Authorization [Siyi minfu taijiao]

[1] In all cases where, without authorization, officials or functionaries of any yamen or emissaries make commoners carry sedan chairs, they shall be punished by 60 strokes of beating with the heavy stick. If the local officials furnish them, the penalty shall be reduced one degree. If powerful or wealthy households make their tenant farmers carry sedan chairs, the penalty shall be the same. For each person and each day, 60 *wen* of labor charge shall be levied and given [to the laborers].

[2] For women, old or ill persons, or those who hire laborers for wages, this provision shall not be applicable.

Article 273   Family Members of Officials Deceased from Illness Returning to Their Home Villages [Bingguguan jiashu huanxiang]

In all cases where incumbent civil or military officials die from illness in a natural way and their family members do not have the means to return to their home villages, the officials having jurisdiction shall send someone to take charge [of sending them home] and to supply the necessary means and verify the distance and [the number of] family members. Government offices shall furnish food for the journey and send them home. For those who violate [this provision] and do not send them home, they shall be punished by 60 strokes of beating with the heavy stick.

Article 274   Receiving Assignments but Hiring or Sending Others to Perform Them [Chengchai zhuan guji ren]

[1] In all cases where those who receive assignments to transport government property, prisoners, or animals do not personally take charge of

the matters and transport them but hire or send others to act for them in performing the missions, they shall be punished by 60 strokes of beating with the heavy stick. If, as a result, the government property is damaged or animals or prisoners are lost, in each case they shall be punished by the heavier penalty according to the *Code* [i.e., Arts. 145, 414, 416]. The penalty for those who are hired or sent shall be reduced one degree.

[2] If those who receive assignments together mutually substitute for each other and release each other, they shall each be punished by 40 strokes of beating with the light stick. If they take property, calculate the value of the illicit goods; they shall be punished on the basis of [accepting property] without subverting the law [Art. 367]. If there are damages or losses, they shall also be levied and punished in accordance with the articles on damaging or losing government property [Art. 145] or losing prisoners [Arts. 414, 416]. The provision of reducing penalties shall not be applicable.

Article 275 Carrying Private Goods While Riding on Government Animals, Carriages, or Boats [Cheng guan chuchan chechuan fu siwu]

[1] In all cases where those who are sent on public missions ride on government horses, cattle, camels, mules, or asses, the personal goods carried, apart from the clothing and arms they are wearing or carrying, shall not exceed 10 *jin*. Any violations, for up to 5 *jin*, shall be punished by 10 strokes of beating with the light stick. For each additional 10 *jin*, the penalty shall be increased one degree. The punishment shall be limited to 60 strokes of beating with the heavy stick. (This is not applicable to the article on riding post horses [Art. 271].)

[2] If they ride on [government] carriages or boats, the private goods carried shall not exceed 30 *jin*. Any violations, for up to 10 *jin*, shall be punished by 10 strokes of beating with the light stick. For each additional 20 *jin*, the penalty shall be increased one degree. The punishment shall be limited to 70 strokes of beating with the heavy stick. All family members who accompany [those sent on public missions] shall not be punished. If they receive and carry private goods for other persons, the persons who ship the goods shall be punished the same. Their goods shall all be forfeit to the government. If the officials having jurisdiction know the circumstances and connive at the actions, they shall be punished the same. If they do not know, they shall not be punished. If [officials'] family members should be sent, this provision shall not be applicable.

Article 276 Borrowing Post Horses without Authorization [Sijie yima]

In all cases where post officials borrow post horses for their own use without authorization or lend them to others, they and those who borrow [the animals] shall each be punished by 80 strokes of beating with the heavy stick. For post asses, the penalty shall be reduced one degree. Calculate the number of days, levy for the rent, and send it to the government. If the calculated rent entails a heavier penalty, in each case they shall be punished for illicit goods obtained through malfeasance [Art. 368], with the penalty increased two degrees.

NOTES

1. Articles 214–16 are organized under the same title, "Intruding into the Imperial Procession." I follow Edward Farmer's example and add subtitles to the three articles in brackets (Farmer, *Zhu Yuanzhang and Early Ming Legislation,* 216).

2. Articles 259–61 are organized under the same title, "Delivering Government Documents." I follow Edward Farmer's example and add subtitles to the three articles in brackets (Farmer, *Zhu Yuanzhang and Early Ming Legislation,* 218).

CHAPTER 6

Laws on Penal Affairs [Xinglü]

Section 1 Violence and Robbery [*Zeidao*]
[Twenty-eight Articles]

Article 277   Plotting Rebellion and Great Sedition [Moufan dani]

In all cases of plotting rebellion (this means to plot to endanger the Altars of Soil and Grain) or great sedition (this means to plot to destroy the Imperial Ancestral Temple, mausoleums, or palaces), those who jointly plot shall all be sentenced to death by slicing [*lingchi chusi*], without distinction of principals and accessories. Their paternal grandfather, father, sons, sons' sons, brothers, those living in the same household whether or not their surnames differ [from the criminal's], paternal uncles and brothers' sons whether or not they are in different family registers, and [male] relatives of 16 years of age or older, including those who are incapacitated or disabled, shall all be punished by decapitation. Their [male] relatives of 15 years of age or younger, mother, daughters, wives, concubines, sisters, and sons' wives and concubines shall be enslaved into families of meritorious officials. Their property shall be confiscated by the government. Their daughters who have been betrothed may return to their husbands. Their sons and sons' sons who have been adopted by others, and their wives who have been betrothed but the marriages have not yet been consummated shall all not be punished. (This provision also applies to the next article.) Those who know the circumstances and deliberately connive at the actions or conceal the offenders shall be punished by decapitation. For those who capture the offenders, civilian official positions will be bestowed upon the civilians; military commissions will be bestowed upon the military; they will be rewarded with all of the property of the offenders. Those who know the circumstances and report them so that the government arrests the offenders will be rewarded only with the property. Those who do not report shall be punished by 100 strokes of beating with the heavy stick and life exile to 3,000 *li*.

Article 278   Plotting Treason [Moupan]

[1] In all cases of plotting treason (this means to plot to betray this country or to go over to other countries), those who jointly plot shall all be pun-

ished by decapitation, without distinction of principals and accessories. Their wives, concubines, sons, and daughters shall be enslaved into the families of meritorious officials. Their property shall all be confiscated by the government. Their parents, paternal grandfather, sons' sons, and brothers, whether or not they are in different family registers, shall all be punished by life exile to 2,000 *li* to settle there. Those who know the circumstances and deliberately connive at the actions or conceal the offenders shall be punished by strangulation. Those who report the offenses and capture the offenders will be rewarded with all of the offenders' property. Those who know the circumstances but do not report them shall be punished by 100 strokes of beating with the heavy stick and life exile to 3,000 *li*. If plots are made but have not yet been carried out, the principals shall be punished by strangulation; the accessories shall be punished by 100 strokes of beating with the heavy stick and life exile to 3,000 *li*. Those who know the circumstances but do not report them shall be punished by 100 strokes of beating with the heavy stick and penal servitude for three years.

[2] Those who flee and hide in the mountains or in the marshes and do not submit to government exhortations to surrender shall be punished on the basis of plotting treason that has not yet been carried out. If they resist government troops, they shall be punished on the basis of plotting treason that has been carried out.

Article 279   Making Magical Inscriptions and Magical Incantations
[Zao yaoshu yaoyan]

In all cases of making magical inscriptions or magical incantations or of propagating and using [them] to confuse people, the offenders shall all be punished by decapitation. ("All" refers to making no distinction between principals and accessories. They shall all be punished. References to "all" in other articles shall comply with this provision.) For those who privately possess magical inscriptions but do not turn them over to the government, they shall be punished by 100 strokes of beating with the heavy stick and penal servitude for three years.

Article 280   Stealing Sacred Objects of the Spirits Devoted to the Great Sacrifices [Dao Dasi shenyumu]

In all cases of stealing sacred objects of the spirits such as sacrificial utensils and curtains that are devoted to the Great Sacrifices, or of stealing sacrificial offerings such as jade, silk, livestock, and vessels, the offenders shall all be punished by decapitation. (This means that the theft takes place within the palace and after [the sacred objects] have already arrived at the place of sacrifice.) For those who steal objects that have not yet been presented to the spirits or that have not yet been completed or that have already been offered in sacrifices, or who steal other government objects, they shall all be punished by 100 strokes of beating with the heavy stick and penal servitude for three years. If, in calculating the value of the illicit goods, [the penalty for stealing property of that value] is heavier than this penalty, in each case add one degree to the penalty for robbery. (This means that the penalty for robbery by supervisors or custodians [Art. 287] or by ordinary persons [Art. 288] shall be increased one degree.) Moreover, there shall be tattooing.

Article 281   Stealing Imperial Decrees [Dao zhishu]

[1] In all cases of stealing imperial decrees or imperial seals or orders for the dispatch of troops or tallies for transferring ships, the offenders shall all be punished by decapitation.

[2] In cases of stealing official documents of any yamen, the offenders shall all be punished by 100 strokes of beating with the heavy stick and tattooed. If there is a scheme to circumvent the law, the heavier penalty shall be awarded. If the matters involve money or supplies for military actions, the offenders shall all be punished by strangulation.

Article 282   Stealing Seals [Dao yinxin]

In all cases of stealing seals of any yamen or brass night-patrol tallies, the offenders shall all be punished by decapitation. Those who steal *guanfang* seals or *yinji* seals shall all be punished by 100 strokes of beating with the heavy stick and tattooed.

Article 283   Stealing Property from the Palace Treasury [Dao Neifu caiwu]

In all cases of stealing property from the Palace Treasury, the offenders shall all be punished by decapitation. (This includes stealing imperial seals, clothes, or other objects.)

Article 284   Stealing Keys to City Gates [Dao chengmen yao]

In all cases of stealing keys to the gates of the capital city, the offenders shall all be punished by 100 strokes of beating with the heavy stick and life exile to 3,000 *li*. Those who steal keys to the gates of cities that are the government seats of prefectures, subprefectures, or counties and defense commands shall all be punished by 100 strokes of beating with the heavy stick and penal servitude for three years. Those who steal keys to granaries and to other gates shall all be punished by 100 strokes of beating with the heavy stick. Moreover, the offenders shall be tattooed.

Article 285   Stealing Military Equipment [Dao junqi]

In all cases of stealing military equipment, calculate the value of the illicit goods, the offenders shall be punished on the basis of theft [Art. 292]. Those who steal forbidden military equipment shall be punished the same as those

Laws on Penal Affairs

who privately possess them [Art. 235]. If military personnel of troops that are on the move or palace guards steal [such equipment] from each other for their own use, they shall be punished as comparable to ordinary theft [Art. 292]. If the military equipment is returned to government use, in each case the penalty shall be reduced two degrees.

Article 286   Stealing Plants or Trees within the Imperial Mausoleum [Dao yuanling shumu]

In all cases of stealing plants or trees within the Imperial Mausoleum, the offenders shall all be punished by 100 strokes of beating with the heavy stick and penal servitude for three years. For those who steal plants or trees within other persons' tomb areas, they shall be punished by 80 strokes of beating with the heavy stick. If the calculated value of the illicit goods should entail a penalty that is heavier than this, in each case the penalty shall be increased one degree over that for robbery [Arts. 287, 288, 292].

Article 287   Supervisors or Custodians Themselves Stealing Money or Grain from Granaries or Treasuries [Jianshou zidao cangku qianliang]

In all cases where supervisors or custodians themselves steal things such as money or grain from treasuries or granaries, they shall, without distinguishing between principals and accessories, be punished on the basis of all illicit goods taken together. ("All illicit goods taken together" refers to cases such as the following. Suppose that 10 persons on several occasions have together stolen 40 *guan* of government copper cash. Although each person appropriates 4 *guan* for himself, [the 40 *guan* of copper cash shall be] calculated together. Therefore, these 10 persons have each stolen 40 *guan* and shall all be punished by decapitation. Or if 10 persons have together stolen 5 *guan* of copper cash, they shall all be punished by 100 strokes of beating with the heavy stick.) Furthermore, the three characters "stole government (grain/money/thing)" shall be tattooed on their right forearms. (Each character shall be one *cun* and five *fen* long. Every stroke shall be one *fen* and five *li* wide. On the top [the tattoo] shall not pass the joint of the elbow, and at the bottom, it shall not go below the wrist. Other articles shall comply with this provision.)

[The punishment shall be inflicted in accordance with the amount of goods stolen as follows:]

> Less than 1 *guan*: 80 strokes of beating with the heavy stick.
> 1 *guan* to 2 *guan* 500 *wen*: 90 strokes of beating with the heavy stick.
> 5 *guan*: 100 strokes of beating with the heavy stick.
> 7 *guan* 500 *wen*: 60 strokes of beating with the heavy stick and penal servitude for one year.

10 *guan:* 70 strokes of beating with the heavy stick and penal servitude for one and one-half years.

12 *guan* 500 *wen:* 80 strokes of beating with the heavy stick and penal servitude for two years.

15 *guan:* 90 strokes of beating with the heavy stick and penal servitude for two and one-half years.

17 *guan* 500 *wen:* 100 strokes of beating with the heavy stick and penal servitude for three years.

20 *guan:* 100 strokes of beating with the heavy stick and life exile to 2,000 *li*.

22 *guan* 500 *wen:* 100 strokes of beating with the heavy stick and life exile to 2,500 *li*.

25 *guan:* 100 strokes of beating with the heavy stick and life exile to 3,000 *li*.

40 *guan:* decapitation.

Article 288   Ordinary Persons Stealing Money or Grain from Granaries or Treasuries [Changren dao cangku qianliang]

In all cases where ordinary persons steal things such as money or grain from granaries or treasuries, if they have not obtained any property, they shall be punished by 60 strokes of beating with the heavy stick and exempted from tattooing. As long as they obtain property, they shall, without distinguishing between principals and accessories, be punished on the basis of all illicit goods taken together. ("All illicit goods taken together" refers to cases such as the following. Suppose 10 persons on several occasions have together stolen 80 *guan* of government copper cash. Although each person appropriates 8 *guan* for himself, [the 80 *guan* of copper cash shall be] calculated together. Therefore, these 10 persons have each stolen 80 *guan* and shall all be punished by strangulation. Or if 10 persons have together stolen 10 *guan* of copper cash, they shall all be punished by 90 strokes of beating with the heavy stick.) Furthermore, the three characters of "stole government (grain/money/thing)" shall be tattooed on their right forearms.

[The punishment shall be inflicted in accordance with the amount of goods stolen as follows:]

Less than 1 *guan:* 70 strokes of beating with the heavy stick.

1 to 5 *guan:* 80 strokes of beating with the heavy stick.

10 *guan:* 90 strokes of beating with the heavy stick.

15 *guan:* 100 strokes of beating with the heavy stick.

20 *guan:* 60 strokes of beating with the heavy stick and penal servitude for one year.

25 *guan:* 70 strokes of beating with the heavy stick and penal servitude for one and one-half years.

30 *guan*: 80 strokes of beating with the heavy stick and penal servitude for two years.

35 *guan*: 90 strokes of beating with the heavy stick and penal servitude for two and one-half years.

40 *guan*: 100 strokes of beating with the heavy stick and penal servitude for three years.

45 *guan*: 100 strokes of beating with the heavy stick and life exile to 2,000 *li*.

50 *guan*: 100 strokes of beating with the heavy stick and life exile to 2,500 *li*.

55 *guan*: 100 strokes of beating with the heavy stick and life exile to 3,000 *li*.

80 *guan*: strangulation.

Article 289 Forcible Robbery [Qiangdao]

[1] In all cases where forcible robbery is committed but no goods are taken, the offenders shall all be punished by 100 strokes of beating with the heavy stick and life exile to 3,000 *li*. As long as goods are taken, the offenders shall, without distinction between principals and accessories, be punished by decapitation.

[2] If drugs are used to dope others with the aim of taking goods, the punishment shall be the same.

[3] If, at the very moment when a theft [Art. 292] is committed, the offenders resist arrest or kill or injure others, they shall all be punished by decapitation. If fornication is committed during the theft, the punishment shall also be the same. If those who participate in the theft do not give their assistance and do not know the circumstances of resisting arrest, killing or injury, or fornication, they shall only be punished for theft [Art. 292].

[4] If, in the course of theft, the owners discover the offenses, and the offenders abandon the goods and run away, and the owners pursue them and they resist arrest, they shall be punished according to the law on criminals resisting arrest [Art. 412].

Article 290 Rescuing Prisoners by Force [Jieqiu]

[1] In all cases of rescuing prisoners by force, the offenders shall be punished by decapitation. ([The offenders shall be] punished as long as they rescue by force. It is not necessary that they obtain the prisoners.) For those who secretly help prisoners escape, they shall be punished the same as the prisoners. If the penalty amounts to death, then reduce one degree. (Although they are relatives within the degrees of mourning, they should be considered the same as ordinary people.) For those who secretly act to release prisoners but do not obtain them, the penalty shall be reduced two degrees. If, as a result, they injure others, they shall be punished by stran-

gulation. If they kill others, they shall be punished by decapitation. For accessories, in each case the penalty shall be reduced one degree.

[2] When government offices send people to collect money or grain, to take care of public matters, or to arrest criminals, those who gather a crowd on the road to strike them and to take [the prisoners] away shall be punished by 100 strokes of beating with the heavy stick and life exile to 3,000 *li*. If, as a result, they injure others, they shall be punished by strangulation. If they kill others, or the crowd is as many as 10, the principal will be punished by decapitation. Those who strike and cause mortal injury shall be punished by strangulation. For accessories, in each case the penalty shall be reduced one degree. If household members are led to strike and take [the prisoners] away, only the superior and oldest [member of the household] shall be punished. If household members also injure others, they shall still be punished according to [the law] for principals and accessories among ordinary persons.

Article 291   Forcibly Taking in Daytime [Baizhou qiangduo]

[1] In all cases of taking away others' goods in daytime, the offenders shall be punished by 100 strokes of beating with the heavy stick and penal servitude for three years. If the calculated illicit goods entail heavier penalties, the offenders shall be punished for theft [Art. 292], with the penalty increased two degrees. If the offenders injure others, they shall be punished by decapitation. For accessories, in each case the penalty shall be reduced one degree. The two characters "forcibly taking" shall be tattooed on their right forearms.

[2] For those who, as a result of a fire or because a ship is driven into the shallows by wind, forcibly take away others' goods or destroy the ship, the penalty shall also be the same.

[3] For those who fight with others or arrest criminals and then steal their goods, calculate the value of the illicit goods; they shall be punished as comparable to theft [Art. 292]. If they forcibly take away the goods, the penalty shall be increased two degrees. The punishment shall be limited to 100 strokes of beating with the heavy stick and life exile to 3,000 *li*. In such cases, tattooing shall be exempted. If they kill or injure others, in each case, the offenders shall be punished in accordance with the rules on deliberate killing or killing in affrays [Art. 313].

Article 292   Theft [Qiedao]

[1] In all cases where theft is committed but goods are not taken, the offenders shall be punished by 50 strokes of beating with the light stick. Tattooing shall be exempted. As long as goods are taken, the penalty shall be based on the one owner who is the most important, and the offenders shall be punished on the basis of all illicit goods taken together. As for accessories, each shall have his sentence reduced one degree. ("Taking one owner as the

Laws on Penal Affairs

most important" means that, if goods are stolen and obtained from two households, adjudge the penalty for the household whose property is greater in value. "All illicit goods taken together" refers to cases such as the following. Suppose 10 persons jointly steal and obtain goods from one household, and the amount of the illicit goods is valued at 40 *guan*; then although each receives 4 *guan*, the illicit goods shall be aggregated [in arriving at the sentence]. Each of the 10 persons shall be punished on the basis of 40 *guan*. Those who formulate the plan are principals and shall be punished by 100 strokes of beating with the heavy stick. The others are accessories, and the penalty for each of them shall be reduced one degree; their punishment shall be limited to 90 strokes of beating with the heavy stick. Other articles shall comply with this provision.) For the first offense, tattoo on the right forearm the two words "secretly stealing" [*qiedao*]. For the second time, tattoo [the same words] on the left forearm. For the third offense, the offenders shall be punished by strangulation. Punish on the basis of the tattoos that have already been applied.

[2] The penalties for pickpocketing shall be the same.

[3] If military personnel commit theft, although tattooing is exempted, they shall all be punished by strangulation after three offenses.

[The punishment shall be inflicted in accordance with the amount of goods stolen as follows:]

> Less than 1 *guan:* 60 strokes of beating with the heavy stick.
> 1 to 10 *guan:* 70 strokes of beating with the heavy stick.
> 20 *guan:* 80 strokes of beating with the heavy stick.
> 30 *guan:* 90 strokes of beating with the heavy stick.
> 40 *guan:* 100 strokes of beating with the heavy stick.
> 50 *guan:* 60 strokes of beating with the heavy stick and penal servitude for one year.
> 60 *guan:* 70 strokes of beating with the heavy stick and penal servitude for one and one-half years.
> 70 *guan:* 80 strokes of beating with the heavy stick and penal servitude for two years.
> 80 *guan:* 90 strokes of beating with the heavy stick and penal servitude for two and one-half years.
> 90 *guan:* 100 strokes of beating with the heavy stick and penal servitude for three years.
> 100 *guan:* 100 strokes of beating with the heavy stick and life exile to 2,000 *li*.
> 110 *guan:* 100 strokes of beating with the heavy stick and life exile to 2,500 *li*.
> 120 *guan:* the punishment is limited to 100 strokes of beating with the heavy stick and life exile to 3,000 *li*.

Article 293   Stealing Horses, Cattle, and Other Livestock
[Dao maniu chuchan]

[1] In all cases of stealing horses, cattle, asses, mules, swine, sheep, chickens, dogs, geese, or ducks, calculate the value of the illicit goods; the offenders shall be punished on the basis of theft [Art. 292]. If they steal government livestock, they shall be punished on the basis of ordinary persons stealing government property [Art. 288].

[2] For those who steal and kill horses or cattle, they shall be punished by 100 strokes of beating with the heavy stick and penal servitude for three years. For those who [steal and kill] asses or mules, they shall be punished by 70 strokes of beating with the heavy stick and penal servitude for one and one-half years. If the calculated value of the illicit goods entails heavier penalties, the offenders shall be punished for theft [Art. 292], with the penalty increased one degree.

Article 294   Stealing Rice and Wheat from Fields [Dao tianye gumai]

[1] In all cases of stealing rice, wheat, vegetables, or fruit from fields, or stealing utensils or objects that no one is guarding, calculate the value of the illicit goods; the offenders shall be punished as comparable to theft [Art. 292]. Tattooing shall be exempted.

[2] For those who, without authorization, take in the mountains or plains firewood, grass, wood, stone, and the like, which have already been cut or gathered by the efforts of others, the penalty shall be the same.

Article 295   Relatives Stealing from Each Other [Qinshu xiangdao]

[1] In all cases where relatives who do not live together steal goods from each other, for stealing from relatives of mourning for one year [second degree], the penalty shall be reduced five degrees from that for ordinary persons; for relatives of the third degree of mourning, reduce four degrees; for relatives of the fourth degree of mourning, reduce three degrees; for relatives of the fifth degree of mourning, reduce two degrees; for relatives outside the mourning relationship, reduce one degree. In all cases, tattooing shall be exempted. In the case of forcible robbery [Art. 289], if superior or older relatives commit offenses against inferior or younger relatives, the penalty shall also be reduced according to the above provision. If inferior or younger relatives commit offenses against superior or older relatives, they shall be punished as ordinary persons. If killings or injuries occur, the offenders shall be punished by the heavier penalty according to the relevant law on killing or injuring superior, older, inferior, or younger relatives [Art. 307].

[2] If inferior or younger relatives living in the same household lead others to steal property from their own households, the penalty shall be two

degrees heavier than that for privately making use of family property [Art. 94]. The punishment shall be limited to 100 strokes of beating with the heavy stick. As for other persons, the penalty shall be reduced one degree from that for ordinary theft [Art. 292]. Tattooing shall be exempted. If killings or injuries occur, the offenders shall be punished according to the relevant law on killing or injuring superior, older, inferior, or younger relatives [Art. 307]. Even though other persons do not know the circumstances, they shall still be punished according to the law on forcible robbery [Art. 289]. If the killing or injuring is committed by other persons, even though inferior or younger relatives do not know the circumstances, they shall still be punished by the heavier penalty according to the relevant law on killing or injuring superior, older, inferior, or younger relatives [Art. 307].

[3] As for slaves or hired laborers living in the same household who steal the property of the household heads or who steal from each other, the penalty shall be reduced one degree from that for ordinary theft [Art. 292]. Tattooing shall be exempted.

Article 296   Obtaining Property by Threats [Konghe qucai]

[1] In all cases of obtaining others' property by threats, calculate the value of the illicit goods; the offenders shall be punished as comparable to theft [Art. 292] increased one degree. Tattooing shall be exempted.

[2] If relatives of the degree of mourning for one year or less threaten each other, when inferior or younger relatives commit offenses against superior or older relatives, they shall be punished as ordinary persons; when superior or older relatives commit offenses against inferior or younger relatives, they shall be punished according to the law on relatives stealing from each other [Art. 295], with penalties progressively reduced.

Article 297   Obtaining Government or Private Property by Deceit or Cheating [Zhaqi guansi qucai]

[1] In all cases of scheming and obtaining government or private property by deceit or cheating, calculate the value of the illicit goods; the offenders shall be punished as comparable to theft [Art. 292]. Tattooing shall be exempted. If relatives of the degree of mourning for one year or less deceive or cheat each other, they shall be punished according to the law on relatives stealing from each other [Art. 295], with penalties progressively reduced.

[2] If supervisors or custodians deceitfully obtain property in areas under their jurisdiction, they shall be punished on the basis of supervisors or custodians themselves stealing [Art. 287]. If they fail to obtain the goods, the penalty shall be reduced two degrees.

[3] For those who obtain the property from others by making false claims

164   Laws on Penal Affairs

to it or by using deceitful schemes or traps, calculate the value of the illicit goods; they shall be punished as comparable to theft [Art. 292]. Tattooing shall be exempted.

Article 298   Kidnapping Persons or Kidnapping and Selling Persons [Lüeren lüemairen]

[1] In all cases of devising tricks and enticing and seizing honorable persons or kidnapping and selling honorable persons as slaves, the offenders shall all be punished by 100 strokes of beating with the heavy stick and life exile to 3,000 *li*. If [they take them] as wives, concubines, sons, or sons' sons, they shall be punished by 100 strokes of beating with the heavy stick and penal servitude for three years. If, as a result, they injure others, they shall be punished by strangulation. If they kill others, they shall be punished by decapitation. The persons kidnapped shall not be punished and shall be returned to be reunited with their families.

[2] For those who, by using the pretext of raising and adopting [children] to have them change households, purchase honorable persons' children and then sell them, the penalty shall be the same.

[3] In the case of enticing others [to agree to be taken into the offenders' households] or, with mutual agreement, selling honorable persons as slaves, the offenders shall be punished by 100 strokes of beating with the heavy stick and penal servitude for three years. If [they take them] as wives, concubines, sons, or sons' sons, they shall be punished by 90 strokes of beating with the heavy stick and penal servitude for two and one-half years. For the persons who are enticed, the penalty shall be reduced one degree. If they are not yet sold, in each case the penalty shall be reduced one degree. If those who are enticed are 10 years old or younger, although they agree, the penalty shall be the same as that for kidnapping and enticing.

[4] For kidnapping, selling, or enticing others' slaves, in each case the penalty shall be reduced one degree from that for kidnapping, selling, or enticing honorable persons.

[5] For those who kidnap and sell sons or sons' sons as slaves, they shall be punished by 80 strokes of beating with the heavy stick. [For kidnapping and selling] younger brothers, younger sisters, brothers' sons, brothers' sons' sons, daughters' sons, [the offenders'] own concubines, sons' wives, or sons' sons' wives, the penalty shall be 80 strokes of beating with the heavy stick and penal servitude for two years. [For selling and kidnapping] sons' concubines or sons' sons' concubines, the penalty shall be reduced two degrees. [For kidnapping and selling] father's brothers' sons or daughters who are younger than the offenders, father's brothers' sons' sons, or father's brothers' sons' sons' sons, the penalty shall be 90 strokes of beating with the heavy stick and penal servitude for two and one-half years. If these relatives are sold by consent, the penalty shall be reduced one degree; if they are not yet

sold, the penalty shall be reduced one more degree. The inferior or younger relatives who are sold shall not be punished and shall be returned to be reunited with their families.

[6] For those who sell wives as slaves, or who sell relatives of the third mourning degree or more distant as slaves, in each case they shall be punished according to the law on enticing or kidnapping ordinary persons.

[7] If those who harbor the persons who are sold and the buyers know the circumstances, they shall be punished by the same penalty as that for the offenders. For broker-guarantors, in each case the penalty shall be reduced one degree; and the prices shall be forfeit to the government. For those who do not know the circumstances, in both cases they shall not be punished; and the prices shall be returned to the owners.

Article 299   Uncovering Graves [Fazhong]

[1] In all cases of uncovering graves, if coffins are reached, the offenders shall be punished by 100 strokes of beating with the heavy stick and life exile to 3,000 *li*. If coffins are opened and corpses appear, they shall be punished by strangulation. If they uncover graves but do not reach coffins, they shall be punished by 100 strokes of beating with the heavy stick and penal servitude for three years. (In cases where spirits are summoned and coffins [without bodies] are buried, it [the offense] is the same.) If graves have already collapsed or coffins have not yet been buried, and the coffins are stolen, the penalty shall be 90 strokes of beating with the heavy stick and penal servitude for two and one-half years. If the offenders open the coffins and corpses appear, they shall be punished by strangulation. If they steal utensils, objects, bricks, or stones, calculate the value of the illicit goods; they shall be punished as comparable to theft [Art. 292]. Tattooing shall be exempted.

[2] If inferior or younger relatives uncover graves of senior or older relatives, they shall be punished as ordinary persons. If coffins are opened and corpses appear, they shall be punished by decapitation. If they discard the corpses and sell the land where the tomb is, the punishment shall be the same. If purchasers or broker-guarantors know the circumstances, they shall be punished by 80 strokes of beating with the heavy stick. The price shall be forfeit to the government; and the land shall be returned to the relatives in the same lineage. If they do not know the circumstances, they shall not be punished. If superior or older relatives uncover graves of inferior or younger relatives, and coffins are opened and corpses appear, if [the deceased] are relatives of the fifth degree of mourning, they shall be punished by 100 strokes of beating with the heavy stick and penal servitude for three years. If [the deceased] are relatives of the fourth mourning degree or closer, the penalty shall be progressively reduced one degree. For those who uncover graves of sons or sons' sons, and coffins are opened and corpses appear, they shall be punished by 90 strokes of beating with the heavy stick.

Those who have reasons and thus transfer and bury [the corpses] in accordance with the rites shall not be punished.

[3] For cutting up or destroying the corpses of other persons or tossing the corpses into water, in each case the offenders shall be punished by 100 strokes of beating with the heavy stick and life exile to 3,000 *li*. (This refers to cases where the corpses are still at home or in the field and have not yet been buried, and then they are burnt, cut up, or otherwise destroyed. If the corpses are already in the coffins or buried, the offenders shall be punished according to the heavier penalties stipulated in the law of uncovering graves, opening coffins, and causing corpses to appear.) For destroying or discarding the corpses of senior or older relatives of the fifth mourning degree or closer, the offenders shall be punished by decapitation. If the corpses are discarded but not lost or hairs are cut off or the corpses are injured, in each case the penalty shall be reduced one degree. [If senior or older relatives commit such offenses against] inferior or younger relatives of the fifth mourning degree or closer, in each case the penalty shall be progressively reduced one degree from that for ordinary persons. For those who destroy or discard the corpses of sons or sons' sons, they shall be punished by 80 strokes of beating with the heavy stick. If sons or sons' sons destroy or discard the corpses of paternal grandparents or parents, or if slaves or hired laborers destroy or discard the corpses of their household heads, they shall be punished by decapitation.

[4] For those who, in digging in the ground, find corpses but do not immediately bury them, they shall be punished by 80 strokes of beating with the heavy stick. For those who burn coffins in others' graveyards for the purpose of smoking out foxes, they shall be punished by 80 strokes of beating with the heavy stick and penal servitude for two years. If they burn the corpses, they shall be punished by 100 strokes of beating with the heavy stick and penal servitude for three years. [If the offenses are committed in the graveyard of] senior or older relatives of the fifth mourning degree or closer, in each case the penalty shall be progressively increased one degree. [If the offenses are committed in the graveyard of] junior or younger relatives, in each case the penalty shall be progressively reduced one degree from that for ordinary persons. If sons or sons' sons [smoke out foxes in the graveyard] of paternal grandparents or parents, or slaves or hired laborers smoke out foxes in the graveyard of their household heads, they shall be punished by 100 strokes of beating with the heavy stick. If they burn coffins, they shall be punished by 100 strokes of beating with the heavy stick and penal servitude for three years. If they burn the corpses, they shall be punished by strangulation.

[5] For those who level others' graveyards for a field or garden, they shall be punished by 100 strokes of beating with the heavy stick. For those who

bury corpses in others' graveyards, they shall be punished by 80 strokes of beating with the heavy stick and they shall be ordered to bury the corpses elsewhere within a stated time period.

[6] If there are dead persons within the community territory, and if the community heads and the residents of the area do not report to the authorities to investigate but without authorization transfer them to other areas or bury them, they shall be punished by 80 strokes of beating with the heavy stick. If their acts result in losing the corpses, they shall be punished by 100 strokes of beating with the heavy stick. If they cut up or destroy the corpses or discard them in water, they shall be punished by 60 strokes of beating with the heavy stick and penal servitude for one year. If the corpses are discarded but not lost or hairs are cut off or the corpses are injured, in each case the penalty shall be reduced one degree. For those who consequently steal clothes, calculate the value of the illicit goods; they shall be punished as comparable to theft [Art. 292]. Tattooing shall be exempted.

Article 300   Entering Others' Houses at Night without Reason
[Ye wugu ru renjia]

In all cases of entering others' houses at night without reason, the offenders shall be punished by 80 strokes of beating with the heavy stick. If at that moment the owners of the households kill the offenders, they shall not be punished. If the owners detain the offenders and without authorization kill or injure them, the penalty shall be reduced two degrees from that for killing or injuring others in affrays [Art. 325]. If death occurs, they shall be punished by 100 strokes of beating with the heavy stick and penal servitude for three years.

Article 301   The Harborers of Thieves and Robbers [Daozei wozhu]

[1] In all cases where the harborers of forcible robbers [Art. 289] formulate plans, even though they themselves do not act, as long as they receive a share of the illicit goods, they shall be punished by decapitation. If they do not act and receive no share of the illicit goods, they shall be punished by 100 strokes of beating with the heavy stick and life exile to 3,000 *li*. For those who collectively plot forcible robbery, if they act but do not receive a share of the illicit goods, or receive a share of the illicit goods but do not act, they shall all be punished by decapitation. If they neither act nor receive a share of the illicit goods, they shall be punished by 100 strokes of beating with the heavy stick.

[2] If the harborers of thieves [Art. 292] formulate plans, even though they themselves do not act, as long as they receive a share of the illicit goods, they shall be punished as principals. If they do not act and receive no share

of the illicit goods, they shall be punished as accessories; those who direct others at the moment of theft shall be punished as principals. If [the harborers do not formulate plans but] act as accessories, [i.e., they] act but do not receive a share of the illicit goods, or they receive a share of the illicit goods but do not act, they shall still be punished as accessories. If they neither act nor receive a share of the illicit goods, they shall be punished by 40 strokes of beating with the light stick.

[3] For those who originally do not make joint plots but happen to meet together and jointly commit robbery, the persons who direct others at the moment of robbery shall be punished as principals; the others shall be punished as accessories.

[4] For those who know the circumstances of kidnapping, selling or enticing others, or forcible robbery or theft and who receive a share of the illicit goods, calculate the value of the illicit goods; they shall be punished as accessories as comparable to theft [Art. 292]. Tattooing shall be exempted.

[5] For those who know that the items are the result of forcible robbery or theft but deliberately purchase them, calculate the value of the things purchased; they shall be punished for illicit goods obtained through malfeasance [Art. 368]. If they know of the illicit goods but still conceal them, the penalty shall be reduced one degree. In each case the punishment shall be limited to 100 strokes of beating with the heavy stick. If they do not know the circumstances but mistakenly purchase or receive for deposit, in both cases they shall not be punished.

Article 302   Jointly Plotting to Commit Robbery [Gongmou weidao]

[1] In all cases where those who jointly plot forcible robbery do not carry it out at the time but rather commit theft, and those who jointly plot receive a share of the illicit goods, the persons who formulate the plan shall be punished as principals for theft; the others shall all be punished as accessories for theft. If they do not receive a share of the illicit goods, the persons who formulate the plan shall be punished as accessories for theft; the others shall all be punished by 50 strokes of beating with the light stick. Those who plan and direct the robbery at the time shall be punished as principals for theft.

[2] If those who jointly plot theft do not carry it out at the time but rather commit forcible robbery, the persons who do not act but who formulate the plan and receive a share of the illicit goods, regardless of whether they know the circumstances, shall be punished as principals for theft. Those who formulate the plan but do not receive a share of the illicit goods, or those other persons who receive a share of the illicit goods, shall all be punished as accessories for theft. Those who direct others at the moment of the act or those who jointly commit forcible robbery shall be punished without distinction of principals and accessories.

Laws on Penal Affairs

Article 303   Taking Goods Openly or Secretly Each Constitutes Robbery
[Gongqu qiequ jiewei dao]

In all cases of robbery, taking goods openly or secretly each constitutes robbery. ("Taking openly" means that the persons who commit robbery take the goods in an open way [i.e., they don't try to disguise either themselves or the deed]. "Taking secretly" means to take the goods stealthily by acting secretly or hiding one's face. They both constitute robbery.) Things such as utensils, money, and silk must have been moved and left the place of the robbery. As for things such as pearls, jade, and other valuable objects, as long as they have been taken into the hands and concealed, it constitutes robbery even though they have not been taken away. As for things such as wood, stones, and other heavy objects which are beyond the power of a person to bear, although they have been moved from their original location, as long as they have not yet been loaded on to carts, it does not constitute robbery. Things such as horses, cattle, camels, and mules must have been taken away from their fenced enclosures; and animals such as falcons and dogs must have come under the offenders' control. Only then does it constitute robbery. (If someone steals one horse but other horses follow it, they shall not be combined in calculating the value to determine the penalty. But if someone steals one mare and her foals follow her, they shall all be combined in calculating the value to determine the penalty.)

Article 304   Removing Tattoos [Qichu cizi]

In all cases where robbers have been tattooed, they shall all be sent back to their places of original registration to be made to serve as police guides. If they are punished by penal servitude, they shall be made to serve as police guides upon fulfilling their sentences. If they are punished by life exile, they shall be made to serve as police guides in the places of exile. For those who remove the tattoos, they shall be punished by 60 strokes of beating with the heavy stick; and the tattoo shall be replaced.

Section 2   Homicide [*Renming*] [Twenty Articles]

Article 305   Plotting to Kill Others [Mousha ren]

[1] In all cases of plotting to kill others, those who formulate the plan shall be punished by decapitation. The accessories who aid in the crime shall be punished by strangulation. Those [accessories] who do not aid in the crime shall be punished by 100 strokes of beating with the heavy stick and life exile to 3,000 *li*. Only if the killing takes place shall they be punished.

[2] If the acts result in injury instead of death, those who formulate the plan shall be punished by strangulation. The accessories who aid in the crime shall be punished by 100 strokes of beating with the heavy stick and life exile to 3,000 *li*. Those [accessories] who do not aid in the crime shall be pun-

ished by 100 strokes of beating with the heavy stick and penal servitude for three years.

[3] If plots are made and the killing is attempted but nobody is injured, the offenders shall be punished by 100 strokes of beating with the heavy stick and penal servitude for three years. The accessories in each case shall be punished by 100 strokes of beating with the heavy stick. All the conspirators shall be punished.

[4] For those who formulate the plan, even though they do not take part in carrying out the crime, they shall be punished as principals. If the accessories do not take part in carrying out the crime, their penalty shall be reduced one degree from that for those who do.

[5] If, by committing the crime, the offenders obtain goods, the penalty shall be the same as that for forcible robbery. All shall be punished by decapitation without distinction of principal and accessories.

Article 306   Plotting to Kill Imperial Emissaries
or One's Own Superior Officers [Mousha zhishi ji benguan zhangguan]

In all cases where officials or functionaries plot to kill emissaries carrying imperial decrees, commoners plot to kill their own prefects, subprefects, or district magistrates, soldiers plot to kill their own commanders, battalion commanders, or company commanders, or functionaries or government runners plot to kill their own officials of the fifth rank or above, if they have already acted, they shall be punished by 100 strokes of beating with the heavy stick and life exile to 2,000 *li*. If they have caused injury, they shall be punished by strangulation. If they have killed them, they shall all be punished by decapitation.

Article 307   Plotting to Kill Paternal Grandparents or Parents
[Mousha zufumu fumu]

[1] In all cases of plotting to kill paternal grandparents, parents, senior or older relatives of mourning for one year, maternal grandparents, husband, or husband's paternal grandparents or parents, if actions have already been taken, the offenders shall all be punished by decapitation. If the killing has already been done, they shall all be sentenced to death by slicing. For those who plot to kill senior or older relatives of the fifth mourning degree or closer, if actions have already been taken, they shall be punished by 100 strokes of beating with the heavy stick and life exile to 2,000 *li*. If injuries have already been inflicted, they shall be punished by strangulation. If the killing has already been done, they shall all be punished by decapitation.

[2] In cases where senior or older relatives plot to kill junior or younger relatives, if actions have already been taken, in each case they shall be pun-

Laws on Penal Affairs

ished in accordance with the penalty for deliberate killing reduced two degrees. If injuries have already been inflicted, reduce one degree. If the killing has already been done, they shall be punished in accordance with the law of deliberate killing. ("In accordance with the law of deliberate killing" means that in each case they shall be punished in accordance with the provisions for senior or older relatives deliberately killing junior or younger relatives [e.g., Arts. 340–41] in the section "Affrays and Batteries.")

[3] If slaves or hired laborers plot to kill their masters or masters' relatives of the second degree of mourning, maternal grandparents, or relatives of the fifth mourning degree or closer, they shall be punished by the same penalty as that for sons or sons' sons.

Article 308   Killing Adulterous Lovers [Shasi jianfu]

[1] In all cases where a wife or concubine commits adultery with another, if [her own husband] himself catches the adulterer and the adulterous wife at the place of adultery and immediately kills them, he shall not be punished. If he only kills the adulterous lover, the adulterous wife shall be punished in accordance with the *Code* [Art. 390] and be remarried or sold by her husband.

[2] If the wife or concubine, because of adultery, plots [with her adulterous lover] and kills her own husband, she shall be sentenced to death by slicing. The adulterous lover shall be punished by decapitation. If the adulterous lover himself kills the husband, the adulterous wife shall be punished by strangulation even if she does not know the circumstances.

Article 309   Plotting to Kill the Parents of a Deceased Husband [Mousha gufu fumu]

[1] In all cases where a wife or concubine plots to kill the paternal grandparents or parents of her deceased husband, she shall be punished the same as for plotting to kill her present parents-in-law [Art. 307].

[2] If slaves plot to kill their former household heads, they shall be punished in accordance with the rule for ordinary persons [Art. 305]. (This refers to the slaves who are sold to others by their own household heads. They shall be punished as ordinary persons. Other articles shall follow this provision.)

Article 310   Killing Three Persons from One Household [Sha yijia sanren]

In all cases of killing three persons from one household who have not committed capital crimes, or of dismembering others, the offenders shall be sentenced to death by slicing. Their property shall be confiscated and given to the family of the decedent. Their wives and children shall be exiled to 2,000 *li*. Accessories shall be punished by decapitation.

Article 311   Extracting Vitality by Dismembering Living Persons
[Caisheng zhege ren]

In all cases of extracting vitality by dismembering living persons, the offenders shall be sentenced to death by slicing. Their property shall be confiscated and given to the families of the decedent. Their wives, children, and those living in the same households shall all be punished by life exile to 2,000 *li* and settled there even though they do not know the circumstances. Accessories shall be punished by decapitation. If the actions have been attempted but no one is injured, the offenders shall still be punished by decapitation. Their wives and children shall be punished by life exile to 2,000 *li*. Accessories shall be punished by 100 strokes of beating with the heavy stick and life exile to 3,000 *li*. If the community heads know the circumstances but do not report the matters, they shall be punished by 100 strokes of beating with the heavy stick. If they do not know, they shall not be punished. Those who report the matters and thus have the offenders captured shall be rewarded with 20 *liang* of silver by the government.

Article 312   Killing Others by Making or Keeping Gu *Poison*
[Zaoxu gudu sharen]

[1] In all cases of making or keeping *gu* poison that can be used to kill others or of training others [to make or keep *gu* poison], the offenders shall be punished by decapitation. The property of those who make or keep [*gu* poison] shall be forfeit to the government. The offenders' wives, children, and those living in the same households shall all be punished by life exile to 2,000 *li* and settled there even though they do not know the circumstances. If the *gu* poison is used to poison those living in the same households, and if the parents, wives, concubines, sons, or sons' sons of the persons who are poisoned do not know the circumstances of the making of the *gu* poison, they shall not be punished by life exile. If the community heads know the circumstances but do not report the matters, in each case they shall be punished by 100 strokes of beating with the heavy stick. If they do not know, they shall not be punished. Those who report the matters and thus have the offenders captured shall be rewarded with 20 *liang* of silver by the government.

[2] For those who inflict captive spirits [*zao yanmei*] or make spells or incantations [*fushu zuzhou*] in order to kill others, in each case they shall be punished for plotting to kill others [Art. 305]. If, as a result, death occurs, in each case they shall be punished in accordance with the relevant law on killing [Art. 305]. If they wish [only] to cause sickness or pain to others, the penalty shall be reduced two degrees. If sons or sons' sons [commit the crime] against paternal grandparents or parents, or if slaves or hired laborers [commit the crime] against their household heads, in each case the penalty shall not be reduced.

Laws on Penal Affairs

[3] For those who use poison to kill others, they shall be punished by decapitation. If they purchase but do not use [the poison], they shall be punished by 100 strokes of beating with the heavy stick and penal servitude for three years. If those who sell the drugs know the circumstances, they shall be punished the same. If they do not know, they shall not be punished.

Article 313   Killing Others in Affrays or by Intention [Douou ji gusha ren]

[1] In all cases of killing others in affrays, regardless of whether [the offenses are committed] with hands, feet, or other objects, or with metal knives, the offenders shall all be punished by strangulation.

[2] Those who deliberately kill others shall be punished by decapitation.

[3] In cases where several persons jointly plot to strike others collectively and therefore death results, the fatal injury shall be considered to be the most serious blow. The persons who strike shall be punished by strangulation. The persons who make the plots shall be punished by 100 strokes of beating with the heavy stick and life exile to 3,000 *li*. The other persons shall each be punished by 100 strokes of beating with the heavy stick.

Article 314   Depriving Others of Clothes or Food [Bingqu ren fushi]

[1] In all cases of placing extraneous objects in others' ears, nose, or other body orifices, or deliberately depriving others of clothes, food, or drink, and therefore causing injuries, the offenders shall be punished by 80 strokes of beating with the heavy stick. (This refers to such actions as taking away others' clothes during the cold months, taking away others' food or drink when they are hungry or thirsty, or secretly taking away others' stepladders or reins when they climb a height or mount horses.) If they cause others to be maimed or disabled, they shall be punished by 100 strokes of beating with the heavy stick and penal servitude for three years. If they cause incapacitation, they shall be punished by 100 strokes of beating with the heavy stick and life exile to 3,000 *li*. Half the offenders' property shall be given to the incapacitated for their support. If death results, they shall be punished by strangulation.

[2] In cases where snakes, scorpions, or poisonous insects are used to sting and thus injure others, the offenders shall be punished on the basis of injuring others in affrays [Art. 325]. If death results, they shall be punished by decapitation.

Article 315   Killing or Injuring Others in Play, by Mistake,
or by Negligence [Xisha wusha guoshi shashang ren]

[1] In all cases of killing or injuring others in play or, because of being in affrays, killing or injuring bystanders by mistake, the offenders shall each be punished on the basis of killing or injuring others in affrays [Arts. 313

and 325]. For those who plot to kill or intend to kill others but who by mistake kill bystanders, they shall be punished on the basis of deliberate killing [Art. 313].

[2] For those who know that river crossings are deep and muddy but deceitfully claim that they are level and shallow, or who know that bridges or ferries are rotten or leak and are not adequate to carry people across but deceitfully claim that they are sturdy, and who by lies cause others to cross so that they fall into the water and die or get injured, they shall also be punished on the basis of killing or injuring others in affrays [Art. 313].

[3] For those who kill or injure others by negligence, in each case they shall be punished as comparable to killing or injuring others in affrays [Art. 313]. Redemption shall be allowed in accordance with the *Code*, and the money shall be given to the families [of those who are killed or injured]. ("Negligence" refers to the circumstances where ears or eyes cannot perceive the result [*ermu suo buji*] or where thought or planning cannot contemplate the consequence [*silü suo budao*]. For example, when one is shooting birds or animals or, for some reason, tossing bricks or tiles, he unexpectedly kills others. Or when one is climbing to a dangerous height, he loses his footing and thus harms his partners. Or when one is sailing a boat, the boat is driven by the wind; when one is riding a horse, the horse runs wildly; when one is driving a carriage at a rapid speed on a descent, he cannot stop. Or when one is carrying a heavy object together with others, the other persons carrying the object are injured because his strength is insufficient to control [the object]. In all such cases, those who initially do not intend to harm others but who accidentally cause death or injury shall all be punished as comparable to killing or injuring others in affrays [Art. 313]. Redemption shall be allowed in accordance with the *Code*. The money shall be given to the families of those who are killed or injured for burial or medical treatment.)

Article 316   Husbands Striking Transgressing Wives or Concubines to Death [Fu ousi youzui qiqie]

[1] In all cases of killing, without authorization, wives or concubines because they strike or curse the husbands' paternal grandparents or parents, the husbands shall be punished by 100 strokes of beating with the heavy stick.

[2] If husbands strike or curse wives or concubines who consequently commit suicide, they shall not be punished.

Article 317   Killing Sons, Sons' Sons, or Slaves and Putting the Blame on Others [Sha zisun ji nubi tulai ren]

[1] In all cases where paternal grandparents or parents deliberately kill sons or sons' sons, or household heads deliberately kill slaves, and put the

Laws on Penal Affairs

blame on others, they shall be punished by 70 strokes of beating with the heavy stick and penal servitude for one and one-half years.

[2] If sons or sons' sons take the bodies of their deceased paternal grandparents or parents, or if slaves or hired laborers take the bodies of their deceased household heads, and put the blame on others, they shall be punished by 100 strokes of beating with the heavy stick and penal servitude for three years. If [they take the bodies of] their senior or older relatives of the second degree of mourning, they shall be punished by 80 strokes of beating with the heavy stick and penal servitude for two years. If [they take the bodies of] their relatives of the third, fourth, or fifth degree of mourning, in each case the penalty shall be progressively reduced one degree.

[3] If senior or older relatives take the bodies of their deceased junior or younger relatives or of other persons and put the blame on others, they shall be punished by 80 strokes of beating with the heavy stick.

[4] If complaints are made to the government, the offenders shall, according to the seriousness of the complaints, be punished on the basis of falsely accusing law-abiding persons [Art. 359].

[5] If the offenders, as a result, deceitfully obtain property, calculate the value of the illicit goods; they shall be punished as comparable to theft [Art. 292]. If they forcibly take property, they shall be punished as comparable to forcibly taking in daytime [Art. 291]. Tattooing shall be exempted. In each case the heavier penalty shall be inflicted.

Article 318   *Injuring Others with Bows and Arrows* [Gongjian shangren]

In all cases of deliberately slinging bullets, shooting arrows, or throwing bricks or stones toward urban areas or places where people live, the offenders shall be punished by 40 strokes of beating with the light stick. If people are injured, they shall be punished for injuring others in affrays [Art. 325] reduced one degree. If people are killed, they shall be punished by 100 strokes of beating with the heavy stick and life exile to 3,000 *li*.

Article 319   *Killing or Injuring Others with Carriages or Horses* [Chama shashang ren]

[1] In all cases of driving carriages very fast or galloping on horses in streets, markets, or towns without good reason, and thus injuring others, the offenders shall be punished for injuring others in affrays [Art. 325] reduced one degree. If as a result they kill others, they shall be punished by 100 strokes of beating with the heavy stick and life exile to 3,000 *li*. For those who drive carriages very fast or gallop horses in the countryside where no one lives and who consequently injure others and cause death, they shall be punished by 100 strokes of beating with the heavy stick. In all cases 10 *liang* of silver shall be levied for burial expenses.

[2] For those who, because of official business, hurry and gallop and

thus kill or injure others, they shall be punished on the basis of negligence [Art. 315].

Article 320   Incompetent Physicians Killing or Injuring Others
[Yongyi shashang ren]

[1] In all cases where incompetent physicians use medicines or needles to treat others and mistakenly do not follow proper prescriptions and, as a result, cause death, other physicians shall be ordered to examine the medicines and the acupuncture points. If there is no evidences of deliberate harm, [the incompetent physicians] shall be punished on the basis of killing by negligence [Art. 315] and shall not be permitted to [continue to] practice medicine.

[2] For those who deliberately violate the proper prescriptions, fraudulently treat others' diseases, and receive goods, calculate the value of the illicit goods; they shall be punished as comparable to theft [Art. 292]. If they, as a result, cause death or for some reason deliberately use medicines to kill others, they shall be punished by decapitation.

Article 321   Killing or Injuring Others with Spring Bows
[Wogong shashang ren]

In all cases where hunters in the deep mountains or the wilds, where wild animals appear and disappear, dig pits or set up spring bows but do not put up warning poles or ropes, they shall be punished by 40 strokes of beating with the light stick. If, as a result, they injure others, they shall be punished for injuring others in affrays [Art. 325] reduced two degrees. If, as a result, they cause death, they shall be punished by 100 strokes of beating with the heavy stick and penal servitude for three years. Ten *liang* of silver shall be levied for burial expenses.

Article 322   Using Coercion to Cause Others to Die [Weibi ren zhisi]

[1] In all cases of, because of some matters, using coercion to cause others to die, the offenders shall be punished by 100 strokes of beating with the heavy stick. If officials or functionaries or other persons in official service, because of nonofficial business, use coercion to cause commoners to die, the penalty shall be the same. In each case 10 *liang* of silver shall be levied for burial expenses.

[2] For those who use coercion to cause superior or older relatives of the second mourning degree to die, they shall be punished by strangulation. If the relatives are of the third mourning degree or more distant, the penalty shall be progressively reduced one degree.

[3] For those who, because of fornication or robbery, use coercion to cause others to die, they shall be punished by decapitation.

Article 323 Making Private Settlements When Superior or Older Relatives Are Killed by Others [Zunzhang weirensha sihe]

[1] In all cases where paternal grandparents, parents, husbands, or household heads are killed by others, if sons, sons' sons, wives, concubines, slaves, or hired laborers make private settlements, they shall be punished by 100 strokes of beating with the heavy stick and penal servitude for three years. If superior or older relatives of the second mourning degree are killed, but inferior or younger relatives make private settlements, they shall be punished by 80 strokes of beating with the heavy stick and penal servitude for two years. For relatives of the third mourning degree or more distant, in each case the penalty shall be progressively reduced one degree. If inferior or younger relatives are killed but superior or older relatives make private settlements, in each case the penalty shall be reduced one degree. If wives, concubines, sons, sons' sons, wives of sons or sons' sons, slaves, or hired laborers are killed but paternal grandparents, parents, husbands, or household heads make private settlements, they shall be punished by 80 strokes of beating with the heavy stick. For those who receive goods, calculate the value of the illicit goods; they shall be punished as comparable to theft [Art. 292] by the heavier penalty.

[2] If ordinary persons make private settlements about homicide cases, they shall be punished by 60 strokes of beating with the heavy stick.

Article 324 Knowing Companions Plot to Harm [Tongxing zhiyou mouhai]

In all cases where those who know their companions plot to harm others but do not immediately stop them and help [the victims], or after [the victims] are harmed do not report to the authorities, they shall be punished by 100 strokes of beating with the heavy stick.

Section 3 Affrays and Batteries [*Douou*] [Twenty-two Articles]

Article 325 Affrays and Batteries [Douou]

[1] In all cases of affrays and batteries (Quarreling together constitutes an affray. Mutual striking constitutes a battery.), for those who strike others with hands or feet but do not cause injury, they shall be punished by 20 strokes of beating with the light stick. If they cause injury, or if they strike people with other objects but do not cause injury, they shall be punished by 30 strokes of beating with the light stick. If they cause injury, they shall be punished by 40 strokes of beating with the light stick. Blue or red swelling constitutes "injury." Anything other than hands or feet is "another object."

Thus, a weapon can also be ["another object"] if its blade is not used. If a square *cun* of hair or more is pulled out, the penalty shall be 50 strokes of beating with the light stick. If blood comes from the ears or eyes, or if there is an internal injury and [the victim] spits blood, the penalty shall be 80 strokes of beating with the heavy stick. For those who use dirty objects and soil others' heads or faces, the penalty shall also be the same.

For those who break others' one tooth or one finger or toe, wound others' one eye, injure others' one ear or nose, injure others' bones, or injure others with boiling liquid, fire, molten copper or iron, they shall be punished by 100 strokes of beating with the heavy stick. If they pour dirty things into others' mouths or noses, they shall also be punished the same.

For those who break two or more teeth or fingers or completely shave the hair off, they shall be punished by 60 strokes of beating with the heavy stick and penal servitude for one year.

For those who break others' ribs, wound others' two eyes, cause a miscarriage, or injure others with the blade of a metal implement, they shall be punished by 80 strokes of beating with the heavy stick and penal servitude for two years. ("Causing a miscarriage" means that the child dies within the period of responsibility [Art. 326] and that the fetus is more than 90 days old and that the child is formed. [Only under such circumstances shall the offenders] be punished. Although [the miscarriage] is caused by the affray and battery, if the child dies beyond the period of responsibility, or if the fetus is less than 90 days old and the child is not formed, in each case the offenders shall be punished in accordance with specific provisions on striking and injuring. They shall not be punished for "causing a miscarriage.")

For those who break others' one limb, dislocate one joint, or blind one eye, they shall be punished by 100 strokes of beating with the heavy stick and penal servitude for three years.

[2] For those who blind others' two eyes, break others' two limbs, cause others two or more injuries, cause others to become incapacitated because of an old injury, cut off others' tongues, or destroy others' sexual organs, in each case they shall be punished by 100 strokes of beating with the heavy stick and life exile to 3,000 *li*. Moreover, half of the offenders' property shall be confiscated and given to the persons who are injured and become incapacitated for their support. ("Two or more injuries" refers to such cases as striking others so as to blind one eye and break one limb. "Causing others to become incapacitated because of an old injury" refers to such cases as where previously a person was blind in one eye and was thus maimed, and [now] the person's other eye is also blind and thus he becomes incapacitated; or where previously a person's foot was broken and was thus disabled, and [now] the person's one eye is blind and thus he becomes incapacitated. "Cutting off others' tongues" means cutting off a person's tongue and thus making him unable to speak at all. "Destroying others' sexual organs" refers

to such cases as cutting off a male's penis or damaging his testicles, for which the offenders shall be punished by 100 strokes of beating with the heavy stick and life exile to 3,000 *li*, and half of their property shall be confiscated and given to the persons who become incapacitated for support. For those who, contrary to reason, injure women's exterior genitalia, they shall only be punished [by 100 strokes of beating with the heavy stick and life exile to 3,000 *li*]; the provision for confiscating half of the property shall not be applied.) For those who jointly plot and collectively strike and injure others, in each case the persons who cause the most serious injury shall be punished by the heavier [i.e., the above-stipulated] penalty. The penalty for the original plotters shall be reduced one degree.

[3] If, during affrays, people strike and injure each other, in each case investigate the seriousness of the injury and determine the penalty. The penalty for those who strike subsequently and who have reasons shall be reduced two degrees. If they cause deaths or strike older brothers or sisters or paternal uncles, the penalty shall not be reduced.

Article 326   The Period of Responsibility for Crimes [Baogu xianqi]

[1] In all cases concerning the period of responsibility for crimes, order the offenders to have medical treatment provided. If, within the period, [the victims] die as a direct result of their injuries, the offenders shall be punished on the basis of killing in affrays [Art. 313]. (This means that in cases of striking and injuring others, the offenders shall, within the period assigned, care for the victims of the offenses. They shall be punished only if the victims [die] as a direct result of the injury. For example, someone strikes another and injures the head, and in consequence the wind goes from the sore on the head into [the body] and causes death. The offender then shall be punished on the basis of killing in affrays [Art. 313].)

[2] If [the victims] die after the period of responsibility, or although they are within the period of responsibility, their injuries have already been cured and [the recovery] is clearly recorded in the official documents, and they die from other causes, in each case the offenders shall be punished according to the original law on striking or injuring others [Art. 325]. ("Other causes" refers to such cases as someone strikes another and injures the head, but the victim dies, not from getting wind through the head sore, but from another illness. Then in each case the offenders shall be punished according to the original injuries.) If the injury is a fracture or worse and if it is treated medically and cured within the period of responsibility, in each case the penalty shall be reduced two degrees. (The penalty for causing a miscarriage shall not be reduced.) If, even though they recover during the period of responsibility, the persons who are injured become maimed, disabled, or incapacitated, or if, within the period of responsibility, the injuries are not cured, in each case the offenders shall receive the full penalty according to the *Code*.

[3] In cases of striking and injuring others with hands, feet, or other objects, the period [of responsibility for the offense] shall be limited to 20 days.

[4] In cases of injuring others with the blade of a metal implement, boiling liquid, or fire, the period shall be limited to 30 days.

[5] In all cases of breaking limbs, dislocating joints, breaking bones, or causing miscarriages, regardless of whether [the injuries are caused by use of] hands, feet, or other objects, the period shall be limited to 50 days.

Article 327   Quarreling within the Palace [Gongnei fenzheng]

In all cases of quarreling within the palace, the offenders shall be punished by 50 strokes of beating with the light stick. If the sound reaches the place where the emperor is present, or if mutual strikes occur, the penalty shall be 100 strokes of beating with the heavy stick. For injuries of fracture of bones or worse, the penalty shall be increased two degrees from that for injuring others in affrays [Art. 325]. If the offenses take place within the palace halls, the penalty shall be progressively increased one degree.

Article 328   Striking the Imperial Relatives within the Sixth Degree of Mourning [Huangjia tanwen yishang qin beiou]

In all cases of striking the imperial relatives of the sixth mourning degree, the offenders shall be punished by 60 strokes of beating with the heavy stick and penal servitude for one year. If they cause injuries, they shall be punished by 80 strokes of beating with the heavy stick and penal servitude for two years. If the injuries are fractures or worse and thus the penalty is heavier [than 80 strokes of beating with the heavy stick and penal servitude for two years], then the penalty shall be increased two degrees from that for ordinary affrays [Art. 325]. For striking the imperial relatives of the fifth mourning degree or closer, in each case the penalty shall be progressively increased one degree. If the offenders cause incapacitation, they shall be punished by strangulation. If they cause death, they shall be punished by decapitation.

Article 329   Striking Imperial Emissaries or One's Own Head Officials [Ou zhishi ji benguan zhangguan]

[1] In all cases where [emissaries] receive imperial orders to go on missions and officials or functionaries strike them, or where commoners strike their own prefects, subprefects, or district magistrates, or where soldiers strike their own commanders, battalion commanders, or company commanders, or where functionaries or runners strike their own head officials of the fifth rank or above, the offenders shall be punished by 100 strokes of beating with the heavy stick and penal servitude for three years. If they cause injuries, they shall be punished by 100 strokes of beating with the heavy stick and

life exile to 2,000 *li*. If they cause fractures, they shall be punished by strangulation. For striking head officials of the sixth rank or below, in each case the penalty shall be reduced three degrees. For striking associate officials or staff supervisors, in each case the penalty shall again be progressively reduced one degree. If the reduction causes the penalty to be too light, add one degree to the penalty for ordinary affrays [Art. 325]. If the offenders cause incapacitation, they shall be punished by strangulation. If they cause death, they shall be punished by decapitation.

[2] If unranked officials, soldiers, civilians, functionaries, or runners strike officials of the third rank or above who are not their own superior officials, they shall be punished by 80 strokes of beating with the heavy stick and penal servitude for two years. If they cause injuries, they shall be punished by 100 strokes of beating with the heavy stick and penal servitude for three years. If they cause fractures, they shall be punished by 100 strokes of beating with the heavy stick and life exile to 2,000 *li*. For striking and injuring officials of the fifth rank or above, the penalty shall be reduced two degrees. If the reduction causes the penalty to be too light, or if they strike and injure officials of the ninth rank or above, in each case the penalty shall be increased two degrees from that for ordinary affrays [Art. 325].

[3] For those who are sent on official missions outside [their permanent duty stations] and strike officials having authority in those areas, the penalty shall be the same. The offices to which [the officials who are struck] belong should detain and interrogate the offenders.

Article 330   Associate or Other Subordinate Officials Striking Head Officials [Zuozhi tongshu ou zhangguan]

In all cases where, in a yamen, staff supervisors or their subordinate officials strike and injure head officials, in each case the penalty shall be reduced two degrees from that for functionaries or runners striking and injuring head officials [Art. 329]. If associate officials strike head officials, in each case the penalty shall again be reduced two degrees. If the reduction causes the penalty to be too light, the penalty shall be increased one degree to that for ordinary affrays [Art. 325]. If the offenders cause incapacitation, they shall be punished by strangulation. If they cause death, they shall be punished by decapitation.

Article 331   Superior Officials and Subordinate Officials Striking Each Other [Shangsiguan yu tongshuguan xiangou]

In all cases where blows are exchanged between supervisory officials, associate officials, or staff supervisors and subordinate officials whose ranks are higher or commoners within their areas of jurisdiction who are of higher ranks, they shall all be punished as [if they had participated in] ordinary affrays [Art. 325]. If blows are exchanged between officials who are not in the same chain of command and who are of equal rank, they shall also be punished as [if they had participated in] ordinary affrays [Art. 325].

Article 332 *Officials of the Ninth Rank or Above Striking Head Officials* [Jiupin yishang guan ou zhangguan]

In all cases where officials of the ninth rank or above strike officials of the third rank or above who are not in command of them, they shall be punished by 60 strokes of beating with the heavy stick and penal servitude for one year. If they cause fractures or worse, or if they strike and injure officials of the fifth rank or above, or if officials of the fifth rank or above strike and injure officials of the third rank or above, in each case the penalty shall be increased two degrees from that for injuring others in ordinary affrays [Art. 325].

Article 333 *Resisting or Striking Persons Sent to Collect Taxes or to Direct Official Tasks* [Juou zhuisheren]

In all cases where government offices send persons to collect taxes or to direct official tasks but [the households involved] resist and strike or do not obey the persons who are sent, they shall be punished by 80 strokes of beating with the heavy stick. If the injuries are so serious that [the injured persons] suffer internal injuries and thus spit blood or worse, or if the [penalty] for the original offenses is heavier than [those for ordinary affrays], in each case the penalty shall be increased two degrees [from that for ordinary affrays]. The punishment shall be limited to 100 strokes of beating with the heavy stick and life exile to 3,000 *li*. If the offenders cause incapacitation, they shall be punished by strangulation. If they cause death, they shall be punished by decapitation.

Article 334 *Striking Teachers from Whom [the Offenders] Receive Their Education* [Ou shouyeshi]

In all cases of striking teachers from whom the offenders receive their education, the penalty shall be increased two degrees from that for ordinary persons [Art. 325]. If the offenders cause death, they shall be punished by decapitation.

Article 335 *Using Coercion or Physical Strength to Restrain or Bind Others* [Weili zhifu ren]

In all cases where disputes arise, the matters shall be reported to the authorities. Those who use coercion or physical strength to restrain or bind others or torture or lock others up in private households shall all be punished by 80 strokes of beating with the heavy stick. If the injuries are so serious that [the injured persons] suffer internal injuries and thus spit blood or worse, in each case the penalty shall be increased two degrees from that for injuring others in ordinary affrays [Art. 325]. If, as a result, the offenders cause death, they shall be punished by strangulation. In cases of using coercion or physical strength to make other persons strike and thus cause death, those who make [others to strike] shall be punished as principals; and those who strike the blows shall be punished as accessories, whose penalty shall be reduced one degree.

Article 336   Honorable and Mean Persons Striking Each Other
[Liangjian xiangou]

[1] In all cases where slaves strike honorable persons, the penalty shall be increased one degree from that for ordinary persons [Art. 325]. If they cause incapacitation, they shall be punished by strangulation. If they cause death, they shall be punished by decapitation. If honorable persons strike or injure others' slaves [but do not cause death], the penalty shall be reduced one degree from that for ordinary persons. If they cause [the slaves to] die or deliberately kill them, they shall be punished by strangulation. If slaves strike, injure, or kill each other, in each case they shall be punished in accordance with the law on injuring or killing in ordinary affrays [Arts. 313 and 325]. If they take property from each other, this provision shall not be applied.

[2] For those who strike slaves of relatives of the fifth or fourth degree of mourning but do not cause fractures, they shall not be punished. If they cause fractures or worse, in each case the penalty shall be reduced two degrees from that for injuring or killing ordinary persons' slaves. [For injuring or killing slaves of relatives of] the third degree of mourning, the penalty shall be reduced three degrees. If death results, the penalty shall be 100 strokes of beating with the heavy stick and penal servitude for three years. If they deliberately kill [the slaves], they shall be punished by strangulation. If they accidentally kill them, in each case they shall not be punished.

[3] For those who strike hired laborers of relatives of the fifth or fourth degree of mourning but do not cause fractures, they shall not be punished. If they cause fractures or worse, in each case the penalty shall be reduced one degree from that for ordinary persons. [For injuring hired laborers of relatives of] the third degree of mourning, the penalty shall be reduced two degrees. If they cause death or if they deliberately kill [the hired laborers], they shall all be punished by strangulation. If they accidentally kill them, in each case they shall not be punished.

Article 337   Slaves Striking Household Heads [Nubi ou jiazhang]

[1] In all cases where slaves strike their household heads, they shall all be punished by decapitation. If they kill them, they shall all be sentenced to death by slicing. If they accidentally kill them, they shall be punished by strangulation. If they injure them, they shall be punished by 100 strokes of

beating with the heavy stick and life exile to 3,000 *li*. If they strike their household heads' relatives of the second degree of mourning or maternal grandparents, they shall be punished by strangulation. If they injure them, they shall all be punished by decapitation. If they accidentally kill them, the penalty shall be reduced two degrees from that for striking. If they [accidentally] injure them, the penalty shall again be reduced one degree. If they deliberately kill them, they shall all be sentenced to death by slicing. If they strike their household heads' relatives of the fifth degree of mourning, they shall be punished by 60 strokes of beating with the heavy stick and penal servitude for one year. For striking relatives of the fourth degree of mourning, the penalty shall be 70 strokes of beating with the heavy stick and penal servitude for one and one-half years. For striking relatives of the third degree of mourning, the penalty shall be 80 strokes of beating with the heavy stick and penal servitude for two years. If they cause fractures or worse, for relatives of the fifth degree of mourning, the penalty shall be increased one degree from that for striking honorable persons. For relatives of the fourth degree of mourning, increase two degrees; for relatives of the third degree of mourning, increase three degrees. The addition [of degrees] may lead to the death penalty. If they cause death, they shall all be punished by decapitation.

[2] If hired laborers strike their household heads or household heads' relatives of the second degree of mourning or maternal grandparents, they shall be punished by 100 strokes of beating with the heavy stick and penal servitude for three years. If they injure them, they shall be punished by 100 strokes of beating with the heavy stick and life exile to 3,000 *li*. If they cause fractures, they shall be punished by strangulation. If they cause death, they shall be punished by decapitation. If they deliberately kill them, they shall all be sentenced to death by slicing. If they accidentally kill or injure them, in each case the penalty shall be reduced two degrees from that for killing or injuring. If they strike household heads' relatives of the fifth degree of mourning, they shall be punished by 80 strokes of beating with the heavy stick. For relatives of the fourth degree of mourning, the penalty shall be 90 strokes of beating with the heavy stick; and for relatives of the third degree of mourning, 100 strokes of beating with the heavy stick. If the injuries are so serious as to cause internal injuries or spitting of blood or worse, for relatives of the fifth or fourth degree, the penalty shall be increased one degree from that for ordinary persons; and for relatives of the third degree, increase two degrees. If they cause death, in each case they shall be punished by decapitation.

[3] If slaves are guilty of crimes and their household heads or the household heads' relatives of the second degree of mourning or maternal grandparents do not report to the authorities but strike and kill them, they shall be punished by 100 strokes of beating with the heavy stick. If [the slaves]

Laws on Penal Affairs 185

are not guilty of crimes but they kill them, they shall be punished by 60 strokes of beating with the heavy stick and penal servitude for one year. The members of the [slave] households shall all be freed and become honorable persons.

[4] If household heads or household heads' relatives of the second degree of mourning or maternal grandparents strike their hired laborers, if they do not cause injuries, they shall not be punished. If they cause fractures or worse, the penalty shall be reduced three degrees from that for ordinary persons. If, as a result, they cause death, they shall be punished by 100 strokes of beating with the heavy stick and penal servitude for three years. If they deliberately kill them, they shall be punished by strangulation.

[5] If [slaves or hired laborers] disobey orders and [their household heads or household heads' relatives of the second degree of mourning or maternal grandparents], according to the law, punish them and unexpectedly cause death, or accidentally kill them, in each case they shall not be punished.

Article 338   Wives or Concubines Striking Husbands [Qiqie ou fu]

[1] In all cases where a wife strikes her husband, she shall be punished by 100 strokes of beating with the heavy stick. If the husband wishes to divorce her, he may do so. (She shall be punished only if the husband himself makes the accusation to the authorities.) If she causes fractures or worse, in each case the penalty shall be increased three degrees from that for injuring others in ordinary affrays [Art. 325]. If she causes incapacitation, she shall be punished by strangulation. If she causes death, she shall be punished by decapitation. If she deliberately kills her husband, she shall be sentenced to death by slicing.

[2] If a concubine strikes the husband or the principal wife [zhengqi], in each case the penalty shall again be increased one degree. The addition may lead to death.

[3] If a husband strikes his wife and does not cause fractures, he shall not be punished. If he causes fractures or worse, the penalty shall be reduced two degrees from that for ordinary persons [Art. 325]. (He shall be punished only if the wife herself makes the accusation to the authorities.) First hear the case: If the husband and wife are willing to divorce, decide on the penalty and decree the divorce. If they are not willing to divorce, [the husband's] penalty shall be determined and then redeemed. If he causes death, he shall be punished by strangulation. If he strikes and injures concubines and causes fractures or worse, the penalty shall be reduced two degrees from that for striking and injuring his wife. If he causes death, the penalty shall be 100 strokes of beating with the heavy stick and penal servitude for three years. If a wife strikes and injures a concubine, she shall be punished the same as for the husband striking his wife. (She shall also only

be punished if the concubine herself makes the accusation to the authorities.) For accidental killings, in each case they shall not be punished.

[4] If [the husband] strikes his wife's parents, he shall be punished by 100 strokes of beating with the heavy stick. If he causes fractures or worse, in each case the penalty shall be increased one degree from that for injuring others in ordinary affrays [Art. 325]. If he causes incapacitation, he shall be punished by strangulation. If he causes death, he shall be punished by decapitation.

Article 339   Relatives of the Same Surname Striking Each Other
[Tongxing qinshu xiangou]

In all cases where relatives of the same surname strike each other, although they are beyond the five degrees of mourning, as long as the relationships of superior and inferior still exist, the penalty for the superior or older relatives shall be reduced one degree from that for ordinary persons [Art. 325]. For the inferior or younger relatives the penalty shall be increased one degree [from that for ordinary persons]. If death occurs, they shall all be punished on the basis of the rules for ordinary persons.

Article 340   Striking Superior or Older Relatives of the Third
Mourning Degree or More Distant [Ou dagong yixia zunzhang]

[1] In all cases where inferior or younger persons strike older male or female relatives of the same generation in the fifth degree of mourning who are in the same lineage or who are in the maternal line or who are relatives by marriage, they shall be punished by 100 strokes of beating with the heavy stick. [If they strike older relatives of the same generation in] the fourth degree of mourning, they shall be punished by 60 strokes of beating with the heavy stick and penal servitude for one year. [If they strike older relatives of] the third degree of mourning, they shall be punished by 70 strokes of beating with the heavy stick and penal servitude for one and one-half years. For superior relatives, in each case the penalty shall be increased one degree. ("Superior relatives" refers to the relatives who are in the same generation with parents such as father's brothers and their wives, father's sisters, and mother's brothers and sisters.) If they cause fractures or worse, in each case the penalty shall be increased one degree from that for injuring others in ordinary affrays [Art. 325]. If they cause incapacitation, they shall be punished by strangulation. If they cause death, they shall be punished by decapitation.

[2] If superior or older relatives strike inferior or younger relatives but do not cause fractures, they shall not be punished. If they cause fractures or worse [to inferior or younger relatives of] the fifth degree of mourning, the penalty shall be reduced one degree from that for ordinary persons. For fourth degree of mourning, reduce two degrees. For third degree of mourn-

ing, reduce three degrees. If they cause death, they shall be punished by strangulation. If they strike and kill younger male or female relatives of the same generation on the father's side [i.e., father's brothers' sons or daughters], children of father's brothers' sons, or children of father's brothers' sons' sons, they shall be punished by 100 strokes of beating with the heavy stick and life exile to 3,000 *li*. If they deliberately kill them, they shall be punished by strangulation.

Article 341   Striking Superior or Older Relatives of the Second Mourning Degree [Ou jiqin zunzhang]

[1] In all cases where younger brothers or sisters strike older brothers or sisters, they shall be punished by 90 strokes of beating with the heavy stick and penal servitude for two and one-half years. If they cause injuries, they shall be punished by 100 strokes of beating with the heavy stick and penal servitude for three years. If they cause fractures, they shall be punished by 100 strokes of beating with the heavy stick and life exile to 3,000 *li*. If they injure [the older brothers or sisters] with knives, break one limb, or blind one eye, they shall be punished by strangulation. If they cause death, they shall all be punished by decapitation. For those who strike father's brothers or their wives, father's sisters, maternal grandparents, in each case the penalty shall be increased one degree. If they accidentally kill or injure them, in each case the penalty shall be reduced two degrees from that for the killing or injuring. If they deliberately kill them, they shall all be sentenced to death by slicing. (In cases of plotting to kill or of killing deliberately [the superior or older] relatives with outsiders, the outsiders shall be punished in accordance with the laws on deliberately killing others by ordinary persons under the circumstances in which they [the outsiders] formulate the plan and carry out the killing, aid in the crime as accessories, or do not aid in the crime as accessories. Other articles shall follow this provision.)

[2] In cases where older brothers or sisters strike and kill younger brothers or sisters, where father's brothers or their wives strike and kill the father's children or the father's sons' children, or where maternal grandparents strike and kill their daughters' children, they shall be punished by 100 strokes of beating with the heavy stick and penal servitude for three years. If they deliberately kill them, they shall be punished by 100 strokes of beating with the heavy stick and life exile to 2,000 *li*. If they accidentally kill them, they shall not be punished.

Article 342   Striking Paternal Grandparents or Parents [Ou zufumu fumu]

[1] In all cases where sons or sons' sons strike paternal grandparents or parents, or where wives or concubines strike husbands' paternal grandparents or parents, they shall all be punished by decapitation. If they kill them,

they shall all be sentenced to death by slicing. If they accidentally kill them, they shall be punished by 100 strokes of beating with the heavy stick and life exile to 3,000 *li*. If they [accidentally] injure them, they shall be punished by 100 strokes of beating with the heavy stick and penal servitude for three years.

[2] If sons or sons' sons disobey instructions [*weifan jiaoling*], and paternal grandparents or parents, contrary to a reasonable manner, strike and kill them, they shall be punished by 100 strokes of beating with the heavy stick. If they deliberately kill them, they shall be punished by 60 strokes of beating with the heavy stick and penal servitude for one year. If their proper mothers, stepmothers, carrying mothers, or adoptive mothers kill them, in each case the penalty shall be increased one degree. If they cause the extinction of a line of descent, they shall be punished by strangulation. If they [superior relatives], contrary to a reasonable manner, strike wives of sons or of sons' sons or strike the adopted sons or sons' sons of different surnames to the point of disability, they shall be punished by 80 strokes of beating with the heavy stick. If they cause incapacitation, the penalty shall be increased one degree. [The wives of sons or of sons' sons and the adopted sons or sons' sons of different surnames] shall all be returned to their own lineages. The wives of sons or of sons' sons shall require the return of their dowry and be given 10 *liang* of silver for their support. The adopted sons or sons' sons shall be given their share of the property for their support. If [the senior relatives] cause death, in each case they shall be punished by 100 strokes of beating with the heavy stick and penal servitude for three years. If they deliberately kill them, in each case they shall be punished by 100 strokes of beating with the heavy stick and life exile to 2,000 *li*. If the victims are concubines [instead of wives], in each case the penalty shall be reduced two degrees.

[3] If sons or sons' sons strike or curse paternal grandparents or parents, or wives or concubines strike or curse husbands' paternal grandparents or parents, and they [i.e., sons, sons' sons, wives, or concubines] are struck to death, or if they disobey instructions and are disciplined according to the law and deaths happen to result, or they are killed accidentally, then in each case there shall be no punishment.

Article 343   Wives or Concubines and Husbands' Relatives Striking Each Other [Qiqie yu fu qinshu xiangou]

[1] In all cases where wives or concubines strike their husbands' superior or older relatives of the second mourning degree or more distant, or of the fifth mourning degree or closer, they shall be punished the same as husbands who strike them [the relatives] [Arts. 340–41]. If they cause death, in each case they shall be punished by decapitation.

[2] If wives strike and injure [husbands'] inferior relatives, they shall be punished the same as husbands who strike them [the inferior relatives] [Art. 340]. If they cause death, they shall be punished by strangulation.

[3] If [wives] strike and kill husbands' brothers' sons, they shall be punished by 100 strokes of beating with the heavy stick and life exile to 3,000 li. If they deliberately kill them, they shall be punished by strangulation. If concubines commit such crimes, they shall be punished in accordance with the law on ordinary affrays [Art. 325].

[4] If superior or older relatives strike and injure wives of inferior or younger relatives, the penalty shall be reduced one degree from that for ordinary persons [Art. 325]. If the victims are concubines, the penalty shall be reduced one more degree. If death results, the offenders shall be punished by strangulation.

[5] If younger brothers or sisters strike older brothers' wives, the penalty shall be increased one degree from that for ordinary persons [Art. 325].

[6] If older brothers or sisters strike younger brothers' wives, or if wives strike husbands' younger brothers or sisters or younger brothers' wives, in each case the penalty shall be reduced one degree from that for ordinary persons [Art. 325]. If the victims are concubines, the penalty shall be reduced one more degree.

[7] For those who strike the husbands of older or younger sisters, the older or younger brothers of wives, or the husbands of husbands' older or younger sisters, they shall be punished on the basis of ordinary affrays [Art. 325]. If concubines commit such crimes, in each case the penalty shall be increased one degree.

[8] If concubines strike the sons of husbands' concubines, the penalty shall be reduced two degrees from that for ordinary persons [Art. 325]. If they strike sons of wives, they shall be punished as ordinary persons. If sons of wives strike and injure their father's concubines, the penalty shall be increased one degree from that for ordinary persons. If sons of concubines strike and injure their father's concubines, the penalty shall be increased two more degrees.

[9] If death results, in each case the offenders shall be punished as ordinary persons [Art. 325].

Article 344 Striking Sons of Wives by Their Former Husbands
[Ou qi qianfu zhi zi]

[1] In all cases of striking sons of wives by their former husbands (this refers to those who previously lived in the same household, but who now live apart), the penalty shall be reduced one degree from that for ordinary persons [Art. 325]. If they live together, the penalty shall be reduced one more degree. If death results, the offenders shall be punished by strangulation.

[2] For those who strike stepfathers (this also refers to those who previously lived in the same household, but who now live apart), they shall be punished by 60 strokes of beating with the heavy stick and penal servitude for one year. If they cause fractures or worse, the penalty shall be increased one degree from that for ordinary affrays [Art. 325]. If they live together,

the penalty shall be increased one more degree. If death results, the offenders shall be punished by decapitation.

[3] For deliberate killing, or for those who have never lived together, in each case they shall be punished as ordinary persons [Arts. 313, 325].

Article 345 Wives or Concubines Striking Parents of Deceased Husbands [Qiqie ou gufu fumu]

[1] In all cases where wives' or concubines' husbands die and they remarry, if they strike the paternal grandparents or parents of the deceased husbands, they shall be punished the same as for striking their parents-in-law [Art. 342]. If the former parents-in-law strike the deceased sons' or sons' sons' wives or concubines who have remarried, they shall also be punished the same as for striking the wives of their sons or sons' sons [Art. 342].

[2] If slaves strike former household heads, or household heads strike former slaves, in each case they shall be punished as ordinary persons [Art. 325].

Article 346 When Father or Paternal Grandfather Is Struck [Fuzu bei ou]

[1] In all cases where paternal grandparents or parents are struck by others and their sons or sons' sons immediately aid them and return the strikes, if they do not cause injuries, they shall not be punished. If they cause fractures or worse, the penalty shall be reduced three degrees from that for ordinary affrays [Art. 325]. If they cause death, they shall be punished in accordance with the ordinary law [Art. 325].

[2] If paternal grandparents or parents are killed by others and their sons or sons' sons, without authorization, kill the offending persons, they shall be punished by 60 strokes of beating with the heavy stick. If they immediately kill the offenders, they shall not be punished.

Section 4 Cursing [*Mali*] [Eight Articles]

Article 347 Cursing Others [Maren]

("*Ma*" refers to humiliating others with bad language; "*li*" refers to slandering each other with lewd words. The intentions of these articles are the same as those in the section "Affrays and Batteries," but the circumstances of cursing are minor. Therefore, the penalties are accordingly light.)

In all cases of cursing others, the offenders shall be punished by 10 strokes of beating with the light stick. For those who curse each other, they shall each be punished by 10 strokes of beating with the light stick.

Article 348 Cursing Imperial Emissaries or One's Own Head Official [Ma zhishi ji benguan zhangguan]

In all cases where [emissaries] receive imperial orders to go on missions and officials or functionaries curse them, or where commoners curse their own prefects, subprefects, or district magistrates, or where soldiers curse their own commanders, battalion commanders, or company commanders, or where functionaries or runners curse their own head officials of the fifth rank or above, the offenders shall be punished by 100 strokes of beating with the heavy stick. For those who curse officials of the sixth rank or below, in each case the penalty shall be reduced three degrees. For those who curse associate officials or staff supervisors, in each case the penalty shall be progressively reduced one more degree. (They shall be punished only if [the officials] themselves hear the curse.)

Article 349   Associate or Other Subordinate Officials Cursing Head Officials [Zuozhi tongshu ma zhangguan]
  In all cases where staff supervisors or their subordinate officials curse head officials of the fifth rank or above, they shall be punished by 80 strokes of beating with the heavy stick. If they curse head officials of the sixth rank or below, the penalty shall be reduced three degrees. If associate officials curse head officials, in each case the penalty shall again be reduced two degrees. (They shall be punished only if [the head officials] themselves hear the curse.)

Article 350   Slaves Cursing Household Heads [Nubi ma jiazhang]
  In all cases where slaves curse their household heads, they shall be punished by strangulation. If they curse their household heads' relatives of the second degree of mourning or maternal grandparents, they shall be punished by 80 strokes of beating with the heavy stick and penal servitude for two years. For cursing relatives of the third degree of mourning, the penalty shall be 80 strokes of beating with the heavy stick; fourth degree, 70 strokes of beating with the heavy stick; fifth degree, 60 strokes of beating with the heavy stick. If hired laborers curse their household heads, they shall be punished by 80 strokes of beating with the heavy stick and penal servitude for two years. If they curse their household heads' relatives of the second degree of mourning or maternal grandparents, they shall be punished by 100 strokes of beating with the heavy stick. For cursing relatives of the third degree of mourning, the penalty shall be 60 strokes of beating with the heavy stick; fourth degree, 50 strokes of beating with the light stick; fifth degree, 40 strokes of beating with the light stick. (They shall be punished only if [the victims] themselves make the accusation.)

Article 351   Cursing Superior or Older Relatives [Ma zunzhang]
  In all cases of cursing older male or female relatives in the same generation of the fifth degree of mourning, the offenders shall be punished by 50 strokes of beating with the light stick. For cursing relatives of the fourth degree of mourning, the penalty shall be 60 strokes of beating with the heavy stick; third degree, 70 strokes of beating with the heavy stick. For cursing

192   Laws on Penal Affairs

superior relatives, in each case the penalty shall be increased one degree. For cursing older brothers or sisters, the penalty shall be 100 strokes of beating with the heavy stick. For cursing father's brothers or their wives, or maternal grandparents, in each case the penalty shall be increased one degree. (They shall be punished only if [the relatives] themselves make the accusation.)

Article 352   Cursing Paternal Grandparents or Parents
[Ma zufumu fumu]

In all cases where [sons or sons' sons] curse paternal grandparents or parents, or where wives or concubines curse husbands' paternal grandparents or parents, they shall all be punished by strangulation. (They shall be punished only if [the relatives] themselves make the accusation.)

Article 353   Wives or Concubines Cursing Husbands' Superior or Older Relatives of the Second Mourning Degree [Qiqie ma fu jiqin zunzhang]

In all cases where wives or concubines curse husbands' superior or older relatives of the second mourning degree or more distant or the fifth degree of mourning or closer, they shall be punished the same as husbands who curse them [Art. 351]. If concubines curse husbands, they shall be punished by 80 strokes of beating with the heavy stick. If concubines curse wives, the penalty shall be the same. If [concubines] curse wives' parents, they shall be punished by 60 strokes of beating with the heavy stick. (They shall be punished only if [the victims] themselves make the accusation.)

Article 354   Wives or Concubines Cursing Parents of Deceased Husbands
[Qiqie ma gufu fumu]

[1] In all cases where wives' or concubines' husbands die and they remarry, if they curse the paternal grandparents or parents of the deceased husbands, they shall be punished the same as cursing their parents-in-law [Art. 352].

[2] If slaves curse former household heads, they shall be punished as ordinary persons [Art. 347].

Section 5   Accusations and Suits [Susong]
[Twelve Articles]

Article 355   Litigation Bypassing Appropriate Jurisdiction [Yuesu]

[1] All lawsuits brought by military personnel or civilians must begin at the lowest authorities and move to the higher authorities. For those who bypass their own superior offices and who, without authorization, bring the suits directly to the higher authorities, they shall be punished by 50 strokes of beating with the light stick.

Laws on Penal Affairs

[2] For those who bring lawsuits by intercepting the sedan chair of the emperor [*ying chejia*] or beating the petitioner's drum [*ji dengwengu*] but who present false statements, they shall be punished by 100 strokes of beating with the heavy stick. If the matters [falsely complained of] entail heavier penalties, the offenders shall be punished by the heavier penalty. If the statements are true, they shall not be punished.

Article 356 Making Anonymous Written Accusations of Offenses against Others [Tou niming wenshu gao renzui]

In all cases of making anonymous written accusations of offenses against others, the offenders shall be punished by strangulation. Those who see the accusations shall immediately burn them. If they [those who see the accusations] deliver them to government offices, they shall be punished by 80 strokes of beating with the heavy stick. If officials accept them and act on them, they shall be punished by 100 strokes of beating with the heavy stick. Those who are accused shall not be punished. For those who can seize both [the accusers and] the written accusations and send them to the authorities, they shall be given 10 *liang* of silver by the government in reward.

Article 357 Not Accepting and Acting on Accusations [Gaozhuang bu shouli]

[1] In all cases where accusations of plotting rebellion, great sedition, or treason are made but the officials do not immediately accept and act on them and attack and arrest the offenders, they shall be punished by 100 strokes of beating with the heavy stick and penal servitude for three years. If, as a result, crowds are gathered to cause disorder, attack and capture cities, or plunder the people, the penalty shall be decapitation. If accusations of contumacy [Art. 2] are made but [the officials] do not accept and act on them, they shall be punished by 100 strokes of beating with the heavy stick. If accusations of killing or forcibly robbing others are made but [officials] do not accept and act on them, they shall be punished by 80 strokes of beating with the heavy stick. If accusations concerning matters such as striking in affrays, marriages, fields, or houses are made but [officials] do not accept and act on them, in each case the penalty shall be reduced two degrees from that for the offenders. The punishment shall be limited to 80 strokes of beating with the heavy stick. For those who accept property, calculate the value of the illicit goods; they shall be punished by the heavier penalty on the basis of [accepting property and] subverting the law [Art. 367].

[2] If the plaintiffs and defendants in the accusations are in two different subprefectures or districts, the plaintiffs may proceed to the officials [who have jurisdiction over] the defendants to make the accusations and to have

the matters settled. If the said officials find excuses and do not accept the accusations and act on them, they shall be punished the same.

[3] If officials in Chief Military Commissions or any ministry, investigating censors, or officials in Surveillance Commissions or their subordinate offices, in places where they go on inspection tours, [find] cases that ought to be heard but that have not yet been brought to the authorities having jurisdiction or that have not yet been decided, they shall establish files and set time limits and send the cases back to the proper offices to conduct the interrogations, obtain the decisions along with their reasons, and settle the cases. If there are delays or errors but they do not immediately proceed to correct them, they shall be punished the same as the responsible officials. If [the accusations] have already been made to the responsible offices but are not accepted and acted on, or the cases have been decided but the decisions are not correct and [the persons involved] complain about the injustice, officials in each [superior] yamen shall immediately investigate them. If they find excuses and do not accept and act on them, transfer them to other offices or send the cases back to the original offices to decide; they shall be punished in accordance with the provision on "not accepting and acting on accusations" [above].

[4] All great or small public matters and all suits where interrogations need to be conducted must be decided by competent offices and shall not be transferred or delegated. Any violations shall be punished according to the seriousness of the matters that are brought to the authorities. (This means that if a public matter that is brought [to a yamen] is punishable by beating with the heavy stick, the offender shall then be punished by beating with the heavy stick. If it is punishable by beating with the light stick, the offender shall then be punished by beating with the light stick. If it is a death penalty and [the accused] has been executed, then the offender shall be punished by the same penalty; if [the accused] has not yet been executed, then the penalty for the offender shall be reduced [one] degree. If the penalty is penal servitude or life exile, the offender shall be punished by penal servitude or life exile.)

Article 358   Withdrawing from Trying Cases [Tingsong huibi]

In all cases where officials or functionaries have mourning-degree relationships with parties to the cases, or if their families are connected by marriage, or if the parties are teachers [from whom the officials or functionaries] receive their education or persons [against whom they] have former enmity, they shall transfer the documents and withdraw themselves from trying the cases. Any violations shall be punished by 40 strokes of beating with the light stick. If the penalty is increased or reduced, they shall be punished on the basis of deliberately exonerating or incriminating others [Art. 420].

Article 359   Making False Accusations [Wugao]

[1] In all cases of falsely accusing others of offenses punishable with beating with the light stick, the penalty shall be increased two degrees over that for the offenses that are falsely accused. If the penalty [for the accused offenses] is life exile, penal servitude, or beating with the heavy stick, in each case the penalty shall be increased three degrees over that for the offenses that are falsely accused. In each case the punishment shall be limited to 100 strokes of beating with the heavy stick and life exile to 3,000 *li*. If the persons falsely accused of offenses punishable with penal servitude have already performed the labor, or if persons sentenced to life exile have already gone to the places of exile, then, although the matters have been corrected, and the said persons have been released and returned home, [it is necessary] to investigate the number of days and then to seize property from the false accusers for the expenses of the journey [of the falsely accused persons]. If [the falsely accused persons] have already sold fields or houses by *dian* mortgage, the offenders shall provide money to redeem them. If, as a result, one of the relatives of a degree of mourning who accompanies [the falsely accused person] dies, [the false accuser] shall be punished by strangulation. Half the offenders' property shall be taken and given to the falsely accused persons. (If one of the relatives of the accused persons dies, although the offenders are punished by strangulation, they shall still compensate [the accused persons] for the expenses of the journey or redeem the fields or houses; furthermore, take half of their property and give it to the accused persons for support.) If the [falsely accused] offenses are punishable with the death penalty, and if the falsely accused persons have already been executed, [the false accusers] shall be punished by a reciprocal death penalty. (If the accused persons have already been executed, although the offenders are punished by the death penalty, they shall also be ordered to compensate [the accused persons] for the expenses of the journey or redeem the fields or houses; take half their property and give it to the accused persons' families for support.) If the penalty has not yet been executed, the offenders shall be punished by 100 strokes of beating with the heavy stick and life exile to 3,000 *li* with an additional three years of labor service.

[2] If the offenders are poor and cannot compensate for the expenses of the journey or redeem the fields or houses or have no property that can be taken and given [to the victims], only the penalty shall be inflicted.

[3] If the persons who are falsely accused do not report the true circumstances and falsely accuse the offenders [the original false accusers], they shall also be punished by the penalty for the falsely accused offenses. The [original] offenders shall be punished only by the original penalty. (This means that if, for example, none of the accused persons' relatives die but they deceitfully claim the death, or they take other persons' corpses and fraudulently claim that they are their relatives, and thus falsely accuse the [orig-

inal] offenders, they shall also be punished by strangulation. The [original] offenders shall be punished only by the penalty for the original offenses. They shall not be responsible for compensating for the expenses of the journey, redeeming the fields or houses, or handing over half their property.) For those who accuse others of two or more offenses, if the more serious is true and the less serious is false, or if the offenses are equally serious but one of the accusations is true, all the penalties shall be exempted.

[4] For those who accuse others of two or more offenses, if the less serious is true and the more serious is false, or if they accuse others of one offense but falsely state a less serious matter to be a more serious matter, in all these cases [the false accusers] shall be punished by the penalties for the excess offenses. If the penalty has been executed [on the falsely accused persons], they shall be punished by [the penalties for] all the excess offenses. If the penalty has not yet been executed, for beating with the light or heavy stick, the punishment may be redeemed; for penal servitude or life exile, the punishment shall be limited to 100 strokes of beating with the heavy stick, and the rest of the penalty may also be redeemed. (This means that if someone accuses another of a more serious offense [when he is guilty of] a less serious one, and the punishment extends to penal servitude or life exile, for every degree of penal servitude, the penalty shall be converted to 20 strokes of beating with the light stick. If the punishment extends from penal servitude to life exile, each of the three degrees of the life exile shall be converted to four years of penal servitude; and in each case one year shall be considered as the excess penalty and be converted to 40 strokes of beating with the light stick. If the punishment extends from a near place to a distant place, each degree of life exile shall be considered one-half year of penal servitude as the excess penalty and shall also be converted to 20 strokes of beating with the light stick. Redeeming means if someone accuses another of two offenses, and one offense entailing 50 strokes of beating with the light stick is false, and the other entailing 30 strokes of beating with the light stick is true, exclude the 30 strokes for the correct accusation from the 50 strokes of beating with the light stick; [the false accuser] may redeem the remaining 20 strokes of the beating with the light stick for the falsely accused offense in the amount of 1 *guan* and 200 *wen* of copper cash. Or if someone accuses another [of two offenses], and one offense entailing 100 strokes of beating with the heavy stick is false, and the other entailing 60 strokes of beating with the heavy stick is true, then exclude the 60 strokes for the correct accusation from the 100 strokes of beating with the heavy stick; [the false accuser] may redeem 40 strokes of beating with the heavy stick for the falsely accused offense in the amount of 2 *guan* and 400 *wen* of copper cash. Or if someone accuses another [of two offenses], and one offense entailing 100 strokes of beating with the heavy stick and penal servitude for three years is false, and the other entailing 80 strokes of beating with the heavy stick is

true, then exclude the 80 strokes for the correct accusation from the 100 strokes of beating with the heavy stick and penal servitude for three years. Thus, the excess penalty of 20 strokes of beating with the heavy stick and penal servitude for three years resulting from the false accusation remains. Furthermore, the five degrees of penal servitude shall be converted to 100 strokes of beating with the heavy stick. Then the total shall be 120 strokes of beating with the heavy stick. The original [false] accuser shall [first] be punished by 100 strokes of beating with the heavy stick and then redeem the remaining 20 strokes of beating with the heavy stick in the amount of 1 *guan* and 200 *wen* of copper cash. Again, if someone accuses another of one offense entailing 100 strokes of beating with the heavy stick and life exile to 3,000 *li*, and in the interrogation, the accused admits only to an offense entailing 100 strokes of beating with the heavy stick, since the three degrees of life exile shall each be converted to four years of penal servitude, the penalty shall be calculated to be 240 strokes of beating with the heavy stick in total. The original [false] accuser shall be punished by 100 strokes of beating with the heavy stick and then redeem the remaining 40 strokes of beating with the heavy stick in the amount of 2 *guan* and 400 *wen* of copper cash. If the penalty has been executed, the offenders shall be punished on the basis of the entire remaining penalty; they shall not redeem it.) As for the death penalty, if the falsely accused persons have already been executed, the false accusers shall also be punished by the death penalty. If the sentence has not yet been executed, the false accusers shall be punished by 100 strokes of beating with the heavy stick and life exile to 3,000 *li*.

[5] If the *Code* provides a limit to the punishment, even if the false accusation is more, there shall be no further reciprocal punishment. (This means, for example, that someone accuses another of taking illicit goods in the amount of 200 *guan* of copper cash without subverting the law [Art. 367]. It is true that the accused person has taken 120 *guan* of copper cash, but the accusation as to the remaining 80 *guan* is false. According to the *Code*, the punishment for taking illicit goods worth 120 *guan* or more without subverting the law shall be limited to 100 strokes of beating with the heavy stick and life exile to 3,000 *li*. Therefore, the [remaining] punishment shall be exempted [i.e., the false accuser will not be punished at all].)

[6] For those who accuse two or more persons, as long as the accusation proves to be untrue for one person, although the offense is minor, they shall still be punished on the basis of false accusation. (This means, for example, that someone accuses three persons. The accusations about two persons whose offenses entail penal servitude prove to be true, but the accusation of one person whose offense entails beating with the light stick proves to be untrue. Then the false accuser shall still be reciprocally punished on the basis of false accusation, and the penalty shall be increased two degrees from beating with the light stick.)

[7] If officials of various yamen falsely accuse others by presenting sealed reports to the throne, or if surveillance officials make false reports to the throne to pursue their private interests, they shall be punished the same. If the reciprocal penalty or the increased penalty is lighter [than 100 strokes of beating with the heavy stick and penal servitude for three years], they shall be punished in accordance with the law on making false reports to the throne [Art. 380].

[8] If prisoners have already confessed to their offenses and there are no errors but their relatives fraudulently bring actions [to appeal the convictions], the penalty shall be reduced three degrees from that for the prisoners. The punishment shall be limited to 100 strokes of beating with the heavy stick. If the prisoners have already been punished [by beating with the light or heavy stick] or sent [to perform labor in the case of penal servitude or life exile], and they themselves fraudulently make accusations of injustice or errors, framing the officials who presided at the original proceedings, their penalty shall be increased three degrees over that for the falsely accused offense. The punishment shall be limited to 100 strokes of beating with the heavy stick and life exile to 3,000 *li*.

Article 360 Violating Status and Offending against Righteousness [Ganming fanyi]

[1] In all cases where sons or sons' sons bring accusations against paternal grandparents or parents, or where wives or concubines bring accusations against husbands or husbands' paternal grandparents or parents, they shall be punished by 100 strokes of beating with the heavy stick and penal servitude for three years. If they make false accusations, they shall be punished by strangulation. For those who bring accusations against superior or older relatives of the second degree of mourning or against maternal grandparents, even if the accusations are true, they shall be punished by 100 strokes of beating with the heavy stick. For relatives of the third degree of mourning, the penalty shall be 90 strokes of beating with the heavy stick; relatives of the fourth degree, 80 strokes; relatives of fifth degree, 70 strokes. The accused superior or older relatives of the third or second degree of mourning, maternal grandparents, or wives' parents shall be exempted from punishment as if they themselves had voluntarily confessed [Art. 24]. The [accused] superior or older relatives of the fourth or fifth degree of mourning shall have their penalty reduced three degrees from that for the original offense [Art. 359]. If the penalty for a falsely accused offense is more serious [than the offense of violating status punished by this article], in each case the penalty [for the false accusers] shall be increased three degrees over that for the falsely accused offenses. (The increased punishment shall not extend to death. If superior or older relatives are falsely accused of offenses punishable with penal servitude and they have already performed the labor,

or if they are falsely accused of offenses punishable with life exile and they have already gone to the places of exile, then although the matters have been corrected, and the said relatives have been released and returned home, still investigate the number of days and seize property from the false accusers for the expenses of the journey [of the falsely accused persons] in accordance with the law of false accusation [Art. 359]. If the relatives have already sold fields or houses by *dian*, the offenders shall provide the consideration to redeem them. If, as a result, one of the relatives of a degree of mourning who accompanies [the falsely accused persons] dies, [the false accusers] shall be punished by strangulation, and they shall still compensate [the accused persons] for the expenses of the journey or redeem the fields or houses. Furthermore, half the offenders' property shall be taken and given to the victims' families for support. If the [falsely accused] offenses are punishable with the death penalty, and if the falsely accused persons have already been executed, [the false accusers] shall be punished by the death penalty. They shall also be ordered to compensate [the accused persons] for the expenses of the journey or redeem the fields or houses; take half their property and give it to the accused persons' families for support. If the penalty has not yet been executed, the offenders shall be punished by 100 strokes of beating with the heavy stick and life exile to 3,000 *li* with an additional three years of labor service.) For those who accuse others of plotting rebellion or great sedition [Art. 277], plotting treason [Art. 278], hiding spies [Art. 246], or accuse proper mothers, stepmothers, carrying mothers, adoptive mothers, or biological mothers [*suoshengmu*] of killing their [the accusers'] fathers, or accuse adoptive parents of killing their [the accusers'] biological parents, or accuse superior or older relatives of the second degree of mourning or below of wrongfully taking their property or striking and injuring their persons and such offenses are supposed to be brought to the attention of the authorities by the victims themselves, the accusations shall be permitted. The provision of violating status and offending against righteousness is not applicable.

[2] If accusations are brought against inferior or younger relatives and the accusations are true, the [accused] relatives of the second or third degree of mourning or sons-in-law shall also be exempted from punishment as if they themselves had voluntarily confessed. The [accused] relatives of the fourth or fifth degree of mourning shall have their penalty reduced three degrees from that for the original offenses. If the accusations are false, for relatives of the second degree of mourning, the penalty [for the false accusers] shall be reduced three degrees from that for the falsely accused offenses. For relatives of the third degree, reduce two degrees. For relatives of the fourth or fifth degree, reduce one degree. If [husbands] falsely accuse wives, or wives falsely accuse concubines, they shall also have their penalty reduced three degrees from that for the falsely accused offenses.

[3] If slaves accuse household heads or household heads' relatives of the fifth degree of mourning or above, they shall be punished the same as sons or sons' sons or other inferior or younger relatives. If hired laborers accuse household heads or household heads' relatives, their penalty shall be reduced one degree from that for slaves. If the accusations are false, the penalty shall not be reduced.

[4] If paternal grandparents or parents falsely accuse sons, sons' sons, daughters' sons, wives or concubines of sons or sons' sons, or their own concubines, slaves, or hired laborers, in each case they shall not be punished.

[5] If there are indeed circumstances that break the bond of righteousness [*yijue*] between sons-in-law and wives' parents, they may accuse each other. In each case they shall be treated as ordinary persons. (The circumstances of breaking the bond of righteousness refer to such cases as those where the husband is in a distant place and his wife's parents marry her to someone else; they drive [the son-in-law] out and call in another son-in-law; they permit others to commit adultery with [the wife]; the husband himself strikes the wife and injures her to the extent of fracture; he forces her to commit adultery; although he is married, he deceitfully claims that he is not and thus fraudulently marries another woman; he makes his wife a concubine; he accepts consideration to sell his wife or concubine by *dian* mortgage or hire her out; or he fraudulently claims his wife or concubine as his sister and marries her to another person.)

Article 361 Sons or Sons' Sons Violating Instructional Orders
[Zisun weifan jiaoling]

In all cases where sons or sons' sons disobey instructional orders of their paternal grandparents or parents, or where they are deficient in support of [paternal grandparents or parents], they shall be punished by 100 strokes of beating with the heavy stick. (This means that the instructional orders can be followed but are deliberately disobeyed, or the support can be provided with the resources of the family but is deliberately not provided. Only when the paternal grandparents or parents themselves bring the accusations to the authorities shall the offenders be punished.)

Article 362 Prisoners Are Not Permitted to Make Accusations Regarding Others' Matters to the Authorities [Xianjinqiu bude gaoju tashi]

[1] No prisoners are permitted to make accusations regarding others' matters to the authorities. However, in cases where they are cruelly treated by the prison wardens or jailers without reason, the accusations shall be permitted. When the prisoners, during interrogation, confess to other offenses in which others are involved, they shall also be permitted to confess, and [the others] shall be interrogated and sentenced in accordance with law.

[2] Those who are 80 years of age or older, 10 years of age or younger,

Laws on Penal Affairs

incapacitated, or women may make accusations in such matters as plotting rebellion, great sedition, treason, or sons or sons' sons lacking filial piety, or when they themselves or those who live with them in the same households have had their property taken away by robbery, fraud, or seizure or have been killed or injured. They are not permitted to make accusations regarding any other matters to the authorities. If officials accept such accusations and act on them, they shall be punished by 50 strokes of beating with the light stick.

Article 363   Instigating Litigation [Jiaosuo cisong]

In all cases of instigating litigation or of writing complaints for others that change the circumstances or nature of the offenses and thus make false accusations, the offenders [the instigators] shall be punished by the same penalty as that for the offenders [the false accusers]. For those who are hired to accuse others falsely, they shall be punished the same as those who themselves falsely accuse others [Art. 359]. If they receive property, calculate the value of the illicit goods; they shall be punished by the heavier penalty on the basis of [accepting property and] subverting the law [Art. 367]. If they are acquainted with some people who are unlearned and who cannot redress their wrongs and they give them advice in accordance with the facts, or if they write complaints for others that do not change the offenses, there shall be no punishment.

Article 364   Coordinating Litigation Involving Military Personnel and Civilians [Junmin yuehui cisong]

[1] In all cases where military officers or soldiers commit homicide, the military yamen having jurisdiction shall make arrangements with the competent civilian authorities to have the cases investigated and tried. In matters such as fornication, robbery, fraud, household, marriage, land, affray, and battery that involve civilians, the cases must be tried by both authorities together. In matters that do not involve civilians, competent military officers may themselves proceed to investigate and try the cases. If the offenders are held and not sent [to relevant authorities], in each case the staff supervisors and functionaries shall be punished by 50 strokes of beating with the light stick.

[2] If military officers exceed their authority and, without authorization, accept civilian litigation, they shall be punished the same.

Article 365   Family Members Lodging Accusations on Behalf of Officials or Functionaries [Guanli cisong jiaren su]

In all cases where officials or functionaries have disputes regarding matters such as marriage, monetary debts, and land, their family members are permitted to lodge accusations to the authorities for trial. [The officials or functionaries] shall not exchange official documents [on such matters].

Any violations shall be punished by 40 strokes of beating with the light stick.

Article 366   False Accusations of Offenses Punishable by Military Exile or Banishment [Wugao chongjun ji qianxi]

[1] In all cases of falsely accusing others of offenses punishable by military exile, if civilians make the accusations, they shall be sentenced to perform military service; if military personnel make the accusations, they shall be sentenced to military exile at distant places.

[2] If officials or functionaries deliberately substitute innocent persons for others [i.e., the offenders] to perform military service, they shall be punished, on the basis of deliberately decreasing or increasing a sentence of exile, by 100 strokes of beating with the heavy stick and life exile to 3,000 *li*.

[3] For those who falsely accuse others of arranging for favors and bribes, which is punished by banishment [Art. 367], their penalty shall first be reduced by half from life exile, which is equivalent to penal servitude for two years; then, add three degrees to the penalty for the falsely accused offenses, [which will entail life exile to 2,000 *li*]. Moreover, combine this sentence with the appropriate number of strokes of beating with the light or heavy stick that the offenders should receive. The offenders shall be punished by both the penalties.

Section 6   Accepting Illicit Goods [*Shouzang*] [Eleven Articles]

Article 367   Officials or Functionaries Accepting Property [Guanli shoucai]

[1] In all cases where officials or functionaries receive property, calculate the value of the illicit goods and decide the penalty accordingly. For those who have no official salary, in each case the penalty shall be reduced one degree. The officials shall have their certificates of appointment revoked and be disenrolled from their official registers. The functionaries shall be dismissed from their employment. Both are not permitted to be reassigned.

[2] For those who arrange for favors and bribes, if they have an official salary [i.e., receive a salary for their position as officials], the penalty shall be reduced one degree from that for the persons who accept money; if they have no official salary, the penalty shall be reduced two degrees. The punishment shall be limited to 100 strokes of beating with the heavy stick. In each case they shall be punished by banishment. For those who accept illicit goods, calculate the value of the illicit goods; they shall be punished by the heavier penalty.

For those who have an official salary:

Laws on Penal Affairs

If they accept illicit goods and subvert the law, calculate the entire amount of the illicit goods from each person and decide the penalty accordingly. (This means that if they accept property from litigants and subvert the law to decide the matters, and if they receive property from 10 persons and the matters are discovered at one time, calculate the entire amount [of illicit goods] together as in a single case and decide the penalty accordingly.)

[The punishment shall be inflicted in accordance with the amount of goods received as follows:]

> Less than 1 *guan*: 70 strokes of beating with the heavy stick.
> 1–5 *guan*: 80 strokes of beating with the heavy stick.
> 10 *guan*: 90 strokes of beating with the heavy stick.
> 15 *guan*: 100 strokes of beating with the heavy stick.
> 20 *guan*: 60 strokes of beating with the heavy stick and penal servitude for one year.
> 25 *guan*: 70 strokes of beating with the heavy stick and penal servitude for one and one-half years.
> 30 *guan*: 80 strokes of beating with the heavy stick and penal servitude for two years.
> 35 *guan*: 90 strokes of beating with the heavy stick and penal servitude for two and one-half years.
> 40 *guan*: 100 strokes of beating with the heavy stick and penal servitude for three years.
> 45 *guan*: 100 strokes of beating with the heavy stick and life exile to 2,000 *li*.
> 50 *guan*: 100 strokes of beating with the heavy stick and life exile to 2,500 *li*.
> 55 *guan*: 100 strokes of beating with the heavy stick and life exile to 3,000 *li*.
> 80 *guan*: strangulation.

If they accept illicit goods without subverting the law, calculate the entire amount of the illicit goods from each person and reduce it by half, and then decide the penalty accordingly. (This means that even though they accept property from litigants, they do not subvert the law to decide the matters. If they accept property from 10 persons and the matters are discovered at one time, calculate the entire amount of property and decide the penalty for half that amount.)

[The punishment shall be inflicted in accordance with the amount of goods received as follows:]

> Less than 1 *guan*: 60 strokes of beating with the heavy stick.
> 1–10 *guan*: 70 strokes of beating with the heavy stick.

20 *guan*: 80 strokes of beating with the heavy stick.
30 *guan*: 90 strokes of beating with the heavy stick.
40 *guan*: 100 strokes of beating with the heavy stick.
50 *guan*: 60 strokes of beating with the heavy stick and penal servitude for one year.
60 *guan*: 70 strokes of beating with the heavy stick and penal servitude for one and one-half years.
70 *guan*: 80 strokes of beating with the heavy stick and penal servitude for two years.
80 *guan*: 90 strokes of beating with the heavy stick and penal servitude for two and one-half years.
90 *guan*: 100 strokes of beating with the heavy stick and penal servitude for three years.
100 *guan*: 100 strokes of beating with the heavy stick and life exile to 2,000 *li*.
110 *guan*: 100 strokes of beating with the heavy stick and life exile to 2,500 *li*.
120 *guan*: the punishment shall be limited to 100 strokes of beating with the heavy stick and life exile to 3,000 *li*.

For those who have no official salary:
If they subvert the law, 120 *guan*, strangulation.
If they do not subvert the law, over 120 *guan*, the punishment shall be limited to 100 strokes of beating with the heavy stick and life exile to 3,000 *li*.

Article 368   Committing Crimes Involving Illicit Goods Obtained through Malfeasance [Zuozang zhizui]

In all cases where officials or functionaries who accept property not because of matters commit crimes involving illicit goods obtained through malfeasance, calculate the entire amount of illicit goods from each person as a whole and reduce it by half. Then decide the penalty accordingly. Those who offer [the property] shall have their penalty reduced five degrees. (This refers, for example, to cases where the persons who are robbed or struck and injured accept property in addition to the compensation for the monetary loss or medical expenses [to which they are entitled]. If the property is accepted from more than one person, it shall be calculated together and reduced to half. Then, decide the penalty accordingly. This [the reduction of the entire value of the illicit goods by half] is because the two parties accept and give by common consent. The persons who offer money shall have their penalty reduced five degrees from that for those who accept it. This refers to cases such as those where the offenders levy property without authority [Art. 374] or collect too much or levy too little money or grain taxes [Art. 128], even though they themselves do not possess the property; or they waste manpower or select unsuitable materials for manufacturing or construction projects [Art. 449]. All the cases where crimes are committed because of such illicit goods are called "committing crimes involving illicit goods obtained through malfeasance.")

[The punishment shall be inflicted in accordance with the amount of goods received as follows:]

> Less than 1 *guan:* 20 strokes of beating with the light stick.
> 1–10 *guan:* 30 strokes of beating with the light stick.
> 20 *guan:* 40 strokes of beating with the light stick.
> 30 *guan:* 50 strokes of beating with the light stick.
> 40 *guan:* 60 strokes of beating with the heavy stick.
> 50 *guan:* 70 strokes of beating with the heavy stick.
> 60 *guan:* 80 strokes of beating with the heavy stick.
> 70 *guan:* 90 strokes of beating with the heavy stick.
> 80 *guan:* 100 strokes of beating with the heavy stick.
> 100 *guan:* 60 strokes of beating with the heavy stick and penal servitude for one year.
> 200 *guan:* 70 strokes of beating with the heavy stick and penal servitude for one and one-half years.
> 300 *guan:* 80 strokes of beating with the heavy stick and penal servitude for two years.
> 400 *guan:* 90 strokes of beating with the heavy stick and penal servitude for two and one-half years.
> 500 *guan* or more: the punishment shall be limited to 100 strokes of beating with the heavy stick and penal servitude for three years.

Article 369   *Accepting Property after Completing the Matters*
[Shihou shoucai]

In all cases where [officials or functionaries] do not accept property beforehand but do so after they complete the matters, if they make the decisions by subverting the law, they shall be punished as comparable to [accepting property and] subverting the law [Art. 367]. If they make the decisions without subverting the law, they shall be punished as comparable to [accepting property] without subverting the law [Art. 367].

Article 370   *Seeking Favorable Decisions of Matters by Offering Property*
[Youshi yicai qingqiu]

In all cases of seeking favorable decisions of matters by offering property, if the offenders cause subversion of the law, calculate the value of the property that is offered; they shall be punished for illicit goods obtained through malfeasance [Art. 368]. If they commit such offenses to avoid difficult matters and seek easy ones, and if the penalty for subverting the law is heavier [than that for offering property], they shall be punished by the heavier penalty. If officials or functionaries manipulatively create difficulties, deliberately complicate issues by force, or use coercion to obtain [the property], the persons who give the money shall not be punished.

Article 371   Officials Extorting or Borrowing Property from Others
[Zaiguan qiusuo jiedai ren caiwu]

[1] In all cases where supervisory officials or functionaries, by taking advantage of their power, or powerful persons extort or borrow property from those within their areas of jurisdiction, calculate the value of the illicit goods; they shall be punished as comparable to [accepting property] without subverting the law [Art. 367]. If force is used, they shall be punished as comparable to [accepting property and] subverting the law [Art. 367]. The property shall be returned to the owners.

[2] If they sell their own goods to those within their areas of jurisdiction or purchase goods at reduced prices to make profits, then calculate the value of the profits; they shall be punished as comparable to [accepting property] without subverting the law [Art. 367]. If force is used, they shall be punished as comparable to [accepting property and] subverting the law [Art. 367]. The goods or their price shall be either forfeit to the government or returned to the owners.

[3] If they purchase goods from those within their areas of jurisdiction but do not immediately pay the price, or if they borrow clothing or articles but do not return the items within one month, they shall be punished for illicit goods obtained through malfeasance [Art. 368].

[4] If they borrow, for private use, items such as horses, cattle, camels, mules, asses, carts, boats, mills, and inns from those within their areas of jurisdiction, in each case calculate the value of the rent by day; they shall also be punished for illicit goods obtained through malfeasance [Art. 368]. The money shall be returned to the owners.

[5] If they accept gifts of local products from those within their areas of jurisdiction, the recipients shall be punished by 40 strokes of beating with the light stick. The penalty for those who offer the gifts shall be reduced one degree. If they accept things because of certain matters, calculate the value of the illicit goods; they shall be punished on the basis of [accepting property] without subverting the law [Art. 367]. If they are provided with food or drink when they pass through certain places, or if they accept presents from relatives or friends, this provision shall not be applied.

[6] If official emissaries, at the places where they are sent, extort or borrow things, or purchase or sell things and thus make profits, or accepts gifts, they shall be punished the same as supervisory officials or functionaries.

[7] If officials who have left the service accept property from those within their former areas of jurisdiction or extort or borrow things from them, in

each case the penalty shall be reduced three degrees from that for those in government office.

Article 372   Household Members [of Officials] Extorting [Property]
[Jiaren qiusuo]

In all cases where household members of supervisory officials or functionaries, within their areas of jurisdiction, accept, extort, or borrow property or use people's labor or purchase or sell things and thus make profits, in each case the penalty shall be reduced two degrees from that for the officials [or functionaries]. If the officials [or functionaries] know the circumstances, they shall be punished the same. If they do not know, they shall not be punished.

Article 373   Surveillance Officials or Functionaries Committing Offenses Involving Illicit Goods [Fengxian guanli fanzang]

In all cases where surveillance officials [censors] accept property or, at the places under their jurisdiction, extort or borrow property or purchase or sell things and thus make profits or accept gifts of local products, in each case the penalty shall be increased two degrees from that for all other officials or functionaries.

Article 374   Making Unauthorized Collections for Public Benefit
[Yingong shan kelian]

[1] In all cases where officials or functionaries in government offices or other persons, without having received written orders from superior authorities, make collections of property within their areas for public benefit without authorization, or where military officers or clerks, platoon commanders, or squad commanders make collections of money, grain, or special rewards from the soldiers, they shall be punished by 60 strokes of beating with the heavy stick. If the value of the illicit goods results in a heavier penalty, they shall be punished for illicit goods obtained through malfeasance [Art. 368]. If they take the goods for themselves, they shall be punished on the basis of [accepting property and] subverting the law [Art. 367].

[2] If they, not because of public matters, make collections of property from others and take the goods for themselves, calculate the value of the illicit goods; they shall be punished on the basis of [accepting property] without subverting the law [Art. 367]. If they offer the goods to others as presents, although they do not take them for themselves, the penalty shall be the same.

Article 375   Privately Accepting Property from Dukes or Marquises
[Sishou gonghou caiwu]

No military guard commanders, battalion commanders, company commanders, military judges, platoon commanders, or squad commanders shall privately or openly accept from dukes or marquises paper currency, gold, silver, silk, clothing, grain, money, or other objects. If they accept such items, the military officers shall be punished by 100 strokes of beating with the heavy stick, removal from the service, and military exile to distant frontiers. The penalty for the platoon commanders and squad commanders shall be the same. If they commit the offense again, they shall be sentenced to death. The dukes or marquises who offer the items shall, for the first and second offenses, be exempted from punishment but have their transgressions recorded. For the third offense, they are permitted to be exempted once from the death penalty. If they receive orders and go on military expeditions, this provision shall be applied to neither the donors nor the recipients.

Article 376   Retaining Stolen Goods [Keliu daozang]

In all cases where officials who are responsible for arresting thieves have seized the thieves but retain the illicit goods and do not deliver them to the government, they shall be punished by 40 strokes of beating with the light stick. If they take the goods for themselves, calculate the value of the illicit goods; they shall be punished on the basis of [accepting property] without subverting the law [Art. 367]. [If part of the stolen goods is delivered,] the penalty for the robbery shall still be decided by combining the value of both [delivered and retained] stolen goods. If soldiers or archers commit such offenses, although the value of the illicit goods is great, the punishment shall be limited to 80 strokes of beating with the heavy stick.

Article 377   Officials or Functionaries Permitting Promises of Property [Guanli tingxu caiwu]

In all cases where officials or functionaries permit promises of property, although they do not accept it, if they subvert the law, they shall be punished as comparable to [accepting property and] subverting the law [Art. 367]. If they do not subvert the law, they shall be punished as comparable to [accepting property] without subverting the law [Art. 367]. In each case, the penalty shall be reduced one degree. If the penalty for the matters as to which the law is subverted is heavier, in each case the offenders shall be punished according to the heavier penalty.

Section 7   Deceiving and Counterfeiting [*Zhawei*] [Twelve Articles]

Article 378   Counterfeiting Imperial Rescripts [Zhawei zhishu]

[1] In all cases of counterfeiting imperial rescripts or of adding to or subtracting from [the original provisions of the imperial rescripts], the offenders shall be punished by decapitation. If [the counterfeited or

changed rescripts] have not yet been carried out, the offenders shall be punished by strangulation. If they make mistakes in copying [the rescripts] for transmission, they shall be punished by 100 strokes of beating with the heavy stick.

[2] For those who counterfeit documents of generals, regional commanders, the Five Chief Military Commissions, the Six Ministries, the Censorate, Regional Military Commissions, the military command of each guard in the capital or provinces, or battalions that guard the important passes, or who forge others' signatures, or steal seals and use them, or take blank paper and put seals on them, they shall all be punished by strangulation. [If they commit such offenses involving documents or seals of] the Investigation Bureau, Provincial Administration Commissions, Surveillance Commissions, or the yamens of prefectures, subprefectures, or districts, they shall be punished by 100 strokes of beating with the heavy stick and life exile to 3,000 li. [For documents or seals of] other yamen, the penalty shall be 100 strokes of beating with the heavy stick and penal servitude for three years. [If the counterfeited items] have not yet been used, in each case the penalty shall be reduced one degree. If the offenses of counterfeiting are committed to circumvent the law and this would result in a heavier penalty, the offenders shall be punished by the heavier penalty.

[3] If the officials in charge know the circumstances and connive at the offenses, in each case they shall be punished the same. If they do not know, they shall not be punished.

Article 379   Deceitfully Transmitting Imperial Decrees [Zhachuan zhaozhi]

[1] In all cases of deceitfully transmitting imperial decrees, the offenders shall be punished by decapitation. For the orders of the empress, the heir apparent, or the imperial princes, the penalty shall be strangulation.

[2] For those who deceitfully transmit the spoken orders of the first- or second-rank yamen officials and who command public matters in each yamen to circumvent the law, they shall be punished by 100 strokes of beating with the heavy stick and penal servitude for three years. For spoken orders of the third- or fourth-rank yamen officials, the penalty shall be 100 strokes of beating with the heavy stick. For spoken orders of the fifth-rank yamen officials or below, the penalty shall be 80 strokes of beating with the heavy stick. For accessories, in each case the penalty shall be reduced one degree. If they receive property, calculate the value of the illicit goods; they shall be punished on the basis of [accepting property] without subverting the law [Art. 367]. If they consequently distort the facts and twist the law, they shall be punished on the basis of [accepting property and] subverting the law [Art. 367]. In each case, they shall be punished by the heavier penalty.

[3] If the officials in charge know the circumstances and allow the action

to take place, in each case they shall be punished by the same penalty. If they do not know, they shall not be punished.

[4] If, with regard to public matters such as collecting money or grain and investigating law cases, the yamen officials or functionaries in charge have received the imperial decrees in response to memorials on the proper handling of the matters [to remit the taxes or not to carry on the investigations] but recklessly claim to have received imperial decrees to collect [the taxes] or to conduct the investigations, they shall be punished by decapitation.

Article 380   Replying to or Memorializing the Emperor Untruthfully
[Duizhi shangshu zha bu yishi]

[1] In all cases of untruthfully replying to [duizhi], reporting to [zoushi], or memorializing [shangshu] the emperor, the offenders shall be punished by 100 strokes of beating with the heavy stick and penal servitude for three years. If the matters are not secret but are recklessly claimed to be secret, the penalty shall be increased one degree.

[2] Those who receive the imperial decree to make inquiries [tui], examinations [an], or investigations [wen] but who do not present truthful reports to the emperor shall be punished by 80 strokes of beating with the heavy stick and penal servitude for two years. If the matters entail a heavier penalty, they shall be punished on the basis of implicating the innocent or exonerating the guilty [Art. 433].

Article 381   Counterfeiting Items Such as Seals and Almanacs
[Weizao yinxin liri deng]

In all cases of counterfeiting yamen seals, almanacs, tallies, night patrol bronze tallies, tea licenses, or salt licenses, the offenders shall be punished by decapitation. Those who accuse the offenders and cause them to be seized shall be rewarded by the government with 50 liang of silver. Those who counterfeit guanfang yinji seals [special oblong seals] shall be punished by 100 strokes of beating with heavy stick and penal servitude for three years. Those who accuse the offenders and cause them to be seized shall be rewarded by the government with 30 liang of silver. The accessories or those who know the circumstances and use [the seals] in each case shall have their penalties reduced one degree. For those who have started the counterfeiting and have not completed it, in each case the penalty shall be reduced one more degree. If the officials in charge know the circumstances and allow the action to take place, they shall be punished the same. If they do not know, they shall not be punished.

Article 382   Counterfeiting Treasure Paper Currency [Weizao baochao]

[1] In all cases of counterfeiting treasure paper currency [baochao], as long as the offenders know the circumstances and use the items, they shall,

regardless of principals, accessories, or harborers, all be punished by decapitation. Their property shall all be forfeit to the government. Those who report the cases and cause the offenders to be arrested shall be rewarded with 250 *liang* of silver by the government; and they shall still be given the property of the offenders. If the community heads know the circumstances but do not report, they shall be punished by 100 strokes of beating with the heavy stick. If they do not know, they shall not be punished. If patrolmen or guarding officers or soldiers know the circumstances but deliberately connive at the offenses, they shall be punished the same as [the original offenders]. For those who search out the counterfeited treasure paper currency but conceal it and do not deliver it to the government, they shall be punished by 100 strokes of beating with the heavy stick and life exile to 3,000 *li*. For those who are negligent in apprehension and who consequently let the offenders slip through [the meshes of law], they shall be punished by 80 strokes of beating with the heavy stick; and they shall still be ordered to pursue and seize the offenders according to the time limit for apprehending forcible robbery.

[2] For those who change the treasure paper currency with such methods as picking out, cutting out, patching, assembling, drawing, and altering and who thereby turn the true paper currency into a sham one, they shall be punished by 100 strokes of beating with the heavy stick and life exile to 3,000 *li*. The accessories or those who know the circumstances but use the items shall be punished by 100 strokes of beating with the heavy stick and penal servitude for three years.

[3] If those who collaborate on counterfeiting the paper currency repent and thus capture their partners and report the cases to the authorities, they shall be exempted from punishment and be rewarded as ordinary persons.

Article 383   Privately Casting Copper Cash [Sizhu tongqian]

[1] In all cases of privately casting copper cash, the offenders shall be punished by strangulation. The artisans shall be punished the same. As for the accessories or those who know the circumstances but buy and use the items, the penalty shall in each case be reduced one degree. Those who report the cases and cause the offenders to be arrested shall be rewarded with 50 *liang* of silver by the government. If the community heads know the circumstances but do not report, they shall be punished by 100 strokes of beating with the heavy stick. If they do not know, they shall not be punished.

[2] Those who clip or grind the copper cash that are in circulation and make them thinner or smaller and thus take the copper to make a profit shall be punished by 100 strokes of beating with the heavy stick.

[3] Those who counterfeit gold or silver shall be punished by 100 strokes of beating with the heavy stick and penal servitude for three years. As for

accessories or those who know the circumstances but buy and use the items, the penalty shall in each case be reduced one degree.

Article 384   Deceitfully Impersonating Officials [Zhajia guan]

[1] In all cases of deceitfully impersonating officials or of falsely making others impersonate officials, the offenders shall be punished by decapitation. Those who know the circumstances but accept the false official status shall be punished by 100 strokes of beating with the heavy stick and life exile to 3,000 *li*. If they do not know, they shall not be punished.

[2] If those who are not officials deceitfully claim to be officials in order to obtain something they want, or deceitfully claim to be sent by government offices to make arrests, or deceitfully claim the names of officials, they shall be punished by 100 strokes of beating with the heavy stick and penal servitude for three years. If they deceitfully claim to be the sons, sons' sons, younger brothers, brothers' sons, or foremen of household servants of serving officials, and within the territory over which [the officials] have jurisdiction seek to obtain something, they shall be punished by 100 strokes of beating with the heavy stick. As for the accessories, in each case the penalty shall be reduced one degree. If they obtain property, calculate the value of the illicit goods; they shall be punished as comparable to theft [Art. 292] by the heavier penalty.

[3] If the officials concerned know the circumstances but allow the action to take place, they shall be punished the same. If they do not know, they shall not be punished.

Article 385   Deceitfully Claiming to Be Palace Attendants or Other Officials [Zhacheng neishi deng guan]

[1] In all cases of deceitfully claiming to be palace attendants, officials of Chief Military Commissions, Four Supports, Remonstrance Bureau, or officials of the Six Ministries, investigating censors, or officials of Provincial Surveillance Commissions, and, outside the capital, investigating matters, deceiving government offices, or agitating the people, the offenders shall be punished by decapitation. For those who know the circumstances but who follow them, the penalty shall be reduced one degree. If they do not know, they shall not be punished.

[2] Those who deceitfully claim to be official emissaries and who use postal relay services shall be punished by 100 strokes of beating with the heavy stick and life exile to 3,000 *li*. As for the accessories, the penalty shall be reduced one degree. If the officers of the postal relay stations know the circumstances but provide the services, they shall be punished the same. If they do not know the circumstances but fail to make inquiries, they shall be punished by 50 strokes of beating with the light stick. If they provide services when they are shown tallies, they shall not be punished.

Laws on Penal Affairs 213

Article 386   Court Attendants Deceitfully Claiming to Be on Private Missions [Jinshi zhacheng sixing]

In all cases where court attendants, outside the capital, deceitfully claim to be on private missions and thus investigate matters and agitate the people, they shall be punished by decapitation. (This refers to such officials as supervising secretaries [*jishizhong*], the chief steward of seals [*shangbao*], chief stewards [*fengyu*], palace attendants [*neishi*], officials of the Imperial Regalia Office [Yiluan Si], or commandants.)

Article 387   Deceitfully Making False Auspicious Portents [Zhawei ruiying]

[1] In all cases of deceitfully making false auspicious portents, the offenders shall be punished by 60 strokes of beating with the heavy stick and penal servitude for one year.

[2] If there are disasters or auspicious signs and officials in the Directorate of Astronomy do not report according to facts, the penalty shall be increased two degrees.

Article 388   Avoiding Duties by Feigning Illness, Death, or Injury [Zha bingsishang bishi]

[1] In all cases where officials, functionaries, or other persons feign illness to avoid duties, they shall be punished by 40 strokes of beating with the light stick. If the matter is serious, they shall be punished by 80 strokes of beating with the heavy stick.

[2] If those who have committed offenses and who are awaiting trial deliberately injure or mutilate themselves, they shall be punished by 100 strokes of beating with the heavy stick. If they feign death, they shall be punished by 100 strokes of beating with the heavy stick and penal servitude for three years. If the matters that are avoided entail heavier penalties, in each case the offenders shall be punished by the heavier penalties. If they do not intend to avoid matters but deliberately injure or mutilate themselves, they shall be punished by 80 strokes of beating with the heavy stick. Those who are employed to injure or mutilate others shall be punished by the same penalty as that for the offenders. If they cause death, they shall be punished as for killing others in affrays [Art. 313], reduced one degree.

[3] If the officials in charge know the circumstances but allow the action to take place, they shall be punished the same. If they do not know, they shall not be punished.

Article 389   Deceitfully Enticing Others to Violate the Law [Zha jiaoyou ren fanfa]

In all cases of deceitfully enticing others with tricks or words to violate the law or inducing others to agree to violate the law and then capturing them or accusing them, or ordering others to capture them or accuse them, in order to seek a reward or to cause harm to others by having them punished, the offenders shall be punished by the same penalty as that for the offenders.

Section 8 Committing Fornication [*Fanjian*] [Ten Articles]

Article 390   *Committing Fornication* [Fanjian]

[1] In all cases of fornication with consent [*hejian*], the offenders shall be punished by 80 strokes of beating with the heavy stick. If the women have husbands, the penalty shall be 90 strokes of beating with the heavy stick. For fornication brought about by seduction [*diaojian*], the penalty shall be 100 strokes of beating with the heavy stick.

[2] For those who commit forcible fornication [*qiangjian*], they shall be punished by strangulation. If it is not consummated, the penalty shall be 100 strokes of beating with the heavy stick and life exile to 3,000 *li*.

[3] For those who commit fornication with young girls of 12 years of age or younger, although there is consent, they shall be punished the same as for forcible fornication.

[4] For fornication with consent or by seduction, the men and women shall be punished by the same penalty. If illegitimate boys or girls are born, the men shall bring them up. The adulterous women shall be sold or married [to others] by their husbands. If the husbands wish to keep them, they may do so. If [the adulterous women] are married or sold to the adulterous lovers, the adulterous lovers and the real husbands shall each be punished by 80 strokes of beating with the heavy stick. The women shall be divorced and returned to their own lineages. The property shall be forfeit to the government.

[5] In cases of forcible fornication, the women shall not be punished.

[6] For brokers or those who accept [others in their houses] to engage in fornication, in each case the penalty shall be reduced one degree from that for the offenders. For those who privately settle fornication cases, the penalty shall be reduced two degrees.

[7] For those who are not seized in places where the fornication takes place or who are pointed out as fornicators [without proof], they shall not be punished. If the adulterous women become pregnant, only the women shall be punished.

Article 391   *Facilitating and Tolerating Wives or Concubines to Commit Fornication* [Zongrong qiqie fanjian]

[1] In all cases of facilitating and tolerating wives or concubines to commit fornication with others, the husbands, adulterous men, and adulter-

Laws on Penal Affairs

ous women shall each be punished by 90 strokes of beating with the heavy stick. For those who force wives, concubines, or adopted daughters to commit fornication with others, the husbands or adoptive fathers shall each be punished 100 strokes of beating with the heavy stick. The adulterous men shall be punished by 80 strokes of beating with the heavy stick. The women shall not be punished; and they shall be divorced and returned to their own lineages.

[2] For those who facilitate and tolerate or force their daughters or the wives or concubines of sons or sons' sons to commit fornication, the penalty shall also be the same.

[3] If property is used to buy divorces or to make others sell divorces so that [those who offer property] may marry others' wives with consent, the husbands, wives, and those who buy the divorces shall each be punished by 100 strokes of beating with the heavy stick. The wives shall be divorced and returned to their own lineages. The wedding gifts shall be forfeit to the government. If those who buy the divorces and the wives use tricks to force the husbands to divorce and the husbands do not have other intentions to divorce, the husbands shall not be punished. Those who buy the divorces and the wives shall each be punished by 60 strokes of beating with the heavy stick and penal servitude for one year. The wives' remaining penalty shall be redeemed; and they shall be returned to their husbands, who may marry them off or sell them. For concubines, the penalty shall be reduced one degree. For brokers, in each case the penalty shall be reduced one degree from that for the offenders.

Article 392   *Committing Fornication with Relatives* [Qinshu xiangjian]

[1] In all cases of committing fornication with relatives of the same lineage who are not within the degrees of mourning or the wives of relatives who are not within the degrees of mourning, the offenders shall each be punished by 100 strokes of beating with the heavy stick.

[2] For those who commit fornication with relatives within the fifth degree of mourning or the wives of relatives within the fifth degree of mourning (this refers to mourning relatives both by blood and by marital relationship), daughters of wives' former husbands, or sisters of the same mother and different father, they shall each be punished by 100 strokes of beating with the heavy stick and penal servitude for three years. If force is used, they shall be punished by decapitation. If they commit fornication with paternal grandfather's brothers' wives, paternal grandfather's sisters, paternal great-grandfather's sons' sons' wives, paternal great-grandfather's sons' daughters, paternal grandfather's sons' daughters, mother's sisters, brothers' wives, or brothers' sons' wives, they shall each be punished by strangulation. If force is used, they shall be punished by decapitation. If they commit fornication with father's or paternal grandfather's concu-

bines, father's brothers' wives, father's sisters, their own sisters, sons' or sons' sons' wives, or brothers' daughters, they shall each be punished by decapitation.

[3] If they commit fornication with concubines, in each case the penalty shall be reduced one degree. If force is used, they shall be punished by strangulation. (This means that if they commit forcible fornication with relatives' concubines, they shall be punished by strangulation.)

Article 393   Falsely Accusing Fathers-in-Law of Fornication
[Wuzhi weng jian]

In all cases where sons' wives falsely accuse fathers-in-law or where younger brothers' wives falsely accuse husbands' brothers of fornication by deceit [qijian], they shall be punished by decapitation.

Article 394   Slaves or Hired Laborers Committing Fornication with Household Heads' Wives [Nu ji gugongren jian jiazhang qi]

[1] In all cases where slaves or hired laborers commit fornication with their household heads' wives or daughters, they shall each be punished by decapitation.

[2] If they commit fornication with their household heads' relatives of the second degree of mourning or the wives of the relatives of the second degree of mourning, they shall be punished by strangulation. The penalty for the women shall be reduced one degree. If they commit fornication with their household heads' relatives of the fifth degree of mourning or closer or the wives of the relatives of the fifth degree of mourning or closer, they shall each be punished by 100 strokes of beating with the heavy stick and life exile to 2,000 *li*. If force is used, they shall be punished by decapitation.

[3] If they commit fornication with concubines, in each case the penalty shall be reduced one degree. If force is used, they shall also be punished by decapitation.

Article 395   Committing Fornication with Wives or Daughters of Subordinates [Jian bumin qinü]

[1] In all cases where military or civil officials or functionaries commit fornication with the wives or daughters of the people within their areas of jurisdiction, the penalty shall be increased two degrees from that for ordinary fornication [Art. 390]. They shall each be removed from offices or employment and shall not be reassigned. The women shall be punished for ordinary fornication [Art. 390].

[2] If they commit fornication with imprisoned women, they shall be punished by 100 strokes of beating with the heavy stick and penal servitude

Laws on Penal Affairs

for three years. The imprisoned women shall only be punished for the original offenses.

Article 396 Committing Fornication during the Period of Mourning or by Buddhist or Daoist Clergy [Jusang ji sengdao fanjian]

In all cases of committing fornication during the period of mourning for parents or husbands, or by Buddhist priests or nuns or Daoist priests or nuns, the penalty in each case shall be increased two degrees from that for ordinary fornication [Art. 390]. Those who fornicate with them shall be punished for ordinary fornication.

Article 397 Honorable and Mean Persons Committing Fornication with Each Other [Liangjian xiangjian]

In all cases where male slaves commit fornication with honorable persons' wives or daughters, the penalty [for the slaves] shall be increased one degree from that for ordinary fornication [Art. 390]. If honorable persons commit fornication with others' female slaves, the penalty shall be reduced one degree [from that for ordinary fornication]. If male and female slaves commit fornication with each other, they shall be punished for ordinary fornication [Art. 390].

Article 398 Officials or Functionaries Sleeping with Entertainers [Guanli suchang]

[1] In all cases where officials or functionaries sleep with entertainers, they shall be punished by 60 strokes of beating with the heavy stick. As for the go-betweens, the penalty shall be reduced one degree.

[2] If officials' sons or sons' sons sleep with entertainers, the penalty shall also be the same. Their transgressions shall be recorded. On the day when they inherit official titles, they shall be demoted one class and be employed at distant frontiers.

Article 399 Purchasing Honorable Persons to Be Entertainers [Mailiang weichang]

In all cases where entertainers, dancers, or musicians purchase sons or daughters of honorable persons to be entertainers or dancers, or take them in marriage as wives or concubines, or adopt them as sons or daughters, they shall be punished by 100 strokes of beating with the heavy stick. For those who know the circumstances and who sell them or marry them off, the penalty shall be the same. As for the go-betweens, the penalty shall be reduced one degree. The wedding gifts shall be forfeit to the government. The boys or girls shall be returned to their lineages.

Section 9 Miscellaneous Offenses [Zafan]
[Eleven Articles]

Article 400 Destroying Exhibition Pavilions [Chaihui shenming ting]

In all cases of destroying exhibition pavilions or notice placards, the offenders shall be punished by 100 strokes of beating with the heavy stick and life exile to 3,000 *li*.

Article 401 Furnishing Medical Care and Medicine to Artisans and Soldiers Who Are Sick [Fujiang junshi bing ji yiyao]

In all cases where soldiers get sick in their places of guard duty or laborers or artisans get sick in the places where they perform services, if the officials in charge do not request physicians and medicines to treat them, they shall be punished by 40 strokes of beating with the light stick. If, as a result, death occurs, they shall be punished by 80 strokes of beating with the heavy stick. If the request has already been sent to relevant officials, but the said officials do not provide good physicians or appropriate medicines to treat them, the penalty shall be the same [for the said officials].

Article 402 Gambling [Dubo]

[1] In all cases of gambling for property, the offenders shall be punished by 80 strokes of beating with the heavy stick. The gambling devices and money shall be forfeit to the government. Those who run gambling halls shall be punished the same. Only those who are seen and discovered on the spot shall be punished. If officials in service gamble, the penalty shall be increased one degree.

[2] For those who gamble for drink or food, they shall not be punished.

Article 403 Castrating Others [Yange huozhe]

No official or civilian households shall adopt others' sons and castrate them. Any violations shall be punished by 100 strokes of beating with the heavy stick and life exile to 3,000 *li*. The sons shall be returned to their parents.

Article 404 Seeking Favors in Public Matters [Zhutuo gongshi]

[1] In all cases where officials, functionaries, or any other persons distort the law and seek favors in public matters, they shall be punished by 50 strokes of beating with the light stick. As long as they seek the favors, they shall be punished. (This means that as long as they seek favors to distort the law they shall be punished, whether or not the requests are granted or favors are carried out.) If the officials or functionaries in charge grant the favors, they shall be punished the same. If they do not grant the favors, they shall not be punished. If the favors have already been carried out, the penalty shall be 100 strokes of beating with the heavy stick. If the penalty for sub-

verting the law is heavier, the officials or functionaries shall be punished on the basis of deliberately exonerating the guilty and implicating the innocent [Art. 433]. For those who seek favors for others or for relatives, the penalty shall be reduced three degrees from that for officials or functionaries. For those who seek favors for themselves, the penalty shall be increased one degree from their original penalty.

[2] If supervisors or influential persons seek favors for others, they shall be punished by 100 strokes of beating with the heavy stick. If the penalty for subverting the law is heavier, the penalty shall be the same as that for the officials or functionaries in charge. If the penalty amounts to death, reduce one degree. (This means that as long as the supervisors or influential persons seek favors they shall be punished by 100 strokes of beating with the heavy stick. If officials or functionaries [in charge] grant the favors, they shall still be punished by 50 strokes of beating with the light stick. If the favors have already been carried out, they shall also be punished by 100 strokes of beating with the heavy stick. If the penalty for subverting the law is heavier than 100 strokes of beating with the heavy stick, the officials or functionaries and the supervisors or influential persons shall all be punished on the basis of deliberately exonerating the guilty or implicating the innocent [Art. 433]. If the officials or functionaries shall be sentenced to death in accordance with the *Code*, the supervisors or influential persons shall have the death penalty reduced one degree.) If they accept illicit goods, calculate the value of the illicit goods; they shall all be punished on the basis of [accepting property and] subverting the law [Art. 367].

[3] If officials or functionaries do not fear the supervisors or influential persons but take the evidence of seeking favors in public matters to the superior offices and make accusations, they shall be promoted one rank.

Article 405   Privately Settling Public Matters [Sihe gongshi]

In all cases of privately settling public matters, the penalty shall be reduced two degrees from that for the offenders. The punishment shall be limited to 50 strokes of beating with the light stick.

Article 406   Accidentally Setting Fires [Shihuo]

[1] In all cases of accidentally setting fires and burning one's own houses, the offenders shall be punished by 40 strokes of beating with the light stick. If the fires spread to and burn government or private houses, the penalty shall be 50 strokes of beating with the light stick. If, as a result, death occurs, the penalty shall be 100 strokes of beating with the heavy stick. The punishment shall be inflicted on those who accidentally set fires. If the fires spread to and burn the Imperial Ancestral Temple or imperial palace, the offenders shall be punished by strangulation. As for the Altar of the Soil, the penalty shall be reduced one degree.

[2] For those who accidentally set fires within the area of imperial tombs, they shall be punished by 80 strokes of beating with the heavy stick and penal servitude for two years. If the fires spread to and burn trees, the penalty shall be 100 strokes of beating with the heavy stick and life exile to 2,000 *li*. For those who accidentally set fires within government buildings, granaries, or warehouses, they shall also be punished by 80 strokes of beating with the heavy stick and penal servitude for two years. If the custodians, because of [the fires], fraudulently take property, calculate the value of the illicit goods; they shall be punished on the basis of supervisors or custodians themselves stealing [Art. 287]. If the fires are accidentally set outside and spread and burn, in each case, the penalty shall be reduced three degrees.

[3] For those who light fires inside warehouses or granaries, they shall be punished by 80 strokes of beating with the heavy stick.

[4] Those who are on guard at the imperial palace, imperial audience halls, granaries, or warehouses or who are guarding prisoners shall not leave their posts when they see fires break out. Any violations shall be punished by 100 strokes of beating with the heavy stick.

Article 407   Deliberately Setting Fires and Burning Others' Houses [Fanghuo gushao ren fangwu]

[1] In all cases of deliberately setting fires and burning one's own houses, the offenders shall be punished by 100 strokes of beating with the heavy stick. If the fires spread to and burn government or private houses or stores of goods, they shall be punished by 100 strokes of beating with the heavy stick and penal servitude for three years. If the offenders consequently steal and take property, they shall be punished by decapitation. If [the fires] kill or injure others, the offenders shall be punished on the basis of deliberately killing [Art. 313] or injuring [Art. 325] others.

[2] For those who deliberately set fires and burn government or private houses, government offices, granaries, warehouses, or stores of government goods, they shall all be punished by decapitation. (They shall be punished only when they are apprehended at the spots where they set the fires and there is clear evidence.) If they deliberately set fires and burn others' unoccupied houses or goods that are stored in fields, in each case the penalty shall be reduced one degree.

[3] Moreover, calculate the diminished value of the damaged property, and take the offenders' property sufficient to compensate [for the damages] and give it to the government or the private owners.

Article 408   Theatrical Performances [Banzuo zaju]

In all cases of theatrical performances, musicians shall not be permitted to dress up as former emperors, empresses or other imperial consorts, loyal ministers, martyrs, sages, or worthies. Any violations shall be punished by

100 strokes of beating with the heavy stick. If the households of officials or commoners allow them to dress up this way for the performances, the penalty shall be the same. As for acting as immortals, righteous husbands, chaste wives, filial sons, or obedient sons' sons with the aim of motivating others to be good, it shall not be prohibited.

Article 409   Violating the Commandment [Weiling]

In all cases of violating the *Commandment,* the offenders shall be punished by 50 strokes of beating with the light stick. (This refers to the cases where the *Commandment* has a prohibition but the *Code* does not stipulate a penalty.)

Article 410   Doing What Ought Not to Be Done [Buying wei]

In all cases of doing what ought not to be done, the offenders shall be punished by 40 strokes of beating with the light stick. (This refers to the cases where neither the *Code* nor the *Commandment* has an article dealing with the act, but the act shall not be done according to reason [*li*].) If the circumstances are serious, the penalty shall be 80 strokes of beating with the heavy stick.

Section 10   Arrests and Escapes [*Buwang*] [Eight Articles]

Article 411   Pursuing and Arresting Criminals by Those Who Are Charged with the Duty of Arrest [Yingburen zhuibu zuiren]

In all cases where those who are charged with the duty of arrest receive orders to pursue and arrest criminals but make pretexts and do not set out, or if they know where the criminals are but do not arrest them, they shall be punished one degree less than the criminals. Set a time limit of thirty days: If they themselves are able to arrest one-half of the criminals or more, or although the total number of criminals seized does not reach one-half but those who are seized commit the most serious crimes, all who are charged with the duty of arrest shall be exempted from punishment. If only one person seizes the criminals, the others shall also be treated the same. If the criminals are already dead, or they voluntarily confess all their crimes, [those who are charged with the duty of arrest shall] also be exempted from punishment. If the criminals do not confess all the crimes, [those who are charged with the duty of arrest shall] be punished only for the crimes that are not confessed. For those who are not originally charged with the duty of arrest but who are temporarily sent after the criminals, in each case the penalty shall be reduced one degree from that for those who are charged with the duty of arrest. As for those who receive property and deliberately connive at the acts, no time limit for arrest shall be given; in each case they shall be punished the same as the criminals. If the value of the illicit goods entails a heavier penalty, calculate the value of the illicit goods; they shall be punished by the heavier penalty on the basis of [accepting property and] subverting the law [Art. 367].

Article 412   Criminals Resisting Arrest [Zuiren jubu]

[1] In all cases where criminals run away or resist arrest, in each case the penalty shall be increased two degrees from that for the original crime. The punishment shall be limited to 100 strokes of beating with the heavy stick and life exile to 3,000 *li*. If the criminals strike the arresting persons and cause injuries of fracture or worse, they shall be punished by strangulation. If they kill the arresting persons, they shall be punished by decapitation. As for accessories, in each case the penalty shall be reduced one degree.

[2] If the criminals use weapons to resist arrest and the arresting persons kill them in the struggle, or prisoners run away and the arresting persons pursue and kill them, or prisoners kill themselves in despair, in none of these cases shall the arresting persons be punished.

[3] If the criminals have already been caught or they do not resist the arrest but the arresting persons kill them or injure them to the extent of fracture, in each case they shall be punished on the basis of killing or injuring others in affrays [Arts. 313, 325]. If the criminals whose original crimes entail the death penalty are killed without authorization, the penalty shall be 100 strokes of beating with the heavy stick.

Article 413   Imprisoned Criminals Escaping from Prisons or Using Force to Break out of Prisons and Running Away [Yuqiu tuojian ji fanyu zaitao]

[1] In all cases where imprisoned criminals escape from prisons [through doors] or free themselves from their fetters and handcuffs and escape from prisons [over the wall] and run away, in each case the penalty shall be increased two degrees from that for their original crimes. If they stealthily release other prisoners whose penalties are heavier than theirs, they shall be punished the same as the other [released] prisoners. The punishment shall be limited to 100 strokes of beating with the heavy stick and life exile to 3,000 *li*. If their own crimes entail the death penalty, the regular rules in the *Code* shall be followed.

[2] If imprisoned criminals use force to break out of prisons and run away, they shall all be punished by decapitation. If those who are confined in the same prisons do not know the circumstances, they shall not be punished.

Article 414   Criminals under Penal Servitude or Life Exile Running Away [Tuliuren tao]

[1] In all cases where the prisoners who are sentenced to penal servitude, life exile, or banishment run away during the period of service, for one day,

they shall be punished by 50 strokes of beating with the light stick. For each additional three days, the penalty shall be increased one degree. The punishment shall be limited to 100 strokes of beating with the heavy stick; they shall still be sent back to the places to which they were sentenced. As for the prisoners who are sentenced to penal servitude, the years of penal servitude of the original sentence will begin again from his new capture; past servitude shall not count.

[2] If the prisoners who are sentenced to penal servitude, life exile, banishment, or military exile have begun their journey and run away before they reach the place of sentence, the penalty shall also be the same.

[3] If custodians or escort guards do not discover that the prisoners have run away, for one person, they shall be punished by 60 strokes of beating with the heavy stick. For each additional person, the penalty shall be increased one degree. The punishment shall be limited to 100 strokes of beating with the heavy stick. They shall all be allowed 100 days to pursue and capture [the escaped prisoners]. The penalty for the officials in charge or escort officers shall be reduced three degrees from that for custodians or escort guards. If, within the time limit, the prisoners are captured by [responsible officials or guards] themselves or others, or the prisoners have died or voluntarily surrender themselves, in all cases the punishment shall be exempted. If [the officials or guards] deliberately connive at the acts, in each case they shall be punished the same as the prisoners. If they receive property, calculate the value of the illicit goods; they shall be punished by the more serious penalty on the basis of [accepting property and] subverting the law [Art. 367].

Article 415   Delaying in Sending Prisoners [Jiliu qiutu]

[1] In all cases where prisoners have been sentenced to penal servitude, life exile, banishment, or military exile, the responsible officials shall, within 10 days and according to the rules, have them [the prisoners] put in fetters and handcuffs, send persons to guard and escort them, keep a careful watch over them, and send them to the places designated for serving the sentence. If, beyond the authorized time limit, they delay in sending the prisoners without reason, for 3 days, they shall be punished by 20 strokes of beating with the light stick. For each additional 3 days, the penalty shall be increased one degree. The punishment shall be limited to 60 strokes of beating with the heavy stick. If the prisoners consequently run away, the responsible officials or functionaries shall be sent to substitute for the offenders in serving the original sentence. After the offenders are captured and sent to the authorities to replace [the officials or functionaries] for serving the sentence, then from the day [when the offenders] arrive, the [officials or functionaries] shall be released and appointed elsewhere. ("To substitute for the offenders in serving the original sentence" means that the responsible officials or func-

tionaries shall be sent to serve the sentence that is assigned to the original offenders. They shall serve penal servitude if penal servitude is originally sentenced. They shall serve life exile if life exile is originally sentenced. They shall serve banishment if banishment is originally sentenced. They shall serve military exile if military exile is originally sentenced. After the offenders are captured and sent to the authorities, the officials or functionaries will be released and appointed elsewhere.)

[2] If prisoners are delivered to the neighboring territories but the local officials delay and do not immediately transfer them, the penalty shall be the same.

[3] If, at the time of sending [prisoners to serve sentences], the responsible officials or functionaries do not affix fetters and handcuffs in accordance with the rules and, as a result, the prisoners free themselves en route from their fetters and handcuffs and run away, [the responsible officials or functionaries] shall be punished the same as the escort guards [Art. 414].

[4] In all cases the penalty shall be inflicted only on those who are responsible. If they receive property, calculate the amount of the illicit goods; they shall be punished by the more serious penalty on the basis of [accepting property and] subverting the law [Art. 367].

Article 416   Custodians Not Discovering the Escape of Prisoners
[Zhushou bujue shiqiu]

[1] In all cases where jail guards do not discover the escape of prisoners, they shall be punished two degrees less than the prisoners. If the prisoners break out of prison and run away, the penalty [for the jail guards] shall be reduced two more degrees. They will be given 100 days to pursue and arrest [the prisoners]. If, within the time limit, they themselves or others capture [the prisoners], or the prisoners have already died or voluntarily surrender themselves, in all such cases the punishment shall be exempted. The penalty for the warders and functionaries in charge of the prison [*siyu guandian*] shall be reduced three degrees. If the prison-inspecting officials themselves have already counted the prisoners one by one and the cangues, fetters, or handcuffs are all according to the rules, and if they have received written statements from the warders and jail guards that the prisoners are securely imprisoned, they shall not be punished. If they have not counted [the prisoners] and subsequently the prisoners run away, they shall be punished the same as the warders. For those who deliberately connive at the acts, they shall not be given the time limit for capturing [the prisoners], and in each case they shall be punished the same as the prisoners. If they themselves capture [the prisoners] before [the penalty for the prisoners] has been executed, or if others capture [the prisoners], or if the prisoners have already died or voluntarily surrender themselves, in each case the penalty shall be reduced one degree. For those who receive property, calculate the value of

Laws on Penal Affairs

the illicit goods; they shall be punished by the heavier penalty on the basis of [accepting property and] subverting the law [Art. 367].

[2] If outlaws break into prisons from outside and rescue prisoners and their force is too strong to be resisted, [the officials and guards] shall not be punished.

[3] When escorting prisoners who are being transferred, if the escort guards do not discover the loss of prisoners en route, they shall be punished the same.

Article 417   Knowing the Circumstances and Concealing Criminals
[Zhiqing cangni zuiren]

[1] In all cases where those who know that others have committed crimes, which have been discovered, and that government offices have sent people to pursue and capture [the criminals] conceal [the criminals] in their houses and do not arrest them and make accusations to the authorities, or they point out to them the route or give them food and clothing and send them to hiding places, in each case the offenders shall be punished by one degree less than the criminals' penalty. When criminals are successively transferred from place to place, if the persons who conceal the criminals know the circumstances, they shall all be punished; if they do not know the circumstances, they shall not be punished.

[2] For the persons who know that the government offices are pursuing and capturing criminals but who leak the information so that the criminals are able to run away, they shall be punished one degree less than the criminals. If they themselves capture the criminals before [the penalty for the criminals] has been executed, they shall be exempted from the punishment. If others capture [the criminals], or if the criminals have already died or voluntarily surrender themselves, in each case the penalty shall be reduced one more degree.

Article 418   Time Limit for Arresting Robbers and Thieves
[Daozei buxian]

[1] In all cases of arresting robbers and thieves, take the day when the matter is discovered as the beginning, if the arresting constables do not capture forcible robbers within one month, they shall be punished by 20 strokes of beating with the light stick. For two months, the penalty shall be 30 strokes of beating with the light stick; for three months, 40 strokes of beating with the light stick. The arresting officials shall be punished by a fine of two months' salary. If the constables do not capture thieves within one month, they shall be punished by 10 strokes of beating with the light stick. For two months, the penalty shall be 20 strokes of beating with the light stick; for three months, 30 strokes of beating with the light stick. The arresting officials shall be punished by a fine of one month's salary. If, within the time limit,

they capture as many as one-half of the robbers or thieves, they shall not be punished.

[2] If [the victims of the forcible robbery or theft] delay 20 days or more and then report [the cases] to the authorities, there shall be no arresting time limit. The time limit for arresting criminals of homicide shall be the same as the limit for forcible robbers.

Section 11 Judgment and Imprisonment [*Duanyu*] [Twenty-nine Articles]

Article 419   Not Imprisoning Criminals Who Should Be Imprisoned
[Qiu yingjin er bujin]

[1] In all cases where criminals who should be imprisoned are not imprisoned, or who should be put in cangues, fetters, and handcuffs are not put in cangues, fetters, and handcuffs, or [the criminals' cangues, fetters, and handcuffs are] removed, if the criminals are guilty of crimes punishable by beating with the heavy stick, [the judging officials] shall be punished by 30 strokes of beating with the light stick. If it is penal servitude, the penalty shall be 40 strokes of beating with the light stick. If it is life exile, the penalty shall be 50 strokes of beating with the light stick. If it is death, the penalty shall be 60 strokes of beating with the heavy stick. If the criminals should be put in cangues but are put in fetters, or if they should be put in fetters but are put in cangues, in each case the penalty shall be reduced one degree.

[2] If the criminals themselves remove the instruments of restraint, or the warders and functionaries in charge of the prison or jail guards privately remove the cangues, fetters, or handcuffs, the penalty shall also be the same. If the prison-inspecting officials know the circumstances but do not report to the authorities, they shall be punished the same. If they do not know, they shall not be punished.

[3] If the criminals should not be imprisoned but are imprisoned, or if they should not be put in cangues, fetters, or handcuffs but are put in cangues, fetters, or handcuffs, in each case the penalty shall be 60 strokes of beating with the heavy stick.

[4] If [the judging officials, prison-inspecting officials, warders or functionaries in charge of the prison, or jail guards] receive property, calculate the value of the illicit goods; they shall be punished by the heavier penalty on the basis of [accepting property and] subverting the law [Art. 367].

Article 420   Deliberately Imprisoning or Interrogating Innocent Persons
[Gujin gukan pingren]

[1] In all cases where officials or functionaries cherish private enmity and therefore deliberately imprison innocent persons, they shall be punished

by 80 strokes of beating with the heavy stick. If they consequently cause death, they shall be punished by strangulation. If the prison-inspecting officials, warders or functionaries in charge of the prison, or jail guards know the circumstances but do not report to the authorities, they shall be punished the same. If they do not know, they shall not be punished. If they mistakenly imprison innocent persons who are indirectly involved due to public matters and who make no confessions to the authorities, and consequently they cause them to die, they shall be punished by 80 strokes of beating with the heavy stick. If those persons should be imprisoned in accordance with official documents, there shall be no punishment.

[2] If [officials or functionaries] deliberately interrogate innocent persons, they shall be punished by 80 strokes of beating with the heavy stick. If they cause injuries of fracture or worse, they shall be punished for ordinary affrays [Art. 325]. If they cause death, they shall be punished by decapitation. If officials in the same office or jail guards know the circumstances and jointly conduct the interrogation, they shall be punished the same. If death results, the penalty shall be reduced one degree. If they do not know the circumstances or interrogate or torture in accordance with the law, they shall not be punished. When innocent persons are indirectly involved due to public matters and should be interrogated by the authorities, if they refuse to make an avowal even though the evidence for the criminals such as illicit goods or weapons is clear, set up files for them and interrogate them with torture according to the law. If death results incidentally, there shall be no punishment.

Article 421   Prolonging Imprisonment [Yanjin]

In all cases where the circumstances and [nature of the] offenses committed by prisoners have been determined clearly, and the investigating censors or provincial surveillance commissioners have reviewed the record [and determined that] there is no injustice and nothing else needs to be investigated and that [the punishment] should be executed, then the punishment shall be executed within the time limit of 3 days. The prisoners who should be deported shall be deported within the time limit of 10 days. If after the time limit has expired the punishment is not executed or the deportation is not commenced, for 3 days, the responsible officials or functionaries shall be punished by 20 strokes of beating with the light stick. For each additional 3 days, the penalty shall be increased one degree. The punishment is limited to 60 strokes of beating with the heavy stick. If death results because of the prolongation of imprisonment and the prisoners are guilty of capital crimes, [the responsible officials or functionaries] shall be punished by 60 strokes of beating with the heavy stick. If it is life exile, the penalty shall be 80 strokes of beating with the heavy stick. If it is penal servitude, the penalty shall be 100 strokes of beating with the heavy stick. If it is beating with the heavy stick or below, the penalty shall be 60 strokes of beating with the heavy stick and penal servitude for one year.

Article 422 Mistreating Prisoners [Lingnüe zuiqiu]

In all cases where jail guards without reason mistreat and injure prisoners within the jail, they shall be punished for ordinary affrays [Art. 325]. If they reduce clothing or food, calculate the value of the illicit goods; they shall be punished on the basis of supervisors or custodians themselves stealing [Art. 287]. If consequently death results, they shall be punished by strangulation. If the warders or functionaries in charge of the prison or prison-inspecting officials know the circumstances but do not report to the authorities, they shall be punished the same. If death results, the penalty shall be reduced one degree.

Article 423 Giving Prisoners Edged Metal Tools That Can Be Used to Free Themselves [Yuqiu jinren jietuo]

[1] In all cases where jail guards give prisoners edged metal tools or other objects that can be used to kill themselves or to remove their cangues or fetters, they shall be punished by 100 strokes of beating with the heavy stick. If as a result the prisoners run away or injure themselves or injure others, the penalty shall be 60 strokes of beating with the heavy stick and penal servitude for one year. If the prisoners kill themselves, the penalty shall be 80 strokes of beating with the heavy stick and penal servitude for two years. If as a result the prisoners break out of prison or kill others, the penalty shall be strangulation. If the prisoners run away and, before [the jail guards] have been sentenced, they [the jail guards] themselves capture the prisoners or others capture them, or the prisoners have died or voluntarily surrender themselves, in each case the penalty shall be reduced one degree.

[2] If ordinary persons give prisoners objects that can be used to free themselves, or sons or sons' sons give [such objects] to [imprisoned] paternal grandparents or parents, or slaves or hired laborers give to household heads, in each case the penalty shall be reduced one degree.

[3] If the warders or functionaries in charge of the prison or prison-inspecting officials know the circumstances but do not report to the authorities, they shall be punished the same. If this amounts to death, the penalty shall be reduced one degree.

[4] For those who receive property, calculate the value of the illicit goods; they shall be punished by the heavier penalty on the basis of [accepting property and] subverting the law [Art. 367].

[5] If jail guards fail to inspect [the prison] so that prisoners commit suicide, the jail guards shall be punished by 60 strokes of beating with the heavy stick. The warders or functionaries in charge of the prison each shall be pun-

ished by 50 strokes of beating with the light stick. The prison-inspecting officials shall be punished by 40 strokes of beating with the light stick.

Article 424   Custodians Instructing Prisoners to Contradict Their Confessions [Zhushou jiaoqiu fanyi]

[1] In all cases where warders or functionaries in charge of the prison or jail guards instruct prisoners to contradict their confessions and therefore change and confuse the facts, or transmit messages so that the penalty is increased [for others] or reduced [for the prisoners], they shall be punished on the basis of deliberately exonerating the guilty or implicating the innocent [Art. 433]. If outsiders commit the offense, the penalty shall be reduced one degree.

[2] For those who permit outsiders to enter the prison or to transmit information to the prisoners but this does not lead to an increase or a reduction in [the penalty], the penalty shall be 50 strokes of beating with the light stick.

[3] For those who receive property, calculate the value of the illicit goods; they shall be punished by the heavier penalty on the basis of [accepting property and] subverting the law [Art. 367].

Article 425   Prisoners' Clothing and Food [Yuqiu yiliang]

[1] In all cases where warders or functionaries in charge of the prison or jail guards should request clothing, food, medical treatment, or medicine for prisoners who need such items but do not request, or they should remove sick prisoners' cangues, fetters, or handcuffs but they do not remove them, or they should release [sick prisoners] under security but do not release them, or they should allow prisoners' family members to visit [the prisoners] but do not allow them to visit, they shall be punished by 50 strokes of beating with the light stick. If as a result death occurs, and if the criminals are guilty of capital crimes, the penalty shall be 60 strokes of beating with the heavy stick. If it is life exile, the penalty shall be 80 strokes of beating with the heavy stick. If it is penal servitude, the penalty shall be 100 strokes of beating with the heavy stick. If it is beating with the heavy stick or below, the penalty shall be 60 strokes of beating with the heavy stick and penal servitude for one year. If the prison-inspecting officials know the circumstances but do not report to the authorities, they shall be punished the same.

[2] If the request has already been made to the superior offices but [the superior officials or functionaries] do not immediately act on the request, for one day, they shall be punished by 10 strokes of beating with the light stick. For each additional day, the penalty shall be increased one degree. The punishment shall be limited to 40 strokes of beating with the light stick. If as a result death occurs, and if the criminals are guilty of capital crimes, the

penalty shall be 60 strokes of beating with the heavy stick. If it is life exile, the penalty shall be 80 strokes of beating with the heavy stick. If it is penal servitude, the penalty shall be 100 strokes of beating with the heavy stick. If it is beating with the heavy stick or below, the penalty shall be 60 strokes of beating with the heavy stick and penal servitude for one year.

Article 426 When Meritorious Officials Are Imprisoned, Their Relatives May Visit Them [Gongchen yingjin qinren rushi]

In all cases where meritorious officials or officials of the fifth rank or above commit crimes and should be imprisoned, their relatives are allowed to visit them. If they commit crimes punishable by penal servitude or life exile, their relatives are allowed to accompany them. If they die of illness when they are imprisoned [before they are sentenced] or after they arrive at the place of sentence or when they are en route [to the place of sentence], the judging officials at the capital or officials with jurisdiction outside the capital shall write out the report on the cause of death. Then they shall send someone to conduct the relatives to the "watchtower" [the imperial palace] and petition the emperor that they be set free. Any violations shall be punished by 60 strokes of beating with the heavy stick.

Article 427 Prisoners Sentenced to Death Ordering Others to Kill Them [Siqiu lingren zisha]

[1] In all cases where prisoners who are sentenced to death have already admitted their crimes and they order relatives by blood or marriage or friends to kill them or order [relatives or friends] to hire others to kill them, the relatives, friends, or the persons who conduct the killing shall each be punished two degrees less than the killing that is stipulated in the law [i.e., Arts. 338–45 on striking and killing relatives and Art. 313 on killing ordinary persons in affrays]. If the prisoners have already admitted their crimes but have not ordered relatives or friends to kill them, or although they ordered [their relatives or friends] to kill them, they have not admitted their crimes, and [their relatives or friends] kill them without authorization or hire others to kill them, the relatives, friends, or the persons who conduct the killing each shall be punished on the basis of killing or injuring in affrays [Art. 313].

[2] If, although the prisoners have already admitted their crimes, their sons or sons' sons commit such an act for their paternal grandparents or parents, or slaves or hired laborers commit such an act for their household heads, they shall all be punished by decapitation.

Article 428 Old and Young Persons Are Not Put to Judicial Torture [Laoyou bu kaoxun]

In all cases involving persons who have the privileges of the Eight Deliberations [Art. 3] or who are 70 years of age or more, 15 years of age or less, or disabled, judicial torture shall not be allowed. Their crimes shall all be determined by the testimony of a group of witnesses. Any violations shall be punished on the basis of deliberately or negligently implicating the innocent [Art. 433]. As for those who are allowed mutual concealment according to the *Code* [Art. 31] or who are 80 years of age or more, 10 years of age or less, or incapacitated, they shall not be ordered to serve as witnesses. Any violations shall be punished by 50 strokes of beating with the light stick.

Article 429 Detaining Prisoners during Interrogations to Wait for Direct Confrontation [Juyu tingqiu daidui]

[1] In all cases where judging officials detain criminals during interrogations to wait for direct confrontation because the criminals' partners in the same case are in other jurisdictions, although the judging officials are not in the same chain of command with the officials of other jurisdictions, they shall all deal with each other directly to have [the criminals' partners] brought [to the place where the interrogations are taking place]. [The officials in other jurisdictions shall] send [the wanted persons] within three days after the request documents arrive. If they violate the time limit and do not send [the wanted persons], for one day, they shall be punished by 20 strokes of beating with the light stick. For each additional day, the penalty shall be increased one degree. The punishment shall be limited to 60 strokes of beating with the heavy stick. [Official documents] shall be sent to the superior offices of those responsible officials [in other jurisdictions] to request that their crimes [of violating the time limit] be punished and [the wanted persons] be sent and transported [to the place where the interrogations are taking place].

[2] If in the same case the criminals' accomplices should be questioned by confrontation but their crimes have already been discovered at other subprefectures or districts and they are being interrogated there, then transfer the criminals guilty of less serious crimes to the place where the criminals guilty of more serious crimes are located. [If the criminals' crimes are of the same degree,] transfer the smaller number of criminals to the place where the larger number of criminals is located. If the numbers of the criminals are the same, transfer the criminals who are discovered later to the place where the criminals who are discovered first are located for interrogation. If the two districts are more than 300 *li* apart, each case shall be judged in the place where it is discovered. Any violations shall be punished by 50 strokes of beating with the light stick. If [the officials] violate the law and transfer the criminals guilty of more serious crimes to the place where the criminals guilty of less serious crimes are located, or transfer the larger number of criminals to the place where the smaller number of criminals is located, the local officials shall immediately receive and interrogate [the criminals]; and they shall still report to the [guilty officials'] superior officials, who shall

investigate and punish their subordinates' crime of transferring criminals contrary to law. If the criminals arrive [but the officials having proper jurisdiction] do not receive [them], for one day, they shall be punished by 20 strokes of beating with the light stick. For each additional one day, the penalty shall be increased one degree. The punishment shall be limited to 60 strokes of beating with the heavy stick.

Article 430 Judging Cases in Accordance with the Specifications in the Complaints [Yi gaozhuang juyu]

[1] In judging all cases it is essential that the interrogation be conducted in accordance with the specifications in the complaints. If [the judging officials] go beyond these specifications and seek information about other matters and increase the number of crimes, they shall be punished on the basis of deliberately implicating the innocent [Art. 433]. If the officials' colleagues in the same office have not signed the documents, they shall not be punished.

[2] If, because of the specifications of the complaints or because [the law] requires arrest and investigation, other crimes are consequently discovered and the matters should be investigated, this provision is not applicable.

Article 431 Complainants Not Being Released after the Trial Is Completed [Yuangaoren shibi bu fanghui]

In all cases of [handling] proceedings based on complaints, when the facts have been obtained at the interrogation and the defendants have admitted their crimes, if there are no other matters requiring the complainants to wait for confrontation, [the complainants] shall be immediately released. [Those who] hold [the complainants] without reason for three days and do not release them shall be punished by 20 strokes of beating with the light stick. For each additional three days, the penalty shall be increased one degree. The punishment shall be limited to 40 strokes of beating with the light stick.

Article 432 Prisoners Falsely Accusing Innocent Persons [Yuqiu wuzhi pingren]

[1] In all cases where prisoners falsely accuse innocent persons, they shall be punished on the basis of falsely accusing others [Art. 359]. If their original crimes are more serious, they shall be punished in accordance with the more serious crimes.

[2] If officials or functionaries while interrogating prisoners unlawfully torture them and deliberately instruct them to accuse innocent persons falsely, they shall be punished on the basis of deliberately implicating the innocent [Art. 433].

[3] If [officials] in collecting [owed] money or grain taxes force [the fam-

ilies that owe the taxes] to state falsely that other, innocent persons should pay for them, calculate the value of unlawfully collected property; they shall be punished on the basis of obtaining illicit goods through malfeasance [Art. 368]. The property shall be returned to the owners.

[4] If [officials], without reason, detain the falsely accused innocent persons for three days and do not release them, they shall be punished by 20 strokes of beating with the light stick. For each additional three days, the penalty shall be increased one degree. The punishment shall be limited to 60 strokes of beating with the heavy stick.

[5] If, in interrogating prisoners, witnesses do not speak truthfully but deliberately give false evidence, or if persons beyond the pale of civilization have committed crimes but the interpreters, when translating foreign languages, do not respond correctly so that the penalty for the crimes is either reduced or increased, the witnesses shall be punished two degrees less than the original criminals. (This refers to cases such as those where the witnesses do not speak the truth so that the offenders completely evade punishment; they shall be punished two degrees less than the penalty for the offenders. If, [because of the witnesses' false evidence,] the penalty for the offenders is either increased or reduced, the witnesses shall also be punished two degrees less than the increased or reduced penalty for the offenders.) The interpreters shall be punished the same [as the persons beyond the pale of civilization]. (This refers to cases such as those where persons beyond the pale of civilization have committed crimes but the interpreters collude with them and mistranslate [the language] so that the offenders completely evade punishment; [the interpreters] then shall be punished by the entire penalty that the offenders should receive. If the interpreters by mistranslating increase or reduce the penalty for the persons beyond the pale of civilization, they shall be punished by the increased or reduced penalty. For instance, if the persons beyond the pale of civilization have admitted crimes punishable with 60 strokes of beating with the heavy stick but the interpreters in translating increase the penalty to 100 strokes of beating with the heavy stick, the interpreters then shall be punished by 40 strokes of beating with the heavy stick. Again, if the persons beyond the pale of civilization have admitted crimes punishable with 100 strokes of beating with the heavy stick but the interpreters in translating reduce the penalty to 50 strokes of beating with the light stick, the interpreters then shall be punished by 50 strokes of beating with the heavy stick.)

Article 433 *Officials Exonerating the Guilty or Implicating the Innocent* [Guansi churu renzui]

[1] In all cases where officials deliberately exonerate the guilty or implicate the innocent, for complete acquittal or complete conviction, they shall

be punished on the basis of the whole penalty. (This refers to cases such as those where, because they receive others' property or use extralegal torture, officials or functionaries deliberately inflict punishment upon innocent persons or deliberately exonerate guilty persons; they shall all be punished on the basis of the whole penalty. "Extralegal torture" refers to cases such as applying heated iron on others or pouring cold water on others' bodies during winter months.)

[2] If they increase a lighter penalty to a heavier one, or reduce a heavier penalty to a lighter one, they shall be punished on the basis of the increased or reduced penalty. If the penalty amounts to death, they shall be punished on the basis of the death penalty. (This means, for instance, that the penalty for the crime that someone commits is 10 strokes of beating with the light stick, but it is increased to 20 strokes. This is called "increasing a lighter penalty to a heavier one." [The officials or functionaries then shall] be punished by the increased 10 strokes of beating with the light stick. If someone should be punished by 50 strokes of beating with the light stick but the penalty is reduced to 30 strokes, this is called "decreasing a heavier penalty to a lighter one." [The officials or functionaries then shall] be punished by the reduced 20 strokes. Other articles shall follow this provision. When a lighter penalty is increased to a heavier one, if the penalty is increased to penal servitude, each degree of penal servitude shall be converted into 20 strokes of beating with the heavy stick. If the penalty is increased to life exile, each degree of life exile shall be converted into one-half year of penal servitude. If the penalty is increased to death and the death penalty has already been carried out, [the offenders shall] be sentenced to death. When a heavier penalty is reduced to a lighter one, the penalty shall also be [computed] the same.)

[3] If, in judging cases, [officials or functionaries] negligently implicate innocent persons or increase a lighter penalty to a heavier one, in each case their penalty shall be reduced three degrees [from that for the original criminals]. If they negligently exonerate guilty persons or reduce a heavier penalty to a lighter one, in each case their penalty shall be reduced five degrees. (This means that [the officials or functionaries], in interrogating prisoners, reduce or increase the penalty because the witnesses give false evidence, or [the accused persons] confess to the false charges when [the officials or functionaries] conduct judicial torture in accordance with the law, or [the officials or functionaries] only make mistakes in deliberating the sentence and have not committed such transgressions as accepting illicit goods or using extralegal torture. If they negligently increase a lighter penalty to a heavier one or reduce a heavier penalty to a lighter one, they shall also be punished on the basis of the excess.) In all these cases, the functionaries shall be punished as principals; the staff supervisors shall have their penalty reduced one degree from that for the functionaries; the associate officials shall have their

penalty reduced one degree from that for the staff supervisors; the head officials shall have their penalty reduced one degree from that for associate officials.

[4] If the penalty for the prisoners has not been executed, the prisoners have not been released, the prisoners have been captured again after they are released, or the prisoners have died, in each case the penalty shall be reduced one degree. (This means that if [the officials or functionaries] deliberately or negligently increase the penalty to beating with the light stick, beating with the heavy stick, penal servitude, life exile, or death but the penalty has not been executed; or if they deliberately or negligently reduce the penalty of beating with the light stick, beating with the heavy stick, penal servitude, life exile, or death but the prisoners have not been released; or although the prisoners are released but they have been captured again; or the prisoners have themselves died; in each case, the penalty for [the officials or functionaries] shall be reduced one degree from that for deliberately decreasing or increasing or negligently decreasing or increasing others' penalty.)

Article 434   Reversing Unjust Judgments [Bianming yuanwang]

[1] In all cases where investigating censors or provincial surveillance commissioners reverse unjust judgments, it is essential that they write down all of the evidence of unjust judgments and report by memorial under seal to the throne. If the officials designated to do so pursue the investigation of the injustices and find them to have occurred, the sentence for the wrongfully accused persons shall be rectified in accordance with the *Code*. The punishment shall be inflicted on the original complainants [Art. 359] and the original investigating officials or functionaries [Art. 433].

[2] If the judgments are not unjust but [the investigating censors or provincial surveillance commissioners] fraudulently reverse them, they shall be punished by 100 strokes of beating with the heavy stick and penal servitude for three years. If the penalty for the falsely accused crimes is heavier, they shall be punished on the basis of deliberately exonerating the guilty or implicating the innocent [Art. 433]. If the persons whose judgments are reversed know the circumstances, they shall be punished the same; if they do not know, they shall not be punished.

Article 435   The Degrees of Competence of Officials Having Jurisdiction for Executing [Sentences] of Prisoners [Yousi jueqiu dengdi]

[1] In all cases where prisoners have been interrogated clearly and the investigation and examination have been handled completely, penalties of penal servitude, life exile, or below shall be carried out by the prefecture, subprefecture, or district. For the death penalty, the investigating censors in the capital or provincial surveillance commissioners outside the capital

shall examine the case to see if there is injustice. They shall deliberate on the sentence in accordance with the *Code* and then submit [the judgment] to the Ministry of Justice. The Ministry of Justice shall prepare a decision and then report by memorial to the throne and wait for the imperial reply. [If the death penalty is approved by the throne,] it shall be executed, in the capital, jointly by the officials delegated by the Ministry of Justice and the investigating censors or, outside the capital, jointly by the officials delegated by the Provincial Administration Commissions and the Provincial Surveillance Commissions.

[2] If the offenders object to the original judgments or their family members complain of injustice, [the officials who are reviewing the records] shall immediately investigate the matters. If the judgments have indeed violated [the law], [the reviewing officials shall] meet with the original investigating and judging officials and together they shall review the case and change the sentence.

[3] If the records have been examined and no injustice has been found but [the reviewing officials] deliberately procrastinate and do not execute the sentence, they shall be punished by 60 strokes of beating with the heavy stick. If [the prisoners] clearly state that they are victims of injustice and oppression but [the reviewing officials] do not handle the cases for them, they shall be punished on the basis of deliberately or negligently increasing the penalty [Art. 433].

Article 436 *Examining Wounds on Corpses and Making Untrue Reports* [Jianyan shishang bu yishi]

[1] In all cases of examining wounds on corpses, if written commissions have arrived but [the examining officials] make excuses and do not immediately conduct the examination so that the corpses decompose, or if they do not personally go to [the places where the corpses are] and superintend [the examination] but send functionaries or runners [to conduct the examination], or if the initial examining or reviewing officials or functionaries together view the corpses and harmonize [their statements regarding] the conditions of the corpses, or if they do not examine diligently but make untrue reports regarding the nature, severity, and number of the wounds on the corpses and consequently determine an inaccurate cause of death, the senior officials shall be punished by 60 strokes of beating with the heavy stick. The staff supervisors shall be punished by 70 strokes of beating with the heavy stick. The functionaries shall be punished by 80 strokes of beating with the heavy stick. If the coroners do not examine correctly but harmonize [their statements regarding] the conditions of the corpses together with [the examining officials or functionaries], they shall be punished the same. If as a result the penalty is increased or reduced, [the officials, functionar-

Laws on Penal Affairs

ies, or coroners] shall be punished on the basis of negligently exonerating the guilty or implicating the innocent [Art. 433].

[2] If [the officials, functionaries, or coroners] receive property and deliberately make untrue reports on the examination, they shall be punished on the basis of deliberately exonerating the guilty or implicating the innocent [Art. 433]. If the value of the illicit goods entails a heavier penalty, calculate the value of the illicit goods; in each case they shall be punished by the heavier penalty on the basis of [accepting property and] subverting the law [Art. 367].

Article 437   Administering Penalties Not in Accordance with the Law
[Juefa bu rufa]

[1] In all cases where officials do not administer penalties in accordance with the law, they shall be punished by 40 strokes of beating with the light stick. If as a result death occurs, they shall be punished by 100 strokes of beating with the heavy stick. They shall all be levied 10 *liang* of silver for the burial expenses. For those who inflict the beatings, the penalty shall be reduced one degree. ("Not in accordance with the law" means that light sticks should be used but heavy sticks are used, or heavy sticks should be used but [the bigger] interrogating sticks are used, or the buttocks should be beaten but the waist is beaten, or the thighs should be beaten but the back is whipped.) For those who inflict the beatings, if they do not touch the skin, they shall be punished in accordance with the examined number of beatings [that do not touch the skin]. In all the cases only those who are responsible shall be punished. For those who receive property, calculate the value of the illicit goods; they shall be punished on the basis of [accepting property and] subverting the law [Art. 367].

[2] If supervisory officials, because of public matters, unlawfully strike vulnerable parts of others' bodies or themselves strike others with large sticks, edged metal tools, or hands or feet and cause injuries of fractures or worse, they shall be punished two degrees less than injuring others in ordinary affrays [Art. 325]. If as a result death occurs, they shall be punished by 100 strokes of beating with the heavy stick and penal servitude for three years. They shall be levied 10 *liang* of silver for the burial expenses. For those who receive the orders and inflict the beatings, in each case the penalty shall be reduced one degree. In all the cases, only those who are responsible shall be punished. (This refers to cases such as those where [the officials] do not cherish private interests and the matters do not affect them personally. For instance, when officials having jurisdiction collect money or grain taxes, investigate public matters, oversee manufacturing works, or supervise construction projects, they strike subordinate officials, functionaries, or artisans. Or when commanding military officers train troops and horses, direct

the practice of military arts, supervise military operations, or manage repairs of city walls and moats, they strike platoon commanders, squad commanders, or soldiers.) If they inflict beatings in accordance with the law on the buttocks or thighs that are designated for the infliction of penalty and unexpectedly cause death, or [the prisoners] commit suicide, in each case there shall be no punishment.

Article 438 Head Officials or Emissaries Committing Offenses [Zhangguan shiren youfan]

In all cases where head officials of any yamen outside the capital or emissaries commit offenses at the places where they are sent, their subordinate officials shall not conduct the interrogation without authorization. All the cases shall be sent up to [the offenders' own] superior officials to take action. If the crimes are punishable with the death penalty, [the officials in the same office] shall take control [of the offenders] and wait for replies [from the superior officials]. The seals and the locks and keys shall be turned over to the official's second in command to take charge. For offices that do not have head officials, the official's second in command who is in charge of the seals shall be considered the same as a head official. Any violations shall be punished by 40 strokes of beating with the light stick.

Article 439 Citing the Code and the Commandment in Deciding Penalties [Duanzui yin Lüling]

[1] In all cases of deciding penalties, [the officials] shall all cite [the articles of] the Code and the Commandment. Any violations shall be punished by 30 strokes of beating with the light stick. If several crimes are stipulated in one article, it is permitted to cite only the portions regarding the specific crimes.

[2] The imperial decrees that decide penalties for individual cases as temporary expediencies and that are not promulgated as [a part of] the established Code shall not be cited analogically as [articles of] the Code. If they are cited analogically without authorization so that penalties are decreased or increased, [the officials] shall be punished on the basis of deliberately or negligently [exonerating the guilty or implicating the innocent] [Art. 433].

Article 440 Obtaining Prisoners' Acceptance of Punishment or Petition for Revision [Yuqiu qu fubian]

[1] In all cases where prisoners are punished by penal servitude, life exile, or death penalty, [the officials] shall summon the prisoners and their relatives to announce the penalty and obtain from the prisoners written statements that they accept the punishment or petition for revision. If they do not accept the punishment, they may themselves set out the reasons; and [the cases] shall be carefully reexamined. For crimes punishable with penal

servitude or life exile, any violations shall be punished by 40 strokes of beating with the light stick. In the case of the death penalty, violations shall be punished by 60 strokes of beating with the heavy stick.

[2] If the prisoners' relatives are 300 *li* or more distant, only obtain from the prisoners written statements that they accept the punishment or petition for revision. It is not required to announce the penalty to the relatives.

Article 441 Incorrectly Deciding Penalties before Amnesties
[Sheqian duanzui budang]

In all cases where penalties are not correctly decided before amnesties, if lighter penalties are decided to be heavier ones, they shall be corrected to the lighter ones. If heavier penalties are decided to be lighter ones, and if the crimes are those that are not exempted from punishment by ordinary amnesties [Art. 16], the penalties shall be increased in accordance with the *Code*. If the officials or functionaries deliberately reduce or increase the penalties [Art. 433], although amnesties are issued, they shall not be exempted from punishment.

Article 442 Hearing That There Will Be Amnesties and Deliberately Committing Crimes [Wenyou enshe er gufan]

[1] In all cases of hearing that there will be amnesties and deliberately committing crimes, the criminals shall be punished one degree more severely than for ordinary crimes. Although amnesties are issued, they shall not be exempted from punishment.

[2] If officials hear that there will be amnesties and deliberately decide and then execute penalties for prisoners, they shall be punished on the basis of deliberately implicating the innocent [Art. 433].

Article 443 Prisoners Sentenced to Penal Servitude Failing to Perform Labor Services [Tuqiu bu yingyi]

[1] In all cases where prisoners sentenced to penal servitude who are assigned to perform services in the salt pits or iron foundries do not perform the services, or where prisoners sentenced to penal servitude who have been excused [from work] because of illness are not, after illness is cured, ordered to calculate the lost days and make up the missed services, for more than three such days, [the prisoners or the responsible officials] shall be punished by 20 strokes of beating with the light stick. For each additional three days, the penalty shall be increased one degree. The punishment shall be limited to 100 strokes of beating with the heavy stick.

[2] If the years of service of prisoners sentenced to penal servitude have not been fulfilled, but the supervisors or custodians deliberately permit them to flee and return home or allow them to hire others to replace them, then [the officials or custodians] shall serve the uncompleted number of days

and months which remain in the original sentence of penal servitude. Only those who are responsible shall be punished. If they receive property, calculate the value of the illicit goods; they shall be punished by the heavier penalty on the basis of [accepting property and] subverting the law [Art. 367]. Moreover, the prisoners sentenced to penal servitude [who have fled or hired substitutes] shall be punished in accordance with the [above] law, and they shall make up the services.

Article 444   Women Committing Crimes [Furen fanzui]

[1] In all cases where women commit crimes, for fornication and capital crimes they shall be imprisoned; for all other miscellaneous crimes they shall be put in the charge of their husband for supervision. If they have no husband, they shall be put in the charge of their relatives within the degrees of mourning or of the neighborhood for supervision. They shall be held at the disposition of the yamen to be called [to appear]. They shall not be imprisoned generally. Any violations shall be punished by 40 strokes of beating with the light stick.

[2] If pregnant women commit crimes and should be judicially tortured or beaten [with the light or heavy stick], they shall be put in charge as above [Sec. 1]. They shall all be judicially tortured or beaten 100 days after the delivery. If they are judicially tortured or beaten before the delivery and as a result they abort, officials or functionaries shall be punished for injury in ordinary affrays [Art. 325] reduced three degrees. If as a result death occurs, the penalty shall be 100 strokes of beating with the heavy stick and penal servitude for three years. If the judicial torture or beating is administered after they have given birth but before the term [of 100 days] has passed, the penalty shall be reduced one degree.

[3] If [pregnant women] commit capital crimes, allow midwives to come to the prison and examine them. The penalty shall also be executed 100 days after the delivery. If the penalty is executed before the delivery, the offenders shall be punished by 80 strokes of beating with the heavy stick. If the penalty is executed after they have given birth but before the term has passed, they shall be punished by 70 strokes of beating with the heavy stick. If the penalty is not executed after the term has passed, they shall be punished by 60 strokes of beating with the heavy stick.

[4] If [judicial torture or beating is administered to the women] negligently, in each case the penalty shall be reduced three degrees.

Article 445   Awaiting Replies to Memorials
concerning Prisoners Sentenced to Death [Siqiu fuzou daibao]

[1] In all cases where [officials or functionaries] do not await replies to the memorials requesting permission [to administer the death penalty] but

Laws on Penal Affairs 241

proceed without authorization to carry out the execution of the prisoners sentenced to death, they shall be punished by 80 strokes of beating with the heavy stick. If they have received replies to the memorials requesting permission and the execution has been approved, they shall not administer the death penalty until three days have elapsed. If the penalty is administered before that time period is over, or if the penalty is not administered after that time period is over, in each case they shall be punished by 60 strokes of beating with the heavy stick.

[2] If the death penalty is administered between the beginning of spring and the autumn equinox, [the officials or functionaries] shall be punished by 80 strokes of beating with the heavy stick.

[3] In the case of any of the Ten Abominations [Art. 2] entailing the death penalty or forcible robbery [Art. 289], although [the criminals] must be executed immediately without waiting for the correct season [*juebu daishi*], if the execution is administered on days when punishment is prohibited [*jinxing ri*], [the officials or functionaries] shall be punished by 40 strokes of beating with the light stick.

Article 446   Deciding Penalties Incorrectly [Duanzui budang]

[1] In all cases of deciding penalties, if the execution [of the penalties of beating with the light or heavy stick, penal servitude, or life exile] is required but redemption is allowed, or if redemption is required but the execution [of the penalties] is ordered, in each case [the officials] shall be punished for deliberately or negligently exonerating the guilty or implicating the innocent [Art. 433] with the penalty reduced one degree.

[2] If strangulation is required but decapitation is ordered, or if decapitation is required but strangulation is ordered, [the officials] shall be punished by 60 strokes of beating with the heavy stick. If the sentence is given negligently, the penalty shall be reduced three degrees. If [the officials] mutilate the corpses after the death penalty has been executed, they shall be punished by 50 strokes of beating with the light stick.

[3] If [the officials] release those who should be enslaved by the government as a result of rebellion, great sedition, or collective prosecution, or if they enslave those who should not be enslaved by the government, in each case they shall be punished on the basis of deliberately or negligently exonerating those who are guilty of crimes punishable by life exile or increasing penalties to life exile [Art. 433].

Article 447 Functionaries Writing Confessions for [the Accused]
[Lidian daixie zhaocao]

In all cases where investigations and interrogations into crimes and penalties are conducted in each yamen, if functionaries amend or write confessions for [the accused] and change the facts or circumstances and as a result cause the penalties to be reduced or increased, they shall be punished for deliberately exonerating the guilty or implicating the innocent [Art. 433]. If the offenders are indeed illiterate, those who are not involved in the cases may be allowed to write for them.

CHAPTER 7

Laws on Public Works [Gonglü]

Section 1 Constructions and Manufactures [*Yingzao*] [Nine Articles]

Article 448 Engaging in Constructions and Manufactures without Authorization [Shan zaozuo]

[1] In all cases where civil or military officials engage in constructions and manufactures, if they should report to the superiors but they do not do so, or if they should await [the superiors'] replies but they do not do so, and they levy labor services without authorization, in each case calculate the wages of the hired laborers, they shall be punished for obtaining illicit goods through malfeasance [Art. 368].

[2] If [the officials] engage in constructions in violation of the law or levy laborers to engage in constructions at wrong times, the penalty shall be the same.

[3] If, when city walls collapse or granaries, treasuries, or other public buildings are damaged, [the officials] immediately dispatch laborers or military soldiers to make repairs, this provision shall not be applied.

[4] When [the officials] engage in constructions, if the estimated or petitioned amount of materials and labor is not correct, they shall be punished by 50 strokes of beating with the light stick. If the property has been damaged or labor has been wasted, in each case combine and calculate the price of the damaged property and the amount of money paid for the labor. If the penalty [for obtaining illicit goods] is heavier [than 50 strokes of beating with the light stick], [the officials] shall be punished as obtaining illicit goods through malfeasance [Art. 368].

Article 449 Wasting Labor in Procuring [Things] That Cannot Be Used [Xufei gongli caiqu bu kanyong]

In all cases where [officials] use labor to procure materials such as wood and stone or to bake objects such as bricks and tiles, if they waste labor [on making things] that cannot be used, calculate the amount of money paid for the labor; they shall be punished for obtaining illicit goods through malfeasance [Art. 368]. If, when constructing or demolishing things, proper

243

measures are not taken, and as a result people are inadvertently killed, [the officials or laborers] shall be punished on the basis of killing others by negligence [Art. 315]. The artisans and proctorial officials shall each be punished on the basis of the acts for which they are responsible.

Article 450   Engaging in Constructions and Manufactures Contrary to the Law [Zaozuo bu rufa]

[1] In all cases where [officials] engage in constructions and manufactures contrary to the law, they shall be punished by 40 strokes of beating with the light stick. If they manufacture military articles contrary to the law or weave rolls of silk that are too coarse or too thin, they shall be punished by 50 strokes of beating with the light stick. If the things are completely unusable or must be remade [to be usable], in each case combine and calculate the value of the damaged property and the amount of money paid for the labor. If the penalty [for illicit goods] is heavier, [the officials] shall be punished for obtaining illicit goods through malfeasance [Art. 368]. For articles that are produced for imperial use, the penalty shall be increased two degrees. In each case the artisans shall be punished on the basis of the acts for which they are responsible. The penalty for the officials in charge of the services [juguan] shall be reduced one degree from that for the artisans.

[2] The penalty for the proctorial officials or functionaries [tidiao guanli] shall be reduced one more degree from that for the officials in charge of the services. In all the above cases, the price of the things and the money paid for the labor shall be jointly paid [by the artisans, officials in charge of the services, and proctorial officials and functionaries] back to the government.

Article 451   Fraudulently Taking Excessive Materials [Maopo wuliao]

[1] In all cases where the foremen or artisans of manufacturing or construction services or institutes [yuan] use an excessive quantity of materials and appropriate them, calculate the value of the illicit goods; they shall be punished on the basis of supervisors or custodians themselves stealing [Art. 287]. The property shall be levied and returned to the government.

[2] If officials in charge of the services or officials and functionaries who are delegated to check the facts know the circumstances but allow the actions to take place, they shall be punished with the same penalty. If they fail to discover, the penalty shall be reduced three degrees. The punishment shall be limited to 100 strokes of beating with the heavy stick.

Article 452   Bringing in [Private] Materials and Manufacturing Them into Silk Cloth [Daizao duanpi]

In all cases where supervisory or custodial officials or functionaries bring their own materials without authorization into government establishments and have them manufactured into silk cloth, they shall be punished by 60 strokes of beating with the heavy stick. The silk cloth shall be forfeit to the government. The artisans shall be punished by 50 strokes of beating with the light stick. If the officials in charge of the services know the circumstances but do not report, they shall be punished with the same penalty. If they fail to discover, the penalty shall be reduced three degrees.

Article 453   Weaving Silk Cloth with Prohibited Designs of Dragons and Phoenixes [Zhizao weijin longfengwen duanpi]

[1] In all cases where common people weave and sell coarse silk or gauze with prohibited designs of dragons or phoenixes, they shall be punished by 100 strokes of beating with the heavy stick. The silk cloth shall be forfeit to the government.

[2] The weavers and the artisans who embroider and who [create designs by] knotting the pile shall be punished with the same penalty. They, together with their family members, shall be sent to the capital and registered as artisans of government services.

Article 454   Exceeding Time Limits for Manufacture [Zaozuo guoxian]

[1] In all cases where regular quotas are established to manufacture silk cloth and military articles, if government agencies exceed the time limits and fail to produce the adequate amount, take [the quota as] 10 portions; for 1 portion [that is short], the artisans shall be punished by 20 strokes of beating with the light stick. For each additional portion, the penalty shall be increased one degree. The punishment shall be limited to 50 strokes of beating with the light stick. The penalty for the officials in charge of the government services shall be reduced one degree from that for the artisans. The penalty for the proctorial officials or functionaries shall be further reduced one degree from that for the officials in charge of the government services.

[2] If materials are not distributed [to the artisans] in the prescribed time period, the officials in charge of the government services shall be punished by 40 strokes of beating with the light stick. The penalty for the proctorial officials or functionaries shall be reduced one degree.

Article 455   Repairing Granaries or Treasuries [Xiuli cangku]

In all cases where damages occur to public buildings such as offices, granaries, treasuries, services, and institutes, responsible officials or functionaries shall immediately send dispatches to the competent officials having authority to make repairs. Any violations shall be punished by 40 strokes of beating with the light stick. If, as a result, government property is damaged, [the officials] shall be punished in accordance with the *Code* [for illicit goods (Art. 368)], and they shall pay compensation for the damaged property. If dispatches have already been sent but the competent officials having authority fail [to make repairs], they shall be punished.

Article 456 Officials or Functionaries Having Authority but Not Residing in Public Office Buildings [Yousi guanli buzhu gongxie]

[1] In all cases where officials or functionaries having authority do not reside within official quarters in public office buildings but live in private houses in the community, they shall be punished by 80 strokes of beating with the heavy stick.

[2] For those who cause articles of public use to disappear, they shall be punished on the basis of destroying or losing government property [Art. 104].

Section 2 Dikes [Hefang] [Four Articles]

Article 457 Breaching Dikes through Theft [Daojue hefang]

[1] In all cases where dikes are breached through theft [of water], the offenders shall be punished by 100 strokes of beating with the heavy stick. For those who breach levees or reservoirs through theft, they shall be punished by 80 strokes of beating with the heavy stick. If, as a result, houses are harmed, property is washed away and lost, or the fields or crops are soaked and destroyed, calculate the value of the lost property. If [the value of the property regarded as illicit goods entails] heavier penalties, they shall be punished for obtaining illicit goods through malfeasance [Art. 368]. If, as a result, people are injured or killed, in each case the penalty shall be reduced one degree from that for killing or injuring others in affrays [Art. 313].

[2] For those who deliberately breach dikes, they shall be punished by 100 strokes of beating with the heavy stick and penal servitude for three years. For those who deliberately breach levees or reservoirs, the penalty shall be reduced two degrees. If, [when the value of] what is washed away [is calculated], the penalty for illicit goods of that amount [Art. 368] is heavier, they shall be punished as comparable to theft [Art. 292]. There shall be no tattooing. If, as a result, people are injured or killed, the offenders shall be punished on the basis of deliberately killing or injuring others [Art. 313].

Article 458 Failing to Repair Dikes at the Proper Time [Shishi buxiu difang]

[1] In all cases where dikes are not repaired, or although they are repaired, they are not repaired at the proper time, the proctorial officials or functionaries shall each be punished by 50 strokes of beating with the light stick. If houses are destroyed or property is washed away and lost, the penalty

Laws on Public Works 247

shall be 60 strokes of beating with the heavy stick. If, as a result, people are injured or killed, the penalty shall be 80 strokes of beating with the heavy stick.

[2] If levees are not repaired, or although they are repaired, they are not repaired at the proper time, the penalty shall be 30 strokes of beating with the light stick. If, as a result, the fields or crops are soaked and destroyed, the penalty shall be 50 strokes of beating with the light stick.

[3] If violent waters or continuous rains damage dikes, which are circumstances beyond human control, there shall be no punishment.

Article 459   Encroaching on Public Streets and Roads [Qinzhan jiedao]

In all cases of encroaching on streets, alleys, or roads and erecting houses or making gardens, the offenders shall be punished by 60 strokes of beating with the heavy stick. In each case the offenders shall be ordered to restore the original conditions. For those who make holes in walls to let out filth to the streets or alleys, they shall be punished by 40 strokes of beating with the light stick. If they only let out water, they shall not be punished.

Article 460   Repairing Bridges and Roads [Xiuli qiaoliang daolu]

[1] In all cases where the associate officials of prefectures, subprefectures, and districts supervise [the maintenance of] bridges and roads, they shall, during slack seasons, frequently inspect them one by one and repair them. [The bridges] must be durable and solid, and [the roads must be] level and smooth. If there are damages [to the bridges and roads], repairs are not made, and traffic is hindered, the proctorial officials or functionaries shall be punished by 30 strokes of beating with the light stick.

[2] If, at ferries, bridges should be built but they are not built, or ferryboats should be provided but they are not provided, the penalty shall be 40 strokes of beating with the light stick.

Glossary

an 按 examine
ancha si 按察司 Provincial Surveillance Commissions
Anhui 安徽
Ao Ying 敖英

Bachi hangshi 把持行市 "Monopolizing Markets" (Art. 173)
baidai zhi zhunsheng 百代之準繩 yardstick for one hundred generations
baidou 拜斗 worship the Dipper
baifu zhang 百夫长 centurions
baihu 百户 company commander
Bailian She 白莲社 White Lotus Society
Baiyun Zong 白雲宗 White Cloud School
Baizhou qiangduo 白晝搶奪 "Forcibly Taking in Daytime" (Art. 291)
bangwen 榜文 placard
Banzuo zaju 搬做雜劇 "Theatrical Performances" (Art. 408)
baochao 寶鈔 Treasure paper currency
Baochao Ku 寶鈔庫 Treasury of Treasure Paper Currency
Baogu xianqi 保辜限期 "The Period of Responsibility for Crimes" (Art. 326)
baojing lou 抱經樓 the building that embraces the classics
baozhang 保长 security group heads
baxian lizu 罢闲吏卒 discharged functionaries and runners
Bayi 八議 "The Eight Deliberations" (Art. 3)
bazhi buxu 罢职不叙 dismiss from one's appointment and do not reassign
Beiping 北平
beiyou 卑幼 inferior or younger family members
Beiyou sishan yongcai 卑幼私擅用財 "Inferior or Younger Family Members Making Use of Family Property without Authorization" (Art. 94)
benguan yamen 本管衙门 one's own offices
benlü 本律 basic law
Bentiao bieyou zuiming 本條別有罪名 "Specific Articles Having Different Regulations for Punishment" (Art. 37)
benzui 本罪 basic punishment
bian 編 compilation

249

Bianjing shensuo junxu 邊境申索軍需 "Requesting Military Supplies at the Frontiers" (Art. 224)

Bianming yuanwang 辯明冤枉 "Reversing Unjust Judgments" (Art. 434)

bianyuan 邊遠 distant frontiers

Biaolü panxue xiangshi 標律判學詳釋 Explanations of the Code and Judgments

biaowen 表文 yellow-paper prayers

bici juzui zhi zang 彼此俱罪之贓 illicit goods that criminate both parties

Bieji yicai 別籍異財 "Establishing Separate Household Registers or Dividing the Family Property" (Art. 93)

biexu 別敘 reassign to other posts

Binggu guan jiashu huanxiang 病故官家屬還鄉 "Family Members of Officials Deceased from Illness Returning to Their Home Villages" (Art. 273)

Binglü 兵律 "Laws on Military Affairs" (Chapter 5)

Bingqu ren fushi 屏去人服食 "Depriving Others of Clothes or Food" (Art. 314)

binli 賓禮 rituals for guests

biqu qiusuo 逼取求索 solicit through extortion

Bo Hua 柏樺

Boshang nihuo 舶商匿貨 "Maritime Merchants Hiding Goods" (Art. 166)

boshu fumu 伯叔父母 father's brothers and their wives

boshu zufumu 伯叔祖父母 father's father's brothers' and their wives

Boyang 鄱陽

bu 卜 diviners

Bu caolian junshi 不操練軍士 "Failing to Train Soldiers" (Art. 230)

bu tongju jifu 不同居繼父 stepfather who does not live together [with stepson]

bu yishi 不依事 does not make judgment in accordance with the facts

budao 不道 depravity

buke 卜課 making divination

bumu 不睦 discord

Buwang 捕亡 "Arrests and Escapes" (Chapter 6, Section 10)

buxiao 不孝 lack of filial piety

buyi 布衣 common people

buyi 不義 unrighteousness

Buying wei 不應為 "Doing What Ought Not to Be Done" (Art. 410)

Buzheng Si 布政司 Provincial Administration Commission

buzhunshu sizui 不准贖死刑 unredeemable capital crimes

caisheng 採生 extracting vitality

Caisheng zhege ren 採生折割人 "Extracting Vitality by Dismembering Living Persons" (Art. 311)

cang 倉 granaries

Glossary

Cangku 倉庫 "Granaries and Treasuries" (Chapter 3, Section 4)
Cangku bujue beidao 倉庫不覺被盜 "Failing to Discover Theft in Granaries and Treasuries" (Art. 139)
Chaihui shenming ting 拆毀申明亭 "Destroying Exhibition Pavilions" (Art. 400)
chang 嘗 once
chang 場 works
Chang Wei-jen 張偉仁
Chang Yuchun 常遇春
changfa 常法 permanent law
Changren dao cangku qianliang 常人盜倉庫錢糧 "Ordinary Persons Stealing Money or Grain from Granaries or Treasuries" (Art. 288)
Changshe suo buyuan 常赦所不原 "Crimes That Shall Not Be Pardoned under the General Amnesty" (Art. 16)
Chaofa 鈔法 "Rules of Paper Currency" (Art. 125)
chaohe 朝賀 imperial audiences and congratulatory ceremonies
Chaojian liunan 朝見留難 "Obstructing Others from Attending Court Audiences" (Art. 189)
Chayuan 察院 Investigation Bureau (in the Censorate)
chejia 車駕 Carriage (i.e., the emperor)
chelie 車裂 tearing the body by carts
Chema shashang ren 車馬殺傷人 "Killing or Injuring Others with Carriages or Horses" (Art. 319)
Chen Jing 陳敬
Chen Min 陳敏
Chen Wenhui 陳汶輝
Chen Xing 陳省
Chen Youding 陳友定
Chen Youliang 陳友諒
Cheng chengyu chejia 稱乘輿車駕 "The Terms 'Sedan Chair' and 'Carriage'" (Art. 39)
Cheng daoshi nüguan 稱道士女冠 "The Terms 'Daoist Priests' and 'Daoist Nuns'" (Art. 44)
Cheng guan chuchan chechuan fu siwu 乘官畜產車船附私物 "Carrying Private Goods While Riding on Government Animals, Carriages, or Boats" (Art. 275)
Cheng guanchu jipo lingchuan 乘官畜脊破領穿 "Injuring Government Livestock on Their Backs or Necks When Riding Them" (Art. 252)
Cheng jianlin zhushou 稱監臨主守 "The Terms 'Supervisors' and 'Custodians'" (Art. 42)
Cheng jiqin zufumu 稱期親祖父母 "The Terms 'Relatives of Mourning for One Year' and 'Paternal Grandparents'" (Art. 40)
Cheng Kongzhao 程孔昭

Cheng rizhe yi baike 稱日者以百刻 "The Term 'Day' as Being One Hundred Units" (Art. 43)

Cheng Xu 程徐

Cheng yima zhai siwu 乘驛馬齎私物 "Carrying Private Articles While Riding on Post Horses" (Art. 271)

Cheng yu tongzui 稱與同罪 "The Term 'Shall Be Punished by the Same Penalty'" (Art. 41)

chengchai 承差 runners

Chengchai zhuan guji ren 承差轉雇寄人 "Receiving Assignments but Hiring or Sending Others to Perform Them" (Art. 274)

Chengxuan Buzheng Shi Si 承宣布政使司 Provincial Administration Commission

chengyu 乘輿 Sedan Chair (i.e., the emperor)

Chengyu fuyu wu 乘輿服御物 "Clothing or Personal Objects of the 'Sedan Chair'" (Art. 183)

chengzu 承祖 becomes the heir of one's paternal grandparents

chi 尺 unit of length

chi 笞 beating with the light stick

chongjun 充軍 military exile

Chongjun tiaoli 充軍條例 Regulations concerning Military Exile

Chongtu yizhang 衝突儀仗 "Intruding into the Imperial Procession" (Arts. 214–16)

Chuchan yaoti ren 畜產咬踢人 "Livestock Biting and Kicking People" (Art. 255)

Chujue panjun 處決叛軍 "Executing Military Personnel Guilty of Treason" (Art. 33)

chuming 除名 disenroll someone from official register

Chuming dangchai 除名當差 "Disenrollment and Labor Service" (Art. 14)

chumu 出母 repudiated mother (i.e., natural mother who is repudiated by father)

Chuna guanwu youwei 出納官物有違 "Violating [Rules] in Issuing or Receiving Government Goods" (Art. 141)

chunqiu yishe 春秋義社 spring and autumn sacrificial societies

chuqi 出妻 repudiate wives

chuqi 出妻 "Repudiating Wives" (Art. 123)

churu renzui 出入人罪 exonerate the guilty and incriminate the innocent

Chushi bu fuming 出使不復命 "Not Returning after Being Sent on Missions with Imperial Edicts" (Art. 69)

cimu 慈母 carrying mother (i.e, after one's natural mother dies, the father makes a concubine raise the child)

cizi 刺字 tattoo

cong jimu jia 從繼母嫁 following the stepmother who remarries after father dies

Glossary

Congjia jiwei 從駕稽違 "Delaying in Escorting the 'Carriage'" (Art. 205)
Congzheng shouyu guanjun tao 從征守禦官軍逃 "Officers or Soldiers Fleeing from Campaigns or Defense" (Art. 238)
Congzheng weiqi 從征違期 "Violating the Time Limit in Following [Orders] to Go on Campaigns" (Art. 226)
congzu zugu 從祖祖姑 father's father's sister
cuan 攢 bookkeepers, account keepers
Cui Liang 崔亮
Cui Yongtai 崔永泰
cun 寸 unit of length
cunliu yangqin 存留養親 remain at home to care for relatives

da bujing 大不敬 great irreverence
Da gao 大誥 *Grand Pronouncements*
Da Ming huidian 大明會典 *The Collected Institutes of the Great Ming*
Da Ming ling 大明令 *Great Ming Commandment*
Da Ming lü 大明律 *The Great Ming Code*
Da Ming lü, fu Da Ming ling, wenxing tiaoli 大明律附大明令問刑條例 *The Great Ming Code, with the Great Ming Commandment and Itemized Regulations for Pronouncing Judgments Attached*
Da Ming lü fuli 大明律附例 *Great Ming Code with Regulations*
Da Ming lü fuli zhujie 大明律附例註解 *The Great Ming Code with Regulations Attached and Commentaries*
Da Ming lü gao kao 大明律誥攷 *An investigation on the Great Ming Code with Pronouncements*
Da Ming lü jijie 大明律集解 *Commentaries to the Great Ming Code*
Da Ming lü jijie fuli 大明律集解附例 *The Great Ming Code with Commentaries Attached by Regulations*
Da Ming lü shiyi 大明律釋義 *Commentary to the Great Ming Code*
Da Ming lüli fujie 大明律例附解 *Great Ming Code and Regulations with Commentaries*
Da Ming lüli juhui xizhu 大明律例據會細注 *Detailed Commentaries to the Great Ming Code and Regulations*
Da Ming lüli linmin baojing 大明律例臨民寶鏡 *Precious Mirror for Governing the People: The Great Ming Code and Regulations*
Da Ming lüli tianshi pangzhu 大明律例添釋旁注 *Commentaries and Interlinear Notes on the Great Ming Code and Regulations*
Da Ming lüli xiangxing bingjian 大明律例祥刑冰鑑 *Lucid Commentaries to the Great Ming Code and regulations*
Da Ming lüli zhijun qishu 大明律例致君奇術 *Marvelous Methods for the Ruler: The Great Ming Code*
Da Ming lüshu fuli 大明律疏附例 *Commentaries to the Great Ming Code with Regulations*

Da Qing lüli tongkao jiaozhu 大清律例通考校註 *A Comprehensive Investigation of the Great Qing Code and Regulations, Collated and Annotated*

Dachen zhuanshan xuanguan 大臣專擅選官 "Selecting Officials by High Officials without Authorization" (Art. 49)

Dadu 大都

dagong 大功 relatives of the third mourning degree

Daizao duanpi 帶造緞匹 "Bringing in [Private] Materials and Manufacturing Them into Silk Cloth" (Art. 452)

Dangtu 當塗

dao 盜 robbery

Dao dasi shenyuwu 盜大祀神御物 "Stealing Sacred Objects of the Spirits Devoted to the Great Sacrifices" (Art. 280)

Dao chengmen yao 盜城門鑰 "Stealing Keys to City Gates" (Art. 284)

Dao gengzhong guanmin tian 盜耕種官民田 "Fraudulently Cultivating Government or Private Land" (Art. 102)

Dao junqi 盜軍器 "Stealing Military Equipment" (Art. 285)

Dao maniu chuchan 盜馬牛畜產 "Stealing Horses, Cattle, and Other Livestock" (Art. 293)

Dao neifu caiwu 盜內府財物 "Stealing Property from the Palace Treasury" (Art. 283)

Dao tianye gumai 盜田野穀麥 "Stealing Rice and Wheat from Fields" (Art. 294)

Dao yinxin 盜印信 "Stealing Seals" (Art. 282)

Dao yuanling shumu 盜園陵樹木 "Stealing Plants or Trees within the Imperial Mausoleum" (Art. 286)

Dao zhishu 盜制書 "Stealing Imperial Decrees" (Art. 281)

Daojue hefang 盜決河防 "Breaching Dikes through Theft" (Art. 457)

Daomai tianzhai 盜賣田宅 "Fraudulently Selling Fields and Houses" (Art. 99)

daoshi 道士 Daoist priests

Daozei buxian 盜賊捕限 "Time Limit for Arresting Robbers and Thieves" (Art. 418)

Daozei wozhu 盜賊窩主 "The Harborers of Thieves and Robbers" (Art. 301)

dapi 大辟 death penalty

Dasi 大祀 Great Sacrifices

Daxue 大學 Great Learning

Daxue yanyi 大學衍義 *Expanded Meaning of the Great Learning*

De yishi wu 得遺失物 "Finding Lost Objects" (Art. 170)

dedai 得代 replacement

Deng Yu 鄧愈

di ci zisun 嫡次子孫 wife's younger sons and sons' sons

di zhang zisun 嫡長子孫 wife's eldest son and eldest sons' sons

dian 典 conditional sale, mortgage

Glossary

Dianchai yuzu 點差獄卒 "Appointing Prison Guards" (Art. 91)
Diangu qinü 典雇妻女 "Mortgaging or Renting Out Wives or Daughters" (Art. 108)
dianjia 佃甲 chief tenant farmers
Dianmai tianzhai 典買田宅 "Purchasing Fields or Houses by Mortgage" (Art. 101)
diaojian 刁姦 fornication brought about by seduction
diaosang 吊喪 condole the bereaved
dijian 遞減 reduce progressively
dimu 嫡母 proper mother (i.e., father's wife)
Dingfu chaiqian buping 丁夫差遣不平 "Unequally Assigning [Corvée Services to] Able-Bodied Adult Males" (Art. 87)
dingyou 丁憂 take leave to observe mourning for the death of parents
Disong gongwen 遞送公文 "Delivering Government Documents" (Arts. 259–61)
Disong taojun qinü chucheng 遞送逃軍妻女出城 "Sending Wives or Daughters of Military Deserters out of Cities" (Art. 244)
disun 嫡孫 son's son by the proper wife
disun fu 嫡孫婦 proper wife's son's son's wife
Dong Yu 董裕
douji 斗級 granary keepers, measurers
Douou 鬬毆 "Affrays and Batteries" (Chapter 6, Section 3; Art. 325)
Douou ji gusha ren 鬬毆及故殺人 "Killing Others in Affrays or by Intention" (Art. 313)
Du Chayuan 都察院 Censorate
Du lü suoyan 讀律瑣言 *Miscellaneous Notes on Reading the Code*
Du Zhihui Shi Si 都指揮使司 Regional Military Commission
duangong 端公 proper lord
duanshiguan 斷事官 judges
Duanyu 斷獄 "Judgment and Imprisonment" (Chapter 6, Section 11)
Duanzui budang 斷罪不當 "Deciding Penalties Incorrectly" (Art. 446)
Duanzui wu zhengtiao 斷罪無正條 "Deciding Penalties without Specific Articles" (Art. 46)
Duanzui yi xinban lü 斷罪以新頒律 "Deciding Penalties in Accordance with the Newly Promulgated *Code*" (Art. 45)
Duanzui yin lüling 斷罪引律令 "Citing the *Code* and the *Commandment* in Deciding Penalties" (Art. 439)
Dubo 賭博 "Gambling" (Art. 402)
Dudu Fu 都督府 Chief Military Commission
duiwen 對問 confrontational interrogation
duizhi 對制 reply to the throne
Duizhi shangshu zha bu yishi 對制上書詐不以實 "Replying to or Memorializing the Emperor Untruthfully" (Art. 380)

duji 篤疾 incapacitated

Duocheng yima 多乘驛馬 "Excessively Using Postal Horses" (Art. 266)

duoqing qifu 奪情起復 return to government service by curtailing sentiment

Duoshou shuiliang humian 多收稅糧斛面 "Collecting Too Much Grain Tax above the Level of the Grain Measures" (Art. 128)

Duozhi linji 多支廩給 "Accepting Excessive Supplies" (Art. 267)

Duqun Suo 都群所 Herd Office

eni 惡逆 contumacy

ermu suo buji 耳目所不及 ears and eyes cannot perceive the result

erzui jufa 二罪俱發 two crimes are discovered together

erzui jufa yi zhong lun 二罪俱發以重論 "Sentencing on the Basis of the Punishment for the More Serious Crime When Two Crimes Are Discovered Together" (Art. 25)

fafeng 罰俸 fine of salary

fan shisan tiao 凡十三條 13 articles altogether

Fan Xianzu 范顯祖

Fan Yongluan 范永鑾

Fan Zugan 范祖幹

Fang Guozhen 方國珍

Fanghuo gushao ren fangwu 放火故燒人房屋 "Deliberately Setting Fires and Burning Others' Houses" (Art. 407)

fangzu boshu 房族伯叔 father's male second cousins

fangzu xiongdi 房族兄弟 paternal male third cousins

fanhui 犯諱 violate name taboos

Fanjian 犯姦 "Committing Fornication (Chapter 6, Section 8; Art. 390)

fanni yuanzuo 反逆緣坐 collective prosecution for rebellion or sedition

Fanzui cunliu yangqin 犯罪存留養親 "Committing Crimes and Remaining at Home to Care for Relatives" (Art. 18)

Fanzui de leijian 犯罪得累減 "Committing Crimes for Which Penalties May Be Cumulatively Reduced" (Art. 11)

Fanzui gongtao 犯罪共逃 "Fleeing Together after Committing Crimes" (Art. 26)

Fanzui shi wei laoji 犯罪時未老疾 "Committing Crimes before Becoming Aged or Maimed" (Art. 22)

Fanzui shifa zaitao 犯罪事發在逃 "Fleeing When Crimes Are Discovered" (Art. 30)

Fanzui zishou 犯罪自首 "Voluntary Confession of Crimes" (Art. 24)

fawai 法外 extralegal

Faxue gailun 法學概論 Introduction to Jurisprudence

Fazhong 發塚 "Uncovering Graves" (Art. 299)

Glossary

Feibao junqing 飛報軍情 "Reporting Military Information at Full Speed" (Art. 223)
feiji 廢疾 disabled
Feiyong shouji caichan 費用受寄財產 "Consuming Property Received in Deposit" (Art. 169)
fen 分 unit of length
feng 封 enfeoff official titles during one's lifetime
fengshui 風水 geomancy
Fengxian guanli fanzang 風憲官吏犯贓 "Surveillance Officials or Functionaries Committing Offenses Involving Illicit Goods" (Art. 373)
Fengyang 鳳陽
fengyu 奉御 chief stewards
Fengzhang yinxin 封掌印信 "Covering Up and Keeping Seals" (Art. 76)
fensi 分司 branch offices
fenxun yushi 分巡御史 regional inspectors
fu 府 prefecture
fu 輔 assist
fu boshu fumu 夫伯叔父母 husband's father's brothers' and their wives
fu boshu zufumu 夫伯叔祖父母 husband's father's father's brothers' and their wives
fu gao zufumu 夫高祖父母 husband's father's father's father's parents
Fu Huan 傅瓛
Fu Minxue 傅敏學
Fu ousi youzui qiqie 夫毆死罪妻妾 "Husbands Striking Transgressing Wives or Concubines to Death" (Art. 316)
fu qingu 夫親姑 husband's father's sister
fu tang boshu fumu 夫堂伯叔父母 husband's father's father's brother's son
fu tang xiongdi 父堂兄弟 father's father's brother's son
fu tang xiongdi ji qi 夫堂兄弟及妻 husband's father's brother's son and his wife
fu tang zhi 夫堂姪 husband's father's brother's son's son
fu tang zhifu 夫堂姪婦 husband's father's brother's son's son's wife
fu tang zhinü 夫堂姪女 husband's father's brother's son's daughter
fu tang zhisun 夫堂姪孫 husband's father's brother's son's son's son
fu tang zhisunnü 夫堂姪孫女 husband's father's brother's son's son's daughter
fu tang zimei 夫堂姊妹 husband's father's brother's daughter
fu tang zimei 父堂姊妹 father's father's brother's daughter
fu tang zugu 夫堂祖姑 husband's father's father's brother's daughter
fu tanggu 夫堂姑 husband's father's father's brother's daughter
fu xiongdi ji qi 夫兄弟及妻 husband's brothers and their wives
fu zaicong xiongdi 夫再從兄弟 husband's father's father's brother's son's son
fu zaicong zhi 夫再從姪 husband's father's father's brother's son's son's son

fu zaicong zhinü 夫再從姪女 husband's father's father's brother's son's son's daughter
fu zaicong zimei 夫再從姊妹 husband's father's brother's son's daughter
fu zeng zhisun 夫曾姪孫 husband's brother's son's son's son
fu zeng zhisunnü 夫曾姪孫女 husband's brother's son's son's daughter
fu zeng zufumu 夫曾祖父母 husband's father's father's parents
fu zeng zugu 夫曾祖姑 husband's father's father's father's sister
fu zhi 夫姪 husband's brother's son
fu zhifu 夫姪婦 husband's brother's son's wife
fu zhinü 夫姪女 husband's brother's daughter
fu zhisun 夫姪孫 husband's brother's son's son
fu zhisunfu 夫姪孫婦 husband's brother's son's son's wife
fu zhisunnü 夫姪孫女 husband's brother's son's daughter
fu zimei 夫姊妹 husband's sister
fu zimei 父姊妹 father's sister
fu zu boshu fumu 夫族伯叔父母 husband's father's father's father's brother's son's son
fu zu xiongdi 夫祖兄弟 husband's father's father's father's brother's son's son's son
fu zu zeng zufumu 夫族曾祖父母 husband's father's father's father's brothers and their wives
fu zu zimei 夫族姊妹 husband's father's father's father's brother's son's son's daughter
fu zufumu 夫祖父母 husband's father's parents
fu zugu 夫族姑 husband's father's father's father's brother's son's daughter
fu zugu 夫祖姑 husband's father's father's sister
fuguo huanzhi 附過還職 record transgressions and return to appointments
Fujian 福建
Fujiang junshi bing ji yiyao 夫匠軍士病給醫藥 "Furnishing Medical Care and Medicine to Artisans and Soldiers Who Are Sick" (Art. 401)
fuluan daosheng 扶鸞禱聖 invoke spirits by sand-writing séance
fumu 父母 parents
Fumu qiujin jiaqu 父母囚禁嫁娶 "Marrying Off or Taking in Marriage While Parents Are Imprisoned" (Art. 112)
Furen fanzui 婦人犯罪 "Women Committing Crimes" (Art. 444)
Fushe weishi 服舍違式 "Violating Sumptuary Regulations on Clothing and Houses" (Art. 194)
fushu zuzhou 符書詛咒 make spells and incantations
fuyan 符驗 authority tallies
Fuyi bujun 賦役不均 "Unequally Levying Taxes and Corvée Services" (Art. 86)
Fuyu qianliang sixia bushu 附餘錢糧私下補數 "Secretly Using Excess Money or Grain to Make Up Deficits" (Art. 132)

Glossary

fuzai 附載 attach
Fuzu bei ou 父祖被毆 "When Father or Paternal Grandfather Is Struck" (Art. 346)

gaichu 改除 transference
Ganming fanyi 干名犯義 "Violating Status and Offending against Righteousness" (Art. 360)
Ganxian 贛縣
gao zufumu 高祖父母 father's father's father's parents
gaoming 誥命 certificates of appointment
gaotian 告天 pray to Heaven
Gaozhuang bu shouli 告狀不受理 "Not Accepting and Acting on Accusations" (Art. 357)
ge 各 each
gong 工 artisans
gong fanzui 共犯罪 commit joint crimes
Gong fanzui fen shoucong 共犯罪分首從 "Distinguishing Principals and Accessories in Joint Crimes" (Art. 29)
gongbing 弓兵 archers
Gongchai renyuan qiling zhangguan 公差人員欺凌長官 "Official Messengers Insulting Senior Officials" (Art. 193)
Gongchen tiantu 功臣田土 "Meritorious Officials' Fields" (Art. 98)
Gongchen yingjin qinren rushi 功臣應禁親人入視 "When Meritorious Officials Are imprisoned, Their Relatives May Visit Them" (Art. 426)
gongdian 宮殿 palaces and halls
Gongdian men shanru 宮殿門擅入 "Entering the Gates of Palaces and Halls without Authorization" (Art. 203)
Gongdian zaozuo ba buchu 宮殿造作罷不出 "Failing to Leave Palaces or Halls after the Constructions or Manufactures Are Completed" (Art. 208)
Gonghou siyi guanjun 公侯私役官軍 "Employing Military Officers or Soldiers by Dukes or Marquises without Authorization" (Art. 237)
Gongjian shangren 弓箭傷人 "Injuring Others with Bows and Arrows" (Art. 318)
gongju 共居 dwell together
Gongju fei qiren 貢舉非其人 "Recommending Inappropriate Persons" (Art. 53)
Gonglü 工律 "Laws on Public Works" (Chapter 7)
Gongmin di 恭閔帝
Gongmou weidao 共謀為盜 "Jointly Plotting to Commit Robbery" (Art. 302)
Gongnei fenzheng 宮內忿爭 "Quarreling within the Palace" (Art. 327)
Gongqu qiequ jiewei dao 公取竊取皆為盜 "Taking Goods Openly or Secretly Each Constitutes Robbery" (Art. 303)

Gongshi 公式 "Official Documents" (Chapter 2, Section 2)
Gongshi rending suojie mapi 公使人等索借馬匹 "Government Messengers Demanding to Borrow Horses" (Art. 258)
Gongshi shicuo 公事失錯 "Making Errors in Public Matters" (Art. 28)
Gongshi yingxing jicheng 公事應行稽程 "Delaying Government Affairs That Should Be Carried Out" (Art. 269)
Gongwei 官衛 "Guarding Palaces" (Chapter 5, Section 1)
Gongyuehu ji furen fanzui 工樂戶及婦人犯罪 "Committing Crimes by Government Artisans, Musicians, and Women" (Art. 19)
gongzui 公罪 public crimes
gu 姑 father's sisters
gu 蠱 insect poison
gu 故 deliberately
gu zhi sun 姑之孫 father's sister's son's son
gu zhi zi 姑之子 father's sister's son
guan 貫 copper currency unit
guan 觀 Daoist monasteries
guanfang 關防 seal
Guanfang neishi churu 關防內使出入 "Controlling Identification Passes of Palace Eunuchs Who Enter or Leave" (Art. 210)
Guangde 廣德
Guangdong 廣東
Guangxi 廣西
Guanjin 關津 "Guard Posts and Fords" (Chapter 5, Section 3)
Guanjin Liunan 關津留難 "Causing Difficulties at Checkpoints" (Art. 243)
guanjun yamen 管軍衙門 offices that command troops
Guanli cisong jiaren su 官吏詞訟家人訴 "Family Members Lodging Accusations on Behalf of Officials or Functionaries" (Art. 365)
Guanli jiyou 官吏給由 "Career Records of Officials or Functionaries" (Art. 59)
Guanli qingxu caiwu 官吏聽許財物 "Officials or Functionaries Permitting Promises of Property" (Art. 377)
Guanli shoucai 官吏受財 "Officials or Functionaries Accepting Property" (Art. 367)
Guanli suchang 官吏宿娼 "Officials or Functionaries Sleeping with Entertainers" (Art. 398)
Guanma bu tiaoxi 官馬不調習 "Failing to Break and Train Government Horses" (Art. 253)
Guansi churu renzui 官司出入人罪 "Officials Exonerating the Guilty or Implicating the Innocent" (Art. 433)
Guanwenshu jicheng 官文書稽程 "Delaying Transmitting Official Documents" (Art. 71)

Glossary

Guanyuan furen guoxian 官員赴任過限 "Exceeding the Time Limit by Officials When Going to Their Posts" (Art. 56)
Guanyuan xiyin 官員襲廕 "Officials' Protection Privilege" (Art. 51)
guanzhuang 管莊 bailiffs
gufu 姑夫 paternal aunts' husbands
guibi 規避 circumvent the law
Guizhou 貴州
Gujin gukan pingren 故禁故勘平人 "Deliberately Imprisoning or Interrogating Innocent Persons" (Art. 420)
Guo Huan 郭桓
Guo Zixing 郭子興
guojia 國家 the reigning dynasty
Guoque 國榷 *An Evaluation of the Events of Our Dynasty*
Guozi Jian 國子監 Directorate of Education
Guozi Xue 國子學 National University

Hami 哈密
Han 漢 ethnic and government name
Han Liner 韓林兒
Han Shantong 韓山童
Hanlin Yuan 翰林院 Hanlin Academy
Hao Zhicai 郝志才
haomin 豪民 influential individuals
He Guang 何廣
Hefang 河防 "Dikes" (Chapter 7, Section 2)
Hehe yuyue 合和御藥 "Preparing Imperial Medicine" (Art. 182)
hejian 和姦 fornication with consent
Hongwu 洪武 grand military achievement (reign name)
Hongwu falü dianji kaozheng 洪武法律典籍考證 *Textual Research on Legal Documents of the Hongwu Period*
Hongwu yuzhi quanshu 洪武御製全書 *Complete Imperial Writings during the Hongwu Reign*
Hu Qiong 胡瓊
Hu Weiyong 胡惟庸
Huai 淮
Huai Xiaofeng 怀校峰
Huang Chang-chien 黃彰健
Huang Miantang 黃冕堂
Huang Ming zhaoling 皇明詔令 *Imperial Edicts of the August Ming*
Huang Ming zuxun 皇明祖訓 *Ancestral Instructions of the August Ming*
huang taihou 皇太后 empress dowager
huang taizi 皇太子 heir apparent
Huang Yunmei 黃云眉

huangce 黄册 yellow books
Huangcheng 皇城 Imperial City
huanghou 皇后 empress
Huangjia tanwen yishang qin beiou 皇家袒免以上親被毆 "Striking the Imperial Relatives within the Sixth Degree of Mourning" (Art. 328)
Huangjue si 皇覺寺 Huangjue Temple
Huangwu tiandi 荒蕪田地 "Allowing Land to Go Uncultivated" (Art. 103)
huansu 還俗 return to lay status
huawairen 化外人 persons beyond the pale of civilization
Huawairen youfan 化外人有犯 "Committing Crimes by Persons beyond the Pale of Civilization" (Art. 36)
Hui dasi qiutan 毀大祀丘壇 "Destroying Mounds or Altars for Great Sacrifices" (Art. 177)
Huiqi junqi 毀棄軍器 "Destroying or Discarding Military Equipment" (Art. 234)
huishe youliu 會赦猶流 enforce life exile even though an amnesty is proclaimed
Hulü 戶律 "Laws on Revenue" (Chapter 3)
hunyin 婚姻 marriage
Hunyin 婚姻 "Marriages" (Chapter 3, Section 3)
Huyi 戶役 "Households and Corvée Services" (Chapter 3, Section 1)
Huzhou 湖州

ji 籍 household register
ji 即 then
ji 及 and/or
ji 疾 maimed
ji dengwengu 擊登聞鼓 beat the petitioner's drum
jia 加 increase
Jiajian zuili 加減罪例 "Principles for Increasing and Reducing Punishments" (Art. 38)
jiajiang xieshen 假降邪聖 pretend to be the mediums of heretical spirits
jiali 嘉禮 auspicious rituals
jiamu 嫁母 remarried mother, i.e., natural mother marries another person due to father's death
jian 姦 fornication
jian 減 reduction
jian 賤 inferior persons
Jian bumin qinü 姦部民妻女 "Committing Fornication with Wives or Daughters of Subordinates" (Art. 395)
jiancha yushi 監察御史 investigating censors
jianchen 奸臣 treacherous officials
jiandang 奸黨 treacherous clique

Glossary

Jiandang 姦黨 "Treacherous Cliques" (Art. 60)
Jiang Yonglin 姜永琳
Jiangdu lüling 講讀律令 "Explaining and Reading the *Code and Commandment*" (Art. 63)
Jiangning 江寧
Jiangxi 江西
jianlin 監臨 supervisors
Jianlin shiyao zhongyan 監臨勢要中鹽 "Supervisory [Officials or Functionaries] or Powerful Persons Engaging in Salt Transactions" (Art. 161)
Jianshou zidao cangku qianliang 監守自盜倉庫錢糧 "Supervisors or Custodians Themselves Stealing Money or Grain from Granaries or Treasuries" (Art. 287)
Jianta zaishang tianliang 檢踏災傷田糧 "Inspecting Fields and Their Produce Damaged by Natural Calamities" (Art. 97)
Jianyan shishang bu yishi 檢驗屍傷不以實 "Examining Wounds on Corpses and Making Untrue Reports" (Art. 436)
Jianyuan 諫院 Remonstrance Bureau
jiao 絞 strangulation
Jiao Hong 焦竑
Jiaojie jinshi guanyuan 交結近侍官員 "Associating with Court Attendant Officials" (Art. 61)
Jiaomin bangwen 教民榜文 *Placard of People's Instruction*
Jiaosuo cisong 教唆詞訟 "Instigating Litigation" (Art. 363)
Jiaqu weilü zhuhun meiren zui 嫁娶違律主婚人罪 "Punishments for Matchmakers and Others Who Arrange Marriages That Violate the *Code*" (Art. 124)
Jiaren qiusuo 家人求索 "Household Members [of Officials] Extorting [Property]" (Art. 372)
jiashou 甲首 tithing chiefs
jiazhang 家長 household heads
jiazhang fumu 家長父母 household head's parents
jiazhang zhangzi 家長長子 household head's eldest son
jiazhang zhongzi 家長眾子 household head's other sons
Jibian liangmin 激變良民 "Provoking Honorable Persons to Revolt" (Art. 231)
jie 皆 all
jie xianren 解現任 remove from the current appointments
Jieqiu 劫囚 "Rescuing Prisoners by Force" (Art. 290)
jieren 解任 dismissal
jigang 紀綱 net-ropes [principles] of administration
jigu lifa 稽古立法 imitate antiquity and establish the law
jili 吉禮 felicitation rituals

Jiliu qiutu 稽留囚徒 "Delaying in Sending Prisoners" (Art. 415)
jilu 紀錄 record of the transgression
Jimo zangwu 給沒贓物 "Restitution and Confiscation of Illicit Goods" (Art. 23)
jimu 繼母 stepmother
jin 斤 unit of weight
Jin jingduanren chong suwei 禁經斷人充宿衛 "Prohibiting Those Who Have Been Convicted from Serving as Imperial Guards" (Art. 213)
Jin Qi 金祈
Jin Zhi 金祉
jing 經 standard provisions
Jingcheng lu 精誠錄 *Record of Absolute Sincerity*
Jinge zhubao lizhang 禁革主保里長 "Prohibition [against Fraudulently Claiming to Be] Security Group Chiefs or Community Heads" (Art. 89)
Jingshi 京師
jingshi 淨室 purified houses
jingtiao 荊條 *Vitex negundo* branch
jinshi 進士 metropolitan graduates, presented scholars
Jinshi zhacheng sixing 近侍詐稱私行 "Court Attendants Deceitfully Claiming to Be on Private Missions" (Art. 386)
jinxing ri 禁刑日 days when punishment is prohibited
Jinzhi shiwu xieshu 禁止師巫邪術 "Prohibiting Sorcery of Wizards and Witches" (Art. 181)
Jinzhi yingsong 禁止迎送 "Prohibition against Greeting and Bidding Farewell" (Art. 192)
jinzi 禁子 jailers
jiqin 期親 relatives of mourning for one year
Jiqing 集慶
jishen 己身 ego
jishizhong 給事中 supervising secretaries
Jisi 祭祀 "Sacrifices" (Chapter 4, Section 1)
jiu zhi sun 舅之孫 mother's brother's son's son
jiu zhi zi 舅之子 mother's brother's son
jiugu 舅姑 husband's parents
Jiumu 廄牧 "Stables and Herds" (Chapter 5, Section 4)
Jiupin yishang guan ou zhangguan 九品以上官毆長官 "Officials of the Ninth Rank or Above Striking Head Officials" (Art. 332)
Jixiang 祭享 "Sacrifices and Imperial Ancestor Worship" (Art. 176)
jiyou 給由 career records
ju 局 services
jue 爵 noble titles

Glossary

juebu daishi 決不待時 execute immediately without waiting for the correct season
Juefa bu rufa 決罰不如法 "Administering Penalties Not in Accordance with the Law" (Art. 437)
juguan 局官 officials in charge of the services
junding 軍丁 military servants
Junguan junren fanzui mian tuliu 軍官軍人犯罪免徒流 "Committing Crimes by Military Officers or Soldiers Who Shall Be Exempted from Penal Servitude or Life Exile" (Art. 10)
Junguan youfan 軍官有犯 "Committing Crimes by Military Officers" (Art. 6)
junli 軍禮 military rituals
junli 軍吏 military functionaries
junling 峻令 harsh statutes
Junmin yuehui cisong 軍民約會詞訟 "Coordinating Litigation Involving Military Personnel and Civilians" (Art. 364)
junren 軍人 military personnel
Junren tiyi 軍人替役 "Arranging for Substitutes in Service by Military Soldiers" (Art. 227)
Junzheng 軍政 "Military Administration" (Chapter 5, Section 2)
junzi 君子 gentlemen
Juou zhuisheren 拒毆追攝人 "Resisting or Striking Persons Sent to Collect Taxes or to Direct Official Tasks" (Art. 333)
juren 舉人 provincial graduates
Jusang ji sengdao fanjian 居喪及僧道犯姦 "Committing Fornication during the Period of Mourning or by Buddhist or Daoist Clergy" (Art. 396)
Jusang jiaqu 居喪嫁娶 "Marrying Off or Taking in Marriage during the Mourning Period" (Art. 111)
Juyong youguo guanli 舉用有過官吏 "Recommending Officials or Functionaries Who Have Transgressed" (Art. 54)
juyou 具由 reasons for judgment
Juyu tingqiu daidui 鞫獄停囚待對 "Detaining Prisoners during Interrogations to Wait for Direct Confrontation" (Art. 429)

kaoman 考滿 time due for scrutiny
ke 刻 [time] units (1/100 day)
Kecheng 課程 "Taxes" (Chapter 3, Section 5)
kelian 科斂 levy tax excessively
Keliu daozang 剋留盜贓 "Retaining Stolen Goods" (Art. 376)
konghe 恐嚇 threat
Konghe qucai 恐嚇取財 "Obtaining Property by Threats" (Art. 296)

kongyin 空印 prestamped document

ku 庫 treasures

Kucheng guyi qinqi 庫秤雇役侵欺 "Deceitfully Embezzling by Weighers in Granaries and Employees" (Art. 136)

kunxing 髡刑 penal servitude

kuzi 庫子 storehousemen, collectors

lan 攔 checkers, watchers

Lan Yu 藍玉

Lanna shuiliang 攬納稅糧 "Monopolizing Payment of Tax Paid in Grains" (Art. 130)

Lanshe guanli 濫設官吏 "Appointing Too Many Officials or Functionaries" (Art. 52)

Laoxiao feiji shoushu 老小廢疾收贖 "Redeeming Punishment by Those Who Are Aged, Juvenile, or Disabled" (Art. 21)

Laoyou bu kaoxun 老幼不拷訊 "Old and Young Persons Are Not Put to Judicial Torture" (Art. 428)

Lei Menglin 雷夢麟

leijian 累減 cumulative reduction

leixuan quanzhu 類選銓注 select [the candidates] in different categories and appoint them

li 里 unit of length

li 理 reason

li 厘 unit of length: 1/1,000 of *chi* (approx. 0.00123 inch)

li 例 regulation

Li dizi weifa 立嫡子違法 "Illegally Designating Wives' Sons [as Heirs]" (Art. 84)

Li Qing 李清

Li Shanchang 李善長

Li Shoukong 李守孔

Li Wenzhong 李文忠

Li Yumin 李裕民

liang 良 honorable people

Liang 梁 dynastic name

Liangjian wei hunyin 良賤為婚姻 "Marriages between Honorable and Mean Persons" (Art. 121)

Liangjian xiangjian 良賤相姦 "Honorable and Mean Persons Committing Fornication with Each Other" (Art. 397)

Liangjian xiangou 良賤相毆 "Honorable and Mean Persons Striking Each Other" (Art. 336)

liangyi zhi zi 兩姨之子 mother's sister's son

liangzhang 糧長 tax captain

lianzuo 連坐 implicate together

Glossary

Liao 遼 dynastic name
Lidai diwang lingqin 歷代帝王陵寢 "The Mausoleums of Rulers of Previous Dynasties" (Art. 179)
Lidai xingfa kao 歷代刑法考 *An Investigation on the Penal Laws of the Previous Dynasties*
lidian 吏典 functionaries
Lidian daixie zhaocao 吏典代寫招草 "Functionaries Writing Confessions for [the Accused]" (Art. 447)
lijia 里甲 community and tithing
Lilü 禮律 "Laws on Rituals" (Chapter 4)
Lilü 吏律 "Laws on Personnel" (Chapter 2)
Linchuan 臨川
Ling 令 *The Commandment*
ling 令 commandment, orders
lingchi chusi 凌遲處死 sentence to death by slicing
Lingnüe zuiqiu 凌虐罪囚 "Mistreating Prisoners" (Art. 422)
Linhao 臨濠
liu 流 life exile
Liu Chengzhi (a) 劉承直
Liu Chengzhi (b) 劉丞直
Liu Feng 劉鋒
Liu Futong 劉福通
Liu Hainian 劉海年
Liu Ji 劉基
Liu Junwen 劉俊文
Liu Weijing 劉惟敬
Liu Weiqian 劉惟謙
liu you wuxing 流宥五刑 exile can be used to pardon those who are punished by one of the five punishments
liuguan 流官 ranked officials
liuqing 六卿 six ministers
Liuqiu jiashu 流囚家屬 "Families of Those Punished by Life Exile" (Art. 15)
liuzhu fa 留住法 law on remaining in original places
Lixue leibian 理學類編 *The Classified Encyclopedia on the Learning of Principle*
lizhang 里長 community heads
lizu 吏卒 functionaries
Lizu fan sizui 吏卒犯死罪 "Committing Capital Crime by Functionaries" (Art. 32)
Longfeng 龍鳳 dragon and phoenix (reign name)
Loushi yinxin 漏使印信 "Omitting to Affix Seals" (Art. 77)
Louxie junqing dashi 漏泄軍情大事 "Divulging Important Military Information" (Art. 70)

Louyong chaoyin 漏用鈔印 "Omitting to Employ Seals on Paper Currency" (Art. 78)
Lu Yongzhen 逯永貞
lü 律 *Code*, law
Lü gao 律誥 *The Code with Pronouncements*
Lü jie bianyi 律解辯疑 *The Code with Commentaries and Explication of Questions*
Lü jie bianyi, Da Ming lü zhijie ji Ming lü jijie fuli sanshu suozai Ming lü zhi bijiao yanjiu 律解辯疑，大明律直解，及明律集解附例三書所載明律之比較研究 *A Comparative Study on The Ming Code Which Is Seen in the Three Books "The Code with Commentaries and Explication of Questions," "The Great Ming Code with Directed Explanations," and "The Ming Code with Commentaries and Regulations Attached"*
Lü ling zhijie 律令直解 *The Code and Commandment Directly Explained*
lüeren lüemai heyou renkou 略人略賣和誘人口 kidnap or kidnap and sell or seduce persons
Lüeren lüemairen 略人略賣人 "Kidnapping Persons or Kidnapping and Selling Persons" (Art. 298)
Lütiao shuyi 律條疏議 *Commentaries to the Code*

Ma 馬
ma 罵 curse with bad language
Ma zhishi ji benguan zhangguan 罵制使及本管長官 "Cursing Imperial Emissaries or One's Own Head Official" (Art. 348)
Ma zufumu fumu 罵祖父母父母 "Cursing Paternal Grandparents or Parents" (Art. 352)
Ma zunzhang 罵尊長 "Cursing Superior or Older Relatives" (Art. 351)
Mailiang weichang 買良為娼 "Purchasing Honorable Persons to Be Entertainers" (Art. 399)
mali 罵詈 curse
Mali 罵詈 "Cursing" (Chapter 6, Section 4)
mao 冒 falsely claim
Mao Peiqi 毛佩琦
Mao Yilu 毛一鷺
maoai 冒哀 conceal the mourning
Maopo wuliao 冒破物料 "Fraudulently Taking Excessive Materials" (Art. 451)
Maozhi guanliang 冒支官糧 "Fraudulently Issuing Government Grain" (Art. 137)
Maren 罵人 "Cursing Others" (Art. 347)
meiji leijue 每季類決 execute in different categories every season
Menggu semuren hunyin 蒙古色目人婚姻 "Marriages by Mongols and Semu People" (Art. 122)

Glossary

menglong baoju 朦朧保舉 misleadingly recommend others
Mengshuizhai cundu 盟水齋存牘 *Court Opinions at Mengshuizhai Studio*, a casebook written by Yan Junyan
Menjin suoyao 門禁鎖鑰 "Locking Gates through Which Passing Is Prohibited" (Art. 219)
miaoxiang 廟享 imperial ancestor worship
Mile Fu 彌勒佛 Buddha Maitreya
Ming 明 brightness, radiance (dynastic name)
Ming Dagao junling 明大誥峻令 *The Severe Punishments in the Grand Pronouncements*
Ming Dagao yanjiu 明大誥研究 *A Study of the Grand Pronouncements*
Ming Dagao yu Mingchu zhengzhi shehui 明大誥与明初政治社會 *The Grand Pronouncements and Politics and Society in the Early Ming*
Ming Hongwu Yongle chao de bangwen junling 明洪武朝的榜文峻令 "The Placards and Harsh Regulations in the Ming Hongwu and Yongle Reigns"
ming li 名例 punishments and general principles
Ming lü 明律 *The Ming Code*
Ming lü mu jian 明律目箋 "An Exegesis of the Articles in *The Great Ming Code*"
Ming Qing shi jiangyi 明清史講義 *Lectures on Ming and Qing History*
Ming Qing shi yanjiu conggao 明清史研究叢稿 *Draft Studies on the Ming and Qing Histories*
Ming Taizu 明太祖
Ming Taizu shilu 明太祖實錄 *Veritable Records of Ming Taizu*
Ming Taizu shilu jiaokan ji 明太祖實錄校勘記 *Comparative Notes on the Veritable Records of Ming Taizu*
Ming Taizu yuzhi wenji 明太祖御制文集 *The Collected Writings of Ming Taizu*
Ming Yuzhen 明玉珍
Mingdai chongjun yanjiu 明代充軍研究 *Military Exile in the Ming*
Mingdai liuxing kao 明代流刑考 "Life Exile in the Ming"
Mingdai lü li huibian 明代律例彙編 *Compendium of the Code and Regulations in the Ming Dynasty*
Mingdai zhouxian yashu de jianzhi yu zhouxian zhengzhi tizhi 明代州縣衙署的建置与政治體制 "The Yamen Complex and Political Institution of Subprefecture and District during the Ming"
Mingjiao 明教 Manicheism
Mingli lü 名例律 "Laws on Punishments and General Principles" (Chapter 1)
Mingshi 明史 *The History of the Ming Dynasty*
Mingshi kaozheng 明史考證 *Verification of the History of the Ming Dynasty*
Mingshi renming suoyin 明史人名索引 *Index to Names in the History of the Ming Dynasty*

Mingwang 明王 Prince of Radiance

Mingzun Jiao 明尊教 Light-honoring Sect

Mokan juanzong 磨勘卷宗 "Reviewing Documentary Files" (Art. 73)

mou 謀 plot

moudani 謀大逆 plotting great sedition

moufan 謀反 plotting rebellion

Moufan dani 謀反大逆 "Plotting Rebellion and Great Sedition" (Art. 277)

Moupan 謀叛 "Plotting Treason" (Art. 278)

Mousha gufu fumu 謀殺故夫父母 "Plotting to Kill the Parents of a Deceased Husband" (Art. 309)

Mousha ren 謀殺人 "Plotting to Kill Others" (Art. 305)

Mousha zhishi ji benguan zhangguan 謀殺制使及本管長官 "Plotting to Kill Imperial Emissaries or One's Own Superior Officers" (Art. 306)

Mousha zufumu fumu 謀殺祖父母父母 "Plotting to Kill Paternal Grandparents or Parents" (Art. 307)

Mu Ying 沐英

mu zhi xiongdi 母之兄弟 mother's brothers

mu zhi zimei 母之姊妹 mother's sisters

mu zufumu 母祖父母 mother's father's parents

mujiu 母舅 maternal uncles

Muyang chuchan bu rufa 牧養畜產不如法 "Raising Livestock Contrary to Law" (Art. 248)

muyifu 母姨父 maternal aunts' husbands

naixing 耐刑 penal servitude

Nanjing 南京

Nannü hunyin 男女婚姻 "Marriages of Men and Women" (Art. 107)

Neifu gongzuo renjiang tiyi 內府工作人匠替役 "Substituting Services by Craftsmen Working in the Palace Treasury" (Art. 207)

neiluan 內亂 incest

neishi 內使 palace attendants

ni 尼 Buddhist nuns

Ni fumu fu sang 匿父母夫喪 "Concealing the Death of Parents or Husbands" (Art. 198)

Niduan zangfa budang 擬斷贓罰不當 "Deciding the Seizure of Illicit Goods Improperly" (Art. 146)

Nishui 匿稅 "Evading Taxes" (Art. 165)

Nu ji gugongren jian jiazhang qi 奴及雇工人姦家長妻 "Slaves or Hired Laborers Committing Fornication with Household Heads' Wives" (Art. 394)

Nubi ma jiazhang 奴婢罵家長 "Slaves Cursing Household Heads" (Art. 350)

Nubi ou jiazhang 奴婢毆家長 "Slaves Striking Household Heads" (Art. 337)

Nuoyi chuna 那移出納 "Diverting [Items] in Expenditures or Receipts" (Art. 135)

Glossary

nupu 奴仆 bond servants
nü zhi sun 女之孫 daughter's son's son
nü zhi zi 女之子 daughter's son
nüguan 女冠 Daoist nuns

ou 偶 accidentally
Ou dagong yixia zunzhang 毆大功以下尊長 "Striking Superior or Older Relatives of the Third Mourning Degree or More Distant" (Art. 340)
Ou jiqin zunzhang 毆期親尊長 "Striking Superior or Older Relatives of the Second Mourning Degree" (Art. 341)
Ou qi qianfu zhi zi 毆妻前夫之子 "Striking Sons of Wives by Their Former Husbands" (Art. 344)
Ou shouyeshi 毆受業師 "Striking Teachers from Whom [the Offenders] Receive Their Education" (Art. 334)
Ou zhishi ji benguan zhangguan 毆制使及本管長官 "Striking Imperial Emissaries or One's Own Head Officials" (Art. 329)
Ou zufumu fumu 毆祖父母父母 "Striking Paternal Grandparents or Parents" (Art. 342)

Pan Tingjian 潘庭堅
Panjie jianxi 盤詰奸細 "Interrogating Spies" (Art. 245)
panshu 判署 make judgments and sign documents
peichang 賠償 repayment
Pushe sunhuai 鋪舍損坏 "Damaged Postal Relay Station Buildings" (Art. 263)
Puyang yandu 莆陽讞牘 *Court Opinions from Xinghua Prefecture*

qi 其 but
Qi Biaojia 祁彪佳
qi boshu 妻伯叔 wife's father's brother
qi fumu 妻父母 wife's parents
qi wai zufumu 妻外祖父母 wife's mother's parents
qi xiongdi ji fu 妻兄弟及婦 wife's brother and his wife
qi zhi gu 妻之姑 wife's father's sister
qi zimei zi 妻姊妹子 wife's sister's son
qi zufumu 妻祖父母 wife's father's parents
qian 錢 unit of weight
Qian Tang 錢唐
Qian Yongren 錢用壬
Qianfa 錢法 "Rules of Coinage" (Art. 126)
qiang maimai you yuli 強買賣有餘利 gain excessive profits through forcing purchase or sale
Qiangdao 強盜 "Forcible Robbery" (Art. 289)

qiangjian 強姦 forcible fornication, rape

qianguan 遷官 reassign to other posts

Qiangzhan liangjia qinü 強占良家妻女 "Forcibly Seizing Wives or Daughters of Honorable Families" (Art. 118)

qianhu 千戶 battalion commander

qianhu suo 千戶所 battalion

Qianliang huxiang juecha 錢糧互相覺察 "Watching Each Other for Money and Grain" (Art. 138)

qianshi 僉事 assistant commanders

qianxi 遷徙 banishment

qianxi anzhi 遷徙安置 banish someone to settle in remote regions

Qianzhai 錢債 "Monetary Obligations" (Chapter 3, Section 6)

qiaoyan lingse 巧言令色 give clever talks in an ingratiating manner

qichu 七出 seven causes for repudiation

Qichu cizi 起除刺字 "Removing Tattoos" (Art. 304)

qichuan fuyan 起船符驗 authority tallies for using post boats

qideng 七燈 seven lamps

qiedao 竊盜 theft, secretly stealing

Qiedao 竊盜 "Theft" (Art. 292)

Qihui qiwu jiase deng 棄毀器物稼穡等 "Discarding or Destroying Things Such as Utensils or Crops" (Art. 104)

Qihui zhishu yinxin 棄毀制書印信 "Discarding or Destroying Imperial Edicts or Official Seals" (Art. 65)

qijian 欺姦 fornication by deceit

Qijie jinyin zuse 起解金銀足色 "Delivering Gold or Silver in Standard Purity" (Art. 143)

qilao 耆老 village elders

qima yubao shengzhi 起馬御寶聖旨 imperial decrees stamped with imperial seals for using post horses

qin 侵 encroach upon

Qin ding lü gao tiaoli 欽定律誥條例 *The Imperially Approved Regulation of the Code and Pronouncements*

Qing 清 purity (dynastic name)

qing 請 petition

qingci 青詞 black-paper charms

qingfeng sili 請俸司吏 staff foremen who request a salary

qinmu 親母 natural mother

Qinshu xiangdao 親屬相盜 "Relatives Stealing from Each Other" (Art. 295)

Qinshu xiangjian 親屬相姦 "Committing Fornication with Relatives" (Art. 392)

Qinshu xiangwei rongyin 親屬相為容隱 "Mutual Concealment by Relatives" (Art. 31)

Glossary

Qinzhan jiedao 侵占街道 "Encroaching on Public Streets and Roads" (Art. 459)

Qiqie ma fu jiqin zunzhang 妻妾罵夫期親尊長 "Wives or Concubines Cursing Husbands' Superior or Older Relatives of the Second Mourning Degree" (Art. 353)

Qiqie ma gufu fumu 妻妾罵故夫父母 "Wives or Concubines Cursing Parents of Deceased Husbands" (Art. 354)

Qiqie ou fu 妻妾毆夫 "Wives or Concubines Striking Husbands" (Art. 338)

Qiqie ou gufu gumu 妻妾毆故夫父母 "Wives or Concubines Striking Parents of Deceased Husbands" (Art. 345)

Qiqie shixu 妻妾失序 "Disordering Wives and Concubines" (Art. 109)

Qiqie yu fu qinshu xiangou 妻妾與夫親屬相毆 "Wives or Concubines and Husbands' Relatives Striking Each Other" (Art. 343)

Qiqin zhiren 棄親之任 "Abandoning Relatives to Take Government Offices" (Art. 199)

qishi 棄市 display the executed body in the market

Qiu yingjin er bujin 囚應禁而不禁 "Not Imprisoning Criminals Who Should Be Imprisoned" (Art. 419)

qiusuo 求索 solicitation

qiutan 丘壇 mounds and altars

Qiyin tianliang 欺隱田糧 "Fraudulently Concealing Fields and Their Produce" (Art. 96)

Qiyong bujuan bu rufa 器用布絹不如法 "Failing to Manufacture Utensils and Textiles in Accordance with the Rules" (Art. 175)

qizha 欺詐 fraud

Qu bumin funü wei qiqie 娶部民婦女為妻妾 "Marrying Women or Daughters of Those under [the Officials'] Jurisdiction as Wives or Concubines" (Art. 116)

Qu qinshu qiqie 娶親屬妻妾 "Marrying Relatives' Wives or Concubines" (Art. 115)

Qu taozou funü 娶逃走婦女 "Marrying Runaway Women" (Art. 117)

Qu yueren wei qiqie 娶樂人為妻妾 "Marrying Musicians as Wives or Concubines" (Art. 119)

quan 權 expedient provisions

quanke 全科 whole penalty

queben 闕本 document concerning vacancies

quyu buhe 取與不和 take or give without consent

Renhu kuidui kecheng 人戶虧兌課程 "Households Failing to Pay Taxes" (Art. 167)

Renhu yiji weiding 人戶以籍為定 "Households Should Be Established according to the Registers" (Art. 82) *renman* 任滿 completion of service terms

Renming 人命 "Homicide" (Chapter 6, Section 2)

Rensuo zhimai tianzhai 任所置買田宅 "Purchasing Fields or Houses [by Officials or Functionaries] in the Locations of Their Service" (Art. 100)

ruguan 入官 confiscation by the government; being forfeit to the government

rumu 乳母 wet nurse, i.e., the father's concubine who nurses the child

ruo 若 if

ruwu qingliang 入伍請糧 join the army and request rations

sanbuqu 三不去 three restrictions on divorce

sanguan 散官 titular officials

Sangzang 喪葬 "Funerals" (Art. 200)

Sanshi nian tiaoli 三十年條例 Regulation of Hongwu 30

sansi 三司 three provincial offices

Santai Minglü zhaopan zhengzong 三臺明律招判正宗 Standard Formats for Making Judgments according to The Ming Code

sanzhai 散齋 partial abstinence

seng 僧 Buddhist priests

Sengdao bai fumu 僧道拜父母 "Buddhist and Daoist Priests Honoring Parents" (Art. 195)

Sengdao quqi 僧道娶妻 "Buddhist or Daoist Priests Taking Wives" (Art. 120)

Sha yijia sanren 殺一家三人 "Killing Three Persons from One Household" (Art. 310)

Sha zisun ji nubi tulai ren 殺子孫及奴婢圖賴人 "Killing Sons, Sons' Sons, or Slaves and Putting the Blame on Others" (Art. 317)

Shaanxi 陝西

Shahai junren 殺害軍人 "Killing Military Personnel" (Art. 34)

Shan zaozuo 擅造作 "Engaging in Constructions and Manufactures without Authorization" (Art. 448)

Shandiao guanjun 擅調官軍 "Moving Government Troops without Authorization" (Art. 221)

Shandong 山東

shangbao 尚寶 chief steward of seals

Shangou shuguan 擅勾屬官 "Summoning Subordinate Officials without Authorization" (Art. 58)

shangshu 上書 memorialize the throne

Shangshu chenyan 上書陳言 "Sending Memorials or Making Statements to the Throne" (Art. 190)

Shangshu zoushi fanhui 上書奏事犯諱 "Mistakenly Violating Name Taboos in Memorials or Statements to the Throne" (Art. 67)

Shangsiguan yu tongshuguan xiangou 上司官與統屬官相毆 "Superior Officials and Subordinate Officials Striking Each Other" (Art. 331)

Glossary

Shangyan dachen dezheng 上言大臣德政 "Memorializing in Praise of the Virtues and Achievements of High Officials" (Art. 62)
Shanli zhiyi 擅離職役 "Leaving Official Appointments or Employments without Authorization" (Art. 55)
Shanshi tianyuan guaguo 擅食田園瓜果 "Eating Melons or Fruits of Gardens or Orchards without Authorization" (Art. 105)
Shanxi 山西
Shanyong diaobing yinxin 擅用調兵印信 "Employing Seals of Transferring Troops without Authorization" (Art. 79)
Shasi jianfu 殺死姦夫 "Killing Adulterous Lovers" (Art. 308)
she 赦 amnesty
sheji 社稷 Altars of Soil and Grain
shejiao 設醮 establish [Daoist] sacrificial altars
Shen Jiaben 沈家本
Shen Shirong 沈士榮
Shen Shixing 申時行
Shenbao junwu 申報軍務 "Reporting Military Matters" (Art. 222)
Sheng Yuanfu 盛原輔
shenglao 牲牢 sacrificial beasts
shenming ting 申明亭 exhibition pavilions
Sheqian duanzui budang 赦前斷罪不當 "Incorrectly Deciding Penalties before Amnesties" (Art. 441)
Shi yingzou buzou 事應奏不奏 "Not Memorializing Matters That Ought to Be Memorialized" (Art. 68)
Shichan 市廛 "Markets" (Chapter 3, Section 7)
Shie 十惡 "The Ten Abominations" (Art. 2)
Shihou shoucai 事後受財 "Accepting Property after Completing the Matters" (Art. 369)
Shihuo 失火 "Accidentally Setting Fires" (Art. 406)
shipo 師婆 grand instructress
Shisan jing zhushu 十三經註疏 *Thirteen Classics with Annotations and Commentaries*
Shishi buxiu difang 失時不修堤防 "Failing to Repair Dikes at the Proper Time" (Art. 458)
Shisi ping wujia 市司評物價 "Assessing Prices of Merchandise by Market Authorities" (Art. 172)
shiwu 師巫 wizards and witches
shiwu 失誤 make errors
Shiwu chaohe 失誤朝賀 "Making Errors in Imperial Audiences or Congratulatory Ceremonies" (Art. 186)
shiwu junji 失誤軍機 losses and mistakes in military operations
Shiwu junshi 失誤軍事 "Losses or Mistakes in Military Operations" (Art. 225)

Shiyi 失儀 "Misbehaving during Ceremonies" (Art. 187)

Shizhan tianxiang 失占天象 "Failing to Prophesy Heavenly Portents" (Art. 196)

shou 收 take in

shou 首 principals

shou shijie 受誓戒 start the abstinence period

shoucai wangfa 收財枉法 accept property and subvert the law

shoucang jinshu 收藏禁書 collect and keep proscribed books

Shoucang jinshu ji sixi tianwen 收藏禁書及私習天文 "Collecting and Keeping Proscribed Books and Practicing Astronomy without Authorization" (Art. 184)

Shouliang weixian 收糧違限 "Violating the Time Limits in Collecting Grain Taxes" (Art. 127)

shouling guan 首領官 staff supervisors

Shouliu mishi zinü 收留迷失子女 "Taking Stray Children" (Art. 85)

shoushu 收贖 redemption

Shouyang gulao 收養孤老 "Supporting Orphans and Elderly Persons" (Art. 95)

shouye shi 受業師 the teacher from whom one has received his education

shouyu guan 守禦官 commandant

Shouzang 受贓 "Accepting Illicit Goods" (Chapter 6, Section 6)

Shouzhang zaiguan caiwu 守掌在官財物 "Guarding Goods in the Hands of the Government" (Art. 147)

Shouzhi liunan 收支留難 "Creating Obstructions in Receiving or Issuing [Government Goods]" (Art. 142)

Shouzhi qianliang ji shankai guanfeng 守支錢糧及擅開官封 "Waiting for Money and Grain to Be Expended and Opening Official Seals without Authorization" (Art. 140)

shu 贖 redemption [of punishment]

shu zhang zisun 庶長子孫 concubines' eldest sons and sons' sons

shufu zhoushui 書符咒水 draw magical signs or recite incantations over water

shuiliang 稅糧 grain taxes

shumu 庶母 secondary mother, i.e., father's concubine who has borne a child

Shushi wangyan huofu 術士妄言禍福 "Soothsayers Recklessly Predicting Disaster or Good Fortune" (Art. 197)

Shuzui tiaoli 贖罪條例 The Regulation on Redemption of Crimes

si 死 death penalty

si 寺 Buddhist temples

si zhuqian 私鑄錢 privately minting copper currency

Sicang yingjin junqi 私藏應禁軍器 "Possessing Prohibited Military Equipment without Authorization" (Art. 235)

Sicha 私茶 "Illegal Transactions in Tea" (Art. 163)

Glossary

Sichong yahang butou 私充牙行埠頭 "Filling Positions of Commission Agents or Port Masters without Authorization" (Art. 171)

Sichu waijing ji weijin xiahai 私出外境及違禁下海 "Crossing Frontiers without Authorization or Going to Sea in Violation of the Prohibitions" (Art. 246)

Sichuan 四川

Sichuang anyuan ji sidu sengdao 私剏庵院及私度僧道 "Establishing Buddhist or Daoist Monasteries without Authorization and Ordaining Buddhist or Daoist Priests without Authorization" (Art. 83)

Sidian 祀典 *The Sacrificial Canon*

sidu guan 私度關 pass checkpoints without authorization

Sifan 私礬 "Illegal Transactions in Alum" (Art. 164)

Sifu 四輔 Four Supports

Sihe gongshi 私和公事 "Privately Settling Public Matters" (Art. 405)

Sijie guan chechuan 私借官車船 "Borrowing Government Carriages or Boats without Authorization" (Art. 106)

Sijie guan chuchan 私借官畜產 "Borrowing or Lending Government Livestock without Authorization" (Art. 257)

Sijie guanwu 私借官物 "Borrowing Government Objects without Authorization" (Art. 134)

Sijie qianliang 私借錢糧 "Borrowing Money or Grain without Authorization" (Art. 133)

Sijie yima 私借驛馬 "Borrowing Post Horses without Authorization" (Art. 276)

silü suo budao 思慮所不到 thought or planning cannot contemplate the consequence

sima 緦麻 relatives of the fifth mourning degree

Simai junqi 私賣軍器 "Selling Military Equipment without Authorization" (Art. 233)

Simai zhanma 私賣戰馬 "Selling Military Horses without Authorization" (Art. 232)

Siqiu fuzou daibao 死囚覆奏待報 "Awaiting Replies to Memorials concerning Prisoners Sentenced to Death" (Art. 445)

Siqiu lingren zisha 死囚令人自殺 "Prisoners Sentenced to Death Ordering Others to Kill Them" (Art. 427)

sishan yongcai 私擅用財 use property without authorization

Sishou gonghou caiwu 私受公侯財物 "Privately Accepting Property from Dukes or Marquises" (Art. 375)

Sishu Wujing daquan 四書五經大全 *The Great Compendium of the Four Books and Five Classics*

sixi tianwen 私習天文 privately practice astronomy

siyan 私鹽 smuggle salt

Siyi bumin fujiang 私役部民夫匠 "Privately Employing Commoners or Government Artisans under One's Jurisdiction to Perform Services" (Art. 92)

Siyi gongbing 私役弓兵 "Employing Constables without Authorization" (Art. 247)

Siyi minfu taijiao 私役民夫抬轎 "Making Commoners Carry Sedan Chairs without Authorization" (Art. 272)

Siyi pubing 私役鋪兵 "Employing Postal Relay Station Soldiers without Authorization" (Art. 264)

siyu guandian 司獄官典 warders and functionaries in charge of the prison

Siyuemao du guanjin 私越冒渡關津 "Passing Guard Posts or Fords without Authorization, by Circumvention, or by Deception" (Art. 241)

Sizao hu dou cheng chi 私造斛斗秤尺 "Manufacturing Volume Measures, Weights, or Linear Measures without Authorization" (Art. 174)

Sizhu tongqian 私鑄銅錢 "Privately Casting Copper Cash" (Art. 383)

sizui 私罪 private crimes

Song 宋 dynastic name

Song Lian 宋濂

Sui 隋 dynastic name

susong 訴訟 accusations and suits

sun 孫 son's son

sun 損 harm

Sun Zhong 孫忠

sunfu 孫婦 son's son's wife

Sunhuai cangku caiwu 損壞倉庫財物 "Damaging Goods in Granaries or Treasuries" (Art. 144)

suo 所 offices

suoshengmu 所生母 biological mothers

Susong 訴訟 "Accusations and Suits" (Chapter 6, Section 5)

Suwei ren bingzhang 宿衛人兵仗 "Arms of Imperial Guards" (Art. 212)

Suwei shouwei ren sizi daiti 宿衛守衛人私自代替 "Substituting Imperial Bodyguards or Palace Guards without Authorization" (Art. 204)

Suzhou 蘇州

tai huang taihou 太皇太后 grand empress dowager

taibao 太保 grand guardian

taichang 太常 grand banner

Taimiao men shanru 太廟門擅入 "Entering the Gates of the Imperial Ancestral Temple without Authorization" (Art. 202)

taishe 太社 Altar of the Soil

Taiyuan 太原

Tan Qian 談遷

Tan Zhang 譚章

Glossary

tang boshu fumu 堂伯叔父母 father's father's brother's sons and their wives
Tang He 湯和
Tang lü shuyi 唐律疏議 *The Tang Code with Commentaries*
Tang lü shuyi jianjie 唐律疏議箋解 *Explanations to the Tang Code with Commentaries*
tang xiongdi 堂兄弟 father's brother's son
tang xiongdi qi 堂兄弟妻 father's brother's son's wife
tang zhi sunnü 堂姪孫女 father's brother's son's son's daughter
tang zhinü 堂姪女 father's brother's son's daughter
tang zhisun 堂姪孫 father's brother's son's son's son
tang zhisun fu 堂姪孫婦 father's brother's son's son's son's wife
tang zimei 堂姊妹 father's brother's daughter
tanggu 堂姑 father's father's brother's daughter
tangjiu zhi zi 堂舅之子 mother's father's brother's son's son
tangyi zhi zi 堂姨之子 mother's father's brother's daughter's son
tangzhi 堂姪 father's brother's son's son
tangzhi fu 堂姪婦 father's brother's son's son's wife
tanwen 袒免 relatives of the sixth mourning degree
Tao An 陶安
Taobi chaiyi 逃避差役 "Fleeing to Evade Corvée Services" (Art. 90)
Teng Ssu-yü 鄧嗣禹
Teng Yi 滕毅
tiandeng 天燈 celestial lamp
tianwen 天文 astronomical prophecy
tianxia 天下 all under Heaven
tianzhai 田宅 "Fields and Houses" (Chapter 3, Section 2)
tidiao guanli 提調官吏 proctorial or inspecting officials or functionaries
tiebang 鐵榜 iron placard
tieye 鐵冶 iron smelters
Tingsong huibi 聽訟迴避 "Withdrawing from Trying Cases" (Art. 358)
Tingxing Ancha Shi Si 提刑按察使司 Provincial Surveillance Commission
tongcai 同財 have common property
tongguan 通關 invoices
tongju 同居 people who live together
tongju jifu 同居繼父 stepfather who lives together [with the children]
tongliao 同僚 members of the same office
Tongliao dai panshu wenan 同僚代判署文案 "Colleagues Affixing Dates or Signatures to Documentary Files on Others' Behalf" (Art. 74)
Tongliao fan gongzui 同僚犯公罪 "Committing Public Crimes by Those in the Same Office" (Art. 27)
tongpai 銅牌 bronze warrants
tongshe suoshu 統攝所屬 be in charge of subordinates

Tongxing qinshu xiangou 同姓親屬相毆 "Relatives of the Same Surname Striking Each Other" (Art. 339)

Tongxing weihun 同姓為婚 "Marrying Persons with the Same Surname" (Art. 113)

Tongxing zhiyou mouhai 同行知有謀害 "Knowing Companions Plot to Harm" (Art. 324)

tongzhi 同知 associate commanders

Tou niming wenshu gao renzui 投匿名文書告人罪 "Making Anonymous Written Accusations of Offenses against Others" (Art. 356)

tu 徒 penal servitude

tuchen 圖讖 augural diagrams

tui 推 make inquiries

tuisuan xingming 推算星命 cast horoscopes

Tuliu qianxi difang 徒流遷徙地方 "Places for Penal Servitude, Life Exile, and Banishment" (Art. 47)

Tuliu rentao 徒流人逃 "Criminals under Penal Servitude or Life Exile Running Away" (Art. 414)

Tuliuren you fanzui 徒流人又犯罪 "Committing Crimes Again by Those Punished by Penal Servitude or Life Exile" (Art. 20)

Tuliuren zaidao huishe 徒流人在道會赦 "Those Punished by Penal Servitude or Life Exile Are En Route When the Amnesty Is Proclaimed" (Art. 17)

Tuolou hukou 脫漏戶口 "Ommitting to Register Households or Household Members" (Art. 81)

Tuqiu bu yingyi 徒囚不應役 "Prisoners Sentenced to Penal Servitude Failing to Perform Labor Services" (Art. 443)

wai zufumu 外祖父母 mother's parents

waisun 外孫 grandson in the female line

Wang Guangyang 汪廣洋

Wang Kentang 王肯堂

Wang Nan 王楠

Wang Yibu xiansheng jianshi 王儀部先生箋釋 Wang Kentang's Commentaries [to The Great Ming Code]

Wang Zao 王藻

Wanli 萬曆 reign name

wanshi zhi changfa 萬世之常法 the permanent law of ten thousand generations

wei 衛 guard, garrison

wei qi zi 為其子 for one's own son

Weibi ren zhisi 威逼人致死 "Using Coercion to Cause Others to Die" (Art. 322)

weicong 為從 accessories

Glossary

weifan jiaoling 違犯教令 violate instructions
Weijin quli 違禁取利 "Taking Interest in Violation of Prohibitions" (Art. 168)
Weili zhifu ren 威力制縛人 "Using Coercion or Physical Strength to Restrain or Bind Others" (Art. 335)
Weiling 違令 "Violating the *Commandment*" (Art. 409)
weiru liupinguan 未入流品官 unranked officials
weisuo 衛所 guard-battalion
Weizao baochao 偽造寶鈔 "Counterfeiting Treasure Paper Currency" (Art. 382)
Weizao yinxin liri deng 偽造印信曆日等 "Counterfeiting Items Such as Seals and Almanacs" (Art. 381)
wen 文 unit of copper currency
wen 問 investigate
Wen Yuanji 文元吉
Wenguan buxu feng gonghou 文官不許封公侯 "Civil Officials Shall Not Be Designated as Dukes or Marquises" (Art. 50)
wenji 問疾 visit the sick
Wenshu ying jiyi er buji 文書應給驛而不給 "Documents That Should Be Provided with Postal Relay Station Services [for Delivery] but Are Not Provided" (Art. 268)
Wenwuguan fan gongzui 文武官犯公罪 "Committing Public Crimes by Civil or Military Officials" (Art. 7)
Wenwuguan fan sizui 文武犯私罪 "Committing Private Crimes by Civil or Military Officials" (Art. 8)
Wenyou enshe er gufan 聞有恩赦而故犯 "Hearing That There Will Be Amnesties and Deliberately Committing Crimes" (Art. 442)
Wogong shashang ren 窩弓殺傷人 "Killing or Injuring Others with Spring Bows" (Art. 321)
Wu 吳 government and reign name
wu 務 agencies
Wu Chen 吳沉
Wu Han 吳晗
Wu Quji 吳去疾
Wu Tan 吳墰
Wu Tong 吳彤
Wu Yanhong 吳艷紅
wu zhengtiao 無正條 without specific articles
Wu Zumou 吳祖謀
Wuchang 武昌
Wufu 五府 Five Commissions
wufu zhi qin 無服之親 relatives beyond the mourning system

Wugao 誣告 "Making False Accusations" (Art. 359)

Wugao chongjun ji qianxi 誣告充軍及遷徙 "False Accusations of Offenses Punishable by Military Exile or Banishment" (Art. 366)

Wugu bu chaocan gongzuo 無故不朝參公座 "Failing to Attend Audiences at the Court or to Fill Official Posts without Reason" (Art. 57)

Wuguan fanzui 無官犯罪 "Committing Crimes by Those Who Have Not Yet Become Officials" (Art. 13)

Wujun Dudu Fu 五軍都督府 Five Chief Military Commissions

Wuxing 五刑 "The Five Punishments" (Art. 1)

Wuzhi weng jian 誣執翁姦 "Falsely Accusing Fathers-in-Law of Fornication" (Art. 393)

xi 襲 inheritance privilege

Xia 夏 dynastic name

xian 縣 district

Xiang gongdian shejian 向宮殿射箭 "Shooting Arrows at Palaces or Halls" (Art. 211)

Xiang yinjiu li 鄉飲酒禮 "Community Wine-Drinking Ceremonies" (Art. 201)

Xianjinqiu bude gaoju tashi 見禁囚不得告舉他事 "Prisoners Are Not Permitted to Make Accusations regarding Others' Matters to the Authorities" (Art. 362)

xianren 賢人 worthy men

xianren 見任 incumbent officials

Xianrenguan zhezi libei 見任官輒自立碑 "Incumbent Officials Erecting Stele without Authorization" (Art. 191)

xiao lizhang 小里長 deputy community heads

xiao ming wang 小明王 young prince of radiance

xiaogong 小功 relatives of the fourth mourning degree

xiaoqi 小旗 squad commanders

xiaoshou 梟首 exposing the decapitated head

xiaowei 校尉 commandants

xiedu shenming 褻瀆神明 profaning the spirits

Xiedu shenming 褻瀆神明 "Profaning the Spirits" (Art. 180)

xing zhongshu sheng 行中書省 branch secretariat

Xingbu 刑部 Ministry of Justice

Xinggong yingmen 行宮營門 "The Camp Gates of the Imperial Traveling Palaces" (Art. 217)

Xingli daquan 性理大全 The Great Compendium of the Philosophy of Human Nature

Xinglü 刑律 "Laws on Penal Affairs" (Chapter 6)

xingsha wenshu 刑殺文書 documents concerning punishments or the death penalty

Xingshu juhui 刑書據會 Essentials of the Code
Xinpai 信牌 "Warrants" (Art. 80)
xiongdi 兄弟 brothers
xiongdi nü 兄弟女 brother's daughters
xiongdi qi 兄弟妻 brother's wife
xiongdi zi 兄弟子 brother's sons
xiongli 凶禮 rituals at the time of ill omen
Xisha wusha guoshi shashang ren 戲殺誤殺過失殺傷人 "Killing or Injuring Others in Play, by Mistake, or by Negligence" (Art. 315)
xiucai 秀才 cultivated talents
Xiuli cangku 修理倉庫 "Repairing Granaries or Treasuries" (Art. 455)
Xiuli qiaoliang daolu 修理橋梁道路 "Repairing Bridges and Roads" (Art. 460)
xiuzhai 修齋 establish [Buddhist] fasting altars
Xu Ben 徐本
Xu Changzuo 徐昌祚
Xu Cunren 許存仁
Xu Da 徐達
Xu Shouhui 徐壽輝
Xuandai guanfang paimian 懸帶關防牌面 "Carrying Identification Tablets" (Art. 220)
xuansun 玄孫 son's son's son's son
xuansun fu 玄孫婦 son's son's son's son's wife
xuanxiang qiwu 玄象器物 celestial instruments
Xuanyong junzhi 選用軍職 "Selecting Military Posts" (Art. 48)
Xuchu tongguan zhuchao 虛出通關硃鈔 "Fraudulently Issuing Invoices or Receipt" (Art. 131)
Xufei gongli caiqu bu kanyong 虛費工力採取不堪用 "Wasting Labor in Procuring [Things] That Cannot Be Used" (Art. 449)
xunjian 巡檢 police chiefs

Yan chuchan bu yishi 驗畜產不以實 "Verifying Livestock Incorrectly" (Art. 250)
Yan Junyan 顏俊彥
yanchang 鹽場 salt farms
Yanfa 鹽法 "The Salt Rules" (Arts. 149–60)
Yang Xian 楊憲
Yang Yifan 楊一凡
Yange huozhe 閹割火者 "Castrating Others" (Art. 403)
Yangliao shoubing chuchan bu rufa 養療瘦病畜產不如法 "Raising or Treating Emaciated or Sick Livestock Contrary to Law" (Art. 251)
yangmu 養母 adoptive mother
yanjin 淹禁 prolong imprisonment
Yanjin 淹禁 "Prolonging Imprisonment" (Art. 421)

yanjing 鹽井 salt wells
yanmei 魘魅 practice sorcery
Yanyu gao 讞獄稿 *Records of Judging Cases*
Yao Siren 姚思仁
Yaoqu shifeng gongwen 邀取實封公文 "Intercepting Sealed Government Documents" (Art. 262)
Ye wugu ru renjia 夜無故入人家 "Entering Others' Houses at Night without Reason" (Art. 300)
Yejin 夜禁 "Curfews" (Art. 240)
yexun tongpai 夜巡銅牌 bronze warrant for night patrol
yi 醫 physicians
yi 以 on the basis of
yi 驛 post couriers
yi 役 employment
yi 義 bond of righteousness
yi dao lun 以盜論 punished on the basis of robbery
Yi gaozhuang juyu 依告狀鞫獄 "Judging Cases in Accordance with the Specification in the Complaints" (Art. 430)
yi wangfa lun 以枉法論 punished on the basis of subversion of law
yi zhi sun 姨之孫 mother's sister's son's son
yibin 議賓 deliberation for guests
yidai fa 一代法 the law of the whole dynasty
yigong 議功 deliberation for meritorious subjects
yigu 議故 deliberation for old retainers
yigui 議貴 deliberation for subjects of high position
yijue 義絕 extinguish the bond of righteousness
Yili quguan 以理去官 "Leaving Offices for Legitimate Reasons" (Art. 12)
Yiluan Si 儀鸞司 Imperial Regalia Office
yin 蔭 protection privilege
Yinbi chaiyi 隱蔽差役 "Hiding [Persons from] Corvée Services" (Art. 88)
yineng 議能 deliberation for talents
ying chejia 迎車駕 intercept the carriage of the emperor
Ying Jia 應檟
Yingburen zhuibu zuiren 應捕人追捕罪人 "Pursuing and Arresting Criminals by Those Who Are Charged with the Duty of Arrest" (Art. 411)
Yingong shan kelian 因公擅科斂 "Making Unathorized Collections for Public Benefit" (Art. 374)
Yingtian 應天
Yingyizhe fanzui 應議者犯罪 "Committing Crimes by Those Entitled to the Eight Deliberations" (Art. 4)
Yingyizhe zhi fuzu youfan 應議者之父祖有犯 "Committing Crimes

Glossary

    by the Parents or Paternal Grandparents of Those Entitled to the Eight Deliberations" (Art. 9)
yingzao 營造 construction and manufacture
Yingzao 營造 "Constructions and Manufactures" (Chapter 7, Section 1)
yinji 印記 seal
yinlü bifu 引律比附 cite the *Code* and decide the case by analogy
Yinman ruguan jiachan 隱瞞入官家產 "Concealing Household Goods That Go to the Government" (Art. 148)
Yinni feiyong shuiliang kewu 隱匿費用稅糧課物 "Concealing or Consuming Tax Paid in Grain or Other Taxable Materials" (Art. 129)
Yinni zisheng guan chuchan 隱匿孳生官畜產 "Hiding Newborn Government Livestock" (Art. 256)
yiqin 議親 deliberation for relatives
yiqin 議勤 deliberation for diligent subjects
Yishi jicheng 驛使稽程 "Government Messengers Delaying in Their Mission" (Art. 265)
Yishi zhishu 遺失制書 ["Losing Imperial Edicts"] (Art. 66)
yixian 議賢 deliberation for worthies
yixiang 移鄉 relocation
Yizhi 儀制 "Ceremonial Regulations" (Chapter 4, Section 2)
Yizhi Si 儀制司 Bureau of Ceremonies
Yongle 永樂 eternal happiness (reign name)
yongqiang shengshi 用強生事 use force and make trouble
Yongyi shashang ren 庸醫殺傷人 "Incompetent Physicians Killing or Injuring Others" (Art. 320)
you wenan xiang guanshe 有文案相關涉 dealing with official documents
youlu ren 有祿人 salaried officials
Youshi yicai qingqiu 有事以財請求 "Seeking Favorable Decisions of Matters by Offering Property" (Art. 370)
Yousi guanli buzhu gongxie 有司官吏不住公廨 "Officials or Functionaries Having Authority but Not Residing in Public Office Buildings" (Art. 456)
Yousi jueqiu dengdi 有司決囚等第 "The Degrees of Competence of Officials Having Jurisdiction for Executing [Sentences] of Prisoners" (Art. 435)
Youxu junshu 優恤軍屬 "Treating Military Dependents Preferentially" (Art. 239)
Youyi 郵驛 "Postal Relay Stations" (Chapter 5, Section 5)
yu 御 imperial
yu tongzui 與同罪 punish with the same penalty
yu yanyan 與筵宴 attend feasts
Yuan 元 origin or greatness (dynastic name)
yuan 院 institutes
Yuan dianzhang 元典章 *The Institutes of the Yuan Dynasty*

Yuangaoren shibi bu fanghui 原告人事畢不放回 "Complainants Not Being Released after the Trial Is Completed" (Art. 431)
yuanzuo 緣坐 collective prosecution
yucheng 獄成 case is established
Yuci yiwu 御賜衣物 "Clothing and Objects Bestowed by the Emperor" (Art. 185)
yue 樂 musicians
Yuecheng 越城 "Climbing over City Walls" (Art. 218)
yuedu guan 越度關 pass checkpoints by circumvention
Yuesu 越訴 "Litigation Bypassing Appropriate Jurisdiction" (Art. 355)
yulin tuce 魚鱗圖冊 fish-scaled plot books
Yunnan 雲南
Yuqiu jinren jietuo 與囚金刃解脫 "Giving Prisoners Edged Metal Tools That Can Be Used to Free Themselves" (Art. 423)
Yuqiu qu fubian 獄囚取服辯 "Obtaining Prisoners' Acceptance of Punishment or Petition for Revision" (Art. 440)
Yuqiu tuojian ji fanyu zaitao 獄囚脫監及反獄在逃 "Imprisoned Criminals Escaping from Prisons or Using Force to Break out of Prisons and Running Away" (Art. 413)
Yuqiu wuzhi pingren 獄囚誣指平人 "Prisoners Falsely Accusing Innocent Persons" (Art. 432)
Yuqiu yiliang 獄囚衣糧 "Prisoners' Clothing and Food" (Art. 425)
Yushi Tai 御史臺 Censorate
Yuzhi dagao 御製大誥 *The Imperial Grand Pronouncements*
Yuzhi Dagao sanbian 御製大誥三編 *Third Imperial Grand Pronouncements*
Yuzhi Dagao xubian 御製大誥續編 *Supplementary Imperial Grand Pronouncements*
Yuzhi wenji bu 御製文集補 *The Imperial Writings, Supplemented*
yuzu 獄卒 prison guards

Zafan 雜犯 "Miscellaneous Offenses" (Chapter 6, Section 9)
zafan chaiyi 雜泛差役 miscellaneous corvée services
zafan sizui 雜犯死罪 miscellaneous capital crimes
zaicong xiongdi 再從兄弟 father's father's brother's son's son
zaicong xiongdi qi 再從兄弟妻 father's father's brother's son's son's wife
zaicong zhi 再從姪 father's father's brother's son's son
zaicong zhi fu 再從姪婦 father's father's brother's son's son's wife
zaicong zhinü 再從姪女 father's father's brother's son's son's daughter
zaicong zimei 再從姊妹 father's father's brother's son's daughter
Zaiguan qiusuo jiedai ren caiwu 在官求索借貸人財物 "Officials Extorting or Borrowing Property from Others" (Art. 371)
Zaijing fanzui junmin 在京犯罪軍民 "Military Personnel and Civilians Residing in the Capital Who Commit Crimes" (Art. 35)

Glossary

Zaisha maniu 宰殺馬牛 "Slaughtering Horses and Cattle" (Art. 254)
zang 贓 illicit goods
Zang Lihe 臧勵龢
zao 竃 salt workers
zao yanmei 造魘魅 inflict captive spirits
Zao yaoshu yaoyan 造妖書妖言 "Making Magical Inscriptions and Magical Incantations" (Art. 279)
zaoxu gudu 造蓄蠱毒 make or keep insect poisons
Zaoxu gudu sharen 造畜蠱毒殺人 "Killing Others by Making or Keeping *Gu* Poison" (Art. 312)
zaoyi 造意 formulate the plan
Zaozuo bu rufa 造作不如法 "Engaging in Constructions and Manufactures Contrary to the Law" (Art. 450)
Zaozuo guoxian 造作過限 "Exceeding Time Limits for Manufacture" (Art. 454)
zazhi 雜職 miscellaneous offices
Zeidao 賊盜 "Violence and Robbery" (Chapter 6, Section 1)
zeng 贈 award posthumous official titles
zeng gao 曾高 paternal great-grandparents and great-great-grandparents
zeng xuan 曾玄 great-grandsons and great-great-grandsons in the male line
zeng zhisun 曾姪孫 brother's son's son's son
zeng zhisun fu 曾姪孫婦 brother's son's son's son's wife
zeng zufumu 曾祖父母 father's father's parents
Zengjian guanwenshu 增減官文書 "Adding to or Subtracting from Official Documents" (Art. 75)
zengsun 曾孫 son's son's son
zengsun fu 曾孫婦 son's son's son's wife
zha 詐 deceitfully claim
Zha bingsishang bishi 詐病死傷避事 "Avoiding Duties by Feigning Illness, Death, or Injury" (Art. 388)
Zha jiaoyou ren fanfa 詐教誘人犯法 "Deceitfully Enticing Others to Violate the Law" (Art. 389)
Zhacheng neishi deng guan 詐稱內使等官 "Deceitfully Claiming to Be Palace Attendants or Other Officials" (Art. 385)
Zhachuan zhaozhi 詐傳詔旨 "Deceitfully Transmitting Imperial Decrees" (Art. 379)
Zhajia guan 詐假官 "Deceitfully Impersonating Officials" (Art. 384)
Zhamao gei luyin 詐冒給路引 "Deceitfully Issuing Travel Passes" (Art. 242)
zhan 斬 decapitation
zhang 丈 unit of length
zhang 杖 beating with the heavy stick
Zhang Chang 張昶
Zhang Chuncheng 張純誠

Zhang Dexin 張德信
Zhang Jinfan 張晉藩
Zhang Kai 張楷
Zhang Kentang 張肯堂
Zhang Meihe 張美和
Zhang Shicheng 張士誠
Zhang Tingyu 張廷玉
Zhang Yi 章溢
Zhang Yin 張引
zhangguan 長官 head official
Zhangguan shiren youfan 長官使人有犯 "Head Officials or Emissaries Committing Offenses" (Art. 438)
zhangzi 長子 eldest son
zhangzi fu 長子婦 eldest son's wife
Zhansu yishe shangfang 占宿驛舍上房 "Occupying the Best Rooms of Postal Relay Stations" (Art. 270)
zhao 詔 decree
Zhao Lin 趙麟
Zhaoshua wenjuan 照刷文卷 "Inspecting Documentary Files" (Art. 72)
Zhaqi guansi caiwu 詐欺官私取財 "Obtaining Government or Private Property by Deceit or Cheating" (Art. 297)
zhawei 詐偽 deception and counterfeit
Zhawei 詐偽 "Deceiving and Counterfeiting" (Chapter 6, Section 7)
Zhawei ruiying 詐為瑞應 "Deceitfully Making False Auspicious Portents" (Art. 387)
Zhawei zhishu 詐為制書 "Counterfeiting Imperial Rescripts" (Art. 378)
Zhe churu gongdian men 輒出入宮殿門 "Leaving or Entering Palace or Hall Gates without Authorization" (Art. 209)
zhehao 折耗 extra allowance
Zhejiang 浙江
Zhen Dexiu 真德秀
zhenfan 真犯 true crimes
zhenfan sizui 真犯死罪 true capital crimes
Zhenfan zafan sizui tiaoli 真犯雜犯死罪條例 *Regulation concerning True and Miscellaneous Capital Crimes*
zhenfu 鎮撫 judges
Zheng Rubi 鄭汝璧
Zheng Tianting 鄭天挺
zhengfan 正犯 responsible criminals
zhengguan 正官 regular officials; principal officials
zhengqi 正妻 principal wife
Zhenjiang 鎮江
Zheyu xinyu 折獄新語 *New Talks on Judging Cases*

Glossary

zhi 職 appointments
zhi 姪 brother's son
zhi 制 imperial decree
zhi fu 姪婦 brother's son's wife
zhi sunnü 姪孫女 brother's son's daughter
zhi zeng sunnü 姪曾孫女 brother's son's son's daughter
zhifu 知府 prefect
Zhiguan youfan 職官有犯 "Committing Crimes by Officials" (Art. 5)
zhihou 祗候 ushers
zhihui 指揮 guard commander
Zhiji sidian shenqi 致祭祀典神祇 "Performing Sacrifices to Spirits Recorded in *The Sacrificial Canon*" (Art. 178)
zhijie ren 支解人 dismember persons
zhili fuzhou 直隸府州 prefectures and subprefectures directly under the central government
zhinü 姪女 brother's daughter
Zhiqing cangni zuiren 知情藏匿罪人 "Knowing the Circumstances and Concealing Criminals" (Art. 417)
zhishi 執事 officiator
zhishi 致仕 retirement
zhishiguan 職事官 active-duty officials
zhishu 制書 imperial edicts
Zhishu youwei 制書有違 "Violating Imperial Edicts" (Art. 64)
zhisun 姪孫 brother's son's son
zhisun fu 姪孫婦 brother's son's son's wife
zhixian 知縣 magistrate
Zhixing yudao 直行御道 "Walking on the Imperial Pathway" (Art. 206)
zhiyin 知印 seal keepers
zhiyu zhi zhunsheng guiju 治獄之準繩規矩 rules and criteria for judging law cases
Zhizao weijin longfengwen duanpi 造違禁龍鳳文緞匹 "Weaving Silk Cloth with Prohibited Designs of Dragons and Phoenixes" (Art. 453)
zhizhai 致齋 full abstinence
Zhizheng 至正 utmost uprightness (reign name)
Zhizhi 職制 "Administrative Institutions" (Chapter 2, Section 1)
zhizhou 知州 subprefect
zhong 眾 group
Zhongguo fazhi shi 中國法制史 *Chinese Legal History*
Zhongguo fazhi shi shumu 中國法制史書目 *Bibliography of Chinese Legal History*
Zhongguo fazhi tongshi 中國法制通史 *General History of Chinese Legal Systems*
Zhongguo lishi da cidian 中國歷史大辭典 *Dictionary of Chinese History*

Zhongguo renming da cidian 中國人名大辭典 *A Comprehensive Dictionary of Chinese Names*

Zhongguo shi gao 中國史稿 *A Draft History of China*

Zhongguo zhenxi falü dianji jicheng 中國珍稀法律典籍集成 *Collection of Rare Works of Chinese Law*

Zhongshu Sheng 中書省 secretariat

zhongsi 中祀 medium sacrifices

zhongsun 眾孫 son's other sons

zhongsun fu 眾孫婦 son's other son's wives

zhongzheng 眾証 three or more witnesses

zhongzi 眾子 other sons

zhongzi fu 眾子婦 other sons' wives

zhou 州 subprefecture

zhou 咒 swear by spells

Zhou Zhen 周禎 chief minister

Zhou Zhen 周湞 assistant minister

Zhouli 周禮 *The Institutes of Zhou*

Zhu Biao 朱標

Zhu Di 朱棣

Zhu Jingxun 朱敬循

Zhu Yuanzhang 朱元璋

Zhu Yuanzhang pingzhuan 朱元璋評傳 *Biography of Zhu Yuanzhang*

Zhu Yuangzhang zhuan 朱元璋傳 *A Biography of Zhu Yuanzhang*

Zhu Yunwen 朱允炆

Zhuanjiie guanwu 轉解官物 "Transmitting Government Goods" (Art. 145)

zhubao 主保 security group chiefs

zhuchao 硃鈔 receipts

zhuchi 住持 abbots

zhuiduo 追奪 revoke one's certificates of appointment

Zhujiang bu gushou 主將不固守 "Commanding Officers Failing to Defend [Their Positions] Tenaciously" (Art. 228)

zhun 准 as comparable to

zhunshu sizui 准贖死刑 redeemable capital crimes

zhushou 主守 custodians

zhushou 主首 tithing chief managers

Zhushou bujue shiqiu 主守不覺失囚 "Custodians Not Discovering the Escape of Prisoners" (Art. 416)

Zhushou jiaoqiu fanyi 主守教囚反異 "Custodians Instructing Prisoners to Contradict Their Confessions" (Art. 424)

Zhutuo gongshi 囑託公事 "Seeking Favors in Public Matters" (Art. 404)

Zhuxu jianü 逐婿嫁女 "Expelling Sons-in-Law and Marrying Off Daughters" (Art. 110)

zi 子 son; children

Glossary

zi jueju 自覺舉 discover and report the errors on one's own
zimei 姊妹 sisters
Zisheng mapi 孳生馬匹 "Breeding Horses" (Art. 249)
Zishi tongxun 資世通訓 *Instructions to Aid the World*
zishou 自首 voluntary confessions
Zisun weifan jiaoling 子孫違犯教令 "Sons or Sons' Sons Violating Instructional Orders" (Art. 361)
zong 宗 lineage
zongbing jiangjun 總兵將軍 generals of regional command
Zongfang junren xieyi 縱放軍人歇役 "Allowing Military Soldiers to Abandon Service" (Art. 236)
zongheng zhi tu 縱橫之徒 persuasive persons
Zongjun lulüe 縱軍虜掠 "Allowing Troops to Pillage" (Art. 229)
zongqi 總旗 platoon commanders
Zongrong qiqie fanjian 縱容妻妾犯姦 "Facilitating and Tolerating Wives or Concubines to Commit Fornication" (Art. 391)
Zoudui shixu 奏對失序 "Failing to Observe the Proper Procedure in Making Responses to the Throne" (Art. 188)
zoushi 奏事 report to the throne
zu boshu fumu 族伯叔父母 father's father's father's brother's son's sons and their wives
zu boshu zufumu 族伯叔祖父母 father's father's father's brother's sons and their wives
zu xiongdi 族兄弟 father's father's father's brother's son's son's son
zu xiongdi 祖兄弟 father's father's brother
zu xiongdi qi 族兄弟妻 father's father's father's brother's son's son's son's wife
zu zeng zufumu 族曾祖父母 father's father's father's brothers and their wives
zu zeng zugu 族曾祖姑 father's father's father's sister
zu zimei 族姊妹 father's father's father's brother's son's son's daughter
zu zimei 祖姊妹 father's father's sister
zu zugu 族祖姑 father's father's father's brother's daughter
zufumu 祖父母 father's parents
zugu 族姑 father's father's father's brother's son's daughter
Zuhuai yanfa 阻壞鹽法 "Obstructing the Salt Laws" (Art. 162)
Zuiren jubu 罪人拒捕 "Criminals Resisting Arrest" (Art. 412)
zuizhi 罪止 maximum punishment
zunbei shixu 尊卑失序 the senior or junior order is violated
Zunbei weihun 尊卑為婚 "Marrying Superior or Inferior Relatives" (Art. 114)
zunshu 尊屬 senior relatives
zunzhang 尊長 senior or elder relatives
Zunzhang weirensha sihe 尊長為人殺私和 "Making Private Settlements When Superior or Older Relatives Are Killed by Others" (Art. 323)

zuodao luanzheng zhi shu 左道亂政之術 heterodox teachings that create disturbances

zuoer guan 佐貳官 associate officials

zuoxing 作刑 penal servitude

Zuozang zhizui 坐贓致罪 "Committing Crimes Involving Illicit Goods Obtained through Malfeasance" (Art. 368)

Zuozhi tongshu ma zhangguan 佐職統屬罵長官 "Associate or Other Subordinate Officials Cursing Head Officials" (Art. 349)

Zuozhi tongshu ou zhangguan 佐職統屬毆長官 "Associate or Other Subordinate Officials Striking Head Officials" (Art. 330)

zuzhi 祖制 ancestral instructions

Bibliography

The following abbreviations are used in the notes:

DMB   Goodrich and Fang, *Dictionary of Ming Biography*
DML   *Da Ming ling*
HMZS Zhang Lu, *Huang Ming zhishu*
JF   Gao, *Da Minglü jijie fuli*
MS   Zhang Tinyu, *Ming shi*
TS   *Da Ming Taizu Gao Huangdi shilu*

Andrew, Anita. "Zhu Yuanzhang and the *Great Warnings* (*Yuzhi dagao*): Autocracy and Rural Reform in the Early Ming." Ph.D. diss., University of Minnesota, 1991.
Bo Hua. "Mingdai zhouxian yashu de jianzhi yu zhouxian zhengzhi tizhi" (The yamen complex and political institution of subprefecture and district during the Ming). In Chen Huairen, ed., *Mingshi lunwen ji* (Collected articles on Ming history), 351–69. Hefei, China: Huangshan Shushe, 1997.
Bodde, Derk, and Clarence Morris. *Law in Imperial China: Exemplified by 190 Ch'ing Dynasty Cases*. Philadelphia: University of Pennsylvania Press, 1967.
Brook, Timothy. *The Confusions of Pleasure: Commerce and Culture in Ming China*. Berkeley and Los Angeles: University of California Press, 1998.
Bünger, Karl. "The Punishment of Lunatics and Negligence according to Classical Chinese Law." *Studia Serica* 9 (1950): 159–91.
Chan, Hok-lam. "The Chien-wen, Yung-lo, Hung-hsi, and Hsüan-te Reigns, 1399–1435." In Mote and Twitchett, eds., *The Cambridge History of China*, 7.182–304.
———. "The Rise of Ming T'ai-tsu: Facts and Fictions in Early Ming Historiography." *Journal of the American Oriental Society* 95 (1975): 679–715.
Chan, Wing-tsit. "The Ch'eng-Chu School of Early Ming." In William Theodore de Bary, ed., *Self and Society in Ming Thought*, 29–51. New York: Columbia University Press, 1970.
Chang, George Jer-lang. "The Village Elder System of the Early Ming Dynasty." *Ming Studies* 7 (1978): 53–62.
Chen Xing. *Da Ming lüli fujie* (*The great Ming code* and regulations with commentaries). Ming edition.
Ch'u T'ung-tsu. *Law and Society in Traditional China*. Paris: Mouton, 1961.
Da Ming ling (The great Ming commandment). 1367. In *HMZS*, 1.1–117.

Da Ming lü (The great Ming code). 1397. In *HMZS*, 4.1605–2205.

Da Ming lüli juhui xizhu (Detailed commentaries to *The great Ming code* and regulations). Author unknown. Ming edition.

Da Ming lüshu fuli (Commentaries to *The great Ming code* with regulations). Author unknown. Ming edition.

Da Ming Taizu Gao Huangdi shilu (Veritable records of the great Ming Taizu). Ed. Huang Chang-chien. 8 vols. Taipei: Academia Sinica, 1955.

Dardess, John W. *Confucianism and Autocracy: Professional Elites in the Founding of the Ming Dynasty*. Berkeley and Los Angeles: University of California Press, 1983.

———. *Conquerors and Confucians: Aspects of Political Change in Late Yuan China*. New York: Columbia University Press, 1973.

Dong Yu. *Da Ming lüli xiangxing bingjian* (Lucid commentaries to *The great Ming code* and regulations). 1599. Ming edition.

Dreyer, Edward L. *Early Ming China: A Political History*. Stanford: Stanford University Press, 1982.

———. "Military Origins of Ming China." In Mote and Twitchett, eds., *Cambridge History of China*, 7.58–106.

Eisenstadt, S. N. "The Study of Oriental Despotisms as Systems of Total Power." *Journal of Asian Studies* 17.3 (1958): 435–46.

Elman, Benjamin. *A Cultural History of Civil Examinations in Late Imperial China*. Berkeley and Los Angeles: University of California Press, 2000.

Fan Yongluan. *Da Ming lü* (Great Ming code). Reprint, Jinan: Qilu shushe, 1996. Siku Quanshu Cunmu Congshu edition, 276.469–730.

Farmer, Edward L. *Early Ming Government: The Evolution of Dual Capitals*. Cambridge: East Asian Research Center, Harvard University, 1976.

———. "The Great Ming Commandment (*Ta Ming Ling*): An Inquiry into Early-Ming Social Legislation." *Asia Major*, 3rd ser., 6.1 (1993): 181–99

———. "The Prescriptive State: Social Legislation in the Early Ming Dynasty." In *Proceedings of the Second International Conference on Sinology* [Section on Ming Ching and Modern History], 161–87. Taipei: Academia Sinica, 1989.

———. "Social Regulations of the First Ming Emperor: Orthodoxy as a Function of Authority." In Kwang-ching Liu, ed., *Orthodoxy in Late Imperial China*, 103–25. Berkeley and Los Angeles: University of California Press, 1990.

———. *Zhu Yuanzhang and Early Ming Legislation: The Reordering of Chinese Society following the Era of Mongol Rule*. New York: E. J. Brill, 1995.

Feng Han-yi. *The Chinese Kinship System*. Cambridge: Harvard University Press, 1948.

Franke, Wolfgang. *An Introduction to the Sources of Ming History*. Singapore: University of Malaya Press, 1968.

Gao Ju, ed. *Da Minglü jijie fuli* (*The great Ming code* with commentaries attached by regulations). Wanli edition. 5 vols. Reprint, Taipei: Taiwan Xuesheng Shuju, 1970.

Goodrich, L. Carrington, and Chaoying Fang, eds. *Dictionary of Ming Biography*. New York: Columbia University Press, 1976.

He Guang. *Lüjie bianyi* (*Code* with commentaries and explication of questions). 1386(?). Ming edition. The text of the *Code* contained in this book is also collected in Liu Hainian and Yang Yifan, eds., *Zhongguo zhenxi falü dianji jicheng*, ser. 2, 1.275–395.

Hu Qiong. *Da Minglü jijie* (Commentaries to *The great Ming code*). Ming edition.
Huai Xiaofeng, ed. *Da Ming lü, fu Da Ming ling, wenxing tiaoli* (*The great Ming code*, with *The great Ming commandment* and itemized regulations for pronouncing judgments attached). Shenyang, China: Liaoshen Shushe, 1990.
Huang Chang-chien, ed. "Da Ming lü gao kao" (An investigation on *The great Ming code with pronouncements*). In Huang Chang-chien, ed., *Ming Qing shi yanjiu conggao* (Draft studies on the Ming and Qing histories), *juan* 2, 155–207. Taiwan: Shangwu Yinshuguan, 1977.
———. *Da Ming Taizu gao huangdi shilu* (Veritable records of the great Ming Taizu). Taipei: Academia Sinica, 1955.
———. "Lüjie bianyi, Da Ming lü zhijie ji Ming lü jijie fuli sanshu suozai Ming lü zhi bijiao yanjiu" (A comparative study on *The Ming code* which is seen in the three books *The Code with explanations and answers to questions*, *The great Ming code with directed explanations*, and *The Ming code with commentaries and regulations attached*). In Huang Zhangjian, ed., *Ming Qing shi yanjiu conggao* (Draft studies on the Ming and Qing histories), *juan* 2, 208–86. Taiwan: Shangwu Yinshuguan, 1977.
———. "Ming Hongwu Yongle chao de bangwen junling" (The placards and harsh regulations in the Ming Hongwu and Yongle reigns). In Huang Zhangjian, ed., *Ming Qing shi yanjiu conggao* (Draft studies on the Ming and Qing histories), *juan* 2, 237–86. Taiwan: Shangwu Yinshuguan, 1977.
———. *Ming Taizu shilu jiaokan ji* (Comparative notes on *The veritable records of Ming Taizu*). 2 vols. Taipei: Academia Sinica, 1962.
———. *Mingdai lü li huibian* (Compendium of the *Code* and regulations in the Ming dynasty). 2 vols. Taipei: Academia Sinica, 1979.
Huang Miantang and Liu Feng. *Zhu Yuanzhang pingzhuan* (Biography of Zhu Yuanzhang). Nanjing: Nanjing Daxue Chubanshe, 1998.
Huang, Ray. "The Ming Fiscal Administration." In Mote and Twitchett, eds., *Cambridge History of China*, 8.106–71.
———. *Taxation and Government Finance in Sixteenth-Century Ming China*. Cambridge: Cambridge University Press, 1974.
Huang Yunmei. *Mingshi kaozheng* (Verification of the history of the Ming dynasty). Vol. 3. Beijing: Zhonghua Shuju, 1984.
Hucker, Charles O. 1966. *The Censorial System of Ming China*. Stanford: Stanford University Press.
———. *A Dictionary of Official Titles in Imperial China*. Stanford: Standard University Press, 1985.
———. *The Ming Dynasty: Its Origins and Evolving Institutions*. Michigan Papers in Chinese Studies, no. 34. Ann Arbor: Center for Chinese Studies, University of Michigan, 1978.
———. "Ming Government." In Mote and Twitchett, eds., *Cambridge History of China*, 7.9–105.
Jiang Yonglin. "Defending the Dynastic Order at the Local Level: Central-Local Relations as Seen in a Late-Ming Magistrate's Enforcement of the Law." *Ming Studies* 43 (2000): 16–39.
———. "*The Great Ming Code*: A Cosmological Instrument for Transforming 'All under Heaven.'" Ph.D. diss., University of Minnesota, 1997.
Jiang Yonglin, and Wu Yanhong. "'Satisfying Both Sentiment and Law': Fairness-Centered Judicial Reasoning as Seen in Late Ming Casebooks." Manuscript.

Jiao Hong. *Biaolü panxue xiangshi* (Explanations of the *Code* and judgments). Ming edition.
Johnson, Wallace, trans. *The T'ang Code*. 2 vols. Princeton, N.J.: Princeton University Press, 1979–97.
Jones, William C., with the assistance of Tianquan Cheng and Yonglin Jiang, trans. *The Great Qing Code: A New Translation with Introduction*. New York: Oxford University Press, 1994.
Ko Sa-Kyong and Kim Chi, eds. *Taemyong yul chehae* (The great Ming code directly explicated). 1395. Collected in Liu Hainian and Yang Yifan, eds., *Zhongguo zhenxi falü dianji jicheng*, ser. 2, 1.397–632.
Langlois, John D., Jr. "The Code and *ad hoc* Legislation in Ming Law." *Asia Major*, 3rd ser., 6.2 (1993): 85–112.
―――. "The Hung-wu Reign, 1368–1398." In Mote and Twitchett, eds., *Cambridge History of China*, 7.107–81.
―――. "Ming Law." In Mote and Twitchett, eds., *Cambridge History of China*, 8.172–220.
Langlois, John D., Jr., and Sun K'o-k'uan. "Three Teachings Syncretism and the Thought of Ming T'ai-tsu." *Harvard Journal of Asiatic Studies* 43.1 (1983): 97–139.
Legge, James, trans. *The Chinese Classics*. 5 vols. Oxford: Clarendon Press, 1893. Reprint, Hong Kong: University of Hong Kong Press, 1960.
Lei Menglin. *Du lü suoyan* (Miscellaneous notes on reading the *Code*). 1563. Ed. Huai Xiaofeng and Li Jun. Beijing: Falü Chubanshe, 1999.
Li Qing. *Zheyu xinyu* (New talks on judging cases). Changchun: Jilin Renmin Chubanshe, 1987.
Li Yumin, ed. *Mingshi renming suoyin* (Index to names in *The history of the Ming dynasty*). 2 vols. Beijing: Zhonghua Shuju, 1985.
Liu Chongri et al. *Zhongguo shi gao* (A draft history of China). Vol. 6. Beijing: Renmin Chubanshe, 1987.
Liu Hainian and Yang Yifan, eds. *Zhongguo zhenxi falü dianji jicheng* (Collection of rare works of Chinese law). 14 vols. Beijing: Kexue Chubanshe, 1994.
Liu Junwen, ed. *Tanglü shuyi jianjie* (Explanations to the *Tang Code* with commentaries). 2 vols. Beijing: Zhonghua Shuju, 1996.
Long Wenbin. *Ming huiyao* (Essentials of the Ming institutions). 2 vols. Beijing: Zhonghua Shuju, [1956].
MacCormack, Geoffrey. *Traditional Chinese Penal Law*. Edinburgh: Edinburgh University Press, 1990.
Mao Yilu. *Yunjian yanlüe* (Court opinions from Songjiang Prefecture). Ming edition.
McKnight, Brian E. *Law and Order in Sung China*. New York: Cambridge University Press, 1992.
Meng Seng. *Ming Qing shi jiangyi* (Lectures on Ming and Qing history). 2 vols. Beijing: Zhonghua Shuju, 1981.
Mote, Frederick W. "The Growth of Chinese Despotism: A Critique of Wittfogel's Theory of Oriental Despotism as Applied to China." *Oriens Extremus* 8.1 (1961): 1–41.
―――. "The Rise of the Ming Dynasty, 1330–1367." In Mote and Twitchett, eds., *Cambridge History of China*, 7.11–57.
Mote, Frederick W., and Denis Twitchett, eds. *The Cambridge History of China*.

Vol. 7, *The Ming Dynasty, 1368–1644*, pt. 1. New York: Cambridge University Press, 1988.

———. *The Cambridge History of China*. Vol. 8, *The Ming Dynasty, 1368–1644*, pt. 2. New York: Cambridge University Press, 1998.

Naito Kenkichi. "Dai Min ryō kaisetsu" (An explanation of *The great Ming commandment*). In Naito Kenkichi, *Chugoku hōseishi kōshō* (Chinese legal history, studies on evidence), 90–116. Tokyo: Yuhikaku, 1963.

Peng Yingbi. *Xingshu juhui* (Essentials of the *Code*). Ming edition.

Qi Biaojia. *Puyang yandu* (Court opinions from Xinghua Prefecture). Ming edition.

Ruan Yuan, ed. *Shisan jing zhushu* (Thirteen classics with annotations and commentaries). 2 vols. Reprint, Beijing: Zhonghua Shuju, 1980.

Shen Jiaben. "Ming Dagao junling" (The severe punishments in *The grand pronouncements*). In Deng Jingyuan and Bian Yuqian, eds., *Lidai xingfa kao* (An investigation on the penal laws of the previous dynasties), 4.1897–1947. Beijing: Zhonghua Shuju, 1985.

———. "Ming lü mujian" (An exegesis of the articles in *The great Ming code*). In Deng Jingyuan and Bian Yuqian, eds., *Lidai xingfa kao* (An investigation on the penal laws of the previous dynasties), 4.1783–1896. Beijing: Zhonghua Shuju, 1985.

Shen Zhiqi. *Da Qing lü jizhu* (Collected commentaries to *The great Qing code*). Ed. Huai Xiaofeng and Li Jun. 2 vols. Beijing: Falü Chubanshe, [1998].

Su Maoxiang. *Da Ming lüli linmin baojing* (Precious mirror for governing the people: *The great Ming code* and regulations). 1632. Ming edition.

Sun, E-tu Zen. *Ch'ing Administrative Terms: A Translation of the Terminology of the Six Boards with Explanatory Notes*. Cambridge: Harvard University Press, 1961.

Tan Qian. 1958. *Guoque* (An evaluation of the events of our dynasty). Collated and punctuated by Zhang Zongxiang. 6 vols. Reprint, Beijing: Guji Chubanshe, 1958.

Tang lü shuyi (*The Tang code* with commentaries). Ed. Liu Junwen. Beijing: Zhonghua Shuju, 1983.

Taylor, Romeyn. *Basic Annals of Ming T'ai-tsu*. San Francisco: Chinese Materials Center, 1975.

———. "Chinese Hierarchy in Comparative Perspective." *Journal of Asian Studies* 48.3 (1989): 490–511.

———. "Yüan Origins of the Wei-so System." In Charles Hucker, ed., *Chinese Government in Ming Times: Seven Studies*, 23–40. New York: Columbia University Press, 1969.

Teng Ssu-yü. "Ming *Dagao* yu Mingchu zhengzhi shehui" (*The grand pronouncements* and politics and society in the early Ming). *Yanjing xuebao* 20 (1936): 455–83.

Wang Kentang. *Wang Yibu xiansheng jianshi* (Wang Kentang's commentaries [to *The great Ming code*]). Beijing: Beijing Chubanshe, 2000. Siku weishoushu jikan edition, 1st ser., 25.264–749.

Wang Mingde. *Du lü peixi* (Bodkin [for unpicking knots] to be worn on the girdle when reading the *Code*). Ed. He Qinhua et al. 1674. Reprint, Beijing: Falü Chubanshe, 2000.

Wang Nan. *Da Minglü jijie* (Commentaries to *The great Ming code*). Ming edition.

Wang Zao. *Da Ming lüli fujie* (*Great Ming code* and regulations with commentaries). Ming edition.

Wu Han. 1980. *Zhu Yuanzhang zhuan* (A biography of Zhu Yuanzhang). 1965. Reprint, Beijing: Shenghuo Dushu Zhishi Sanlian Shudian.

Wu Tan. *Da Qing lü li tongkao jiaozhu* (A comprehensive investigation of *The great Qing code* and regulations, collated and annotated). Ed. Ma Jianshi and Yang Yutang. Beijing: Zhongguo Zhengfa Daxue Chubanshe, [1992].

Wu Yanhong. *Mingdai chongjun yanjiu* (Military exile in the Ming). Beijing: Zhongguo Shehui Kexue Wenxian Chubanshe, 2003.

———. "Mingdai liuxing kao" (Life exile in the Ming). *Lishi yanjiu* 6 (2000): 33–43.

Wu Zumou, ed. *Faxue gailun* (Introduction to jurisprudence). Beijing: Falü Chubanshe, 1984.

Xu Changzuo. *Da Ming lüli tianshi pangzhu* (Commentaries and interlinear notes on *The great Ming code* and regulations). Ming edition.

Xue Yunsheng. *Tang Ming lü hebian* (A combined text of Tang and Ming codes). Ed. Huai Xiaofeng and Li Ming. Beijing: Falü Chubanshe, [1998].

Yan Junyan. *Mengshuizhai cundu* (Court opinions at Mengshuizhai studio). Beijing: Zhongguo Zhengfa Daxue Chubanshe, [2002].

Yang Yifan. *Hongwu falü dianji kaozheng* (Textual research on legal documents of the Hongwu period). Beijing: Falü Chubanshe, 1992.

———. *Ming Dagao yanjiu* (A study of *The grand pronouncements*). Jiangsu: Jiangsu Renmin Chubanshe, 1988.

Yao Siren. *Da Ming lü fuli zhujie* (*The great Ming code* with regulations attached and commentaries). Reprint, Beijing: Beijing Daxue Chubanshe, 1993.

Ying Jia. *Yanyu gao* (Records of judging cases). Ming edition. Tianjin: Guji Chubanshe, [1981].

Yu Yuan. *Santai Minglü zhaopan zhengzong* (Standard formats for making judgments according to the *Code*). Ming edition.

Zang Lihe et al. *Zhongguo renming da cidian* (A comprehensive dictionary of Chinese names). Taipei: Taiwan Shangwu Yinshu Guan, 1964.

Zhang Dexin and Mao Peiqi, eds. *Hongwu yuzhi quanshu* (Complete imperial writings during the Hongwu reign). Anhui: Huangshan Shushe, 1995.

Zhang Jinfan, ed. *Zhongguo fazhi shi* (Chinese legal history). Beijing: Qunzhong Chubanshe, 1982.

Zhang Jinfan and Huai Xiaofeng, eds. *Zhongguo fazhi tongshi* (General history of Chinese legal systems). Vol. 7, *Ming*. Beijing: Falü Chubanshe, 1999.

Zhang Kai. *Lütiao shuyi* (Commentaries to the *Code*). 1471. Ming edition.

Zhang Kentang. *Xunci* (Court opinions that touched people's hearts). 2 vols. [1634?] Reprint, Taipei: Xuesheng Shuju, 1970.

Zhang Lu, ed. *Huang Ming zhishu* (Regulatory documents of the august Ming). 6 vols. 1579. Reprint, Taipei: Chengwen Chubanshe, 1969

Zhang Tinyu. *Ming shi* (History of the Ming dynasty). 28 vols. 1736. Reprint, Beijing: Zhonghua Shuju, 1974

Zhang Weiren, ed. *Zhongguo fazhi shi shumu* (Bibliography on Chinese legal history). 3 vols. Taipei: Zhongyang Yanjiuyuan Lishi Yuyan Yanjiusuo, 1976.

Zheng Rubi. *Da Ming lüjie fuli* (*The great Ming code* with commentaries attached by regulations). Ming edition.

Zheng Tianting et al., eds. *Zhongguo lishi da cidian* (Dictionary of Chinese history). 2 vols. Shanghai: Shanghai Cishu Chubanshe, 2000.

Zhu Jingxun. *Da Ming lüli zhijun qishu* (Marvelous methods for the ruler: *The great Ming code*). Ming edition.

Zhu Yuanzhang. *Huang Ming zhaoling* (Imperial edicts of the august Ming) [Hongwu reign]. In Liu Hainian and Yang Yifan, eds., *Zhongguo zhenxi falü dianji jicheng*, ser. 2, 3.1–91.

———. *Huang Ming zuxun* (Ancestral instructions of the august Ming). In Zhang Dexin and Mao Peiqi, eds., *Hongwu yuzhi quanshu*, 387–410.

———. *Ming Taizu yuzhi wenji* (The collected writings of Ming Taizu). Reprint, Taipei: Xuesheng Shuju, 1966.

———. *Taizu baozun* (Precious instructions of Ming Taizu). In Zhang Dexin and Mao Peiqi, *Hongwu yuzhi quanshu*, 412–605.

———. *Yuzhi dagao* (The imperial grand pronouncements). In Yang Yifan, *Ming Dagao yanjiu*, 195–452.

———. *Yuzhi Dagao sanbian* (Third imperial grand pronouncements). In Yang Yifan, *Ming Dagao yanjiu*, 339–421.

———. *Yuzhi Dagao xubian* (Supplementary imperial grand pronouncements). In Yang Yifan, *Ming Dagao yanjiu*, 255–338.

———. *Yuzhi wenji bu* (The imperial writings, supplemented). In Zhang Dexin and Mao Peiqi, *Hongwu yuzhi quanshu*, 252–361.

———. *Zishi tongxun* (Instructions to aid the world). In Zhang Lu, *Huang Ming zhishu*, 3.1449–84.

Index

abstinence, 110
academies, xxxvii
accessories, 40–41, 63, 80, 158, 187; exempt from punishment, 59; interrogation of, 231; punished as, 89, 167–68, 169, 183; punishment for, 24, 131–32, 144, 154–55, 159, 160–61, 170–72, 209, 211–12, 222. *See also* criminals; principals
accomplices. *See* accessories
account books and keepers, 46, 93–94
accusations, 100, 192–202, 219; personal, 185–86, 191–92; to made authorities, 18–19, 34–35, 76, 127, 213, 225; false, 100, 175, 195–202, 216, 232–33
accused persons, 234–35
accusers, 104, 114, 195–98
acquittal, 233
acupuncture points, 176
administrative institutions, 52–59
adoption, 53, 217–18
adulterers, 171, 214–15
affrays: and batteries, 171, 177–90, 201; crimes punished as, 145, 160, 174, 213, 227, 228, 230, 237, 240, 246; punishment for, 40, 43, 173, 175, 176, 189
age: as legal standard, 46–47, 69, 72, 84, 89
aged persons, 29–32, 40, 82, 118–19, 130, 148, 151, 200, 230–31
agencies, 55, 64
agreements, 105, 108
"all"(*jie*), lxvii, 41, 46, 155
alleys, 247
almanacs, 210
altars, 18, 111, 119, 120, 124, 154, 219
alum, 104
amnesty, lxv, lxxxiv, 26–30, 33, 87, 90, 239
amputation, lxxxii
analogy, principle of, lxi, 47
ancestral tablets, 81
Anhui, xxxiii
animals, 33, 100, 104, 106, 111, 125, 145, 151–52, 169, 174, 176. *See also* livestock
archers, 54, 208

archives, 57
area limits, 103
armies, 19, 129, 150
arms. *See* military, weapons; weapons
arrest, 24, 100, 137, 154, 159–60, 193, 208, 211–12, 221–26, 232
arson, 27
artisans, xxxviii, 26, 71, 73, 115, 123, 218, 237; punishment of, 29, 59, 75, 108, 114, 117, 211, 244, 245
as comparable to (*zhun*): as criminal distinction, lix
asses, 141–46, 149, 151–52, 162, 206
astronomy, xliii–xliv, 29, 35, 114, 213
audiences at court, 56, 114–15, 126–27
augural diagrams, 114
August Ming Ancestral Instruction, xl, lxxviii, lxxxii
aunts, 18, 23, 83, 89, 118, 186–87, 192, 216
auspicious portents, 213
authorities, 53, 56, 61, 62, 95; criminals sent to, 35–37, 42, 193; fail to report to, 77–78, 88, 112, 127, 140, 177, 184, 226, 227, 228, 229; and interrogation, 23, 43; make accusations to, 185–86, 192, 194, 200–201, 223–24, 225; punishment for, 73, 75, 79; report to, 126, 182, 199, 211; and revenue crimes, 71, 72, 92, 93, 107
authorization, lack of: and laws on revenue, 79, 81–82, 94, 96, 98, 101, 106, 107, 108; and laws rituals, 116; and laws on personnel, 52, 55, 56, 59, 60, 62, 63, 67; and laws on punishments, 21, 23, 47; and military affairs, 120–28, 131, 133–34, 135, 138, 139, 140–41, 145–46, 148, 150, 151, 152–53; and penal affairs, 167, 174, 190, 192, 207, 222, 238, 240–41; and public works, 243, 244–45
authorization tallies, 60, 63
awards. *See* rewards

baggage, 148
bailiffs, 23, 78

301

bandits, 127
banishment, 26, 28, 54, 74, 92, 202, 222–24
banners, 133–34
banquets, 118–19
"barbarian counties," lxii
battalions, xxxvi, 128, 209
batteries, 177–79
bearers, 141
beasts, 110–11
beating with the heavy stick: and accusations, 193, 194–200, 202; and affrays, 178–79; and counterfeiting, 210–11; and cursing, 191–92; and deceiving, 209–10, 212–13; degrees of, 17; *80* strokes, 17, 22, 43, 54, 56, 60–61, 63, 65–67, 69–73, 76–77, 81–83, 86–88, 98, 103, 105–8, 110–13, 116, 118–19, 122–23, 125–27, 130–36, 138–40, 143, 149–50, 152, 157–58, 161, 164–67, 173, 175, 177–78, 182, 184, 188, 191–93, 196, 198, 202–3, 205, 209, 211, 213–15, 218, 220–21, 227, 229–30, 236, 240–41, 246–47; and errors in judging, 39; and fields, 77–78, 81; and fornication, 214–17; *40* strokes, 197; and graves, 165–67; and guard posts, 138–41; and households, 69–76; and illicit goods, 94–95, 98, 168, 202–5, 207–8; and interrogation, 21–22; and joint crimes, 41, 158; and kidnapping, 164; and killing, 169–70, 172–77; and laws on personnel, 52–55, 57, 59–67; and laws on punishments, 17, 22, 24, 29–30, 32, 35–37, 41, 43–44; and laws on rituals, 110–14, 116–19; and livestock, 141–44, 146; and markets, 107–8; and marriage, 82–84, 86–89; and military administration, 129–36; and miscellaneous offences, 218–21; monetary obligations, 106; *90* strokes, 17, 22, 59, 81, 84, 88, 102, 116, 120, 131, 136, 138, 140, 157–58, 161, 165, 184, 198, 203–5, 214–15; and palaces, 120–27; and multiple crimes, 36–37; *100* strokes, 17, 22, 24, 29–30, 36–37, 44, 52–55, 57, 59–67, 69–74, 76, 78, 83–84, 86, 88–92, 94, 96, 101, 103–4, 106, 108, 110–14, 116–22, 124–25, 129–33, 136, 139–41, 143, 147–48, 150, 156–58, 161, 166–68, 170, 172–76, 178, 180, 184–86, 188, 191–93, 196–98, 200, 203–5, 208–9, 211–15, 217–22, 227–30, 233, 237, 245–46; *120* strokes, 197; and postal relay stations, 146–52; and prisoners, 222–23, 226–30, 233, 235–36, 239–41; and public crimes, 22, 26, 63, 66; and public works, 245–47; redemption for, 29, 32, 196–97; and recidivism, 30; and salt, 101–3; *70* strokes, 17, 22, 36, 41, 60, 62, 82, 102, 108, 116, 130, 138, 149, 158, 161, 191, 198, 203, 205, 236, 240; *60* strokes, 17, 22, 61–63, 65, 67, 69, 72, 74–76, 78, 83, 87, 91–92, 95–96, 101–3, 107–8, 113–14, 116–18, 121, 124, 132–33, 138, 142, 146–47, 149, 151–52, 158, 161, 169, 190–92, 196, 203, 205, 207, 213, 217, 223, 226–30, 233, 236, 239–41, 245, 247; and stealing, 96, 156–59, 161, 168; and striking, 180–90; and taxes, 90–92, 104–5; *20* strokes, 197, 234; *240* strokes, 197
beating with the light stick: and accusations, 192, 194–98, 201–2; and affrays, 175, 177–78; and coinage, 91; and community heads, 74; and corvée services, 70, 73, 75; and cursing, 190–91; and deceit, 211, 213; and fields, 77–80; *50* strokes, 17, 22, 44, 57, 60, 62, 64, 70, 79, 81, 83, 94, 97, 101–2, 105, 107, 109–10, 113, 117, 119, 124, 135, 137, 139, 142–43, 146, 148, 151, 160, 168, 178, 180, 191–92, 196, 201, 205, 211, 218–19, 221, 223, 226, 229, 231, 233–34, 241, 243–47; *40* strokes, 17, 22, 41, 44, 54–57, 59, 61–63, 65–67, 70, 74–76, 78–80, 84, 91, 97, 101–5, 108, 112–14, 120–22, 124, 133, 135, 139, 141–43, 145–48, 150, 152, 168, 175, 177, 191, 194, 196, 202, 205–6, 208, 213, 218–19, 221, 225–26, 229, 233, 237–41, 244–45, 247; and governmental affairs, 150; and illicit goods, 94, 168, 205–6, 208; and increasing or reducing penalties, 44, 194, 234–35; and joint crimes, 40–41; and knowledge of the *Code*, 59; and livestock, 141–46; and markets, 107–9; and marriage, 83–84; and military affairs, 124, 133, 135, 137, 139; and not administering in accordance with the law, 237, 241; and official documents, 59–67; and officials, 26, 54–57, 238; and palaces, 120–22, 180; and postal relay stations, 146–48, 150; and property, 76, 152; and prisoners, 223, 226–27, 229, 231, 233, 239; and public crimes, 21–22; and public works, 243–47; redemption for, 17, 241; and rituals, 110, 112–14, 117, 119; and salt, 101–3; and seeking favors, 218–19; and taxes, 97, 104–5; *10* strokes, 17, 55–57, 63–64, 67, 73, 75, 105, 152, 190, 225, 229, 234; and theft, 96, 160; *30* strokes, 17, 54, 64, 66, 70, 77, 80, 105, 137, 141–42, 144, 147, 177, 196, 205, 225–26, 234, 238, 247; and time limits, 225; and trials, 232; *20* strokes, 17, 40, 54–55, 57, 61, 64, 70, 73, 75–76, 78, 80, 96, 105–

Index

6, 137, 139, 143, 146–48, 150, 177, 196–97, 205, 223, 225, 227, 231–34, 239, 245; and violating the *Commandment*, 221
Beiping, xxxvi, xcii *n.83*
bells, 91, 107
benefit, public, 207
betrothal, 82–83, 154
beyond the pale of civilization, lxii, 43, 233
birds, 174
birth, 137, 145
blame, 174–75
boats, 33, 60, 81, 98, 100, 103, 107, 114, 139, 149, 152, 206
bodies, "extralegal torture" of, 234
bodies, parts of: back, 237; blood, 178; bones, 178, 180; buttocks, 237–38; ears, 173–74, 178; eyes, 174, 178; feet, 177, 180, 237; fingers, 178; hands, 177, 180, 237; hair, 178; head, 178–79; joints, 178; mouth, 178; nose, 173, 178; sexual organs, 178, 179; skin, 237; thighs, 237–38; toes, 178; waist, 237
bodies, search of, 124
bond of righteousness, 25, 200
bond servants, 23
bookkeepers, 95, 96, 104
books, 32, 35, 114
borders, 131, 134
borrow, 81–82, 94–95, 98–99, 105, 113, 116, 127, 145–46, 152–53
boundaries, 19
boys, 214, 217
Branch Secretariat, xxxvii
bribes, 27, 32, 202
bricks, 165, 174–75, 243
bridges, 68, 174, 247
broker-guarantors, 103, 165
brokers, 72, 100, 104, 214–15
brothers, 23, 154–55, 186, 216; and marriage, 83, 86, 87, 89; older, 18, 40, 118, 187, 189, 192; and property, 41, 76; younger, 40, 53, 69, 73, 130, 164, 187, 189, 212
Buddha Maitreya, Society of, 112
Buddhist and Buddhism, xxxiv, xxxviii, 26, 47, 71, 87, 112, 117, 119, 217
buildings, public, 243, 245–46
Bureau of Ceremonies, 115
Bureau of Evaluations, 57
burial, 119, 166–67, 174–76, 237
business, 83, 123, 134, 175–76
buyers, 72, 80, 103–4, 133, 165, 173
bypass appropriate jurisdiction, 192–93

calamities, 68, 77
camels, 33, 141–44, 152, 169, 206
cangues, lxxxii, 226, 228–29

capital, 117, 126, 136, 140; crimes committed by officials in the, 20–21, 43; officials in the, 54–56, 59, 66, 115, 129, 209, 212–13, 230, 235–36, 245; officials outside the, 55–56, 59, 66, 129, 147, 151, 212–13, 230, 235–36, 238
captive spirits, 172
Carriage (emperor), 18, 45, 121–22, 125
carriages, 81, 113, 116, 152, 174–75
carters, 141
carts, 33, 206
cases, 41, 42, 56, 61, 64, 65–66, 136, 201; judging of, 64, 232; review of, 236; withdraw from, 194
castration, lxxxii, 218
cattle, 33, 111, 140, 141–45, 152, 162, 169
celestial instruments, 114
celestial lamp, 112
Censorate, xxxvi, xli, xliii–xliv, lxxviii, 148, 209
Censor-in-Chief, xlvii
censors, xli, 207
censors, investigating, xxxvii, xliii, 64, 115–16, 227; and accusations, 194; claim to be, 212; deliberation of, 20; judgments of, 235–36; and knowledge of the *Code*, 59
centurions, 100
ceremonies, 110, 113–19, 125
certificates, 104
Chang Yuchun, xxxiv
checkers, 46
checkpoints. *See* guard posts
Cheng Kongzhao, xliii, xciii *n.92*
Chen Jing, xciii *n.88*
Chen Min, xliii, xciii *n.88*
Chen Youding, xxxv
Chen Youliang, xxxiv–xxxv
chickens, 162
chief legislator, xlii
Chief Military Commissions (Dudu Fu), xxxvi, 129, 194, 212. *See also* Five Chief Military Commissions
chief minister, xliii, xlv
children, 45, 53, 58, 72, 99, 171, 172, 187, 214
chimes, 91
Chinese, xxxiii, xxxvii–xl, xlv, xlvii, lxxxii, 88
circumstances: beyond human control, 247; that break the bond of righteousness, 200; deliberate the seriousness of, 59; of marriage, 82; in official reports, 62
circumvent the law, 43, 54, 56–58, 60–66, 118, 126–27, 139–40, 147, 156, 209
cities, 107, 116, 124, 126, 128, 131–32, 137, 140, 193, 238

civilians, xxxviii, 26, 43, 70, 71, 112, 138, 139–40, 154, 181, 192, 201
civil service examinations, xxxvii, lxxxii
Classified Encyclopedia on the Learning of Principle, xxxix
cliques, 27, 58, 99
clothes, 18–19, 94, 114, 116–18, 133, 152, 173, 208, 225, 228–29
Code: and analogy, lxi, lxxxvii; articles of, liv, lvi, lxxxiv, lxxxvii, 43, 47, 68, 221; characteristics of, xlix–l; codification of, xl–lv; and confession, lxxiv–lxxv; councilors of, xci *n.75*; and criminal liability, lxi–lxvii; and death penalty, 20, 58, 219, 222; diagrams of, xcvi *n.143*, 5–16; drafting commission of, xlii–xliv; as dynastic law, lxxvii–lxxxviii; holism of, lxxvii–lxxix; Imperial Preface of, xlv, lv, 3; knowledge of, 59; legal interpretation of, lx–lxi; legal principles of, xli; and the Ming legal system, lxxvii–lxxxviii; and mutual concealment, 231; as penal code, lv–lxxvii; penalties of, lviii–lix, 47, 221, 238–39; and period of responsibility, 179; and persons beyond the pale of civilization, 43; and private crimes, lxvii–lxviii, 26; and provisional sentences, 21, 23; and public crimes, lxvii–lxviii, 56, 67–68; and punishments, lxx–lxxvii, 43, 197; and recidivism, lxxv–lxxvi, 30; and redemption, lxxi–lxxii, 174; reward clauses of, lix–lx; special statutes of, lxxxv–lxxxviii; structure of, xliv–xlvii, lv–lxi; and unjust judgments, 235–36. *See also Commandment; Code with Commentaries and Explication of Questions; Grand Pronouncements; Great Ming Code Directly Explained*
Code and Commandment Directly Explained, xliv–xlv, xc *n.62*
[Code of the] Nine Chapters, xliv
Code with Commentaries and Explication of Questions, xlvii–xlix, xcvii *n.160*
Code with Pronouncements, lii, lxxxiii
Code of 1368, lxxviii
coercion, 176, 182–83, 206
coffins, 165–66
coinage, 90–91
Collected Rituals of the Great Ming, xc *n.49*
collective prosecution, xlii, xliv, lxiv, lxviii–lxix, 23, 28–30, 33, 35, 45, 241
collectors, 95
collusion, 56–58, 61, 65
colony farms, xxxvi, 140
commandants, 24, 42, 116, 126, 213

Commandment, 28, 92; compiled, xxxix, xli, xciv *n.110*; relationship with the *Code*, xlv–xlvi, lvii, lxi, lxxxv, lxxxvii, ci *n.230*, 47, 59, 221, 238; as Zhou Zhen's book, xliv
commands, lxxxv
commerce, 104
commission agents, 107–8
commission of acts, lxi
commoners, xxxvii, 79, 151, 176; crimes of, 19, 58, 72, 84, 116–17, 122, 170, 180, 190–91, 221, 245
"communities and tithings," xxxvii
community heads, 74, 77–78, 80, 91–92, 99, 112, 136, 167, 211
community wine-drinking ceremonies, lvii, 119
companies, xxxvi
companions, 177
compensation, 35, 81, 94, 133, 142, 144–45, 148–49, 195–96, 204, 220, 245
compilers, xxxviii
complaints, 175, 201, 232, 235
concealment, 65, 112; of crimes, l, 55, 57, 95, 134, 148; of criminals, 42, 154, 225; of deaths, 18, 19, 118; of goods, 76–77, 92, 98, 99, 105, 145, 168, 169, 211; mutual, 231
concubines, 19, 26, 73, 154, 155, 172, 177; accusations of, 198–200; children of, 53, 71, 82; crimes of, 171, 174, 185–90, 192, 214–17; and marriage, 83–84, 86–87, 200; as property, 72, 106, 164, 200; as victims, 177, 188–89
"conditions," lvi–lviii
confessions, 20, 42, 198, 200, 229, 234, 241–42; voluntary, lxviii, lxxiv–lxxv, 24, 34–37, 100, 117, 198–99, 221
confiscation, 32–33, 36, 58, 68, 99, 104, 171–72, 178–79
Confucianism, xxxiii, xxxv–xl, lxxvii
conspirators, lxiv, 170
constables, 141, 225
constructions, 56, 122–23, 205, 237, 243–46
consumption, 104, 106
contracts, 78, 104
contumacy, 18, 193
conviction, 233
convicts, 150
cooks, 113, 126
copper, xli, 21, 33, 34, 79, 90–91, 140, 178, 211; redemption by, 17–18, 29, 32, 196–97; stealing of, 157–58
coroners, 236
corpses, 119, 165–67, 175, 195, 236–37, 241
corvée services, xxxviii, 69–76, 78

Index 305

cotton, 81, 91
counterfeit, 18, 27, 208–14
Court of Judicial Review, xliii, xlv
Court of the Imperial Stud, 142–43, 145
courts, 58, 95
craftsmen, 115, 122
crimes: accidental, 183–84, 186–88, 219; and accusations, 196, 235; and the aged, 30–32; and amnesty, xlix–l, 27, 239; as "capital crimes," liii, 42, 171, 227, 229, 240; as a concept, lxi–lxii; and confession, 24, 34–35; and criminal liability, lxi–lxvi; and the eight deliberations, l, lxxiii, 20, 23, 230; and the Imperial City, 43, 124; joint, 24, 37, 168; and knowledge of the *Code*, 59; and military personnel, 21–22, 42–43, 128, 132–33, 135–36, 201, 208; mistaken, 18, 27, 60–61, 81, 110–11, 113, 126, 133, 143–44, 149, 168, 176, 227; multiple, 22, 36–37, 232; and mutual concealment, 34, 41–42; of negligence, 24–25, 27, 35, 38–39, 47, 55, 59, 66, 108–9, 113, 120–21, 124, 135, 138, 140–41, 145, 147, 174, 211, 231, 234–41; and officials, 20–22, 38–39, 54–55, 74, 79, 86, 101–2, 204–5, 218, 235, 238, 242; original, 37, 182, 196, 198–99, 222, 232, 239; and period of responsibility, 179–80; and persons beyond the pale of civilization, 43, 233; and prisoners, 227, 229, 230, 231; and recidivism, 29–30, 54, 208; and redemption, 31, 57; and slaves, 184–85; and the Ten Abominations, lxxiii–lxxiv, 20, 23; and women, 29, 86, 240. *See also* names of individual crimes
criminal legal norm, lvi–lviii
criminals, 36–37, 46, 226; arrest of, 221–22, 225; concealment of, 41–42, 225; confessions of, 34–36, 241–42; escape/flight of, 37–38, 159, 222–25; punishments for, 43, 44–46, 53, 107, 233. *See also* accessories; principals
crops, 81, 246–47
Cui Liang, xlix
Cui Yongtai, xliii
"cultivated talents," xxxvii
curfews, 137
currency, 67, 90–91, 126, 208, 210–11
curse, 18, 174, 188, 190–92
custodians, 46, 81, 97, 113, 220, 223, 224, 229
cymbals, 91

Dadu, xxxvi
dancers, 217
Dangtu, xciii *n.89*
Daoists and Daoism, xxxviii, 26, 47, 71, 87, 91, 112, 117, 119, 217
daughters, 83, 87, 106, 112, 140, 154, 155, 187, 216; and marriage, 84, 86
day(s): and laws on personnel, 55–57, 59–60, 62–64, 67; and laws on punishments, 28, 32, 33; and laws on revenue, 75, 82, 94, 97, 103, 106–7; and laws on rituals, 118; and military affairs, 122, 130, 133, 136–37, 139, 145–58, 150–53; and penal affairs, 178–80, 195, 199, 206, 217, 221–27, 229, 231–32, 239–41; reference for, 46
Dazhong coins, 90
death, 195, 218–19, 225; cause of, 236; and coercion, 176, 183; of criminals, 33; feign, 213; and funerals, 119; investigation of, 167, 179; of livestock, 141–42; mourn, 18–19, 118; and period of responsibility, 178–79; of prisoners, 224, 227–30, 235, 237, 240; for striking, 180–90. *See also* killing; miscarriage
death by slicing, lxxxii, xcix–c *n.199*, 154, 170–72, 183–85, 187–88
death penalty, 17–18, 20, 30–32, 46, 58, 89, 222, 226, 238–39; and accusations, 194–97, 199; and amnesty, 27–28; and confession, 35; degrees of punishment, 44–45, 87, 184, 188, 219, 234–35; and errors in judging, 39, 241; execution of, 235–36, 240–41; history of, xcix *n.198*; and joint crimes, 37; and military officers, 61, 135, 208; and official documents, 66, 110; and "Seven Homicides," xlii; for striking, 186–88. *See also* death by slicing; decapitation; strangulation
debts, 105–6, 201
decapitation, 127, 209–10, 213, 220, 241; and accusations, 193, 195; and counterfeiting, 208, 210–11; and the eight deliberations, 20; and fornication, 215–16; and graves, 165–66; and illicit goods, 94, 100; and interrogation, 227; and increasing or reducing punishments, 44–46; and killing, 164, 169–73, 176, 180–82, 186–88, 190, 222, 227, 230; and knowledge of the *Code*, 59; and military affairs, 63, 124–25, 128, 129–33, 137, 141, 148, 150; and official documents, 59, 148; and officials, 53, 58, 131, 212; and prisoners, 159–60, 222; and public matters, 62, 210; and rebellion, 154, 193; redemption for, 18; and robbery, 159, 167; and sedition, 154, 193; and slaves, 183–84; and spying, 140; and stealing,

decapitation (continued)
   155–58; and striking, 180–82, 184, 186–88, 190; and treacherous cliques, 58; and treason, 155, 193. *See also* death by slicing; death penalty; strangulation
deception, 56, 59, 71, 77, 163, 208–14
decrees, lxxxv
deficits, 93–94
delays: and laws on personnel, 56, 59–60, 63–66; and laws on revenue, 73, 105–6; and military affairs, 115, 121–22, 129, 130, 133, 137, 147, 148, 150; and penal affairs, 223–24
deliberation, lxii–lxv
Deng Yu, xxxiv
deportation, 227. *See also* life exile
destruction, 36, 37, 60, 81, 111, 133, 166
dian mortgage, 78–80, 83, 195, 200
dikes, 68, 246–47
diligent subjects, 19–20
Dipper, 112
Directorate of Astronomy, 29, 117, 213
Directorate of Education, xxxvii
Directorate of Paper Currency, 67
disabled, 30–32, 69, 82–83, 130, 137, 154, 173, 178–79, 188, 231
disasters, 61, 117, 213
discarding, 60, 81, 133, 165–66
discord, 18–19
diseases, 176
dismemberment, 18, 171–72
districts (counties), xxxvii, 38–39, 56, 74, 98, 126, 147, 156, 193, 231, 247; punishment for officials in, 21, 24, 64, 67–68, 80, 86, 209
diviners, xxxviii, 117
divorce, 88, 185, 214–15
documents, official, 35, 46, 54, 59–68, 110, 179, 194, 201, 227, 231–32; alter, 65–66; counterfeit, 109; delays of, 27, 39–40, 63, 129, 149–50; mistakes in, 27, 38–39, 61; stealing of, 156
dogs, 145, 162, 169
donors, 79, 208
donkeys, 33
dowry, 188
drinks, 113, 173, 206, 218
drugs, 113, 124, 159, 173
Du Chayuan, xxxvi
ducks, 162
dukes, 53, 135, 207–8
duties, 88, 213

East Hall, xxxix
eight deliberations, l, lxvi, lxxiii–lxxiv, 19–20, 23, 230

elderly, 76. *See also* aged persons
elders, xxxvii, 74
embezzlement, 95, 98–99, 105
emissaries, 62, 151, 206, 212, 238
emoluments, 53, 64, 74, 79, 116
emperor, 18–19, 23–24, 113–14, 120–22, 124–25, 180, 193, 210, 220, 230
employees, 95
employments, 59, 79, 101–2, 216; dismissed from, 22, 26, 36–37, 52, 55, 63, 67, 114, 117–18
empress, 19, 45, 209, 220
enemy, 19, 128, 130–31, 150
enslavement, 58, 71, 88, 154, 155, 241. *See also* slaves
entertainers, 217
enticement, 164–65, 213–14
equinox, 241
errors: and laws on punishments, 39–40; and laws on personnel, 56–57, 59, 64–66; and laws on rituals, 114; and penal affairs, 194, 198. *See also* mistakes
eunuchs, 58, 123–24, 126
evidence, 37, 42, 98, 106, 176, 219–20, 227, 223–35
execution, 43. *See also* death penalty
exhibition pavilions, 218
exile. *See* life exile
exoneration, 24–25, 27, 39, 58, 65, 107, 233–35
Expanded Meaning of the Great Learning, xxxix
expenditures, 94, 96
express stations, 68, 147–48
extortion, 34

facts: distortion of the, 65, 209, 229, 242; ignore the, 83; judgment made according to the, 55, 62, 201; reported, 20–21, 23, 58, 98, 115, 141; verified, 21, 131
false pretenses, 56
failure: and laws on personnel, 56, 57; and laws on punishments, 18, 37; and laws on revenue, 75, 78, 94, 95–96, 100, 102, 104, 109; and laws on rituals, 110, 111, 115, 117; and military affairs, 122–23, 125, 131, 132, 143; and penal affairs, 212, 223, 228, 239–40; and public works, 244–45, 246–47
fairs, 112
falcons, 169
family, xxxviii, 29, 72, 119, 164–65, 188, 200; of artisans, 117, 245; crimes committed by, 40–41; and marriages, 82–90; of military, 53, 112; of officials, 25, 53, 112, 151–52, 154–55, 194, 201; and property, 76, 163; registers of, 18, 76, 154–55

famine, 150
Fang Guozhen, xxxiv–xxxv
Fan Xianzu, xliii, xcii *n.81*
Fan Zugan, xxxix
farewell, bidding of, 116
Farmer, Edward, xl
farmers, tenant, 151
farming, 135
fasts, 119
fathers, 26, 40, 43–44, 82–83, 86, 154, 190, 199, 215
fathers-in-law, 216
favors, 19, 202, 205, 218–19
feasts, 110
females. *See* women
Fengyang, xxxiii
ferries, 174, 247
festivity, 75
fetters, 222–24, 226, 228–29
fields, 166, 193, 220; concealment of, 99; destroyed, 247; inspection of, 77–78; products of, 73, 76–77, 162; purchase of, 79–80; redemption of, 196, 199; sale of, 78–79, 195, 199
files: establish, 22, 62, 70, 94–96, 125, 139, 194, 227; false, 98; review, 64–65
filial piety, 18
fine, 21, 59, 90, 92, 110, 114–15, 225
fires, 27, 98, 106, 112, 160, 180, 219–20
fish-scaled plot books, xxxviii
Five Chief Military Commissions (Wujun Dudu Fu), lxxviii, 20, 21, 42, 115, 128, 148, 209. *See also* Chief Military Commissions
Five Classics, xxxix
Five Punishments, xlvii, xlix, lxix, 6, 17
five relationships, li
flags, 19, 133
flight, 42, 74, 128; after committing crimes, 35, 37–38, 41, 155; from duty, 121–22, 131, 132, 135–36, 139; from marriage, 88–89
floods, 98, 106, 148
food, 81, 113, 119, 162, 173, 206, 218, 225, 228–29
forbidden articles, 32, 35
force, use of: and fornication, 215–16; to escape from prison, 159–60, 222, 225; and robbery, 27, 34, 35–36, 96, 159, 162–63, 167–68; 170, 193, 211, 226, 241; to take property, 106, 128, 206
fords. *See* guard posts
foreign: countries, 63; languages, 233; territories, 138
foreigners, lxii, 131–32, 140
foremen, 212, 244

forests, 80
forfeit to the government, 107, 109, 117, 151; gifts, 82–83, 86, 90, 215, 217; goods, 92, 100, 103–4, 141, 143, 152, 206, 245; money, 103, 107, 122, 131, 133, 135, 165, 206, 218; property, 172, 211, 214
fornication, 23, 35, 37, 41, 82, 87, 159, 176, 201, 214–17; by force, 214; by women, 29, 240; with relatives, 19, 86, 215–16; as "true crime," 27
Four Books, xxxix
Four Supports, 20, 212
foxes, 166
fractures, 137, 179–87, 189–90, 200, 222, 227, 237
fraud, 27, 32, 34, 35, 58, 65, 83, 93, 201
friends, 206, 230
frontiers, 66, 67, 129, 131–32, 140–41, 150; distant, 42, 49–51, 53, 132, 217
Fu Huan, xlii, xcii *n.77*
Fujian, xxxv
Fu Mingxue, xliii
functionaries: and administration of the law, 98, 201, 224, 226–69, 237; appointments of, 54; career records of, 57–58; and capital crimes, 42; and cases, 194, 234–35; and coercion, 176; collective prosecution of, lix; and corpses, 236–37; and corvée services, 70, 73–75; and counterfeiting, 210; and cursing, 190–91; and deceit, 95–99, 213; dismissed, 52, 55, 74, 202; and documents, 46, 59–67, 147; and fields, 77–79; and fornication, 216–17; and illicit goods, 93, 95, 98, 101, 103, 202–7; and increasing or reducing penalties, 234, 239; and knowledge of the *Code*, 59; leave employment, 55; make false reports, 236–37, 241–42; and marriage, 87; and measures, 96, 108; and messengers, 146; and military posts, 52; and mourning, 118; negligence of, 234; and postal relay stations, 147–50; and prisoners, 232–35, 240–41; and property, 206–8; public crimes of, 21–22, 24–27, 38–40, 56, 57, 58, 79, 96–97, 151, 170, 180–81, 190–91; and public works, 244–47; private crimes of, 19, 22, 26; and seeking favors, 218–19; and striking, 180–81; and supporting others, 76; and taxes, 91–93; and time limits, 130; and travel passes, 139. *See also* officials
funerals, 119

gambling, 218
gardens, 80–81, 166, 247

gates: of altars, 111, 120; of cities, 104, 121, 126, 156; guarding the, 94, 123–24, 140; of the Imperial City, 41, 120–22, 124–26
geese, 162
geomancy, 119
gifts, 82, 90, 206–7
girls, 214, 217
gods. *See* spirits
gold, 33, 79, 91, 94, 97, 208, 211
gongs, 112
good fortune, 117
goods, 31–36, 67, 90, 93, 99, 104, 108, 141, 152, 160–63, 169–70, 176–77, 206–8, 220
goods, illicit, 45, 156, 163, 227; accept, 27, 58; and accusations, 193, 201; and amnesty, 33; and arrest, 221–22; borrowed, 94, 98, 105; conceal, 105; and confession, 35–36; confiscation of, 36–37; and crops, 81; damaged, 97–99, 244; delivered, 90; and grain, 92–95, 157; and graves, 81, 157, 165, 167; and livestock, 142–45, 162; and measures, 95, 108; and money, 93–95, 105–6, 157; and officials, 65, 70, 74, 75, 98–99, 139, 202–8, 219, 226, 232–34, 237; and price, 107–8, 142, 146, 153; and property, 105–7, 140, 152, 164, 175, 206–7, 212, 220, 233, 246; and prisoners, 223–25, 228–29, 240; and public works, 243–44, 246; received, 176–77, 193, 209; and rent, 82, 146, 153; restitution of, xlix–l, 31–34; and salt, 101–2; seizure of, 99; and taxes, 73, 78, 91–92; and theft, 79–80, 160, 167–68, 208; types of, xlix–l, 15
government, 19, 58, 126, 175; agencies, 95, 140, 155, 244–45; artisans, 29, 114, 117, 245; buildings, 126, 220, cheat or deceive the, 59, 93, 95, 98, 105, 108, 134; confiscated by the, 32–34, 99, 154–55; copper, 91, 157–58, 211; documents, 123, 146–48, 153 *n*.2; examinations, lxxxii, 107; goods, 32–34, 81, 92, 94–99, 104, 148, 157–59, 107–8, 244; houses, 219–20; interrogation, 23, 140; livestock, 141–46, 150, 162; local, 21, 28, 101, 111; money paid to the, 79–82, 94, 106, 146, 148, 149, 153, 157–60, 207, 244; offices, 38–39, 64, 116, 129, 139, 193, 220, 225; postal relay stations of, 148–53; property of the, 27, 60, 79, 81–82, 94–95, 106–7, 144–45, 149, 208, 211, 244; rewards, 172, 210–11; runners, 23, 170, 236; salt, 102–3; service, 26, 83, 118, 206; stealing from the, 95, 155–58; taxes, 92, 97, 104–5, 182; troops, 127–28, 131–32, 136, 155. *See also* forfeit to the government

grain, 56, 61, 64–66, 90, 92–96, 103, 110, 136, 157–60, 207–8, 210
granaries, 46, 55, 64, 90–100, 156–58, 220, 243, 245
grand academician, xxxix
Grand Canal, xxxiv
Grand Court of Revision, lxxviii
grand empress dowager, 19, 45
"grand guardian," 112
"grand instructress," 112
grandparents, 23, 41, 45; arrange marriages, 83, 89; care of, 28–29, 118–19, 200; crimes against, 76, 172, 174, 177, 191–92; crimes of, 119, 174–75, 185, 188, 228; of criminals, 26, 154, 155; death of, 166, 175; disobey instructions of, 188, 200; plotting to kill, 18, 170–71; striking of, 18, 184, 187–88, 190
Grand Pronouncements, xxxix, lii, lv, lxxxi–lxxxv, lxxxviii
grandson, 41. *See also* sons' sons
grass, 162
graves, 27, 165–67
Great Compendium of the Four Books and Five Classics, xc *n*.53
Great Compendium of the Philosophy of Human Nature, xc *n*.53
Great Learning, xxxix
Great Ming Code. *See Code*
Great Ming Code Directly Explicated, l–li
Great Ming Code with Commentaries Attached by Regulations, 68 *n*.1
Great Ming Code with Pronouncements, lii, lxxxiii
Great Ming Code with Regulations, lxxxiv
Great Ming Commandment. *See Commandment*
Great Qing Code, xlvi, 68 *n*.1
Great Sacrifices, 18, 43, 111
great sedition. *See* sedition
Great Wall, xxxvi
"group," 47
gu (insect) poison, 18, 26, 28–30, 172–73
Guangde, xcii *n*.82
Guangdong, xxxvi, xcii *n*.78, xcii *n*.85
Guangxi, xxxvi, xciii *n*.86
Guanxian, xciii *n*.91
guarantors, 37, 56
guardians, 104
guard posts, 35, 41, 138–41
guards, xxxvi, 113, 121, 223–24
guests, 20
guides, 100
Guizhou, xxxvi
Guo Huan, xl

Index

Guo Ying, c *n.211*
Guo Zixing, xxiv

halls, 120–24
handcuffs, 222–24, 226, 229
Hanlin Academy, xxxviii, xxxix, xliii, xlvi, xlix
Han Liner, xxxiv, xxxv
Han regime, xxxv, xl
Han Shantong, xxxiv–xxxv
"happy medium," xlii, xlvii, liv, lxxxviii
Heaven, 112
Heavenly Portents, 117
Heavenly will, xli
He Guang, xlviii–xlix, xcv *n.134*, xcvii *n.160*
heirs, 71–72
hemp, 80–81, 117
hired laborers, 183; crimes of, 163, 171, 172, 184, 216, 230; and household heads, 43, 41, 166, 175, 177, 185, 191, 200, 228; wages of, 33, 243
History of the Ming Dynasty (Mingshi), xliv, xlviii, xlix–l, li–lii
home: hide items in, 72, 135; and marriage, 84; remaining at, 28–29, 166; return to, 26, 89, 137, 151
homicide, 23, 30, 169–77, 226; as a "true crime," 27. *See also* killing
Hongwu reign, xxxv–xl, lxxvii–lxxxviii, 75, 87, 90–91
Hongzhi reign, ciii *n.264*
honorable people, 72–73, 88, 132, 164, 183, 185, 217
horoscopes, 117
horses: care of, 113, 141–45; and military affairs, 128, 133, 138, 140, 145–56, 237–38; post, 60, 148–49, 152–53; value of, 33, 162, 169, 206
households, 35, 54, 91, 99, 114, 119, 151, 164, 171, 177; and corvée services, 69–76; crimes of, 112, 117, 134, 160–62, 167; members of, 124–15, 138; of officials, 118, 207, 221; registers, xxxviii, 41, 46, 56, 69–71, 76, 130; and property, 76, 80, 107, 161; and servants, 86, 87, 212; and slaves, 87–89, 166, 174–75, 183–85, 190–92, 200, 216, 228; and taxes, 92–93, 182
houses, 76–82, 119, 167, 193; and dian mortgage, 195, 199; and fires, 219–20; hide in, 91, 99, 225; and military affairs, 135; and public works, 246, 247; redemption of, 165–96, 199; and sumptuary regulations, 116–17
Huai River region, xxxiv
Huang Chang-chien, xlvii–xlviii, li, lxxxiv

Huangjue Temple, xxxiv
Hucker, Charles, xlv
husbands, 82, 88, 101, 104, 118, 154, 171, 177, 221; and fornication, 214–15, 240; relatives of, 18, 23, 170, 188–89, 192, 200; and striking, 18–19, 174, 185, 188–90, 200; and wives or concubines, 25, 83, 86–89, 171, 174, 185, 188–89, 192, 199–200
Hu Weiyong, xxxvi, lx, xlvii, ci *n.229*
Hu Zhou, xcii *n.82*

identification, 107, 122–24, 126–27, 139
illegitimate children, 214
illness, 79, 137, 151, 213, 230, 239. *See also* sickness
immortals, 221
impeachment, 123
imperial, lxxxiii, 37, 61, 125, 236, 244; audiences, 56, 114, 127; carriages, 113, 121–22; consorts, xc *n.211*, 220; court, 52–53, 56, 63, 127–28, 150; decrees, 45, 52, 60–61, 156, 170, 209–10; edicts, 59–60, 62, 114; emissaries, 116, 170, 180–81, 190–91; food, 18, 113; guards, 121, 123–25; halls, 120–24, 126, 180, 220; mausoleums, 18, 111, 114, 120, 154, 157; medicine, 18, 113; "old retainers," 19–20; orders, 156, 180, 190; palaces, 18, 120–26, 154–55, 180, 219–20; personal objects, 113–14, 156; Regalia Office, 213; relatives, c *n.211*, 19–20, 180; rescripts, 20–21, 23, 124–28, 135, 208–9; seals, 18, 60, 156; Storehouse, 122; tombs, 220
Imperial City, 120–21, 124–26
Imperially Approved Code and Pronouncements, liii, lxxxiii, xcvii *n.163*
Imperially Approved Regulation of the Code with Pronouncements, lxxxiv, lxxxvi
imprisonment, 226–42. *See also* prisoners
incantations, 112, 172
incapacitated, 30–32, 40, 76, 118–19, 154, 173, 178–83, 185–6, 188, 201, 231
incest, 19
"incorporated commentary," lxxxi
infirm, 118, 148. *See also* disabled; incapacitated
information, leak, 58, 141
inheritance, 53
injuries, 35, 130, 149, 166–67; in affrays, 177–90; feign, 213; by husbands, 185–86, 200; internal, 178, 182, 184; and interrogation, 227; in joint crimes, 37, 40; and livestock, 141–45; and military affairs, 128, 131, 139; and negligence, 27,

310 *Index*

injuries *(continued)*
  173–74; by an object, 178, 180, 237; and plots to kill, 169–72; and prisoners, 159–60, 200, 222; and redemption, 30–31; by relatives, 186–87, 189, 199; by slaves, 183–84; and robbery, 159; by a weapon, 175–79; by wives, 185–86. *See also* fractures
injustice, 42, 227, 235–36
innocent, 100–102, 202, 226–27; implication of, 25, 27, 38–39, 58, 65, 100, 107, 194, 210, 219, 231–35, 237, 239, 241–42
inns, 33, 81, 206
inquests, 68
Institutes of the Yuan Dynasty, xlv, lxxviii
Institutes of Zhou, lxxviii
institutions, 61, 244–45
insurrection, 127
interest, on loans, 105–6
interests, private, 38–39, 198, 237
interlinear notes, lx–lxi, lxiii
interpreters, 233
interrogating sticks, 237
interrogation: and accusations, 194, 197, 200; authorization for, 20–21, 23; and confession, 34, 241–42; of innocent persons, 226–27, 233–34; and military operations, 148; and officials, 42, 58, 62, 181; and principals, 41; of prisoners, 200, 231–35; of spies, 140
Investigation Bureau, 21, 59, 209
invoices, 93, 96
iron, 48, 79, 140, 178, 239
irrigation works, xxxviii

jade, 110, 155, 169
jail, 46
jail guards, 42, 46, 116, 200, 224, 226–29. *See also* prison warders
Japan, xxxiii
Jiajing reign, cii *n.253*
Jiangnan area, xl
Jiangning, xcii *n.85*
Jiangxi, xcii *n.85*, xciii *n.87*, xciii *n.90*, xciii *n.91*, xciii *n.93*, xcv *n.134*
Jiaxing, lxxxvi
Jingshi, xxxv
Jinhua, xxxix
Jin Qi, xcvi *n.145*
Jin Zhi, xcvi *n.145*
Jiqing, xxxiv–xxxv
joint crimes, 24, 154–55, 161, 168, 173, 179; and family members, 40–41; and flight, lxvii, 37–38. *See also* accessories; principals
judges, 20, 56, 132, 134

judgments, 20–21, 55, 110, 235–36
juveniles, 30–31, 32

kidnap, 27, 164–65
killing, 139, 159, 220, 227, 247; accusations of, 193, 201; in affrays, xlii, 160, 167, 173–76, 179, 183, 185, 213, 230, 246; and amnesty, 26–28; with intention, xlii, 35, 139, 173–74, 246; and joint crimes, 40; livestock, 143–45, 162; by mistake, xlii, 173–74; by negligence, xlii, 27, 173–74, 176, 244; in play, xlii, 173–74; plots to, xlii, 170–71; and prisoners, xlii, 222, 230; redemption of, 28–30; relatives, 18, 162–63, 170–71, 174–76, 185–90, 230; and slaves, 174–75, 183–85; and striking, 182–86, 230; three persons from one family, 18, 26, 28–30, 171; with weapons, 176
Kim Chi, l–li, xcvi *n.145*
kneecaps, removal of, lxxxii
knowledge, lack of, lxii–lxv
Korea, xxxiii, xxxvi, l–lii
Ko Sa-Kyong, l–li

labor, 26, 29–32, 46, 207; fees, 135, 151; and penal servitude, 39, 195, 198, 239–40; wasted, 243–44
laborers, 59, 122, 151, 218, 243
land, 79–81, 93, 107, 111, 165, 201
Langlois, John, lxii
Lan Yu, xl
law(s): in accordance with the, 237–38; and "all," 155; not applicable, 59; and arrest, 232; articles of the, 29, 42, 45, 68, 111, 121, 157, 161, 221; and capital crimes, 42; circumvention of, 43, 54, 56, 58, 60–66, 109, 118, 126–27, 139–40, 147, 156; and confession, 35; contrary to the, 132, 142, 244; and deciding by analogy, 47; distortion of, 218; and enforcement, 58; and execution, 42, 43; and increasing punishment, 45; and mutual concealment, 34; and sentencing, 200; special, lxxxv–lxxxviii; and torture, 227, 234; violations of the, 24, 213–14, 231, 236, 243
law, provisions of, 30–32, 43, 151, 206, 243; and accusations, 194, 199; and amnesty, 22, 28; and confession, 34; and errors in judging, 39; and military affairs, 42, 208; and officials, 26, 206; and "original places," 29; and penalties, 27, 152, 234; and rebellion, 154; and repayment, 36; and sacrifices, 111; and sedition, 154; and slaves, 171, 183; and soldiers, 136;

Index

and stealing, 157, 161; and striking, 178–79, 183; and taxes, 104; and treason, 42, 154–55

law, subversion of: and accusations, 193, 197, 201; "as comparable to," 46; and bribes, 32; and confession, 34; and construction, 65; and corveé services, 73–75; and fields, 78; and fraud, 36–37; and household registers, 70; and illicit goods, 107, 139–40, 150, 152, 193, 197, 201, 203, 209, 222–26, 228–29, 237, 240; and interest, 105; and property, 205–8; and robbery, 36–37; and salt, 100–102; and seeking favors, 218–19; and soldiers, 134; and taxes, 73, 91–93; and the Ten Abominations, 23, 27

lawsuits, 192–93

legal norms, lv–lxi, lxxxi, lxxxv

legal privileges, lxvi

lending, 94–95, 98–99, 113, 116, 127, 145–46

leniency, xli, xlvii

levees, 246–47

life exile, 29–30, 37, 79, 111–12, 165–66, 218, 220, 224, 226; and accusations, 194–99, 202; and affrays, 178–79; and amnesty, 27–28; and counterfeiting, 209, 211; and errors in judging, 39, 124, 241; and fornication, 214; history of, xcix *n.197*; and the Imperial City, 126, 156; and illicit goods, 158–61, 167; increasing or reducing punishment of, 44–45, 99, 234–35; and kidnapping, 164; and killing, 169–73, 175; and military exile, 22, 24; and officials, 181, 212; places for, 49; prisoners' acceptance of, 238–39; redemption of, 17, 29, 30–31; and rebellion, 154; and relatives, 26–27, 29, 58, 155, 171, 239; and running away, 222–23; and striking, 183–84, 187; three degrees of, 17, 44–45, 49; and treason, 154–55; 2,000 *li*, 17, 44, 58, 111, 155, 158–59, 161, 171–72, 202–4; 2,500 *li*, 17, 44, 158–59, 161, 203–4; 3,000 *li*, 17, 28–29, 37, 44–46, 112, 124, 126, 154–56, 158–61, 164–67, 169, 172–73, 175, 178–79, 183–84, 187–89, 195, 197–99, 202–4, 209, 211–12, 214, 219, 222

Light-Honoring Sect, 112

Linchuan, xciii *n.93*

lineage, 71–72, 90, 165, 186, 188, 214–15, 217

Li Qing, civ *n.269*

Li Shanchang, xxxiv, xli–xlii, xliv

litigants, 203

litigation, 192–93, 201

Liu Chengzhi, xliii, xciii *n.91*

Liu Futong, xxxiv

Liu Ji, xxxv, xliii–xliv, xcii *n.79*

Liu Weijing, xliii, xciii *n.86*

Liu Weiqian, xlvi, xciii *n.86*

Liuqiu, xxxvi

livestock, 99, 141–46, 155, 162. *See also* animals

Li Wenzhong, xci *n.76*, c *n.211*

Li Xiang, xliii

Longfeng, xxxv

losses: of corpses, 167; of dynastic policies, 115; of imperial decrees, 60; of livestock, 141–42; and military affairs, 129–30, 131, 132, 133, 148, 150, 152; of prisoners, 152, 225

Lu Yongzhen, xliii

lü ling, xlv

Ma, Empress, xxxiv

magic, 112, 155

magicians, 117

magistrates, district, 19, 170, 180, 191

maimed, 29, 31–32, 173, 178–79

malarial regions, 28

Manchuria, xxxvi

Manchus, xxxiii

Manicheism, xxxiv–xxxv, xxxviii

manufactures, 108–9, 122–23, 134, 205, 237, 243–46

Mao Yilu, ciii *n.267*, civ *n.269*

mares, 142, 169

markets, 90, 107–9, 175

marquises, 53, 135, 207–8

marriages, 18, 82–90, 154, 214, 217; and accusations, 193, 201; and concubines, 200, 215; and relatives by, 186, 194

martyrs, 111, 220

matchmakers, 89–90, 217

mausoleums, 111, 114

measures, 95–96, 108

medical expenses, 204

medical treatment, 174, 176, 179, 217

mediums, 112

memorials, 20–21, 61–62, 115, 127–28, 240–41

men, 33, 40, 119; able-bodied adult, 29, 69–70, 73, 75, 77, 93, 99, 101, 112, 118; and fornication, 214–17

Mengshuizhai cundu, civ *n.269*

merchants, 104, 107

Meridian Gate, lii, 122

messengers, 56, 116, 128–29, 146, 148–50

Metropolitan Coinage, 91

midwives, 240

military: administration, 127–37; articles, 244–45; battalions, 52, 128, 209; campaigns, 128–31, 133, 135–37, 139; com-

312 Index

military (continued)
  missions, 132, 154; equipment, 129, 133–34, 141, 156; functionaries, 24, 95, 134, 170; guards, 19, 24, 43, 52, 71, 128, 135–36, 209; households, xxviii; information, 63, 127, 129, 141, 150; offices, 101, 116; operations, 60–61, 66–67, 129–30, 148, 150, 238; provisions, 60, 66, 129, 150; service, 43, 71, 130–32, 134–35, 202, 212; supplies, 95, 98, 129, 137, 150; training, 132, 237; troops, 127, 132, 135; weapons, 35, 91, 100, 103, 121, 123, 132, 133, 152. See also weapons
military exile, 53, 71, 74, 121, 124, 126, 127, 140; for abandoning service, 122, 134–35, 136; for crimes, 22, 24, 43, 140, 156, 207, 208; and distant frontiers, 49–51; for failure to train, 132; for false accusations, 202; history of, lxxxii; as military guards, 22, 24; for pillaging, 131–32; and prisoners, 223, 224; for selling equipment, 133
military personnel, xli, lxxv; battalion commanders, 19, 52, 102, 132, 134–35, 137, 170, 180, 191, 207; and the capital, 43; commanders, 116, 129–32, 170, 180, 191; company commanders, 19, 52, 102, 121–22, 124, 132, 134–35, 137, 170, 180, 191, 207; crimes of, 21–22, 24, 42, 61, 157, 161, 170, 201; demotion of, 22; dismissal of, 22, 130–36; escorting officers, 125, 223; generals, 63, 67, 127–29, 131–32, 133, 150, 209; guarding officers, 120–24, 135, 138, 211; families of, 53, 112, 137, 140, 151; and inheritance of titles, 53; killing of, 43; and lawsuits, 192, 211; officials, 19, 20, 126, 212, 243; platoon commanders, 22, 52, 95, 131–32, 134–37, 207–8, 238; regional commanders, 128, 130, 209; return to status as, 26; squad commanders, 52, 95, 131–32, 134–36, 207–8, 238; and travel passes, 139
mills, 80–81, 206
Ming Code. See Code
Ming dynasty: founding, xxxiii–xl; and codification of the Code, xl–lv
Ming History. See History of the Ming Dynasty
Mingjiao, xxxv
Ming Taizu. See Zhu Yuanzhang
Ming Yuzhen, xxxvi
ministries, 147, 194
Ministry of Justice, xxxvi, xlvi, xlix, lxi, lxxxvii, 20, 42, 47, 58, 236
Ministry of Personnel, xxxvi, 57
Ministry of Public Works, xxxvi

Ministry of Revenue, xxxvi, lxxxvi, 94
Ministry of Rites, xxxvi, xxxix
Ministry of War, xxxvi, 128
mirrors, 91
miscarriage, 178–80, 240
missions, 62, 213
mistakes: and laws on personnel, 61; and laws on punishments, 18, 38; and laws on rituals, 110, 113; and penal affairs, 173, 209, 234. See also errors
monetary obligations, 105–7, 201
money, 61, 64, 66–67, 72–73, 91, 94–95, 98, 103, 107, 218; and bribery, 208; and counterfeiting, 210–11; and dian mortgage, 78, 195; and extortion, 139, 206; and interest, 105–6; and labor, 122, 131, 243–44; and repayment, 81, 174; and reward, 126–27; and robbery, 169; and stealing, 156, 157–59; and taxes, 56, 64–65, 90, 93, 160, 104, 207
Mongolia, Outer, xxxvi
Mongols, xxxiii–xxxvi, xxxviii, xl, xliv, xcv, 88
months, 65, 118, 124, 147, 173, 206, 234; and debt, 105–7; and delays, 115–16; and fines, 110, 115; and penal servitude, 32, 240; and time limits, 225
mortgage, redemption of, 80
mother, 25, 45, 154, 188, 199.
mounds, 111
mourning, 18, 19, 56, 75, 76, 110, 118, 217
mourning degrees, l, lxxii–lxxiii; beyond the, 35, 41–42, 162, 186, 215; diagrams, 8–14; fifth degree, 18–19, 86, 110, 162, 165–66, 170–71, 175, 180, 183–84, 186, 188, 191–91, 198–200, 215–16; fourth degree, 19, 34, 42, 86, 162, 165, 175, 183, 184, 186, 191, 198–99; one year, 45, 76, 89, 118, 162, 163, 170; second degree, 162, 171, 175–77, 184–85, 187–88, 191–92, 198–99, 216; third degree, 18–19, 34, 41, 89, 162, 165, 175–77, 183–84, 186–87, 191, 198–99; within the, 42, 80, 195, 215, 240; sixth degree, 19, 180. See also relatives
mulberry, 80–81
mules, 33, 138, 141, 143–46, 152, 162, 169
music, 18–19, 118–19
musicians, 29, 71, 75, 87, 217, 220
mutilation, 18, 26, 28–30
Mu Ying, c n.211

names, taboos about, 61
Nanjing, xxxv, xxxviii, xliv
National University, xxxvii, xxxix
negligence, lxii–lxv, 25, 173, 176, 244

Index

neighborhood, 240
nephews, 43, 69, 73
night watchmen, 96, 137
Nine Chapters, Code of the, xliv
noble titles, 20, 26, 53
norms, legal, lv–lviii, lxxxi, lxxxv

objects, 106–7, 111, 114
obstructions, 97, 115
offenders. *See* criminals
offenses. *See* crimes
offerings, 110–11
Office of Transmission, lxxviii
offices, public, 67, 245–46
officials: and accusations, 193–94, 198, 201–2; and administering the law, 237–38; appointments of, 22, 25–26, 36, 52, 55–56, 63, 202; associate, 25, 38, 66, 181, 191, 234–35; career records of, 57, 61, 96; and chain of command, 56, 182, 231; civil offices of, 116; classes of, 38; collective prosecution of, lix; competence of, 235–36; and construction, 122, 243; and corvée services, 70, 73–75; and the court, 52, 56, 58, 63, 213; crimes committed by, 20–22, 24–26, 38–39, 54–55, 116, 238; and cursing, 190–91; as custodians, 46; and deceit, 209–10, 212–13; demotion of, 22, 25, 217; dismissal of, 22, 25–26, 54, 216; disputes of, 201–2; district, 80; and dukes or marquises, 53, 208; emissaries, 62, 151, 206, 212, 238; emoluments of, 53, 64, 74, 79, 116; and errors, 39–40; evaluations of, 26; and extortion, 206–7; family of, 22–24, 52, 78, 152, 154–55, 207, 221, 230; and fields, 77, 79–80; and gates, 121, 123–24; and grain, 92–93, 96, 108, 232–33; and illicit goods, 97–98, 100–101, 105, 150; incumbent, 25, 116, 151; and inspections, 108, 194; judging, 226, 230–32, 235–36; and killing, 170; and knowledge of the *Code*, 59; and leaving office, 25–26, 55; and livestock, 141–43, 145; local, 67–68, 151, 224; and marriage, 86; and memorials, 58, 115; and messengers, 116, 146, 148–50; meritorious, 23–24, 74, 78–79, 154–55, 230; and military affairs, 21–22, 52, 125, 243; and the Ministry of Justice, 58; and money, 93, 96, 98, 105, 108, 232–33; and mourning, 26, 118; and official documents, 52, 54, 59–68; and palaces, 122, 124–25, 212–13; and postal relay stations, 147–49; and prisoners, 75, 198, 223–24, 226–29, 231–39; privilege of, 23, 53; and property, 105, 206–8, 237; and public works, 243–45; rank of, 19–20, 22–23, 26, 56, 87, 170, 182, 191, 209, 219, 230; and rituals, 110–11, 113–17; salaries of, 36; and seeking favors, 218–19; status of, 212; and stealing, 76; and striking, 180–82, 237; and successors, 56, 96, 219; and taxes, 73, 92, 97, 104, 182, 232–33; and time limits, 56; titles of, 25, 53, 87, 217; and travel passes, 139; and treacherous cliques, 58
officiators, 110
old retainers, 19–20
omission of acts, lxi
omit, 57, 64–67, 69
on duty, 55, 96, 120–21, 138
on the basis of (*yi*): as criminal distinction, lix
orchards, 81
orphans, 76
outlaws, 225
outsiders, 40–41, 187, 229
overseers, 75, 123

palaces, 120–27, 157
Palace Treasury, 94, 122, 156
Pan Fu, xliii, xciii *n.89*
Pang An, lxxxvi
Pan Tingjian, xciii *n.89*
parents, 71, 117, 166, 199, 218; accusations of, 76, 199, 200; care of, 28–29, 118–19, 200; crimes of, 119, 174–75, 188, 228; of criminals, 155, 172; cursing of, 174, 192; death of, 118, 170, 175, 177, 199; and the eight deliberations, 23; of husbands, 18, 170, 171, 174, 187–88, 190, 198; and marriage, 83, 86, 89; plot to kill, 18, 170–71; striking of, 187–88; of wives, 41, 174, 198, 200
parents-in-law, 171, 190, 192
patrolmen, 211
pearls, 169
penal instruments, 7
penal servitude, 31–32, 86, 141, 143, 220, 224, 238–39; for accepting illicit goods, 36, 103–5, 246; and accusations, 185, 193, 194–98, 199, 202; for affrays, 167, 178; and amnesty, 27–29; and care of prisoners, 228–30; and corpses, 165–67; for cursing, 191; for fornication, 215–17; four years, 29–30, 196–97; history of, xcix *n.196*; and imprisonment, 226, 227; increasing or reducing penalty of, 44–45, 134–35; and joint crimes, 37, 40; for kidnapping, 164;

penal servitude *(continued)*
　for killing, 169–70, 173, 175, 176, 177; and labor, 30, 31, 39, 195, 198, 199, 239–40; and laws on personnel, 53, 60, 63; and laws on revenue, 72–73, 97; and laws on rituals, 111, 114, 117, 118; and military affairs, 120, 126, 127, 138–39; and military exile, 22, 24; one and one-half years, 17, 44, 143, 158, 161–62, 175, 184, 186, 203–5; one year, 17, 30, 32, 44, 86, 97, 118, 120, 126, 157–58, 161, 166–67, 178, 180, 182, 184–86, 188–89, 203–5, 213, 215, 229–30; one-half year, 196, 234; and penal affairs, 155, 156, 157, 209–13, 220, 237; penalties decided incorrectly, 241; places for, 47–48; prisoners' acceptance of, 238–39; redemption of, 17, 29, 32, 196, 241; for repeat offenders, 29–30; running away during, 222–23; and salt, 100–103; and slaves, 72–73; for stealing, 79, 157–59, 161–62; for striking, 175, 180–81, 182, 183, 184–85, 186, 187–88, 189; three years, 17, 29–31, 36, 44, 45, 53, 63, 72–73, 79, 100–103, 111, 114, 117, 127, 138–39, 141, 155–62, 164–67, 169–70, 173, 175–78, 180–81, 183–85, 187–88, 193, 196–98, 203–5, 209–13, 215, 217, 220, 235, 237, 240, 246; two and one-half years, 17, 40, 44, 60, 72–73, 100, 158–59, 161, 164–65, 187, 203–5; two years, 17, 72, 100, 158–59, 161, 164, 166, 175, 177–78, 180–81, 191, 202–5, 210, 220, 228; and women, 29–30, 240
penal system, lxix–lxx
penalties: administration of, 237–38; and amnesty, 27, 239; basic rules for, lxx, 40, 44; conversion of, lxxvi–lxxvii, 29–30, 32, 196–97, 234; "cumulatively reduced," lxxi, 24; excess, 196–97; execution of, 235–36; exempt from, 26, 34–40, 58–60, 74–75, 78, 100, 117, 125, 135–36, 197–99, 208, 211, 221, 223–25, 239; extralegal, lxxxii–lxxxiii; and the *Grand Pronouncements*, lxxxii; incorrectly deciding, 239, 241; increasing or reducing, 44–45, 152, 234, 239; not stipulated in the *Code*, 221; remaining, 29, 32, 196–97, 215; reciprocal, 197–98; for specific articles, 43; supplemental, lxix–lxx. *See also* accessories; banishment; beating with a heavy stick; beating with a light stick; death by slicing; death penalty; decapitation; emoluments; life exile; military exile; penal servitude; penalties, redemption of; period of responsibility; principals; salaries; strangulation; tattooing
period of responsibility, 178–80
persons: law-abiding, 175; mean, 183, 217. *See also* aged persons
persons, ordinary, 35, 42, 43, 192, 228; and the eight deliberations, 23; and killing, 171, 187; and mourning degrees, 117, 162–63, 165–66, 184, 186; and rewards, 36, 211; rules for, 186; and stealing, 94, 144, 158–59, 162–63; and striking, 182–83, 185–86, 189–90; powerful, 79, 87, 103, 106, 139, 206, 219
persons beyond the pale of civilization, lxii, 43, 233
petitioner's drum, 193
petitions, lxvi, lxxiii–lxxiv
physicians, xxxviii, 70, 113, 131, 176, 218
pickpocket, 161
pictorial signs, 114
Placard of People's Instruction, xl, lxxxvi
placards, lxxxv–lxxxvi, 3, 218
plaintiffs, 193
play, 173
"plots," 47; to harm, 177; to kill, 18–19, 169–70, 171, 172, 174, 187; to strike, 173
plotting great sedition. *See* sedition, great
plotting rebellion. *See* rebellion
plotting treason. *See* treason
poison, 18, 26, 28–30, 172–73
police, 64, 101, 139, 169
population survey, xxxviii
portals, 120
ports, 104, 107
post couriers, 70
postal relay stations, 68, 146–53, 212
prefects, 19, 116, 170, 180, 191
prefectures, 75, 124; crimes in, 38–39, 156, 209; and examinations, xxxvii–xxxviii; officials of, 21, 64, 67–68, 86, 98, 147, 235, 247; and military affairs, 24, 129; and penalties, 48–51
prices, 104, 133, 165; of animals/livestock, 104, 106, 142–44, 146; of goods, 33, 91, 97, 106, 107–8, 206; of property, 79–80, 106, 243–44
prime minister, lxxviii
princes, 59–60, 209
principals, 40–41, 63, 80, 112, 158; confession of, 37; punished as, 38–39, 89, 167–68, 183; punishment for, 24, 131–32, 154–55, 159, 160, 170, 211. *See also* accessories; criminals
prisoners: and acceptance of punishment, 238–39; accusations of, 200, 232–33;

Index

and appeals, 198; and confession, 198, 229; and death penalty, 230, 239, 240–41; delay in sending, 223–24; escape, 222–25, 228; guarding of, 220, 225; imprisonment of, 226–42; interrogation of, 226–27, 231–34; kill themselves, 228, 230; and labor services, 239–40; rescued, 159–60, 225; sentences of, 235–36; transport of, 151–52; treatment of, 228–30
prison guards, 75
prisons, 46
prison warders, 226, 228–29
processions, 112
profits, 80, 108, 206–7, 211
prohibitions, 74, 88, 105–6, 112–13, 116, 124–26, 132–33, 137, 140–41
"proper lord," 112
property, 41, 46, 105, 128, 215, 218, 234, 243–44, 246; family, 18, 76, 163; forfeit to the government, 58, 94, 154–55, 211, 214; given as reward, 141; given to victims' families, 171–73, 178–79, 188, 199, 195–96; government, 81, 106–7, 144–45, 152, 162; obtain by deceit, 163–64, 175, 212; stolen, 79, 93, 106, 156, 158, 161, 163, 183, 201, 220; and subversion of the law, 101–2, 134, 139–40, 150, 193, 201–9, 221–22, 223–24, 226, 228–29, 237, 240; and taxes, 204, 233
prophecy, 114
provinces, 20–21, 43, 46, 115–16, 209
Provincial Administration Commissions, xxxvii, 38–39, 42, 98, 129, 209, 236; commissioners of, 227, 235
Provincial Surveillance Commissions, xxxvii, xli, 64, 115–16, 209, 212, 236; and cases, 20–21, 194; and knowledge of the Code, 59; and military affairs, 42, 129
public matters, 56, 62–63, 237; and collections, 74, 207, 210; and interrogations, 20–21, 194; mistakes in deciding, 38–40; and prisoners, 160, 227; seeking favors in, 218–19
punishments. *See* penalties
purified houses, 110
Puyang yandu, civ n.269

Qian Yongren, xliii, xcii n.82
Qi Biaojia, civ n.269
Qincha Muslims, 88
Qing dynasty, xxxiii
Que Jing, xlviii

race, 88
reappointment, 129

reassignment: and laws on personnel, 55, 57, 63, 67; and laws on punishments, 22, 25; and laws on revenue, 78; and laws on rituals, 114, 117, 118; and penal affairs, 202, 216
rebellion: accusations of, 35, 193, 199, 201; and amnesty, 26, 28–30, 33; and concealment, 42; and confession, 35; and knowledge of the Code, 59; and military affairs, 63, 127; penalties for, 42, 46, 154, 241; and the Ten Abominations, 23, 99
rebels, 70, 127, 132
receipts, 93–94, 96
recidivists, lxxv–lxxvi
recommendations, xxxvii, 54–55
Record of Absolute Sincerity, xxxix
Red Armies, xxxiv
Red Turbans, xxxiv–xxxv
redemption of penalties, lxxi–lxxii, 57, 215, 241; for the aged, 30–32; by amnesty, 30, 37–38; by copper currency, 17–18, 29, 32, 196–97; in accordance with the Code, 174; by merit, 130; by officials, 21–22
Regional Military Commissions, xxxvii, 42, 52, 67, 129, 209
registers, 107
registrar, xliii
registration, 74
Regulation concerning True and Miscellaneous Capital Crimes, lxxxvi
Regulation of Hongwu 30, lxxxvi
Regulation on Crime Redemption, lii, lxxxiii–lxxxiv
regulations, liii–lv, lxxi, lxxxiii–lxxxviii, ciii n.254, 116–17
Regulations concerning Military Exile, lxxxvi
reimbursement, 97–98
relatives: and accusations, 34–35, 76, 198–200; care for, 28, 118–19; collective prosecution of, lxviii–lxix; and concealment, 34, 41–42; of criminals, 154, 238–39; and cursing, 191–92; and degrees of mourning, 18–19, 76, 89, 159, 165–66, 170–71, 175–77, 183, 186, 187, 192, 198–200; and the eight deliberations, 19, 23; and fornication, 215–16; of household heads, 184–85, 191, 200, 216; and killing, 18–19, 170–71, 175–77; and living separately, 41, 162, 189; and living together, 34, 41, 124, 130, 162; and marriage, 86, 89; by marriage, 23–24, 186, 215, 230; offending against righteousness, 198–99; and officials,

relatives *(continued)* 206, 219; of officials, 23–24, 52, 230; returned to, 72, 87; and stealing, 162–63; and striking, 183, 186–87, 188–90
remarriage, 19, 84–86, 88–89, 171, 190, 192
Remonstrance Bureau, 20, 212
rent, 33, 82, 146, 206
repayment, 36, 133
repudiation, 86, 88–89
reservoirs, 246
reward: for capturing offenders, 36, 100, 154–55, 193; for confession, 117; for finding lost objects, 106, 126; punishment for seeking, 213–14; for reporting crimes, 54, 58, 104, 114, 127, 141, 172, 210–11
rice, 91, 93, 162
righteousness, 198–200
Right Office, xlii
rituals, xli, xli, xciii, xc *n.49*, 82, 110–19
Rituals, 119
rivers, 64, 174
roads, 247
robbers, 98, 167–68, 225–26
robbery, 23, 30–31, 40, 46, 82, 176, 201; and government goods, 98, 106; penalties for, 156, 157, 208; reference, 169; as a "true crime," 27. *See also* force, use of
runners, 54, 74, 170, 180–81, 191

sacrifices, 110–13, 155–56
Sacrificial Canon, 111
sages, 111, 220
salaries, 24, 60, 97, 116, 141, 202–4; and fines, 21, 59, 110, 115, 225; reduced, 102, 136–37
sale, 109, 173, 215, 245; of goods, 91, 108, 206; of government property, 133, 145; of houses or fields, 78–80, 195, 199; of persons, 18–19, 27, 72, 164–65, 171, 200, 214, 217; of salt, 100–104
salt, xli, 34; licenses, 102–3, 210; rules about, 100–105, 109 *n.1*; sites, 48, 100–101, 103, 105, 239; taxes on, 90, 104; workers, 26, 70, 100, 103, 239
sanction, lvi–lviii
scholars, 58
sea, 140–41
seals, 54, 66–67, 107, 114, 210, 238; destroyed, 35, 60; opening of, 96, 146–47; stealing of, 156, 209
seasons, 21, 241, 247
Secretariat, xxxvi, xli–xlii, lxxviii
security groups, 74

sedan chairs, 45, 151, 193
sedition, great: accusations of, 193, 199, 201; and amnesty, 26, 28–30, 33; and concealment, 42; and confession, 35; and knowledge of the *Code*, 59; and military affairs, 63; and the Ten Abominations, 23
Semu people, 88
sentences, 36–37, 234, 236, 240; place of, 223, 230; provisional, 20–21, 23
settlements, 155, 171–72, 177
Seven Homicides, xlii, liv
seven lamps, 112
Shaanxi, xxxvi, xcv *n.134*
Shandong, xcii *n.83*
Shanxi, xxxvi
sheep, 33, 111, 141–44, 162
Sheng Yuanfu, xliii, xcii *n.83*
Shen Jiaben, xciv *n.105*
ships, 104, 107, 141, 156, 160
shops, 33, 81, 103–4
Siam, xxxvi
Sichuan, xxxvi
sickness, 56, 69, 82, 110, 172, 218. *See also* illness
silk, 91, 94, 98, 117, 140, 169, 208; manufacture of, 244–45; offerings of, 110, 155
silver, 33, 79, 91, 97, 188, 108; for burial expenses, 175–76, 237; as reward, 58, 114, 117, 172, 193, 210–11
simplicity, xli, xlvii
sinew, lxxxii
sisters, 154, 216; and the eight deliberations, 23; and marriage, 82, 83; older, 18, 82, 89, 118, 187, 189, 192; of relatives, 186, 189, 215; younger, 82, 164, 187, 189
Six Illicit Goods, xlix–l, 15. *See also* goods, illicit
Six Ministries, xxxvi, xlv, lxxvii–lxxviii, 21, 61, 115, 148, 209, 212
slaves, 175, 177, 185; female, 88, 217; and fornication, 216, 217; killed, 174–75, 177; and household heads, 41, 163, 166, 171, 172, 183–84, 190–92, 200, 228, 230; and marriage, 87–88; runaway, 72, 88–89; sold as, 72, 164
soldiers, 71, 125, 130, 133, 218, 243; abandon service, 134–37; crimes committed by, 19, 24, 101–2, 131, 170, 180–81, 191, 201, 208; on guard, 121, 122–24, 138, 140; and postal relay stations, 146–48; and training, 132, 238
solicitation, 33, 34
Song dynasty, xxxix
Songjiang, xlviii
Song Lian, xxxv, xxxix, xlvi

Index

sons, 73, 76, 106, 130, 177; adopted, 53, 71–72, 82–83, 154, 164, 188, 217, 218; of concubines, 53, 71, 82, 189; and corpses, 119, 165, 166, 175; crimes of, 187–88, 192; of criminals, 26, 101, 154, 155, 172, 228, 230; disobey instructions, 188, 200; and the eight deliberations, 23; and filial piety, 201, 221; killed, 174–75, 177; of officials, 25, 53, 87, 212, 217; and marriage, 82, 86; of relatives, 23, 53, 71, 86–87, 130, 154, 164, 187, 189–90, 200, 212; and slaves, 72, 171, 200

sons-in-law, 23, 41, 69, 199–200

sons' sons, 73, 76, 130, 177, 188, 201, 221; accusations of, 198–200; adopted, 154, 188; and corpses, 119, 165, 166; crimes of, 187–88, 192, 230; of criminals, 26, 154, 155, 172, 228, 230; and the eight deliberations, 23; killed, 174–75, 177; and marriage, 86; of officials, 53, 87, 212, 217; reference, 45; of relatives, 164; slaves punished as, 171, 200; sold as, 72, 164

soothsayers, 117

sorcery, 18, 112

spells, 172

spirits (gods), 43, 111, 112, 155–56, 165

spies, 140, 199

staff foreman, 24

stamps, 96

status, violation of, 198–200

statutes, lxxxv–lxxxvi, 115

stealing, 40, 220; goods, 160–61, 162–63; government property, 18, 95, 144, 145, 155, 156–57; from graves, 165, 167; livestock, 34, 162, 169; punishment for, 157–59; sacred objects, 18, 156–57; seals, 18, 156, 209; and supervisors, 76, 81, 93–95, 98–99, 105, 142, 220, 222, 228, 244

stele, 116

stepfathers, 189

stepmothers, 45, 188, 199

stone, 33, 162, 175, 243; and tombs, 81, 165

storehouses, 46, 55, 95, 220

strangulation, 61, 112, 165–66, 203–4, 211, 219, 222; and accusations, 193, 195–96, 199; and cursing, 191–92; as death penalty, 20, 241; and fornication, 214–16; and increasing or reducing punishments, 44–45, 46, 241; for kidnapping, 164; and killing, 169–71, 173; and military affairs, 120–27, 134, 136, 138, 141; and marriage, 86, 87, 88; and prisoners, 159–60, 227–28; redemption for, 18; and seals, 60, 209; and sentencing, 36; and stealing, 36, 141, 155–56, 161; and striking, 180–90; and taxes, 92, 182; for treason, 155

streets, 175, 247

striking, 137, 160, 177–80, 193, 222; and concubines, 174, 185–86; and hired laborers, 184, 185, 190; and husbands, 18, 185–86; and husbands' relatives, 18, 174, 187–90; and officials, 149, 180–82, 237–38; and relatives, 18–19, 40, 179, 186–87; and slaves, 183–85, 190; and wives, 174, 185–86; and wives' relatives, 18, 186–90

subjects, 19–20, 111

subprefects, 19, 116, 170, 180, 191

subprefectures, xxxvii; and laws on personnel, 56, 64, 67–68; and laws on punishment, 21, 24, 38–39, 48–51; and laws on revenue, 74, 86, 98; and military affairs, 126, 129, 147; and penal affairs, 156, 193, 209, 231, 235; and public works, 247

suicide, 174, 228, 230, 238

Sun Zhong, xliii

supervisors, 97, 156, 239–40; and cheating the government, 93, 98; and borrowing government property, 81–82, 94, 145–46; and stealing, 76, 81, 93–95, 98–99, 105, 142, 145, 157–58, 163, 220, 228, 244

support: from the government, 53, 76; for victims' families, 173–74, 179, 188, 195, 199

surnames, 154, 186; and adoption, 53, 71–72, 188

surrender, 19, 223–25, 228

surveillance commissions, xliii

Suzhou, xxxiv–xxxv

swine, 144, 162

tablets, 111

taboos, 61

Taiyuan, xci *n.76*

talents, xxxvii, 19–20, 54

tallies, xlviii, 94–95, 107, 114, 156, 210, 212

Tang Code, xlii, lxii; and the *Ming Code*, xliv, xlvi, li, lxxxviii, 68 *n.1*; structure of, xlv–xlvii, xlix, c–ci *n.217*

Tang dynasty, xliv, lv, lxxvii

Tang He, c *n.211*

Tao An, xxxix, xliii, xcii *n.84*, xciii *n.89*

tattooing, lxxxii–lxxxiii, 36–37, 46; exempt from, 24, 29, 46, 80–81, 92–95, 107–8, 144, 167–68, 175, 246; of "forcibly taking," 160; and military personnel, 24, 161; removal of, 169; of "secretly stealing," 161; of "stole government

tattooing *(continued)*
(grain/money/thing)," 157–58; and taxes, 92–93; for theft, 80, 92, 94–95, 107–8, 144, 156, 162–64, 167–68, 175, 246
taxes, 54, 65, 76, 90, 95, 100–5; collection of, 74, 78, 90, 92–93, 97, 182; on grain, xxviii, 56, 73, 77, 81, 90–93, 210, 232–33, 237; on land, xxviii, 69, 79–80; levies for, 33–34, 73, 105, 204; and money, 56, 210, 232–33
Taylor, Romeyn, lxxix
tea, xxxi, 79, 90, 104, 105, 210
teachers, 182, 194
Ten Abominations, l, lxvi–lxvii, lxxiii, 18–19, 20, 23, 27, 99, 241
Teng Yi, xliii, xcii *n.83*, xciii *n.90*
testimony, 231
textiles, 109
theatrical performances, 220–21
theft, 29, 41, 43, 60, 80–82, 96, 160–62; as comparable to, 92, 157, 162–65, 176–77, 212, 246; confession of, 34–36; of illicit goods, 95, 106–8, 143–44, 156–57, 167–68, 175, 177, 212, 246; punishment for, 80–81, 160, 162; tattooing for, 37; as "true crime," 27
thieves, 56, 167–68, 208, 225–26
threats, 32, 163
Three Provincial Offices, xxxvii
throne, 147, 150, 198; appeal to the, 116; decision by the, 67, 113–15; execution by, 27, 58, 236; memorialize or petition to the, 20–21, 23–24, 29–32, 42, 47, 61, 67, 123, 128, 235; selection by, 52, 125
tiles, 174, 243
timber, 81
time limits, lxi–lxii, 28, 121–22; to arrest criminals, 211, 221, 223–26; to collect taxes, 91–92; and government property, 60, 106, 145, 150, 245; and military affairs, 130, 136, 148–49; and officials, 39–40, 55–57, 67, 194, 231
tin, 79
tithings, xxxvii, 74, 77–78
Toghto, xxxiv
tombs, 81, 111, 157, 165
tools, 94
torture, 34, 227, 230–31, 233–34, 240
towns, 126–27, 175
trade, xxxviii, 90, 108
transgressions, 54–57, 110; record, 21–22, 25–26, 56–57, 59, 74, 79, 87, 101–2, 116, 132, 135, 217
travel pass/permit, 107, 138–39
treason, 18, 154–55; accusations of, 35, 193, 199, 201; and amnesty, 26, 28–30; and knowledge of the *Code*, 59; punishment for, 42, 46; and the Ten Abominations, 99; and troops, 127
treasuries, 64, 90–100, 157–58, 243, 245
Treasury of Treasure Paper Currency [Baochao Ku], 67
tribute students, xxxvii
tripods, 107
troops, 19, 21, 42, 63, 66–67, 95, 127–28, 130–32, 135–36, 150, 155–57, 237

uncles, 18, 23, 43, 69, 83, 89, 118, 154, 186–87, 192
unrighteousness, 19
urban areas, 175
ushers, 42, 54, 116
utensils, 81, 94, 109, 162, 165, 169

Veritable Records of the Ming, xlv, xlvii–xlviii, xlix, li, xciii *n.91*
Veritable Records of Ming Taizu (Ming Taizu shilu). See *Veritable Records of the Ming*
vessels, sacred, 155
vice censor-in-chief, xliii–xliv
Vietnam, xxxiii, xxxvi
village, 81, 107, 151
vinegar, 104

wages, 33, 151, 243
wagons, 100, 141
walls, 81, 126, 238, 243, 247
Wang Guangyang, xlvii, xci *n.76*
Wang Zao, xliii
warehouses, 103, 220
warrants, 56, 60, 67–68
watchers, 55, 95, 96, 131
"watchtower," 230
weapons, 32, 124, 152, 175–76, 178, 222, 227. See also military, weapons
weavers, 245
wedding gifts, 86, 90, 215, 217
weights, 95, 108
weisuo, xxxvi
Wen Yuanji, xliii, xcii *n.80*
wheat, 91, 93, 162
White Cloud School, 112
White Lotus Society, xxxiv, 112
widowers, 76
widows, 53, 76
wine, 104, 119
witches, 112
witnesses, 41, 231, 233–34
wives, 71, 73, 87, 99, 106, 112, 171, 174, 177,

Index

221; accusations of, 198–200; and concubines, 83–84, 171, 185–86, 199–200; crimes of, 25, 171, 174, 185–86, 187–90, 192; of criminals, 26, 140, 154–55, 171–72; and the eight deliberations, 23; and fornication, 214–17; and marriage, 83–90; of officials, 53, 58; of relatives, 19, 41, 45, 86, 90, 154, 164, 188, 190, 200, 215–16; and remarriage, 171, 215; repudiated by husband, 25, 86, 88–89; runaway, 86–88; and slaves, 72, 88, 164–65; sold, 72, 88, 164–65, 171
wizards, 112
women, 25, 45, 84, 87, 112, 119, 151, 179, 201; crimes of, 29, 40, 86, 101, 240; and fornication, 19, 214–17; and marriage, 82–90, 101, 200; and pregnancy, 214, 240; runaway, 86–87
wood, 162
worthies, xxxvii, 19–20, 111, 220
wounds, 236–37
wrongs, 125, 201
Wuchang, xxxv, xl
Wu Chen, xxxix
Wu Quji, xliii
Wu Tong, xliii, xciii *n.93*

Xia regime, xxxvi
Xie Ruxin, xliii
Xu Ben, xlii, xcii *n.78*
Xu Cunren, xciii n.92
Xu Da, xxxiv, c *n.211*
Xunci, civ *n.269*
Xu Shouhui, xxxiv

yamen, 55, 57, 110, 139, 181, 201; and accusations, 194, 198; crimes of, 238, 240; dissolution of, 25; and memorials, 58, 62, 115–16; and money, 90, 93–94; and official documents, 59, 61, 63–64, 147–48, 150, 156, 209–10; and seals, 60, 66; and warrants, 56, 68
Yang Xian, xlii, xci–xcii *n.76*
Yang Yifan, lxxxii, lxxxiv, lxxxvi
Yangzi (River/Valleys), xxxiv
Yan Junyan, civ *n.269*
Yanyu gao, cii *n.253*, ciii *n.267*, civ *n.269*
years, 22, 30, 32, 44–45, 47, 59, 115, 119; reference for, 46. *See also* penal servitude
"yellow books," xxxviii. *See also* household registers
Yellow River, xxxiv
Yi dynasty, l
Ying Jia, cii *n.253*, ciii *n.267*, civ *n.269*
Yingtian, xxxiv–xxxv
Yi Song-gye, l
Yongle period, xxxix
Yuan dynasty, xxxiii–xxxiv, xl–xli, lv
Yunjian yanlüe, ciii *n.267*
Yushi Tai, xxxvi

Zhang Chuncheng, xliii
Zhang Kentang, ciii *n.269*
Zhang Meihe, xxxix
Zhang Shicheng, xxxiv–xxxv, xl
Zhang Yin, xliii
Zhao Lin, xliii
Zhejiang, xxxiv–xxxv
Zhen Dexiu, xxxix
Zhenjiang, xciii *n.90*
Zheyu xinyu, civ *n.269*
Zhou Zhen (assistant minister), xliii, xcii–xciii *n.85*
Zhou Zhen (chief minister), xliii–xlv, xciii *n.87*
Zhu Biao, lii
Zhu Yuanzhang, xxxiii–xl, xciii *n.92*; and codification of the *Code*, xl–lv
Zhu Yunwen, li–lii